THOROUGHBRED

CYCLES

MARK CRAMER

THOROUGHBRED

CYCLES

How the Form Factor Affects Handicapping

ECHO POINT BOOKS & MEDIA, LLC

Published by Echo Point Books & Media
Brattleboro, Vermont
www.EchoPointBooks.com

Thoroughbred Cycles
ISBN: 978-1-62654-286-0 (paperback)
        978-1-62654-287-7 (casebound)

Interior book design by Bernard Schleifer

Cover design by Rachel Boothby Gualco,
Echo Point Books & Media

Editorial and proofreading assistance by Ian Straus,
Echo Point Books & Media

Printed and bound in the United States of America

To my uncle Arthur

Acknowledgments

DICK MITCHELL, for his insight and solidarity. The students in my horse-racing classes, for their challenging participation. Our friends in El Masnou, Barcelona, and Avignon, France, for their hospitality and support. Copy editor Peter Weissman, who saw each and every tree while never losing sight of the forest.

Contents

Preface

MY MOST BELOVED passengers have united in criticizing me for driving a different route every trip in order to arrive at the same place. I say, "Okay, you drive," and they answer, "Sorry, we can't drive; it's been impossible to learn the way because you've gone a different route every time." I suppose that the word "routine" comes from "route," so my driving habits represent a symbolic attempt to fight off the persistent incursions of routine into my life.

Why, I ask, does a man from Massachusetts, traveling in West Virginia, feel comfort and relief when he encounters an outlet of a national hamburger chain, which allows him to eat the exact same burger and fries that he has been accustomed to in his hometown? Or, why does a normally intelligent woman fear walking away from a bad marriage even after her child-raising responsibilities have been fulfilled? Is it that a return to the same nightly arguments is safer than a confrontation with the unknown in the outside world?

The more I bet and see others bet, the more I am convinced that there is an attitudinal relationship between lifestyle and handicapping style. In particular, attitude toward *routine* may have a vital impact upon handicapping methodology. During a period of research, a dear colleague and I faced a conflict over a particular speed figure. The horse in question showed its most recent race over a sloppy track. The methodology we were testing asked users to enter the most recent speed figure whenever possible.

My colleague wrote in a number for the sloppy track race, in which the horse in question had run dismally. I said, "Wait, we need to go back to a fast-track race."

He said: "No, we don't. The variant was zero that day." (For us, a zero variant meant that the final times of the races on that day were normal.)

He probably noted by my voice that I was astounded by his decision: "But this horse obviously hates the slop. The zero variant means to me simply that some horses that day improved in the slop to a similar degree that others declined. The variant is only an average." It was a desperately long-winded argument.

"If the variant says zero," he countered, "then we are *supposed* to enter the race."

Clearly he was arguing in favor of the letter of the law, which in this case seemed to me like bureaucratic routine. I maintained that I argued in favor of the spirit of the law, which in this particular instance required that we depart from the normal route of the method in order to be faithful to its intrinsic purpose. His allegiance to a flawed routine was parallel in some ways to the married lady's decision to return home to an inevitable argument.

I suppose that the need for routine has something to do with a positive effort to create a safe microworld within a hostile external world. We are condemned to live and die in a setting of transportation accidents, viruses, natural disasters, burglars, and bombs. So we create routines to protect us from these abrupt changes. Some routines are rational (using seat belts, for example) while others are irrational (totally avoiding motor travel). We try to manufacture an existence in which "the best surprise is no surprise."

Even the vocabulary of routine-oriented people differs from that of people who seek change. One person's "strange language" is another's "exotic tongue." In general, handicappers fit into two broad categories: those who look for and expect repetition, and those who search for change. The ones who are guided by continuity attempt to impose a safe routine upon the handicapping process. It is uncomfortable for them to imagine that the horse that just ran a 1:12 may tomorrow run a 1:13 or a 1:11. A radical form reversal would prompt my colleague to complain that the game was unfair, which really meant that it didn't adjust to his routine. In the same way that routine-oriented bureaucrats run the affairs of state, routine-oriented handicappers often determine the odds.

Both continuity and change play important roles in the dynamics that produce race results. However, the realities of pari-mutuel life reduce payoffs of overbet factors while increasing payoffs of underbet factors; as an underbet procedure, the projection of change is superior, in terms of investment, to the identification of continuity. To project is dynamic; to identify is static. Handicappers who project are taking certain risks, like musicians who play by ear; simple identification is like reading the music, safer and less rewarding.

Handicappers are no different than other forms of the human species. Horseplayers will seek comfort in the expectation of repetition as the traveler will feel at ease with his hamburger ritual. As a bureaucracy, the betting public attempts to turn the other way in the face of change. Yet ups and downs, not steady lines, are the feature of the brittle careers of most thoroughbred horses.

In this context, attitude is a vital component of handicapping and is inherently related to the type of horses we choose. At the racetrack it is the norm to expect the past to repeat in current performance. To win at the track, it is pari-mutuelly necessary to go against the norm, to avoid the illusory comfort that comes with following an accepted routine. Damon Runyan was totally wrong in characterizing the losing horseplayers of his stories and plays as being abnormal. The best way to lose at the races is to be normal, to follow the racetrack routine, to begin with the daily double, to write in religiously "two pounds over," to practice a literal interpretation of the handicappers' "Bible," to fervently attempt to standardize visits to the track as if they were visits to McDonald's.

The best way to avoid a ritual that inevitably will be decimated by the track "take" is to make the *projection of change* a handicapping priority. The most fundamental changes in horse performance relate to what is called, in racetrack terminology, *performance cycles*. The term is used loosely in that it does not necessarily involve a "pure" definition of "cycle," which implies a return to an original starting point or a symmetrical path. Long imprinted in handicapping language, "cycle" refers to patterns of ups and downs in the trajectory of a horse's career.

While most horseplayers will recognize the existence of performance cycles, to most players the projection of cycles is like a foreign language. Here, part of the attempt to label the different types of cycles will involve the use of a descriptive language that is intended to translate abstractions into intimate and familiar images.

Ironically, in seeking to categorize form cycles and develop methods for their projection, *Thoroughbred Cycles* must create a routine. This routine must be dynamic rather than static. It must be flexible and resilient in that it accepts an inherent contradiction: the recurrence of change. Variation and not sameness is the foundation of this methodology.

I guess that what I am saying is, not all routine equals sameness. There is something exciting about creating a new order out of chaos. Even the so-called avant-garde artists who took pride in being different followed a certain routine which involved the custom that each generation make a complete rupture with the past. By making change their icon, they created a new protocol. In going against one type of regimentation, they created another.

While the judgment of an artist's work is subjective, our work is measured by the most objective judge of all time: *return on investment* (ROI). We can take risks and explore new modes of thinking, but we cannot afford to be capricious in our experiments.

Nor can we afford to be dogmatic. Continuity and change are no different than light and dark, tall and short, the chicken and the egg; they need each other. For pari-mutuel reasons we make *change* the foundation of our methodology, but we recognize continuity as the opposite force in a delicate balance. When everything in the past performances points to radical change, we must search for the hidden continuity.

A form-cycle approach to handicapping sees past performances as histories and not merely as a series of moments in time. Some of these histories will involve romantic revivals, others tragic declines. There will be stories of heroes and antiheroes. The life passages of some of our featured competitors would have qualified for literary and historical prominence had the protagonists been people instead of horses.

I'm sorry to say that *Thoroughbred Cycles* will not be presenting a rigid routine that can be followed mechanically and bureaucratically. It will present a collection of typical horse and trainer cycles, each of which has its theme and variations. Variations will be discovered by the process of critical and judgmental handicapping which will fit within the workshop portion of the book, where readers will be asked to actively participate.

Not only do horses and trainers play a star role in this book. We the handicappers have our own cycles to confront. By becoming better aware of the orbits that whirl around us, our own orbit should find an improved trajectory. Hopefully, *Thoroughbred Cycles* will create a roller coaster in reverse, in which the horseplayers' downs will be tempered and cushioned while the ups will soar with exhilaration, overpowering the gravitational pull of the track take.

There will be one mechanical routine relating to the form-cycle methodology. At the end of each month the handicapper will need to sit down, take out a ledger, and add in the profits.

Part I
Words and Numbers

CHAPTER 1

Moving Past

As I WALKED IN I passed a uniformed guard who hardly noticed my arrival. The first thing I noticed was the climate. It seemed to adjust perfectly to the requirements of my body. Rows of desks, each with a comfortable cloth chair and individual lamp. The carpet under my feet was firm enough to make walking effortless and soft enough to cushion my lower back.

On the wall in front of the room were several monitors which changed periodically from live moving pictures to displays of words and numbers. Beneath the monitors was a row of windows, apparently for the purchase of tickets. I walked up to one of the windows and asked a lady where I could buy a *Racing Form*.

"There's no charge. Which do you want?"

I looked up at the monitors. They showed Monmouth, Saratoga, Hawthorne, and Del Mar. "Eastern and Western, please." The Eastern form was my favorite. Perhaps it was the smell of the paper or its larger page size, which related better to the infinite nature of its content.

I sat down. If you'd have seen me at that moment, as I opened the *Form*, I'd have looked like a kid opening up a Christmas present. Inside, the greatest mystery in the world. What would Einstein have discovered within these pages; why had he chosen physics instead of horse-race handicapping?

A lady came by, dressed in an unearthly costume. She asked with a tender voice if there was anything I would like. I noticed

21

that the people around me were being served by similar ladies, fresh coffee, soft drinks, mixed drinks. I asked for a tomato juice. She returned a few minutes later.

"How much is it?" I asked.

"Compliments of the house."

I took a deep breath to see if I was still alive. Could this be heaven? Was the guy at the door Saint Peter? Could these ladies be the angels?

I gave a tip to the angel.

Later I discovered other wonders about this magical place. I could construct my own bets, parlays, quinellas, almost anything I thought would fit the circumstances. At the track the possibilities were limited. I'd often come up with a fine exacta bet, only to realize that it was the first race of the triple and there was no exacta betting. Here I could "Q it."

Here, too, the monitors were larger and clearer and the call of the races was crisp and intimate. As if Trevor Denman's voice were right here in this room rather than five hundred miles away, where one could be standing right under his press box and not hear a word of his race call.

After a few days I noticed that some of the people I had seen did not return. It was then that I realized that this could not be the same heaven I had heard about as a kid. In the heaven people talk about, you earn the right to enter. In this heaven, you earn the right to stay. No wonder the uniformed guard at the entrance did not check my credentials.

So, I was still alive. I asked myself, What if I lived a good and correct life and qualified for heaven? How were they going to offer an improvement from this place here on earth? No doubt they'll have climate control and low overhead, but action at tracks across the country? I doubt it.

Several years later I walked out of a Lake Tahoe race book as the sun was setting. Back inside there was still night action from New Jersey. A short walk and I was settled on the same rocks I had seen year after year. From this position on the rock formation the ripples on the lake seemed to move inward and disappear. As the sun vanished behind the mountains I marveled at how I had found such stillness, so near to so much action.

The light that remained after the sun had gone covered everything with softness. The mountains were now fading purple profiles outlined by a delicate thread of light. They had lost their jagged edges. The water seemed to lose its movement as the last soft ripple went under and the surface faded from distant pink into slate black. The stillness and silence of a boat on the horizon suggested that the people inside lived a timeless existence. The stones under my feet contributed to my feeling of continuity and security.

Everything had become solid and immobile, as if an eternal present tense had arrived and nothing would ever change.

But at this very moment of stillness the lake and its nearby underground springs were tearing away at the mountains and the soil. The rock under my feet was vulnerable, not destined to be there forever.

And here, under my arm, were the past performances, which were much like the rocks in the mountains around Lake Tahoe. They presented an illusion that reality was immobile, that numbers represented fixed abilities of horses. They emphasized that horses were to be expected to continue performing at a certain capacity, but they deemphasized that horses were also expected to change their performance levels.

Three years for the rocks under my feet represented a minute period in geological time. Ten races in the past performances of a horse represented an inadequate period within which to observe the *movement* and *pattern* of its career. A horse's previous peak performance period may have occurred 14 races ago. And 15, 16, and 17 races ago may give us a clue as to how this horse arrives at its peak, abruptly or gradually. Thirteen and 12 races back may tell us how long this horse can maintain its top form. And its first career race may tell us how he will run today, following a layoff. Eighteen races back may show us that today's rider won with the same horse, the only time he ever rode him. Or it may tell us that the horse's last victory came stretching out from six furlongs to 1⅛ miles, precisely the distance of today's race.

As the underground mountain springs make an impact on the visible terrain, undercurrents affecting the direction of a horse's career may be hidden between the lines of the past performances or buried in separate sources of information. For example, what a particular trainer has achieved with other horses may have a direct bearing on the chances of the horse he runs today. And within the past performances themselves, which of the ten listed races is most representative of how the horse will do today? The answer is right there in the *Form*, and yet you can't see it unless you can read the secret signs that reveal the direction in which the horse's performance pattern is moving. The racetrack itself, an apparent passive witness, may at time become a primary participant in determining the rise and fall of certain horses, the way the soft and caressing tide nonchalantly changes the shore and the mountains around it.

The format of the *Racing Form* encourages a static reading of the past, as if history were a series of chronological but isolated events rather than an ebbing and flowing of interrelated currents. The past is fractured, as significant pieces of information are confined to chronological order instead of conceptual order.

One way to miss the inner flow of the past is to overemphasize numbers. In the past performances, numbers function like the stones on the shore. They are hard data, but they are not as "hard" as they seem, and sometimes become brittle. The same numbers that sometimes produce great handicapping may create an illusion that they represent unchanging truths, that yesterday's number translates literally into tomorrow's reality. Numbers may become the icon of the handicapper.

Horseplayers find refuge in the belief in numbers for several reasons:

1. We live in a number-oriented society in which narrative truths are overshadowed by numerical truths. Unemployment statistics are a good example. Homeless people are not included in the percentage of unemployed because they are simply not part of the same statistic. So they become a footnote when unemployment is referred to on the news. We give more value to a number that is distorted than to a sensible observation.

2. Numbers encourage averaging. An average is a static figure that evens out the ups and downs. "Average earnings per race" is the gross national product of horse racing. One big win distorts the image represented by the number in the way that one successful industry—such as military hardware—may create the illusion that all of us are living well, when it is averaged together with other less successful industries.

   "Best average earnings per race" as a handicapping factor yields a terrible flat-bet loss because it obliterates the whole form-cycle factor. Many a washed-up Breeders' Cup winner will suck in millions of dollars in bets based on his past earnings, which mask the fact that the horse is presently on the decline.

3. Numbers are easier to use literally than analytically. For this reason, finish position and lengths behind are overbet factors. They appear to tell us an obvious truth with overwhelming finality when, in fact, they only give a one-dimensional picture, and a distorted one at that! The maiden that finished second twice in a row may be no nearer to the winners' circle than the one that finished fourth as a first-time starter. Which of these two is most likely to improve? Numbers just don't give us enough information. "Finish position last race" and "lengths behind" are like stones on the side of a mountain, above a sign that reads Beware of Falling Rocks.

4. Numbers, in the format of statistics, highlight the characteristics of *sets*, which portray a very generalized "truth." But all sets are composed of *subsets*. Horse racing does not differ from any other sector of reality; its subsets are often opposites or antagonists in the groups they belong to, yangs within a yin. Consider some powerful examples of statistics in relationship to the subsets they hide within:

	Set	Subset
Layoffs	Horses run poorly following a layoff	A particular type of horse runs its best race after a layoff
Cold Jockeys	Slumping riders are bad bets, even on good horses	The same rider who can't seem to win for most stables, can't lose for one particular trainer
Maiden, 2nd in Last Race	Wins more than fair share of races	Hanger, chronic seconditis horse, terrible bet
Class Drop	Wins more than fair share of races	Rapidly declining horses, up for sale, bad bet
Low-Percentage Trainer	Virtual tossout in handicapping	Has high-percentage success rate in one particular category, makes an excellent bet
Dull Current Form (Out-of-$ Chronically)	Terrible bet	Several types of horses sharply improve in this context because of unique form cycles
Best Adjusted Speed Figure	Wins more than fair share of races	Certain types of form cycles project poor races following peak efforts as elsewhere

This represents but a partial list of the many subsets that will contradict the general statistic they belong to. These apparent exceptions are viewed by the crowd as abnormal or irrational events that make horse racing an irrational game. This point of view is not only philosophically wrong, it is pari-mutuelly fatal. In horse racing, no statistic is monolithic and all numbers are like atoms with counteracting forces. When a contradictory outcome knocks us out of a Pick 6, it does not mean that our numbers were "wrong," only that they were insufficient, that a subset came to the surface at a particular moment.

Most profitable subsets relate to unique form cycles. Here, whenever possible, we will search for new, more specialized numbers to describe and categorize winning subsets. If the meteorologist can predict a sunny day in Seattle, then we should be able to forecast layoff winners. If the medical researcher can discover medicinal value in a poisonous plant, we should be able to isolate the winning moments of no-win horses.

In other words, thoroughbred cycles' methodologies will not be antinumber, simply opposed to the deceptive and demagogic use of numbers. Ultimately, all natural phenomena have a material explanation. If ghosts have truly appeared, then there will be a material explanation for their appearance. If Vilzak, 2 for 27 lifetime, can enter and win a Grade 1 stakes race, there will be a rational reason.

The language of numbers, in its current format, is not yet imaginative enough to capture certain concepts. In these cases our form-cycle methods will resort to narrative techniques of analysis to uncover profitable subsets. At this current stage in the development of horse-race handicapping, both numbers and words are vital tools for the handicapper. In the grammar of horse-race analysis, both numbers and words are integral parts of speech that contribute to the clarity of thought essential to successful handicapping.

PAST PERFORMANCES: POP ART WITH A MESSAGE

In my office you will find a work of art, an enlargement of past performances, framed and hung where you can see it when you walk in. Numbers play a prominent role in this work of art, for, in spite of my diatribe against numerical determinism, numbers are the basis of handicapping. Past performance numbers are graceful and should be valued for their imagery more than for the mathematics they encourage.

Framed in my numerical masterpiece are images of courage and cowardice, images of power and weakness, images of grace and pride, triumph and tragedy.

For the horseplayer these numbers represent great drama. Consider the following numerical image:

$$4^3 \qquad 7^8 \qquad 6^4 \qquad 1^2$$

as it compares with:

$$1^2 \qquad 1^3 \qquad 1^1 \qquad 2^{\frac{1}{2}}$$

The first represents a heroic drama with a happy ending, while the second tells of a heartbreaking tragedy. The personalities of the actors in these dramas are often so associated with their numerical running lines that experienced handicappers could conceivably play "Name That Horse" when shown particular running lines. Even the casual racegoer might associate

$$9^{17} \qquad 8^{12} \qquad 5^6 \qquad 1^2$$

with the famous Silky Sullivan, while old-timers might relate the same numbers to Maxwell G, who in his teens was still repeating the lines of the above drama, at Sportsmans Park, Cicero, Illinois.

Numbers in Movement

In the same way that the Lake Tahoe landscape seemed immobile, my past performance landscape appears to hang still. For handicappers who deal with numbers statically, it represents a still life. For those who see numbers in movement, it tells a story.

Consider two horses that have just faced each other twice and are entered in the same race for the third time today:

A	19Apr	6^4	4^3	3^2	3^3	1:12.2
	6Apr	4^3	3^3	2^1	2^2	1:12.1
B	19Apr	3^2	3^3	4^3	4^4	1:12.3
	6Apr	8^7	7^5	6^4	6^5	1:13

A won both matches, earning the best speed figure each time, but B is an improving horse. On April 6, A got the jump on B. But B showed superior early speed on April 19. B's final times and finish positions are improving while A is going nowhere and showing signs of decline.

Handicappers who use final time as a foundation for their selections need to decide which particular running line best represents the horse's chances in today's race; if speed figures are seen statistically and not as part of a progression, there is a higher risk of extracting a running line *out of context*, and thus arriving at a false number. In the case of the improving B, one could argue that a most representative speed figure might be extracted from his previous peak performance rather than from his last race, since his numbers are currently ascending.

In the case of A, what shall we do if his most recent speed figure turns out to be the best of the field? The personality that is embedded in his running lines is that of a horse with talent but no punch, a horse that may lose no matter how slow the rest of the field runs. The *image* of A hanging in the stretch speaks louder than the apparent proficiency of the *numbers* that represent his final times.

Context

On the other hand, this apparently negative sign in A's running lines may have been taken out of context. What if the April 6 race had followed a layoff? As we shall study later, a sharp comeback race is frequently followed by a letdown or "bounce." If this were the case with A, then the handicapper should be projecting a number that will be superior to the figures earned on April 19 and April 6. The context broadens even more if it is discovered that, throughout his career, a peak effort can be expected from A in the third race following the layoff. Now the context of pertinent information may extend beyond the ten races listed in the past performances. Two opposite patterns are possible: the one that projects a past performance third time back, and an opposite pattern which tells us that A runs his best races *right after a layoff*. If the first case is true, A will improve today, but if the latter proves true, today's race will produce a declining number.

Horseplayers who extract numbers out of context will come

up with brittle numbers. And when the race produces a change and the expected number crumbles, the bettor will complain that it's all a crapshoot. For this type of player the latest par times, variants, and sophisticated speed-figure methodologies will be rendered useless; he would do better to choose horses at random and, in that way, only lose 16 percent of his total investment.

Superior handicappers who are practitioners of methodologies based on final time, pace, or class, as different as they are from each other, will have the common need to choose the appropriate running line from within a logical context of the progression of form. Choosing the proper running line is the least mechanical and most analytical component of the handicapping trade. It is based on the contextual evaluation of potentially contradictory running lines.

The concept of form cycle offers a perspective for viewing numbers in movement, within a context. As the most dynamic factor in handicapping, form cycle can also be the foundation for successful methodologies in which pace, class, and adjusted final times play important but secondary roles. These form-related methodologies will be studied in very concrete terms in the workshop portion of this book, which will follow a series of foundational chapters that will research, analyze, and categorize the types of form-cycle patterns most typical for thoroughbred race horses.

The concept of form cycle covers the total picture of ups and downs in race-horse careers, and overlaps, too, with the ups and downs in the careers of trainers. Form-cycle analysis has an important economic foundation in handicapping, as it anticipates and projects peak moments of horses and their trainers *before they become obvious*, before they lose their pari-mutuel value. The more static of final-time and class methods will tend to identify these peaks after they become evident to the public, when they are already in the process of losing their pari-mutuel value. In the worst cases, these methods will point to a momentary reality at the time it is already in process of decomposition.

The material information that is the basis of form-cycle analysis resides in the dynamic flow of numbers and events. These moving pictures can be best understood in the context of a diverse set of prototypical horse and trainer patterns that make up the core of this book. The major component of handicapping as an *art* can thus relate best to music, which moves, rather than painting or sculpture, which are fixed. The component of cycle analysis, which is a *science*, can best relate to meteorology or economics, sciences of probability, rather than chemistry or algebra, which are deterministic. Class, pace, and final times gravitate toward deterministic analysis, while form-cycle handicapping sees reality as made up of different potential scenarios.

ASCENDING NUMBERS

Here are some typical situations in which the flow of numbers from previous races points to a peak performance today. Although there are more esoteric ways of calculating fractional and final times, we shall use the standard "⅕ second = 1 length" formula. To seek a more precise calculating method based on *Racing Form* calls, which are not precise to begin with, may lead to a false idolatry of numbers. We are not interested so much in the number itself as the flow in which it occurs, the image that the number creates.

1. Horse shows successive improvement in final times, perhaps accompanied by a parallel improvement in finish position. Be careful that the reason for the improvement is not simply the result of better pace opportunity. For example, a front runner who finds a paceless field will improve its final time without necessarily improving its form.
2. Early speed is carried for progressively longer distances.

2^1	1^1	3^4	7^8
2^2	2^3	7^8	8^{12}
1^1	6^8	8^{11}	8^{14}

3. Sudden improvement in fractions.
   a. Four-furlong fraction improves several ticks (for example, from 46^4 to a 46^1).
   b. Improved *turn time* (second call of a six-furlong race, at most tracks). The following horse, which we shall study later, triple-jumped to a long-shot victory off these lines:

Fractions of leader

21^1	44^1	1:10	7Feb88	3^2	3^{nk}	$1^{1/2}$	1^{nk}
22	45^2	1:16.4	24Jan88	$2^{1/2}$	$1^{1/2}$	1^2	$1^{2 1/2}$

While the first-call fraction of our horse went from 22^1 in his first race to a 21^3 in his second ($2^{1/2}$ ticks improve), the second-call fractions went from 45^2 to 44^1 (6 ticks improve). This horse's turn time on January 24 was approximately 23^2, while its turn time one race later was a fabulous 22^3 (a 4-tick improvement). Turn time is probably the most underrated and therefore most valuable of fractions. But in spite of the impressive times, if these two races had been reversed chronologically, we'd have been dealing with a declining horse.

  c. Six-furlong fraction within a route is faster than previous 6F sprint times of the same horse. (Generally, interior fractions should be slower, since the longer the race, the slower the pace.)

There are many types of variations on the theme of fractions, for the obvious reason that there are so many types of interior fractions. For example, a horse shortening up from 6½ to six furlongs may have run an improved six-furlong fraction in its previous race and then eased up for the final sixteenth. This and other fractional times don't appear in the past performances but are clearly denoted in the results charts. For example, the quarter-mile fraction of a route is another piece of information that appears in charts but not in past performances. Any number that does not show up in the pps becomes enhanced in value because it is scarce knowledge. Fractional times that are ignored by the public function like powerful undercurrents which impact the topography without ever being seen. Handicappers looking for hidden form improvement will relish experimenting with interior fractions.

4. Workout improvements (especially powerful impact upon maidens).

  a. The recent six-furlong workout is faster than the horse's 6F race times that preceded the work.

  b. The recent four-furlong workout is faster than the 4F fraction of the race that preceded it.

Of course, all of these numbers are gross figures that may need adjustments according to track bias and variant information. Personally, I do not use track variants in a systematic way, for I find that by working with too many numbers—often secondary numbers which turn out to be of little use—I may miss one important number, the way a beautiful tree may be lost in an immense forest.

Instant variants

When I see a fraction or final time that strikes me as atypical, I automatically do an "instant variant." For example, if I were to doubt the validity of the turn time we have just highlighted, I would turn to my charts from the two racing days in question and compare my horse's fractions/final times with those of superior and inferior fields from the same card. If I had discovered, for example, that maiden claimers had run a 44.1 half-mile on February 7, then I would conclude that my horse's 44.1 was a mirage. On the other hand, if I had discovered that stakes horses that same day had run 44.4, then suddenly I'd see my horse's 44.1 in neon lights on my personal marquee. When doing daily variants, numbers file by in an abstract parade. By doing instant variants, numbers become vibrant images.

Bias

This is one of the most misinterpreted concepts in horse racing. Three favorites win in a row, wire to wire, and pay $3.60, $4.40, and $4.80, and you'll hear hundreds of guys around the grandstand repeating the same cliché: "the speed is sticking." This is nonsense. The odds clearly tell us that it was simply a case of the best horses winning; they happened to have been front runners.

The only time a bias exists is when horses that *shouldn't win* are winning. Then a common running style or post position may be more than coincidental. A series of front-running long shots in the winners' circle along with a bunch of off-the-pace favorites somewhere "up the track" means there is a bias favoring front runners. The odds tell the story. The reverse would mean a bias in favor of closers (long-shot closers winning, front-running favorites failing).

While the reasons for bias may be mysterious, there is no mystery about its identification. It is the track, playing a major role now in the races, which favors one running style or post/ part of the track. There are two ways to make money from a bias situation.

1. Bet the running style favored by the bias until the bias has subsided.
2. Follow up by betting the horse whose running style was defeated by the bias (after there is a fair track, of course).

The toughest part about track bias is not keeping up with it; any competent observer can do that, with a good memory or with clear note taking. What is difficult is to be willing to bet on horses that "look bad." Psychologically we have been so conditioned to look for the best horse, that we must confront some powerful anxieties in order to put our money on another horse, one which is inherently inferior. Often the horse favored by the bias may have a no-win rider or a terrible recent record. Consequently, many a $1000 exacta will include horses that were carried to victory by a bias or that ran against the undertow in their previous race, horses that don't figure unless the handicapper comes to terms with the fact that on many occasions the track itself becomes the primary handicapping factor.

This means that the context in which numbers are interpreted will be altered. It also means that horse and trainer cycles may encounter a wobble in their orbit as the track cycle exerts its force. Turf courses may begin a meet with tall grass which favors closers and end the meet in a pounded-down condition which favors early speed. At some tracks there is little or no discrimination against running styles or post positions, but others, such as Del Mar, go through phases and are never without some sort of slant. Even at Santa Anita, which is supposed to have outlawed discrimination, I have seen three weeks go by without one rail horse winning; then the bias disappears, the way the common cold arrives irrationally and then subsides and is gone.

The literature of horse-race handicapping is laden with insightful expositions on track bias and variant, so the reader is directed toward the classic works of Beyer, Davidowitz, and Quirin, as well as the recent discoveries of Sartin and Brohamer; the theme of bias and variant is tangential to the core material of *Thoroughbred Cycles*, so we shall deal with it at appropriate points throughout the book. While we are on the theme of numbers in movement, we have emphasized the point that bias and variant may induce a glitch in the normal upward or downward progression of a horse's performance figures.

DESCENDING NUMBERS

Betting favorites are generally horses in top form. They usually display high speed ratings and/or top earnings. They lose 67 percent of the time. There are two possible reasons for the defeat of a betting favorite:

1. *Internal.* The horse itself had already peaked and is now on the decline in its form cycle.
2. *External.* Bad luck, trouble, bad ride, wrong setting (distance, surface), sudden change in track conditions.

Go to the grandstand and take a voice vote as to whether 1 or 2 is the primary cause of defeat, and the clear majority will vote for the second:

"Shoemaker's a bum. The human anchor."

"They stiffed him. They're goin' for a big price next time."

"Got into traffic . . . bad luck."

Some horseplayers believe the reason is totally external. They blame their wife, their biorhythm. "The favorite won the last race, so he was 'due' to lose."

"Whenever I bet on Delahoussaye, he loses. Whenever I don't bet on him, he wins. I'm gonna move to another track where he's not riding."

I've heard all this and more. But very rarely does one hear comments to the effect that the beaten favorite must have passed his peak form. If the public is correct and form cycle is of little consequence in the defeat of a favorite, the next time out the same horse should be a profitable investment.

In order to tell whether favorites are beaten because of internal form decline or external reasons of no bearing on form, I studied a random sample of 500 beaten favorites in the next race. A form-cycle decline would mean that the next race should be poor; a loss due to extenuating circumstances should mean that the next race would show an improvement.

In order to test the public's ability to judge beaten favorites, I divided the original sample into two subsets, those horses supported by the public (odds of 7–2 or less) and those rejected by the crowd (odds of above 7–2). In theory, those beaten favorites that receive action in their next race should outperform those the public has decided are no longer fit to bet. The results of the study were as follows:

Sample:	500 horses
Winners:	93 (just under 19%)
Invested:	$1000 (based on minimum $2 wager)
Return:	760
Loss:	$ 240
ROI:	−24%

This percentage of loss makes the betting favorite an investment inferior to random selection.

Beaten Favorites Receiving Action (253 horses)
Winners: *68* (nearly 27%)
Beaten Favorites Not Getting Action (247 horses)
Winners: *25* (a bit over 10%)

Apparently, the public knows what it is doing. Only apparently, for both subsets came out with virtually the *same return on investment*, once more, minus 24%. In other words, horses from both subsets ran worse than their odds, to the same degree.

Beaten favorites simply do not produce at the level that their performance numbers say they should. The implication is that when a favorite loses, declining form is more to blame than extenuating circumstances. Two thirds of all favorites will lose because all too often the public expects a previous peak in form to continue. The public has spotted these horses after the fact, when it is too late.

In the realm of numbers, watch for mild declines in speed and pace figures as if they are the first raindrops preceding the storm.

DECEIVING NUMBERS

A type of horse we call the "proven loser" will be a featured antihero in later chapters, but let him make his first appearance while the discussion is focused on numbers. By "proven loser" we don't mean a horse that can't win, but one that keeps trying at a particular level and cannot break through the invisible barrier the class of competition holds before him.

This type has an intriguing personality worthy of the lead role in a feature film or a great stage tragedy. He is blessed with some measure of talent, occasionally with brilliant skills. But somewhere in the stretch drive he politely moves over and lets at least one of his rivals pass by. For the proven loser, it's not whether you win or lose but how you play the game. The herding instinct in this character tells him to be a follower rather than a leader.

Most proven losers will be found at the bottom rung of a particular class category, which means they can't be dropped any lower without having to ship out or risk being claimed.

   a. Lowest level of maiden claimers
   b. Lowest level of claiming ranks
      (These two groups have nowhere to drop, unless they leave their current racing circuit and attempt to be a bigger fish in a smaller pond.)
   c. Lowest levels of allowance conditions
      (These horses can be dropped, but with the risk of being purchased for a claiming price.)

Occasionally you'll find proven losers at other levels, where by chance or design of the trainer they've remained over a period of time without being dropped. They may be paying their bills, at least at subsistence level, with minor purses for in-the-money finishes, so there will be more to lose by dropping them in class. Many of these types are talented, so they will finish races deceivingly near and yet so far from actually winning.

James Quinn, in his *Handicapper's Condition Book*, did the pioneer studies that led to the identification of this type of horse. Convinced of the validity of Quinn's work, I still need to recheck the concept in my own way in order to acquire a more intimate understanding and to update the validity. Specifically, I wanted to study a particular type of proven loser, one that displays the performance numbers of an improving horse, which figures to attract betting action. I was searching for an objective type of elimination, one that would allow me to throw out apparent contenders and thus gain a percentage advantage.

In theory, going into a race, the proven loser will often have the best speed figures from a recent losing effort and may appear to be the sharpest horse in the field. The theory says that this character has the talent to earn successful numbers but possesses a type of class consciousness that prohibits him from fighting it out against his peers; he will run but not duel. If the theory is correct, the class factor will now eclipse the speed and form factors.

I took a random sample of 100 proven losers, only using those horses that were *peaking in form*, by demanding an in-the-money and competitive last race. Horses must have:

1. Lost at least 3 recent races *at today's level*
2. Finished *in-the-money* and run competitively in their *last race*

Sample:	100 horses
Winners:	15 (15%)
Invested:	$200 (based on minimum $2 wager)
Return:	110
Loss:	$ 90
ROI:	−45%

Here we have rediscovered a fabulous elimination, one that will clearly lead to an investment advantage. Reason: this type of horse gets heavy action. Only seven horses in the sample went off at 8–1 or up. Thirty-one of them were 3–1 or below. Of five odds-on "locks," only one of them won. The average but infrequent mutuel was $7.33.

There are several lessons here for the form-cycle handicapper.

1. With this type of horse, *improving numbers* don't usually progress to a winning peak.
2. A one-level drop to class levels that contain most proven losers becomes especially potent because (a) Dropper encounters easy pickings, horses that don't belong, and (b) the public perceives a one-level drop to the bottom as insignificant, since the lesser dollar amounts of the class drop cover up its extraordinary class advantage.
3. We will later discover what is implied by this study, that many of these proven losers can win at lower levels. Bottom-of-the-barrel losers who ship and drop will fre-

quently discover what it is like to win and gain a new feeling of competitiveness. This revival will sometimes take them back up to the class level at which they were failures and find them beating the same horses to whom they had previously lost.

In the intricate web of currents and countercurrents that coalesce to produce the ups and downs of thoroughbred cycles, numbers only represent some of the threads, only one dimension of a very complex and often contradictory story. As human beings, we may think of horses as simple beings with few psychological variations; but the profusion of distinct types of performance cycles implies that horse psychology is far more complex than we've assumed. Horses can't talk, but they can express their feelings in the way they run a race.

NARRATIVE HISTORIES: THE EPIC OF RACING

Even the most fanatical of numerical handicappers will recognize that there are intangibles and undercurrents that affect the phases of a thoroughbred's career; since this is evident, perhaps words might better express the realities of the past performances than numbers. I listen to the experts around me who share their analysis of a race, and even the ones with computers and complex algorithms use words rather than numbers for the foundation of their arguments.

Although horses lack human intelligence, they are closer to being people than they are to being automobiles. A car does miles per hour, a horse gallops. Granted that some horses "run out of gas" in the stretch, but other become "fainthearted" or "quit." True, some horses "accelerate" on the far turn, but others "charge gallantly" into the stretch. Did Alysheba recover from a stumble caused by "traffic" in the Kentucky Derby because he had "good shock absorbers" or did he rebound from the interference because of "competitive spirit"?

While automobile vocabulary is used on occasion by sports writers as a metaphor for events in horse racing, human-related vocabulary sounds less like a cliché and is nearer to realistic expression than the language of cars. Since horses are living creatures, perhaps language rather than arithmetic will bring us closer to the essence of thoroughbred behavior.

When analyzing the past performances, handicappers are more likely to translate numbers to words than the other way around, because words are more likely to uncover the mysteries of living creatures. If intelligent beings from outer space were to take back a copy of the *Racing Form* to their planet, their anthropologists would be more likely to label it as an example of epic poetry than mathematics.

We have seen how numbers come together to form graceful images of the history of thoroughbred race horses. Now let us explore the past performances through the medium of language. Perhaps through the approach of a story we might understand the nature of thoroughbred cycles from a new dimension.

In the *Racing Form* as it is currently structured, language functions as an adjunct of numbers. At the base of the results charts are brief narrative descriptions of races which may or may not include comments on all horses entered. Within the past performances, brief trip and trouble comments such as "wide" and "took up" are notable in their economy of language and can be related to the numbers that represent the horses' pace lines.

On separate pages of the *Form* we find articles that involve interviews with trainers and riders or "human" interest commentary on horse careers. On some occasions this information is vital to handicappers; trainer Smith comments that he has just gelded this horse, and subsequent workouts show great improvement. Other articles simply function as racing's society pages and are of little or no value to the horseplayer.

It is clear that the *Racing Form* publishers have made conscientious efforts to organize numerical information while leaving narrative data in disarray. It is enlightening to compare this perspective with that found in French racing forms. Perhaps the French culture is more narrative and less numerical than ours. Various racing papers such as *Paris-Turf* and *Week-End* are lacking in some basic numerical data that U.S. horseplayers expect to have available, such as running lines and lengths behind at interior sectors of the race. On the other hand, French publications set "word" information within a much more meaningful format.

1. Each past performance race names the six instead of the three top finishers.
2. Listed past performance races are not as spare in their pace and trip comments.
3. For the more important races, most papers include each

horse's trainer's analysis—specifically, form comments—
within past performances; candid comments such as "My
horse is not quite at his peak" take some of the guesswork
away from form-cycle analysis.
4. Results charts include a lengthier narrative description of
the race, highlighting pace comments with words—the
way our charts suggest with numbers—and charts include
a photograph of the field at the finish line.
5. Numerically, the only factor with which the French racing
papers outdo ours concerns trainer and jockey stats. First,
all trainers and riders are listed. Second, for followers of
trainer and rider cycles, current losing streaks are listed for
each entry. An "O," for example, means that the rider or
trainer has won his/her last race; a 46 means that he has
lost that many races in a row. At one glance handicappers
can tell who's cold and who may be hot.

Surprisingly, trainers are candid about crucial form-cycle factors that in the U.S. are often shrouded in mystery. The winner
of the 1988 L'Arc de Triomphe, *Tony Bin*, at 14–1, carried the
following trainer comment in the form: "Luigi Camici has let us
know that he considers his horse stronger than ever, at five years
of age . . . that he is in his best form," a significant commentary,
considering that Tony Bin had finished second to Trempolino in
the previous year's Arc.
A few days later I bet on a horse by the name of Slipalex, to
win. The trainer had commented that his horse was not quite in
an ideal moment and that "an in-the-money finish would satisfy
me." To me that quote seemed like the evasive type of trainer
comment I am used to disregarding in the United States. To my
chagrin, Slipalex finished third and paid the equivalent of $9.20.
Consider one more example of how numbers can be subjective and misleading while words and narration become a more
objective medium of information. November 2, 1988: The day's
trifecta (called *tierce* in French) looks like a cinch, with the three
top choices figuring to be right there at the wire. But in trifectas,
a mystery horse inevitably pops into the top three, with highly
competent handicappers holding losing tickets with a first-third-
fourth finish. The *meat* of the trifecta sandwich is a horse that
just did not figure.
This day's mystery horse was *Quatalinska*. Only 1 in-the-
money finish in her last 10, Quatalinska had shown a mild im-

provement two races back, if you can call eighth place an improvement. In her next race, immediately prior to today's event, she had run a forward race and then dropped completely out of sight. The past performance comment was *"inexistante,"* hardly encouraging. But trainers are interviewed for all trifecta races, and Quatalinska's trainer offered an excuse. "She had had a tough race a short time prior to her last effort, so we *didn't insist.* She's well placed here, and I won't hide the fact that I have been waiting for this particular race. So pay careful attention."

The crowd didn't pay attention and Quatalinska went off at 21–1, finished second in a field of nineteen. The second favorite had won and the third choice came in third. Quatalinska sparked a huge trifecta, and the proper information was available to the handicapper, in the form of words that had explained how the numbers were misleading.

In the U.S. we horseplayers deserve comprehensive narrative information to go along with our well-designed numerical data. We are naive to think that numbers can tell the whole story. If there is any one area in which the horseplayer/consumer is most seriously abused, it is certainly in the poverty of narrative information. And of all types of data formats, the medium of language functions best for the description of form cycle.

What I propose is to extend the medium of words from the descriptive to the narrative, from images to histories. My feeling is that the "story" format helps collect the isolated bits of *Racing Form* information into a meaningful sequence. Consider the following narrative history of a race whose key was found in the form-cycle factor.

Santa Anita, ninth race, January 24, 1988 (Grade 3). This race is but one act in an ongoing drama whose characters confront each other on different terms each time. The winner is the one who feels best at the time, the one who is reaching a peak. A narrative approach helps us to discover where these characters are going and not just where they were at.

Forlitano

Forlitano was the victim of cultural shock when he arrived in New York from his native Argentina in 1985. You'd think the city life of the Big Apple would have been a minor transition from a cosmopolitan place such as Buenos Aires; but Forlitano could not adjust to the opposite hemisphere and finished last in three races. The nearest he came to the leader was seventeen lengths. The fact that one of those three races was a grade 1 implied that great things were expected of Forlitano. It was an understatement to say that he was an underachiever. With his level of performance, he was helping to provide more employment for American horses by making them look better than they were.

The Argentine Embassy refused to help, so Mr. Charles Whittingham, known for his professional care of foreign boarders, took him in and got him used to the way of life of the Northern Hemisphere. Forlitano came back to the races in July 1986, this time in a more hospitable California. The crowd saw he had failed to make any impact in his U.S. races and made him 9–1. Forlitano won that comeback race. But such a competitive effort after such a long vacation might have taken something out of him, because his next four races were mediocre. Then, two second-place finishes led up to a Christmas Eve competition in which Forlitano went off at 14–1. Another surprise victory, followed up with another win on February 5 to celebrate the New Year and establish him as one of the top classified-allowance competitors.

At this crest in his career Forlitano forgot completely that he had suffered through two periods of depression. The American Dream was alive in his competitive spirit, and classified allowance was not enough. He tried restricted stakes twice, coming close both times. The third time he conquered that plateau. But the process of growth is also the process of decline; each day that a living being matures it is also a day nearer its death.

In the rise of Forlitano were the seeds of his decline. Twice during this period of ascent he was a beaten favorite; in the second restricted stakes and in a subsequent try at Grade 2. He continued to leave handicappers with mixed messages as he traveled up to Golden Gate to win with ease a Grade 3 event.

There was no turning back now. On July 27, 1987, Forlitano tried Grade 1, 1½ miles. The crowd made him 7–1 against the favored entry of Rivlia and Swink. These were his grazing companions, his drinking companions, residing in the same Whittingham stable. In order for Forlitano to advance one step further in his American Dream, he would have to topple his roommates.

Fourth at the half-mile, Forlitano made a steady and powerful move to take the lead at the mile and a quarter. He seemed to hold on gamely, putting away Rivlia in a stretch. But a powerful move by Swink left Forlitano in second place, two lengths behind at the finish line. Forlitano had defeated Rivlia, a proven Grade 1 performer, so a second-place finish was no discouragement.

Once again he would try for the highest of glory, traveling to Illinois to run in the Grade 1 Arlington Million. At 22–1, his moment of glory ended before the finish line; at the mile the rest of the field began to catch up with him and he faded to last . . . memories of those bitter days in New York. Still another Grade 1 race saw him face Rivlia, in October 1987 at Santa Anita. Once more things seemed to fall apart. Not only did Rivlia get his revenge, but two other horses of much less status also finished ahead of Forlitano. At 7–2, his fifth-place finish was worse than his odds. He had tried Grade 1 three times now, without ever having won a Grade 2.

When you get so close to your goal and can't make it, life seems cruel. A lowly claimer without the expectations of Forlitano could never understand his unhappiness. Although he seemed to be falling as much as rising, Forlitano was too competitive to give up. On November 24, 1987, at Hollywood Park, he had his chance to go up one notch instead of two, in a Grade 2 event. He won, gamely, cleverly. He was now materially one step closer to his Grade 1 goal; and yet, more seeds of decline were apparent. The time of this Grade 2 win was mediocre, and the second- and third-place finishers were not legitimate Grade 2 horses; in fact, they probably belonged at the classified-allowance level, where, it seemed like ages ago, Forlitano began his climb. Each step upward seemed to be a step downward in a weird geometry of his performance cycle.

Yet Forlitano continued to move upward on what appeared to be a treadmill. He entered the Grade 1 Hollywood Park Turf Cup Invitational. This was his fourth try at Grade 1. In the stretch he captured the lead! Hoofbeats could be heard from behind as Forlitano put away one rival only to be confronted by another. It was only *Vilzak*, a horse with a dismal 2 for 26 record lifetime and 0 for 16 in 1987. In order to win his Grade 1 race, Forlitano had to fight off the rush of a horse that only three months before was a loser of a Keeneland allowance race. The two horses ran in tandem as they crossed the wire. The photo sign flashed, but any guy in the crowd with binoculars could see that Vilzak was the winner.

For what seems like an eternity, Forlitano has been showing signs of improvement and signs of decline simultaneously. A second-place Grade 1 finish seems pretty close to glorious, but a heartbreaking defeat to a horse which was mediocre before today's race and would be mediocre after it is a discouraging sign. Has Forlitano been improving or has the crop of horses he's faced been declining? Depending on your angle of view, he is either going up or down.

And this is the moment in Forlitano's life when he is entered in the Grade 3 San Marcos Handicap. With him in the field are his colleagues Rivlia and Swink, who have just finished in back of the pack in the Vilzak race. Things are tense back at the stable as Forlitano, the newcomer, now rivals his grazing partners.

Rivlia and Swink

These two, as an entry, will go off as the 5–2 favorite in the San Marcos, in spite of their loss to Forlitano. They are the only two Grade 1 winners in the field. They also have the highest average earnings per race. If "class" were equivalent to a lifetime batting average, these two would leave the rest of the field behind; but both have had up-and-down careers and have lost three races in a row. By living together and running together, these two have become like each other. Last summer Swink reached a peak just before Rivlia, and beat his buddy when Forlitano finished second, sandwiched between the two. But now both Swink and Rivlia are declining commodities, with Rivlia descending gradually and Swink plunging; so Rivlia, in losing efforts, has finished ahead of Swink in their last two races. The crowd believes that today Mr. Whittingham will turn it around for these two Grade 1 winners; but in entering them at Grade 3, the trainer has sent a message of declining expectations. The crowd misses the message and chooses to ignore the entire concept of form cycle and the money pours in on these declining stars.

Schiller

I have known Schiller personally for four years now. I first met him when he was a maiden. I had noticed a fair degree of talent; one lazy Hollywood Park afternoon I invested in his fortunes. In the stretch he looked like a winner, as the two horses in front of him were tiring badly. He was right there, but *he did not want to pass*. Was he being polite, or did he feel pity for his rivals? They hit the wire together.

The photo sign went up, but I had seen enough. Schiller was either second or third. From the top deck of the Pavillion at Hollywood Park, it looks like all horses are hanging at the wire. So when Schiller did his act, he looked like heavy, wet blue jeans on a clothesline. I shouted down from the Pavillion: "Schiller, you're a future claimer." Schiller's "Song of Joy" seemed off-key.

I was wrong. I did not consider that Schiller's trainer, Vivian Pulliam, tends to race her horses slightly above their capacity and just waits and hopes to encounter fields of declining horses. Consequently, her horses, such as Le Cid, win about once a year but finish second and third with greater frequency, paying their bills with the quantity of their labors more than with the quality.

Somehow Schiller made it to the stakes ranks and stayed there. In 1986 he went 0 for 16 and nevertheless had a successful year. On September 1, at Grade 2, he finished second by a nose at 77–1. On November 3 he finished second, by only a neck, in a Grade 1 race, at 25–1. His next race, on Christmas Eve, when Forlitano was the winner, Schiller was again finishing in second place, this time at 14–1. While Forlitano persisted in his search for the American Dream, Schiller remained laid back and content to finish second, collect purses, and stay out of the rat race.

The crowd incorrectly judged Schiller to be inconsistent. What really happened was that this guy always showed up for work, but treated his labor as a game, without serious consequences. In the post parade he'd check out his rivals. If they were sharp and competitive, Schiller would simply follow them around the track; but if they were vulnerable, declining horses, Schiller would put forth his best effort.

On April 4, 1987, Schiller won a restricted stakes race. Forlitano, the beaten favorite, was just as surprised to lose as Schiller was to win. The loss made Forlitano more competitive, more ambitious. The win for Schiller was merely a moment in history that happened to coincide with a period of vulnerability for the field of horses he beat.

Since then, Schiller has been a secondary character in three victories by Rivlia and two by Swink. On July 27 he lost contact with the field after a bad start, when the order of finish was Swink, Forlitano, and Rivlia. He was also present on November

29, 1987, to witness Forlitano reach his Grade 2 peak of glory. In that race, too, Schiller was wiped out by a poor start.

As Schiller comes onto the track, January 24, 1988, for the San Marcos Handicap, he has only 4 wins in 49 races, only one win in his last two years (32 races), but with his 8 seconds and 8 thirds, he has earned the right to stay where he is. His poor races seem to occur when he loses contact with the field; but today, when he encounters declining horses, he will also have a good start assured, as the field is absent of early speed. Horses such as Swink and Rivlia, who come from way off the pace, will be joined by others of their kind. In his last three races Schiller has gone off at 36–1, 19–1, and 41–1, and today he will be much higher than that! There will be no group of gate breakers to intimidate Schiller into a poor start.

Great Communicator

The life of Great Communicator has crossed paths on many an occasion with Rivlia, Swink, Forlitano, and Schiller. With no prior graded-stakes victories, Great Communicator had been brash enough to show up for a Grade 1 race on June 14, 1987. It was only a six-horse field, so he went off at 12–1 instead of 50–1. He was facing Rivlia, who was coming back after a Grade 1 third-place finish followed by a Grade 2 victory.

In some ways, Great Communicator's sponsors were more ambitious than those of Forlitano, having decided that their pride and joy would improve more profoundly by facing the best horses as soon as possible. On this particular occasion Great Communicator finished second, four lengths behind Rivlia, aided by the type of slow pace often found in races of 1½ miles. Behind Great Communicator by two lengths was Schiller, who had loomed up right beside the second horse and characteristically failed to pass. These images stay with me forever and are better expressed with narration than with numbers.

The horse that had beaten Great Communicator was at the peak of his performance cycle, while Great Communicator was just getting used to competing at this high level. Like Schiller, Great Communicator came back with many in-the-money finishes at big odds, culminating in his second by a neck in the Grade 1 D.C. International later that year. Also like Schiller, Great Communicator thrived in paceless fields of marathon races, even when overmatched. Unlike Schiller, Great Communicator was an ambitious horse who had not shown a propensity to hang when the going got tough. His second in the D.C. International was all the more impressive because there were twelve horses behind him at the finish.

Great Communicator's latest effort was the very same Grade 1 race in December 1987 that included Forlitano, Rivlia, Swink, and Schiller, the race won by the notorious Vilzak. Of all the horses in that field, Great Communicator ran best *in relation to his odds,* finishing a close fourth at 86–1.

Going into the San Marcos, Great Communicator has never won a graded-stakes race, but his gradually improving form and his pace-control running style are especially favorable for this field.

The Race

The relationship between the participants in the San Marcos is parallel to that of characters in a soap opera. Each race is an episode; in each episode a different character gains the advantage within a distinct set of circumstances. The advantage changes hands endlessly, from race to race, episode to episode, as new characters appear when old ones disappear.

In the San Marcos the only other participant with graded-stakes credentials is The Medic (Grade 3 winner), but as a four-year-old, he is too much of a newcomer and has not yet paid his dues. There is a shipper by the name of Ten Keys who has shown a couple of thirds in Grade 3 races and is 5 for 9 on the turf as a big fish in a small pond.

It becomes a weird race since the "best horses" figure to lose, because they are on the decline, while an overbet Forlitano has been dropping too many hints that his credentials are tainted and that he has reached a vulnerable point in his career. The tool of memory seems more appropriate for this particular race than speed figures and earnings; the personality of these horses, as represented by their life histories and running styles, seems to allow for a clearer view of form cycle. With the numbers of handicapping presenting isolated points of each horse's career, the narration of their life stories seems to set this racing moment in its proper context.

With Rivlia, Swink, and possibly Forlitano as declining

horses, this might be the occasion for the opportunistic Schiller to beat horses he usually loses to. A win bet is nevertheless out of the question, as the image of Schiller hanging in a maiden race, and hanging in a later race to cede second to Great Communicator, is fresh in my mind. I will bet Schiller to place.

But wait. My colleague, Steve Martin (the other Steve Martin), sees tremendous value in betting against the declining horses, in the form of exactas. He sees value in horses such as Great Communicator and Ten Keys inheriting the win. "I really wanted to bet Schiller to place," I tell him.

"Then let's box the three!"

"Tell you what," I respond. "Let's put Schiller in second place to the ones you like, and I'll go along with boxing your two, simply because we agree that the best horses are not going to win."

This is Steve's type of race. Rather than handicapping for a high-percentage hit rate, Steve invests in the most confusing races, looking for high-yield scenarios. This style has earned him the highest return on investment of all racing services monitored in southern California. I bypass my place bet and go along with the exactas.

The 1¼ mile race begins on a turn with an incline, passes over a dirt strip and on to the main turf track, by the grandstand for the first time. At this point the outcome for Rivlia and Swink is unpredictable; they run in the back of the pack, as usual. On the other hand, it is apparent that Forlitano is not running his usual near-the-pace style; in a relatively paceless field, he should be right up there with the leaders, who are Schiller and Great Communicator, in relaxed pursuit. As these two leave the rest of the field behind while running relatively slow fractions, it begins to look like a two-horse race.

They run this way in the backstretch and around the final turn. Schiller is still leading and running gamely. Suddenly it occurs to me that if Schiller holds on, I won't collect a penny, but if I had made my place bet, as I'd intended, I would have collected whether Schiller holds on for first or gives way to Great Communicator. The place price figures to be huge, but that's all over for me. Now, the only way to collect is if Schiller is to do what he's always done, and hangs near the wire so that Great Communicator can pass.

I say, "Don't worry, Steve, Schiller will let him by. I've known Schiller since he was a kid. That's the way he is."

As they move into the stretch, two horses alone, the rest of the field going through the motions, Schiller seems to have decided to hold on. Great Communicator advances, but by inches. In mid-stretch Great Communicator finally does what he's supposed to and passes Schiller to lead by one-half length.

Everything I know about Schiller tells me that we are about to collect on a monster exacta. But then something happens that makes me doubt everything I have learned as a handicapper; Schiller is acting as if he's come out of successful psychoanalysis, coming on again to challenge Great Communicator. He comes up head to head with Great Communicator, and the race is going to be taken by whichever horse truly wants it.

And then Schiller does it! The talent in his body is superseded by the hang-ups in his head. As the two heads come side by side, the secret language of horses is communicated. Any attempt to paraphrase what goes on between these two horses would highlight the weakness of human language. Suddenly, Schiller prefers to admire the talent of his colleague, and he gives way. He hangs. The photo sign goes up, but I know very well what Schiller has done. The $5 exacta payoff is $2438. Without Steve Martin at the table in the clubhouse, I would have missed the exacta and collected on a $35 place price for Schiller.

CHANGING OF THE GUARD

After many months, many races of watching the tails of horses such as Rivlia, Swink, and Forlitano, was this January 24 to be but one fleeting moment of glory for Great Communicator or had the phases of thoroughbred cycles changed so profoundly that a whole new regime of horses would come to power? Swink and Rivlia seemed too classy to subside forever, and yet they had been beaten easily for some time now.

February 15: Great Communicator wins again. His previous win had paid off at 12–1, but the crowd was not convinced that a changing of the guard had taken place and let him go off at 11–1. Rivlia was out of the money; Swink, in a different race, also out of the money.

March 27: These three are reunited. The public now begins to perceive that the class power struggle has led to a new regime. Great Communicator goes down to 5–1, Rivlia up to 9–1. In a moment of profound nostalgia, Rivlia finds inspiration one more time and wins the race.

April 24: A turf marathon today which will decide whether the old guard is actually recapturing power or whether a new class structure has evolved. Rivlia, 7–2; Swink, 9–2; Great Communicator, 6–1. Nostalgia is the primary handicapping factor that determines these odds. Great Communicator clinches his position as the meet's champion marathoner by prevailing in a photo finish. Once more he pays a big price; it's tough for the public to accept change. Swink and Rivlia are not even involved in the photo.

In every peak of a form cycle there are the seeds of change and decline. Great Communicator is king, but how long will his regime last?

EIGHTH RACE
Santa Anita
APRIL 24, 1988

ABOUT 1 ¾ MILES.(Turf). (2:45⅗) 49th Running of THE SAN JUAN CAPISTRANO INVITATIONAL HANDICAP (Grade I). Purse $400,000. 4-year-olds and upward. By invitation, with no nomination or starting fees. The winner to receive $220,000, with $80,000 to second, $60,000 to third, $30,000 to fourth and $10,000 to fifth. Weights to be published Thursday, April 14. The Los Angeles Turf Club will invite a field of the highest-weighted horses to accept. In the event that one more of these decline, those weighted as provisional invitees below them will be invited in weight order to replace them. The field will be drawn by the closing time of entries, Friday, April 22. A trophy will be presented to the owner of the winner.

Value of race $400,000; value to winner $220,000; second $80,000; third $60,000; fourth $30,000; fifth $10,000. Mutuel pool $755,740. Exacta Pool $714,613.

Last Raced	Horse	Eqt.A.Wt	PP	½	1	1¼	1½	Str	Fin	Jockey	Odds $1
27Mar88 8SA2	Great Communicator b	5 119	4	$3^{\frac{1}{2}}$	2^{1}	$2^{1\frac{1}{2}}$	$2^{2\frac{1}{2}}$	$2^{1\frac{1}{2}}$	1^{nk}	Sibille R	6.10
2Apr88 8SA1	Fiction	4 116	2	$1^{3\frac{1}{2}}$	1^{1}	$1^{\frac{1}{2}}$	$1^{\frac{1}{2}}$	1^{2}	2^{nk}	Shoemaker W	10.10
3Apr88 8SA2	Carotene	5 115	3	6^{2}	7	7	$5^{\frac{1}{2}}$	3^{1}	$3^{4\frac{1}{2}}$	Seymour D J	4.80
27Mar88 8SA3	Swink	5 119	6	$5^{2\frac{1}{2}}$	5^{hd}	$6^{2\frac{1}{2}}$	6^{1}	$5^{1\frac{1}{2}}$	4^{3}	Pincay L Jr	4.80
27Mar88 8SA1	Rivlia	6 123	7	7	$6^{2\frac{1}{2}}$	$5^{\frac{1}{2}}$	$3^{\frac{1}{2}}$	$4^{\frac{1}{2}}$	5^{2}	McCarron C J	3.40
12Mar88 8SA1	Putting	5 119	5	2^{hd}	4^{5}	4^{2}	4^{1}	$6^{2\frac{1}{2}}$	$6^{3\frac{1}{2}}$	Stevens G L	2.90
4Apr88 4Fra2	Dahlaan	4 117	1	4^{7}	$3^{\frac{1}{2}}$	3^{1}	7	7	7	Legrix E	6.30

OFF AT 5:07. Start good for all but DAHLAAN. Won driving. Time, :47, 1:11⅗, 1:37, 2:02⅗, 2:28⅖, 2:51⅗, Course good.

$2 Mutuel Prices:				
	4–GREAT COMMUNICATOR	14.20	6.20	4.20
	2–FICTION		9.00	5.00
	3–CAROTENE			4.20

$5 EXACTA 4–2 PAID $368.00.

B. g, by Key to the Kingdom—Blaheen, by Beekeeper. Trainer Ackel Thad D. Bred by Waitress James R (Ky).

GREAT COMMUNICATOR, under a snug rating hold early while being outrun, advanced to get near the lead approaching the finish line the first time, forced the pace while outside FICTION down the backstretch and around the far turn, kept after FICTION in the final furlong after that rival had drawn clear in the upper stretch and finished gamely to get up in the closing yards. FICTION went to the front at once, quickly drew well clear early when somewhat full of run and went the opening quarter in :23 1/5, settled down nicely passing the stands the first time while still in front, continued to set the pace down the backstretch and around the far turn while inside GREAT COMMUNICATOR, drew clear in the upper stretch during the drive, held on stubbornly late but could not quite resist the winner's closing bid. CAROTENE, unhurried while far back early, rallied in the last three furlongs but could not quite get up in a good try. SWINK, also unhurried while far back early, lacked the necessary rally. RIVLIA, patiently handled when far back early while trailing, made a move to look dangerous a quarter of a mile out but failed to sustain his rally in the final quarter. PUTTING, rated early while being outrun, moved up to get within close range of the lead approaching the finish line the first time, stayed in contention to the stretch drive, then lacked the necessary response when called upon in the drive. DAHLAAN broke last when failing to get away in good order, improved his position in the early going, moved up to get within close range of the lead nearing the finish line the first time, remained in contention to the far turn, then gave way. WOLSEY (6) WAS SCRATCHED. ALL WAGERS ON HIM IN THE REGULAR AND EXACTA POOLS WERE ORDERED REFUNDED AND ALL OF HIS PICK SIX, PICK NINE AND DAILY TRIPLE SELECTIONS WERE SWITCHED TO THE FAVORITE, PUTTING (5).

Owners— 1, Class Act Stable; 2, Evergreen Farm; 3, Kinghaven Farms; 4, Hunt N B; 5, Yamamoto S; 6, Sofro D I; 7, Chalhoub Ecurie H.

Trainers— 1, Ackel Thad D; 2, Whittingham Charles; 3, Attfield Roger; 4, Whittingham Charles; 5, Whittingham Charles; 6, Canani Julio C; 7, Biancone Patrick L.

Scratched—Wolsey (10Apr88 3SA6).

A superficial look at the margin of his victory gives the impression that the kingdom of Great Communicator will not be everlasting. He has caught Swink and Rivlia when they were down, and two up-and-coming horses have accompanied him in the same photo. But there is a certain type of competitiveness that does not depend on margin of victory. The style of victory tells a truer story. The great John Henry rarely got away from a field; horses would come deceptively close to John Henry in the stretch. Then he would let them know who was the boss. He thrived on an intimate proximity with his victims. If John Henry had been in a medieval duel and his rival had dropped a sword, John Henry would have waited until his opponent had the chance to recover the fallen sword.

Great Communicator may be this type of horse. He allows Fiction an inside trip and is left to take the longer way around. He lets his rival draw clear in the stretch and then comes back again to wear him down. He has not inherited a victory; he has fought for it. That is his competitive personality, and it is the type of lifestyle of an extended regime.

Another sign that Great Communicator will prolong his period of glory is that his rise to power has not been sudden and opportunistic. He has fought his way up, little by little. A figurative graph of his improvement process will show a gradually ascending line. It is this type of rise that tends to hold its peak for longer periods of time.

This analysis has been written prior to the Breeders' Cup Turf, Churchill Downs, November 5, 1988, where Great Communicator goes to post at 12–1. I've seen several of his European rivals run in France, where at this distance—1½ miles (2400 meters)—races are like waiting games, like harness events, in which the pace is extremely slow in the early going. The presence of the imports in this type of race can only improve the chances of Great Communicator, by lessening the probability of an unrealistic early pace.

On November 5 it is Sunshine Forever, winner of the Laurel Budweiser International, who will play the role of fiction and Schiller by keeping company with Great Communicator. Our hero has proven he does not need to shake loose of the field; a fair early pace will do. When it is all over, Great Communicator has maintained his position as number-one turf marathon horse. The margin of victory is short, but Sunshine Forever is not Schiller, and Great Communicator has earned an extension of his regime.

Taking Turns

Chronology of Common Races

4-24-88	Great Communicator(1), Swink, Rivlia
3-27-88	Rivlia(1), Great Communicator(2), Swink(3), Vilzak
2-15-88	Great Communicator(1), Swink, Rivlia
1-24-88	Great Communicator(1), Schiller(2), Forlitano, Swink, Rivlia
12-13-87	Vilzak(1), Forlitano(2), Great Communicator(3), Rivlia, Swink
11-29-87	Forlitano(1), Schiller
10-11-87	Rivlia(1), Forlitano, Schiller
9-21-87	Rivlia, Great Communicator, Swink
9-7-87	Swink(1); Schiller(4) only 1½ back, bumped start, wide into stretch; Great Communicator
7-27-87	Swink(1), Forlitano(2), Rivlia(3), Great Communicator(4), Schiller
6-14-87	Rivlia(1), Great Communicator(2), Schiller(3)
5-24-87	Rivlia(1), *Forlitano*, *Schiller*
4-19-87	Rivlia(3), Schiller(4)
4-4-87	*Schiller*(1), *Forlitano*(3)
3-14-87	*Forlitano*(2), *Schiller*
2-16-87	*Schiller*(3), Rivlia(4), *Forlitano*
12-24-86	*Forlitano*(1), *Schiller*(2)

Note, too, Great Communicator's emergence over this span of races, which included five of his frequent rivals: Schiller, Forlitano, Swink, Rivlia, and Vilzak. The top four finishing positions in races involving these competitors has been noted.

Pace handicappers are sure to argue that varying pace configurations have more to do with the reason for horses taking turns than performance cycles. I have therefore italicized Schiller and Forlitano over a six-month period in which these two horses with *similar pace styles* alternated in order of finish. In addition, Swink and Rivlia, two horses that both come from behind, regularly take turns beating each other. Scan the chronology in any way you wish and it still shows that horses pass through performance phases that are independent of their running style.

RELATIVITY

Balance in the thoroughbred universe is determined by thousands of horse and trainer orbits whose interrelationship forms a moving geometry far more complex than the linear arithmetic of basic handicapping. Speed and pace figures as well as class calculations remain valid in the way that Newtonian physics coexists with the more fertile reality of relativity.

Horse and trainer cycles are bent one way or another by other lesser but significant forces. Every handicapper has seen that riders go through their own ups and downs. Follow the performance of the offspring of turf or mud sires and you will see that sires, too, pass through phases of hot and cold spells. Indeed, whole crops of horses seem to follow a type of cyclical pattern worthy of study in the *Farmer's Almanac*. For example, one season's entry-level allowance crop may be far superior or inferior to the crop of the following season, and so it goes for every class and surface category.

In each horse race many of these distinct orbits are converging or collapsing to form a new, unique relationship. In this sense, the heroic rise of Great Communicator is the product of a particular convergence of orbits and not merely a one-man show. Let's look back on that moment in time from several perspectives.

1. Horses: Swink, Rivlia, and Forlitano had all beaten Great Communicator with regularity. Meanwhile, Great Communicator had been showing steady but gradual improvement; with his rivals, coincidentally, on the down part of their form cycles, he emerged to beat them on January 24.
2. Some horseplayers will argue that Charles Whittingham is the best trainer in the business, while most will at least rank him within the top ten. Yet at this particular moment his orbit was at one of its lower points. A number of his horses were simultaneously in decline; those mentioned above, as well as Ferdinand, who was losing to Alysheba. Other residents of the same stable, such as Fiction (loser to Great Communicator by a neck), were just short of their peak.
3. Crops: the current crop of turf routers was particularly lacking early speed horses, thus easing the wear and tear on Great Communicator. On other occasions the opposite force is at a peak and the turf-router colony is overpopulated by speedsters. When this happens, closers will win every race.

This was the context of cycles in which the improving Great Communicator fit perfectly. A graph of the horse cycles leading up to January 24 will add a dimension to the picture, although a two-dimensional graph is more of an illustration than a methodology.

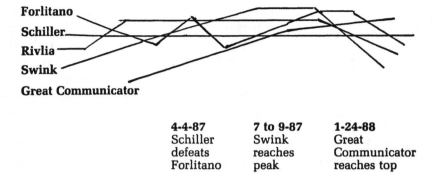

	4-4-87	7 to 9-87	1-24-88
	Schiller defeats Forlitano	Swink reaches peak	Great Communicator reaches top

In this impressionistic and largely symbolic graph, I've given Schiller a straight line, which represents the peak he is always capable of but only tries to reach at opportune moments. The graph makes several points, through its limitations as much as through its strengths.

1. Speed and pace figures function well in providing an isolated still picture of certain moments in a horse's career. Within a graph format, these numbers can be seen more as moving images, which converts them into dynamic projectors of change.
2. If there were ever a truly accurate graph of performance cycles, it would need to incorporate the behavior of horses as "psychological" beings and not merely the progression of performance numbers, as if horses were machines.
3. The narrative process is one tool for approaching these added dimensions of form cycle. For example, in strictly numerical terms, Schiller would look erratic. But his apparently inconsistent performance had nothing to do with his inherent form and was strictly a function of external factors, such as pace configuration and current class of opposition.

We have now observed the phases of some very particular horse cycles, from the perspective of numbers and words. In order to come up with a handicapping methodology, we need to go from the particular to the general. We need to relate past performances to a set of clearly defined *types* of performance cycles. These cycles will represent various horse "cultures" and "lifestyles" of a pluralistic thoroughbred society.

THE PERSONALITY OF CYCLES I

Both numerical and narrative analysis suggests that the trajectory of a horse's career has something to do with its character or behavior traits. A wealth of numerical imagery supports this contention.

1. We have witnessed the running *line* as a sign of "style." The term "running style" is used automatically by handicappers, without ever questioning whether it is possible for an animal to have a style of behavior.
2. Consider two sequences of numbers that represent the last ten finish positions of two horses:

   1, 2, 4, 3, 2, 2, 1, 4, 1, 3

   8, 1, 7, 9, 2, 11, 1, 6, 3, 12

   Now, label each sequence with a one-word description. Around the track you'll hear words such as "consistent-inconsistent" and "dependable-undependable," words that have human overtones. These number sequences suggest, at once, form cycles and modes of behavior that might qualify as personality traits.
3. In the realm of competitiveness, a number of humanizing metaphors are standard to horseplayer vocabulary:

   "ran a *gutsy* race"
   "made a *bold* move"
   "*quit* at the sixteenth pole"

   Consider another set of numbers, now referring to the performance box that lists number of races, wins, seconds, and thirds. What language would you choose to describe the following two records?

	Races	*Won*	*2nd*	*3rd*
Horse P	23	1	7	4
Horse Q	18	7	1	0

When I asked this of my students, a number of respondents used terms that are normally directed toward human beings:

P "gutless," "lacks *heart*"
Q "*spirited* competitor," "*loves* to win"

Like the sequence of finish positions, performance-box numbers seem to point out behavior traits as well as form cycle traits. Each type of numerical image has its own character. Numbers come alive.

4. Two horses find themselves side by side in a stretch duel. Ask the class handicapper which factor will determine the outcome. Naturally, the class advocate considers relative speed ratings as secondary; the inherent class consciousness of these two horses will decide which one prevails. By calling themselves "class" handicappers, these colleagues are highlighting a word that is usually reserved for human beings, not animals.

   But wait! Can't we refer to automobiles and clothing as "classy"? Yes, but cars and clothes are designed *by people*. You won't hear anyone in Yosemite National Park talking about classy trees and mountains.

5. If horseplayers find it comfortable to use humanizing vocabulary to describe horse performance, then perhaps horse handicapping techniques can be used to project the performance of human beings. I tested this hypothesis by using some of my horse form-cycle projection factors to predict the performance of baseball players. I chose baseball because it offers the most comprehensive system of numbers to describe performance, and I specifically chose the position of pitcher, because that position is most susceptible to apparently unpredictable ups and downs.

   We'd be going off on a tangent if I were to get into specifics. The point is, by successfully projecting radical form reversals of baseball players, a methodology developed to work for the horses worked with human beings. (See Addendum G)

What I am proposing here is that there is something that can be labeled "competitive character," which is composed of behavior traits—"personality" traits, if you will—universal to all beings who engage in competition; fighting fish of Thailand, roosters in Mexico, race horses, and human beings. Supporting my contention is the numerical imagery of the past performances in the *Racing Form*, the humanizing metaphors used by horseplayers to describe horse performance, and the applicability of horse handicapping techniques to the projection of human performance.

Let us leave the issue of horse personality open for consideration as we relate it to the ensuing analysis of the prototypes of thoroughbred performance cycles.

Part II
Horses

CHAPTER 2

Vacationers: Back to Work

THE MYTH OF TAMTULIA

I AM LOOKING OUT from my balcony on to the Mediterranean Sea, where each wave that hits the shore deposits ancient particles from the times of Greek mythology. In the dusty tomes of the local library there is nothing to be found on the Myth of Tamtulia.

The Myth of Tamtulia owes its infamy to a forgettable afternoon at the Hippodrome of Del Mar, where the waves from another sea provided the backdrop for a spectacle that began centuries ago on the old continent. A three-year-old filly by the name of Tamtulia was the 8–5 favorite for the seventh race. Coming off a layoff of three and one-half months, Tamtulia ran a mediocre race and finished sixth. Myths are perpetuated by the public, and what better forum for a myth than the grandstand of a racetrack? Following the race, the subject in the minds of the majority of prognosticators who had backed Tamtulia was something like: "She lost after a layoff; that proves you shouldn't bet horses when they return after a layoff."

And thus an isolated event served to perpetuate a horse-racing myth; at the racetrack, lasting impressions are often formed from isolated events. The same bettor we quoted may later observe a victory by a layoff horse. But the $200 he lost on Tamtulia has already registered a lasting impression.

Strange how these profound opinions materialize out of isolated events. A guy could fly in to Los Angeles from Seattle on a February afternoon and hit three consecutive days of rain, conclude that there's too much precipitation in southern California, and return to Seattle. Another gentleman watches the news on TV and learns of an airplane hijacked by a Latin American; next week, the man finds himself in an elevator amid a conversation between two Spanish-speaking men and concludes that they are planning to hijack the elevator, when in reality they are talking about contemporary Puerto Rican poetry.

These two incidents actually happened. So many myths are formed when the anecdotal becomes generalized. While mediocre politicians make decisions based on anecdotal "thoughts" that affect the future of the world, losing horse players eat up their bankroll and rent money by making decisions based on the anecdotal. While most politicians don't pay the consequences of anecdotal thought, most horse players do. Around the racetrack whole subcultures materialize because of common anecdotal experiences. Then there are system peddlers and turf writers who further add to the generalization of the experiential. Most "systems" have a recency clause that penalizes horses coming back after a layoff. Every Tamtulia that comes around reinforces such criteria.

Jack Bederson looks like he's hung around the track for many years. If a movie director were looking for extras for a racetrack grandstand scene, they'd be sure to choose Jack. But Jack doesn't believe in the Myth of Tamtulia. The betting public is a weird entity because many people who are part of the crowd are really different from the crowd. Jack's published a book of poetry and he's also the author of a massive study called *By the Numbers*. One of the observations of this study of thousands of races is that, with the advent of year-round racing, there is no statistical disadvantage against horses coming back after a layoff; this is because many of the horses with recency are overraced and stale, and to be overworked lowers performance ratings as much or more than to be underworked.

I was interested in finding which subsets from the set of layoff horses had the best chance to win at a profitable percentage. I decided on an analytical approach rather than a statistical approach because I feared that statistics might lead to false correlations. For example, higher-class horses win more races after layoffs than lower-class horses. However, higher-class horses win more races in general, and higher-class horses have more opportunity to win after layoffs because they are laid off more frequently (they compete for higher purses, so they don't have to race so often to pay the bills).

I already had Jack's stats, which suggested that the Myth of Tamtulia would lead the public to underbet layoff horses and that some types of layoff situations might be profitable. Jack identified certain trainers who excelled with layoff horses, but I wanted to find a certain type of horse whose performance cycle would make layoff wins predictable. I took a random sample of 50 layoff winners and examined their life histories as if I were doing intake interviews.

Technique: Questions were asked regarding age, sex, distance, previous layoff history, and performance as a first-time starter. Within the fifty case studies, I only allowed for ten horses of foreign upbringing, since in foreign racing horses are acculturated into racing with layoffs because of seasonal rather than year-long racing.

Summary

1. Age, sex, and distance: no conclusive date
2. Previously won after layoff: *13 (26%)*
3. Won as first-time starter: *21 (42%)*
4. Previously won when fresh (either after a layoff or as a first-time starter): *30 (60%)*
5. Won or finished second as a first-time starter: *30 (60%)*
6. Displayed no prior evidence of ability to run well fresh: *12 (24%)*
7. Average mutuel of horse that had history of running well fresh: *$10.80*
8. Of 12 *irrational* winners, at least 6 had trainers with positive record for layoff situations
9. Rationality Index: 76% (means that in 76% of cases, there was a rational reason in horse's previous history for a subsequent layoff victory)
10. Eliminate horses first race after layoff when they:
    a. Did not finish first or second as first-time starters
    b. Have never won after a layoff
    c. Do not have trainer who does well with horses after a layoff

Some numbers are more significant than face value and others less. Although 13 layoff winners out of the 50 studied had *previously won after a layoff,* many of the 37 other winners had

never lost after a layoff, because this win came after their *first
layoff*. On the other hand, obviously all 50 horses studied had
once been first-time starters, so we not only observe that 21 of 50
horses studied had won as first-time starters, but also that 29 of
the 50 had lost as first timers.

The greatest significance about this racing research, as it relates to practical handicapping, is the suggestion that what happens to a horse early in its career has a strong bearing on later
performance. If indeed the whole life history of a horse gives
some message about today's performance, then the ten races
given to us in the *Racing Form* past performances will be inadequate for comprehensive handicapping. We shall see in later
chapters that the layoff factor is but one of several handicapping
factors for which the seeds of later years' performance will have
been planted early in the horses' careers.

Case Histories

Tropical Holiday. Note that on June 21, 1987, after 4½
months of vacation, this filly comes back and wins in a Hollywood Park dirt sprint.

Either the handicapper had a good memory or he needed to go
way back to an old *Form* to discover that, as a first-time starter,
Tropical Holiday won a dirt sprint at Hollywood Park.

Tropical Holiday — B. f. 3, by If This Be So—Holiday Jet, by Tri Jet

MCHARGUE D G — 115 — Br.—Hooper F W (Fla) — Tr.—Fenstermaker L R

Own.—Hooper F W

1986	6	0	0	2	$14,875
1985	4	2	0	1	$22,800
Lifetime	10	2	0	3	$37,675

11May86-4Hol	7f	:22 :45 1:23^{2}ft	16 116	7^6 5^4 5^5 4^6	McHrgDG^5	(F)Aw23000	81-15	Chick OrTwo,MissBenson,Witchery	7
18Apr86-7SA	6½f	:22^1 :45^4 1:17^{1}ft	18 116	5^6 5^{6}½ 5^{5}½ 5^{5}¾	McHrgDG^1	(F)Aw20000	78-21	WintrTrsur,MissBnson,ViolinMlody	5
18Apr86—Veered out start									
12Mar86-7SA	1	:46^2 1:12 1:37 sy	14 116	5^{8}½ 5^{6}½ 4^{7}½ 3^{13}½	McHrgDG^1	(F)Aw35000	78-25	Nture'sWy,SilntArrivl,TropiclHolidy	5
20Feb86-8SA	6½f	:22 :45^3 1:17^{4}m	28 116	7^9 7^{8}½ 6^9 7^{12}	McHrgDG^6	(F)Aw31000	69-27	NervousBb,SilentArrivl,AnEmpress	7
5Feb86-8SA	7f	:22^2 :45^1 1:23^{2}ft	39 116	6^{5}¾ 5^{7}½ 5^8 5^{13}½	McHrDG^8	(F)Sta Ynez	69-19	Sri'sHeroine,AnEmprss,LifAtThTop	8
5Feb86—Grade III									
4Jan86-8BM	6f	:22^1 :45 1:10^{1}sy	10 117	5^{11} 5^{10} 4^{8}½ 3^{10}½	McHrgDG^2	(F)Hl Hlrus	77-29	Sari'sHeroine,Alquizr,Trop'clHolidy	5
18Sep85-11Pom	6f	:22^3 :46 1:11^{2}ft	2¾ 119	6^7 4^{2}½ 3^3 3^{hd}	HsRD^2	(F)Bstls & Bws	— —	MissBnson,ApichBld,TropiclHolidy	9
18Sep85—Run in divisions									
1Sep85-8Dmr	1	:46^3 1:11^2 1:36 ft	3 113	4^{8}½ 4^5 4^{10} 6^{12}	ShomkrW^6	(F)Dmr Deb	76-13	Arewehvingfunyet,Python,WeeLvlir	6
21Aug85-7Dmr	6½f	:21^4 :44^4 1:16^{3}ft	7½ 115	7^{17} 5^{18} 3^7 1^2	McHrgDG^5	(F)Aw21000	93-12	TropiclHoldy,ExubrntEffort,Al'sHln	7
12Jly85-6Hol	5½f	:23 :46^2 1:05^{4}ft	5½ 118	5^{8}¾ 4^4 3^{1}½ 1^{1}½	McHrguDG^4	(F)M50000	— —	Tropical Holiday,Velveteen,Pastreil	8

May 27 Hol 7f ft 1:28^1 h — May 20 Hol 6f ft 1:16^2 h — May 6 Hol 6f ft 1:16^2 h — Apr 28 Hol 5f ft 1:02^1 h

With this information either unavailable to the public or underestimated as a factor by racegoers, Tropical Holiday paid off at 8½–1. Sometimes the correct information is visible in the past performances and the public still errs. Example:

L.B. Jaklin. On February 19, 1988, L.B. Jaklin faced a very weak field of entry-level allowance horses. At the same track where he had won as a first timer, they let him go off at 15–1. Later performances imply that this horse will only win when he's fresh.

L. B. Jaklin — Ro. c. 4, by Jaklin Klugman—Even Dollars, by Rising Market

DOOCY T T — 119 — Br.—Klugman J (Cal) — Tr.—Fanning Brett C

Own.—El Rancho de Jaklin

1988	5	1	1	0	$30,650
1986	2	1	0	0	$12,575
Lifetime	7	2	1	0	$43,225

28Apr88-8GG	6f	:21^2 :43^4 1:08^{4}ft	7½ 113	5^{4}½ 3^{4}½ 3^{3}½ 4^{2}¾	DocyTT^3	[S]Freeway H	88-20	Tomocomo,MchFnGold,FrndlyForc	6
28Apr88—Jostled at start									
9Apr88-7SA	6f	:21^1 :43 1:08 ft	2½ 119	3^2 2^6 2^7 5^{12}¾	Solis A^8	Aw30000	86-13	OlympicProspct,DncForL,LnsMnus	9
25Mar88-5SA	6½f	:21^2 :44^1 1:16 ft	7½ 119	2½ 2½ 2½ 2¾	Solis A^7	Aw30000	89-18	Tomocomo,L.B.Jaklin,DnceForLee	10
13Mar88-7SA	6f	:22 :45^1 1:10 ft	4 118	4^{2}½ 4^2 4^2 4^{3}¾	Toro F^7	Aw35000	84-15	Pewter, Tomocomo, Seniority	9
19Feb88-7SA	6½f	:21^3 :44^4 1:16^{4}ft	15 117	3^{2}½ 3^2 1^1 1^{1}¾	Solis A^3	Aw32000	86-23	L. B. Jaklin, UnderAndOver,Chinati	7
3Dec86-8Hol	6f	:22 :45^2 1:10^{4}ft	8-5 120	3^{1}½ 2^{1}½ 3^4 4^6	DelhoussyeE^4	Aw21000	84-18	SundncSqur,WstrlyWnd,GoldOnGrn	6
22Oct86-6SA	6f	:21^2 :44^3 1:10^{4}ft	*8-5 117	3^2 1^{hd} 1^{1}½ 1^3	Valenzuela PA^4	[S]Mdn	84-23	L.B.Jklin,SwtwtrSprngs,HlrousFlrt	11

May 8 GG 4f gd :48^2 h — Apr 25 SA 4f ft :48^1 h — Apr 18 SA 4f ft :47^2 h — Apr 4 SA 5f ft 1:00^4 h

Bargain Fun and *Marimascus* have understood in a literal sense the term "performance cycle." On opposite coasts with different trainers, they live and relive the same uncanny yearly cycle as if it were the celebration of a secret solstice.

Bargain Fun *
DOOCY T T
Own.—Sawyer J J
112
Dk. b. or br. m. 5, by Bargain Day—Fernofun, by Bobillard
Br.—Upton L W (Cal)
Tr.—Wiberg Steve
Lifetime 18 7 0 4 $65,445
1988 1 1 0 0 $9,250
1987 8 3 0 2 $27,725
17Apr88-3GG 6f :21³ :44 1:08⁴ft 7 116 1hd 1½ 11 1½ Doocy T T7 Ⓕ 25000 95-11 BrgnFn,Hylnd'sHHop,GoodNwsDoll 7
18Oct87-10TuP 6f :21⁴ :44⁴ 1:09²ft 9½ 116 55¾ 64¾ 65½ 612 SmithV1 ⒻSsn's Grl H 75-16 MostPrestigious,Buty'sSis,SbrLind 6
22Aug87-10Stk 5f :21³ :44 :56³ft 3½ 115 46 49 511 49 White C2 ⒻAw11000 96-06 QuickN'Cool,MissPso,ViolinMelody 7
22Aug87—Broke out start
8Aug87-9SR 5½f :21⁴ :45³ 1:03²ft 3½ 110 43½ 55½ 56 34 Tohill K S6 ⒻInvH 90-14 Lovely Candy, Sweepy, BargainFun 7
8Aug87—Lugged out drive
31Jly87-9SR 6f :21⁴ :44² 1:09¹ft *7-5 115 21½ 21½ 2½ 12 WarrenRJJr1 Ⓕ c25000 95-15 BarginFun,ByAnyOtherNme,AmecJ. 8
12Jun87-5Hol 1 :45² 1:11 1:37⁴ft 6½ 116 1hd 11 11½ 33 Sibille R2 Ⓕ 32000 71-16 French Star, Stillou, Bargain Fun 9
21May87-5Hol 6f :22 :45³ 1:10²ft 9-5 116 22 21 1hd 1½ Sibille R4 Ⓕ 25000 91-12 BargainFun,OkPortl,Winsomething 5
4Apr87-7GG 6f :21⁴ :44² 1:10¹ft 2¾ 116 42 32 34 51½ Judice J C8 Ⓕ c25000 87-12 RightCautious,Balimonday,Torktue 8
12Mar87-9GG 6f :21² :44³ 1:11³sy *3 116 33 11 16 15 Judice J C6 Ⓕ 16000 81-28 Bargain Fun, NickolinJean,BlueSilk 8
15Oct86-6BM 6f :22¹ :45² 1:10²ft 5¾ 114 21 22 2½ 68½ Judice J C2 Ⓕ 25000 80-17 OneDrum,NturlBlonde,Blke'sDncer 7
●Apr 26 BM tr.t 5f ft 1:00³ h ●Apr 15 BM 3f m :36¹ hg Apr 5 BM 5f ft 1:00¹ h ●Mar 31 BM 5f ft 1:00⁴ h

Bargain Fun sits out from October 15, 1986, to March 12, 1987 (five months), and then wins first day back from vacation at Golden Gate. The mare then follows a very similar ritual by staying away from the races October 18, 1987, until April 17 of the next year (six months) and returns to the scene of the previous ritual, winning at 7–1.

Marimascus
DAY P
Own.—Shaw J
112
Dk. b. or br. f. 4, by Bailjumper—Mariwitch, by Maribeau
Br.—Peterson John L (Fla)
Tr.—Fernandez Floreano
Lifetime 14 4 1 0 $107,833
1988 1 1 0 0 $40,359
1987 10 2 1 0 $52,874
Turf 11 4 1 0 $107,833
15May88-7Pen 1⅛Ⓣ 1:42¹fm 4 112 2hd 1½ 11½ 11½ AlsRB8 ⒻBudBreedsH 79-21 Marimascus, Chaudennay, Cecina 9
19Nov87-8Aqu 1⅜Ⓣ:49¹1:15 1:53³gd 13 117 2½ 1½ 12½ 23 Antley CW9 ⒻAw35000 64-37 NorlandNanny,Marimascus,RreLed 9
7Nov87-8Med 1⅛[T]:45⁴1:10¹1:42³fm 7 118 2hd 1½ 4¾ 46 PzuJM7 ⒻTiger Heart 84-10 Reassert, Muskrat Love, Tappiano 9
16Oct87-6Med 1⅛Ⓣ:46²1:10³1:42³fm 9¾f 113 2hd 12½ 12½ 11 Pezua J M1 ⒻSabin 87-16 Mrimscus,FlyingKtun,MuskrtLove 14
28Sep87-6Bel 1¼[T]:49 1:38²2:04 fm 18 115 2hd 2hd 1½ 54¾ CordroAJr8 ⒻAw31000 69-24 Strdusk,Brbr'sMomnt,BlnchDuBos 10
17Aug87-6Sar 1⅛[T]:47 1:11⁴1:41⁴fm 10 112 76 75½ 64 45½ Pezua J M7 ⒻAw28000 91-08 Love For All, Purify, Riverquill 8
8Aug87-3Sar 1⅜[T]:47⁴1:12 1:49²fm 11 112 53½ 53 73½ 74½ Cruguet J1 ⒻAw28000 88-13 Lepa, Nastique, Riverquill 11
10Jly87-7Bel 1⅛[T]:49²1:14 1:47¹sf 4¾ 111 31 2hd 22½ 47¾ Cruguet J2 ⒻAw28000 57-35 Debonirly,DremCrek,AntiquMystiqu 8
3Jly87-5Bel 1⅜:50 1:39³ 2:19³m 7½ 112 54 622 650 — Cruguet J6 ⒻAw28000 — — Laughing Lady, Far East, Darbyvail 6
3Jly87—Eased
18Jun87-8Bel 1⅛[T]:47⁴1:11¹1:41²fm 8 109 52½ 53 63½ 79½ Davis R G7 ⒻHcp0 85-10 Fam,PerfectPoint,SmoketheQueen 7
May 13 Bel tr.t 5f ft 1:03 b May 2 Bel tr.t 5f ft 1:02⁴ b Apr 23 Bel tr.t 4f ft :48¹ h Apr 12 Bel tr.t 5f ft 1:01⁴ h

Marimascus
Own.—Sunset Bay Stable
112
Dk. b. or br. f. 3, by Bailjumper—Mariwitch, by Maribeau
Br.—Peterson John L (Fla)
Tr.—Fernandez Floreano
Lifetime 7 2 0 0 $31,680
1987 4 1 0 0 $17,880
1986 3 1 0 0 $13,800
Turf 4 2 0 0 $31,680
10Jly87-7Bel 1⅛[T]:49²1:14 1:47¹sf 4¾ 111 31 2hd 22½ 47¾ Cruguet J2 ⒻAw28000 57-35 Debonirly,DremCrek,AntiquMystiqu 8
3Jly87-5Bel 1⅜:50 1:39³ 2:19³m 7½ 112 54 622 650 — Cruguet J5 ⒻAw28000 — — Laughing Lady, Far East, Darbyvail 6
3Jly87—Eased
18Jun87-8Bel 1⅛[T]:47⁴1:11¹1:41²fm 8 109 52½ 53 63½ 79½ Davis R G7 ⒻHcp0 85-10 Fam,PerfectPoint,SmoketheQueen 7
22May87-3Bel 1⅛[T]:47³1:11³1:44⁴gd 3 112 2½ 1½ 13 14 Cruguet J5 ⒻAw27000 77-22 Marimascus, Starita, Sassy Mama 7
30Nov86-2Aqu 1 :47¹ 1:12³ 1:38³ft 61 121 96 1014 1021 1028 Skinner K2 ⒻAw27000 45-24 MissileMgic,Alyffirm,GrcefulDrby 11
30Nov86—Slow early
3Nov86-4Aqu 1⅛Ⓣ:48⁴1:14¹1:46⁴fm 31 117 84 33 3nk 1hd Skinner K8 ⒻMdn 71-22 Mrmscs,AntqMyst,CrwnAndScptr 10
16Oct86-7Bel 1 :46² 1:12¹ 1:37⁴ft 25 117 85¾ 711 716 719¾ Skinner K10 ⒻMdn 56-19 GrcfulDrby,TurnSwift,MssUnnmbl 10
Jly 30 Bel [T] 5f fm 1:03 b (d) Jun 11 Bel [T] 5f fm 1:01⁴ b (d)

While handicappers at Golden Gate had enough information right there in the past performances, the May 15 crowd at Penn National that considered the chances of Marimascus would have needed to go back to previous *Forms* to discover November to May, the previous layoff leading to victory (1986–87), was precisely the same length and period of time of layoff leading up to the May 15, 1988, comeback race.

Was the pattern relating to the layoffs of Bargain Fun and Marimascus one of destiny, relating to the inherent horse biology of these competitors, or one of design, relating to external trainer strategies based on observations of past performance cycles? Could the April 17 victory of Bargain Fun and the May 15 win of Marimascus have been the result of self-fulfilling prophecies?

The trainer factor is embedded in horse performance cycles to varying degrees. We shall be studying the ups and downs of horse careers from both the horse and the trainer perspective, but I suspect that the best of trainers are not those who try to change a horse's natural life passages but those who adapt to them and make the best use of them.

And what of Tamtulia, the antihero of our story? Tamtulia's Del Mar backers of September 11, 1987, could have easily saved their money if they had seen the research from this chapter. Tamtulia's previous layoff led to a sixth-place finish, seventeen lengths behind the leader. As a first-time starter this filly had finished eighth by twelve lengths at 143–1. Tamtulia did not lose because of some general rule about layoffs; she lost because her own inherent conditioning system did not reach its peak the first day back after a vacation.

THE POST-COMEBACK BLUES

Throughout the clubhouse, grandstand, and infield of Santa Anita on January 8, 1988, "lock" and "sure thing" were primary words in just about everyone's vocabulary. In each instance they were pointing to the number one horse in the sixth race, *Art's Prospector*. Favorite players who tend to overuse such vocabulary were not the only ones to consider the filly a cinch. They found their unexpected allies in long-shot players who supposedly never bet a horse at under 5–1. Now, most of the big-score players were singling Art's Prospector in the Pick 6 and triple.

For once the guy in the plaid sports jacket with tout sheets hanging out of all the pockets had affinities with the guy who carried the briefcase filled with computer printouts and esoteric pace figures. Final time handicappers and followers of speed ratings saw a 1:10.1 time in the filly's last race, which was especially fast in comparison with the times of the rest of the sixth-race competitors, none of whom seemed capable of breaking 1:11.

More sophisticated members of the crowd went deeper into

the subtleties of horse-race handicapping and came up with the same conclusion. The very same day that Art's Prospector had earned her 1:10.1, Bid Us, a member of the stronger sex* had completed the same trip in 1:10.4 (three lengths slower), and that feat occurred in a classified-allowance race that included other older males of distinction that ran to figures even more flattering to Art's Prospector.

Female maidens had run more quickly than a featured field that included several stakes winners. If you were to compare the two races as if they had been one, the allowance-race favorite, Broadway Pointe, would have finished more than five lengths behind Art's Prospector.

SEVENTH RACE
Hollywood
DECEMBER 13, 1987

6 FURLONGS. (1.08⅘) ALLOWANCE. Purse $52,000. 3-year-olds and upward which have not won $20,000 since February 1, 1987. Weights, 3-year-olds, 120 lbs.; older, 122 lbs. Non-winners of $19,000 twice since April 22 allowed 3 lbs.; two such races of $18,000 since then, 5 lbs.; $17,000 since then, 7 lbs. (Claiming and starter races not considered.)

Value of race $52,000; value to winner $28,600; second $10,400; third $7,800; fourth $3,900; fifth $1,300. Mutuel pool $300,871. Exacta pool $352,691.

Last Raced	Horse	Eqt.	A.	Wt	PP	St	¼	½	Str	Fin	Jockey	Odds $1
29Nov87 7Hol3	Bid Us		7	117	1	6	3hd	1hd	1½	1½	Pincay L Jr	2.30
21Nov87 13BM3	Magic Door		3	108	3	4	41	3½	3½	22	Gryder A T5	9.70
11Jan87 8SA3	Broadway Pointe		3	116	2	2	2hd	2hd	2hd	31½	Delahoussaye E	2.10
22Apr87 8GG5	Right Con		5	115	7	5	6hd	6hd	51	41¼	Vasquez J	29.70
24Aug87 8AP7	Gemini Dreamer	b	7	115	4	7	7	7	4hd	53½	Day P	34.50
29Nov87 7Hol4	Orojoya		5	115	6	1	52½	41	61½	61¼	Hawley S	10.40
11Apr87 7Kee5	Faster Than Sound		3	114	5	3	1hd	51	7	7	Cordero A Jr	2.00

OFF AT 4:14. Start good. Won driving. Time, :22⅖, :45⅗, :58, 1:10⅘ Track fast.

$2 Mutuel Prices:

1-BID US	6.60	4.20	2.40
3-MAGIC DOOR		6.20	2.80
2-BROADWAY POINTE			2.60

$2 EXACTA 1-3 PAID $36.40

FOURTH RACE
Hollywood
DECEMBER 13, 1987

6 FURLONGS. (1.08⅘) MAIDEN. Purse $28,000. Fillies and mares. 3-year-olds and upward. Weights, 3-year-olds, 118 lbs.; older, 120 lbs.

Value of race $28,000; [illegible] $15,400; second $5,600; third $4,200; fourth $2,100; fifth $700. Mutuel pool $330,628. Exacta pool $388,554.

Last Raced	Horse	Eqt.	A.	Wt	PP	St	¼	½	Str	Fin	Jockey	Odds $1
	Persona Profit		3	113	3	4	51½	1hd	25	1hd	Gryder A T5	a-2.70
15Nov86 6Hol9	Art's Prospector		3	118	6	2	1hd	21	1hd	28	Hawley S	8.70
20Dec87 6Hol2	Fancy Sauce		3	118	2	3	41	41½	33	33½	Cordero A Jr	3.70
8Aug87 6LA2	Sonic Dream		3	118	5	8	81	6hd	4½	42½	Delahoussaye E	12.00
	Never A Thorn		3	118	4	6	62	72	61½	5½	Meza R Q	15.90
	Cat Call		3	113	8	10	10	94	90	6½	Sherman A B5	a-2.70
5Dec87 4Hol4	Slew Of Fortune	b	3	118	10	7	93½	81½	81½	71½	Pincay L Jr	3.50
20Dec87 6Hol3	Our Amy		3	118	7	1	3hd	31½	51	83	Santos J A	11.10
27Nov87 4Hol4	Mogadora	b	3	118	1	9	2½	5hd	72	912	Valenzuela P A	5.50
9Aug87 4Lga7	Little Chicago		3	113	9	5	7½	10	10	10	Banderas A L5	109.40

a-Coupled: Persona Profit and Cat Call.

OFF AT 2:36. Start good for all but CAT CALL. Won driving. Time, :22⅘, :45⅘, :58, 1:10⅕ Track fast.

$2 Mutuel Prices:

1-PERSONA PROFIT (a-entry)	7.40	4.60	3.20
6-ART'S PROSPECTOR		8.80	5.40
3-FANCY SAUCE			2.80

$2 EXACTA 1-6 PAID $79.60

*Horse racing is one of the rare sports that allows for males and females to compete in the same league. Female riders such as Krone and Aragon have been at the top of the standings, on occasion, while Very Subtle and Winning Colors won the Breeders' Cup Sprint and the Kentucky Derby, respectively, beating the boys fair and square.

Art's Prospector went to post at 3–5, which meant the crowd gave her an incredible 60 percent chance to win (minus track "take"). The only way that horseplayers can neutralize the take and gain an edge is to justifiably eliminate horses, which would be equivalent to eliminating numbered slots on a roulette wheel by dropping antimagnetic powder into certain slots so that the ball would be repelled out. Eliminating an even-money favorite would be the same as slipping that powder into nineteen of the thirty-eight roulette slots and still receiving 35–1 for single-number payoffs. Find a reason for eliminating horses such as Art's Prospector, and a trip to the window would amount to making withdrawals from an infinite bank account, one that contained the inexhaustible funds of the betting public.

Assume for a moment that, after the track take, Art's Prospector is getting 60 percent of the public's action. Assume there is a way to eliminate this type of horse. If so, you could calculate your expected income by subtracting the 17 percent (negative expectation) from the 60 percent advantage you have gained by having eliminated such a popular horse:

60%	Gross Advantage
−17%	Built-in Disadvantage
43%	Net Advantage

With that much of an advantage, in the long run random betting on any other horse in the race would yield a profit equivalent to the net advantage calculated.

On the other hand, if we can't find legitimate reasons for eliminating false favorites, then Scarne would have been right when he wrote in his diatribes that we horseplayers should toss in the towel rather than confront such perversely negative percentages. But then, Scarne knew little about handicapping and less about the predictable ups and downs of thoroughbred race horses.

Here we have one of the many situations in which cycle-oriented handicappers have a material advantage. Art's Prospector had earned his fast time *following a long layoff*, thirteen months to be precise. It is very typical that a *peak effort following a layoff will cause a horse to underachieve in its next race.* During my lusterless career as a college cross-country runner, I remember a teammate named John coming on the team with no prior training and winning a race. He was so far ahead of me that he had already showered and dressed by the time I crossed the finish line. I was ready to toss in my shoes after seeing that so much excruciating training had gotten me nowhere. In the next race, though, John finished near the back of the pack, where I could talk to him during the race. He had come up sore following his premature peak effort. This must have something to do with the logic as to why horses "bounce" after a post-layoff peak effort.

Art's Prospector gave it a good try on January 8, staying close to her inferiors and ultimately finishing third. A lot of money found its way out of the pockets of handicappers who disregarded the fact that for legitimate form-cycle reasons, horses don't run 'em all alike. Next time out, these same handicappers had given up on the filly, as she proceeded to win and pay off in double figures.

The sequence of events, then, in the "bounce" cycle is: *lay-off—peak effort—underachievement—*possible improvement. There is no guarantee of a win in the third race following the layoff; that remains a situation of potential pari-mutuel value which must be analyzed on its own terms. The true value in this sequence of events lies in wagering against overbet horses in their moment of expected underachievement, when they figure to be overbet.

The story of *Little Bolder* has a plot that conforms to the bounce cycle as well as a tangential subplot of interest as a prelude to later chapters on trainer cycles.

Little Bolder	B. f. 4, by Taufan—Stony Ground, by Relko		
DELAHOUSSAYE E	Br.—O'Dwyer & Collins (Ire)	1988 2 1 1 0	$28,500
Own.—Bollinger & Milhous 118	Tr.—Otteson Kimberly	1987 2 1 0 0	$3,427
	Lifetime 7 2 3 1 $33,151	Turf 7 2 3 1	$33,151

20Feb88-5SA 1 ①:46⁴1:10⁴1:36²fm *6-5 118 68½ 52½ 4¹ 2¹⅜ DlhoussyE² ⒸAw38000 91-05 NirobiExprss,LittlBoldr,DrngDoon 10
20Feb88—Wide into stretch
27Jan88-5SA 1⅛①:47²1:12²1:52 fm 19 116 45½ 43½ 2½ 16½ DlhoussyE⁴ ⒸAw38000 67-33 Little Bolder,CleverEdge,Confiture 8
27Jan88—Crowded, check at 1/4
7Jly87◊2Chepstow(Eng) 7f 1:21⁴gd 10 123 ① 1½ NwnsW   ⒻFlur d Lys (Mdn) LittleBolder,AlbynLdy,ExoticSuce 14
22May87◊6Pontefract(Eng) 6f 1:15³fm 5½ 123 ① 49½ RobrtsM   Cedar (Mdn) Praiseworthy, Tarsa,TrapezeDancer 8
3Sep86◊6Bath(Eng) a5½f 1:13³gd 3½ 120 ① 2ⁿᵏ Roberts M   ⒻTog Hill Attempting, LittleBolder,JustKala 15
19Aug86◊1Folkestone(Eng) 6f 1:17²gd 6 123 ① 2½ RbrtsM   ⒹDanes (Mdn) Attempting,LittleBoldr,RipCristin 14
25Jly86◊1Warwick(Eng) 5f :59 gd 16 123 ① 3⁵ BnnerM   ⒻGarick (Mdn) UltrNov,PrdiseCoffee,LittleBolder 11
Feb 15 SA 3f ft 1:02³ h   Feb 5 SA 3f ft :37 h   Jan 21 SA 6f ft 1:16² h   Jan 15 SA 6f ft 1:15² h

February 20 saw, once more, the unholy alliance between the average Joe and the would-be pro. Anyone who scanned the *Form* would have seen a dynamic victory for Little Bolder, who overcame the wrath of the Horse Gods to draw off to a six-length victory. Sophisticated handicappers noted that Little Bolder had just won a race *above her conditions.* On January

27 she had been entered in an "allowance non-winners of two," meaning for horses that had won no more than one allowance race. But Little Bolder had won zero allowance races and could have qualified to enter a race against lesser competition, labeled "nonwinners of one," meaning for horses that had never won an allowance race.

By having won her last race above her conditions, Little Bolder was eligible on February 20 to enter a race at the same class level she had already dominated. Indeed, she was the only horse in that third race that had already won at the designated class level. Most wagerers did not distinguish between the different allowance levels, so many of the pros thought they were on to a good thing.

But Little Bolder's January 27 victory had taken place in a comeback race, one that followed a layoff of greater than six months! Handicappers sensitive to performance cycles could suspect that Little Bolder should run at something less than peak-performance level. And sure enough, while running courageously in order to fulfill the promises of her 6–5 odds, she lost to Nairobi Express, a horse she had beaten the time before by 8½ lengths. Art's Prospector's had also been defeated by a horse he had trounced by eight lengths.

The subplot concerns the trainer-cycle factor, which we will be insisting is usually embedded in some way in horse cycles. The same trainer of Little Bolder, Kimberly Otteson, had pulled off a similar coup more than a year earlier with a foreign import/layoff horse by the name of Thresh It Out, who won its comeback race at huge odds, nosing out the horse I had bet on. Since that race, Thresh It Out had tried numerous times to win another race at the same class level of its layoff win. At this writing, Thresh It Out's losing streak is beginning to look like the inverse of Joe DiMaggio's famous hitting streak.

For the sixth race, January 13, at Aqueduct, a three-year-old colt by the name of *Won Lump* would have rated marquee billing in just about every handicapping textbook. It was an entry-level allowance race, and every other horse except Won Lump should have been an automatic throwout. We're not talking about a future Breeders' Cup champion, but in this setting, Won Lump was the only horse of the field that had triumphed in its maiden race against straight maidens at a major-league track. An added asset was the fact that most of his competition had already proven it couldn't win at the allowance level. Most trainers dream of finding a spot for a recent open maiden winner against claimers and horses from the bush leagues.

The tote board was pulsating with heavy action on Won Lump. Even the colt's less-than-attractive name could not stop any of the money from forging through the windows. But Won Lump's peak effort, which was attracting all the action, had been achieved right after a three-month layoff. As could be expected by followers of horse orbits, Won Lump did not run to his odds, while in his following race he ran competitively, finishing third at 11–1.

Astute horseplayers might suggest that the layoff—sharp-race/dull-race sequence—most logically applies to cheaper horses. Sound reasoning tells us that superior horses should overcome the negative cycle, that the classier the animal, the more likely it can defy the percentages. Observe the past performances of *Girl Powder* and *Rita H.*, both of whom became stakes-placed competitors:

On May 16 Girl Powder came back after a five-month layoff to engage in a head-to-head skirmish with Happy Helen. The rest of the field was left twelve lengths behind. In spite of the layoff, Girl Powder prevailed, but in her next race she joined the club of the beaten favorites.

After an 8½-month vacation, Rita H. came back to the races as a 20–1 unlikely-to-win and startled the crowd by finishing a competitive second. Next time out, the same crowd responded by betting her down to 5–2. Bettors should have refrained, with the expectation that a bounce would be normal in the context of form cycles. She turned in a dull race, for apparently no reason according to advocates of the "continuity" mode of handicapping. Her next effort on April 8 at Keeneland was a winning one, but this time at the profitable odds of 5½–1, as the public shook its collective head in confusion.

Both Girl Powder and Rita H. were classier horses who had failed in races that followed a post-layoff effort. One of the classiest of all horses in recent racing history was equally vulnerable to the post-peak blues.

On December 26, 1986, the mighty *Ferdinand*, winner of the Kentucky Derby, returned to the races after nearly six months of luxurious grazing in green pastures. He was not supposed to win the Malibu Stakes, as that event was a prep for bigger and better races during the Santa Anita meet. Seven furlongs was clearly not the right distance for the long-winded Ferdinand. A sprint win after a layoff will take even more out of a horse than a route event, because the pace is torrid at the shorter distances. The betting public was aware of all these considerations and let Ferdinand get away at over 4–1. He won anyway, with a powerful stretch charge that surprised everyone in Arcadia, including his rider, William Shoemaker.

Ferdinand's next race, as we have by now deduced, called for a underachieving effort. But the public either ignores or underestimates this unique facet of the form factor, and Ferdinand was heavily backed at 6–5. A lot of principled money went down the drain, as believers in continuity were once more questioning their Horse Gods. The great Ferdinand, future Breeders' Cup winner, finished a well-beaten fourth.

Ferdinand Ch. c. 4, by Nijinsky II—Banja Luka, by Double Jay
DELAHOUSSAYE E 126 Br.—Keck H B (Ky) 1987 1 0 0 0 $11,250
Own.—Keck Mrs H B Tr.—Whittingham Charles 1986 8 3 3 2 $981,678
Lifetime 14 4 4 4 $1,171,578

18Jan87-8SA	1⅛	:482	1:121	1:49 ft	6-5	123	54	55	45	46½	ShmkrW1	Sn Frndo	77-19	VarietyRoad,BrodBrush,SnowChief	8
18Jan87—Grade I; Checked 5 1/2															
26Dec86-8SA	7f	:222	:444	1:213ft	4½	123	96½	75½	41½	11½	ShmkrW11	Malibu	92-13	Ferdinand, Snow Chief,DonB.Blue	12
26Dec86—Grade II															
7Jun86-8Bel	1½	:474	2:04	2:294sy	3½	126	33½	3½	2½	31½	ShmkrW7	Belmont	69-16	DnzgConncton,JohnsTrsur,Frdnnd	10
7Jun86—Grade I															
17May86-8Pim	1³⁄₁₆	:472	1:11	1:544ft	3	126	614	612	24	24	ShmkrW5	Preakness	89-18	Snow Chief, Ferdinand,BrcadBrush	7
17May86—Grade I															
3May86-8CD	1¼	:451	1:37	2:024ft	18	126	1620	52	11	12½	ShmkrW1	Ky Derby	83-10	Frdinnd,BoldArrngmnt,BrodBrush	16
3May86—Grade I; Crowded early															
6Apr86-5SA	1⅛	:471	1:11	1:483ft	5½	122	55	54	54½	37	ShmkrW2	S A Dby	79-15	Snow Chief, Icy Groom, Ferdinand	7
6Apr86—Grade I															
22Feb86-8SA	1	:453	1:102	1:353ft	*9-5	116	77½	41½	12	2½	ShmkrW9	Sn Rafael	89-16	VarietyRoad,Ferdinnd,JettingHome	9
22Feb86—Grade II; Wide into stretch															
29Jan86-8SA	1¹⁄₁₆	:462	1:11	1:43 ft	2½	114	64½	64½	32	1½	ShmkrW6	®Sta Ctlna	86-15	Ferdinand,VrietyRod,GrndAllegince	8
29Jan86—Lacked room, steadied at intervals 5/16 to 1/8															
4Jan86-8SA	1	:453	1:103	1:361ft	*4-5	114	32½	3½	11½	2hd	ShoemkrW3	®Ls Feliz	87-13	Badger Land,Ferdinand,CutByGlass	7
4Jan86—3-wide into stretch															
15Dec85-8Hol	1	:443	1:09	1:341ft	34	121	95½	35½	35½	36½	ShomkrW2	Hol Fut	85-09	SnowChief,ElectricBlue,Ferdinand	10
15Dec85—Grade I; Broke slowly															

●Feb 4 SA 5f ft :581 h ●Jan 29 SA 1f ft 1:39 h Jan 24 SA 3f ft :363 h Jan 17 SA 3f ft :362 b

Not only are the classiest horses equally subject to the post-comeback blues, but the best of trainers are not exempt. I recall a cloudy winter day, 1985, Santa Anita, when Mr. Robert Frankel entered a European maiden shipper in an allowance event, on the downhill grass course. Like Little Bolder, the Frankel horse raced above its conditions and won anyway. Also like Ms. Otteson's horse, the Frankel long-shot winner was to bounce the next time out. This was my first experience with a long parade of Frankel's European layoff winners which were to decline in their post-comeback race. Kimberly Otteson is in the best of company. The epic stories of these and other trainers will continue in subsequent pages.

In the meantime, beware of the sharp race following a layoff. The next time on the track, a case of the post-comeback blues is a high probability for horses that will be inevitably overbet. A huge pari-mutuel advantage awaits us if we bet against this type of horse.

Subset

All observations are subject to distortions when based solely on a general set of events. In the case of the horse that has just run competitively following a vacation, it may make a difference whether or not the horse is inherently competitive or whether or not the horse has a good trainer. Perhaps the set of all bad horses with mediocre trainers are more likely to bounce the second race after the layoff than are the better horses with the smarter trainers.

The following sample studies the subset that is most likely to contradict our findings: horse has just run a sharp race following a layoff of three months or more and is either a *proven competent horse* and/or a *better-than-average trainer*.

Sample:	50 races
Wins:	12 (24%)
Invest:	$100
Return:	$69 (31% loss)

Observation

From this elite sample came an apparently fair percentage of winners. However, the average mutuel was so low that the percentage of loss (return on investment) was dismal. My aunt Tillie does twice as well (half as bad) by wagering according to a random method she calls "Pin the Tail on the Program."

CHAPTER 3

Serfdom in the Sport of Kings

WILLY LOMAN MEETS THE DEVIL

"AN OFFER YOU CAN'T REFUSE, Willy. One month, perhaps two or three, in which you will depart from mediocrity and encounter success and prosperity. You'll feel younger and stronger. Your boss will give you an unlimited expense account. People who closed doors in your face will come calling, begging."

"What's the catch?"

"No catch. Simply, one day, unexpectedly, it will come to an end and you will be the same Willy Loman as before, picking up small purses but never finishing first."

"There's got to be something in it for you. I know who you are. I know what you represent."

"Well, yes . . . for me something. But that does not concern you. Put it this way: your transformation will confuse others on my list, disorient, even ruin some who have tried to escape without paying me back. They'll get only what they bargained for."

Most thoroughbreds barely reach Willy Loman's level of mediocrity. Maiden-claiming fields are full of horses that, if you look back at the field a year later, will have never won a race. Most three-year-old claimers are destined to disappear. They won't be forgotten, because they were never known enough in the first place.

Then there are those just good enough to survive. They fill fields in claiming races for older horses but they become known as proven losers. They are the Willy Lomans of horse racing, always hoping their day will come, persisting, here and there finishing in the money, earning barely enough to pay most of the bills but not all of them.

If all of these Willy Loman–type horses were predictable, they would be automatic tossouts, exclusions from the handicapping process. But the pari-mutuel Devil cannot allow horseplayers the luxury of automatic eliminations. So he makes pacts with certain proven losers. Here's the scenario.

July 16, 1987, Monmouth, second race.

Starry Moon has a record of resounding mediocrity. Two wins in 32 races. She wins at 8½–1. We all figure that it must have been a weak field or a track biased in her favor. So two races later she comes back at a higher class and we say, "If it takes her thirty-four races to win only three, she's not going to put two victories so close together!" We know that the stats clearly prove that most horses that win races in clusters have a high win percentage to begin with. So only a month later, Starry Moon wins at 22–1.

March 11, 1986, Santa Anita, first race.

The infamous *T.V. Oil*, 1 for 35 in his illustrious career, wins a race at 5–1. Eleven days later he does it again, this time at 6–1. So where is T.V. Oil today? Same place as Willy Loman.

There is an odd type of form cycle that allows certain mediocre claimers one brief interlude of brilliance and prosperity before they lapse back into mediocrity. The only apparent explanation for this brief-interlude pattern is some strange pact with the Devil. And each time one of these proven losers wins a second or third time, competent horseplayers have rightfully overlooked the horse because of its terribly low win percentage.

Definition. The "brief interlude" pattern calls for:

1. *At least two years of mediocre performance* (most often less than a 10 percent win rate)
2. *A cluster of victories* (rarely more than three)
3. *Remission* (back to mediocrity and oblivion)

A graph of this life cycle will look like a map of the state of Kansas with a strange mountain range cutting through the middle, north-south.

Question. How can the handicapper distinguish between a proven loser whose recent win was a fluke, and a mediocre horse whose recent win ushers in a brief interlude or cluster of wins at high odds?

Analysis. A random sample of 30 horses of this type from diverse racing circuits shows the following:

1. Eighty percent of this type of winner has won its breakthrough race following an identifiable *change.*
2. In one third of the instances of surprise victory, there has been either (a) a rider switch, (b) a change of racetrack, or (c) a significant class drop.
3. In 4 of the 30 cases there has been a significant trainer change.
4. In cases of trainer, rider, or track change, *the same new trainer, rider, or track remains in effect for the horse's second win,* the one we are concerned about.*
5. In cases of class drop, often the horse has found a proper level, discovered how to win, built confidence or competitiveness, and been capable of going up in class for its unexpected second triumph.
6. Of the 80 percent of surprise winners that have exhibited one or more of the four most frequent changes, (a) over 50 percent *needed only one change* to accomplish their feat,

---

*This particular section concentrates on an unexpected second win; the subject of form reversal, which includes many different types of horses, deserves separate treatment and will be featured in Chapter 6.

      (b) 33 percent needed a combination of two changes, and
      (c) 12 percent needed three or more changes.
7. Of the 20 percent surprise winners that did not show any
change, there were several borderline situations in which
the analyst might have indeed interpreted a change; I decided not to count as a change (a) a switch to a rider who
had lost before with the horse, and (b) drops in class to a
level at which the horse had previously lost.
8. Rationality Index: 80 percent (remember, the rationality
index does not mean predictability, but merely means that
somewhere in the realm of horse-racing logic there is a
reason or explanation for the victory).

SMOOTH BID, A MODERN TRAGIC FIGURE

Traditional tragic figures are fallen nobles, persons of fame, fortune, or status who lose their position due to fateful circumstances, conniving schemers, or human frailty. That came from
periods in history when kings, queens, and dukes were people
and the rest of the world didn't count. The masses were faceless
but for a vicarious identification with their paternal leaders.

    Willy Loman represents a period in which members of the
masses are fed rising expectations that are rarely fulfilled. Willy's tragedy is not that he fell from the heights, but that the table
was never set for him to begin with. His expectations were
stretched far beyond his potential. Serfs had little or no hopes
and dreams. Working people like Willy were nourished on hopes
and dreams.

    In the world of thoroughbreds, *Smooth Bid* keeps struggling
for a moment of glory. In the waning months of the sixth year of
his life (getting to be an old-timer), Smooth Bid has only 1 win in
18 attempts. He has been going from fair to fair in search of fame
and fortune on a lesser scale and coming up with nothing. As a
gelding, he has no chance to encounter a traditional romance. As
a five-year-old he earned less than $6000, not really enough for
decent room and board.

    Even if he were successful at the jobs he undertakes, the pay
is low, and it costs just as much for his feed as it does for Ferdinand's.

    October 9, 1987, Santa Anita, first race.

    Smooth Bid's recent failures have been attempts at finding

happiness as a big fish in a small pond. The minor-league fair circuit was the scene of Smooth Bid, the migrant laborer, failing at Pleasanton, failing at Solano, Stockton, and Fairplex.

Smooth Bid is now entered at the $10,000 claiming level, not exactly the big time but certainly a more glamorous setting than the migrant camps.

The crowd sees this as incongruent and finds it even more irrational that Smooth Bid will be carrying a lady passenger, Joy Scott, who rarely ever wins a race at a major circuit. For these very objective reasons, Smooth Bid goes off at 76–1.

From the outset Smooth Bid finds himself in a suicidal pace duel. Never more than one head in front, Smooth Bid puts away one competitor only to find another at his side. Veteran race watchers know that at this track, when Joy Scott gets in a pace duel, the other rider is likely to win.

When Smooth Bid crosses the finish line in a photo with his nearest rival, most grandstand veterans suppose that only a pact with the Devil could produce a victory for the Smooth Bid/Joy Scott combo.

Number 6 lights up on the tote board, and that is Smooth Bid. Then the payoff: $153.60 to win!

November 15, 1987, Santa Anita, first race.

Smooth Bid is entered at $16,000, two levels higher than his 76–1 triumph. Can he do it again? There are two logics. One says that his win was a fluke, one of the many irrational occurrences that seem to be part of horse racing. The other logic says that the horse may be having his once-in-a-lifetime fling, and that the switch to Santa Anita along with the switch to Joy Scott must be considered positives and not negatives because those two factors should have been negatives and weren't. It's a Yogi Berra type of logic but it makes sense: rider switch and track switch, two major factors that seem to usher in radical transformations in horse behavior.

Smooth Bid wins again, this time at 19–1. As so often happens, horses that once pay off at a huge price do it again. Next time out, Smooth Bid goes from $16,000 to $40,000, and with Ms. Scott at 25–1, he finishes a successful second. Could it be that Smooth Bid is about to enter the ranks of the nobility? So thinks his entourage, which enters him in an allowance race on December 30.

Smooth Bid must overcome two major barriers. It has rained this week and the track has come up muddy. With no mud star at age six going on seven, one must suppose that Smooth Bid is not fond of the wet track. Perhaps he should be scratched. Also, is it not asking too much of a horse that has recently won a $10,000 race to be entered in an allowance event? Could the stiff competition damage the newly-found winning spirit of Smooth Bid? He finishes sixth in a field of nine.

Now, as a seven-year-old, our tragic hero is dropped slightly to $40,000, January 27, Santa Anita, ninth race. Instead of the no-win rider Joy Scott, leading jockey Gary Stevens is the pilot. Perhaps the only time in modern history that a switch from Joy Scott to Gary Stevens is a negative switch. Have Smooth Bid's handlers become disenchanted with Scott, or is she simply unavailable? The crowd, still not realizing that a female rider who rarely gets good mounts is probably greatly responsible for the unexpected success of a once-chronic loser, bets down Smooth Bid to 8½–1. We say 'down" because this horse wins at 76–1 and at 19–1.

The horse breaks slowly with Stevens, something he never did with Scott. He's then rushed up, presses the pace for a while, and finishes out evenly.

February 10, 1988, Santa Anita, second race.

After his two surprise wins, Smooth Bid has had three tough races, not under ideal circumstances. It may be too late for such a move, but the horse is dropped to $25,000, a level he would have done well at back in December. Once more Gary Stevens is up and Joy Scott is nowhere to be found. Smooth Bid is now a startling 5–2 in the morning line. The crowd, which failed to accept him with Joy Scott, even after his first surprise win, now bets him down to 3–1, nearly the favorite.

Although he finishes in the money, he is a well-beaten third. It looks as if Smooth Bid has experienced his one lifetime moment of glory and he is now on the road to oblivion.

Was Smooth Bid's brief fling with glory a question of a pact with the Devil? Are we looking at an irrational peak in an otherwise dull form cycle? Or can Smooth Bid be categorized within the 80 percent of surprise peakers whose wins can be rationally associated with a switch of track, rider, or class (drop)? Whatever the reader may conclude about Smooth Bid, at least 20 percent of surprise-win clusters offer no rational explanation, unless you believe in pacts with the Devil.

Elsada's Joy			Dk. b. or br. f. 4, by Weth Nan—Elsada, by Iron Warrior				
			Br.—Yagoda S (NY)		1988	9 2 1 0	$30,300
Own.—Yagoda S		110⁵	Tr.—Boland William	$13,000	1987	18 1 0 0	$5,430
			Lifetime 27 3 1 0 $35,730		Turf	1 0 0 0	
12May88–1Bel	6f :22² :45⁴ 1:10⁴m	19 115	8⁸ 9⁶¾ 9¹⁰ 9¹⁷¼	Bailey J D⁴	Ⓑ 16500	68–14 LizsJoy,Burn'sDncer,InvernssMiss 10
27Apr88–3Aqu	6f :21⁴ :45 1:11 ft	44 108⁷	56½ 88½ 9¹⁰ 89¾	Walker E E²	Ⓑ 22500	75–18 ClssiclMnner,RunGnuin,MiTi'sBby 10
14Apr88–7Aqu	6f :22 :45³ 1:11¹ft	23 114⁷	77¾ 7¹² 69½ 5¹⁰½	WlkerEE⁵ ⒻⒼ Aw32000		73–21 AnthninGrl,NoblWsh,ShnncockL ss11
2Apr88–7Aqu	1 :46⁴ 1:12³ 1:38⁴ft	13 114⁷	5² 64½ 6¹¹ 6¹⁵½	WlkerEE⁵ ⒻⒼ Aw33000		56–22 DvousDutchss,Unsnctond,FmlyFrud⁷
17Mar88–3Aqu	6f :22² :46⁴ 1:12⁴ft	28 112⁵	75½ 6⁵ 2¹½ 1⅔	BolngrG⁸ ⒻⒼ Aw30000		76–22 Elsd'sJoy,MidOfHerts,MindthGold 11
1Mar88–9Aqu	6f ⊡:23 :47¹¹:133ft	16 112⁵	9⁸ 10⁹½ 7⁵ 7⁶	Boulanger G² Ⓑ 13000		70–31 DuckyDuchesse,Ther'sWy,BigBozo 12
3Mar88–9Aqu	6f ⊡:22⁴ :472¹:134ft	9½ 110⁵	55½ 54½ 41½ 1ʰᵈ	Boulanger G² Ⓑ 13000		75–22 Elsad'sJoy,Nikolodi,MightyModel 10
13Feb88–2Aqu	6f ⊡:22¹ :47¹¹:14 ft	19 115	— — — —	Nuesch D 1	Ⓑ 13000	— — HdingNorth,BlivdSunny,Chryl'sJig 11
13Feb88–Lost rider						

Was it coincidental when *Elsada's Joy*, 1 for 20 at the time, switched to Boulanger, won 2 of 3 at high odds, then, with the mysterious disappearance of Boulanger, resumed her custom of finishing out of the money?

In our visit to the lower classes of thoroughbred society, we now step to the bottom rung and visit horses that are so consistent in their mediocrity that they will experience only the most fleeting of positive moments.

SERFDOM IN THE SPORT OF KINGS

In the competitive society of thoroughbreds, for some to be winners, many must be losers. From the beginning it seems to have been inscribed that certain horses will labor more and earn less so that others above them can earn more and labor less. Many from these downtrodden masses are up for sale ever since their first race (maiden claiming). Departing from serfdom will be an occasional John Henry or Snow Chief, while many nobles will soon fall from grace and be forced to share the track with the more humbly bred.

As the class structure solidifies, each class will develop its own bottom tier, comprised of horses that win less than 10 percent of the time or those that once may have been competitive and now, after two calendar years of mediocrity, have proven that they have lost it. Some of these laborers will continue to try at the same class level, unwilling to concede that they "do not belong." Others will attempt to become big fish in small ponds by competing at lesser levels; of these, some will discover how to win, while more will continue to lose as they descend the class ladder.

The manner in which races are carded will affect the class structure. For example, southern California racing cards few grass claiming races, and of those few, none are for cheaper claimers. In this setting, the grass horse that can't win an allowance race is faced with a terrible dilemma: either keep racing and continue losing at an unrealistic level, or drop into lower-class dirt races with the prospect of losing because of an unfriendly surface.

At the claiming levels it is difficult to become a consistent winner unless there is a period of steady improvement that allows a horse to move up the class ladder. To win and not move up in class is to risk being claimed, precisely at the moment when a win streak is possible. Only the elderly and infirm can go on winning lower-level claiming races without being purchased and forced into a higher level of competition. In other words, the class structure of racing is an active variable in the life cycles of a horse.

Horse racing is solvent and growing largely because the bottom rungs of the class structure continue to run and lose so that others may win and collect purses. (I might add that in countries where horse racing has been kept as an exclusive activity of the aristocracy, such as Spain, the sport has not grown at the same pace as in the nations where we the people can participate.) Within the society of horses—and perhaps that of people too—the laboring masses are allowed to barely subsist, just enough to hold up the whole class structure.

When these common laborers of horse society win a race, it is usually to the surprise of thoughtful handicappers, who have never taken the time to study the characteristics of the victories of proven losers because it seems a more efficient use of time to study those types of horses that pay off more regularly. For this same reason, too often the proven-loser-type member of the laboring class is a precipitous elimination in the handicapping process. Usually, at least one of the Pick 6 races is won by this type of horse, leaving many of us with consolation payoffs instead of the big one.

Ironically, it is this type of horse that is most likely, over the span of its career, to produce a pari-mutuel flat-bed profit. Smooth Bid, for example, at the moment in his career we leave him, has yielded a 300 percent profit for those who decided to invest an equal amount of money in each of his races.

The first mistake of many competent handicappers is to assume that all proven losers are of the same ilk; actually, there are three very distinct types.

1. *Consistently Bad.* This type will win only under very unique circumstances, when it is granted an unusual advantage. Consistently bad horses will drop in class and show little or no improvement. A win does not mean a change in form cycle, but merely an occasion in which this type did not need to be competitive in order to win. Basic characteristic: *uncompetitive.*

2. *Inherently Inconsistent.* Occasionally will feel like competing and will run a strong race, usually at an unexpected moment.

3. *Forced to labor at the wrong level.* This type repeatedly fails to win because it is raced above its proper level of competitiveness. Occasional wins occur either with a class drop or when an unusually bad field is assembled for a particular race.

These three categories may occasionally overlap in the life history of particular horses. All three types occasionally share one type of victory in common: they may "back into a win" *when they face an unusually terrible field* in which they have become the *lesser of evils.* When this event occurs, subsequently eliminate all horses that lost to our proven loser the next several times they race.

Type 1: Consistently Bad

Julio N Me											

Julio N Me wins a maiden claimer as a two-year-old at the Pomona Fair (Fairplex). A year later, already having established himself as a chronic loser, he wins a claimer at Fairplex, paying off at 11–1 (see Chapter 7 for horse for course analysis). As a four-year-old Julio N Me tries Pomona once again, races competitively, but loses. Losses at the only scene of success are an omen of a bleak future. The track switch, usually a powerful factor in form reversals, has no effect on Julio N Me as he goes from grade A to grade B to grade C tracks, descending the class ladder each time, yet fails to exhibit significant improvement.

Type 1 proven losers have in common that they have one-dimensional running styles. They either lack early or tactical speed (Julio N Me) or they can only go as front runners, moving as fast as they can until they tire (which nearly always is prior to the finish line). Noon Time's First fits the second description.

Noon Time's First

The mere thought of another horse near or behind him makes Noon Time's First choke with fear. This horse's natural talent has him as a leader, but his herding instinct makes him want to follow. The only way he can win is by being so far ahead of the pack that he feels as if he's running alone. Compare his three Philadelphia races. He runs a 22 flat first quarter each time and a 23.1 second quarter on December 24 and January 24, with a 23.2 second quarter on January 9. On his winning day he was able to run one tick slower during the second quarter, and yet at the half-mile he found himself farther ahead of the rest of the field. His winning race was really no better than his losing races; it was the rest of the field that was worse.

The consistently bad or uncompetitive type of horse tends to pop up most frequently due to an unusual circumstance (thorough pace advantage, Noon Time's First; favored track, Julio N Me).

A thorough pace advantage is clearly the most frequent manner in which proven losers pop up and win races (without really peaking in their dull performance pattern). Many a time such a pace advantage will only materialize *after the race has begun,* when the *other* front runner has bobbled out of the gate, or variations on that theme.

While the lone front runner is the most popular commodity of pace speculators, its popularity will often destroy its pari-mutuel advantage. Other situations, variations on the theme, are more lucrative. For example, when our proven loser is a pace stalker and finds himself unaccompanied in the "garden spot" instead of racing in a competitive formation:

Stressful Trip

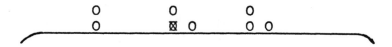

Or when our proven loser finds himself unaccompanied behind a couple of cheap speed horses, a lone front runner *in relation to the rest of the field:*

Unstressful Trip

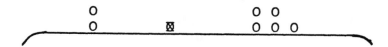

Sometimes this setup is predictable, while on other occasions one of the horses that should have been in the second tier failed to fire and ended up in the third tier, leaving our uncompetitive antihero in a pressureless situation.

Of all the written material I've seen, the Howard Sartin pace methodology is best at identifying this type of horse. This methodology calculates the all-important fractions by feet per second and relates them to prevailing track biases. Occasionally a race is carded that requires no esoteric sophistication to identify the lone garden-spot horse, the type of situation that most allows for bad horses to have one good day.

August 15, 1987, Del Mar, ninth race.

Cutting Wind was once a good horse, but now, after two winless years, he has become a proven loser. Today he is entered in a 1⅜-mile grass race, and has been showing only moderate form against lesser horses, the Canterbury Downs track being several notches below Del Mar. Note that in two of his last three races he has been *within three lengths* at the first two calls. In the other of his last three, he was initially farther back, but that was at a shorter distance, where one expects the pace to be faster. Today he is stretching out; even before considering the other horses, Cutting Wind figures to be closer to the front, since this marathon-type race is characterized by slower early fractions.

Now let us consider the early route fractions, only, of the other horses in this race. In other words, we are isolating the pace factor on the notion that the now mediocre Cutting Wind can only win when there is a highly favorable pace situation. The following table shows each horse's first-call position in its last two route races, with the exception of Rajhaan, who is coming back after a layoff and whose pace positions are taken from his last two Del Mar turf routes.

Migrator	6^9	Plum Certain	10^8
	6^{14}		5^6
Luna Sola	8^{12}	Situada	10^{15}
	6^5		7^{10}
Slane Castle	6^7	Amrapour	6^6
	5^6		8^5
Travet	7^9	Rajhaan	1^{hd}
	5^8		4^{10}

Rajhaan figures to take the lead. Showing two wire-to-wire turf wins in his last ten races plus a better-than-average series of workouts, Rajhaan will either go for the lead or inherit it, and is a serious candidate to steal the race. It seems Cutting Wind will inherit and control the garden spot. Any of these others, deciding to run with Cutting Wind at the early stages, would be huffing and puffing in a too-fast-too-early pace.

The crowd figured to overlook Cutting Wind because of rightfully identifying him as a no-win type of horse (excluding his more successful early life).

There was one more bit of information only available to those handicappers with very sharp memories or a willingness to dig into old *Racing Forms*. Two years back Cutting Wind won a turf race *at Del Mar*. A continuing theme of form-cycle analysis is that what happens a long time ago may have a bearing on today's behavior. Psychoanalysts believe this about their patients, and I believe it about the horses I handicap.

Like Julio N Me, Cutting Wind was a "horse for course." Like Noon Time's First, Cutting Wind had a thorough pace advantage. Since neither Cutting Wind nor Rajhaan was picked first, second, or third by any of the *Racing Form* handicappers, I recommended that the two services I worked for use both horses and bet them both to win. Either scenario was possible at a big price.

As the horses went to post, Rajhaan was 5–1 and Cutting Wind was 38–1. Rajhaan took the lead, as expected, while Cutting Wind initially shared the garden spot with the likely-to-tire-soon Amrapour. At the half-mile Rajhaan led by six lengths, and by the backstretch Cutting Wind had clear control of the garden spot. Going into the stretch, it was Rajhaan by 1½ lengths and Cutting Wind in second, 3½ lengths ahead of the rest of the field, the position of least stress.

Cutting Wind took over in the final sixteenth. He paid $79.40; the exacta with Rajhaan paid $1198. One of my clients called to tell me he had run out of money by the ninth race and didn't bet. Another told me that Cutting Wind looked outclassed so he didn't bet on it. He was probably right; Cutting Wind was outclassed, but not outpaced. Proof that he was right came later when Cutting Wind went back to losing race after race. On August 15 the table had been set, with Cutting Wind at the end of the table. He had not run the race of his life, only been given the opportunity of his life. The two factors that most contribute to pop-up wins for dull horses (pace advantage and horse for course) both materialized in favor of Cutting Wind.

Whether Cutting Wind wins any more races in the next two years will depend on the pace situation. As a long-distance runner, he is more likely to find a pace setup, since marathon races often come up with no early speed or one or two cheap early-speed horses in combination with lethargic come-from-behinders. He is not a neat textbook example of a bad horse, but his type of *opportunistic* victory is very typical of occasions when infrequent winners pop.

Type 2: Inherently Inconsistent

If Cutting Wind will be popping up occasionally, it will not be because he is inconsistent but because the situation or setting of his races changes. External forces will determine if he becomes a no-win horse or a pop-up, occasional winner. External forces will determine the rare occasions when so many horses, such as Julio N Me and Noon Time's First, back into a victory.

The inherently inconsistent, on the other hand, are those who clearly run with different levels of motivation at different times. It is easier to anticipate when a dull horse will inherit a victory than when an inconsistent one will decide to run.

Ernie King has a laid-back lifestyle which calls for much relaxation and occasional odd jobs when he is inspired to be creative or productive. He's great at working in his own garden but he'd hate to be an employee out in the fields. Unfortunately, his job as claimer requires him to labor steadily. When he goes to work he must confront a bias against closers; he lacks early or tactical speed, and this laid-back style offers him little chance at most tracks, which favor the hustling early-speed types. When horse racing is referred to as the "sport of kings," people are not referring to Ernie, who either breaks slowly or is wide into the stretch in 80 percent of his races.

We pick up his career when he is 6 for 59. At one time during his life, from August 7, 1987, through January 18, 1988, he appeared to become a consistent horse, with 2 wins and 3 seconds over the span of 5 races. But that period coincided with a time when the bottom-of-the-barrel claiming colony at southern California was involved in a work slowdown.

Handicappers will be hard pressed to find any patterns linking Ernie King's few victories. Surely there are two wins on wet tracks, but there are also losses in the mud. He was looking like a one-rush sprinter until he won at 1$\frac{1}{16}$ miles on March 7, 1985. The month of March looked like it might become Ernie's personal solstice when he celebrated another victory in March 1986, but that cycle turned out to be coincidental.

Initially he appeared to be a Hollywood Park horse for course, but since then he has shown no special preference for a particular racetrack.

Occasionally he'll throw in a fabulous race and lose, such as on August 7, 1987, at Del Mar, when he had to do the impossible and close against King Apache, a sharp, lone front runner. It's hard to believe he has a true preference for the slop, since his two victories on that type of surface turned out to be against fields of chronic losers who have since faded into oblivion.

After all is said and done, Ernie King has quietly become an unsung hero. Sometimes he makes his move and sometimes he doesn't fire, and most human beings understand what that's all about. Against a perpetual bias, he has outlasted most members of his class, has won both sprints and routes, won on sloppy and fast tracks, won for at least four different riders, and most important, like his colleague Smooth Bid, achieved a flat-bet profit. A $2 investment on each and every race of his career yields nearly a 100 percent profit.

It is the ultimate irony of horse-race handicapping that the most profitable horses are often the ones that look the worst. This is an inherent part of the business. It is built into the pari-mutuel system that most horseplayers must lose. They lose because horses that look good pay less than a fair price when they win. In order for this to happen, some horses that look bad must pay more than a fair price when they win.

In the case of Ernie King and many of his cohorts, these are not bad horses, and their inconsistency often relates to chronic physical problems that plague many claiming horses.

Ultimately, the first four or five furlongs of Ernie King's races are nearly identical; what is different is the final two furlongs. In every race, somewhere on the turn leading to the stretch, Ernie King makes a secret decision to either make an inspired, bold move, or simply jog home.

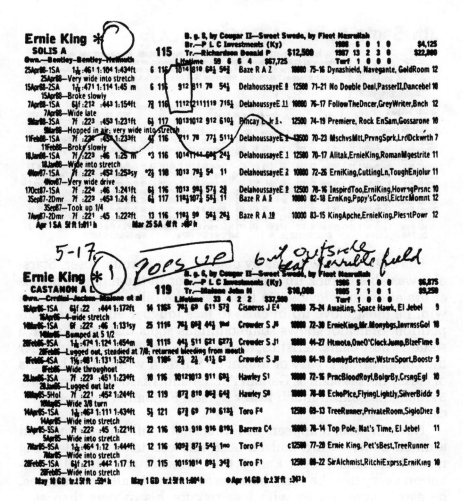

Type 3: Forced Labor at the Wrong Level

Starsalot's recent win occurred when the Horse Gods opened the heavens, forcing the best horses in the field to scratch out and leaving a short field of turf horses (to run on dirt) and horses on the decline.

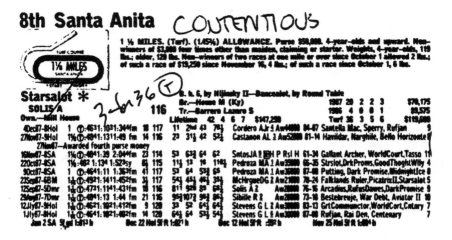

8th Santa Anita CONTENTIOUS

1 ¼ MILES. (Turf). (1.45¾) ALLOWANCE. Purse $50,000. 4-year-olds and upward. Non-winners of $3,000 four times other than maiden, claiming or starter. Weights, 4-year-olds, 119 lbs.; older, 120 lbs. Non-winners of two races at one mile or over since October 1 allowed 2 lbs.; of such a race of $19,250 since November 16, 4 lbs.; of such a race since October 1, 6 lbs.

Starsalot

His October 22 win was by default. As a chronic loser, Starsalot was able to pick up minor purses for in-the-money finishes at the allowance levels. He thus paid the bills. Now, forced to win, he must move up in class to face tougher allowance competition. Starsalot shows some ominous signs that he may have some Type 1 characteristics, for he doesn't seem to care whether the competition is easy or tough; he finished within two lengths of classy horses such as Gallant Archer and Tasso while finishing 5½ lengths behind much lesser horses, Falklands Ruler and Picatrix.

Nevertheless, it appears as if Starsalot would have produced a much better record had he been allowed to run in claiming races. The handicapper knows that Starsalot is a virtual elimination every time he runs, because as a loser in allowance races, he earns more money with less risk for his owners than as a claimer against lesser competition.

Triumvirate went from a grade A track in November 1987 to a grade B track in February 1988, and also made a monumental class drop (perhaps the adjective should be cavernous instead of monumental). In spite of the double change of venue, Triumvirate paid over $100 to win. That win ushered in a new, positive attitude on the part of Triumvirate, and he's been competitive ever since. The problem is that at higher levels, when he has a chance to win, he hangs at the wire.

Triumvirate — Ch. c. 4, by Super Concorde—Pomade, by Prince John
Br.—Elmendorf Farm (Ky)
Tr.—Stutts Charles R
Own.—Boston & Barry — **120**

Lifetime							
23 2 2 2	1988	5	1	2	0	$5,840
$22,970	1987	13	1	0	1	$15,570
	Turf	3	0	0	1	$3,240

3Apr88- 2Crc	fst	7f	:23⅗	:47	1:26⅗	Clm 13000	3	4	4nk	1hd	2hd	2no	Valiente D	116	6.40	83-25	Rexson Vigil 116no Triumvirate 116no Hail totheHour116 1½	Nosed	8
29Mar88- 8Crc	fst	6f	:22⅘	:46⅘	1:13	Clm 16000	1	8	95	96½	64½	64½	Valiente D	b 116	5.80	82-27	Aristocratic Cross 1143½ MasterCatch112nk SirKevan116no	Outrun	10
19Mar88- 5Crc	sly	7f	:23⅗	:48⅕	1:26⅘	Clm 14000	5	7	44	41½	1½	2nk	Valiente D	b 114	2.20	82-17	Ice Jet 116nk Triumvirate 1141½ Swan Point 1165	Lost whip	7
3Mar88- 3GP	fst	6f	:22⅕	:45⅗	1:11⅘	Clm c-10500	10	3	107½	94½	42½	42¾	Castillo H Jr	b 113	5.60	80-22	Slewmobile 105½ Henry's Brother 1172 Showroom 117nk	Late bid	10
18Feb88- 2GP	fst	6f	:22⅕	:45⅗	1:11⅗	Clm 7000	5	8	86½	86½	33	12	Castillo H Jr	b 113	53.90	82-26	Triumvirte1132MedievlInvdr1171NughtyAtNight117hd	Drew clear	12
5Nov87- 1Aqu	fst	1	:46⅘	1:12	1:39⅕	Clm 15500	4	10	109½	1017	1019	1020½	Santagata N	b 113	51.90	49-29	Visible Force 109¾ Rockazado1176½TooToughtoBeat1132¾	Outrun	13
25Oct87- 9Aqu	fst	6f	:22⅘	:46⅗	1:11⅘	Clm 19500	6	11	128½	1013	913	610½	Ortega P Jr5	b 108	46.60	71-20	VisibleForce1085ScreenMaster1153TellItHonestly117nk	No factor	12
28Sep87- 9Bel	gd	1	:46⅕	1:11	1:37⅕	Clm 15500	7	10	912	811	916	919	Vasquez J	b 113	10.50	60-14	Fire Haze 115½ Tell It Honestly 1175 Cayman 1132	Outrun	12
13Sep87- 3Bel	sly	7f	:23	:46⅗	1:25⅗	Clm 17500	4	6	68½	54½	32	44	Guerra W A	b 117	9.50	65-23	Hagabee 1131½ Quietus 1191 Casual Physician 1171½	Steadied	6
15Aug87- 3Sar	fst	1⅛	:46⅗	1:12	1:53⅗	Clm 25000	10	9	817	1015	1112	1114	Santos J A	b 117	6.40	54-18	Cayman 1131½ Balzacian 1172½ Looky Dare 113nk	Outrun	11

LATEST WORKOUTS Apr 13 Crc 1 fst 1:46 b Mar 28 GP 3f fst :35⅗ b Mar 27 GP 4f sly :51⅗ b Mar 13 GP 1 fst 1:43⅘ b

This horse will surely win at lower levels, but if he drops to his win level, he might be claimed.

Eliminante picks up minor purses at the allowance level. If he wins again, he'll be required to race at a level where he may no longer pay the bills. The same owner and trainer have kept this horse ever since he arrived from Argentina with a 1 for 4 record. Eliminante has finished close often enough at allowance levels to suggest that he'd win races in the claiming ranks.

***Eliminante** — Ch. g. 7, by Practicante—Elevacion, by Aristophanes
PEDROZA M A — Br.—Haras La Biznaga (Arg)
116 — Tr.—Borick Robert
Own.—Four Four Forty Farms

Lifetime						
30 2 5 8 $79,473	1988	3	0	1	0	$8,550
	1987	9	1	1	3	$39,050
	Turf	25	2	5	7	$71,500

11Mar88-5SA	1⅛ Ⓣ:46¹1:10⁴1:48²fm	31	116	78½	77¾	34	23	Pedroza MA8	Aw38000	82-15	PleasantVriety,Eliminnte,ProudCt	10
14Feb88-7SA	1¼ Ⓣ:46⁴1:37¹2:02⁴fm	6½	116	27	76	917	919	Meza R Q3	Aw38000	54-23	Uptothehilt, Nilambar, Feraud	10
14Feb88—Veered out start; lugged in backstretch												
17Jan88-7SA	1⅛ :46¹ 1:11 1:50⁴sy	15	116	920	915	58½	55	Sibille R7	Aw38000	78-17	Rupperto,Shigamba,MilleroYMedio	9
26Dec87-7SA	1⅛ Ⓣ:46³1:11²1:49⁴fm	6¾	117	58	55	32½	31	Pedroza MA7	Aw38000	77-22	GeorgiaRiver,Euphrates,Eliminante	9
10Sep87-5Dmr	1⅛ Ⓣ:47 1:12⁴1:50²fm	10	117	811	74	41½	32¼	Pedroza MA6	Aw27000	79-19	PoliticlAmbition,Euphrts,Eliminnt	10
10Sep87—Steadied 5 1/2; crowded 3/8												
29Aug87-7Dmr	1 1/16 Ⓣ:48⁴1:13 1:44 fm	31	116	51¾	52¼	44	75¾	Pedroza MA5	Aw28000	74-18	Bestebreuje, War Debt, Aviator II	10
20Apr87-9SA	1 Ⓣ:46⁴1:10⁴1:35³fm	5	116	31½	3½	31½	63½	Pedroza MA5	Aw35000	93-06	Putting, CherryHill,FabulousSound	8
12Apr87-5SA	1⅛ Ⓣ:46³1:11²1:47²fm	13	117	35	41½	1hd	21	Pedroza MA6	Aw35000	89-15	Havildar, Eliminante, Twice Bold	9
28Mar87-5SA	1⅛ Ⓣ:47¹1:11¹1:47³fm	11	118	42½	42	21½	31½	Pedroza MA8	Aw35000	88-12	Lord Grundy, Starsalot, Eliminante	9
18Mar87-7SA	1⅛ Ⓣ:47²1:11⁴1:49¹fm	14	118	1012	98	77	54¾	Ortega L E1	Aw33000	76-18	Aloma's Tobin, Starsalot, Bananas	10

Mar 19 SA 4f ft :47³ h Mar 5 SA 5f ft 1:02² h Feb 28 SA 4f m :49² h (d) Feb 21 SA 4f ft :47² h

THE ELIMINATOR

I heard the sound of high heels clicking in the dingy hallway outside my third-floor office, which overlooked an adult bookstore on Western, near Santa Monica Boulevard. I thought I had locked my door, but she walked in, put out her cigarette in the ashtray on my desk, placed a thousand-dollar bill under the ashtray, and sat down in a shadowy corner where thin lines of light from between the venetian blinds dimly lit her vague profile.

"Mr. Barlow," she said, "I want you to investigate the mysterious collapse of a number of potentially talented thoroughbred horses."

"Who are you," I asked, "and who do you work for?" I should have said "whom"; she seemed like someone who demanded correct grammar.

"If you want to investigate me, I'll take back your advance and walk out of here the same way I came in"—I wanted to ask her how she came in—"and you'll never see me again."

So it was an advance, I thought. More money coming. I had rent to pay, and alimony.

"I'll take the job. Where can I reach you?"

"Don't call me. I'll find you," she said mysteriously as she deposited a list of horses next to the ashtray, then walked out the door before telling me what I'd get paid. My office was in shadows because I liked it that way; but now I could only get a very dim view of her.

I went down the stairs, two at a time, got my old Pinto started and drove to the *Racing Form* office on Bimini Place, where I asked for a few old *Forms*. I hadn't considered that this was going to be such an expensive investigation until I found out they sold back issues at the same price as current ones. I had no way to contact that mysterious woman with the deep, shadowy voice about my expense account, but I decided to follow through with the investigation.

The horses on my list were:

Thresh It Out
Russian Logic
Parson John
Rodrigue
Grey Writer
Noticiero

A disturbing pattern began to emerge. Prior to its demise, I noticed that each of these horses had finished a race in very close proximity with another horse by the name of Eliminante. I noticed one period of Eliminante's notorious career in which apparently the horse had reached a peak in its performance cycle.

On October 22, 1986, Eliminante finished second in the same picture with *Thresh It Out*. Thresh It Out did not win again in 1986 and was 0 for 16 in 1987, while continuing to lose on into 1988. The third horse, Noticiero, lost a few races and then disappeared from the scene.

***Thresh It Out** — B. g. 5, by Thatch—Last Call, by Klairon
TORO F — 118 — Br.—Wigan J (Eng) — Tr.—Fanning Jerry
Own.—Villa Vista Stable & Potter — Lifetime 31 1 6 4 $48,976

1988	2	0	0	0	
1987	16	0	2	1	$22,985
Turf	26	1	6	4	$46,351

11Feb88-8SA	1⅛ Ⓣ $:46^1\ 1:11^2\ 1:50^1$ fm	20	113	8$^{8\frac{1}{2}}$	4$^{2\frac{1}{2}}$	6$^{2\frac{1}{4}}$	6$^{4\frac{3}{4}}$	Hawley S^1	100000	71-24	AvitorII,TelephoneCnyon,PichErth	8
11Feb88—Wide 3/8 turn												
6Feb88-7SA	a6½f Ⓣ $:21^4\ :44^3\ 1:15^1$ fm	16	116	9^{12}	8^{12}	8^{12}	8^{9}	DelahoussayeE^4	90000	74-26	SprDpont,MyGllntGm,Mrvn'sPolcy	9
6Feb88—Broke slowly												
28Nov87-10Hol	1$\frac{1}{16}$ Ⓣ $:46^4\ 1:10^3\ 1:41^2$ fm	27	116	5^{5}	5$^{3\frac{1}{2}}$	4^{2}	4$^{1\frac{3}{4}}$	Hawley S^1	80000	85-08	PatchyGroundfog,AvitorII,Kensof	12
27Sep87-10Fpx	1$\frac{1}{16}$ $:46\ 1:10^3\ 1:43$ ft	38	115	7^{6}	7$^{7\frac{1}{2}}$	8^{12}	8$^{14\frac{1}{4}}$	SrnsnD^8 Ⓡ	C B Aflbgh	82-13	ForignLgion,Rcognizd,LstCommnd	9
19Sep87-10Fpx	1$\frac{1}{16}$ $:48\ 1:13^3\ 1:45^1$ ft	15	121	9$^{5\frac{3}{4}}$	6$^{2\frac{1}{4}}$	6$^{4\frac{3}{4}}$	5$^{5\frac{1}{4}}$	Corrales J^4	Aw27000	79-18	Bugarian, Proving Spark, Shrewdy	10
10Sep87-5Dmr	1⅛ Ⓣ $:47\ 1:12^4\ 1:50^2$ fm	29	117	6$^{8\frac{1}{2}}$	4^{2}	6$^{4\frac{1}{4}}$	6$^{6\frac{3}{4}}$	Ortega L E^3	Aw27000	74-19	PoliticlAmbition,Euphrts,Eliminnt	10
23Aug87-9Dmr	1⅛ Ⓣ $:47^3\ 1:12^1\ 1:49^3$ fm	14	118	8$^{9\frac{1}{2}}$	8$^{5\frac{1}{2}}$	5$^{5\frac{1}{4}}$	4$^{5\frac{3}{4}}$	Ortega L E^5	Aw24000	79-13	Sobek, Feraud, Euphrates	10
6Aug87-5Dmr	1$\frac{1}{16}$ Ⓣ $:48^1\ 1:11^4\ 1:43^1$ fm	7	117	8^{9}	8^{11}	8$^{7\frac{3}{4}}$	8^{8}	ShoemkerW^9	Aw25000	76-16	WrDbt,MdnghtIc,BooBoo'sBuckroo	9
11Jly87-9Hol	1$\frac{1}{16}$ Ⓣ $:46^4\ 1:10^4\ 1:41^4$ fm	5	116	8$^{8\frac{1}{2}}$	7$^{8\frac{1}{2}}$	7$^{7\frac{1}{2}}$	7$^{3\frac{3}{4}}$	ShoemkerW^3	Aw27000	81-15	FbulousSound,Euphrts,FivDddyFiv	9
11Jly87—Steadied into 7/8												
28Jun87-4Hol	1⅛ Ⓣ $:46\ 1:10^2\ 1:48$ fm	5	115	6^{10}	6$^{5\frac{1}{2}}$	4$^{4\frac{1}{2}}$	3$^{\frac{3}{4}}$	ShoemkerW^2	Aw27000	87-11	WorldCourt,FbulosSond,ThrshItOt	7

Feb 19 SA 6f ft $1:15^3$ h — Feb 3 SA 6f gd $1:14^4$ h — Jan 28 SA 5f ft $1:02$ h — Jan 22 SA 6f ft $1:14^4$ h

On November 8, 1986, a strange race in the annals of thoroughbred history: the photo showed seven horses, all of whom were trying to hang at the wire. Eliminante was the third horse in the photo. The winner that day, Parson John, failed to win again in 1986 and went zero for seventeen in 1987. The second horse in the photo, Rodrigue, lost a few races and then disappeared from the scene. I studied these two photos but could find no apparent weapon near Eliminante or his rider.

Then, on January 3, 1987, Eliminante won a race. The victory took place under suspicious circumstances. The number 4 horse, Disciple, was *pinched back in the opening strides* and never recovered; Disciple had started right next to Eliminante, who left from gate 5! What is worse, it appears that Eliminante had an accomplice to do his dirty work. Top Wing saw Spruce Skipper making his move in the stretch and bumped him approaching the furlong marker.

Top Wing's strongest tactics were employed against the even-money favorite. Was it a coincidence that this favorite, Russian Logic, happened to be one of the horses on my list? Russian Logic was blocked for much of the way and appeared to be *savaged* by Top Wing. Without this severe trouble, he'd have beaten Eliminante and won the race. Of the top four finishers, only Eliminante had what remotely appeared to be a clear trip. *Grey Writer*, another of the horses on my list, finished third. What a scenario! All these horses bumping each other, blocking each other, and miraculously, Eliminante gets a clear path.

FIFTH RACE
Santa Anita
JANUARY 3, 1987

1 ¼ MILES.(Turf). (1.57⅗) ALLOWANCE. Purse $28,000. 4-year-olds and upward which are non-winners of $3,000 other than maiden, claiming or starter. Weights, 4-year-olds, 118 lbs.; older, 120 lbs. Non-winners of a race other than claiming at one mile and one-eighth or over since November 3 allowed 3 lbs. (Non-starters for a claiming price of $20,000 or less since November 3 preferred.)

Value of race $28,000; value to winner $15,400; second $5,600; third $4,200; fourth $2,100; fifth $700. Mutuel pool $371,139. Exacta pool $567,125.

Last Raced	Horse	Eqt.	A.	Wt	PP	¼	½	¾	1	Str	Fin	Jockey	Odds $1
8Nov86 ^{6}Hol^{3}	Eliminante		6	117	5	4^{1}	$4^{1/2}$	$4^{1/2}$	3^{hd}	$1^{1/2}$	$1^{1\frac{1}{2}}$	Pedroza M A	8.50
16Nov86 ^{6}Hol^{10}	Russian Logic		4	116	7	6^{hd}	7^{3}	7^{hd}	$5^{1/2}$	$4^{1/2}$	2no	Delahoussaye E	1.10
18Dec86 ^{8}Hol^{6}	Grey Writer		4	115	3	9^{hd}	10	10	7^{1}	$3^{2\frac{1}{2}}$	$3^{2\frac{1}{2}}$	Baze G	14.00
18Dec86 ^{8}Hol^{5}	Spruce Skipper		4	115	10	$7^{2\frac{1}{2}}$	6^{hd}	6^{hd}	6^{1}	$6^{1\frac{1}{2}}$	4^{hd}	Soto S B	10.80
21Dec86 ^{4}Hol^{5}	Rethymno		4	116	9	$1^{1\frac{1}{2}}$	1^{1}	1^{1}	$1^{1/2}$	2^{1}	5^{3}	Valenzuela P-A	9.50
21Dec86 ^{4}Hol^{4}	Robersky	b	6	117	2	10	$9^{1/2}$	$9^{2\frac{1}{2}}$	$8^{1/2}$	$8^{1\frac{1}{2}}$	$6^{1/2}$	Castanon A L	19.10
18Dec86 ^{8}Hol^{3}	Steamed		5	112	8	$3^{1\frac{1}{2}}$	$2^{1/2}$	2^{2}	2^{1}	$5^{1/2}$	$7^{1\frac{1}{2}}$	Patton D B^{5}	18.90
18Dec86 ^{8}Hol^{4}	Top Wing		4	115	1	$2^{1\frac{1}{2}}$	3^{2}	3^{1}	4^{1}	7^{hd}	8^{hd}	Stevens G L	3.40
30Nov86 ^{9}Hol^{9}	Disciple	b	4	116	4	8^{1}	$8^{1/2}$	$8^{1/2}$	9^{2}	$9^{3\frac{1}{2}}$	$9^{4\frac{1}{2}}$	Toro F	27.90
14Dec86 ^{3}Hol^{5}	Pecos Pippin		5	117	6	5^{2}	5^{2}	$5^{2\frac{1}{2}}$	10	10	10	Olivares F	69.30

OFF AT 2:42. Start good. Won driving. Time, :23⅕, :47⅗, 1:12, 1:37, 2:02⅘ Course firm.

$2 Mutuel Prices:			
5-ELIMINANTE	19.00	5.20	3.60
7-RUSSIAN LOGIC		3.00	2.40
3-GREY WRITER			4.40

$5 EXACTA 5-7 PAID $127.00.

Ch. g, by Practicante—Elevacion, by Aristophanes. Trainer Borick Robert. Bred by Haras La Biznaga (Arg).

ELIMINANTE, never far back, rallied to get the lead near the furlong marker, drew clear in midstretch and was fully extended to prevail. RUSSIAN LOGIC, outrun early, advanced to reach contention on the far turn, was steadied when in heavy traffic approaching the stretch, appeared to be savaged by TOP WING after straightening away for the drive, was steadied when in close quarters approaching the furlong marker, then finished well enough to just get up for the place. GREY WRITER broke against the bit and veered out and checked in the initial strides, was far back early, rallied to menace from along the inner rail a furlong out but lacked the needed further response. SPRUCE SKIPPER, devoid of early speed, began the stretch drive six wide, was bumped by TOP WING approaching the furlong marker and could not gain the necessary ground in the drive. A claim of foul against RUSSIAN LOGIC by the rider of SPRUCE SKIPPER for alleged interference in the stretch drive was not allowed by the stewards when they ruled RUSSIAN LOGIC was not responsible for the interference to SPRUCE SKIPPER. RETHYMNO, away alertly, set the pace for almost nine furlongs, then weakened a bit. ROBERSKY broke slowly and began the stretch drive seven wide. STEAMED forced the early pace, drifted out a bit approaching the furlong marker in the drive to cause some interference to outside rivals and weakened. TOP WING, a bit rank to place early while close up, began the stretch drive five wide, appeared to savage RUSSIAN LOGIC after straightening away for the stretch drive, was steadied when in tight quarters and bumped SPRUCE SKIPPER approaching the furlong marker and gave way. DISCIPLE was pinched back in the opening strides.

Owners— 1, Four Four Forty Farms; 2, Krdjian-McClure-Milch et al; 3, Roy J L-J-Karen Lee; 4, Saron Stable; 5, LaTre-Rbnstn-VkyBthSt et al; 6, Brown B R-D N-T P; 7, Pessin J S & S; 8, Bacharach B; 9, Newport Blue Stables; 10, Fogelson Greer Garson.

Trainers— 1, Borick Robert; 2, Otteson Kimberly; 3, Hutchinson Kathy; 4, Jones Gary; 5, Palma Hector O; 6, Stute Gary; 7, Mollica Michael A; 8, Russell John W; 9, Fulton John W; 10, Whittingham Michael.

Overweight: Russian Logic 1 pound; Rethymno 1; Disciple 1.

Scratched—It's Not My Job (13Dec86 ^{9}BM^{3}).

Top Wing appeared to have left town, and I haven't been able to trace his whereabouts. For Eliminante, this would be his only win in 1987. Russian Logic, the horse that finished second, subsequently tried many times to win, with no success, and then vanished. Grey Writer, third behind Eliminante on that fateful day, tried one more time on January 18, and was out of commission for over a year; he then came back to the races and couldn't win a race.

Grey Writer — Dk. b. or br. g. 5, by Full Out—Baby Julie, by Youth

BLACK C A — 115 — Br.—Sturgis J R (Ky) — Tr.—Sinne Gerald M — $12,500

Own.—Merjoseph J — Lifetime 20 1 6 6 $47,704

1988	5	0	1	2	$8,475
1987	2	0	0	1	$5,025
Turf	7	0	1	3	$15,323

8May88-1Hol	6½f :22 $:45^2$ $1:17^3$ft	5½	115	$6^{4\frac34}$ $6^{4\frac12}$ 5^5 $4^{4\frac34}$	Black C A[2]	12500	85-13	Exotic Motion, Gerril, Zac K.	8
30Apr88-2Hol	1 $:46^1$ $1:11^4$ 1:38 ft	5¾	116	$7^{4\frac34}$ 6^4 $6^{4\frac12}$ $3^{1\frac34}$	Pedroza M A[12]	12500	71-14	D.D.TheKid,Polysemous,GreyWritr	12
23Apr88-1SA	6½f $:21^4$ $:45^1$ $1:17^3$sy	3¼	116	5^5 5^4 4^3 $5^{6\frac34}$	Castanon A L[5]	c10000	75-15	CoursingEgle,Loverue,StrOfAmric	12
7Apr88-1SA	6½f $:21^2$ $:44^3$ $1:15^4$ft	3¼	116	$8^{8\frac12}$ $4^{3\frac12}$ 3^4 $2^{3\frac12}$	Stevens G L[8]	10000	87-17	FollowTheDncer,GreyWriter,Bnch	12
24Mar88-1SA	6f $:21^2$ $:44^3$ $1:09^4$ft	6	116	4^5 3^3 $2^{2\frac12}$ 3^7	Stevens G L[7]	12500	82-17	ClssicQuick,SmulMcIntyr,GryWrtr	12
18Jan87-5SA	1¼ Ⓣ$:46^3$1:36 $2:00^4$fm	6	113	7^{12} $7^{5\frac12}$ 5^8 5^{15}	Shoemaker W[7]	80000	68-15	Keyala, Manzotti, Pas De Choix	8
3Jan87-5SA	1¼ Ⓣ$:47^3$1:37 $2:02^3$fm	14	115	10^{10} 7^4 $3^{1\frac12}$ $3^{1\frac12}$	Baze G[3]	Aw28000	73-24	Eliminnte,RussinLogic,GreyWriter	10
3Jan87—Rough start									
10Dec86-8Hol	1$\frac{1}{16}$ Ⓣ$:48^3$1:12 $1:42^2$fm	3¼	116	3^2 $4^{1\frac12}$ $4^{1\frac12}$ $6^{1\frac34}$	McHrgueDG[3]	Aw24000	80-19	SmoothOpertor,Intuitiveness,Stmd	8
10Dec86—Lugged in stretch									
30Nov86-9Hol	1⅛ Ⓣ$:47^4$$1:12^2$$1:48^3$fm	6¼	114	11^{10} $10^{5\frac34}$ $4^{1\frac12}$ $3^{\frac34}$	Baze G[11]	Aw24000	84-12	Illumineux, Padoue, Grey Writer	12
30Nov86—Wide into stretch									
15Nov86-7Hol	1 Ⓣ$:45^3$$1:09^1$$1:34^3$fm	30	116	9^{15} 8^{14} 8^{12} 3^6	McHrgueDG[9]	Aw24000	88-11	Le Belvedere,RiverMist,GreyWriter	9
Mar 20 SA 5f ft $:59^1$ h									

I began to develop an aversion for this character, Eliminante. In my better days I had investigated hit men of distinction, those who went after men of repute, those who had names less blatant than "Eliminante." This despicable character seems to have specialized in ruining the lives of the most impoverished members of his species, fellow members of the serfdom in the sport of kings. At least Eliminante could have gotten the job done more quickly, instead of allowing his victims to suffer a slow, tortuous, winless demise.

Ultimately, I discovered that at the bottom rungs of thoroughbred society there is a pecking order in which the most unfortunate of the species achieve occasional victories not with a peak in performance cycle, but rather, by doing each other in.

I never did find out who the woman was who had hired me. She sent a messenger, a short guy about five feet tall and one hundred pounds to pick up my report.

I offered him a cigarette; he said he didn't smoke. A glass of cheap wine, which he turned down. A cup of coffee, which he accepted with no cream and no sugar. A doughnut, which he declined. I wondered why a little guy like that would be on a diet.

A theory developed as to who the woman was. When Russian Logic and Thresh It Out raced against Eliminante, they were both trained by the same person, a woman. I thought that the woman who had slipped into my office might have been the same Kimberly who trained those two horses; she was tight-lipped, just like so many trainers. I thought she might have been the one and that she had thrown in the names of other horses so I would not see the pattern.

I asked a colleague who knew more about horse racing if he thought there was something about Eliminante that ruined the horses around him, intentionally or unintentionally. He told me it was coincidental, that it was proof that the only way horses like Eliminante could find a minimum of success is when they find the most lowly of fields.

I'm not sure I agree with him; I still feel there was enough evidence of a conspiracy. But I had learned something from it all. Even in the sport of kings, there is an underclass, an underworld, in which petty bullies pick on each other for the crumbs and leftovers of an opulent society.

Eliminante will be back in later chapters to exert more of his evil influence.

Masters of Their Trade: Steady Horses with a Low Profile

CRAFTSMEN/CRAFTSWOMEN

In Search of the Steady Horse

HORSEPLAYERS WANT A HORSE they can depend on, one that won't drive them crazy with ups and downs in its performance trajectory. In search of this ideal, we must reckon with certain realities of horse racing:

1. No horse wins all races.
2. Dependable horses that win most races yield an unplayably low average mutuel.
3. The closest thing to a truly "consistent" horse is one that loses all its races.

As we've witnessed in the last chapter, there are many ways for proven losers to win by default, so we can't even depend on that type of consistency. So now let's direct our search in a more realistic direction. We want horses whose role is that of secretary: runs the office and gets little recognition while the boss takes the credit. The underpaid employee is equivalent to the underbet horse. Or we search for horses that are like the artist who produces masterpieces in anonymity.

The betting public makes many of its decisions in a commercial way. In other words, it consumes or purchases based on superficial characteristics of the product/horse. This means that many horses are bet on because of the more obvious achieve-

ments in their production, as well as the publicity that surrounds
such achievements, similar to a record purchased because of a
"hook" or a catchy tune, which has been plugged on the radio
while there is a starving musician who plays with artistry in an
obscure club before a crowd of fifteen people.

We're looking for horses that get the job done without being
perceived as having done so by the betting public.

From Antihero to Hero

Tamtulia, the antihero of previous pages, is now observed in
a different light. The first two years of her spotty career now
show Tamtulia as the master of a very defined craft. As a jack-
of-all-trades she is an inconsistent horse, but as a specialist she
turns out a near perfect product. Let's observe the first two years
of her career:

Date	Distance	Finish
1Aug86	6 furlongs	8
21Aug86	6 furlongs	5
3Sept86	two-turn mile	1 (5–1)
10Oct86	6 furlongs	3
13Nov86	one-turn mile	4
11Dec86	one-turn mile	2
7Jan87	two-turn mile	1 (5–2)
11Apr87	6 furlongs	6
20Apr87	two-turn mile	1 (7–2)
6May87	turf 1⅟₁₆ mile	3
25May87	1⅟₁₆ mile	threw rider
11Sep87	turf mile	6
25Sep87	1⅟₁₆ mile	2
15Oct87	two-turn mile	1 (1–1)
21Oct87	two-turn mile	7
18Dec87	1⅟₁₆ mile	3

Tamtulia, the perpetuator of one myth, makes a valiant attempt to disprove another: that female horses in general and
female claimers specifically can't be consistent. In her first 16
races she ran 9 good ones. But more important, she was 4 for 5 in
her specialty, the two-turn dirt mile. The economic feasibility of

her craft declines by October 15, when she won her fourth straight two-turn mile at even money. By April 20, 1987, the handicapper could have identified her steady pattern and collected at 7–2.

I've found that two years of a thoroughbred's life is usually the longest that the bettor can expect this type of specialist horse to be economically feasible. Several things usually happen.

1. It becomes increasingly difficult to find races at the right level carded within the horse's specialty.
2. The public finally recognizes the craft, and payoffs dip too low.
3. With a lack of proper races available, the horse is forced to develop other skills for a more lucrative trade.

Late word on Tamtulia is that she is attempting to develop a new trade. The last time I checked up on her career, she had finished third, only a half length behind the winner, from the outside 10 post in a 1⅛ turf route, at 38–1. We wish her luck. At least, for two years she was the steady and consistent master of her trade.

O Tamtulia, by the time I discover the pattern of your existence, you begin to return low prices and then change your habits. But alas, there are many others like you who are not as elusive or fleeting, and who become more generous to those of us who appreciate their labors.

Like you, Tamtulia, *Lichi* was not always allowed to work within her specialty. Tamtulia, master of the two-turn mile, had to face entire seasons of Hollywood Park in which the mile races were only one turn. And Lichi, supreme master of the turf sprint, was forced to confront meets that had no races of her specialty (Del Mar), and other meets that offered only one or two events within her profession (Hollywood Park). With the demand that these horses run races not of their trade, the illusion is created that presents these competitors as erratic when indeed they are very steady.

Observe first an overview of Lichi's career. Obviously highly competitive, Lichi nevertheless appears to be an in and outer, win one, lose a few, win another.

```
*Lichi                         B. m. 6, by Padereso—Anchisamira, by Snow Track
  BAZE R A               116   Br.—Haras Ocoa (Chile)                    1986 11 4 1 1   $104,950
Own.—Preston Farm              Tr.—Jones Gary                            1985  3 0 0 0
                             Lifetime  24 7 2 2  $130,130                Turf 15 5 2 2   $119,845
8Oct86-5SA   a6½f (T):22^2 :45 1:14^3fm  8¾ 115  31½ 2½ 2½ 1no   Baze G5 (F)Atm Dys H 86-14 Lichi, Tax Dodge, Outstandingly 7
     8Oct86—Run in divisions
6Sep86-7Dmr  6½f :22 :45 1:15^3ft        10 121  6^6 6^4 6^6 57½   Toro F3 (F)Aw40000 86-12 HerRoylty,WinterTresure,WildKitty 6
26Jly86-5Dmr 1 1/16(T):47^4 1:12 1:42^3fm 7¼ 116 3^2 52¾ 7^8 79¾  DlhssyE5 (F)[R]Osnts H 83-05 Loucoum,Felliniana,SeasonlPickup 8
     26Jly86—Run in divisions
4Jly86-5Hol  6f (T):22 :44^4 1:08^3fm    4½ 116  63¼ 53½ 52½ 44½  Toro F1 (F)HcpO 94 — Aberuschka,Loucoum,BoldNSpecial 7
     4Jly86—Altered path early drive
7Jun86-5Hol  6f (T):22^3 :45^2 1:08^4fm  4 115   51½ 2^1 1hd 1no  Toro F1 (F)HcpO 98-02 Lichi, Loucoum, Regal Ties 6
11May86-8Hol 1⅛(T):48^1 1:11^3 1:48 fm   6¼ 115  1^1 1½ 5^4 66½   TrF6 (F)[R]Smthngryl H 85-06 La Koumia, Sauna, Frau Altiva 6
10Apr86-8SA  a6½f (T):22 :44^3 1:14^1fm  30 115  52¾ 42½ 42¾ 22½  Toro F4 (F)[R]Mt Wlsn 85-16 Aberuschka, Lichi, Regal Ties 7
6Feb86-8SA   a6½f (T):22^1 :44^4 1:16 fm 3 116   4^2 32½ 31½ 1¾   DlhoussyE6 (F)Aw34000 79-21 Lichi, Affirming, Wayward Pirate 7
25Jan86-6SA  6f :21^3 :44^1 1:08^3ft     8¾ 116  55½ 6^9 69½ 510¾  DlhoussyE4 (F)Aw40000 84-11 Circular, Tucked Inside, Boldara 7
11Jan86-7SA  a6½f (T):21^2 :44 1:15^1fm  17 115  3^2 32½ 2hd 31½  Meza R Q3 (F)Aw32000 82-20 Loucoum, Pirate's Glow, Lichi 10
  Oct 31 SA (T) 5f fm 1:01^1 h (d)   Oct 22 SA 4f ft :47^1 h   Oct 16 SA 3f ft :35^3 h   Sep 24 SA 5f ft 1:00^3 h
```

```
*Lichi                         B. m. 7, by Padereso—Anchisamira, by Snow Track
  MCCARRON C J           117   Br.—Haras Ocoa (Chile)                    1987  5 1 1 1   $83,475
Own.—Prestonwood Farm Inc      Tr.—Jones Gary                            1986 11 4 1 1   $104,950
                             Lifetime  29 8 3 3  $193,685                Turf 19 6 3 3   $182,445
27Aug87-8Dmr 6f :21^3 :44^2 1:09^1ft     11 119  64½ 53½ 64½ 54½  McCrrnCJ2 (F)Aw35000 87-17 Luisant, Balladry, Joni U. Bar 7
18Apr87-9SA  a6½f (T):21^3 :43^4 1:13^3fm 11 112 31½ 31½ 2^2 31¾  DoglsRR1 Sn Smn H 89-16 BolderThnBold,PrincBobbyB.,Lichi 9
     18Apr87—Grade III
28Mar87-8SA  a6½f (T):21^3 :44 1:14^2fm  10 115  6^4 52½ 31½ 1hd  Baze G2 (F)Ls Cngs H 87-12 Lichi, An Empress, Aromacor 7
     28Mar87—Poor start; bumped 1/8
15Mar87-7SA  a6½f (T):22^1 :44^3 1:15^1gd *2¼ 118 2^1 21½ 22½ 53½ Baze G7 (F)[R]Mt Wlsn 79-24 Firesweepr,AnEmprss,TrudiDomino 8
4Feb87-8SA   a6½f (T):22^2 :45^1 1:15 fm 15 116  31½ 2^1 22½ 2^2  Baze G4 (F)Mnrva H 82-16 Sari's Heroine, Lichi, Aberuschka 7
     4Feb87—Bobbled at start
8Oct86-5SA   a6½f (T):22^2 :45 1:14^3fm  8¾ 115  31½ 2½ 2½ 1no   Baze G5 (F)Atm Dys H 86-14 Lichi, Tax Dodge, Outstandingly 7
     8Oct86—Run in divisions
6Sep86-7Dmr  6½f :22 :45 1:15^3ft        10 121  6^6 6^4 6^8 57½   Toro F3 (F)Aw40000 86-12 HerRoylty,WinterTresure,WildKitty 6
26Jly86-5Dmr 1 1/16(T):47^4 1:12 1:42^3fm 7¼ 116 3^2 52¾ 7^8 79¾  DlssE5 (F)[R]Osunitas H 83-05 Loucoum,Felliniana,SeasonlPickup 8
     26Jly86—Run in divisions
4Jly86-5Hol  6f (T):22 :44^4 1:08^3fm    4½ 116  63¼ 53½ 52½ 44½  Toro F1 (F)HcpO 94 — Aberuschka,Loucoum,BoldNSpecial 7
     4Jly86—Altered path early drive
7Jun86-5Hol  6f (T):22^3 :45^2 1:08^4fm  4 115   51½ 2^1 1hd 1no  Toro F1 (F)HcpO 98-02 Lichi, Loucoum, Regal Ties 6
  Oct 2 SA 4f ft :46^4 h   ●Sep 26 SA 6f ft 1:11^4 h   ●Sep 14 SA 4f ft :47^2 h   ●Sep 7 Dmr (T) 3f fm :35^3 h
```

By January 11, 1986, Lichi had already proven in her past performances that she was a turf sprinter by trade. On January 3, 1986, she earned her southern California turf-sprint credential by winning the fifth race (not shown in above past performances) down the unique Santa Anita Hill Course, and paying off at a prophetic 19–1 in an $85,000 claiming event. Let's chart her career(s) in two separate graphs, one of turf sprints and the other of all races that were not turf sprints. We shall exclude the January 3 coup since handicappers needed to see that win in order to begin to identify Lichi's specialty.

Turf Sprints

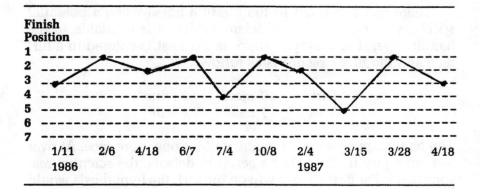

Other Races

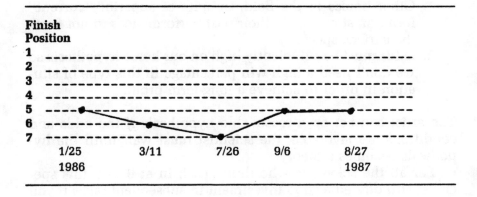

As a turf sprinter, over this span of her career, Lichi achieves 4 wins, 2 seconds, 2 thirds, and 2 out-of-money finishes. In her other races she never gets in-the-money, with 3 fifths, 1 sixth, and 1 seventh. While Tamtulia's win mutuels went down with each successive victory at her specialty, Lichi provided a larger prize each time she won, from 3–1 to 4–1 to 8–1 to 10–1. Even in defeat, Lichi got the job done in virtual anonymity: second at 30–1, second at 15–1, and third at 11–1. Somehow, throughout all this consistent and dynamic performance within her specialty, Lichi managed to keep the type of low profile that allows such masters of their trade to always offer a solid investment.

Far East

There comes a point in the life of a horse when a potential specialty emerges but insufficient evidence is available to the handicapper. For example, suppose Far East is entered in a turf race and the filly's record is as follows:

Dirt	16 races	*2 wins*
Turf	1 race	*1 win*

The handicapper/scientist might wait for one more race. At over 9–1, going up in class after a series of defeats, the scientist reasons that if Far East should win on the turf, the hypothesis would become a solid theory. The handicapper/artist thinks differently; Far East offers enough probability of being a master of the turf to be worth a bet, if two other conditions materialize:

1. Other horses in the field, in spite of superior "current" form, must appear in their past performances to not favor the surface/specialty.
2. Odds must be sufficiently high on our horse/hypothesis so we don't need a high win percentage in this type of situation in order to achieve a long-term profit.

The artist can bet on a reasonable hypothesis *if* the odds and conditions are favorable; the scientist must wait until the hypothesis becomes a theory.

For all the scientists who didn't cash in at 9½–1, this specialist still offered a good investment in subsequent races if you identified her craft as *firm turf* and excluded soft/yielding grass as well as dirt.

Far East — B. m. 5, by Mr Redoy—China Tea, by Round Table
CRUGUET J — 113 — Br.—Forest Retreat Farms Inc (Ky) — 1988 1 0 0 0
Own.—Davis A — Tr.—Moschera Gasper S — 1987 23 7 7 1 $193,751
Lifetime 34 9 7 5 $216,156 — Turf 16 7 3 1 $170,831

14May88-5Bel	1 1/16 (T):47 1:111 1:431fm	9¾	116	55½	66½	67	615¾	Romero R P6	(F)Hcp0	64-24	Fieldy, Small Virtue, Rullah Runner	7
20Nov87-8Aqu	1⅛ (T):491 1:143 1:531yl	4½	119	611	89½	711	615½	Davis R G1	(F)Hcp0	53-34	MuskrtLov,PrnclyProof,LuckyToch	8
8Nov87-4Aqu	1 1/16 (T):491 1:13 1:441fm*4-5		118	64½	45	36	44¾	Davis R G5	(F) 50000	79-16	MyVirginiRl,FirstShot,LuckyTouch	9
17Oct87-6Bel	1 1/16 (T):46 1:104 1:434fm	2¾	119	69	25	2hd	2¾	Davis R G1	(F)Hcp0	76-24	PrincelyProof,FrEst,RllyForJustice	9
12Oct87-8Bel	1⅜ [T]:52 1:434 2:234sf	2¾	116	33½	36½	49	411¾δ	DvisRG2	(F)Athena H	26-62	LdKndlLght,Brbr'sMmnt,SpctclrBv	7
12Oct87—Grade III; δDead heat												
27Sep87-7Bel	1 1/16 (T):482 1:12 1:433gd	7½	118	54	54½	42½	1nk	Davis R G8	(F)Hcp0	78-27	FarEast,Dismasted,MissUnnmeble	10
18Sep87-3Bel	1 1/16 [T]:483 1:13 1:443gd*3-5		122	79	65½	54	11¾	Davis R G5	(F) 100000	78-19	Far East, Lycka Dancer, Debonairly	7
4Sep87-8Bel	1 1/16 [T]:471 1:111 1:424gd	3½	115	77½	33½	21	13¾	Davis R G8	(F)Aw47000	87-23	Far East, Romantic Girl,Subjective	8
27Aug87-1Sar	1⅛ :471 1:123 1:511ft	5½	113	2hd	1½	25	47½	Davis R G7	(F) 70000	71-12	CourgeousKrn,CrownPipr,MdmCrol	9
22Aug87-1Sar	1⅛ (T):502 1:152 1:551sf	2½	122	63	41½	42½	43¾	Davis R G4	(F)Aw45000	47-30	Lead Kindly Light, Fieldy, Carry	7

May 10 Bel tr.t 4f ft :50 b — Apr 27 Bel tr.t 4f ft :484 h — Apr 22 Bel tr.t 3f ft :374 b

Far East — B. f. 4, by Mr Redoy—China Tea, by Round Table
Br.—Forest Retreat Farms Inc (Ky) — 1987 14 4 6 1 $97,200
Own.—Davis A — 122 — Tr.—Moschera Gasper S — 1986 10 2 0 4 $22,405
Lifetime 24 6 6 5 $119,605 — Turf 7 4 2 1 $75,960

14Aug87-5Sar	1⅜ (T):502 2:023 2:391fm	*2½	119	33	2½	22	2-½	Davis R G8	(F)Hcp0	86-08	Slew'sExceller,FarEst,SecretAmie	10
8Aug87-5Sar	1 1/16 (T):473 1:11 1:421fm*6-5		115	31½	31½	32	32¼	Cruguet J6	(F)Aw45000	84-13	Loa, Lake Champlain, Far East	7
23Jly87-8Bel	1 1/16 (T):473 1:111 1:413fm	*2½	119	53¾	1hd	12	13	Antley CW7	(F)Aw31000	88-20	FarEast,LaCavtin,AntiqueMystique	8
17Jly87-7Bel	1 1/16 (T):462 1:102 1:434fm	3	117	52½	34	22	14	Cruguet J1	(F)Aw28000	77-22	Far East, Purify, Rivers Of Mist	8
3Jly87-5Bel	1⅜ :50 1:393 2:193m	2½	117	42	24	25	25	LovatoFJr4	(F)Aw28000	77-24	Laughing Lady, Far East, Darbyvail	6
14Jun87-4Bel	1 (T):473 1:12 1:363fm*7-5		115	21½	21	1½	2nk	Lovato F Jr5	(F) c47500	82-16	Alitina, Far East, Syntonic	12
28May87-1Bel	1 1/16 (T):462 1:102 1:421fm	9½	117	42	42	1½	13	Lovato F Jr10	(F) 35000	85-16	Far East, LadyDictator,Debonairly	11
16May87-3Bel	1⅛ :471 1:121 1:504ft	*9-5	1125	33½	43½	54½	510½	Nuesch D4	(F) 25000	62-18	Dawn Break, Charsky, Nile Flirt	6

Aug 3 Bel 4f ft :482 h — Jly 15 Bel tr.t 4f ft :493 b — Jly 1 Bel tr.t 4f ft :48 h — Jun 24 Bel tr.t 4f ft :50 b

1987	Finish	Odds
6/14	2	7–5
7/17	1	3–1
7/23	1	2–1
8/8	3	6–5
8/14	2	5–2
9/4	1	3–1
9/10	1	3–5
9/27	1	7½–1
10/17	2	5–2
11/8	4	4–5

Far East's record for 1987 looks more like that of a harness horse. The layoff that followed the November 8 race comes with Far East's first out-of-money finish within her craft; had she been overworked and become bored with racing, or did she develop a condition problem? Usually we expect the master of a trade to maintain consistency within the profession for about two racing years; but Far East has crammed two years of labor into the space of one.

Based on a $2 minimum wager: total return of $45 (*excluding* her second turf win at 9½–1) with a total investment of $20, for a return of greater than 100 percent. During the same period, she ran on surfaces that were either dirt or soft/yielding turf and lost every time; if her employers had been fair, she'd not have been forced to labor under adverse conditions. But because of those losing efforts, the steadiness of her performance was disguised just enough to raise her average mutuel.

There are many possible specialties which, if isolated, will uncover a steady, dependable performance record amid apparent inconsistency.

1. Surface (turf, slop, etc.).
2. Specialty distance (one-turn mile, two-turn mile, 7 furlongs, 1¼ miles, etc.).
3. Horse for course (see Chapter 6).
4. Horse for circumference (note that *Time Share* is 3 for 4 on ⅝-mile tracks and 1 for 8 otherwise:

5. Horse always runs well at a particular class level but disguises its perfection by failing when mismatched. *Prime Concord* is one horse who can read the *Racing Form!* He shows in his last 5 claiming races: 3 wins, 1 second, in a photo, and only 1 out of the money; but enter him in an allowance race, even with the best speed and pace figures, and once he's read the "Aw," you can be assured he'll lose. On May 25 he figured to have a clear pace advantage but, unfortunately, the word "allowance" appeared in bold type where Prime Concord could see it, and he lost again.

3rd Hollywood

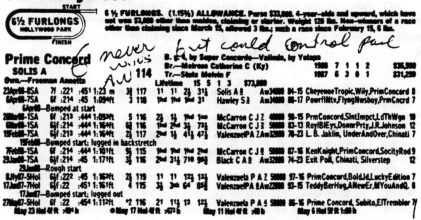

never but could control pace

6. Horse-rider combo (past performances of *Perfect From Afar* are self-explanatory):

7. Horse-trainer combo; horse wins for a particular trainer, loses when claimed away, wins when *reclaimed*.

There are other patterns of consistency, more esoteric, that require a bit of improvisation on the part of the handicapper and can't be reduced to a formula. The final star of the steady horse review happens to be another female.

Auspiciante

In the particular two-year span since she came to the United States, Auspiciante managed to lose 12 of 13 races at below 10–1, while at above 10–1 she earned 4 victories in 5 attempts! It's not that she was stiffed or raced inconsistently; on 15Nov85, 2Nov86,

16Aug87, and 13Sep87, terrible racing traffic cost her victories. In 7 of her losses she was either in the money or within two lengths of the winner at the wire. On November 2, 1986, she raced wide on all three turns while also hitting a traffic jam, and still finished within two lengths of the leader.

***Auspiciante** B. m. 6, by Practicante—Auxey, by Right of Way
TORO F 120 Br.—Haras La Biznaga (Arg) 1987 7 1 1 1 $112,725
Tr.—McAnally Ronald 1986 7 3 1 1 $298,190
Own.—Cooke J K Lifetime 30 8 5 6 $435,482 Turf 29 5 3 4 $411,407
13Sep87-8Dmr 1⅛Ⓣ:49¹1:13²1:50¹fm *2 120 5¾ 5¾ 7¼ 3½ StsGL⁶ ⒻRamona H 81-17 Short Sleeves,Festivity,Auspiciante 9
13Sep87—Grade I; Crowded throughout; forced out, bumped 1/4, 1/8 [redacted]
16Aug87-8Dmr 1 Ⓣ:47²1:11³1:35⁴fm 5½ 120 6⁴½ 8³¾ 7³½ 4½ VIIPA⁹ ⒻPalomar H 90-12 Festivity, AdorableMicol,Secuencia 9
16Aug87—Grade II; Crowded final 3/8; steadied 3/8 [redacted]
5Jly87-8Hol 1⅛Ⓣ:45 1:08²1:46¹fm 12 117 5⁵½ 5⁴½ 4² 1nk VlnlPA⁷ ⒻBv Hls H 97-03 Auspiciante, Reloy, Festivity 8
5Jly87—Grade II
30May87-8Hol 1⅟₁₆Ⓣ:47 1:10⁴1:41 fm 7½ 119 6²¾ 6³½ 6⁵½ 6⁸¾ PncLJr⁴ ⒻWlshre H 82-11 Galunpe,TopSocilite,PerfectMtchII 6
30May87—Grade II
17Mar87-8SA 1⅛Ⓣ:48¹1:11⁴1:48 fm 6 121 4¹½ 5³ 5⁷½ 7⁷¾ Toro F³ ⒻSta Ana H 79-17 Reloy, Northern Aspen, NorthSider 7
17Mar87—Grade I
7Feb87-8SA 1⅟₁₆:46¹ 1:10³ 1:42³ft 7½ 121 6¹⁰ 7⁷ 7⁸½ 7¹⁰½ Toro F³ ⒻS Maria H 78-14 Fran'sVlentine,NorthSider,Infinidd 8
7Feb87—Grade II
19Jan87-8SA 1⅛Ⓣ:48²1:12⁴1:50¹fm 3½ 122 5³½ 6²½ 6²¾ 2¹ ToroF¹ ⒻSn Grgno H 75-29 Frau Altiva, Auspiciante, Solva 7
19Jan87—Grade II; Wide into stretch
13Dec86-8BM a1⅛Ⓣ 1:48 fm*7-5 124 4⁶ 5³½ 6⁶ 6⁸¾ AsssCB⁵ ⒻCa JkyCbH 86-05 Solva, Kraemer, Bonne Ile 7
13Dec86—Grade III
23Nov86-8Hol 1⅛Ⓣ:47³1:11³1:48 fm 15 123 7⁶½ 7⁴¾ 2¹½ 1¹½ AsssCB⁶ ⒻMtrarch Iv 88-13 Auspiciante, Aberuschka, Reloy 12
23Nov86—Grade I
2Nov86-8SA 1¼Ⓣ:46³1:35⁴2:01²fm 6¾ 123 8⁴¾ 3² 4³½ 6¹¾ PcLJr¹² ⒻYlw Rbn Iv 78-20 Bonne Ile, Top Corsage, Carotene 12
2Nov86—Grade I; Wide into drive
Oct 18 SA 1 ft 1:41 h Oct 12 SA 7f ft 1:27² h Oct 6 SA 6f ft 1:13¹ h Sep 30 SA 5f ft 1:00¹ h

Auspiciante B. m. 5, by Practicante—Auxey, by Right of Way
PINCAY L JR 123 Br.—Haras La Biznaga (Arg) 1986 4 2 1 1 $167,190
Tr.—McAnally Ronald 1985 5 2 0 1 $18,678
Own.—Cooke J K Lifetime 20 6 4 5 $209,757 Turf 11 3 2 3 $185,682
5Oct86-10LaD 1⅜Ⓣ:51³1:42¹2:19¹gd *2 118 5³½ 5¹½ 3⁴ 2¹½ ToroF⁴ ⒻGdn Harv H 68-28 NettieCometti,Auspicinte,RoylRgtt 9
5Oct86—Grade II
20Sep86-8BM 1⅛Ⓣ:47²1:11³1:48¹fm *1 117 3¹ 3½ 2¹ 3² StnsGL³ ⒻHlsbrgh H 97 — Justicara,RoyalRegatta,Auspiciante 8
20Sep86—Grade III
7Sep86-8Dmr 1⅛Ⓣ:47¹1:11 1:48²fm 13 114 4⁴ 1½ 1½ 1¹¾ StsGL⁹ ⒻRamona H 92-08 Auspiciante, Justicara, Sauna 9
7Sep86—Grade I
14Aug86-8Dmr 1 Ⓣ:47²1:11⁴1:35¹fm 14 115 5²½ 5¹½ 1½ 1² VlenzulPA⁹ ⒻAw35000 96-04 Auspiciante,RoyalRegatta,Antartic 10
30Nov85-6BM 1⅟₁₆:49 1:14 1:45⁴gd *6-5 115 4⁷ 4⁵ 4⁵½ 3⁴½ CastnedM² ⒻAw22000 58-30 DistantDoll,TraipsinLdy,Auspicinte 6
15Nov85-7Hol 1⅟₁₆Ⓣ:47²1:11²1:41⁴fm 8½e 116 5³½ 6⁵½ 6⁴¼ 5²¾ DlhoussyE⁸ ⒻAw40000 — — CprcornBll,LdydSrn,DncngDsplyII 10
15Nov85—Floated out late
19Oct85-8SA 1⅛Ⓣ:45³1:09⁴1:47¹fm 12 118 10⁹½ 9⁸ 6⁹ 7⁸ DlhssE³ ⒻLs Plms H 83-12 Estrapade, L'Attrayante, Johnica 11
19Oct85—Grade II; Bumped hard start
25Sep85-8BM 1 Ⓣ:48 1:12³1:37⁴fm 5 115 5⁴ 2¹½ 1¹½ 1⁵ CastnedM⁷ ⒻAw18000 91-09 Auspiciante,FinalAssult,TotlWomn 8
25Sep85—Broke slowly
6Jan85♦3Hipodromo(Arg) a1¼ 2:05³ft 2 120 1² LzcnoM ⒻCl Aprtra(Gr3) Auspiciante, Divertida, Nice Love 3
8Dec84♦7SanIsidro(Arg) a1¼ 1:58⁴fm 5½e 119 Ⓣ 2²½ LzcnM ⒻGP Cpa dPlt(Gr1) So Glad, Auspiciante, Poivre 16
Oct 31 SA 4f ft :48³ h Oct 26 SA 1 ft 1:40² h Oct 20 SA 6f ft 1:12³ h Oct 13 SA 4f ft :48³ h

Perhaps the message here is that the public failed to perceive Auspiciante as a consistent tryer. After her 14–1 and 13–1 victories, and following her three-turn-wide valiant loss of November 2, it became clear that this mare would always try to make her investors happy. I bet on her November 23, passed the next two because of the low payoff, also passed on February 7, 1987, because of the wrong surface, and bet her the next four times. That meant 2 winning bets in 5 attempts, with returns of 15–1 and 12–1.

There is no scientific method on this planet that can explain the care with which Auspiciante did her job at above 10–1. Nevertheless, between the lines of the past performances she made it clear that she always could be expected to give it her best, no matter what the odds. In contentious races, with stiff competition, her record is more remarkable. Handicappers looking for a sure winner stayed away from Auspiciante, but those who looked for good value for their investment money had to back her.

In summary, for our investment purposes the definition of a steady horse is not concerned with the Spectacular Bids and John Henrys, for their talent is too obvious to the public. On the other hand, there are many horses that are masters of their trade over extended periods of time (usually about two years), and yet pay off in high figures because they are forced to compete on occasions in situations beyond their craft, thus disguising their professional consistency. The betting public fails to extract their specialty performance record from the illusory ups and downs of their total record.

Only after completing the plans for this chapter did I realize that every one of my primary examples of the craftsman horse was a craftswoman. Every handicapper who continues to believe that fillies and mares are less consistent than their male counterparts will pay for that foolish mythology in the form of a lower return on investment.

In reality, most thoroughbreds of either sex are delicate, spoiled, and inconsistent. The steady performer is a minority in the community of thoroughbreds. The majority of this rare breed runs well only on rare occasions.

JIMMY OLSEN AND LOIS LANE

I have always been fascinated by the popularity of characters such as Superman and Zorro, who lead two lives—one ordinary, bordering on mediocrity, the other impeccable and heroic. Perhaps one can identify with these characters because so many human beings on this earth lead a secretly heroic existence. Consider the farm laborer who takes risks with health and safety while testing the limits of bodily endurance to a maximum degree. According to an old Tex-Mex folk song written by Lalo Guerrero, we the consumer

> know of the tomato
> as it sits on the plate
> but ignore that
> it had to be picked . . .

We are aware of the lifestyles of the rich and famous Secretariats and Risen Stars while ignoring the guy next door who gets the job done with artistry or stamina. It is this trait of ours, as people, that explains how we as horseplayers ignore the masterful performance of the unsung heroes of thoroughbred society.

We see the steady masters of a thoroughbred trade the way Jimmy Olsen and Lois Lane see Clark Kent. Poor races on the wrong surface or at the wrong distance function like Clark Kent's glasses, as a superficial disguise that covers up a dominating competitor. Lois and Jimmy had all the evidence needed to relate Clark Kent to Superman. The betting public possesses all the necessary evidence to relate the Lichi who finishes out of the money every time (in the wrong job) to the Lichi who never runs a dull race (in the right job). Lichi pays superwoman mutuels again and again because she plays the role of Clark (or is it Clarice?) Kent on the days when she is not needed at her trade.

Whenever a horse runs a bad race, make sure he is not role playing in order to cover up his true function at the racetrack. If you can discover these steady masters of their trade, you will likely collect at better than fair payoffs, because there will always be Jimmy Olsens and Lois Lanes in the betting public.

CHAPTER 5

Child Prodigies
and Late Bloomers

CHILD PRODIGIES

Tasso

2-year-old 5 wins, 1 second, including a victory in the
1985 Grade 1 Breeders' Cup Juvenile

3-year-old 2 wins in lesser, ungraded stakes

4-year-old 2 wins in allowance races, beaten favorite five
times!

The decline of Tasso is moderate when compared to the life
cycles of some of his illustrious colleagues.

Capote

2-year-old 3 wins in 4 races, including the 1986 Grade 1
Breeders' Cup Juvenile

3-year-old Out of the money at 7–5 and 6–5, he makes a
symbolic appearance in the Kentucky Derby
and fades into oblivion

At this writing, none of the five Breeders' Cup Juvenile winners
(two-year-old champions) have won the Kentucky Derby as three-
year-olds. Winning Colors, winner of the 1988 Kentucky Derby,
raced only twice as a two-year-old, while other more heavily raced
two-year-olds from the same barn of D. Wayne Lukas, such as Suc-

cess Express (1987 Breeders' Cup Juvenile winner) and Tejano, had nothing to offer when Derby time rolled around.

Alysheba, winner of the 1987 Kentucky Derby, had only one win as a two-year-old and only a maiden victory at the time of the Derby. Ferdinand, winner of the 1986 Kentucky Derby, was only one for five as a two-year-old, that being a very unsensational maiden victory. Ferdinand, Judge Angelucci, and other late bloomers trained by Charles Whittingham continue to win graded stakes as older horses.

Perhaps the structure of today's racing game offers too many financial incentives for patrons to overextend their child prodigies. Perhaps too many individual trainers expect too much of their young talent and literally run it into the ground. Perhaps animals of such big bodies over such thin legs need a slower, more delicate maturation period.

There is too much evidence that premature racing in pressure situations causes a downward-spiral life cycle for racing's child prodigies. Surely each trainer of a two-year-old wonder will have his own unique explanation for the subsequent aborted stardom and decline. Whether these reasons or causes have to do with condition problems, loss of interest in racing, or more esoteric excuses, premature racing activity will often play a major role in catalyzing a quick decline for a would-be star.

For handicappers, "reasons" are not always accessible and are rarely necessary. The pattern in the past performances is clear: a majority of two-year-old champs will have seen their best days before they become mature "adults."

Why did *Bolger Magic* become Bolger Tragic? As a two-year-old he won his first three races, bypassing allowance races in favor of stakes races, perhaps taking advantage of fields composed of horses whose trainers were sacrificing immediate gratification in favor of a more profound future.

At this writing, Bolger Magic is a five-year-old. In the three racing years following his initial binge, he has won but 1 race and lost 22. Did he face stiff competition too early in his career, like the rookie brought up to the major leagues before he's ready? Or was he simply run too much at too early an age, like the kid who is forced to practice the piano when he'd rather be out playing baseball, and thus develops a dislike for Mozart?

The best thing that has happened to many a successful horse is to have failed while heavily bet on as a two-year-old in its first or second attempt to break its maiden. The trainer doesn't like what he sees, or a minor injury is discovered, but the result is the same: the horse is laid off, allowed to grow and mature, and comes back as a three-year-old, often winning first time back. The return to the races of this type of three-year-old often heralds the beginning of a brilliant career that would have been aborted had the horse performed well initially as a two-year-old.

Some gritty horses will survive an overtaxing two-year-old campaign, for sure, but pari-mutuelly it is advantageous to wager against the horse with the flashy "baby" record in favor of the up-and-coming horses that have been slowly nursed toward a racing peak. Ironically, expensive, well-bred horses are more likely to become overextended child prodigies, because there are lucrative races written to tempt their patrons.

As we shall study in the trainer-cycle chapters, the trainer factor is embedded to varying degrees in most horse life cycles. The child-prodigy, rapid-decline cycle will find more Lukas horses than those of Whittingham. But if horse cycles are not completely independent of external factors, neither are trainer angles. Is Wallace Dollase the primary reason why a Bolger Magic starts so early and declines so quickly? Or could it be Bolger, as a sire, which provides the inherent motor for running the cycle? So many of Dollase's horses pass through similar life phases, and yet most of them are sired by Bolger:

```
Sudden Dance                        Dk. b. or br. g. 4, by Bolger—Peignoir, by Windy Sands
                                    Br.—Rowan L & R (Cal)                        1988  2  0  0  0          $900
SOLIS A                        115  Tr.—Dollase Wallace          $12,500         1987  6  0  1  0        $7,850
Own.—Ash-Dollase-Lucian             Lifetime   10   1   2   0    $55,450
12May88-1Hol  7f :222 :452 1:232ft   6½ 115   1¹  2½  22½ 48¾  Meza R Q³      Ⓢ 10000  78-21 ShowerDecree,StrOfAmeric,Dtctor 12
28Apr88-1Hol  6½f :214 :444 1:164ft  7  115   3¹  5⁴  77½ 88   Solis A⁴         10000  86-18 Loverue,SpecilRun,Reinbow'sCup 12
13Dec87-3Hol  6f :222 :46 1:113ft    5½ 115   31½ 32  3⁴  45¾  Valenzuela P A⁵  25000  78-13 SundncSqur,ColdNHrd,Blc'kOrphus 8
28Nov87-2Hol  6½f :214 :444 1:17 ft  9½ 116   31½ 55  98½ 91¹  ValenzuelPA⁵   Ⓢ 32000  82-12 DelVolnte,GretNegotitor,HdlinNws 9
  28Nov87—Bobbled start
18Nov87-6Hol  6f :221 :451 1:103ft   3  111⁵  53½ 55  77. 77½  Gryder A T⁶      40000  81-12 Barnhart, Aranjuez, Naked Jaybird 9
31Oct87-4SA   6½f :213 :442 1:181½y  8  115   66  6¹⁴ 6¹² 49   Solis A ⁵       Aw27000  70-25 Hail Commander, Chinati,DryRidge 6
8Oct87-5SA    6½f :214 :443 1:154ft  2¾ 115   32½ 75½11¹³12¹⁴½ McCrrnCJ⅟    Ⓢ Aw20000  76-19 MiBeso,TimeForSkrto,Bric'sAdvic 12
13Sep87-7Dmr  6f :214 :45 1:10 ft    *6-5 115 2¾  2nd 2nd 22½  McCrronCJ ⅟⁹Aw22000  .85-18 BoldArchon,SuddenDance,Pensco 10
31Aug86-10Cby 6½f :22 :442 1:164ft   *3-5 120 2½  1hd 1¹  2nk  McHrgueDG²  Cby Juv 97-08 StaffRiot,SuddenDance,TexasTrio 14
16Aug86-4Dmr  6f :22 :452 1:094ft    13 117  1²  1¹  1²  13¼  McHargue D G² Mdn  88-13 SuddenDnce,SpcilTrick,LonStrStt 12
     Apr 22 Hol 5f ft 1:02³ h        Apr 10 Hol 5f ft 1:02³ h     ● Apr 4 Hol 4f ft :072 h     Mar 28 Hol 4f ft :49 h
```

Indeed, there are many horses sired by Bolger but not trained by Dollase that pass through similar phases. For example:

He's A Dancing Man. Wins 2 of first 5 races as young three-year-old, then goes 1 for 15, including 0 for 5 through first four months of his fourth year.

Promise Me Luck. All three of her wins come early. Midway through her fifth year she shows no wins as a four-year-old and no wins as a five-year-old.

Banche. Opens his career with two straight wins as a two-year-old, wins four more races as a young three-year-old, then goes into an eight-race losing streak at the end of his third year and beginning of his fourth year.

What materializes from our data is that Bolger tends to produce early winners who decline, and Dollase, independently, tends to excel with younger horses; when these two tendencies combine, the early-peak, rapid-decline cycle is almost inevitable.

Although trainer and sire may be factors that enhance the possibility of an early-peak, rapid-decline cycle, we are really observing a universal phenomenon that, ironically, most affects the better trainers—those maestros who are most capable of preparing their prodigies for immediate stardom. Both Masterful Advocate and Timely Assertion, for example, were fortunate to have the best of trainers (Manzi and Moreno) but still faced the tragedy of the young hero who loses the magic touch.

As a two-year-old, first-time-starter winner, Masterful Advocate rubbed shoulders with Alysheba, and as a young three-year-old was a Grade 2 winner and Kentucky Derby hopeful. Timely

Assertion, winner of her first two races as a two-year-old, competed successfully in the same league as Very Subtle.

These two luminaries made their appearance as four-year-olds and quickly lit up the sky as falling stars, failing to win after repeated tries during the first half of 1988, burning the money of handicappers who based their bets on the good old days of these members of Our Gang, whose performance in adult circles could not come near the level of their childhood achievements.

MUTUEL SAVINGS

Occasionally a child prodigy such as Very Subtle will fulfill the dreams of her mentors, but in the realm of investment, handicappers will protect their bankroll and improve their return on investment by betting against this type of horse as it descends into the valley of mediocrity. Consider the case of *Vamos Al Oro*, who won his first two career races, including the Affirmed Handicap, May 25, 1986, at Rockingham.

The next time out he went off at 2–5 and finished last, 37 lengths behind the winner. The next time out Vamos al Oro was once more favored, this time at 7–5, and once more he finished last, 18 lengths out. It took an extended layoff, eight straight losses, and more than a whole calendar year for Vamos Al Oro to recover a consolatory part of his old form and finally win—at a much lower level, of course.

And what about *Vanslam*, who, as a two-year-old, averaged $3,600 earnings per start? We pick up his career after August 1987, as a three-year-old, where he has just descended another step of the class ladder and is now averaging less than $200 per start.

Vanslam — B. c. 3, by Bold Forbes—Investment, by Vaguely Noble
$12,500 — Br.—Hunt N B (Ont-C) — Tr.—Zappasodi Joseph V — 116
Own.—Grand Pep Stable
Lifetime 15 2 1 0 $16,698 — 1987 11 0 0 0 $2,198 — 1986 4 2 1 0 $14,500 — Turf 4 0 0 0 $315

21Aug87- 2Pna	fst	1 70	:47⅖	1:13⅗	1:45⅘	Clm 12500	3	6	56½	47½	58	46½	Lopez C C	b 116	13.40	61-26	Nicholas R 119nk Driver 1144 Mikey C. 1162	Bobbled st.	8
12Aug87- 9Pna	fm	1	(T):47⅘	1:12⅘	1:39⅕	Clm 17000	7	6	84¾	98½	914	912½	Ayarza I	b 114	59.80	69-20	To Intrepid 116nk Gus Buster 1161 Alabama Smith 119½	Outrun	11
26Jly87- 7Pha	yl	1	(T):47⅘	1:12⅘	1:39	Clm 17000	7	11	1111	913	68¾	511½	Ayarza I	114	29.00	71-10	Alabama Smith 1123½ ToIntrepid1142½RutherGlen1073½	No threat	12
5Jly87- 5Pha	fst	1 1/16	:48⅘	1:13⅘	1:47⅖	Clm 18000	2	7	76½	69	611	59¾	Ayarza I	116	7.80	57-27	Devil's Voodoo 119¾ Mc Forbes 1121NonStopPop1165½	No factor	7
6Jun87- 5GS	fst	6f	:22⅖	:45⅘	1:11⅘	Clm 25000	5	3	69½	612	68	57½	Lopez C C	116	18.70	75-21	AlphBuck114¾LilKell'sBrother1144½HoldYourMoney1161½	Outrun	6
28May87- 8GS	fm	1 70	(T):46⅘	1:11⅗	1:41	Clm 30000	8	4	65½	65	612	613½	Lopez C C	114	29.20	79-06	Bobby's J. S. 1162 Lil Saucy 1161 Mighty Force 1141	Outrun	8
18May87- 9GS	fm	1	(T):47⅘	1:12	1:35⅘	3↑Alw 12500	7	3	53½	74	1019	1029	Lopez C C	114	53.30	67-04	Morewoods 1104½ T. S. Evans 1114½ Tisa Feast 1162½	Tired	10
2May87- 5GS	gd	6f	:22⅕	:45⅕	1:10⅘	3↑Alw 11500	2	7	911	912	813	79½	Lopez C C	b 114	35.20	78-16	Lil Fappi 113nk Hawaiian Buzz 112nk Ruler oftheFleet1084	Outrun	9
13Apr87- 8GS	gd	6f	:22	:45⅗	1:10⅗	3↑Alw 11500	1	9	915	1010	1020	926¾	Madrid A Jr	b 112	25.70	62-26	Capo Cane 1206 Margerine 117¾ Shalmai 1173	Outrun	10
21Feb87- 6Aqu	fst	1 70	[•]:48⅗	1:13⅗	1:43⅗	Alw 28000	6	6	78	713	720	728¾	Graell A	117	42.50	53-24	Mister S. M. 1221½ Forest Fair 1193½ Hoist n' Hail 1123	Outrun	7

LATEST WORKOUTS Jly 18 Pha 4f fst :49 b

The difference between betting thoroughbreds and playing the lottery is that you can't eliminate numbers from the lottery drawings, while you can eliminate horses from the field. Eliminating horses that "look bad" to everyone will do little to reduce the track take (disadvantage) because obviously dull horses account for a small percentage of the betting pools. Eliminating horses that "look good" turns a negative expectation situation into a positive investment.

After Vamos Al Oro's first loss, anyone familiar with the early-peak, rapid-decline cycle would have identified Vamos Al Oro as a prime candidate for defeat. By simply eliminating Vamos Al Oro on July 20 at Philadelphia Park, the investor would have knocked out nearly 40 percent of the betting pool, thus creating a net positive expectation of over 20 percent (after subtracting the negative take from the gross advantage obtained from the elimination of Vamos Al Oro).

Many of these child prodigies continue to receive heavy action for a number of races after the observer of cycles has identified them to be declining horses. Even when a two-year-old is racing at its peak, it is safe to assume that in most instances a decline is imminent. These horses are always overbet; if we take a stand against them, we will watch a few of them win, but the percentages will be strongly in our favor.

LATE BLOOMERS

More mysterious than the definitive decline of the child prodigy is the opposite phenomenon: the proven loser that suddenly turns into a confident winner. As we have seen, many a confirmed failure will have his brief romantic fling of victories, only to depart from the oasis and continue his long trek through the desert.

But another type of proven loser will rise from its barren wasteland to an extended plateau of green meadows. For apparently no reason, the loser will become a winner. A number of case histories of this type will remain an enigma or be explained by a very particular combination of trainer experiments with changes of equipment, rider, distance, and surface until the right combination is arrived at.

On the other hand, study of many case histories uncovers one particular pattern that is common in many instances. Allow me a brief analogy with baseball. Many a career is ruined when a player is brought up to the majors too soon (parallel to the child prodigies of horse racing). Conversely, the minor leagues function as a place where the athlete develops self-confidence through the feeling of success against lesser competition. Some players who flounder in the majors are sent down to the minors, and on occasion they find a level at which the competition is realistic enough for them to do very well. They then work their way back up the ladder with renewed winning spirit until they reach the major leagues and perform with success.

Many an Eliminante, proven loser and dismal failure, if given the chance at lower levels, will discover what it "feels" like to be a winner and will bring that positive self-image to higher levels; this transformed horse may even return to the class level of its chronic failure and now beat the same horses it once lost to.

That many more thoroughbreds are not dropped to their confidence level is a result of the claiming system, in which horses run with a purchase price on their head, as if they were used cars in a lot. The lower the claiming price/level of competition, the more likely they'll be claimed. According to Julio Canani, successful West Coast claiming trainer, many trainers have low win percentages not because they can't handle horses, but because they never risk losing a horse.

It seems a damned-if-you-do-damned-if-you-don't situation; lose at the wrong class level or get claimed. For many horses, such as Julio N Me, a stay in the minors will do nothing to alter their noncompetitive, follower psychology. For others, a chance to compete against lesser horses will lead to a renewed competitive motivation. For the handicapper, it is most difficult to distinguish between these two types.

It now appears that in those cases that allow for rational analysis, two major characteristics separate the brief-fling winners from the late bloomers:

	Late Bloomer	*Brief Flinger*
Type of Win	1st win occurs with improved speed or pace figures	Wins by default vs. lesser of evils field
Claims	Likely to get claimed on the way up in class	Far less likely to get claimed

Majestic Trace

Monumental drop. Wins. Claimed next time on rise.

Winging Missy

Drops in class while going from major track to fair. Begins to win as she goes up in class. Claimed at a much higher level. Continues to win.

Winging Missy — Dk. b. or br. m. 5, by Wing Out—Missy Margie, by Mr Bunker
SHOEMAKER W — 114 — Br.—Cardiff Stud Farm (Cal) — 1987 10 6 1 0 $45,500
Own.—Capitol Clan — Tr.—Stein Roger $45,000 — 1986 12 1 3 1 $15,500
Lifetime 35 10 4 2 $71,110

24Dec87-3Hol 6½f :22¹ :45³ 1:17²ft 4 112 6⁵½ 5⁴½ 3¹½ 1³½ ShoemakerW⁶ Ⓕ 20000 91-10 WngngMssy,FolshLary,DlghtflTwst 8
11Dec87-3Hol 6½f :22¹ :45² 1:17⁴ft 6½ 115 3¹ 3¹½ 3¹½ 4²½ Olivares F⁶ ⒻAw34000 86-18 Survive, Third Down,DreamFeather 7
26Nov87-5Hol 6f :22² :45² 1:11 ft 16 115 2½ 2¹ 2½ 1½ Olivares F⁷ Ⓕ 20000 87-18 WingingMissy,SnFlp'sQun,MmGllo 11
14Nov87-1SA 6½f :22¹ :46 1:18⁴ft *2 117 10⁷½ 9⁸ 9¹⁰ 9¹²½ Pincay L Jr⁵ Ⓕ c16000 64-22 GrySptmbr,AbovThRst,SrchFrHvn 11
22Oct87-7BM 6f :22² :45¹ 1:09²ft 6½ 117 2½ 2¹ 1hd 1¹½ Aragon V A¹⁰ Ⓕ 12500 92-15 WngngMssy,Trsh'sBu,PostvlyPosh 11
11Oct87-9BM 6f :22² :45³ 1:11 ft 2½ 116 5³½ 5⁴½ 3¹½ 1no Aragon V A⁴ Ⓕ 10000 84-14 WingingMissy,BltShos,Gossn'sSwt 10
11Oct87—Drifted in 1/8
17Sep87-10Bmf 6f :22¹ :45¹ 1:10¹ft 5½ 115 9¹⁵ 9¹⁰ 6⁴ 2½ Gonzalez RM⁶ Ⓕ 10000 87-16 PrncssSplndr,WngngMssy,WltArad 9
17Sep87—Hopped in air
30Aug87-8Sac 6f :22 :44³ 1:09³ft 2½ 114 5⁵ 3½ 1¹ 1¹½ Gonzalez R M³ Ⓕ 8000 91-09 WingingMissy,BgddSingr,SisQ.Glmr 8
30Aug87—Drifted out, bumped hard start; steadied 1/2
29Jly87-10SR 5½f :22 :45¹ 1:03³ft 6 115 4¹½ 2hd 1² 1⁷ SchvneveldtCP⁹ Ⓕ 6250 93-12 Winging Missy, Patriotic, QuitaKid 9
16Jun87-2BM 6f :22² :46¹ 1:12⁴ft 7½ 115 5⁶ 5⁵ 4³½ 4¹½ Doocy T T¹ Ⓕ 6250 73-30 PhyllisFeely,DarkSeaBr,Beuty'sSis 11
Dec 21 Hol 4f ft :48² h   Dec 10 Hol 3f ft :35² h   Nov 8 BM 5f ft 1:00⁴ h   Nov 1 BM 5f gd 1:02¹ h

Rowdy Rebel

Wins at his lowest level. Claimed two races later. Goes up the ladder with new trainer. Claimed again; continues to win.

Rowdy Rebel — Ro. h. 7, by On To Glory—Image Of Big Mary, by Sadair
$16,000 — Br.—Sibley Marion E (Fla) — Tr.—Crupi James J — 116
Own.—Martucci W C
Lifetime 63 12 9 11 $74,895 — 1987 17 8 3 2 $35,670 — 1986 10 0 0 1 $2,870 — Turf 3 0 0 0 $1,555

8Aug87- 2Mth fst 1 :46⅘ 1:10⅘ 1:37⅘ 3↑Clm c-10500 6 1 1² 1hd 1½ 1½ Vigliotti M J b 111 *2.20 86-15 Rowdy Rebel 111½ Cannon Royal 115½ AbbeyGrange110½ Driving 7
30Jly87- 2Mth fst 6f :22⅕ :44⅘ 1:10 3↑Clm 9000 6 1 2½ 1½ 1² 1⁵½ Vigliotti M J b 114 4.10 90-14 Rowdy Rebel 1145½ Mr. Mar J. Mar 119½ Ship Mint 116no Driving 7
22Jly87- 2Mth fst 6f :22⅘ :45⅗ 1:11⅖ 3↑Clm 10500 2 4 1hd 2hd 2½ 4¹½ Vigliotti M J b 112 2.70 82-21 Summing All 113½ Storm Warrior 116no Khamfin 119½ Gave way 8
10Jly87- 3Mth fst 6f :22⅘ :45⅗ 1:11 3↑Clm c-7000 7 1 1¹ 1³ 1³½ 1³½ Vigliotti M J b 117 *1.70 85-16 Rowdy Rebel 1173½ Ship Mint 116½ Circle Bound 116³ Ridden out 7
30Jun87- 4Mth fst 6f :22⅘ :45⅗ 1:11⅕ 3↑Clm 6250 8 1 1hd 1² 1³ 1⁴ Vigliotti M J b 119 *1.80 84-13 RowdyRebel1194GemsForSale114hdB.G.'sChrger114½ Ridden out 10
9Jun87- 4Mth fst 6f :22⅘ :46 1:11⅗ 3↑Clm c-5000 7 2 1hd 1¹½ 1² 1³½ Miceli M b 119 *1.60 82-19 RowdyRebl1193½GimmAMrkr1114Rjb'sWillyPop1092½ Ridden out 11
2Jun87- 4Mth fst 6f :22⅘ :45⅗ 1:10⅘ 3↑Clm 6000 6 2 1¹ 1½ 2¹ 3⁵½ Miceli M b 117 3.90 82-16 ChimneySweep1145HiltoOlympus109nkRowdyRebl1171 Weakened 11
15May87- 7GS gd 6f :22⅘ :46⅕ 1:12 3↑Clm 5000 9 1 1¹ 1³ 1³½ 1⁵½ Miceli M b 116 2.60 82-23 Rowdy Rebel 1165½ Intheblack 116nk Anvil Man 116½ Ridden out 11
8May87- 7GS fst 6f :22⅘ :45⅗ 1:11⅘ 3↑Clm 5000 7 1 2hd 2¹½ 2²½ 2² Miceli M b 116 *1.40 81-22 Perfect Match 1222 RowdyRebel1162½Significantly116no Came in 9
27Apr87- 8GS fm 5f Ⓣ:22⅕ :46⅕ :59⅕ 3↑Alw 8500s 6 1 2¹ 2² 3² 4²½ Miceli M b 114 8.80 88-09 AnotherMember1121½SaintMachree114hdKlassySerende1141 Tired 11
LATEST WORKOUTS Aug 22 Mth 4f fst :48⅘ h

A.D.'s Favourite

Wins at her lowest level, claimed next time. Goes up the ladder and continues to win.

A. D.'s Favourite — GRYDER A T — 1115 — Own.—Blasco B

Dk. b. or br. f. 4, by Solid Purchase—Winzaniot, by Crocation
Br.—Domco Management Ltd (BC-C) — 1987 15 5 3 1 $21,198
Tr.—Bell Thomas R II $12,500 — 1986 13 1 3 1 $10,055
Lifetime 28 7 8 4 $80,512

16Dec87-3BM	1 1/8	:472 1:114 1:571ft	3 1/2	115	712 710 69 45	Warren R JJr 7	Ⓕ H6250	73-18	Kviot'sFlight,HiddenAngl,Wlingring	7
26Nov87-3BM	1 1/4	:501 1:39 2:033ft	*2	116	43 1/2 53 1/2 34 34 1/2	Warren R JJr 3	Ⓕ H6250	77-17	Kvot'sFlght,HddnAngl,A.D.'sFvourt	6
6Nov87-3BM	1 1/16	:461 1:112 1:44 ft	*2 3/4	116	911 86 3/4 3nk 16	Hansen R D 2	Ⓕ c10000	72-20	A.D.'sFvourite,VlentinRos,ComicDr	9
29Oct87-3BM	1 1/16	:471 1:124 1:471m	*8-5	119	613 69 56 24	Hansen R D 3	Ⓕ 8000	52-28	BlowDry,A.D.'sFvourit,Mic'l'sSpcil	6
3Oct87-7Lga	1 1/16	:464 1:111 1:434ft	*2	1065	612 59 1/2 44 12	Camargo T 1	Ⓕ 8000	80-17	A.D.'sFvort,TrvlngTropr,MjcPssprt	6
26Sep87-10Lga	1 1/16	:464 1:114 1:44 ft	6 1/2	115	510 45 21 1/2 13	Hansen R D 4	Ⓕ 6250	79-25	A.D.'sFvourite,ImAMck,FightinLil	10
26Sep87—Lost whip 1/8										
5Sep87-7Lga	1 1/16	:47 1:12 1:45 ft	7 1/2	1075	44 45 1/2 69 3/4 58	D'Amico D L 5	Ⓕ 8000	66-18	TrvelingTroopr,T.C.Tryst,FightinLil	8
23Aug87-5Lga	1	:462 1:112 1:374ft	6 1/2	1085	912 912 810 54 1/2	D'Amico D L1	Ⓕ 10000	76-18	RreLegcy,BonneThirteen,SuperTe	10
13Aug87-10Lga	1 1/16	:493 1:162 1:50 m	*2 1/2	1135	89 3/4 42 1/2 13 16	D'Amico DL11	Ⓕ c5000	49-38	A.D.'sFvort,SltwtrMon,FlyngFthrs	12
30Jly87-5Lga	1 1/8	:481 1:124 1:514ft	*4-5	1075	22 1/2 1hd 13 1/2 15	D'Amico D L1	Ⓕ 5000	74-20	A.D.'sFvourit,TndrTlk'n,Ht'y'sSong	7

Dec 14 BM 3f ft :364 h   Dec 8 BM 3f sy :353 h (d)   Nov 28 BM 4f ft :481 h

Ballet Bouquet

Wins at her lowest level, maiden claiming. Makes what is equivalent to a mild rise—statebred to open company, maiden claimer to claimer for winners. Gets claimed on the way up; continues to win.

Ballet Bouquet — KAENEL J L — 118 — Own.—Behman G A

Ch. f. 4, by Splendid Courage—Kate Will Tell, by Taillefer
Br.—Patterson Farms Inc (Cal) — 1988 7 4 0 2 $28,563
Tr.—Arterburn Lonnie $32,000 — 1987 6 M 1 1 $2,100
Lifetime 13 4 1 3 $30,663 — Turf 1 1 0 0 $9,900

28Apr88-7GG	1 1/8 Ⓣ	:48 1:13 1:513fm	7 3/4	118	1 1/2 1 1/2 11 1/2 14	Kaenel J L 1	Ⓕ Aw18000	— —	BlletBouquet,Newscene,SrmyDncr	8
8Apr88-9GG	1 1/16	:462 1:11 1:431ft	5 3/4	116	2hd 2hd 11 1/2 12 1/2	Kaenel J L 5	Ⓕ 16000	83-13	BlletBouquet,ScentedSilerc,Tognll	6
18Mar88-3GG	1 1/16	:464 1:114 1:454ft	3 1/2	116	53 3/4 42 1/2 33 32 1/2	CastanedM 5	Ⓕ c12500	68-23	Bausond,FinllyProved,Blle'Bouquet	6
8Mar88-7GG	1	:472 1:13 1:40 ft	8 1/2	116	1hd 2hd 32 46	Castaneda M 4	Ⓕ 16000	62-30	ProperCraft,K.S.Dncer,EstrellBlnc	10
8Mar88—Ducked in sharply start										
19Feb88-9GG	1	:461 1:104 1:371ft	9	116	1 1/2 1hd 1hd 11 1/2	Castaneda M 3	Ⓕ 10000	82-17	Ballet Bouquet, One Drurr,L'Indian	9
19Feb88—Ducked in start										
5Feb88-5GG	6f	:22 :45 1:102ft	11	118	43 1/2 33 42 1/2 31 3/4	Castaneda M 8	Ⓕ 10000	85-15	FlsConcolor,Funformony,BlltBouqt	8
22Jan88-2BM	6f	:222 :461 1:121ft	*3-2	120	53 31 1/2 11 1/2 13	Baze R A 4	Ⓕ Ⓢ M12500	78-20	BlltBouqt,Clr'sBoldPly,RsonblEln	10
30Dec87-1BM	6f	:223 :454 1:124m	*2 1/2	119	87 3/4 911 913 89 1/2	Baze R A 2	Ⓕ M12500	66-29	Linarullah,SisterRoslie,MerryLore	11
30Dec87—Bumped start										
27Nov87-2BM	6f	:224 :46 1:112ft	3 3/4	119	64 3/4 55 1/2 36 1/2 35	CastnedM 11	Ⓕ M12500	77-22	Whence,SchoolSocil,BlletBouquet	12
8Oct87-2BM	6f	:222 :462 1:113ft	8 1/2	119	32 45 42 1/2 2no	Baze R A 7	Ⓕ M12500	81-23	Frdnkum,BlltBoqt,NoDownPymnt	11

May 12 GG 1 ft 1:41 h   Apr 21 GG 6f gd 1:172 h   Mar 30 GG 5f ft 1:03 h

None of these horses were claimed when initially dropped. In every case the original owner lost his horse *not because of the drop*, but because, following the initial victory, the horse was not moved up in class high enough. In each case the new trainer was beneficiary of multiple wins on the way up in class. The claim was an important message to the handicapper.

The original trainers dropped their horses while in a negative mode of low expectations. The new trainers had high expectations when they made their claims. The significant message here is that most proven losers who have only a brief fling of success in store for them are not going to be claimed, while most late bloomers will be claimed and raised in class.

The venerable Ernie King, for example, was not claimed during or after his 2 for 3 "streak." And claiming trainers were not fooled when, by pact with the Devil, T.V. Oil won two in a row.

In other words, handicappers monitor a potentially reformed horse by the nature of its initial victory, but depend on claiming trainers to confirm the new value of the horse by their willingness to claim it.

Some transformed horses will put together a string of victories with low pari-mutuel payoffs. While there will be little or no value in betting such horses, having identified them as legitimate favorites will save us from fruitlessly betting against them. This methodology will, at least, allow us to know when the proven losers of the past are not the false favorites of the present.

At best, some of these class risers will pay good prices as they improve against stiffer competition. At one point the flashy child prodigy on the down escalator and the late bloomer on the up escalator may face each other in the same field; the former loser may pay a good price because the public bets on the former winner.

CAN A GELDING FIND ROMANCE AT THE AGE OF FIVE?

The only other subset of late bloomers that emerged with common characteristics identifiable to the handicapper concerns a correlation between age and type of horse most likely to become a late bloomer. The following are some examples of the many five-year-old geldings that suddenly became horses of winning spirit (extracted at random points in the fifth year of the racing life of geldings).

Five-year-old geldings that discover how to win should be given extra handicapping points in their subsequent outings, especially when the odds are right, as they were for *Great Communicator*, *Northern Provider*, and occasionally for *Powerful Paul* and *Quick Roundtrip*. By the age of five many geldings have developed such bad credentials that no publicity agent in the world could possibly convince the betting public that these losers have become winners.

Wrapped up in the details of nuts and bolts handicapping, speed figures, and public touts, the people who make the odds on the tote board are generally undereducated in the area of thoroughbred cycles. The child prodigies and late bloomers of thoroughbred society offer ample evidence that horses go through dynamic changes in their racing life; the public expects the past to repeat itself, and often invests in horses that are on

	Races	1st	2nd	3rd	Payoffs as 5-year-old and Comments
Quick Roundtrip					
5-year-old	14	*7*	2	1	7–1, 3–1, 2–1, 4–1, etc.
prior	22	*2*	2	3	(Earned twice as much as 5YO than in rest of career)
Powerful Paul					
5-year-old	9	5	2	1	6–1, 5–1, 3–1, 2–1,
prior	19	3	2	3	even. (Went up the ladder and was claimed several times along the way)
Great Communicator					
5-year-old	4	3	1	0	12–1, 11–1, 7–1 (Winning races at highest class of career, graded stakes)
prior	31	5	5	6	
Northern Provider					
5-year-old	6	3	0	1	Up the ladder, not claimed, paid in double figures each time, incl: $87 and $57
prior	26	4	5	4	

their way down, leaving form-cycle handicappers with profitable payoffs on horses that are on their way up.

Research

The most mysterious of cycle transformations is the late bloomer. The most sensational of late bloomers is the five-year-old gelding, who materialized unexpectedly from my research as a major protagonist in the rags-to-riches drama. What method of handicapping can explain how Travet, a 2 for 38 lifetime horse, can win 2 out of 3, with the old-timer Rudy Campas aboard, at 9–2 and at an amazing 79–1? What system could predict that Parson John, 2 for 38 lifetime, would win twice as a five-year-old gelding, including a 16–1 win, as well as finishing second at 16–1 and at 6–1? Consider Lucky Creation, just become a five-year-old, a gelding with a miserable 3 for 36 record. It's January

2, 1988, Bay Meadows. Fate takes over. Lucky Creation wins at 20–1. Two races later he wins again, at 8–1, only to be disqualified. He loses a few, always competitively, until the chance arises to redeem his name. It's May 1, and this time the disqualification goes in his favor; at 7–1, he is moved up from second to first by the stewards.

Horseplayers in search of a stronger investment portfolio cannot let these sensational observations remain on an impressionistic level.

I dug into my *Racing Forms* and cut out the past performances of as many five-year-old geldings as I could, until my scissors got dulled. My computer colleagues tell me it would have been easier their way, but for me there's something intimate, existential, sensorial, intense, about the touch and smell of the past performances.

This sample is so random that Bugarian goes in, two races before his 20–1 victory would have qualified; I know Bennett Peak to be 4 for 14 as a five-year-old gelding, but my sample gets 0 for 7. This is a good method because it acts as the player who is betting on a system. It may begin action three days after a big long shot has come in, and may miss the big one because of a dentist's appointment.

With tabulations complete and the results looking too good to be true, I intervened for the first and last time, axing out the top two payoffs, expunging mutuels of $160 and $60. As system players are well aware, on the day of the biggest payoff, one is likely to get a flat tire on the way to the track.

First we shall scan the results of the research, and then insert a few comments.

Rule:	horse races as 5YO gelding
Sample:	524 races
Winners:	98 (nearly 19%)
Invested:	$1048
Return:	$1315 (*excluding two biggest long shots*)
Profit:	$267
ROI:	26½% profit

Compare these results with random selection, lottery style. If the five-year-old gelding, as a subset, were no different performancewise from the set of all thoroughbreds, the 26½ percent profit should have been a 17 percent loss. The subset performed

43½ percentage points better than the set it came from. In an average field of ten horses (hypothetical estimate), random selection will win one in ten (10 percent). Compare this approximate figure with the nearly 19 percent winners in random selection of five-year-old geldings, and we find that the subset has performed about 9 percent better than the set it came from. The estimate of a ten-horse average field may be slightly off, but the subset nevertheless shows a clearly superior win percentage. Also, note that the type of horse that is a five-year-old gelding tends to be entered in the type of claiming race that goes to post with a full field of horses.

Now comes the one fundamental question confronted by all researchers: Do we need a larger sample? To develop a betting "system," probably yes. To illustrate a point about late bloomers, probably no. This sample won't convince me that five-year-old geldings perform 43 percent better than horses in general, but the gap is wide enough to assure me that there is a notable difference in favor of this type of late bloomer.

In order to develop a "system," not only is the size of the sample questionable—given the large numbers of five-year-old geldings—but we must also be doubtful about the characteristics of the sample. With horses from New York, San Francisco, and Los Angeles, we have no proof that the same phenomenon exists in New Jersey or at Hawthorne. If readers are impressed by the stats from this survey, their next step is to run the same test at their local tracks. My experience tells me that parallel results at three tracks suggests strongly that the factor will be universal.

Now consider that this particular survey is not a "system." It has no rules. No handicapping principles have been applied. The *average mutuel* in our survey is $13.40, and that impressive number excludes the two highest payoffs. Tamper with this by the intervention of handicapping principles, and risk lowering the average mutuel. Exclude a bad trainer and you may be knocking out your highest pari-mutuel payoff. Exclude horses that look formless by handicapping principles and you may be skimming off the whole top layer of long shots.

Remember that we are dealing with late bloomers. While some of the horses in our original sample had good records to begin with, the ones that contributed the best prices were those who, as four- and three-year-olds, had mediocre records. To convert this into a "system," your standard "rules" of recency, lengths behind, finish position, average earnings per race, and other factors of the same ilk, will be worthless. Just trying to save you some time. We shall return to the theme of the five-year-old gelding at the appropriate moment, Chapter 13, in the section on "Thoroughbred Futures," so stay tuned.

For the time being, we have accomplished our purpose of identifying a particular type of horse that is most likely to become a late bloomer. Two thirds of all the five-year-old geldings examined made a notable improvement during this period of their life. Several horses surveyed showed the improvement signs as late four-year-olds or early six-year-old geldings, cases that, while not conforming to the letter of the law—which is somewhat arbitrary—totally uphold the spirit of the concept.

There are other amazing factors that produce radically positive form reversals, as we shall see as we move on to the next chapter.

Graph. Prototypes of Child Prodigy and Late Bloomer

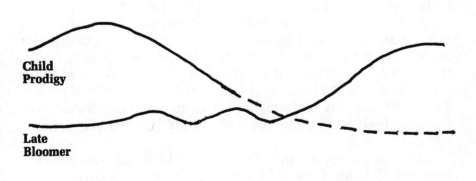

| 2-year-old | 3-year-old | 4-year-old | 5-year-old |

----- Some child prodigies never make it through their fourth or fifth year, since they have little to gain and much to risk with continued racing. Poor performance and injury could diminish or ruin their value as a breeding commodity.

CHAPTER 6

Radicals

REVIVAL MEETING

IT WAS A HOT, humid, subjective afternoon under a huge tent in a mythical southern county. The din of the crickets and cicadas was drowned out by the neighing of a hundred thoroughbred horses who had gotten together to relate the joy of their revival. They all had one thing in common: they had run three terrible races in a row and then, miraculously, to the chagrin of the betting public, had seen the light and won a race.

By definition, the three bad races were *out of the money* and *more than two lengths behind*. For their victory to qualify as a revival—in other words, to have been invited to this gathering—they had to have won with odds of at least 4–1. Most of these horses had won at 15–1, 20–1, and even 100–1. They had looked so bad in the past performances that their transformation had been deemed "miraculous" by the frustrated bettors in the grandstand.

Had my car not run out of gas just past the railroad crossing, near the Cahokie Swamp, I never would have known of this meeting of horses from twenty tracks across the country. I seized the opportunity to investigate the greatest enigma of horse-race handicapping: why completely dull horses wake up and win.

I mingled for some time among the revivalists, eavesdropping as well as I could, but discerning only subjective and supernatural "reasons" for sudden revivals, roughly translating to: "I had seen the light." There had to be a more material explanation for one hundred surprise victories. Then I discovered a stack of *Rac-*

ing Forms representing the histories of the horses present. It was an unexpected opportunity to make a breakthrough, and I dug in, completely forgetting about my abandoned car, which, for all I knew, might have by now been enveloped by the swamp.

After feverish hours of scanning and analyzing, I discovered that ten types of *changes* predominated following the horses' last defeat, in the past performances the day of the horses' wake-up victories.

Type of Change	% of Times Occurred
1. Track Switch	41
2. ClassDrop	39
• one level	24
• more than one level	15
3. Rider Switch	32
• better	14
• little difference	15
• lesser	3
4. Distance Change	22
• stretch-out	16
• shorten up	6
5. Track Condition Change	17
• off to fast	11
• fast to off	6
6. Blinkers	10
• on	7
• off	3
7. Well Bet Last Race(s)	9
8. Claimed	7
• first after claim	4
• second race after	3
9. Surface Switch	6
• grass to dirt	4
• dirt to grass	2
10. Early Speed for First Time Last Race	4

Number of Changes....187
Average Number of Changes Per Revival....2.15
Rationality Index....87%
  (13 revivals showed *no change* prior to victory)

It was too difficult to divide track switch into subcategories of "track upgrade" and "track downgrade" for several reasons. Some changes saw a switch to a classier track accompanied by a drop in class or a switch to a lesser track along with a rise in class. The number of winners going to lesser tracks was greater, but the number of horses going to lesser tracks was also greater; percentagewise, it is hard to make a case for any type of switch, given that each individual instance is so distinct. Nevertheless, the greatest correlation of this whole research project of a hundred surprise winners is: *TRACK SWITCH in combination with CLASS DROP.*

It is not that one-level class drops produce more victories, but that with a 4–1 minimum, many of the multiple droppers, with their victories at low odds, did not qualify for this study.

It would appear that a stretchout is superior to a shortening up, from a handicapping perspective, because horses that are dull because they can't keep up with a fast pace have a chance to adjust to the slower pace of route races. On the other hand, horses that can't keep up with a slower-paced route race will be spotting their rivals too many lengths at the outset of faster-paced sprint races.

When horses switched tracks and there was a mandatory rider switch, this was not counted as a jockey switch. The change of track superseded the change of jockey. These situations did not represent a trainer intention of changing riders. Nevertheless, since a different rider adds a distinct "feel" and a change of running style, somewhere embedded in a track-switch factor is the change of rider.

Well bet last race(s): I suspect that this factor is probably stronger than it appears to be in this study. The researcher would have had to attend each and every one of these wake-up races and have monitored the tote board during the two or three prior races of each horse in order to derive an accurate picture of betting action. For example, a horse that was 10–1 in its last race was assumed to have not received betting action. But what if that horse had opened at 8–5, or what if he had dropped from 10–1 to 6–1 midway through the betting and then gradually moved back to 10–1? These events would have been construed as betting action.

Early speed last race, too, is an undertabulated factor. Redefined to "made bold move last race," several of our distinguished winners would have been added to the list.

I was totally surprised at the very minor impact of the claim in the revival of a horse's form. I shouldn't have been. Research from the previous chapter had already implied that most successful claims are achieved when a horse that has already shown signs of a form revival is purchased.

I would have expected the dirt-to-turf factor to register an impact far superior to the feeble number in this study. The reader may argue that a larger sample was needed. Perhaps. I feel, though, that we are dealing with a very specialized situation. The sample was random, covered a broad cross-section of tracks, and was undertaken in a critical manner. I would bet my worldly possessions that these hundred horses are much closer to the *all* of their category than the most accurate election-poll sample is to the *all* of the potential voters.

Even if we included the off-track situation as a "surface switch," only 23 percent of our form reversals would have contained the surface-switch characteristic, still much less than track switch, class drop, or rider switch. Nevertheless, since there are far fewer surface switches than class drops or rider changes, surface switch remains an important handicapping factor.

On the Right Track

The most powerful factor leading to the form revival of a dull horse is the track switch, a change of venue. But with the average number of changes-per-revival victory at above two, the track-switch factor acquires an extra lift when accompanied by at least one other change.

McGuffey's Reader goes from a major track one notch down, Hollywood to Golden Gate, May 31, 1987. The horse shows five terrible races prior to the track switch. Therefore, the public makes him 25–1. Another factor that allows McGuffey to ' see the light" is the addition of blinkers (underlined number to right of jockey's name). Note that the last time he ran well, he was equipped with blinkers. The following two races with the blinkers look terrible, but when you're fanned wide on the first turn of a route race, you might as well throw in the towel, and that's what happened to our hero on both those occasions.

In sprint races he lacks speed. The stretchout plus the blinks are two changes that should lead to more early speed. The best race shown for McGuffey's Reader (4Dec86) was two furlongs longer than the races that immediately preceded his victory, evidence that the stretchout was positive. *Changes:* track switch, stretchout, blinkers, and last but not least, class drop. The betting public overestimates the factor of finish position last race. In order to make a profit, we need to find horses that looked terrible in their last race(s).

The original *McGuffey's Reader* offered schoolchildren simple solutions and morals for a good life. Horse-racing's McGuffey's Reader needed a complex combination of four changes in order to find a solution.

At the revival meeting there was a separate discussion group for horses that won at 25–1. Joining the group was *High Stepping Girl.*

High Stepping Girl		B. f. 4, by Syncopate—Jeff D Lass, by Jeff D				
BOULANGER G	114	Br.—Miller L R (Ky)		1987 6 1 0 1		$8,950
Own.—Bean Barn		Tr.—Bean Robert A $8,000		Turf 1 0 0 0		$875
		Lifetime 6 1 0 1 $8,950				

5Aug87-9SR	6f :221 :451 1:101ft	23 1105	753 54 45 423	IammrinoMP4 Ⓔ 25000	87-13 Ahmr,PrincessGoodWin,HelloLovly 9
5Aug87—Bumped start					
22Jly87-6Sol	6f :221 :452 1:104ft	25 1115	633 42 31 12	IammrinoMP10 ⓂMdn	89-13 HghStppngGrl,Ktt'sErhr,MndstMn 10
27Jun87-2GG	1⅛Ⓣ:4791:1241:45 fm	19 1095	57 31 553 483	IammarinoMP5 ⓂMdn	68-21 ColorCub,PurityOfLin,MryT.Frnch 11
27Jun87—Bobbled start					
10Jun87-2Hol	6f :22 :462 1:132ft	45 113	653 543 633 623	Ortega L E3 ⓂM28000	73-16 KeepOnFlying,LivelyMiss,CarlotE. 11
22May87-1Hol	6f :221 :461 1:123ft	63 113	533 553 673101½3	Meza R Q3 ⓂM28000	68-17 Pygreene,LittleGirlDoctor,Ridgelit 11
23Apr87-2Hol	6½f :223 :462 1:183ft	73 113	21 21½ 21½ 34	Meza R Q2 ⓂM28000	83-09 Pontd'Esprt,WldDrv,HghStppngGrl 9

May 13 66 4f ft :464 h   May 8 66 6f gd 1:144 h   Apr 30 66 5f ft 1:01²h   Apr 22 66 4f ft :48²h

There was no reason for this filly to go to post at such high odds. Her last race was on the wrong surface, and she was moving down one notch in track level, from Golden Gate to the Solano Fair. In the race prior to her victory, having bobbled at the start, she made a bold move from the first to the second call, perhaps the best move of her short career. Her previous race/out-of-the-money finish was also more competitive than it appeared, since, at 45–1, she came home less than three lengths away from the winner. *Changes:* track switch, surface switch, distance switch, wake-up move last race.

Hesa Frequentflyer also wants to join the 25–1 club. They won't let him join because his two victories were at 23.9–1 and 24.5–1. These revivalists tend to take things by the letter rather than the spirit of the law.

The way Hesa Frequentflyer goes from track to track, he'll soon qualify for every kind of extra-mileage bonus. Meanwhile, he can pay for his flights because he wins at such high odds.

He seems to have an inherent motivation to run his best race when he's just arrived in town. He thrives on change, and loses interest when he's hung around too long. Hesa Frequentflyer is an iconoclast who goes against the grain of reason. While most of the track-change winners are droppers or switchers to a lesser circuit, both of Hesa Frequentflyer's surprise victories have occurred when he faces tougher competition, in the form of a tougher track or higher class.

Even the change-of-surface victory fits into the scheme of things; he wins *first time on turf* as if he is going to make a home on the grass, and then only jogs around the track in his next three grass races. Don't be surprised if he is gone from this revivalist meeting before I am. Don't bet on this horse unless he's changing tracks and going off at odds of at least 20–1.

THE TRACK SWITCH/CLASS DROP

In this investigation of surprise winners at big prices, the leading correlation of factors involves the track switch combined with the class drop. (Class drop is also part of the second strongest correlation, that of the class drop/jockey switch). Many of the track switchers, such as Hesa Frequentflyer, add testimony to the evidence that a switch of surroundings can wake up a horse. These more irrational winners will win without our money on them, but they will bolster our confidence for the times when the change of track is accompanied by some other logical rationale for a wager.

At 4½–1, the victory of *Bett's Beauty* is not as sensational as that of McGuffey's Reader, but the pattern is the same and other handicapping logic beyond the track switch is within the grasp of the handicapper.

Bett's Beauty			B. f. 3, by Beau's Eagle—Bett's Mandy, by Beau Gar					
LAMANCE C			Br.—Mabee Mr-Mrs J C (Cal)		1988 6 2 0 0			$15,325
		116	Tr.—Fierce Ferdell $20,000		1987 1 M 0 1			$3,750
Own.—Golden Eagle Farm			Lifetime 7 2 0 1 $19,075					
1May88-2GG	6f :22 :454 1:104ft	41 116	11 11 14 131	Lamance C4	Ⓕ 12500 85-15	Bett'sButy,MrrigDSport,Kris'sStn	11
12Mar88-1SA	6f :213 :453 1:12 ft	20 117	221 221 441 811½	Meza R Q1	Ⓕ 32000 67-19	MyFirst,LpOfLuxury,Jnie'sGdbout	11
24Feb88-2SA	6f :213 :451 1:122ft	51 118	31½ 34 1014 1115	VlenzuelPA11	Ⓕ 25000 61-24	SummerAllince,CtSnkr,RinbowBrt	11
13Feb88-1SA	6f :214 :451 1:12 ft	17 118	3½ 2½ 23 473	Castanon AL7	Ⓕ 32000 70-22	Bll'sMyStr,SorortyRsh,SmmrAllnc	10
3Feb88-4SA	6f :221 :453 1:121ft	2½ 117	1hd 1hd 1hd 1hd	CstnonAL7	ⒻⓈMdn 77-20	Bett'sBeuty,PreeningEgle,Gil'sTle	11
15Jan88-6SA	6f :213 :451 1:11 ft	3½ 117	44 47 56 712½	Hawley S3	ⒻⓈMdn 70-20	Sadie B. Fast, Stella Rose,SettleIt	12
	15Jan88—Stumbled start; erratic backstretch, lugged out 3/8						
31Dec87-6SA	6f :222 :46 1:113gd	11 117	3nk 32 33 37½	CastanonAL3	ⒻⓈMdn 73-19	Voila, Sadie B. Fast, Bett'sBeauty	10
	31Dec87—Broke slowly, bumped; steadied at 3 1/2						
May 22 GG 3f ft :352 h		May 13 GG 4f ft :463 h		● Apr 15 GG 4f ft :46 h		Apr 9 GG 4f ft :472 h	

Bett's Beauty's previous victory also came with a class drop. Notably, it was a drop to a level she had never raced at before; in other words, she was not a proven loser at that level.

Serious handicappers will always question a multiple class drop; in this case, four levels! It is argued, often accurately, that a monumental class drop may indicate an unfit horse, the kind that the owners hope will be claimed. The beauty of the track-switch factor in combination with the drop in class is that suspicions of a no-try can be dismissed. If owners wanted to get rid of a horse to save money, they would not go to the expense of shipping the horse. Other track switches represent a change of owner through a purchase; the same logic holds true that owners from one circuit will not go out of their way to another racing area in order to buy a horse they want to get rid of.

With serious trainer/owner intention guaranteed, the track-switch/class-drop method will show a profit even when there is little other favorable logic available to the handicapper, especially in maiden races. Under these circumstances it is not far-fetched to cash in on mutuels such as that of *Zab's Hope.*

Zab's Hope			B. f. 3, by Distant Land—Auntie Glo, by War Emperor					
DIAZ A L			Br.—Kelly R & H Lynn (Cal)		1988 5 1 0 0			$4,675
		116	Tr.—Fanning Brett C $18,000		1987 0 M 0 0			
Own.—Kelly L & Royal			Lifetime 5 1 0 0 $4,675					
18May88-5GG	6f :213 :45 1:113ft	41 114	31 32 31½ 11	Diaz A L 3	ⒻM 20000 81-19	Zab'sHope,AlohaCru,DelOfADecde	11
6May88-2Hol	6f :22 :46 1:112ft	33 115	107½ 911 712 716½	Solis A1	ⒻⓈM 32000 68-20	Shaw Say, I'mFlexible,Tali:haKum	12
14Apr88-4SA	1⅟₁₆:471 1:131 1:474gd	13 117	42 42 76½ 811½	Solis A3	ⒻⓈM 32000 50-21	EarlsLdyJy,CjunGem,NughtyPirte	11
29Mar88-6SA	6f :214 :453 1:103ft	106 115	75½ 68 811 715	Solis A9	ⒻM 45000 70-18	RnssncLdy,TchOfSplndr,Brndy'NP	12
28Jan88-4SA	6f :221 :46 1:132ft	14 112½	1111 1115 913 66½	ShermanAB3	ⒻM 32000 64-23	HdToSpd,Ppp'sSdKck,OrFrstTntol	11
	28Jan88—Green down backstretch						
May 3 SA 6f ft 1:144 h		Apr 25 SA 4f ft :474 h		Apr 8 SA 6f ft 1:143 h		Apr 1 SA 5f ft 1:01 h	

One would think that after so much as been written about the power of the drop from straight maiden to maiden claimer, it would be impossible to find a good bet on that maneuver. Not so;

there is plenty of action, especially when the dropper is switching tracks. April 22, 1977, saw *Rule The Land* ship from Philadelphia to Pimlico while dropping from maiden special weight to maiden claiming.

Rule The Land — Br. c. 4, by Iron Ruler—Mundy's Landing, by Burning On
Own.—Scott D W II — $23,500 — Br.—Scott D W II (Ky) — Tr.—Christenson Ralph — 114
Lifetime 16 1 1 1 $13,545 — 1988 3 0 0 0 $840 — 1987 7 1 1 0 $10,235

19Apr88- 8Pim my 1 1/16	:46⅘	1:11	1:44⅘	Clm 23500	7	4	46	43	54½	58¾	Lloyd J S	114	7.00	71-18	Conte De Montee 115⁵ Jusavik 114½ Furzy 114nk	Even try	7
4Apr88- 1Pim fst 1 1/16	:47⅘	1:12⅕	1:44⅘	Clm 18500	6	5	55½	53½	54½	45	Lloyd J S	114	13.50	75-22	Warm Season 114¹ Phenotype 114³ Swift Wind 114¹	No threat	7
21Mar88- 9Pim fst 6f	:23⅘	:47⅘	1:12⅘	Alw 15000	7	9	97	97¾	89¾	811½	Lloyd J S	114	57.00	70-29	AlomSnow119¾SpntAbunch1152½JtSchool1141½	Unruly pre-start	9
10Dec87- 8Lrl fst 6f	:22⅘	:46⅘	1:11⅘	Clm 25000	7	6	77	79	710	610	Douglas F G	114	19.00	75-22	Village Runner 114¾ Mr. Diaz 114³ Wiskers Said 114¹	Checked	7
28May87- 6Pim fst 1 1/16	:48	1:12⅘	1:46	Clm 25000	1	4	33½	35	23	21½	Desormeaux K J⁵	109	3.70	73-23	Prince'sPunch1141½RulThLnd109¾ChifOfHrts1141	Altered course	6
7May87- 9Pim fst 6f	:23	:46⅘	1:12⅘	Alw 14000	3	10	95½	74½	73	63	Desormeaux K J⁵	107	37.60	79-20	Zachman1141½Thespis1121½MinuteNChnge107no	Needed response	10
22Apr87- 5Pim fst 6f	:23⅕	:47	1:12⅘ 3+	Md 30000	2	8	74½	73¾	21	11½	Desormeaux K J⁵	107	21.70	84-17	RuleTheLand1071½Gramp'sFvorite115¾SurpriseLunch1121½	Driving	12
5Feb87- 3Pha fst 6f	:22⅘	:46⅘	1:12⅘	Md Sp Wt	5	2	67¾	68	69	611½	Marquez A	118	8.30	67-23	Rollicking George 1181½ Baybuck 1182½ Rachel'sBeau118¾	Outrun	7
28Jan87- 6Pha fst 6½f	:22⅘	:46	1:17⅘	Md Sp Wt	4	6	54½	54½	46	49¾	Marquez A	118	12.80	76-16	Chank A Chank 1182½ Pertsemlidis 1184¾ David J. 1182½	Even try	10
7Jan87- 1Pha fst 6f	:22⅘	:46⅕	1:12⅘	Md Sp Wt	4	4	53½	77¾	68¾	511½	Lopez C C	118	12.40	66-31	Babar'sBrothers118¾CoreAApple1181½Rachel'sBeau1181½	Outrun	12

LATEST WORKOUTS Apr 25 Lrl 4f fst :52⅕ b ●Apr 16 Lrl 6f fst 1:14⅘ h Apr 10 Lrl 3f fst :38 b Apr 2 Lrl 5f fst 1:06 b

Rather than elaborate on this theme, which is amply covered in many popular books on handicapping (the straight-maiden to maiden-claimer drop), let's go beyond the boundaries of textbook cases.

Variations on a Theme

At this point I anticipate a question from the reader. Is the author sensationalizing by choosing examples with especially high pari-mutuel returns? The answer is no. Please recall that all horses starring in this section have won a wake-up race *following three or more dull races*. All of these horses "look bad" to the public. Also recall that the *most powerful wake-up factor is the track switch,* and that the public tends to underestimate and underbet *unfamiliar horses*.

In addition, track switch proves to be a very significant factor even when there is no drop and even, in some cases, with a rise in class. It stands to reason that if this factor is now accompanied by a class drop (in itself another powerful wake-up factor), we are increasing the chances of a surprise win. Now add to that the finding that in maiden races this combination of factors is deadly, and you've got some very special investment situations. Psychologically it is hard for the public to bet on horses with sixes, sevens, and eights in their running lines and finish positions, so the average mutuel goes up a few more points.

On some occasions the track switch will be obvious but the class drop will be disguised. Both *Program Search* (19Feb88) and *Laconic* (16Apr88) appeared to be maidens going up in class, as they were entered in races facing winners; but the track switch in each case was so significant, that they were facing lesser competition:

Program Search

WARREN R J JR   117

Own.—Hi Card Ranch & Leevers

Dk. b. or br. g. 3, by Government Program—Dr Dorothy, by Jim White
Br.—Leevers T A (Cal)
Tr.—Dutton Jerry $8,000

Lifetime 12 1 0 1 $4,857

Laconic

SIBILLE R   119

Own.—Bacon & Lewis

Dk. b. or br. g. 4, by Matsadoon—Never Speak, by Speak John
Br.—Evans T M (Va)
Tr.—Persinger Jim $20,000

Lifetime 8 1 0 0 $5,825

On other occasions, the track switch itself and the corresponding class designations imply superficially that the competition will be tougher. On February 27 *Boston Doc* ran exactly the way his 50–1 odds said he would. On November 7 the crowd was right in making *Really Virginia* 25–1. But when these two horses changed venue, instead of their odds going up, they went down. The unwarranted odds drop flashed a message that the track switch was positive and not negative, as first assumed.

Really Virginia

Own.—Van Andel P   114

B. f. 3, by Five Star Flight—Virginia Girl, by Olden Times
Br.—Vanandel P (Fla)
Tr.—Zito Nicholas P $22,500

Lifetime 7 1 0 0 $8,770

Boston Doc

Own.—Vaccaro Anthony   1125

Dk. b. or br. c. 3, by Far North—Swoonmist, by Never Bend
Br.—Jones Mrs J G Sr (Ky)
Tr.—Hirsch Marilyn $25,000

Lifetime 5 1 0 0 $8,745

There will always be contradictory messages in the past performances of horses that are about to undergo a form revival. Many handicappers want it both ways: they want the past performances to show an "all systems go," and they want a huge pari-mutuel payoff. Life itself is based on many inherent contradictions, which we live with as citizens, employees, physiological beings, parents, homeowners, renters, drivers, walkers. Horseplayers should expect no different. And if we want simplistic answers, then we should go to revival meetings instead of racetracks.

System?

People who go to revival meetings have something in common with people who search for horse-race systems. Both types are looking for a simple answer. I, too, would love to find a simple solution, and sometimes when I should be playing with my kid or fixing things around the house, I am instead studying thousands of races in search of the perfect system, even knowing that the creative process involved in winning at the races is far too intricate to be reduced to a set of rules.

Can the *track-switch/class-drop* analysis be reduced to a system? Probably not. As we have seen with horses such as Bett's Beauty and McGuffey's Reader, the handicapper could discover, through comprehensive analysis, a complex set of circumstances that served as flesh around the skeletal format of track switch/class drop.

Nevertheless, I will share the results of a systematic tabulation of random occurrences of this format. Even systems with 10,000 race samples have been known to work one year and fail the other. Therefore, I took a much smaller sample, 76 races. Through years of research, I've found that small samples are just as useful as large ones, if: (a) there are many second-place and third-place finishes in the set of losing events, (b) many of the losers win next time out, (c) the sample is truly random, and (d) one or two atypical payoffs are not allowed to distort the results. Another useful technique for research with small samples is to actually use two separate sources and then compare them. So much for the rationale behind this madness. Here are the results.

Rules

1. Horse must have finished *out of the money* and *more than two lengths behind* in its *last three races*
2. *Class drop*
3. *Track switch*
4. Must go off at *4–1 or above*

Tabulation

Sample: 76 races
Winners: 10 (approximately 13½%)
Invested: $152 (based on minimum $2 bets)
Return: $344
Profit: $192 (approximately *127% ROI*)
ROI *excluding largest payoff: 80%*

An average mutuel of $34.40 seems unreal, but remember: we have excluded all short-priced horses to begin with. Excluding the highest payoff, the average mutuel goes down to $29.00. We are dealing with miraculous wake-up horses, the kind that pay the biggest prices. The sample included 6 second-place finishes at odds above the adjusted average mutuel, including two horses that would have paid over $100.

The *revival* of dull horses has more to do with handicapping logic than with supernatural occurrences such as fixes and pacts with the Devil.

By the way, two factors we did not include in this survey are first/second-time Lasix and first/second-time gelded. Performance of Lasix horses tends to be cyclical; there are periods in which they win races in bunches, and there are other periods when fifty or sixty Lasix losers in a row destroy all hopes of those who look for a solution in a drug. Ultimately, the percentage of winners *because of* the addition of Lasix is low. Certain types of runners benefit most, especially those that show early speed and seem to stop on a dime midway through the race. Good handicappers will learn to identify the running line of a bleeder and anticipate the addition of Lasix before it is announced. Similar to the other wake-up factors in this study, the addition of Lasix becomes more significant when accompanied by other revival factors.

Recently-gelded horses often show radical revivals. However, it is impossible to study this factor in the same context as other revival factors because it arises with much less frequency. With both the Lasix and gelded factors, my research has found that success is greatly enhanced when a leading trainer is responsible.

Major form revival factors, then, in order of potency, are: track switch, class drop, and rider switch. Class drop, in combination with either track switch or rider switch (to a better jocky) implies a positive trainer intention.

One of the variations of track-switch revivals relates most specifically to the concept of "cycles." The proverbial *horse for course* is a major player in the drama of thoroughbred cycles and deserves top billing in a separate chapter.

CHAPTER 7

Small-Town Heroes

RETURN TO THE SCENE

HESA FREQUENTFLYER THRIVED on life on the road. While horses for courses also win when changing tracks, they do so for the opposite reason. There is one particular track where they feel at home, and if they had it their way, they'd never leave town. A graph of the life passages of a horse for course would most closely resemble a cycle, in the traditional sense of the word. He makes an annual migration back home; then there is the celebration, as if it were an anniversary or a festival of the solstice. And then he is forced out of town for economic reasons. There is no work.

The horse-for-course phenomenon is most distinct in shorter meets. Consider that in longer race meets horses of all persuasions and origins have ample time to acclimate and acculturate. In shorter meets, however, horses not readily comfortable in the environment have little time to get to feel at home. A short meet is like a small town; it is a closed society, and for the outsider, it is not easy to break through invisible barriers which function like the walls of medieval towns. Those horses whose basic nature fits perfectly in the setting of the short meet will be the local heroes and will win in a way that is as predictable as the coming of the Fourth of July.

No one has ever been able to talk to a horse, but clearly, animals feel "comfortable" in certain settings. When I lived in the country, I remember trying to get my hens to nest in a certain place that was convenient to me. I tried to construct a perfectly comfortable environment. They disregarded my considerable efforts to make them happy and chose a different place to nest.

It took me a while to accept their rebellious behavior. But then I thought about it and concluded that I, as a human being, had something in common with these strange beings. In college I remember that with unassigned seats, I found myself unconsciously sitting in the exact same section of the lecture hall every day. Same thing at the dinner table, the beach, or the park. It is no wonder, with the modern industrial settings in which hens, against their basic nature, reside perpetually in tiny cubicles, that the eggs we get have half their natural flavor. (The theme of one of the earliest of the Disney cartoons was that of hens going on strike.)

It is reasonable to believe that race horses, too, will produce an improved product when they are in a comfortable setting. This goes beyond just the "surface" of the track. It may relate to the angle of the sun in relation to the grandstand, the textures and sounds of the immediate environs, and other intangible influences of the type that cause a student to unconsciously gravitate to a very particular part of the lecture hall.

The reality of horses' preferences for certain racetracks means the potential for radical form reversals, pari-mutuel payoffs far beyond fair value.

CASE STUDY: THREE YEARS AT DEL MAR

Of the three major tracks in the southern California racing circuit, Del Mar has the shortest meet, an annual late-summer get-together by the Pacific Ocean, just north of San Diego. This study measures the impact of the horse-for-course factor not only as it relates to individual horses, but also how it fits in with the total handicapping process.

Each year at Del Mar new track biases affect the outcome of races in a way that led me to hypothesize that the bias factor might seriously disrupt the continuity of horse-for-course domination. During some meets there is a powerful bias in favor of inside post positions, while the following year the extreme outside has dominated. The short stretch and flatter turns tend to favor early-speed horses, and yet for many a period of time closers suddenly and inexplicably dominate. Some years radical shifts in bias occur in the middle of the meet, from one moment to the next, and it seems to be an inherent characteristic of this track that within the same racing day (some people say because of the tides affecting the subsoil), a sudden shift on the bias can be a frightful reminder to overconfident handicappers that we live in a world of contradictions.

In this setting the horse-for-course factor faces the strongest of crosscurrents. Nevertheless, Del Mar seems to house a closed society in which certain horses belong while others remain outsiders.

1. On the average, *26 winners per meet* have won at this track in a prior meet, usually the previous year.
2. Excluding maiden races, where horse for course is a non-factor, 26 winners means about *10 percent of all winners*.
3. At least half the races carded have fields that do not include horses for courses. This means that horses that *won before* at the track account for the winner of at least *20 percent of those races in which previous years' winners are entered*.
4. This does not count horses that fit so well with the track that they become multiple winners the same meet; some of these are simply at the peak of their performance cycle, while others are truly at home at Del Mar and prove it by failing at other tracks. Horses whose initial victory at the meet comes with no prior form improvement signs have a high likelihood of repeating and then returning next year to do the same.
5. Compared with the impact of other major handicapping factors, the horse-for-course factor occurs with the greatest frequency as a characteristic of a Del Mar winner.
6. Horses that did not win last year but finished second at high odds—in other words, had a positive form reversal at Del Mar—also win frequently upon returning to this track. If these near winners are added to the pool of horses who like the track, the horse-for-course impact will measure to be even more powerful.
7. If you bet an equal amount on each entered horse that has previously won at the track, you would have a considerable flat-bet profit.
8. The reason for this is an extremely high average mutuel, since a good number of winners of this type are sudden form revivals. In 1987 the *average mutuel* for all Del Mar winners who *won during a previous Del Mar meet* was $17.00.

PREPARING FOR A SHORT MEET

With the day's *Racing Form* in hand, it's tough to simultaneously handicap and look up the past histories of all the horses on the card. Most of the time races from last year's meet do not show up in today's *Form*. Even if the time were available to rummage through old *Racing Forms*, mechanical tasks on the day of the races may interfere with analytical and creative thinking necessary for a profound understanding of the day's card.

Before the meet begins, compile an alphabetical list of all potential horses for courses. You don't want the type of list that is so byzantine that you have an overwhelming task to look up information. To qualify for the list, a horse must fulfill at least one of the three following characteristics:

1. Won at high odds (5–1 or up) at this track, which means that the horse won, while not "looking good" by conventional handicapping standards, probably won because of a special circumstance.
2. Has won only at this track or most of its wins have been at this track.
3. Was a multiple winner at this track.

To each horse's name, add abbreviated or shorthand notations that identify the type of victory. Was it a specialty distance or surface? Was there a unique pace situation? Was there a significant jockey switch? Did the horse need a prep race over the track? Had a particular trainer just claimed the horse, and does that same trainer today have the horse? Did the horse win with/against a bias?

This seems like a lot of information, but each category should have a one- or two-letter code, and not the type of code that Maxwell Smart invents and then forgets how to use. If circumstances prevent you from having your own file of old *Racing Forms*, most breeders' associations have libraries near the local track with ready access to old *Forms*.

Saratoga

In July 1987 I was hired as a handicapper for a selection outfit in New York. I was to be their Del Mar handicapper. I knew nothing about the company I was to work for, but the person who recommended me had a decent reputation, so I assumed the working conditions would be good and the service to the public fair and square.

They gave me an 800 number to call in my daily selections. This allowed me to call from anywhere I wanted, including Lake Tahoe, where I had planned to do some betting. The first surprise came after several days of Del Mar had become history.

"Can you do Saratoga?" asked Brad (name slightly changed to protect the yet-to-be-proven-guilty).

The town I was born in, Schenectady, New York, is near Saratoga, and I love everything about that part of the country. I told Brad the truth, though:

"I can't promise you I can be prepared on time."

"How long will it take you?"

I had been planning to spend a couple of days at the California Thoroughbred Breeders' Association Library, across from the backstretch of Santa Anita, before my trip to Tahoe. I told Brad I'd see what I could come up with. Of course, one of my tasks at the library is to compile my horse-for-course list. Handicappers who have not done this type of research are missing out on a treat; at the library there are no phone calls, no emergencies, no errands, no interruptions. At this refuge from the contradictions of "normal" life, the chance for human beings to reach new heights of lucidity and discovery is increased geometrically.

After going through several years of Saratoga, I felt very positive about the upcoming meet, both objectively and subjectively. I took the job with my standard commitment, not for a high percentage of winners, but for a flat-bet profit. By August 11 my performance was mediocre on both counts, with only a $12.60 steeplechase winner, Mickey Free (a horse for course, by the way), saving me from total bumhood. On a flat-bet basis, though, my loss was under 10 percent, and a few close seconds at high odds received no appreciation from my employers.

Conversation

From a telephone at Caesar's Palace in Tahoe, I phoned in my August 12 selection:

Mark: I think *Quick Dip* is worth an investment in the second.
Brad: You're testing my patience. He looks terrible. How much do you like him?

M: He's not a "most probable winner," but he'll definitely be the best value.

B: Don't give me that. . . ! I told you we need winners. Is he gonna win?

M: I told you when you hired me that I could only give you the probability of a flat-bet profit. I told you I could give you 38 percent winners and have a loss and I could give you 21 percent winners and have a profit.

B: Our clients don't understand that stuff. Just give me a winner. What do you like about Quick Dip? He looks awful.

M: He won here last year, same inner turf course! He only won once last year, which means he likes Saratoga better than other tracks.

B: That's all?

M: Well, if too many things look good, you won't get a good price. Besides, the field looks mediocre, so anything can happen.

B: The clients would rather have a winner at 2–1 than a loser at 10–1. This is not enough to go on. Give me something in another race that has a better chance.

M: Listen, the research I did points to this race. What can I do?

B: What's Quick Dip's chances of winning?

M: About 20 percent.

B: Twenty percent? (Phone explodes) I want something at least with a 40 or 50 percent chance.

M: The one I'm betting on is Quick Dip. Use him if you like. Otherwise, here are two other horses that look good but that I'm not betting on.

Quick Dip won and paid $15.20. I collected, but I wouldn't know until the next morning whether the handicapping service used him or not. The other two horses lost. I reflected that in the case of shippers, you need more than one factor or you'll be on thin ice. But with horses for courses, the thinner the ice, the bigger the price.

Next morning

    B: What did you see in that horse?

    M: I told you yesterday. Did you use him?

    B: No. When I heard the results, I got sick. I couldn't sleep last night. Why didn't you argue more strongly for the horse?

    M: It's your fault, not mine. (A frustrating situation for me, I thought. The man wants desperately for his clients to win. Is that a bad trait or a good one? Probably more good than bad.)

    B: I'm sorry. Now give me a winner for today.

Quick Dip ended up becoming the turning point of the meet. That very day I gave him another horse for course, Crivitz, who won and paid $11.80. Needless to say, Brad gave out Crivitz to his clients.

Variation on a Theme

At Saratoga every season it will rain a few times, at least. It rains enough so that at least several of last year's winners in the Saratoga mud and slop will this year once again have the chance to compete on their preferred surface. You're dealing with a very unique situation: the horse likes the particular mud of a particular track. This is truly a system. You won't get a lot of plays, but it's an automatic bet at Saratoga when last year's slop or mud winner gets a sloppy or muddy track this year. Some of these horses don't even have mud stars because they've done poorly in the mud of other tracks. During the same meet, horses that win once on the wet surface and are fortunate enough to get another chance on the wet track will have an extraordinary repeat-win percentage.

My term of employment at Saratoga ended up with 41 percent winners, with little thanks to my handicapping since a large portion of the winners came on the muddy tracks during the second half of the meet. There are many powerful variations on the horse-for-course theme that the reader will likely discover at his/her local racing circuit.

Unfortunately for those handicappers culturally wed to the customs of basic handicapping, it will be difficult to bet on horses that look bad. The head will tell you to invest, and the heart will prevent you from doing so. Most readers may have to prove it themselves with their own research. Others have already experienced the culture of form reversals and adjusted accordingly. Naturally it is easier to bet on a track switch when the new track is one of several factors. With the horse for course, though, the biggest mutuels usually arise when the track factor is the only factor.

What better way to test the universality of the horse-for-course factor than to observe it in another country. In Spain, for example, where nearly all racing takes place in Madrid, there is a short summer meet at Lasarte in the Basque country, where the horses run clockwise instead of counterclockwise.

On July 3, 1988, the first racing day at Lasarte, three of the six races that comprise the Quiniela Hipica (Spanish version of the Pick 6) included horses that had previously run well at Lasarte. All three of these races were won by the horse for course. Only one of the three was a favorite.

Del Mar, Saratoga, and Lasarte are yearly meets. Many horses have performance cycles with an annual high at these meets. No doubt, a liking for the track plays a greater role than the season of the year in producing the high. For handicappers to cash in on these circumstances, reasons and explanations may remain a mystery, and that's fine with us. We need to know *what* is likely to happen more than *why* it will happen. Whatever the primitive origins of these annual Rites of Summer, let's participate in the festivities.

THEY'VE GROWN ACCUSTOMED TO A PLACE

If you like the horse-for-course celebrations but are disenchanted with the long waits from year to year, come to France, where the various tracks take turns, not by meet, but on a daily basis. Find a huge field that contains only one or two course specialists, and you'll get more than fair value. Look for a horse that has reasonable current form and is switching to the track of its last victory. Make sure you are dealing with the same trip, as most tracks have their main course and their *grande piste* for longer events.

Since thoroughbreds are more universal than human beings (with fewer cultural variations), sound and logical handicapping should function successfully regardless of the venue. And of all handicapping factors, horse for course may be the most universal.

October 13, 1988, Evry's featured race, the Long John International 1600 meters (one mile). Only one horse in the thirteen-horse field shows a victory at this track, this distance, in the past performances: number 11, *Pharsala*. The filly has current form, with two thirds and a close sixth in her last three races, in fields of 13, 14, and 18 respectively.

One player's negative is another's positive. Pharsala is only 1 for 17 in her career and looks like a "proven loser." But the one victory was precisely her last Evry race, the only race from today's track showing in her past performances. Horse-for-course handicappers love it when the winner at the target track is a loser at other tracks.

Another negative: the filly shows two recent losses to members of today's field:

Longchamp, October 1, 1988
1. Luxieux
2. *Ultimate Ruler*
3. Pharsala
One neck behind Ultimate Ruler, 1600 meters

Saint Cloud, June 30, 1988
1. Sardinella
2. *Pres Du Ciel*
3. Pharsala
A head behind Pres Du Ciel, a length behind Sardinella, 1600 meters

Now let's go back one more race in the past performances:

Evry, June 20, 1988
1. Pharsala
2. Sardinella
Pharsala is 1½ lengths ahead of Sardinella, 1600 meters

With clean trips for both Pharsala and Sardinella on both occasions, Pharsala improves by 2½ at Evry. It stands to reason, in the context of a 2½ length differential, that Pharsala at her favorite venue can defeat the two horses she lost to by a neck or less at unfavorable racetracks.

Here in the town of Avignon, at the PMU (French version of OTB), I can't see the tote odds and must bet blindly. But only one of the thirty-five public handicappers summarized in my *Form* has chosen Pharsala, so an overlay is highly probable. Some people like French culture because of Cezanne or Sartre; for me it's culturally advanced because the feature race is broadcast every day on national TV. This is the sign of a civilized nation.

As the horses enter the gate, the announcer enumerates the odds of the favored horses, getting all the way up to 11–1 without mentioning Pharsala. The filly is in stalking distance all the way, makes her move in the stretch, and prevails at the wire by a neck, confirming the universality of the horse-for-course methodology. Final odds: 14–1.

The thoroughbred cycle of horses for courses is *determined in space and not in time.*

THE MANY CYCLES OF PRANKSTRESS

For the grand finale to the section on horse cycles, Prankstress has volunteered to demonstrate several of the most typical patterns, all in one career. The following illustration extracts the essential details from a career that seems to have been developed explicitly in order to corroborate the theories of *Thoroughbred Cycles.*

5Nov87	1–1	3^3	Restricted Stakes (5-horse field)
28Oct87	4–5	4^3	Handicap
10Sep87	5½–1	$1^{3⁄4}$	Aw35,000
1Nov86	33–1	11^{21}	Breeders' Cup Juvenile Fillies
24Aug86	2–5	1^3	Stakes
10Aug86	6–5	1^{nk}	Stakes
20July86	3–1	1^{nk}	Stakes, vs. boys
26Jun86	4½–1	1^2	Maiden

Child prodigy. It looks as if Prankstress has been overextended as a two-year-old. Following her maiden win, this filly went against the boys, bypassing allowance conditions for a stakes race. Coming from four sprint victories at smaller tracks, she was then asked to deal with a Breeders' Cup level of competition in her first try at a route (November 1). Prankstress's last two races show all the signs of a burned-out child prodigy; twice-beaten favorite at odds of even money or below!

High-percentage *layoff pattern.* As a first-time-starter winner, Prankstress immediately qualified for a better-than-average chance to win following a layoff. Sure enough, on September 10, 1987, at Del Mar, she surprised the crowd by outrunning a field that included the horse for course, Balladry, to accomplish a layoff victory.

The *bounce.* Following a sharp comeback race, horses can be expected to underachieve in their next effort. In spite of a freshening period, Prankstress willingly demonstrated the bounce pattern by failing at odds-on, October 28, 1987, at Santa Anita.

Track switch/class drop. We are probably stretching our own logic a bit if we were to call the September 10 victory a "track switch/class drop," since it followed one terrible effort rather than the three bad races used as our research criteria for horse revivals. Nevertheless, Prankstress has illustrated three, perhaps four, typical thoroughbred behavior patterns associated with horse performance cycles. Prankstress, you may step down from the stage; we wish you the best in overcoming child prodigy burnout. Perhaps another long layoff will set up your next victory, as it appears you are far off on some extended vacation. Best of luck on your return.

Now that we have covered the most typical horse-performance cycles, we shall study a species that is even less communicative than the horse, namely, the trainer. Behind the scenes, shrouded in mystery, the trainer intervenes as best he can in the performance of his horses. The orbit of trainer performance exerts its unique forces on the orbits of the thoroughbred, adding new dimension and complexity to the scenario of form cycle. What happens when the high in the trainer cycle overlaps with the low in the horse cycle? What happens when a cold trainer sends a hot horse to post? When are trainer cycles independent of horse cycles, and when and how do they overlap? Are there times when the horse bettor can invest in the performance of the human partner of the horse rather than the horse itself? Is the trainer a conspiratorial being or merely one who goes about his job in a tight-lipped style?

These are some of the intriguing questions *Thoroughbred Cycles* will examine as it moves into the section dedicated to trainers and their performance patterns.

Part III

Trainers

C H A P T E R 8

Totalitarians

THE HORSE IS RIGHTFULLY the leading star of the drama whose title bears his name. At times, though, the horse is, at best, a supporting actor, and at worst an extra, as the trainer becomes Henry VIII and determines the fate of all those in his kingdom and those in the kingdoms of others.

HOT AND COLD TRAINERS

Handicappers must assume that the truly hot trainer exerts total control over his subjects. Cold jockeys win races for hot trainers. Horses in dull form suddenly come alive. Hot trainers win route races even when they are sprint specialists, and they win on the turf with horses that have preferred the dirt. And if you want to win the lottery, get a hot trainer to buy you the ticket. In the shadow of a hot trainer, handicapping analysis of the pros and cons of horses is rendered an irrelevant sideshow.

At the other end of the spectrum, cold trainers can be expected to lose no matter how much their horses dance and prance. And when the best trainers hit hard times, their story is the Book of Job in the horseplayers' Bible. You will usually find no reason why bad things happen to good trainers, but when the situation arises, to bet against the cold trainer is to eliminate the disadvantage of the track take.

While horse cycles can be explained in biological or situational terms, and player cycles can be reasoned in mathematical or psychological terms, the rise and fall of trainers will often remain a mystery. Somebody please explain how a Vladimir Cerin could move from years as a no-win trainer and automatic elimination, to one year in which no other trainer on his circuit with similar stock outperformed him. After an extended series of long-shot winners, there reached a moment when Mr. Cerin managed to penetrate the public's consciousness, just after he won with a foreign import at nearly triple figures.

Now the betting public is on to Mr. Cerin; his horses start to get action, and lose. Little by little his win percentage has dropped, until once more he is a rare visitor to the winners' circle. This is what musicians of pop music and sonatas alike call the a-b-a form, and many a trainer fits this pattern: (a) dull melody, (b) lively chorus, (a) return to dull melody. The only way these guys survive comes through the hope and replenishment of the occasional chorus. Yet they fulfill a vital role within the industry by filling fields in claiming races. (Maybe they should get a piece of the handle.) While some of these are bad trainers, many of them, like Cerin, are good trainers with bad stock. Give them a Precisionist and they'll win.

Sometimes the main difference between a successful trainer and a field filler is a willingness to run horses at their proper level. Better to lose horses from time to time than to keep horses who lose. Most claiming trainers whose performance cycle is relatively steady will have stables that change personnel more than the Yankees of Steinbrenner.

Total Control

To identify when the trainer eclipses the horse as the primary handicapping factor will require two of the following signs:

1. Has begun to win races at 5–1 and above
2. Has had recent winners that were not typical of his/her specialty
3. Has won recently with form reversals

In other words, we are looking for a trainer who has not only begun to win races in a cluster, but whose victories have been unexpected or atypical. These are the signs of a hot trainer, one who will be in control of the outcomes of races.

The cold trainer can be identified by inverting the above three signs:

1. Has begun to lose with favorites
2. Has been losing races within her/his specialty
3. Has failed recently with apparently sharp horses (negative form reversals)

(The cold trainer should not be confused with the no-win trainer, for whom the frigid zone is a normal habitat.)

Horses of a truly hot trainer can be bet on regardless of their past performances. Horses of a truly cold trainer can be avoided no matter how good they look. In these extreme situations, the normal handicapping process can be bypassed because the trainer has become *the* determining factor. The trainer *dictates* the results of races. Under these circumstances, handicappers who do their figures and choose the "best" horse will finish "best of the rest," second to the hot trainer's unexpected winner.

CASE STUDIES

Santa Anita, 1987

On January 1, 1987, a horse by the name of *Happy In Space* won the sixth race and paid $15.60. Trained by Brian Mayberry, Happy In Space had broken its maiden in its second career start, with no class drop and following a mediocre debut with a slow speed figure. One expects improvement from a second-time starter, but not a twelve-length victory with a speed figure way above par.

With Happy in Space's form reversal, Mayberry's name was block printed in the M section of my alphabetical long-shot trainer standings. I enter pertinent data for each win in my own shorthand; McH meant jockey McHargue, M2 referred to second-time maiden: MAYBERRY 1/1 McH M2.

On January 15 another Mayberry horse, *Eighty Below Zero*, produced another entry on the long-shot trainer list with a $20.20 victory. This horse had won going *up in class* and switching from Pedroza to McHargue.

15Jan87	SA	$1^{1\frac{1}{2}}$	1^2	1^4	1^3	McHargue	Aw26,000
8Nov86	Hol	$1^{\frac{1}{2}}$	$1^{\frac{1}{2}}$	2^3	4^6	Pedroza	25,000

The Mayberry entry in the longshot trainer listings now looked as follows:

> MAYBERRY   1/1   McH M2
>
>   1/15   Pedr-McH   ↑ ↑ ↑

with the upward arrows signifying a triple jump.

Once there are two entries for a particular trainer, the potential arises for an automatic trainer bet. Ordinarily I like to see two or more wins within one week's time, rather than two (the above case), but Mayberry had a small stable, and with few races, he could not be penalized. We now confront a situation similar that of stock-market speculators who face the continuing decision of when to get on a rising item and when to get off. In the hot-trainer market, I like to get on as soon as possible; with long-shot trainer listings, I am more likely to discover the type of pattern required for early investment.

On January 21 a potential wager emerged because certain patterns seemed to have materialized. The horse was *No Double Deal,* a *second-time starter,* going up *in class* from maiden 50,000 to straight maiden and switching from *Pedroza to McHargue.* With three possible pattern matches, No Double Deal became a hot-trainer bet, even though this only represented Mayberry's third long shot. (In the absence of the pattern parallels, we'd have had to wait it out, especially in a field of sharp horses.) In the case of No Double Deal, some pace and class analysts might have discovered some handicapping positives in the horse itself, but our rationale for a wager fell strictly within the parameters of hot-trainer investment.

No Double Deal won and paid $17.80. At this juncture Brian Mayberry's name was boldened and his horses now became automatic bets, providing, of course, that potential payoffs were in double figures. Since McHargue was the supporting actor in this drama, I would expect to see him aboard. This type of hot-trainer bet would continue until Mayberry horses began to run worse than their odds.

The next day the same trainer offered another investment, in the name of *Live By The Sword.* McHargue was the rider. He paid $14.00. When, on January 24, Happy In Space became a repeat winner at $11.00, it was expected that the other Mayberry winners would also do an encore.

January 25 another Mayberry horse by the name of *Hairless Heiress* appeared for the first time in the new year, in an allowance event. Pedroza was off and McHargue on, and you'd think, by now, the crowd would have seen the pattern. But most handicappers that day preferred to approach the race with speed and pace figures as well as class analysis, thus allowing Hairless Heiress to pay off at $17.40.

At some time during the rest of the meet, all of the above-named Mayberry winners did a repeat performance, with the exception of No Double Deal, who did not race again during the meet. Miraculously, the crowd refused to accept the fact that hot trainers make their own rules and do not abide by the laws of the *Racing Form* past performances. The result was a continuation of this extraordinary binge of high payoffs: Live By The Sword, $10.20; Hairless Heiress, $22.00 and $20.80; Eighty Below Zero, $17.00, *all with McHargue!* The same rider also came through with *Five Daddy Five*, another Mayberry horse, at $12.40, while failing to achieve similar success with any other trainer.

"How Do I Know when to Stop?"

"Listen," said a student of mine. "It looks great on paper, but how do you know when to stop? It's like when you own a stock that's on an upward binge and you don't know when to sell, and then the market collapses and you lose all your profits. Sounds more like a guessing game to me."

The stock-market analogy is reasonable but imperfect. In the market, factors external to the company itself affect its stock, including trader psychology and world economic trends. Hot and cold trainer streaks can be mapped by observing trainer performance itself. Sure, subjectivity (guesswork) is involved to a certain extent, but there are objective signs which tell us to get off.

1. Public discovers what is happening, and the odds drop below fair value even before the binge has subsided.
2. Meet ends. This sounds like an arbitrary separation, especially where the same horses continue to run at another track on the same circuit. History shows, though, that each new meet offers something different in the way of balance of trainer power.

3. Pattern that produces the original cluster of wins no longer materializes.
4. Pattern produces a couple of losers who run worse than their odds (in other words, at a lower performance level than their past performances warranted).

The student was not satisfied with my explanation: "Those rules are too vague."

He wants to discover a process that requires no judgmental intervention on the part of the handicapper. A simple formula. But it's an art, not a science. You can't read the music, you have to play by ear. It's the same theme but with all new variations: the trainer and not the horse dictates handicapping procedure in cases when hot trainers take the law into their own hands with no respect for the past performances.

Rules are also impossible because trainer cycles do not lend themselves to categorization the way horse cycles do; animals can't change their style, but trainers can. Example: For years, Richard Mandella was featured in everyone's computer trainer studies as a first-time starter specialist. Horses that could not win their debut races were doomed to fail second time out. Then, without warning, Mandella proved that good trainers cannot be analyzed in the same way that horses are. He went through a period in which his first-timers would lose and his second-timers would hit the winners' circle at a high percentage. Suddenly, Mandella the second time around was a new specialty. And when the trainer studies caught the pattern, Mandella went back to his old ways. Perhaps bad trainers can be more readily classified, but the good ones defy all stereotypes.

Santa Anita, 1988

Until the 1988 Santa Anita meet most southern California handicappers respected Bill Spawr as a competent but unsensational trainer. Only occasionally would he make an appearance in the leading-trainer standings. He did a good job with many an ailing horse but always kept a low profile.

With the new year, all that changed, as if Mr. Spawr had made a very serious resolution on the evening of December 31, 1987. In January 1988, in a competitive racing circuit where many trainers never win and many good ones are fortunate if they win 15 percent of the time, Bill Spawr became a 50 percent winner. Those handicappers sensitive to hot-trainer cycles began betting Spawr's entries automatically. They were rewarded with a number of generous payoffs. If they were taking good notes when Romantic Jet won on January 1 at 10–1, and if they kept up with Spawr through the month, by January 29 they would have collected on Samuel McIntyre at 15–1.

By March 27, about a month from the end of the meet, Spawr had remained near to that impossible 50 percent mark with 14 wins in 31 tries. At that point he was "tied" in the standings with Ron McAnally, who had 14 wins in 104 tries (so much for trainer standings). And with 45 percent winners, Spawr had doubled the success rate of his nearest rival (22 percent winners).

Mysteriously, the betting public went one way in 1987 and the other in 1988. There are $2 bettors and there are high rollers; the big money never caught on to Brian Mayberry in 1987, but in 1988 Bill Spawr became firmly implanted in the public consciousness, or at least within the betting souls of some major movers. The racetrack is like any other marketplace. Some products catch on and others, sometimes superior ones, never make it. I first realized that the party was over when I sent out a bet on a Spawr first-time starter. It was a terrible field, for sure, but in a route race, you expect to get back a good price on a first-timer. I got back only 2–1.

Each and every Spawr horse was getting overbet. My student should have seen clearly that it was time to get off. Romantic Jet won again in January at nearly 7–1, but by February and March, Romantic Jet was a beaten favorite at 9–5 and even money. On March 11, fifth race, I was at the track prepared to bet on a Spawr horse by the name of Madame Sisca, but only if I could get my price of at least 5–1. For a while it appeared that I'd get at least that price. Then the money came in heavily, sending Madame Sisca down to 3–1. Clearly overbet, she got none of my money and proceeded to run up the track.

Bill Spawr, the trainer/craftsman, used to be an understatement in the public consciousness. People couldn't pronounce his name. He gave the bettor his money's worth. But Bill Spawr the trainer/sensation became an overstatement. He began to lose when his horses began to get bet. The investor in hot trainers was rewarded by Spawr during January and much of February. Then, he finished off the meet going 1 for 10. The last time I checked, he was no longer in the standings. But the tote board told the hot-trainer investor when to get off on time.

The hot-trainer methodology is universal in that it can be applied at all tracks, all racing circuits. You can walk into Pimlico, Calder, Fairmount, or Albuquerque, and if you keep up with your trainer lists, you'll find races in which the hot-trainer factor totally eclipses all other handicapping factors.

Under normal circumstances it makes no sense to prove a point with evidence from an atypical source. But I'm insisting that the hot-trainer factor is universal, so why not choose a track where my ignorance of the trainers is total and where the rules of the game are so different as to suggest that previous research should not count?

So we return to Lasarte, Spain, where a gentleman by the name of Maroto (his first name begins with L) wins two races of the six-race opening day card. It's only a three-Sunday meet, so we've got to act quickly. Maroto's winners, Macho Perdiz and Rokin Girl, were both form reversals. The first had been out of the money in his previous three races, and the second was a maiden with two terrible races for her whole career. Rokin Girl was the second-longest shot in a field of thirteen. Remember that hot trainers are not those who win a few at even money; they must produce unexpected winners. Even with my limited knowledge of the Spanish racing form—whose only resemblance to ours is its initials, Recta Final—I could tell that Maroto qualified.

I scanned the final standings for the lengthy Madrid meet and saw that the same Maroto was a 9 percent winner. That suggested that he had found the change of venue to his liking. The following Sunday, Maroto gave you two winners for your Pick 6, which they call Quiniela Hipica. The third Sunday, Maroto went one winner in three attempts, for a profitable afternoon. The three winners that came after Maroto had been identified as the hot trainer beat fields of 12, 15, and 17 horses. The huge fields at Lasarte made it all the more difficult for any trainer to dictate the results of races. Furthermore, Maroto is not the Peter Ferriola of Spain, so evidence for his binge was not public domain.

During periods in which the Mayberrys, Spawrs, or any of their peers exercise totalitarian control, many a sharp and ready horse will lose only because it encountered a rival from a hot barn. As we introduce the trainer in the picture of horse-racing cycles, we go from a solar system with its set of divergent but clear paths, to a galaxy, whose innumerable and contradictory orbits collect clashing forces into a delicate balance.

As we shall see clearly in the workshop section of *Thoroughbred Cycles*, most races will contain several orbits/horse cycles that appear to be reaching a peak performance. It could be a trainer pattern vs. a late bloomer, or a horse for course vs. a track switch/class drop; diverse positive logics from different channels of thought converge at the same spot. The process of handicapping, as we shall see, involves placing a value on each logic and then betting the one(s) that offer the most advantageous investment.

Horseplayers who handicap without considering trainer cycles live a relatively tranquil existence, but they miss many a dynamic opportunity by not crossing the border into more turbulent and contradictory terrain.

"There is no contradiction," countered one such handicapper. "There are twelve months in a year, and a trainer has a twelve-horse stable. The odds that in each month a different horse will peak are exactly the same as the odds that all twelve horses will peak in the same month. A hot trainer simply means a bunch of hot horses!"

I try to get in a word, but he's like an atheist who has cornered a believer on a park bench.

"You say there are horse cycles. That's fine. And if trainers ran around the track, then I'd say there were trainer cycles too. But for two cycles to overlap upon the same horse, one cycle would have to nullify the other. If you argue that a hot trainer does as he pleases and dictates the horse's performance, then you have just obliterated the horse cycle."

There is a look on his face that says, "Hah, what do you think of that!" I actually get the chance to speak, probably because he assumes there is no possible rebuttal to his argument.

"My friend, you are even more correct than you think," I say. "Precisely because trainers *do* exert a force over horse orbits." I try to sound as pedantic as possible, because this type of person respects that brand of argument. "Indeed, trainers can and do obliterate horse cycles. Explain how certain trainers win with first-time starters when it is well-documented that neither people nor animals usually do things right the first time.

"And explain why a claimed horse that was not capable of winning with a particular trainer, changes stables, goes *up in class*, and wins several races!"

He tries to say something, but I take out Athlone's past performances from my back pocket:

2 for 31, lifetime,

gets claimed,

wins 3 straight,

beats the same horses
that used to defeat him.

He reacts: "That's an isolated incident."

"Yes, indeed," I respond, agreeing for the second time. "And to the same measure that trainer dictatorships are isolated or uncommon incidents, they become valuable pari-mutuel investments, because people like you choose to ignore them."

We have just agreed that hot-trainer cycles can obliterate horse cycles and that trainer dictatorships are uncommon occurrences. The problem with our argument on this park bench is not one of different points of view, but of different views of reality. I believe there are several, he believes there is one. I can agree with his arguments at the same time he disagrees with mine.

In one sense, these polemics are beneficial, if ideas are shared or thought processes clarified. But today's type of argument reminds me too much of my days in the world of academia, when supposed colleagues would try to outargue each other and would base promotions and dismissals on such verbiage. What a relief for me that in the world of racetracks, arguments are decided at the betting windows; where participants must put their money where their mouths are; where in one minute and eleven seconds, disagreements are resolved; where at the end of the month the profit/loss tally tells each horseplayer who wants to know, just how right or wrong he has been; where two handicappers of different persuasions can both profit if they have a clear idea of what they are doing.

My colleague on the park bench may have found other reasons for the victories of the Mayberry and Spawr horses, and if he did, wonderful; that takes nothing away from those who cashed in because they followed the cycles of hot and cold trainers. My educated guess, though, is that given the odds of these hot-trainer items, conventional handicapping did not help very many of those players who chose to ignore the importance of long-shot trainer binges.

As we move on to the subject of the partial-trainer dictatorship, it will become more evident that one particular species which does not even run around the track sometimes controls the fate of another species which seems to do all the labor.

CHAPTER 9

Dictators:
Partial Control

SOME TRAINER DICTATORSHIPS are highly specialized and occupy only one region of the vast handicapping landscape, one facet of race-track life. By not exercising a totalitarian grasp over everything around them, they will often escape the attention of the keenest of handicappers while they carry on their esoteric operation.

The partial-control trainer dictatorship is similar to the total control regimes in that:

1. Trainer becomes the primary and sometimes only reason for a wager, while the horse itself is of little consequence.
2. Resulting trainer-bet situation occurs in peak phases within the trainer's unique professional life cycles.
3. These phases may be totally ignored by comprehensive trainer studies of the type that identify long-term trainer specialties, for the reason that we are dealing with short-term phenomena.

Most intriguing of these partial-control phases are those that recur annually, satisfying a strict interpretation of the term "cyclical." Jonathan Sheppard's annual domination of Saratoga stee-plechase events may have stalled in 1987 because it had become commonplace. (Two wins, 2 seconds, and 2 thirds in 9 races would have been fine by any other trainer.) John Gosden's usual May-June binge of foreign import/layoff winners suffered a similar abatement in 1987. The previous year, the Gosden spring ritual had reached notoriety when it reverberated across the continent with winners such as Dan Thatch ($19.00, May 10, 1986, Hollywood Park) and Teased ($22.20, May 29, 1986, Belmont); both those horses and more than a few others like them were victorious first time out in the U.S. after considerable layoffs since their previous European races. At this writing, the Gosden Spring Festival of Europe in America is in full swing at Hollywood Park, 1988, with Sky Ninski ($10.60, April 28), Wakitai ($8.40, April 30), and Angelina Ballerina ($16.80, May 6), all of these winning first time in the U.S. following a layoff and immigration from Europe.

While seasonal considerations often merit the attention of European handicappers, in U.S. racing the seasonal factor is the most elusive of all cycles. The impact of the time of year is either camouflaged or diluted by year-round racing and the economic consequences of long layoffs.

A survey of 8 Gosden spring winners results in a picture in which a trainer of European origins has established his own European racing schedule in the U.S. Seven of the 8 horses studied had been warm-weather winners in England or Ireland (the eighth came to the U.S. as a maiden, with several good warmweather European races).

Seven of the 8 winners showed a layoff of between eight and ten months leading up to their win. The exception had spent 1½ years on the sidelines. In the U.S. a layoff of eight or more months is an automatic sign of physical problems. But by allowing time off for his horses, Gosden was simply respecting the United Kingdom custom of an extended winter vacation.

Notably, 5 of the 8 winners had shown their best European efforts in sprints and were coming back in routes. The pace style of U.S. routes is similar to the rationing of energy in European sprints. A fast pace is not kind to comeback horses in general, nor European horses in particular.

If human beings can be possessed by spring fever, then why not horses? In the U.S. a conditioning process is in high gear, which tends to dull the seasonal horse senses. The climates of Florida and southern California seem to participate in this dulling process. The history of Gosden European imports is our best evidence that the season of the year can still play a role in the form cycles of thoroughbred race horses.

At this point it is proper to pay tribute to another unsung hero of horse-race research. David McCormick began his studies of foreign imports at a time when European horses had begun to make a profound impact on U.S. racing, at the same time when foreign cars had changed the dynamics of the U.S. auto industry.

David discovered, among other things, that European form and past records became a secondary factor in handicapping foreign imports, a factor superseded by the U.S. trainer performance. He also observed that trainers who were well-known for success with foreign horses did not yield a flat-bet profit; most significantly, Charles Whittingham and John Gosden. He discovered that four southern California trainers in particular—Darrell Vienna, Robert Frankel, George Scott, and Richard Cross—produced flat-bet profits with European horses, first outing in the U.S., over extended periods of time and with a fair volume of horses. Especially in the case of Vienna, European form had absolutely no correlation with U.S. success.

It was David's study that helped me discover the Gosden Spring Festival. Since the McCormick study, which remains unpublished, both Cross and Vienna have departed from the list, Cross by having cooled off, and Vienna from an indiscriminate increase in volume of horses. Scott never stopped being profitable to his backers, but strangely phased himself out, at least temporarily, from the training craft he had mastered so well.

Remaining on the list is Robert Frankel, who will receive special attention in the trainer "futures" section (Chapter 13). Also remaining on the separate list that I derived from the original data is John Gosden, as a spring phenomenon. Hopefully, an updated version of David McCormick's work will appear in print. In the meantime, a major observation of his study that remains valid is that there are circumstances in horse-race handicapping when the trainer dictates the outcome of races.

DIATRIBE ON MEMORY

One methodology for traditional trainer computer studies is to throw in as much as you can and then let the computer correlate. Throw in fractions, riders, class designations, distance, surface, claims, recency, and a few hundred other major and minor variables. So you come up with Joe Claimer, 136 percent flat-bet profit going from seven furlongs to 1$\frac{1}{16}$ miles when the odds are between 9–2 and 8–1. Some of these correlations are hard to digest. What happens at 4–1 or 9–1? It seems like the computer has the soul of an arbitrary opportunist. I'll bet the computer can find a hundred-race sample that shows Lukas has a flat-bet profit if you bet him on Thursdays between races five and nine.

These type of correlations I call "neoesoteric." Neos are people who follow. They find an original artist and then bureaucratize his work. Most truly esoteric trainer cycles somehow manage to involve factors that are not among the thousands fed to computers in quantitative fashion. Each day's past performances and results charts contain thousands of bits of information, and not all of it can be included in your data bank.

That's too bad, because six months later, maybe a year later, things we thought insignificant suddenly turn out to be vital factors. I believe in data banks and I've worked on them, but like all modern conveniences, they can dull the senses. Specifically, a dependence on too much written information can dull one's memory. I know guys who write down trip notes for all the races; once the image has gone on to a piece of paper, the mind automatically relaxes as it is assured that all is in order . . . then a horse from one of the significant trip notes appears on the track and the note taker fails to relate the notes to today's race. The mental error costs him a big score. Had he not written everything down laboriously and converted it into an archival document, the original incident would have remained as an image in his mind, to flash before him as soon as he saw the horse in question in the past performances: "Yeah, that's Bold Bolder, scraped outside rail on turn."

Similarly, handling sixty pages of small-type, single-spaced trainer studies is like trying to speak a new language by carrying a dictionary. And with this massive amount of information, you'll be at least twenty-five hours a day looking up each pattern for each trainer in the past performances. The fact that someone else did the study further removes the handicapper from the experiential part of the process. Become too dependent on the written document, which is organized with no context (like a dictionary), and you'll begin to lose touch with your own valuable experiences.

The first type of memory mistake that prevails rampantly in clubhouses and grandstands across the world is that of recalling each and every big exacta and long shot we collect on and forgetting everything else. This is equivalent to the proverbial Monday-morning quarterback only reviewing the good plays from the films on Sunday's game. This obvious memory shortcoming needs no further explanation; nostalgia distorts the past, always to the detriment of the future.

The second mistake affects serious and competent handicappers, who try to remember what is important and discard what is not important. In dealing with trainer cycles or phases, often the most insignificant (at the time) event will become the crucial yardstick for later situations involving valuable trainer patterns.

Damned if you do, damned if you don't, for if you try to remember everything, serious problems will arise. I learned this from a story by the Argentine writer, Jorge Luis Borges, called *"Funes El Memorioso."* Funes is a guy who does not have the ability to forget. Incidents, images, dates, faces, accumulate in his mind until he is overburdened and loses a perspective on reality.

I didn't want to suffer the fate of Funes, so I decided to make my memories selective by forgetting things such as birthdays, anniversaries, words of patriotic hymns, names of celebrities, and everything I learned in college.

My wife says, "Mark, remember we ate at this Chinese restaurant before? It was years ago."

"Sure," I respond. I happen to remember through association. "How could I forget? When we were driving into the parking lot, we had the radio on to the call of the first race and One Eyed Romeo was wiring the field in a ten-thousand-dollar claiming race."

CASE STUDY: MICHAEL WHITTINGHAM

By no handicapping principle could any reasonable, rational human being bet on this horse:

7th Santa Anita

ABOUT 6 ½ FURLONGS. (Turf). (1.11⅘) ALLOWANCE. Purse $29,000. 4-year-olds and upward which are non-winners of $3,000 twice other than maiden, claiming or starter. Weights, 4-year-olds, 121 lbs.; older, 122 lbs. Non-winners of two races other than claiming since November 3 allowed 3 lbs.; of a race other than maiden or claiming since then 5 lbs.; of such a race since October 1, 7 lbs.

Not only does this colt have dull form, but he is entered above his conditions. He qualifies for entry-level allowance (horses that have never won an allowance), but he's entered in a field that includes winners of one allowance.

No chance. Precisely the same situation as another no-chance Michael Whittingham horse, which won on this downhill specialty course after he had lost allowance races of lesser caliber in Canada. *Aromacor* was not without positive credentials on December 31, but her form was dull.

Was Aromacor's win part of a pattern or was it an isolated occurrence? This is the question that directly affects the appraisal of Stratford East. If I had my own data base, it would include a complete record of each trainer, without the precategorizations that break up the order of things like a cubist painting. I needed his record on the downhill turf course, not his overall turf record. I needed to see if he'd win in short clusters, not a general win percentage or even a specified track win percentage. I'd rather scan the raw information to see what materialized than have prepared answers in categories that may or may not fit today's situation.

So now, memory must be allowed to intervene, imperfect memory, but memory that is capable of the skill of synthesis, the discovery of hidden forms in scattered pieces of information. My recollections said that:

1. M. Whittingham's trainer cycle was usually that of pop-up wins. His horses reached a peak in a sequence of *bad-bad-bad-good*, rather than one of *bad-better-better-good*. I recalled frequent high mutuels that implied form reversals.
2. He seemed to win on the Santa Anita downhill turf course. An image came to my mind saying that these downhill wins occurred in the first part of the meet. Specifically, I recalled a February victory for a horse of his called Truce Maker, which paid over $18, on the downhill sprint course.

```
Aromacor                              Dk. b. or br. f. 4, by Bold Ruckus—Tamara, by Up Spirits
OLIVARES F                            Br.—Frostad G C (Ont-C)              1986  16  4  5  0      $79,585
Own.—Ventura Stable Inc      118      Tr.—Whittingham Michael              1985  10  1  0  1      $16,291
                                      Lifetime   26   5   5   1   $95,876   Turf   7  2  2  0      $40,065
31Dec86-8SA  a6½f ①:213 :4341:152fm  27 113   76½ 66  33½ 11     Olivares F⁵ ⒻAw45000 82-18 Aromacor, Tax Dodge, Sign Off  10
30Nov86-8BM  7½f ①:23 :4621:293fm    13 113   79  76½ 76½ 78     OlrsF¹⁰ ⒻMs UnvrseH 88-04 Goldenita,TxDodge,Abstrc'Energy 10
1Nov86-9SA   1   ①:4631:1041:363fm   96 113  103½ 41½ 94½ 96½    OlivrsF¹² ⒻMidwick H 88-07 Aberuschka, Duckweed, Sclva    12
13Oct86-2WO  7f ,:233 :464 1:25 sl   5½ 120   2½ 21  21½ 21      King R Jr³  ⒻHcpO 83-22 White Lotus, Aromacor,FoxyAlexis  5
27Sep86-9WO  1¼:48  1:13 1:43²gd     3½ 114   54  54½ 59½ 611½   KRJr⁵ ⒻLa Prevoyant 74-20 Cuntlmer,MissTressette,RegncySilk 8
18Sep86-8WO  7f ,:232 :463 1:25 ft  *8.5 115   76  76½ 53½ 52½   King RJr³ ⒻAw24000 82-26 MissTressette,DoubleBundles,Relit  8
6Sep86-9WO   1  ⓉⒼ4831:1411:40 yl   12 113   94  74  21  21½    KRJr⁶ ⒻⒼOnt Colleen 75-23 MssEnchntd,Armcr,DncngOnACld  10
             6Sep86—Grade II-C; Steadied; Run in Divisions
27Aug86-9WO  7f ,:233 :46 1:242ft    5 115   43  44½ 33  23      King R Jr⁵ ⒻAw24000 84-21 White Lotus,Aromacor,NonnaMaria 7
4Aug86-10WO  6f  ①:222 :45 1:092fm   4½ 115  104½ 79  36  1nk    King R Jr⁹ ⒻAw15500 97-03 Aromcor,PrkAvenuPrls,RgncySilk  12
27Jly86-10WO 7f  ①:231 :4621:23 gd  14 115  107  85½ 27  22½     King R Jr¹³ ⒻAw15500 92-11 Hear Music, Aromacor, Cote Nord 13
    Jan 1 SA 3fm :36²h            ● Dec 23 SA ① 6f fm 1:14³ h (d) ● Dec 17 Hol ① 3f fm :36¹ h (d)  Dec 12 Hol 5f ft 1:01⁴ h
```

Hypothesis: Surprise wins down the hill could be an annual occurrence for M. Whittingham, a less sensational version of the Gosden ritual. All of these thoughts were not powerful enough to get me to bet on *Stratford East*, although on several occasions I started to get up to go to the window. When Stratford East won, coincidentally paying off at 27–1—Aromacor's payoff on December 31—the hypothesis had become a theory, and my opinion about the importance of memory in handicapping was strengthened.

And so, on January 15, 1987, having just missed a 27–1 winner, rather than berate myself, I inserted a piece of information in my mind, a whole year before it would be useful: sometime early in the 1988 Santa Anita meet, Michael Whittingham could be expected to produce a long-shot winner on the downhill turf course. In order to make space for this information in my memory, I had to forget a few birthdays of uncles and aunts. I would be awaiting the arrival of M. Whittingham's downhill turf winner the way an astronomer awaits the arrival of Halley's Comet. (If I could come up with enough bets of this anticipation variety, the kind that require no *Racing Form* analysis, I could move to Avignon and wake up to fresh crusty bread, hard smelly cheese, and espresso coffee, take a walk on medieval streets and not worry about the day's scratches. I could simply leave a bankroll with friends in Las Vegas and wait for monthly checks.)

Twelve months passed. Birthdays, anniversaries, patriotic holidays, and other trivial annual occurrences. But now, on January 28, 1988, my binoculars became a telescope, and Michael Whittingham's Aromacor became the only hope for the arrival of my annual comet. This trainer had few horses in his stable, and most did not fit the conditions for the downhill races.

Aromacor's current form was questionable enough for me to get a fair price; she had lost her most recent race—on December

27, on the downhill course—but was only two lengths behind, a horse for course, in that race. Her fifth-place finish represented an improvement over her previous three races. The crowd saw the apparently dull form and sent her off at slightly under 7–1.

At the top of the hill the horses entered the gate, far off from the noise of the crowd. Aromacor broke from the gate in a crowd of horses and quickly went to the lead. As she led by a length at the quarter, I contemplated how frequently front runners die on this particular course. They cross the strip of dirt from the main track, and at that point some horses seem to accelerate while others lose interest. As Aromacor hit the dirt strip, I waited for her well-bet follower to wipe out the one-length advantage. But they seemed to go around this time in merry-go-round style. Benzina gained a half length near the wire, but Aromacor won the race as if she were a marionette being guided from above.

EIGHTH RACE
Santa Anita
JANUARY 28, 1988

ABOUT 6½ FURLONGS.(Turf). (1.11⅗) CLASSIFIED ALLOWANCE. Purse $50,000. Fillies and mares. 4–year–olds and upward. Non–winners of $19,500 other than closed or claiming since September 1. Weights, 4–year–olds, 120 lbs.; older, 121 lbs. Non–winners of $17,000 twice since then allowed 3 lbs.; of $19,250 since November 16, 5 lbs.; of $18,000 since September 10, or $22,000 since June 1, 7 lbs. (Claiming races not considered.)

Value of race $50,000; value to winner $27,500; second $10,000; third $7,500; fourth $3,750; fifth $1,250. Mutuel pool $266,585. Exacta pool $279,127.

Last Raced	Horse	Eqt.	A.	Wt	PP	St	¼	½	Str	Fin	Jockey	Odds $1
27Dec87 7SA5	Aromacor		5	111	5	4	1^{1}	1^{1}	1^{1}	$1^{\frac{1}{2}}$	Gryder A T5	6.90
6Jan88 3SA7	Benzina		6	116	7	1	$3^{\frac{1}{2}}$	$2^{1\frac{1}{2}}$	$2^{2\frac{1}{2}}$	2^{2}	Delahoussaye E	3.40
11Dec87 8Hol9	Loucoum		6	114	1	8	$6^{\frac{1}{2}}$	9^{1}	5^{1}	3no	Velasquez J	10.10
7Jan88 8SA5	Daring Doone		5	115	8	5	$7^{\frac{1}{2}}$	5^{2}	3^{hd}	4^{hd}	Valenzuela P A	5.00
6Dec87 3Hol3	Beseya		4	117	11	2	8^{2}	4^{1}	4^{1}	$5^{3\frac{1}{2}}$	Stevens G L	3.70
27Dec87 7SA6	Tropical Holiday		5	114	3	6	$2^{\frac{1}{2}}$	$3^{\frac{1}{2}}$	6^{2}	6^{hd}	Shoemaker W	10.20
2Jan88 8SA5	Toulange		4	117	4	7	$4^{\frac{1}{2}}$	$6^{\frac{1}{2}}$	$7^{1\frac{1}{2}}$	$7^{2\frac{1}{4}}$	Hawley S	7.50
13Jan88 3SA6	La Feria	b	4	113	6	10	11	10^{3}	8^{2}	$8^{\frac{1}{2}}$	Stevens S A	90 10
21Aug87 5Dmr9	Myra's Special		5	115	2	9	$10^{\frac{1}{2}}$	11	$9^{\frac{1}{2}}$	9^{3}	Castanon A L	95.00
21Nov87 8Hol6	Ice Stealer	b	6	114	9	11	9^{hd}	7^{1}	10^{4}	$10^{6\frac{1}{2}}$	Olivares F	78.00
15Jan88 8SA3	Comparability		5	115	10	3	5^{hd}	$8^{\frac{1}{2}}$	11	11	McCarron C J	7.00

OFF AT 4:24. Start good. Won driving. Time, :22⅕, :45⅕, 1:09⅗, 1:15⅘ Course firm.

$2 Mutuel Prices:

5–AROMACOR	15.80	6.40	3.60
7–BENZINA		5.20	3.40
1–LOUCOUM			7.20

$5 EXACTA 5–7 PAID $188.50

Dk. b. or br. m, by Bold Ruckus—Tamara, by Up Spirits. Trainer Whittingham Michael. Bred by Frostad G C (Ont–C).

AROMACOR carved out all the fractions and fought it out gamely to hold safe over BENZINA. The latter stalked the winner the entire trip, made a strong bid through the final fulong but could not get up. LOUCOUM saved ground and rallied for the show. DARING DOONE split horses and could not muster the needed rally. BESEYA was wide and finished with some interest. TROPICAL HOLIDAY and TOULANGE tired. COMPARABILITY was finished early.

The victory was not as sensational as M. Whittingham's previous yearly fetes, but the weird cycle continued to materialize. Even Halley's Comet, though, will someday burn up, never to return.

THE LONG AND THE SHORT OF IT

Trainers can dictate the results of races within their unique specialties, in long and short cycles. *Long cycles* are those that recur at infrequent intervals, such as those yearly peaks of Gosden and Whittingham which relate to highly specialized patterns. *Short cycles* are brief clusters of winners that display common characteristics (the Stratford East victory culminated a two-race short cycle for the same M. Whittingham, downhill turf wins for apparently dull horses at 27–1). This last-mentioned short cycle is not typical, in that it was not a readily identifiable pattern match, as most short cycles are.

From the atypical to the typical, from the particular and peculiar to the universal, we now move to a trainer short cycle that can be found at all racetracks, highlighted in Larry Goldstein's first-time starter studies of the mid-1980s which are now, unfortunately, out of print. In compiling a total picture of the characteristics of first-time starter winners, Goldstein discovered that, with high frequency, when a trainer had one winner of this type, he would follow it up soon with another similar winner. Furthermore, the researcher discovered that what he termed "short cycles" often arise with trainers who are not known for winning with first-timers, trainers who would not be identified in encyclopedic studies of trainer patterns and specialties.

Nowhere in horse-race handicapping is it more evident that a trainer can "dictate" the results of a race than with first-time starters. A talented horse in the hands of one patient trainer may not win until its third or fourth try, while a horse of parallel talent in the hands of a trainer who gears up horses for their debut will win first time out. Goldstein reasoned that these cluster winners often had similar work patterns and must have followed the same training regimen. Sometimes they even worked out in tandem prior to their debuts. He recommended that handicappers keep a log of all trainers who win with first-timers. Trainers who make the list are to be bet on if they enter more first-time starters within the next week or two, excluding those trainers with such a high volume of debutants that investment is pari-mutuelly unfeasible.

If a follow-up debutant has a workout pattern similar to its victorious stablemate, it becomes a priority investment. Note that with these criteria, one is wagering on a trainer and not a horse. Like the total-control trainer dictatorships, partial-control situations produce winners in clusters. Unlike the totalitarian situations, though, partial dominions take place within one highly specialized racing situation.

Trivial Pursuit

The memory tool in handicapping is crucial for short as well as long cycles. I recall a binge of three winners, within a brief period of time, in which trainer Donald Warren brought maiden-claiming winners right back against winners, a very *low probability* situation, and won all three times! Since every handicapper knows that maiden-claimer winners are poor investments in their next race, all three Warren winners paid generous prices. This type of factor does not fit in voluminous trainer studies nor is it the type of event you'd keep tabs of in a notebook. It's one odd occurrence among many that you keep in the back of your mind, if you can.

So after Warren had achieved the first against-the-grain score, the short-cycle watcher needed to be on the lookout for a return of the pattern. The situation materializes and the question is, to bet or not to bet? You need another dimension of information, something that gives some evidence that the weird event may be part of a pattern.

It's time to look up Warren's first winner of this odd type. You discover he's using the same apprentice rider and making the same track switch: the fair to major-league track. The pattern is the same, so the short cycle is possible. The trainer is hot with his other horses too. The field looks mediocre. You're getting 16–1. Many things have materialized that point to a bet, but it all started because of a mental note from the back of your mind.

After the horse wins and pays $35.00, the third time the same situation materializes, it has become an automatic bet. You collect again and you wait for the same situation to pop up, but it has disappeared, maybe forever. Short cycles are valuable precisely because they are hard to find and their orbit only passes briefly before the naked eye, too briefly even for the radar of computer trainer studies.

You wait for this particular Warren orbit to return, but there are no signs. Meanwhile, other bits and pieces collect: seems that this particular trainer does all his winning in cycles, in clusters. On the radio he sounds like a laid-back, whatever-will-be type of individual who takes things as they come, speaks in understatements, and seems to value steadiness over extremism, continuity over intensity. The performance of his stable leaves the opposite impression. His wins come in clusters, binges, and then he is quiet for long periods of time, as if his stable went through periods of introspective brooding alternating with brief periods of elation and sensationalism.

This may be the work of a true artist, one who needs to provide a *form* for the content of his work. Isolated winners would be formless; winners in meaningful clusters, with similar patterns, would be the structure of a work of art. I notice other trainers, here and there, who followed the Warren model in fashioning their craft. Maintaining a low profile, they would surface from time to time, like graffiti artists, make their peculiar splash, and disappear for a while.

Too bad I can't decipher the enigma of more of these types of trainers, for when I discover their pattern, I rarely miss their winners.

It was a muddy February 25, 1987, at Santa Anita, when the signs of a Donald Warren coup materialized. There as no handicapping involved, for when a trainer is about to dictate the outcome of a situation, all other forces in the universe of horse racing are momentarily paralyzed. Warren had entries in the seventh and eighth races. Both had the same sire, Somethingfabulous, who is not bad at producing mud runners. Both had the same rider, Laffit Pincay, Jr., Warren's top jockey at the time. Only incidentally, their names were *Some Sensation* and *Something Lucky*. For any other trainer this set of circumstances should have been construed as a coincidence, but in the case of Warren, two winners in a row with common characteristics is a more likely scenario than one winner and one loser; the guy has always won in clusters, always with horses of similar characteristics.

I am self-conscious about writing these few pages because, to those who don't know me, I must surely sound subjective, bordering on superstitious. I assure you this is not the case. When a trainer exerts a partial dictatorship, all the forces in the universe of horse racing are not enough to shut him down. Here was a rare occasion when the parlay form relates to the race content. One of the few times I've ever chanced a two-horse parlay.

All of the forces from above and below were united in trying to prevent the Warren coup d'etat. In the seventh Some Sensation needed to come out four wide to make her move. Then she started lugging in. She still won the race, paying $16.60. The Horse Gods were not yet defeated, though. As the horses left the gate in the eighth, with Something Lucky at 5–2, the Warren horse was jostled, then forced to move up along the rail, not the best place to be.

Nearing the stretch, he was totally boxed in. What's more, he got bumped by a rival—Mount Laguna, the favorite—at the top of the stretch. But Pincay found a narrow hole and guided Something Lucky through, to a $7.40 victory.

If mud caulks in some way relate to trainer intentions, in the seventh race 4 of the 8 horses did not wear them. In the eighth 3 of the 7 starters were without mud caulks. Both Some Sensation and Something Lucky had been equipped with mud caulks. The trainer was using all available measures. The work of art was completed, but Donald Warren left it without a signature, choosing to lay low and remain just that far from the spotlight. His short cycles remain too avant-garde to fit within the realm of traditional trainer research.

While an abundance of contemporary examples of short cycles could be highlighted here, I'd like to feature a particular incident from the past which is a most sensational illustration of the importance of *indiscriminate memory* in identifying short cycles.

Saturday, September 13, 1986. Meadowlands, first race. I had just arrived at Las Vegas and was anxious to dig into the Eastern *Form*. New Jersey past performances offered a byzantine experience, with shippers, hidden class angles, and distance changes converging into a complex galaxy of contradictory forces. My common sense was stronger than my hunger for action, and I passed the first race due to insufficient information.

My head was buried in the *Form* when I barely noticed the results. The first race had been won by a first-time starter. Glad I passed. I spent no more than thirty seconds scanning the past performance records of the winner . . . works every four days, trainer, Gleaves. Then I stashed that information in a remote corner of my mind and went on with business.

Sunday, September 14. Belmont, fourth race. Maiden special weight. Yours truly was down a fair chunk of his bankroll. My only research preparation for Belmont had been for sloppy tracks. I had prayed for rain, but the track was fast. That called for passing the card. It was Sunday and there was no Jersey racing. Let's scan the Belmont card; see if anything materializes.

Fourth race. There it was. A first-time starter trained by Philip Gleaves. The Goldstein short cycle functioning on both sides of the Hudson River. That's right . . . remember last night's first race, Gleaves's first-time starter, works every four days. Adrenaline flows as I see that the Gleaves entry in today's fourth race,

Snow How, also shows works every four days. Could this be in the computer studies? I doubted it. And how many Belmont players were at the Meadowlands last night? And of those, how many would remember the past performances of the first-race winner? And of those, how many were into "short cycles"? Check the works again, make sure I'm not seeing things:

Snow How

> Sep 10 Bel 4F fst :49 hg
> Sep 6 Bel 4F my :49 1/5 b
> Sep 2 Bel 6F fst 1:16 b
> Aug 29 Bel 4F fst :48 3/5 bg

There it was, the same pattern as last night, same trainer. Two of the works out of the gate, more reason for the horse to be schooled and ready. Weak field, ideal for a debutant.

Here comes Snow How, passing the field in the stretch. Thank you, Jorge Luis Borges, for "*Funes El Memorioso.*" Thank you, Goldstein, for your creative research. The key here was to have remembered something that had no predetermined importance, something that would have been discarded prematurely had racing information been sorted into a hierarchy of values.

Snow How won, paid off big, and turned things around, converting a losing trip into a winning one. More important, for the long run, Snow How taught me that horse-race handicapping is too complex and dynamic to be prefabricated into rigid structures and formulae, that horse and trainer cycles are orbits in an expanding universe with no finite boundaries.

REIGN OF TERROR

Dictatorships arise when collective reason based on educated decisions ceases to have influence on the powers that be, and one man or woman can control many destinies. At the racetrack collective reason is represented by the past performances and their relationship to future outcomes. The day that these past performances cease to relate to future race results will be the day that horse racing as we know it dies.

On one particular afternoon at Hollywood Park a reign of pari-mutuel terror caused many a horseplayer to fear the imminent destruction of their constitution (yes, the *Racing Form* is the constitution and not the Bible of horseplayers, because it is a document of reason and not faith). My partner, Frank Cotolo, and I were so devastated by the awesome show of brute power that the exact date of the disaster is blocked out of our minds. We had 4 winners that day in the Pick 6 along with 2 seconds, on a small ticket. If we'd have added a couple of thousand dollars to our ticket, we still would have ended up with 4 winners and 2 seconds because the two horses that beat us were both first-time starters with dull works, ridden by a low-percentage rider (Fernandez) and trained by Richard Matlow. Matlow handles such a small stable that you'll never have enough of a sample to do a "scientific" study of his specialties. And yet here he was, dictating and sealing the fate of thousands of rational handicappers.

Racing Form fundamentalists beware. Your Bible is not the only source of information that explains the meaning of thoroughbred racing.

Since then I've followed Matlow the best I can, observing a few first-timers come very close but fail, at other tracks, to obliterate the rational channels of handicapping. I began to suspect that the peak in Matlow's long cycle would most likely recur at Hollywood Park. If that was the scene where he muscled his way in and trampled upon the public, that's where he'd most likely return.

I waited. As a citizen, I know I will always take the side against dictatorial abuses of power. But as a horseplayer I might just tag along with the autocrat and pick up a few of the pieces.

Long Cycle

The situation materialized on May 6, 1988, Hollywood Park, sixth race. Everything pointed to the fact that this was the return of the tyrant:

6th Hollywood

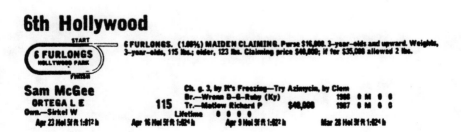

Track: Hollywood
Rider: Ortega, in the throes of an incredibly long losing
            streak, *Matlow's kind of guy*
Works: Dull and without signs of speed, just like on that
            fateful day!

Richard Matlow began to look like an inside-out version of
Philip Gleaves. Gleaves, good works; Matlow, bad. Gleaves, gate
works; Matlow, who needs a gate? Gleaves, good riders; Matlow,
down-and-outers. Gleaves, benevolent dictator; Matlow, sinister,
sly. And Matlow comes from the school of tyrants who profess to
get their power from divine sources. Proof: there was a bias favoring the inside on May 6. It felt great to have this tyrant on my
side as I went up to the window to invest in his horse.

Sam McGee was 15–1 in the morning line. My clear vision of
the past reminded me that on that fateful afternoon, one of Matlow's winners had paid a big price while the other had been
hammered down way below its morning-line odds. I feared that
in this weak field, Sam McGee, too, might get all kinds of action.
But that never happened. The Matlow cycle was not in the minds
of the bettors, while the Ortega losing streak was.

Sam McGee was off slowly, but Ortega got him through on the
inside (the "diamond lane," as they say in California). The cold
jockey had gotten off slowly, as is his style, but took advantage of
the inside bias. Once more I considered that jockey cycles are
more a by-product of trainer cycles and relate specifically to the
types of mounts they are getting. And since rider cycles are secondary while trainer cycles are primary, in cases of contradiction
between two opposite cycles, trainer supersedes rider.

SIXTH RACE **Hollywood** **MAY 6, 1988** — **6 FURLONGS. (1.08⅘) MAIDEN CLAIMING. Purse $16,000. 3-year-olds and upward. Weights, 3-year-olds, 115 lbs.; older, 123 lbs. Claiming price $40,000; if for $35,000 allowed 2 lbs.**

Value of race $16,000; value to winner $8,800; second $3,200; third $2,400; fourth $1,200; fifth $400. Mutuel pool $31[illegible],375.

Last Raced	Horse	Eqt.	A.Wt	PP	St	¼	½	Str	Fin	Jockey	Cl'g Pr	Odds $1
	Sam McGee		3 115	1	11	1^{hd}	2^{hd}	1^{2}	$1^{1\frac{1}{2}}$	Ortega L E	40000	12.80
14Apr88 $^{2}SA^{3}$	Somekindaguy	b	3 108	5	4	2^{hd}	1^{hd}	2^{hd}	2^{2}	Corral J R[5]	35000	4.00
25Apr88 $^{4}SA^{4}$	Explosive Wing		3 115	12	2	4^{1}	$3^{2\frac{1}{2}}$	3^{2}	3^{nk}	Castanon A L	40000	2.00
24Apr88 $^{4}SA^{5}$	Pieds Power	b	3 115	9	7	11^{4}	$11^{3\frac{1}{2}}$	8^{1}	4^{nk}	Sherman A B	40000	6.90
29Jan88 $^{4}SA^{7}$	Star Vesco	b	3 113	2	10	9^{hd}	$9^{1\frac{1}{2}}$	5^{3}	$5^{\frac{1}{2}}$	Meza R Q	35000	68.40
25Apr88 $^{4}SA^{3}$	Rocket Rod	b	3 115	3	6	5^{1}	$4^{1\frac{1}{2}}$	4^{1}	6^{2}	Pedroza M A	40000	3.60
	Zaca Zambia		4 123	7	8	8^{hd}	$7^{\frac{1}{2}}$	$7^{\frac{1}{2}}$	$7^{1\frac{3}{4}}$	Patterson A	40000	41.90
	Zaida's Best Man		3 115	10	1	3^{hd}	$5^{1\frac{1}{2}}$	$6^{\frac{1}{2}}$	$8^{\frac{1}{2}}$	Solis A	40000	23.90
7Apr88 $^{2}SA^{11}$	Re Payment		3 113	6	9	10^{3}	$10^{1\frac{1}{2}}$	9^{1}	$9^{\frac{1}{2}}$	Black C A	35000	51.20
17Mar88 $^{4}SA^{2}$	May B. Time	b	3 115	11	3	7^{1}	6^{hd}	11^{8}	$10^{1\frac{1}{2}}$	Olivares F	40000	6.60
	Lucky Amadeus		3 115	4	5	6^{2}	8^{hd}	10^{hd}	11^{12}	Sibille R	40000	123.80
	William McDoo	b	3 113	8	12	12	12	12	12	Fernandez A L	35000	130.60

OFF AT 4:09. Start good. Won driving. Time, :22, :45⅘, :58⅕, 1:12 Track fast.

$2 Mutuel Prices:				
	1–SAM MCGEE	27.60	13.00	6.60
	5–SOMEKINDAGUY		6.80	4.20
	12–EXPLOSIVE WING			3.20

Ch. g, by It's Freezing—Try Azimycin, by Clem. Trainer Matlow Richard P. Bred by Wrenn D–G–Ruby (Ky).

SAM MCGEE broke a bit slowly, moved up quickly along the inside early to engage for the lead before going a furlong, dueled for the lead around the far turn, drew clear in the upper stretch and had the needed further response in the final furlong to prove best. SOMEKINDAGUY dueled for the lead to the stretch, could not catch SAM MCGEE in the last furlong but finished willingly for the place. EXPLOSIVE WING, wide early, vied for the lead to the stretch, then weakened a bit. PIEDS POWER, devoid of early speed and wide down the backstretch, came into the stretch six wide and finished strongly. ROCKET ROD, in contention early, lacked the needed response in the final quarter. ZACA ZAMBIA was four wide into the stretch. ZAIDA'S BEST MAN had early speed, gave way and was four wide into the stretch. MAY B. TIME, wide down the backstretch, was five wide into the stretch. LUCKY AMADEUS, in contention early, faltered. WILLIAM MCDOO broke slowly.

Owners— 1, Sirkel W; 2, SaberEdge Thbds & PiggottJr; 3, Citro J & F; 4, Nelson & Townson; 5, Duckett-Hinds-Robbins; 6, Murray G & Carol; 7, Bowman-Shidaker-Witthauer(Lessees); 8, El Rancho De Jaklin; 9, Newman B; 10, Beckett & Hersh; 11, Persinger J; 12, Comaianni-Labellarti-Miano.

Trainers— 1, Matlow Richard P; 2, King Hal; 3, Stute Warren; 4, Nelson Kathleen S; 5, Robbins Jay M; 6, French Neil; 7, Shidaker Duff; 8, Fanning Jerry; 9, Stidham Michael; 10, Bernstein David; 11, Persinger Jim; 12, Call Val Dean.

Short Cycle

The previous Matlow invasion had seen him come into town with two first-time-starter winners. Now, to complete the cycle, one more Matlow debutant should be surfacing within a short period of time. Both long cycle and short cycle converged upon this one awaited first-time starter. Did he exist or had there been a shift in the Matlow orbit?

On May 18, after having been scratched off the also-eligible list on a previous day, Matlow's other first-time starter got into the fourth race. Once more it was a weak field, but this time the clockers caught a 1:11.3 workout, so we might have been looking at a favorite. Indeed, *Clev*'s six-furlong work was *faster than the race times* of the other horses in the field. With the fabulous workout and the long and short cycles converging upon this race, line makers should have put Clev at even money and been ready to take the low price.

(Clev) MATLOW / ORTEGA

Clev Dk. b. or br. c. 3, by Clev Er Tell—Spring in Virginia, by Flit-to
ORTEGA L E — 115 — Br.—Tackett P & McMillin Bros (Ky) 1988 0 M 0 0
Own.—R G M Stable — Tr.—Matlow Richard P $50,000 1987 0 M 0 0
Lifetime 0 0 0 0
May 14 SA 4f ft :47³ h May 5 SA 6f ft 1:11³ hg Apr 23 Hol 5f ft 1:02² hg ●Apr 6 Hol 6f ft 1:15² h

The public, however, did two things that helped the Clev investors. First, Ortega was "correctly" assumed to be an ice-cold jockey (even though with Matlow he was one for one). Second, the crowd chose to completely ignore this trainer cycle, preferring to see each race as a strictly isolated event having no part in an overall passage of past performance history.

Clev should have been even money, so at more than 4–1, you were getting him on sale with quadruple coupons. Ortega held off the charge of his nearest rival, and as he crossed the finish line, he must have thought that, with live mounts, he'd be right up there with the leading riders.

FOURTH RACE Hollywood MAY 18, 1988 — **6 ½ FURLONGS. (1.15⅘) MAIDEN CLAIMING. Purse $18,000. 3-year-olds and upward. Weights, 3-year-olds, 115 lbs.; older, 123 lbs. Claiming price $50,000; if for $45,000 allowed 2 lbs.**

Value of race $18,000; value to winner $9,900; second $3,600; third $2,700; fourth $1,350; fifth $450. Mutuel pool $267,481. Exacta pool $251,387.

Last Raced	Horse	Eqt.	A.Wt	PP	St	¼	½	Str	Fin	Jockey	Cl'g Pr	Odds $1
	Clev		3 115	10	2	$2^{1½}$	1^{2}	$1^{1½}$	1^{hd}	Ortega L E	50000	4.30
24Apr88 ^{4}SA^{2}	Devine Boy		3 115	6	6	$5^{½}$	3^{1}	$2^{2½}$	$2^{5½}$	Meza R Q	50000	6.10
	My Son Bret		3 117	7	10	9^{2}	$7^{1½}$	$6^{1½}$	$3^{½}$	Pincay L Jr	50000	7.10
1Jly87 ^{6}Hol^{6}	Watch Tim Go		4 116	3	8	7^{1}	6^{hd}	$5^{½}$	4^{1}	Banderas A L^{5}	45000	14.50
30Apr88 ^{9}Hol^{10}	Toe River		3 116	1	5	$4^{½}$	5^{2}	$4^{1½}$	$5^{1½}$	Delahoussaye E	50000	1.30
1May88 ^{6}Hol^{7}	Brave Chief		3 115	2	3	$1^{½}$	$2^{½}$	$3^{½}$	$6^{2½}$	Stevens G L	50000	5.50
4May88 ^{4}Hol^{9}	Mon Benefactor	b	3 108	9	1	10^{hd}	$10^{3½}$	9^{3}	$7^{¾}$	Corral J R^{5}	45000	117.20
14May87 ^{6}Hol^{8}	Apache Magic	b	4 123	5	4	3^{hd}	4^{hd}	$7^{1½}$	8^{1}	Gryder A T	50000	50.00
15Apr88 ^{6}SA^{9}	Combat Pilot	b	3 115	4	11	11^{4}	9^{hd}	8^{hd}	9^{5}	Cisneros J E	50000	191.40
28Apr88 ^{6}Hol^{6}	Cruiser Manet	b	3 115	8	7	$6^{1½}$	$8^{2½}$	10^{7}	10^{9}	Toro F	50000	18.30
	Traditionally Rich		3 116	11	12	12	12	11^{4}	11^{4}	Cruz J B	50000	188.30
6May88 ^{6}Hol^{12}	William McDoo	b	3 113	12	9	8^{hd}	$11^{1½}$	12	12	Sherman A B	45000	147.10

OFF AT 3:03. Start good. Won driving. Time, :21⅗, :44⅗, 1:10⅗, 1:17⅕ Track fast.

$2 Mutuel Prices:			
10–CLEV	10.60	5.80	6.00
6–DEVINE BOY		5.60	4.20
7–MY SON BRET			5.60

$2 EXACTA 10–6 PAID $65.20

Dk. b. or br. g, by Clev Er Tell—Spring in Virginia, by Flit-to. Trainer Matlow Richard P. Bred by Tackett P & McMillin Bros (Ky).

CLEV took over nearing the end of the backstretch, settled into the stretch with a clear lead, maintained a clear advantage to deep stretch and just lasted. DEVINE BOY, never far back, made a determined late run at CLEV and just missed getting up. MY SON BRET, outrun early after being slow to begin, came into the stretch four wide, improved his position in the drive but failed to threaten. WATCH TIM GO was four wide into the stretch. TOE RIVER, slow to begin, advanced to get in contention early while along the inner rail and lacked the needed response in the last quarter. BRAVE CHIEF set or forced the pace for a half and gave way MON BENEFACTOR was wide down the backstretch. APACHE MAGIC, closed up early, faltered. CRUISER MANET, wide down the backstretch, was four wide into the stretch. TRADITIONALLY RICH broke slowly and was wide down the backstretch. WILLIAM MCDOO was wide down the backstretch.

Owners— 1, R G M Stable; 2, Golden Eagle Farm; 3, Johnson-Stacey-StonebrakerEtal; 4, Wild Plum Farm; 5, Greene H F or Janet; 6, Zuckerman D S; 7, Dean & Ribar; 8, 3 Plus U Stable; 9, Delaplane E E; 10, St George C A B; 11, Hickman & McBrayer; 12, Comaianni-Labellarti-Miano.

Trainers— 1, Matlow Richard P; 2, Stute Melvin F; 3, Warren Donald; 4, Tuck Mary Lou; 5, Stute Warren; 6, Stute Melvin F; 7, Jackson Ronald D; 8, Luby Donn; 9, Guiney Irv; 10, Gosden John H M; 11, McBrayer C H; 12, Call Val Dean.

Some trainers deserve a bet because their horse is sharp and it compares favorably with other horses in the field. Other trainers deserve investing in regardless of who their horse is or what its past performances suggest. The second type of trainer becomes dictator of race results when his performance cycle reaches its unique plateau.

With Richard Matlow's first-time starters, memory of past incidents allowed the handicapper to *anticipate* future outcomes before they ever coalesced into specific fields of horses on a particular day of races.

First-time-starter short cycles are but one of many possible trainer-control situations. They happen to best illustrate how the trainer supersedes the horse in certain situations. We have referred to two other partial-control situations, those of M. Whittingham (specialty surface/distance/time of year) and John Gosden (foreign horses/layoff). Another partial-control situation that arises more frequently than those mentioned, and may manifest itself in both short and long cycles, involves the claiming trainer. At least there is logic behind first-timers winning in clusters, since they have trained together. But with an amazing frequency founded on no clear logic, trainers who win with a claimed horse, especially going up in class while "in jail" (in a mandatory class-rise period within thirty days following the claim), seem to come right back with one or more follow-up winners, also claimed horses. Since these winners most often have come from different stables, the in-tandem training rationale does not apply.

That's the short cycle. The long cycle involves a particular specialty claim that occurs infrequently. For example, trainer Mike Mitchell, who occasionally goes on a short-cycle claiming binge, has one particular type of claim that is highly selective, infrequent, but deadly accurate. For many years now, the horseplayer could cash in more than 50 percent of the time when Mitchell claimed horses *out of maiden-claiming races*. Prices in that type of race are inflated in order to protect the owners, sort of a cushion to compensate for the first years, when horses eat but don't race. Fifty percent sounds like even money, but you're guaranteed to get much more, for these claimed horses rarely look good in the past performances.

One of the more recent peaks in this cycle of long intervals was Jokers Jig, April 29, 1988, Hollywood Park, third race.

Jokers Jig

6Apr88	SA	9^5	5^3	4^4	5^5	Mc40,000
		Lugged out, wide/lugged in				
12Mar88	SA	5^5	5^6	8^8	9^{10}	Mdn
28Feb88	SA	8^{11}	7^7	7^6	5^2	Mdn (lgths behind rounded off)

Not a very distinguished beginning for the career of Jokers Jig. But now Mitchell has him, and he takes advantage of a quirk in the maiden class structure, escaping the class rise to straight maiden because a race for $50,000 claimers satisfied the mandatory class jump. This colt had been bet down to 2–1 favorite in its last race, implying he might have some latent talent which was wasted by lugging in and lugging out; not often that you see a horse lug both ways in the same race. For many horses, the addition of blinkers represents an experiment in wishful thinking, but for Jokers Jig today, they represent a corrective measure to counter the self-destructive habit of lugging in and out. A by-product of the blinkers experiment may be added early speed, which will be an asset in this race of slow-paced horses.

I hadn't had time to analyze all these things because I had expected to arrive at Las Vegas by around the sixth or seventh race and had set aside the earlier races for leisurely consultation that evening. It was four minutes to post time as I walked into the Barbary Coast Race Book, luggage in hand, with no time to handicap the third race. My hotel was a block away and I was not hungry for action, so I decided to watch the race, then get rid of my luggage and return with a clear head and empty arms.

I scanned the past performances so that I might know just enough to learn from watching the race. It was then that I saw the little C between the M and the 40,000 next to Jokers Jig's last race. No time to handicap the race, two minutes to post, this was a trainer-dictator situation. The lines are never long at the race books, and I got in the bet. The colt was 4–1 on the board.

He walked away from the field. By the stretch, the rest of the horses were too far back to fit on the monitor. Post-race ritual: when I lose, I tell myself what I did right, but when I win, I go over my mistakes. Mistake: I'd been too casual about the card and had almost missed one of my favorite bets by not having gone over the whole card at the proper time.

Graph. The Long and the Short of It

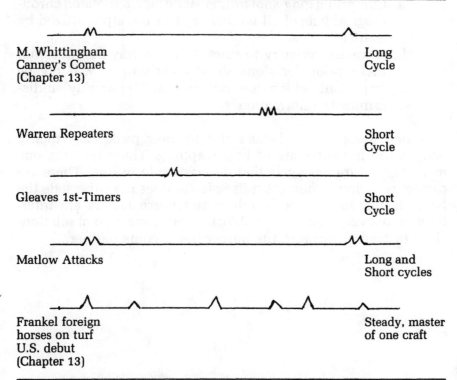

M. Whittingham
Canney's Comet
(Chapter 13) — Long Cycle

Warren Repeaters — Short Cycle

Gleaves 1st-Timers — Short Cycle

Matlow Attacks — Long and Short cycles

Frankel foreign
horses on turf
U.S. debut
(Chapter 13) — Steady, master of one craft

Note: We await more work from Larry Goldstein on the theme of long and short cycles. His terms "long" and "short" refer to the interval between winners.

Summary

1. There are occasions in handicapping when *trainer cycles* rather than horse past performances dictate the results of races.
2. Trainer dictatorships arise in the context of:
   a. *Total control*, when a trainer reaches an extended hot period and dominates a meet, as his whole stable is sharp at the same time
   b. *Partial control*, when a trainer determines the results of a certain type of race, within his specialty
3. Partial control is manifested in:
   a. *Long cycles*, peaks with long intervals in between
   b. *Short cycles*, clusters of winners with little or no intervals in between that show some common characteristic or pattern

4. Handicappers can successfully anticipate these cycles by:
   a. Compiling *long-shot trainer standings*, annotated chronological lists of all winners 5–1 or up, alphabetized by trainer
   b. Allowing *memory* to store data in a way that does not make prior decisions about what will or will not be important, which does not edit out "apparently" indiscriminate information

When these trainer factors rise to their peak, they totally eclipse the horse factors of handicapping. There remains one more type of trainer cycle that deserves solo billing. There are certain occasions when the trainer factor does not supersede the horse factor. In fact, both trainer and horse factors are intertwined in a very dynamic symbiosis, a yin-yang type of relationship. Instead of dictator, the trainer has become partner.

CHAPTER 10

Partners

ALL RACES ARE PREP RACES

MEET AFTER MEET millions of dollars, invested on horses that are not intended to win, make a one-way trip into the betting windows. The horses represented by these losing tickets are similar to baseball players in the month of March. But unlike baseball's spring-training games, the prep races of these horses count in the standings.

When a classy horse loses a prep race, the cry of "stiff" is heard flapping about the grandstand like a balloon running out of air. Would-be consumer advocates take up where the balloon ran out and petition for an inquiry about this alleged foul against handicappers, when there are so many more serious issues that represent true abuse against the horseplayer (breakage, high take in exotics, long lines, poor concessions, poor distribution of handicapping information).

Prep races do not represent abuse against the handicapper for the simple reason that they can be identified through a competent reading of the past performances. Prep races may be turf horses running on the dirt, routers in a sprint, claimers with no recency in allowance races, stakes horses with no recency in allowances races, or any horse not entered in a situation where it is expected to excel.

It is common knowledge that most horses cannot be brought up to their peak performance through works alone and that most trainers prefer to race their horses into shape. For completely different reasons, dull horses and layoff horses both "need racing." The harness-racing industry uses "qualifying races" for this purpose, but the institution of the qualifying race has not cleaned up the industry; furthermore, standardbred racing needs qualifiers more than the thoroughbreds, for the simple reason that with most racing done on the same surface at the same distance, it would be more difficult in harness racing to identify prep races by past performances alone. In harness racing you can't sharpen a horse in a "sprint," nor can you let a dirt horse try a race on the turf.

Students of handicapping with the most rudimentary understanding of past performances can identify the most obvious examples of preps. No elaboration is necessary here; you know what's going to happen with a turf router who is entered in a dirt sprint after a six-month layoff. On the other hand, the most sensational of prep races is also the one most likely to fool the handicapper.

For one moment play the role of the trainer. You own a classy, Grade 1/Grade 2 candidate. There are some $200,000 and $500,000 races down the road. Your horse seems ready for competition but is returning after a layoff of more than a few months. At what level do you enter your horse and what instructions do you give your jockey?

Consider, too, what we have studied: that a sharp race following a layoff often brings with it negative consequences, with layoff winners often "bouncing" next time around.

You'll probably look for an overnight handicap or classified-allowance race with a purse of only about 20 percent of what will be offered in later races you are headed for. If you, the trainer, are protecting the investment of the owners you work for, it would be blatantly unprofessional—bordering on malpractice toward owner, and inhumane treatment toward animal—to "send" your horse at 100 percent capacity. You will be sure to remind the rider to protect this investment. It's in the rider's interest, financially, to protect the horse for the bigger purses, and it's in the horse's interest to protect himself from injury due to overexertion.

Yet classy horses fitting the above description are bet heavily, with even the public handicappers adding wood to the fire. And then, as James Quinn has made clear in his *Handicapper's Condition Book*, these horses usually lose. Occasionally, on class alone, by default, without being extended, they'll win. A few horses fitting this category may thrive on layoffs and run hard with no negative consequences, but most of these will be entered at the proper level to begin with. The stakes horse prepping in an allowance race will usually finish second or third at 1–2, and is not even a good show bet (if you like parlays, like I do). Bet this type of horse to win in its prep races and your return on investment will be on a par with that of keno and lottery players, and many points below random horse-race selection methods of astrologers and numerologists.

Trainers who work in partnership with their horse will be aware of its form cycle and are more likely to nurture it to a peak performance. Sometimes this nurturing process will be reflected in the running lines and finish positions of the past performances. Consider *Some Sensation*, who came back on February 13 following a nine-month vacation. Consider that her one turf victory was a rout and in her comeback race she was entered in a sprint.

Bettors were lucky to collect $11.00 on Some Sensation (May 6, Hollywood Park, eighth race). Her steady improvement should have appeared obvious. Not only did each successive race following the long layoff show an improvement in finish position,

25Apr88	$3^{2¼}$
17Mar88	$5^{4¾}$
5Mar88	$7^{4¾}$
13Feb88	$8^{9½}$

but there were also successive first-call improvements.

In reality, after the fact, all races leading toward a peak performance are prep races, and all races situated in a phase of decline are *inverted* prep races which lead to either a bottoming out or a layoff. This broad view of prep races allows us to view a horse's form phases in dynamic progression. It also accepts the fact that some prep races result from decisions of the trainer to run the horse according to a training need. Other prep races are decisions of the horse, who tells his trainer and the bettors *by the way he runs* that he needs the race. The type of prep race to be featured involves those significant occasions when horse and trainer come to an unwritten and unspoken accord about the process of prep races that will lead to a peak performance.

These situations of partnership are often not as obvious as your classical prep situations and therefore lead to better-than-fair mutuels. They represent a unique partnership, no oral agreement necessary, in which the trainer-controlled regimen meshes perfectly with the horse's internal performance cycle.

Fill in the Blanks

My colleague Brian calls this type of handicapping situation a "pattern match." What do *All In Tune*'s last two victories have in common? First the raw data as it appeared in the past performances of the *Racing Form*:

Now the pattern, extracted:

		Distance	Finish	Rider
19June86	Hol	mile	?	Shoemaker
13June86	GG	6F	4	Baze
13Mar86	SA			
2Jan86	SA	mile	1	Shoemaker
23Dec85	BM	6F	3	Mena
23Sep85	Pom			

From September 23 to December 23, 1985, there is a three-month layoff, followed by a prep race in northern California (Bay Meadows). Then there is a move south, along with a switch to Shoemaker, accompanied by a stretchout to a mile. This combination of circumstances, prep race, stretchout, rider switch, track switch, has led to a victory.

Now observe a subsequent layoff, once more, very precisely three months, March 13 to June 13, 1986. Once more the layoff is followed by a prep race in northern California (Golden Gate). The trainer has intentionally followed the training pattern that led to All In Tune's last victory, with the precision of an artisan. Once more, a move down south, once more a switch to Shoe, and again a stretchout to a mile.

Naturally, inevitably, All In Tune wins. Odds of 3–1 are more than reasonable, given the cyclical return that is as precise and predictable as the rising and setting of the sun. Here we have a "cycle" within the strict definition of the word. Did the trainer create the cycle arbitrarily, like a sculptor who carves a form out of a piece of wood; did Neil French carve the cycle out of a piece of time? Or did he merely discover, almost by accident, the natural performance phases of the horse, and then merely facilitate their repetition? Philosophically it's an exciting question, but from a handicapping point of view, it need not be answered. Following All In Tune's victory, I told Brian that we'd never again get to see a pattern as precise as this one. (I was wrong, as we shall see in a later chapter.)

Little Ignat

Mares like Little Ignat give racing a bad name. By running their best races following their worst races, they lend credence to arguments that the results of thoroughbred races are irrational and unpredictable, that "you can beat the race but you can't beat the races." While the outward appearance of the Little Ignats of racing is disorganized and anarchistic, underneath they are conformists with a repetitive lifestyle, in the avant-garde tradition.

The trainer of Little Ignat has discovered the mare's favorite routines and has developed a regimen that allows her to repeat life cycles according to natural rhythms. Consider one slice of her life, as represented by the following past performances:

Little Ignat * B. m. 6, by Full Intent—Chuck's Raider, by Prince Jay or Busher's Sheik
$5,000 Br.—Gentile C A (Md) 119 Lifetime 1988 4 1 2 0 $6,320
Own.—Susini Phyllis Tr.—Mitchell H Steward 30 7 6 6 1987 10 4 4 2 $10,820
$35,857

9Apr88- 3Pim fst 6f :23⅗ :48⅕ 1:14 ⓕClm 5000 7 3 67½ 65½ 41 1no Desormeaux KJ b 114 3.20 76-21 Little Ignat 114no Partida 118¾ Avie Gate 109nk Shuffled st., up 9
6Mar88- 2Pim fst 1 1/16 :47⅘ 1:13⅘ 1:47⅘ ⓕClm 6000 2 5 33 21 3½ 42¾ Muino D R5 b 107 3.30 63-21 DistilleryRod109½BrownBg114noPrincssJuli1142 Well up, no resp. 8
20Feb88-12Lrl my 6½f :22⅘ :46⅕ 1:18⅘ ⓕClm 5000 5 8 711 55 34 21½ Sides K L5 b 109 *1.00 86-17 Bake 1141½ Little Ignat 1092 Ami Patrice 1144½ Slow st. 8
9Feb88- 3Lrl fst 6f :22⅘ :46⅘ 1:11⅘ ⓕClm 5000 2 8 87½ 88½ 22½ 2no Johnson W C7 b 109 6.30 85-15 Alexandra's Tower 119no LittleIgnat1094½K.K.'sDream1121 Nosed 9
7Dec87- 1Lrl fst 1 :47⅕ 1:13⅕ 1:40⅘ 3+ⓕClm 5000 7 5 54½ 37 34½ 44 Muino D R5 b 112 5.90 66-24 Star Dancing 1171½ Bake 1141 Bourse Grise 1122½ Rallied 9
21Nov87- 1Lrl fst 6½f :23⅘ :48⅘ 1:21⅘ 3+ⓕClm 5000 8 8 75½ 54 2hd 12 Sides K L7 b 110 5.90 72-25 Little Ignat 1102 Rustic Roman 1122½ V. R. Swift 1172½ Driving 10
16Oct87- 2Pim fst 1 1/16 :47⅘ 1:13 1:46⅘ 3+ⓕClm 5000 6 6 56½ 65 75½ 85 Ladner C J Jr b 117 5.20 66-22 Island Treasure 117nk Second Marphe 114hdHandyFare1132 Tired 8
8Oct87- 2Pim fst 6f :24⅕ :48⅘ 1:14⅕ ⓕClm 5000 3 4 32 31½ 1hd 22 Hutton G W b 114 5.00 73-24 Brush 1092 Little Ignat 1144½ Kallistre 114no Weakened 8
27Sep87- 2Pim fst 6f :24 :48 1:14 ⓕClm 5000 7 10 105½ 79 44½ 2nk Ladner C J Jr b 114 4.80 76-19 Whiskey Mama 115nk Little Ignat 1142½ Ellen's Baby 119nk Hung 11
17Sep87- 1Pim fst 6f :24 :48⅘ 1:14 ⓕClm 5000 6 6 46 45 31½ 2no Ladner C J Jr b 114 4.80 76-24 Centipede 115no Little Ignat 1141 Kallistre 1142 Lost whip 6

Clearly, she rebels against the handicapping principle that a second-place finish is an indication of a rounding into form. Extracting her pattern from the past performances, we observe the traits of a dedicated nonconformist. She belittles "recency" while she chooses the path of "route-to-sprint" because most of her colleagues find that situation displeasurable.

	Distance	*Finish*
9Apr88	6F	1no
6Mar88	1 1/16M	$4^{2\frac{3}{4}}$
9Feb88	6F	2no
7Dec87	mile	4^{4}
21Nov87	6½F	1^{2}
16Oct87	1 1/16M	8^{5}

In order to fire her best shot, Little Ignat seems to need a freshening period (short layoff)—relative to her usual schedule of a race every ten days or so—as well as a prior route race to set up the sprint. She shows a nearly identical vacation period of slightly over a month prior to each of her victories. Can a horse remember that its previous race over a month ago had the slower pace characteristics of a route? The pattern seems more coincidental than founded on handicapping logic.

But Little Ignat is a nonconformist; perhaps her route races served a function of prep *before* a freshening period. Horses remember images and stimuli; perhaps the slower-paced route races functioned as going-away parties to usher in a vacation so that her "racing memory" going into the comeback race would be positive.

Let not my reputation as a horse-race handicapper rest on this farfetched speculation. In concrete terms, the trainer has created or uncovered a training pattern that is very effective for Little Ignat and reinforces the special understanding between horse and trainer. Prior to creating (or stumbling upon) this winning pattern, the trainer was aware that sprint races with recency did not lead to victory; so he inverted the pattern into route race plus no recency to lead up to a peak sprint performance.

The best explanation for Little Ignat's adjustment to the odd training pattern comes from a quote by Yogi Berra: for Little Ignat "it was déjà vu all over again."

Winning Pattern for a Losing Horse

When thoroughbred talent and health were partitioned out by the Horse God, *Equal Share* did not get a fair portion. We pick up his career after 21 starts. In 13 of those efforts, Equal Share finished eight or more lengths behind. Twice he went to post above the tote-board limit of 99–1. Many a horse in the image of Equal Share will never win a race. In order for this kind to reach the winners' circle, a superb training effort is required.

What we want to understand is how Equal Share won on April 21, 1988, and why the public allowed him to pay off at 22–1. We go back to his previous victory and observe that he won while moving from *sprint to route*. The only other time in his up-and-down career that he had gone from sprint to route (from prior past performances), he finished *second by only ¾ lengths at 22–1*.

Following the October 21 victory, Equal Share moves down south and loses his edge, lapsing into a phase of horrendous races that parallel other skid-row periods of his career. A layoff and aborted comeback race tell his trainer/partner that only a special sequence of events can lead to a victory. In order to follow the prescribed sequence, perhaps by coincidence but more likely by design, he chooses a path in harmony with the horse's natural performance cycle. That should mean *sprints to route*, and the trainer will respect the spirit of that law while at the same time contradicting the letter of the law. On March 28 and April 13, Ferreyra gets Equal Share to run two sprints, but within two routes. The poor finish position of the two route races covers up the fact that the sprints within are parallel to the two sprints that led to Equal Share's previous route victory.

Narrative Chronology:

Equal Phases in Equal Share's Career

A1 Horrendous races
A2 Improved sprints (including mediocre maiden win at bottom level)
A3 Peak performance, moves right into allowance, sprint to route, second by ¾ at 22–1 in a race far superior to his maiden victory

B1 Horrendous races
B2 Improved sprints (Oct 10, Oct 21)
B3 Peak performance in route, wins at 3–1

C1 Horrendous races
C2 Improved sprints, *within routes* (March 28, April 13)
C3 Peak performance in route (wins at 22–1)

Was phase C2 a stroke of genius on the part of the trainer or was it the horse, running faithful to his cycle in spite of the trainer? I'd like to think it was the trainer's intention, preferring to believe that the horse alone could not have dreamed up such a brilliant sequence. We do have one piece of objective evidence: Equal Share did not choose to enter himself (April 21) at precisely the same specialty distance (1^{70}) of his previous victory!

From the horseplayer's point of view, if prep phase C2 had been composed of sprint races instead of sprints within routes, both the form improvement and the pattern match would have been more obvious and 22–1 would have been an impossible dream.

Dictatorships vs. Partnerships

In trainer dictatorships the same successful-training pattern is imposed on different horses. In trainer-horse partnerships the training pattern is generated from the inherent performance cycle of the particular horse. In the abstract, one might divide these two categories into external and internal.

It has already been clarified that even when the inherent horse cycle is relatively independent of trainer intervention, trainer sensitivity (or lack of sensitivity) to the horse's natural performance phases will be to a greater or lesser extent embedded in the resulting form cycles.

ACCOMPLICES

In media coverage of horse racing, the rider usually receives more publicity than the trainer. After all, it's more romantic to guide an animal as it breaks from the gate, hustles into position, weaves in and out of horses, and charges down the stretch at thirty-five miles per hour than it is to plan for the horse's diet, equipment, accounts, and racing schedule.

But it is more likely for a hot trainer to win with a cold rider (Matlow/Ortega) than the reverse. It was Brian Mayberry who chose Darryl McHargue for his mounts, not the other way around, and during the amazing Mayberry long-shot binge, McHargue's record for other trainers was no more than mediocre. Neil French put William Shoemaker aboard All In Tune when that filly was ready to win.

When the trainer is ready to dictate the results of a race, the rider is an accomplice who, like a skilled press secretary, stands before the prime-time audience so that the guy who wields the true power can remain tight-lipped and enigmatic, hiding his power in the early-morning shadows of shed row.

In every speed and pace figure, in every "objective" numerical image in the past performance, the presence of a trainer is somewhere secretly embedded.

CLAIMS

The fact that there are certain trainers who excel with recently-claimed horses is evidence of the partial trainer dictatorship. The trainer uses the same technique with different horses. The pattern is a reflection of the trainer and not the horse. Within this claim-dictatorship category, my favorite patterns involve: (a) claimed out of maiden race (recall Jokers Jig, Chapter 9) and (b) claimed, rested a whole month through the mandatory class-rise period ("jail"), then entered *above the price of the claim*. In these situations we now know that the trainer was not obligated to make a class jump. I had observed the Arterburn clan use this tactic in northern California, so when *Jaklin And Hide* fit the pattern, May 18, 1988, Hollywood Park, fifth race, this dictatorial move was more familiar to me than to southern Californians who had not bet the horses upstate. The horse was at a peak in form cycle, so the board odds of 20–1 seemed more than fair value.

Note that the date of today's race is only two days past the jail period. Also note that there is an excuse in the filly's last race. Tim Arterburn is not the only trainer to send handicappers a message about this filly; she has been claimed in three of her last four races.

What resulted in an extremely confusing race from a handicapping perspective offered a clear signal from the backstretch, where messages are usually enigmatic and contradictory. The rider, Mr. Corral, was a positive accomplice in the picture, as he had been producing a flat-bet profit as the meet's hot apprentice. At 5–1, Jaklin And Hide would have had to share the spotlight with four other legitimate contenders, but at 20–1, her trainer asset superseded the pace, class, and speed assets of the other contenders.

If trainer-dictatorship patterns sometimes contradict or supersede handicapping principles, trainer-partnership patterns tend to uphold the horse factors in the past performances.

FIFTH RACE
Hollywood
MAY 18, 1988

6 ½ FURLONGS. (1.15⅘) CLAIMING. Purse $21,000. Fillies and mares. 4-year-olds and upward. Weight, 121 lbs. Non-winners of two races since April 5 allowed 3 lbs.; of a race since then, 6 lbs. Claiming price $25,000; if for $22,500 allowed 2 lbs. (Races when entered for $20,000 or less not considered.)

Value of race $21,000; value to winner $11,550; second $4,200; third $3,150; fourth $1,575; fifth $525. Mutuel pool $282,556. Exacta pool $303,601.

Last Raced	Horse	Eqt.A.Wt	PP	St	¼	½	Str	Fin	Jockey	Cl'g Pr	Odds $1
16Apr88 2SA3	Jaklin And Hide	b 4 108	5	6	51½	31½	23½	12¾	Corral J R5	22500	21.60
30Apr88 4Hol3	Fancy Fogarty	b 4 115	6	5	2½	1½	1½	21¾	Stevens G L	25000	4.60
30Apr88 4Hol10	Encroach	b 4 117	12	1	101½	7½	61	3no	Pincay L Jr	25000	19.70
16Apr88 2SA1	Dear Morgana	4 115	1	12	9½	6hd	4½	42	Meza R Q	25000	13.00
3Apr88 2SA8	Egyptian Verdict	4 115	9	10	113	111½	7½	51½	Black C A	25000	53.80
30Apr88 4Hol2	Buy More	b 4 110	8	11	12	12	8½	61¾	Medero F5	25000	8.90
4May88 9Hol6	Oak Portal	b 5 115	7	4	1hd	2½	3hd	7½	Solis A	25000	6.80
24Apr88 1SA1	Lady Helcha	5 118	10	2	6hd	5½	91	82¾	Olivares F	25000	1.70
4May88 9Hol5	Many Passes	b 4 115	4	9	81	9½	102½	95	Castanon A L	25000	9.70
25Apr88 3SA8	Dynamite Kiss	b 4 116	3	8	3hd	41	51½	101¾	Delahoussaye E	25000	9.30
23Apr88 2SA1	Foxies Ego	4 115	2	7	41½	81½	111	111½	Sibille R	25000	25.10
6Mar88 5SA11	Zha Zhana	4 115	11	3	7½	101½	12	12	Patterson A	25000	121.80

OFF AT 3:37. Start good. Won driving. Time, :21⅗, :45, 1:10⅘, 1:17⅘ Track fast.

$2 Mutuel Prices:

5–JAKLIN AND HIDE	**45.20**	**19.60**	**10.20**
6–FANCY FOGARTY		**5.20**	**4.60**
12–ENCROACH			**10.80**

$2 EXACTA 5–6 PAID $261.80.

Gr. f, by Jaklin Klugman—Zaida S B, by True Knight. Trainer Arterburn Tim. Bred by El Rancho de Jaklin (Cal).

JAKLIN AND HIDE, never far back, got the lead a sixteenth out and drew clear. FANCY FOGARTY, a pace factor to the sixteenth marker, could not stay with JAKLIN AND HIDE in the last sixteenth. ENCROACH, outrun early and wide down the backstretch, came into the stretch four wide and finished willingly. DEAR MORGANA, outrun early, just missed the show. EGYPTIAN VERDICT was bumped in the intitial strides. BUY MORE, far back early while trailing and wide down the backstretch after being bumped in the opening strides, entered the stretch six wide and failed to menace. OAK PORTAL vied for the early lead and gave way. LADY HELCHA, outrun early, lacked a sufficient response when asked after a half and was five wide into the stretch. MANY PASSES had no apparent mishap. DYNAMITE KISS and FOXIES EGO, prominent early, faltered. ZHA ZHANA, wide down the backstretch, entered the stretch five wide and was bleeding from the nostrils when she returned to be unsaddled following the finish.

In the realm of claims, we find concrete evidence that winning patterns are more likely to be a discovery, rather than a creation, of the trainer. Whenever there is a claim, look carefully for an intent to enter the purchased horse in a context that mirrors its best previous efforts. In this way, as a new partner of the horse, the trainer tries to repeat the techniques of the old partner. Trainer intention and horse performance are integrated.

For example, Ronald Ellis claims a filly by the name of Symbolically, and for moire than symbolic reasons, he enters her at the precise seven-furlong specialty distance of two of her last three victories. Result: an $11.00 mutuel (April 17, 1987, SA, 5th). Oscar Barrera claims a horse by the name of Cedar Creek, who has just won going from dirt to turf. Barrera wheels him right back on the turf. One would expect a low payoff for a trainer who is known for such maneuvers, but Cedar Creek pays off at 22–1 (June 8, 1987, Bel, 3rd).

A most clever example of trainer-horse partnership where the claiming trainer spots the winning-horse pattern can be observed in the performances on page 194.

3rd Hollywood

START
6 FURLONGS
HOLLYWOOD PARK
FINISH

6 FURLONGS. (1.08¾) CLAIMING. Purse $21,000. Fillies. 3-year-olds. Weight, 122 lbs. Non-winners of two races at a mile or over since March 15 allowed 3 lbs.; such a race since then, 5 lbs. Claiming price $32,000; if for $28,000 allowed 2 lbs. (Races when entered for $25,000 or less not considered.)

Sanctify
Dk. b. or br. f. 3, by Great Above—Patrick's Eve, by Mr Leader
STEVENS G L 116 Br.—Folkerth T L & Judy (Cal) 1988 1 1 0 0 $9,350
Own.—Folkerth T L Tr.—Hendricks Dan L $32,000 1987 0 M 0 0
Lifetime 1 1 0 0 $9,350
18Mar88-2SA 6f :21⁴ :45⁴ 1:12³ft *2½ 117 2½ 1hd 11½ 16 StevensGL 10 ⒻM32000 75-18 Snctify,Thebndplyson,ElvnMystry 12
18Mar88—Bumped early
Apr 29 Hol 6f ft 1:13h Apr 17 Hol 6f ft 1:16²h Mar 17 SA 3f ft :36hg Mar 11 Hol 4f ft :48³hg

Monterey Pearl
Gr. f. 3, by Inverness Drive—Laguna Pearl, by Deep Diver
GRYDER A T 119 Br.—Chandler W C (Cal) 1988 3 1 1 1 $15,500
Own.—Chandler & Zimmerman Tr.—Ellis Ronald W $32,000 1987 0 M 0 0
Lifetime 3 1 1 1 $15,500
13Apr88-4SA 6f :21³ :45³ 1:12²ft 3½ 117 1½ 13 13½ 14 GrydrAT11 ⒻⓈM32000 76-22 MonteryPrl,MjsticLook,SNoFrckls 12
4Mar88-4SA 6f :21⁴ :45² 1:11³ft 6½ 117 1¹ 2hd 22½ 23½ GryderAT6 ⒻⓈM32000 76-19 PrningEgl,MontryPrl,AuntChrlott 12
11Feb88-2SA 6f :21³ :45³ 1:12²ft 3½ 112⁵ 2½ 1hd 21 35¾ Gryder A T3 ⒻM32000 71-23 CrystlSlew,MissCbriole,MontryPrl 11
Apr 25 SA 4f ft :48⁴h Apr 8 SA 5f ft 1:01¹h Apr 1 SA 6f ft 1:13¹h Mar 26 SA 5f ft 1:02²h

Cat Sneaker
Ch. f. 3, by Sunny North—Hi Heel Sneakers, by Phantom Pleasure
MCCARRON C J 119 Br.—Saunders D Jr (Tex) 1988 6 1 1 1 $19,425
Own.—Collins C & Saunders D Jr Tr.—Tinsley J E Jr $32,000 1987 4 1 0 1 $6,550
Lifetime 10 2 1 2 $25,975
7Apr88-6SA 6f :21⁴ :45³ 1:11²ft 4¾ 114 11 1½ 11½ 1no Hawley S2 Ⓕ 28000 81-17 CatSneaker,Gail'sTale,DistntHour 12
25Mar88-1SA 6f :21⁴ :45⁴ 1:11⁴ft *3 114 11½ 11½ 12½ 32½ Stevens G L12 Ⓕ 22500 76-18 Distant Hour, Tis Fast,CatSneaker 12
25Mar88—Bumped late
12Mar88-1SA 6f :21³ :45³ 1:12 ft 4 108⁵ 12½ 12½ 11½ 55¾ BanderasAL11 Ⓕ 28000 72-19 MyFirst,LpOfLuxury,Jnie'sGdbout 11
24Feb88-2SA 6f :21³ :45¹ 1:12²ft 51 109⁵ 11½ 11½ 12 2nk Banderas AL5 Ⓕ 22500 76-24 SummerAllince,CtSnkr,RinbowBrt 11
27Jan88-3SA 6f :21³ :45¹ 1:12 ft 49 114 2hd 67 913 916¾ Black C A5 Ⓕ 25000 61-19 Bill'sMyStr,SorortyRush,AlohStks 10
14Jan88-3SA 6f :21³ :45² 1:11⁴ft 25 114 32½ 45 79½1115½ Hawley S4 Ⓕ 32000 64-21 Akalli, My Native Moon, Valhalla 12
30Dec87-5SA 6f :21⁴ :45¹ 1:12¹m 12 109⁵ 52½ 910 913 915¾ Banderas AL7 Ⓕ 40000 61-23 Tami'sSecret,Invierno,SexyNaskra 10
12Dec87-5Hol 6f :22² :46³ 1:12⁴ft 32 110⁵ 22½ 1hd 1hd 32¾ Banderas AL3 Ⓕ 35000 75-18 Rveneux,MeghnMcLeod,CtSneker 10
4Oct87-8Beu 6f :21⁴ :45⁴ 1:13²ft 5½ 116 2hd 21 44½ 67 Hughes S K7 ⒻAw6250 78-17 BsicllyLoveble,RceyRoutte,JetstDin 8
13Sep87-5Tdn 5f :22⁴ :47³ 1:00³sl 2 117 2hd 21½ 2hd 13 Rivera H Jr6 ⒻMdn 84-23 CatSneaker,PrincessRaquel,ElvirYo 9
Apr 30 Hol 4f ft :50¹h Apr 23 SA 4f ft :51h Apr 16 SA 3f gd :37²h Apr 2 SA 3f ft :36³h

Showerstime
Ch. f. 3, by Forget the Showers—Lovertime, by Old Time Nonsense
DELAHOUSSAYE E 116 Br.—Steele V M (Cal) 1988 3 0 0 1 $3,450
Own.—Friendly Natalie B Tr.—Fulton Jacque $32,000 1987 1 1 0 0 $8,250
Lifetime 4 1 0 1 $11,700
12Mar88-1SA 6f :21³ :45³ 1:12 ft *3½ 115 34 33 55½ 911¼ Sibille R 4 Ⓕ c32000 67-19 MyFirst,LpOfLuxury,Jnie'sGdbout 11
12Mar88—Lugged in 3/8-1/8
27Feb88-1SA 6f :22¹ :45³ 1:11 ft 26 115 1hd 2hd 22 36½ Sibille R 11 Ⓕ 40000 77-17 Bll'sMyStr,MyNtvMoon,Showrstm 11
14Feb88-6SA 6½f:21⁴ :44⁴ 1:17¹ft 52 115 44 44½ 69 711¼ Sibille R 10 ⒻAw32000 72-20 SuperAvie,WrningZone,TwiceTitld 10
14Feb88—Bumped start
19Dec87-4Hol 6f :22 :45³ 1:11²gd *8-5 118 1½ 11 12½ 12½ VlenzuelPA 5 ⒻM32000 85-10 Showerstim,PrningEgl,Trn'sFlight 12
Apr 25 SA 5f ft 1:00h Apr 17 SA 5f ft 1:01h Apr 10 SA 5f ft 1:01¹h Apr 3 SA 5f ft 1:01³h

Gail's Tale
Ro. f. 3, by Go to Sundown—Compra, by Promulgation
NORTH M J 107⁵ Br.—Searing Stock Farm (Cal) 1988 6 1 2 1 $18,000
Own.—Delaplane E E Tr.—Guiney Irv $28,000 1987 3 M 1 0 $3,000
Lifetime 9 1 3 1 $21,000
7Apr88-6SA 6f :21⁴ :45³ 1:11²ft 5½ 118 42½ 2½ 21½ 2no DelhoussyeE1 Ⓕ 32000 81-17 CatSneaker,Gail'sTale,DistntHour 12
7Apr88—Broke slowly
25Mar88-1SA 6f :21⁴ :45⁴ 1:11⁴ft 3½ 118 75½ 75½ 77 68 Sibille R3 Ⓕ c25000 71-18 Distant Hour, Tis Fast,CatSneaker 12
25Mar88—Broke slowly, bumped start; wide into stretch
4Mar88-2SA 6f :22¹ :45⁴ 1:11²ft 3½ 110⁵ 31½ 1hd 11½ 13½ BndersAL8 ⒻⓈM28000 81-19 Gail'sTle,CliforniPepper,LivelyLss 12
15Feb88-4SA 1⅛:47 1:13 1:47¹ft 4½ 117 44 87½ 917 1022½ Hawley S1 ⒻⓈM32000 42-22 CrelessFling,Cor'sScor,Trn'sFlight 10
15Feb88—Checked 1st turn
3Feb88-4SA 6f :22¹ :45³ 1:12¹ft 4½ 117 41½ 31½ 32½ 32 HawleyS11 ⒻⓈM32000 75-20 Bett'sBeuty,PreeningEgle,Gil'sTle 11
20Jan88-3SA 6f :22¹ :46 1:12³ft *7-5 115 53½ 24 22 22½ Hawley S6 ⒻⓈM28000 72-22 Jnie'sGdbout,Gil'sTle,StlthBombr 10
20Jan88—Bumped 5 1/2
31Dec87-6SA 6f :22² :46 1:11³gd 10 117 41¾ 44 711 719¾ Hawley S9 ⒻⓈMdn 60-19 Voila, Sadie B. Fast, Bett'sBeauty 10
13Dec87-6Hol 6f :22³ :45⁴ 1:11 ft 9½ 117 2hd 32½ 46½ 69¾ CastanonAL4 ⒻⓈMdn 77-13 Pirt'sAngl,SdiB.Fst,DsigningChris 10
26Nov87-4Hol 6½f:22 :45 1:19 ft 7½ 118 43 33 32½ 23 CstnonAL6 ⒻⓈM32000 80-18 MeghnMcLeod,Gil'sTle,BetTheHet 12
Apr 25 SA 5f ft 1:01¹h Apr 14 SA 5f ft 1:02²h Apr 3 SA 3f ft :35¹h Mar 14 SA 3f ft :35³h

Pleasing Hostess
Ch. f. 3, by Native Host—Please Snow, by Think Snow
PEDROZA M A 115 Br.—Guest W D (Cal) 1988 2 1 0 1 $12,450
Own.—Guest W D Tr.—Andersen Laurie N $28,000 1987 0 M 0 0
Lifetime 2 1 0 1 $12,450
22Apr88-2SA 6f :21³ :45² 1:12 gd 6 115 2hd 1hd 12½ 12¾ PdrozMA3 ⒻⓈM28000 78-20 PlsngHostss,RdLghtDsc,CctsKtty 12
16Mar88-4SA 6f :22 :45⁴ 1:13 ft 28 115 31 2hd 21½ 34 PdrzMA11 ⒻⓈM28000 69-23 Ldy'sJkln,RunwyBlus,PlsngHostss 12
Apr 18 SA 5f ft 1:00⁴hg Apr 11 SA 5f ft 1:01³h Apr 4 SA 5f ft 1:04¹h Mar 28 SA 5f ft 1:02h

The trainer of *Showerstime*, Jacque Fulton, has claimed a horse that is one for one at Hollywood Park, *just before the meet of the horse's victory*. She gives the filly a freshening period of nearly two months; Showerstime has already shown evidence of running well fresh by having won as a first-time starter. It's a new trainer but two patterns match with the filly's previous career: recency and track.

While horse for course is not usually a factor at the longer meets, these are younger competitors who have never had the chance to acculturate to this particular racetrack. Turns out that Showerstime is the only participant in today's event to have won before at this venue.

THIRD RACE
Hollywood
MAY 4, 1988

6 FURLONGS. (1.08⅗) CLAIMING. Purse $21,000. Fillies. 3-year-olds. Weight, 122 lbs. Non-winners of two races since March 22 allowed 3 lbs.; a race since then, 6 lbs. Claiming price $32,000; for each 2,000 to $28,000, allowed 2 lbs. (Races when entered for $25,000 or less not considered.)

Value of race $21,000; value to winner $11,550; second $4,200; third $3,150; fourth $1,575; fifth $525. Mutuel pool $219,574. Exacta pool $283,808.

Last Raced	Horse	Eq	A.Wt	PP	St	¼	½	Str	Fin	Jockey	Cl'g Pr	Odds $1
12Mar88 ^{1}SA^{9}	Showerstime	b	3 116	4	3	3^{1}	2^{1}	1^{hd}	$1^{2\frac{3}{4}}$	Delahoussaye E	32000	3.50
7Apr88 ^{6}SA^{1}	Cat Sneaker		3 119	3	1	$2^{1\frac{1}{2}}$	1^{hd}	$2^{2\frac{1}{2}}$	$2^{1\frac{1}{2}}$	McCarron C J	32000	4.60
7Apr88 ^{6}SA^{2}	Gail's Tale		3 109	5	5	5^{1}	$4^{\frac{1}{2}}$	$4^{1\frac{1}{2}}$	3^{nk}	North M J^{5}	28000	2.00
18Mar88 ^{2}SA^{1}	Sanctify	b	3 116	1	6	6	6	5^{hd}	4^{nk}	Stevens G L	32000	3.30
22Apr88 ^{2}SA^{1}	Pleasing Hostess		3 115	6	2	$4^{\frac{1}{2}}$	$5^{1\frac{1}{2}}$	3^{hd}	5^{7}	Pedroza M A	28000	8.70
13Apr88 ^{4}SA^{1}	Monterey Pearl		3 119	2	4	1^{hd}	3^{hd}	6	6	Gryder A T	32000	7.10

OFF AT 2:36. Start good. Won driving. Time, :22⅕, :45⅕, :58, 1:12⅘ Track fast.

$2 Mutuel Prices:			
4-SHOWERSTIME	9.00	4.80	3.40
3-CAT SNEAKER		5.00	3.00
5-GAIL'S TALE			2.80

$2 EXACTA 4–3 PAID $53.40.

Ch. f, by Forget the Showers—Lovertime, by Old Time Nonsense. Trainer Fulton Jacque. Bred by Steele V M (Cal).

Watch carefully for claims just prior to a meet where the claimed horse has had its previous success. In general, handicappers should monitor all claims for those occasions when the new trainer enters the horse in a context that displays a sensitivity to the horse's inherent form cycle.

Successful horse-trainer partnerships that have followed claims suggest that trainers are more likely to discover successful performance cycles than to create them.

SUMMARY: THE CONCEPTUAL PAST PERFORMANCES

As we approach the Workshop section of *Thoroughbred Cycles*, we have now observed that many horse and trainer cycles do not obey the order of the past performances. Most trainer-horse partnerships have discovered and developed unique trajectories of horse performance. The chronological format of the past performances is the best friend of form-cycle handicappers because it tends to hide the more nonchronological patterns. The horse for course is a prime example, since it is a manifestation of space rather than time.

Other typical cycles also defy the linear mode of time. Past performances provide a camouflage for the master of a trade by covering up his consistent performance with irrelevant "exhibition" or practice races, which are inserted chronologically but not logically in between the races that truly count. Horses that display seasonal peaks, and those that win after layoffs, often will have their peak performances totally missing from the listed past performances.

In a show of respect for the form-cycle factor, several French racing papers display the past performances in conceptual order rather than within a strictly chronological format. These pps don't seriously disrupt the temporal order of things, as most recent races appear in their correct sequence. However, some races are omitted, replaced by more meaningful past performances.

Strategic insertions include "Best Performance this Track" (horse-for-course factor), "Best Performance this Distance" (when specialty distance becomes a factor), and "Best Performance this Season" (when a seasonal factor may be pertinent). Finish positions of the excluded races are footnoted in their proper chronological sequence.

Ironically, such a format tends to reduce the pari-mutuel value of certain form-cycle factors by increasing their visibility. On the other hand, a good clocker with reasonably accurate variants might achieve a successful ROI with pace handicapping because fractions are absent from French racing papers.

For my purposes, then, let the *Racing Form* continue to obstinately assume that chronological order is the best format. That way, I don't have to share conceptual order with the whole grandstand. Essentially, as form-cycle practitioners, we must reconstruct our own pps, in conceptual order. With a data base similar to the one used by the *Racing Form*, we could make some startling improvements, with some very simple changes.

Conceptual past performances: Exclude those races that, for one reason or another, are not illustrative of the horse's cycle, in order to go back farther and include:

Layoff Horses: first-time-starter race and any comeback races not appearing in the past ten race lines

Specialty Races: race lines of today's specialty distance/surface (turf sprint, dirt marathon, etc.)

Short Meets: races from the same meet, last year

Shippers: previous races at today's track

Distance and Surface Switches: last time horse made the same switch

Horse that Won Last Race: previous occasions when attempting to repeat

Horse Just Claimed: previous best race with today's trainer *if* this represents a "reclaim"

Rider Switch: previous race with today's rider if none in past ten races

We expect that the *Racing Form* bureaucracy will continue its strictly chronological format; the above changes are simple, and all involve accessible information. The less it's used by the public, the more it's valuable to us. For the form-cycle practitioner, chronologic is not the only logic.

Part IV

Handicappers

CHAPTER 11

Natural Highs, Natural Lows

NATURAL DISASTERS

HORSEPLAYERS LIVING IN FLORIDA hurricane territory, midwest tornado zones, and on the San Andreas fault in California, have one thing in common. From Hawthorne to Hialeah to Hollywood Park, the natural disaster most feared by horseplayers is the losing streak.

In the drama of player-performance cycles, the Monsoon of Bankroll Erosion always occupies center stage. Confronted with a funnel cloud on every horizon, most sensible and successful handicappers find refuge by taking irrational protective measures. I say "irrational" because the very strategies that flatten out the normal ups and downs of betting life will inevitably reduce return on investment.

Followers of Dr. Howard Sartin's pace methodology call for betting two horses to win in most races, thereby burdening their highly successful pace methodology with automatic losing bets. In William Scott's *Investing at the Racetrack*, the workout for his successful "ability time" method tallies win-place wagers, even though, as Dick Mitchell once pointed out, Scott's return on investment would have improved by going for two units to win rather than one unit win, one unit place.

If we knew precisely whether we were 23, 28, or 34 percent handicappers, we could mathematically calculate our longest expected losing streak, as Dick Mitchell has spelled out in his works on money management. However, many highly competent handicappers with eclectic approaches will employ distinct methodologies simultaneously with varying win percentages, thus making it more difficult to anticipate the longest probable losing streak. The point that Mitchell makes is nevertheless relevant to a healthy and rational *betting attitude*: no matter what your mathematical expectation of hit rate in the long run, you can be sure to encounter losing streaks that will greatly exceed the normal distribution of losers.

The "natural disaster" of the horseplayer, then, is a mathematical phenomenon that is a function of the long-term percentage of winners. The classical recommendation for confronting the natural upward and downward cycle is to bet more when you are winning and less when you are losing. Many players do the opposite, pressing after a few losses, trying to get it all back in one stroke, applying the Martingale principle of increasing the bet after each loss. In the same way that panic will multiply the casualty rate during catastrophes, "pressing" will increase the impact of a losing streak beyond its natural proportions.

MAN-MADE DISASTERS

There are two types of losing streaks, the "natural" or mathematical, and the "man-made" or psychological. The second may reflect the inability to cope with the first or it may be independently generated. If my interpretation of Dr. Sartin's two-horse strategy is correct, players who collect more steadily are less prone to lapses in judgment that arise out of fear or desperation. In essence, this type of leveling-out strategy gives away a few points in ROI in exchange for the psychological well-being needed to ward off judgmental errors.

That makes a lot of sense. A good long-shot handicapper who only needs to collect 20 percent of the time for a substantial return on investment can expect *with mathematical certainty* to encounter losing streaks well beyond ten races. There are so many undercurrents of psychological pressures that can wash away the firm footing of the steadiest and most cold-blooded of horseplayers. No horseplayer in the world is completely exempt from momentary losses of self-confidence which result in the need to "press."

For example, consider a player who has now had nine losers in a row. In the next race he figures two contenders, a 5–2 "most likely winner" and a 10–1 long shot. The presser, aware that the

5–2 type will win more often, goes for that one. He needs to collect. If the 10–1 should win, the player will feel devastated. The two-horse methodology would have saved him from a deep psychological wound that might impair his handicapping over a nightmarish period of time. And, of course, had he subscribed to the two-horse concept prior to the nine-race disaster, he might never have encountered the losing streak to begin with. We are assuming, of course, a reasonable level of handicapping competence; poor handicappers will do poorly no matter what their method of money management. For them, losing is so normal that there is no such thing as a losing streak.

BIG BROTHER WATCHES

What happens when a monitoring service comes into town and argues that horse-race handicapping services should be monitored in the same way that sports betting services are overseen? Finally, a monitoring publication came to southern California and functioned as a *Consumer Report* for the horseplayer/consumer. To their credit and integrity, most of the professional touts signed up. Handicappers prone to self-flagellation during losing streaks should observe that these top handicappers were all subjected to long and sometimes embarrassing losing streaks. What Mitchell had proven with computer simulation had been reaffirmed by the monitor's "laboratory" tests.

Good handicappers with bad streaks would do well to feel that they are in the best of company, rather than allowing their egos to magnify the personal nature of a bad streak. Significantly, the one handicapping service that escaped extended losing periods and achieved the highest hit rate of all services monitored, failed to show a profitable return on investment three meets in a row.

That's not all. During one meet the folks with the highest hit rate (an amazing 40 percent of bets collected) had the greatest percentage of loss. At the same time, the service with one of the lowest hit rates (22 percent) came out with the highest percentage of profit (Steve Martin, Spectrum Sports). While this service was one of the most likely to suffer losing streaks, it was also the only monitored selection service to show a profit for three consecutive meets.

Now you tell me the reason for going to the track: to walk up to the window and collect regularly while little by little your pockets empty and thread by thread the shirt comes off your back, or to finish the meet with a profit? As a consumer advocate, the monitoring service failed to highlight the difference between return on investment and percentage of winners. The monitors came from the culture of sports betting, where there is a direct correlation between hit rate and return on investment.

The lesson for us is that we tend to confront losing streaks subjectively and out of context, magnifying their importance and thereby risking adverse psychological consequences.

The ultimate irony is that those services with a high hit rate plus negative ROI are more likely to keep their clients from one meet to the next. Most clients don't keep records. The slow leak of funds is less sensational than the longer losing streaks characteristic of the profitable service. Obviously this is but one case history. There are many ways to win at the races, and you are not obligated to ride the Steve Martin roller coaster. You can choose methods with a higher percentage of winners. The point is, though, that losing streaks are a natural phase in the inevitable ups and downs of horseplayer cycles. A losing streak for a good handicapper will not turn into a man-made disaster unless there is intervention of an unhealthy psychological attitude, which may be manifest in:

1. Chasing lower than fair prices
2. Increasing rather than decreasing the size of the wager
3. Flippantly chasing impossible combinations in order to "get it all back" at once
4. Overhandicapping

Point 3 involves underhandicapping. The player has lost confidence, and so there is no need to use analytical procedures that have not been working. This rejection of self leads to shortcuts that are "other directed," with greater attention directed to public handicappers and tote-board angles. Deep down inside, the horseplayer knows that this superficial process will get him nowhere in the long run, but he hopes that in the short run it will bail him out. To compensate for the one-dimensional approach, he will compound the nightmare by doing combination wagers which include more horses and also ensure more automatic losing tickets.

Point 4 deserves special attention because the best handicappers, those who are wise enough to avoid 1, 2, and 3, are susceptible to the type of overhandicapping that compounds a natural losing streak geometrically into catastrophic proportions.

THE NIGHTMARE OF DQ

Don Quick's friends call him DQ because, in cases of inquiry, it's usually his horse that's disqualified. On Sunday, May 8, 1988, DQ is at the track with his buddy Sancho. DQ is the optimist who heroically puts his capital on long shots, while Sancho is the realist who will only bet when everything looks perfect.

DQ has been in a prolonged slump, as reflected by the results of the first race, in which his long shot at 28–1 finished second to Sancho's $3.80 favorite. Both pass the second race, Sancho, out of fear of losing his slim profit, and DQ because of temporary paralysis. The two are standing near the rail, midstretch, studying the past performances of horses in the third race. It is a maiden race, which brings out the fear of the unknown in Sancho. DQ loves maiden races because they represent a time of hope and romantic expectation in the careers of potential champions.

Between races there is always time to think. Sometimes too much thinking creeps into the head. Don Quick's losing streak is magnified by the mind, grows out of proportion, like the piles of *Racing Forms* in his bedroom, on his desk, on the floor, in the closet. He thinks . . .

His daughter and son-in-law begged him to go to the amusement park today with his granddaughter. Today's invitation is not an isolated event but part of his daughter's master plan to take him away from what she calls his "madness." Yes, she thinks he is a madman, waking up in the morning at seven-thirty to get the scratches, as if he were young and didn't need the sleep. His daughter goes into his bedroom to finish her housecleaning and she stumbles over a pile of *Racing Forms* from two years ago. She cries out, "When are you going to stop this folly?"

The bugle has not yet sounded for the post parade, and Don Quick continues to ponder. His slump has debilitated his self-confidence. Between flashes of the tote board, there is a flash in his head . . . "Maybe my daughter is right, maybe I am insane."

He considers the alternative. Instead of his personal betting roller coaster, there are the amusement-park rides, which create fantasy, adventures, imaginary dangers. But here at the track it is the real thing, a true challenge, his youthful mind in his old body battling against giant odds.

Sure, he loves his granddaughter dearly, loves to watch the joy of her discoveries. But that is a vicarious satisfaction. He has passed up the chance to have a day of safe entertainment, a day in which he would feel like an outsider, a watcher, a man who lets things happen instead of creating. That kind of safety is not rewarding enough to give up the precarious adventures of the racetrack.

Between flashes of the tote board these thoughts have dented the armor of DQ's confidence as a handicapper. What he doesn't realize is that this moment of weakness is about to cause him to *overhandicap*. He looks down again at the past performances with a temporary renewal of confidence.

"*Heed The Storm* has one of my favorite form cycle angles," comments DQ. "As a two-year-old she was raced once and *bet heavily*. When she didn't run as expected, the trainer, not wanting to create a child-prodigy disaster, laid the horse off until she matured. Here's the angle: well-bet two-year-old, runs poorly, laid off, comeback race as a three-year-old."

As usual, DQ speaks in a long-winded manner, while his partner is more blunt about things:

"She can't run. I like Tizzy Spree."

Once more Sancho is backing a horse that will go off at less than 2–1. Who needs a betting public? Sancho could serve as a one-man survey for discovering ahead of time which horses will be well bet by the crowd. His affinity with the public is so well-documented that track representatives might consider using him to set the odds, thus saving all the electricity and computer hours that go into running the tote board.

DQ, Sancho's unlikely partner, never fails to oppose the will of the crowd. He proceeds to analyze the race:

"Both Princess Decree and Tizzy Spree are proven losers against maiden claimers; they won't beat straight maidens. Piquant Miss is bred for the turf, so she won't win on the dirt, especially as a first-time starter at two turns. Skim has a similar pattern as Heed the Storm, but she didn't get the same degree of action as Heed the Storm. Both Runaway Barb and Splendid Cause have run terribly recently, which is worse than running terribly many months ago prior to a layoff."

Sancho is amazed how DQ could say all that in the same

3rd Golden Gate

GOLDEN GATE
1 MILE

1 MILE. (1.33) MAIDEN. Purse $15,000. Fillies and mares. 3-year-olds and upward. Weights, 3-year-olds, 114 lbs.; older, 123 lbs.

Princess Decree — Dk. b. or br. f. 4, by Verbatim—Supper, by Noble Decree
CAMARGO T 1185 — Br.—Roca Linda Thoroughbreds (Ky) 1988 3 M 1 0 $2,800
Tr.—Pierce Donald 1987 3 M 0 0
Own.—Escobar-Risdon-Risdon Lifetime 6 0 1 0 $2,800
17Mar88-2SA 1⅛ :473 1:131 1:524ft 40 1115 1hd 2hd 22½ 21¾ Sherman A B 2 Ⓕ 10000 63-20 TipASou,PrincessDecre,FistMoon 10
10Mar88-6SA 1 1/16 :471 1:122 1:461ft 94 1115 911 913 914 912¼ ShermnAB10 ⒻM45000 58-19 Fluttry,SurrndrDorothy,Chumcum 11
10Mar88—Wide
15Feb88-6SA 1 1/16 :472 1:124 1:454ft 34 117 57½ 713 817 719¼ FerndezAL6 ⒻM45000 52-22 Vigora, Cat Call, Bea's Luck 12
3Dec87-2Hol 1 1/16 :472 1:124 1:444ft 36 118 810 911 817 823¼ FernndezAL2 ⒻM32000 55-16 BldArrgnc,CtfshLdy,EvnngElswhr 10
14Nov87-4SA 1 1/16 :46 1:124 1:452ft 69 115 912 919 926 931¼ Baze G 8 Mdn 43-22 Syrian Wind, Silver Dude, Vysotsky 9
14Nov87—Broke slowly, bumped
14Oct87-6SA 6f :22 :452 1:094ft 60 117 814 814 817 818¾ Baze G2 ⒻMdn 70-16 SwetrThnSugr,TblFrolic,JstInnocnt 9
May 4 Hol 4f ft :52 h May 1 Hol 6f ft 1:143 h Apr 16 SA 6f gd 1:15 h Apr 9 SA 6f ft 1:162 h

Tizzy Spree — Ch. f. 3, by In Tissar—Buying Spree, by To Market
DIAZ A L 114 — Br.—Semler R H (Cal) 1988 6 M 3 0 $7,700
Tr.—Jenda Charles J 1987 0 M 0 0
Own.—Semler R H Lifetime 6 0 3 0 $7,700
24Apr88-3GG 1 :462 1:111 1:37 ft 5½ 114 12 11½ 2hd 22 Diaz A L7 ⒻMdn 81-14 YukonLiz,TizzySpree,SpiritualFntsy 7
31Mar88-4GG 6f :22 :451 1:111ft 3½ 117 32 31½ 2hd 2hd Diaz A L4 ⒻⓈM20000 83-20 LikGlorious,TizzySpr,NturllyFinicky 8
8Mar88-3GG 6f :221 :46 1:13 ft 2½ 117 79½ 710 613 611¾ Diaz A L 1 ⒻM32000 62-30 SherryLynnB.,LodiRed,SilverSabina 7
8Mar88—Lugged out turn
17Feb88-4GG 6f :22 :45 1:103ft 8½ 117 43 31 21 2½ Diaz A L8 ⒻM32000 85-13 ColorConnection,TizzySpre,CgyOn 11
17Jan88-7BM 6f :23 :48 1:143sy 4 117 2hd 4nk 44½ 511½ Diaz A L3 ⒻMdn 54-32 RdThCrds,CntssActn,ThrghThCrcks 7
17Jan88—Broke slowly
3Jan88-6BM 6f :222 :461 1:124sy 11 117 810 611 58 411½ Doocy T T7 ⒻMdn 63-28 Tellimr,ThroughThCrcks,RdThCrds 9
May 2 GG 1 ft 1:432 h Apr 22 GG 4f ft :484 h Apr 16 GG 4f ft :48 h Apr 10 GG 4f ft :473 h

Heed The Storm — Dk. b. or br. f. 3, by Storm Bird—Daeltown, by Dictus
CASTANEDA M 114 — Br.—Three Farms & Hewitt (Ky) 1987 1 M 0 0
Tr.—Drysdale Neil
Own.—Warren Mr-Mrs W K Jr Lifetime 1 0 0 0
24Oct87-3BM 6f :224 :462 1:122gd 4½ 118 68½ 78½ 814 814 Castaneda M7 ⒻMdn 63-20 AmyLouise,FaceCard,LittlePssword 8
May 3 Hol 5f ft 1:022 h Apr 28 Hol 3f ft :371 h Apr 23 Hol 5f ft 1:03 h Apr 13 Hol 6f ft 1:153 h

Piquant Miss — Ch. f. 3, by Bold Tropic—Mischievously, by Decidedly
KAENEL J L 114 — Br.—Cardiff Stud Farm (Cal) 1987 0 M 0 0
Tr.—Fanning Brett C
Own.—Cardiff Stud Farm Lifetime 0 0 0 0
Apr 27 SA 6f ft 1:142 h Apr 21 SA 5f sy 1:032 h (d) Apr 14 SA 5f ft 1:022 h Apr 8 SA 5f ft 1:02 h

Skim — B. f. 3, by Nijinsky II—Pass a Glance, by Buckpasser
BAZE R A 114 — Br.—King Ranch Inc (Ky) 1987 2 M 0 0 $600
Tr.—Drysdale Neil
Own.—King Ranch Lifetime 2 0 0 0 $600
5Dec87-7Hol 6f :221 :454 1:111m 6½ 118 98½ 77 56 510 Vasquez J1 ⒻMdn 76-17 FlorlMgic,GrriNJoGo,WlkInThPrk 10
22Nov87-2Hol 6f :214 :451 1:104ft 8½ 117 911 89 75½ 68½ Pincay L Jr11 ⒻMdn 82-14 LittleBrFly,GoldSel,LittlePssword 12
22Nov87—Bumped hard start
May 4 Hol 4f ft :471 h Apr 29 Hol 6f ft 1:142 h Apr 10 Hol 6f ft 1:131 h Mar 19 Hol 7f ft 1:273 h

Runaway Barb — Dk. b. or br. f. 3, by Runaway Groom—Barbsie, by T V Lark
WARREN R J JR 114 — Br.—New Horizon Parnership Xiv (Cal) 1988 2 M 0 0 $1,350
Tr.—Fierce Fordell 1987 0 M 0 0
Own.—CloverRcingStbl(Lessee)etl Lifetime 2 0 0 0 $1,350
24Apr88-3GG 1 :462 1:111 1:37 ft 5 114 68½ 58 48 511½ Warren R J Jr5 ⒻMdn 71-14 YukonLiz,TizzySpree,SpiritualFntsy 7
10Mar88-4GG 6f :214 :443 1:11 ft 34 117 818 815 812 41¾ Warren R J Jr2 ⒻMdn 82-13 Balclutha, Bodhisottva, Rousing 8
May 4 GG 5f ft 1:003 h Apr 16 GG 4f ft :504 h Apr 6 GG 5f ft 1:011 h Mar 13 SA 4f ft :514 h

Splendid Cause — Dk. b. or br. f. 4, by Caucasus—Passing Fair, by Buckpasser
MAPLE S 123 — Br.—Sorensen Heather D (Cal) 1988 3 M 0 0 $1,050
Tr.—Offield Duane 1987 1 M 0 0 $275
Own.—Sorensen Heather D Lifetime 4 0 0 0 $1,325
24Apr88-3GG 1 :462 1:111 1:37 ft 12 123 48 610 719 621½ Maple S 2 ⒻMdn 61-14 YukonLiz,TizzySpree,SpiritualFntsy 7
1Mar88-1GG 1 :473 1:131 1:392ft 11 120 21½ 3nk 32½ 43 Maple S 2 ⒻMdn 68-24 CatfishLady,SpiritualFantsy,LChrc 7
23Jan88-5GG 6f :213 :443 1:111sy 18 120 714 712 716 77¾ Fuentes F P3 ⒻMdn 75-19 Druidin,TouchThSpindl,RfrshngPus 7
23Jan88—Broke slowly
28Dec87-5BM 6f :222 :453 1:104ft 52 119 88½ 88 67 56 Fuentes F P3 ⒻMdn 80-18 FlThMusic,RfrshingPus,ScrtWhispr 8
28Dec87—Broke slowly
Apr 10 GG 5f ft 1:013 h Apr 1 GG 6f ft 1:16 h Mar 18 GG 6f ft 1:181 h Mar 12 GG 4f ft :484 h

breath. He is quick to respond: "But shouldn't Heed The Storm be getting more action? She's only 14–1."

DQ suffers another bout of momentary paralysis, this time laced with fear. The image of his losing streak coupled with the piece of sound logic from his friend are too much to bear. He recalls the extensive research he's done on this maiden comeback angle, and sure enough, the average mutuel is considerably lower than 14–1.

The battle against the odds is a lonely one. No loneliness is worse than that which one feels in a crowd. No one in the multitude, not even Sancho, can warn DQ that he'll be *overhandicapping* if he inflates the value of Sancho's piece of logic. Rarely does a specific case conform neatly, precisely to the general rules. Only a DQ debilitated by a losing phase in his performance cycle could possibly allow a tote-board phenomenon to supersede other factors.

Ordinarily DQ would find a way to rebut his partner. Most railbirds are now familiar with their daily arguments. During a normal period in DQ's handicapping life, he would say: "Of course, Sancho, you are indeed correct." And he would add, pompously, "But with long-shot handicapping, there is always something that looks wrong, something to stop the more cowardly among us from betting. If there weren't something *wrong* about the horse, you'd never get a good price."

But DQ has forgotten his normal argument because he has been rendered extremely vulnerable in the face of his current losing streak. Sancho has now disappeared as the strange dialogue of these two opposite beings comes to an end. As usual, there is something of truth in the convictions of both Sancho and DQ, for in horse-race handicapping the opposite of one profound truth is often another profound truth.

With Sancho gone, DQ begins to find other reasons for not betting on Heed The Storm. Perhaps Tizzy Spree isn't a proven loser. Perhaps she hates to sprint, and so her only route race against straight maidens may indicate her true potential. Once more DQ is overhandicapping; the fear of one more losing ticket leaves him wanting to see all factors in perfect confluence. For one moment he has become his partner, Sancho.

The horses go to post. They're in the gate. They're off. Heed The Storm, off a bit slowly. Sancho arrives as the horses round the far turn into the backstretch. Heed The Storm has taken the lead. DQ's fear of external forces has turned inward and become disgust. He has not bet on Heed The Storm, and now the onward charge of that filly is parallel to a fall when one is dreaming, a fall through the air that the dreamer is impotent to stop. The nearer Heed The Storm comes to the finish line, the nearer DQ is to hitting bottom.

As they reach the stretch, Heed The Storm begins to draw off. As she passes directly in front of Sancho and DQ, Sancho reaches into his pocket and draws out a ticket which shows $5 win on number 2, Heed The Storm. Sancho holds up the ticket in front of DQ's horror-stricken eyes.

"Don't tell me *you* bet it."

"Only a fiver. But it was worth a small bet after hearing your argument."

DQ does not have a losing ticket, and yet at this moment he has hit bottom. A bet on Heed The Storm would have expunged his losing streak from the record. It *would have* put him within the realm of his expected success level. He has overhandicapped and at the same time been vulnerable to the ideas of others. He has turned a natural low into a man-made catastrophe. He has boxed himself in psychologically because he did not recognize that his losing streak had been a normal mathematical phenomenon, until he tampered with it and made it worse.

THIRD RACE **1 MILE. (1.33) MAIDEN. Purse $15,000. Fillies and mares. 3-year-olds and upward. Weights, 3-year-olds, 114 lbs.; older, 123 lbs.**

Golden Gate

MAY 8, 1988

Value of race $15,000; value to winner $8,250; second $3,000; third $2,250; fourth $1,125; fifth $375. Mutuel pool $152,590.

Last Raced	Horse	Eqt.A.Wt	PP	St	¼	½	¾	Str	Fin	Jockey	Odds $1
24Oct87 3BM[8]	Heed The Storm	3 115	2	6	$1^{1\frac{1}{2}}$	$1^{\frac{1}{2}}$	$1^{1\frac{1}{2}}$	1^5	1^7	Castaneda M	14.20
24Apr88 3GG[6]	Splendid Cause	b 4 123	6	2	4^{hd}	$3^{\frac{1}{2}}$	3^1	2^2	$2^{3\frac{1}{2}}$	Maple S	16.00
24Apr88 3GG[5]	Runaway Barb	3 114	5	3	6	6	5	3^{hd}	$3^{1\frac{1}{2}}$	Warren R J Jr	7.00
5Dec87 7Hol[5]	Skim	b 3 115	4	4	5^5	4^1	4^3	4^1	$4^{3\frac{1}{2}}$	Baze R A	1.30
24Apr88 3GG[2]	Tizzy Spree	3 114	1	1	2^2	2^5	2^3	5	5	Diaz A L	1.60
	Piquant Miss	b 3 116	3	5	3^3	5^5	—	—	—	Kaenel J L	6.50

Piquant Miss, Eased.

OFF AT 1:36. Start good. Won handily. Time, :22⅘, :46⅕, 1:11⅘, 1:24⅘, 1:37⅗ Track fast.

$2 Mutuel Prices:

2-HEED THE STORM	30.40	12.80	5.80
6-SPLENDID CAUSE		11.60	4.80
5-RUNAWAY BARB			4.20

DQ left the track without saying good-bye to Sancho. On the way over the bridge into San Francisco, he contemplated what had happened. It was not a handicapping mistake, but rather, a decision-making error caused by overhandicapping. This city he was driving through seemed a natural place for a horseplayer, with its drastic hills, its incessant ups and downs.

That night DQ's granddaughter asks him to tell her a bedtime story. He turns off the light and picks up the story where he left off the night before, hoping to forget the races by losing himself in a fictional fantasy. Last night the main character had been hanging from a cliff . . . "and he hung from the edge," resumed DQ, "and he was losing his grip and he couldn't hold on anymore and he fell six thousand feet to the bottom of the canyon. The whole canyon trembled as he hit the ground."

"Hey," protested the girl. "That's not the way it should go."

"You're right, baby. Look, your mom will finish it for you. I've got to go out and get a *Racing Form* for tomorrow."

And he picked himself up off the floor of the canyon.

While DQ was on the way down toward the bottom, a guy standing a few feet away was in the midst of a hot streak. The hot handicapper fell prey to the opposite psychological phenomenon. He forgot that streaks are part of a natural sequence of events. Suddenly believing himself invincible, and miraculously forgetting he had ever lost a race, he begins to think that "luck" is on his side. As a consequence, he *underhandicaps*. He is now betting more money, as he is supposed to do when he's hot. But the whole reason he is riding high stems from the fact that his thorough and conscientious handicapping is bound to hit high periods. So now he's betting more money (which is right) and doing less handicapping (which is wrong). The result of this fateful equation is rapid erosion of bankroll. Very soon, as this unfortunate horseplayer rides down an escalator of his own making, two opposite escalators will cross paths. He will look over to the up escalator and see his colleague DQ. If you take a look at the grandstand, it appears that most people are either sitting or standing, but in reality they are either going up or down.

In some strange way, each and every one of these horseplayer cycles are related to diverse horse and trainer cycles which are part of the amazing thoroughbred universe.

If this universe were structured in a deterministic way, each time we as horseplayers reached a high point, certain horses or trainers would have had to converge at that same point. That vision is reserved for people who believe in fate and destiny. I believe that horseplayers can determine their own fate by not allowing natural highs and lows to turn into man-made disasters.

In the realm of thoroughbred cycles, the horseplayer can maintain a high plateau or stop a slump by being aware of horse and trainer cycles and taking advantage of them. Conceivably, a player at Santa Anita in 1987 who was at a low point in his personal handicapping could have salvaged the whole meet and even achieved a substantial profit by neutralizing his own slump and superimposing the hot streak of Brian Mayberry. The negative return on investment in his slumping handicapping could have been more than compensated for by the positive return on investment of the Brian Mayberry long-shot binge.

And if this player were aware of the coexistence of opposite cycles, he should have been betting less on those selections generated from his slumping handicapping and more on those wagers relating to the hot-trainer factor.

Handicappers who are critical thinkers will be able to distinguish between hot and cold factors within their own handicapping and adjust accordingly. Horseplayer cycles don't have to be a function of other forces around them. They can be modified in a positive direction as long as negative psychological attitudes are under restraint.

INDEPENDENT BANKROLLS

The most objective method for prolonging highs and minimizing lows in the handicapper's performance trajectory is to maintain a distinct bankroll for each type of investment. In each handicapper there are several handicappers. We are like department stores with several sections, some of which are doing better business than others.

For the owner of a business, it is common sense to keep separate records for distinct products. When the auto industries went into a terrible slump, it was one of their products, the gas guzzler, that threatened to obliterate their bankrolls. If these industries have survived, it is because they have been betting much less on gas guzzlers and more on factors that are doing well, such as economy cars and military vehicles. One day military vehicles will be sitting around gathering dust, and even South American dictators won't want to buy any. When this happens, the industries have a choice. They can start "pressing"—try to sell these things to amusement parks, desert ranches—or change production priorities, making subway cars for the city of Los Angeles.

This is common sense. And yet most handicappers consider all of their bets as part of the same bankroll. A cold streak may simply mean that one particular method is not functioning well. For example, lightly-raced allowance horses, usually a good bet, may be performing poorly because the whole generation of younger horses represents a mediocre "crop." Here is an objective reason for reducing or temporarily refraining from this type of wager. It is not the handicapper who was in a slump; a particular methodology was performing far below expectation because of temporary racing trends.

The player with separate bankrolls for distinct methodologies is in a good position to prevent the natural low from turning into a man-made disaster. Conversely, a portfolio of independent bankrolls will allow for maximum leverage when one particular factor is at a natural high. During a power outage, a general store will emphasize its candle and battery business; during a bias against closers, handicappers should promote their lone front-runner investments.

There are two ways to divide the handicapper's investment portfolio into compartments. The first relates to *form* and the second relates to *content*. In the first formal portfolio, divisions can be made according to type of bet (win, place, Pick 6, etc.) or type of race (dirt sprint, turf route, etc.). While the formal portfolio is better than no portfolio at all, it is less effective in reducing slumps and prolonging hot streaks than the second type of portfolio, based on content and *concept*. Most of the time, hot and cold streaks relate to something far more substantial than distance or type of bet.

An eclectic or comprehensive handicapper might wish to divide his portfolio into compartments based on pace, class, form, final time, and trainer, among other factors. The handicapper who follows the fundamentals of this particular book will most certainly have distinct bankrolls based on the different types of form cycles. The track switch/class drop, for example, deserves a completely separate bankroll. Bets on horses racing after a layoff would be another compartment. A particular hot trainer would demand a completely separate investment record.

Ultimately, each handicapper will create his own unique set of bankrolls, in which the form of each portfolio compartment will relate to the content of a handicapping factor or methodology. It is extremely difficult for one person to intervene in the subjective ups and downs of a colleague/handicapper. Subjectively, we must be self-critical enough to take our own corrective measures. But objectively, the use of independent bankrolls will enhance the value of hot factors while minimizing the lows.

CHAPTER 12

Workshops

LINES

THE PURPOSE OF the Workshop portion of *Thoroughbred Cycles* is to involve the reader as an active participant and colleague in unraveling the mystery of performance cycles. The reader is asked to handicap the following "card" of races, confronting the past performances in relation to the preceding chapters and making "investment" decisions based on the analysis of these races. The format will encourage the participant to do this work prior to the author's intervention.

Format

1. Past performance and selected support information for each race
   Reader's Analysis
2. Approximate post-time odds for each horse in the field
   Reader's Investment Decisions
3. Results of each race, with author's comments

Instructions

Step One involves eliminating noncontenders and isolating contenders. For practical reasons, we shall establish an easy-to-use, *abbreviated* betting-line procedure in which the participant will express the probability for each contender in terms of odds. The probability/odds relate to the definitive reality that in every horse race there is 100 percent probability that there will be a winner. Tote-board odds are purposely adjusted/distorted to add up to a 117 percent probability that a horse will win. That extra 17 percent (take varies from state to state) equals the track take and means that the odds on each horse are 17 percent lower than what the betting pools have made them. Seventeen percent lower odds falsely implies a 17 percent greater probability of winning (greater than each horse's "true" probability as it is appraised by the betting public). When the public is accurate, as it often is, that 17 percent is also equivalent to what is known as the player's *disadvantage*. By adhering to a 100 percent betting line, we negate that disadvantage. The 100 percent line gives each horse less of a probability, by 17 percent than with a 117 percent line. When you translate probabilities into odds, which we will do for you, lower probability means higher odds.

Example: We make a horse 5–2 (28 percent chance) on a 117 percent line. But if we have only 100 instead of 117 percentage points to distribute among all the horses in the field, we must lower the percentage probability on our 5–2 horse, as well as on each other horse. Assume that in this particular field a proportional lowering of each horse's probabilities now leaves our horse with a 25 percent chance. Twenty-five percent equals 3–1.

Now, if we are following the correct strategy, which is: "Demand your price; if you don't get it, don't bet it," then we will need higher odds in order to bet our 3–1 probable than we would have needed to bet our 5–2 probable. In other words, the 100 percent line assures that the player will only bet when there is value, when there is a true advantage. (Sometimes, in big races such as the Kentucky Derby, the program line adds up to over 130 percent, meaning that many horses will seem like overlays when they are not.)

To many readers these arguments may seem strange. To others, too complicated. To still others, too questionable. And to still others, too thought provoking to digest right on the spot and go directly into the workshop races. No problem. First of all, the workshop will function even if you don't agree with or don't immediately understand the betting-line concept. Secondly, by handicapping the workshop races and then reading the author's discussion, the betting-line concept will clarify itself. And third,

I have prepared a table with rigidly mechanical rules for attaching odds to your contenders. This table will be functional for handicappers who have never used a betting line; and those of you who have your own line technique or have read Barry Meadow, Dick Mitchell, or yours truly on the subject, may wish to make your own adjustments of this simple table.

The table assumes that competent handicappers will pick the winner between 67 and 80 percent of the time when allowed to choose up to four contenders.

Abbreviated Betting Line			
ranked contenders infield	*your line %*	*your line odds*	*odds needed for bet**
One Contender			
1	67	1–2	1–1
(rest of field)	(33)		
	100%		
Two Contenders			
1	40	3–2	2–1
2	35	9–5	5–2
(rest)	(25)		
	100%		
Three Contenders			
1	33	2–1	3–1
2	25	3–1	9–2
3	20	4–1	6–1
(rest)	(22)		
	100%		
Four Contenders			
1	28	5–2	7–2
2	22	7–2	5–1
3	16	5–1	8–1
4	14	6–1	9–1
(rest)	(20)		
	100%		

*(must be clearly higher than line)

Obviously there are all kinds of variations possible, especially in the spread between one contender and another. For example, a field of two contenders may find you rating them equally, or, in the field of four contenders you might feel stronger about your top choice and weaker about your second choice. For the purposes of the workshop, though, it is more practical to keep the odds lines as simple as possible, with one clear table for reference, so as not to distract from the theme of the book. Step One, then, finds the participant isolating the contender(s), referring to the odds-line table, and attaching betting-line odds to each contender.

Step Two involves a simple comparison of the contenders' line odds (your odds) to the tote-board odds at post time. With this comparison, it will become apparent which horse(s) will become investments. Example:

Your odds	Tote Odds	
Top Choice	2–1	7–5
Second Choice	3–1	5–1
Third Choice	4–1	4–1

This hypothetical situation finds your top choice as an underlay, meaning that its payoff is below fair market value. Your second choice becomes a wager because its payoff is considerably greater than what you judged to be fair. Your third choice is no bet since it offers no advantage. In order to make a profit at the races, you need your selections to pay off at over fair value, hence the term "overlay." If no horse is over fair value, there is no bet. Pass.

In Step Three, observe the outcome of the race and compare your analysis with the author's. In some instances you will have discovered something that the author missed. Pat yourself on the back and send me a letter. That way, I benefit from the dialogue. In other situations, you may have missed some important patterns or details. Don't be discouraged. It's not a test but a learning process. Good handicappers never stop learning. Remember, too, that I chose the races for the workshop and that would give me an unfair advantage if we had been in competition. Hopefully, the keen sense of competition typical of horseplayers will not enter into the process of Step Three. Your true competition is with yourself, to improve your ROI. And that is precisely my own position. Since we both are out to improve our ROI, we become colleagues. This may seem obvious to most of you, but I have witnessed workshop situations in many professions in which the participants' final goal becomes outdoing other participants instead of improving themselves. The more you learn about horse-race handicapping, the more it teaches you to be humble; the best horseplayers are those with the talent to learn from others.

Step Three should allow for dialogue. I have been fortunate to meet many of my readers and continue the dialogue. Hopefully, this will continue as a natural extension of these workshops.

Summary of Betting-Line Concepts

1. The only way to overcome the approximate 17 percent take is to base our own odds line on a true 100 percent total probabilities.
2. The only way to win at the races is by betting horses that will pay off at more than fair value. The betting line helps us to identify these overlays.
3. Line odds represent fair value. Theoretically that equates to breaking even. Therefore, we demand odds that are clearly above our line, or we don't bet.
4. Conceivably we can bet on second, third, or fourth choices, if their odds are clearly above our line odds.
5. Passing races is not easy; the line methodology helps us because it tells us numerically when to bet and when not to bet.
6. The betting-line procedure is analogous to living on a fixed income with the option of buying food, gas, clothes at a discount (overlay) and having money left over at the end of the month (profitable ROI) instead of buying everything at convenience-store prices (underlays) and running out of money at the end of the month.
7. Betting on second or third choices is surprisingly hard to understand for many competent handicappers, even though they do the same thing in their daily lifestyle. Example: You're looking for a three-bedroom, two-bath house where such houses should cost $150,000 (fair value-line odds). One day you find the perfect house (top choice), but it is selling for $300,000. No one in his right mind would buy (bet on) this unfair price (underlay). Why should investing on horses be any different than investing in

houses? You may end up buying no house (passing the race in a sellers' market) or buying a decent house (your second or third choice) at a much more favorable price.

How Thoroughbred Cycle Analysis Fits the Betting-Line Concept

The only way to find overlay situations in horse racing is to use (1) a method of analysis that is underestimated by the public, or (2) information underestimated or not used by the crowd. It is inherent to the pari-mutuel system that if you handicap in the same mode as the public, you will get less than fair odds and, regardless of your win percentage, you will end up with a flat-bet loss.

On the other hand, the betting public as an entity is an outstanding handicapper, achieving 33 percent winners year after year. Once you realize that your adversary is not dumb, and uses powerful weapons such as speed figures, pace analysis, class angles, and trainer stats, you'll accept the fact that you can't confront this enemy head on, that you must use strategies that circumvent the power of your sophisticated adversary.

This calls for employing a handicapping methodology that relies on information and analysis that is underused and therefore underbet by the majority. Performance-cycle analysis will produce built-in overlays because it will point to horses with a higher average mutuel. The betting lines in this workshop offer a way to document and quantify the dynamics of this betting advantage inherent in cycle handicapping.

Horses you select through classical handicapping will less likely be overlayed than horses pointed out through performance-cycle analysis. The workshops and corresponding betting lines will provide a powerful image of this reality.

Ten races obviously will not cover the infinite variations on the theme of horse and trainer cycles. The achievement of workshops is to involve the reader, to provide hands-on experience to accompany the theoretical and statistical illustrations of prior chapters. The workshops also allow the author to share the profound joy that this most challenging lifestyle has to offer.

Without the workshops the expository sections of this book would be in danger of vanishing into the world of abstractions. The workshops represent a second time around the course, an experiential connection, under fire, to the conceptual exposition.

WORKSHOP ONE

May 8, 1988

5th Golden Gate

6 FURLONGS. (1.07¾) CLAIMING. Purse $10,000. 4-year-olds and upward. Weight, 122 lbs. Non-winners of two races since February 15 allowed 3 lbs.; a race since then, 5 lbs. Claiming price $12,500; if for $10,500 allowed 2 lbs. (Races when entered for $10,000 or less not considered.)

Norway Bay
CHAPMAN T M — 119
Own.—Plemmons J H
B. c. 4, by Belted Earl—Rhine Queen, by Rheingold
Br.—Lynnhaven Farm (Va) — 1988 3 1 0 0 $3,925
Tr.—Murphy G T — $12,500 — 1987 1 M 0 0
Lifetime 4 1 0 0 $3,925 — Turf 1 0 0 0
28Apr88-9GG 1 :452 1:103 1:364ft 27 116 1hd 2hd 32 59¾ Hansen R D8 10000 74-20 AlDeNskr,FrerJcqus,TkAGoodLook 8
16Apr88-5GG 1 1/16 ①:4741:1221:452fm 28 119 54 74½117½118¾ ChapmnTM10 Aw18000 66-25 TrveldInSrch,Robigus,CbinvtBridg 12
6Apr88-1GG 6f :214 :451 1:11 ft 5 120 11 13 16 15 Chapman TM7 M12500 84-20 NrwyBy,RhythmcSn,AmblsAmrcn 11
10Oct87-2Lga 6f :221 :452 1:102ft 3 120 95½ 811 818 913 Mills J W 7 M32000 71-18 Kiwiland,Dr.RickC.,LydirdTregoze 12
Apr 23 GG 5f m 1:05 h (d) — Apr 12 GG ① 5f fm 1:031 h (d) — Mar 30 GG 6f ft 1:132 h — Mar 24 GG 6f ft 1:142 h

***Mutown**
DIAZ A L — 117
Own.—Rubin S
B. c. 4, by Georgetown—Muya, by Venusto
Br.—Haras La Bernardina (Arg) — 1988 5 0 1 0 $1,500
Tr.—McAnally Ronald — $12,500 — 1987 4 1 0 0 $11,456
Lifetime 10 2 1 0 $18,500 — Turf 5 2 0 0 $17,000
16Apr88-7GG 6f :211 :434 1:092ft 9 117 45½ 57½ 710 75¼ Chapman T M 5 12500 87-13 FrOutPlsr,‡ScootrWfr,MnOfThHor 8
16Apr88—Placed sixth through disqualification; Bumped 4 1/2
20Mar88-5GG 6f :213 :442 1:092ft 14 117 35 32 35½ 25 Chapman T M 2 10000 87-15 Court Wizard, Mutown, Togiak 10
4Mar88-7GG 6f :214 :444 1:102ft 30 117 85½ 97¾ 913 88¼ Castaneda M 5 16000 78-26 VictoryPoise,PrfctFool,GloryQust 12
23Jan88-7SA a6½f ①:214 :4441:163fm 149 116 65¾111312191217¾ Meza R Q11 Aw35000 58-28 King Hill,Illumineux,JazzMusician 12
3Jan88-5SA a6½f ①:22 :45 1:154fm 86 116 53½1110¾11141117¼ Meza R Q11 Aw35000 63-23 Crystal Run,KingHill,GloryForever 12
14Nov87-6SA 6f :213 :45 1:11 ft 124 115 121511131112101 2¼ Baze G4 Aw31000 71-22 HppyInSpc,HICmmndr,SprbMmnt 12
12Sep87-7Dmr 1 ①:47 1:1141:373fm 14 116 68 712 819 821 Meza R Q6 Aw25000 62-16 OnTheCrpet,DerDingwll,Uptothhilt 8
12Sep87—Broke out, bumped; erratic down backstretch, 3/8 turn
27Feb87♦6Hipodromo(Arg) a5f :573hy 2½ 121 612 Caro J Cl G Kemmis(Gr2) Punk, LuckyNote, Effective 9
31Jan87♦6SanIsidro(Arg) a5f :572gd 4 121 ① 14 Caro J Cl Congreve(Gr3) Mutown, Lucky Note, Comisionada 5
22Dec86♦4SanIsidro(Arg) a4½f :512fm 14 121 ① 12 Caro J Pr Mudo(Mdn) Mutown, Sabatino, Queluz 7
May 4 GG 4f ft :482 h — Apr 27 GG 4f ft :501 h — Apr 9 GG 5f ft 1:001 h — Apr 3 GG 3f ft :38 h

Summa Sol SCRATCH
THOMAS D S — 119
Own.—G and G Stable & Knight
B. g. 4, by Mikinatool—Rae C Bee, by Kinstar
Br.—Decker Patricia A (Cal) — 1988 2 1 0 1 $3,638
Tr.—Knight Tom — $12,500 — 1986 0 M 0 0
Lifetime 2 1 0 1 $3,638
24Apr88-6GG 6f :213 :443 1:094ft 12 119 2hd 1hd 12 31½ Thomas D S7 8000 88-14 IrishBalcony,GreatSpirit,SummaSol 8
8Apr88-4GG 6f :22 :451 1:10 ft 3 120 11 1hd 1½ 11½ ♦ Thomas D S2 ⊞M12500 89-13 SummSol,GlintShuttl,Cptn'sEnvoy 12
♦ 8Apr88—Dead heat
May 6 GG 3f ft :361 h — Apr 2 GG 7f ft 1:273 h — Mar 26 GG 6f ft 1:14 h — Mar 19 GG 5f ft 1:011 h

Balmondancer
CAMARGO T — 112[5]
Own.—Hjelm Susan
B. g. 5, by Gray Dancer—Balimondo, by Balance of Power
Br.—Doebler J F (Wash) — 1988 5 3 0 1 $3,829
Tr.—Livingston Donald H — $12,500 — 1987 8 0 0 1 $1,160
Lifetime 25 4 2 4 $10,044
30Apr88-6GG 6f :22 :45 1:101ft 38 1125 1½ 21 41¾ 57 Camargo T 11 16000 81-17 ScootrWfr,AckAck'sJy,MnOfThHr 11
26Mar88-10PM 6f :221 :454 1:12 sy 3½ 122 12 12 11 1hd Youngren R 7 10000 87-20 Balmondncer,BoldMexicn,KingKos 8
9Mar88-8PM 6f :222 :461 1:121sy 7½ 122 1½ 1½ 13 14 Southwick W E 2 8000 86-28 Blmondncr,Brtt'sWtch,JustALttlRb 9
21Feb88-8YM 6f :224 :453 1:102ft 3½ 122 11 13 1hd 33½ Bryson D 2 Aw1100 86-15 SpanishLad,Sonaskra,Balmondncer 9
14Feb88-2YM 5f :223 :451 :572ft 3½ 119 11 12 13 17 Bryson D 2 5000 93-12 Blmondncr,BrutusBld,Amric'sPrinc 7
4Oct87-2Lga 6½f :214 :45 1:164ft 14 116 31½ 52½ 918 915¾ Gonsalves F A4 5000 69-14 JyBrBld,FirlyFstFrddy,Jon'sMmory 9
19Sep87-10YM 6f :222 :451 1:101ft 4½ 1145 3½ 2hd 78 717½ Romeo J6 Aw1000 73-15 J.B.Greesyheels,SuSu'sWy,ShstTim 7
7Sep87-9YM 6f :222 :444 1:103ft 6½ 1155 2hd 2½ 22 33½ Romeo J6 Aw1100 85-12 PlsntAppl,Pul'sAboutIt,Blmondncr 7
23Aug87-8Pla 6f :213 :443 1:101ft 12 117 57½ 57½ 411 512½ Stocke M D3 Aw2500 85-09 WynChampion,FalsePss,ElPuntero 7
20Jun87-1Hol 6f :214 :451 1:103ft 39 115 32½ 45½ 69 910 Valenzuela P A4 10000 80-11 SrEdgrAlln,Dn'sTryst,DmndCttrII 11
Apr 27 BM tr.1 4f ft :503 h

Agent Todd *
KAENEL J L — 117
Own.—Boston Garden West
Dk. b. or br. g. 5, by Capt Don—Gaelic's Image, by Gaelic Dancer
Br.—Simon Sandra M (Wash) — 1988 8 2 1 0 $12,400
Tr.—Fuller Richard — $12,500 — 1987 17 3 2 0 $17,502
Lifetime 33 8 3 0 $42,762
22Apr88-7GG 6f :213 :441 1:092ft 9-5 117 22 21 11½ 11 Kaenel J L 2 c10000 92-14 Agent Todd, CuttingLine,K.L'sPapa 9
14Apr88-3GG 6f :214 :443 1:093ft 2½ 117 21½ 11½ 11½ 14 Kaenel J L 7 8000 91-16 AgentTodd,FelthorpeMrinr,K.Gibrn 7
3Apr88-1SA 6½f :22 :451 1:171ft 6 116 52½ 53½ 46½ 89¾ DelahoussayeE 7 12500 75-18 Dr.Relity,AmAllChrgedUp,Michdill 12
12Mar88-7GG 6f :214 :443 1:09 ft 8½ 117 31 41½ 61¾ 63½ Hansen R D 4 16000 90-10 CuttingLin,StrtchItOut,BiscynBoy 11
27Feb88-7GG 6f :214 :45 1:104ft 12 119 68½ 79 511 55½ Fox W I Jr3 Aw16000 80-15 ShurSplendid,NorthwestTst,NtivFr 8
6Feb88-3GG 6f :214 :443 1:083ft 11 117 3nk 31½ 44½ 58½ Fox W I Jr2 25000 86-09 Mr.Medi,AckAck'sJoy,GentlemnJov 7
25Jan88-7GG 6f :214 :45 1:101ft 5½ 117 54 53½ 68 58 Fox W I Jr 5 c20000 82-15 Mr.Medi,HoveringPrsnc,NvdSwingr 7
17Jan88-3BM 6f :23 :461 1:121sy 8½ 117 44½ 44½ 45 2no Aragon V A 2 16000 78-32 K.L'sPapa,AgentTodd,StretchItOut 7
20Dec87-6BM 6f :223 :453 1:102ft 6 119 64½ 64½ 52½ 1hd Aragon V A 8 12500 87-18 AgentTodd,LordBlodgett,BenRdmd 8
20Dec87—Broke in a tangle
11Dec87-7BM 6f :222 :453 1:104gd 9 117 44 55½ 57 68½ Aragon V A 2 16000 75-30 K. L's Papa,NorthwestTest,Bledsoe 9
May 2 GG 4f ft :473 h — Mar 30 GG 6f ft 1:14 h — Mar 23 GG 5f ft :593 h — Mar 10 GG 4f ft :483 h

K. L's Papa *
Dk. b. or br. g. 6, by Pappagallo—K L's Lady, by Admiral's Voyage
NICOLO P 117
Br.—May H A (Wash) 1988 9 1 0 2 $9,000
Tr.—Yaka Roy $12,500 1987 16 4 5 2 $32,428
Own.—Snodgrass R Lifetime 55 11 12 7 $86,758

22Apr88-7GG 6f :213 :441 1:092ft 8½ 117 33 32½ 21½ 32½ Nicolo P 3 10000 89-14 Agent Todd, CuttingLine,K.L'sPapa 9
22Apr88—Ducked out start; drifted out stretch
7Apr88-7GG 6f :213 :44 1:091ft 8½ 117 65 910 1113 1014 SchvneveldtCP 2 16000 79-19 Mjsty'sRod,CourtWizrd,CrigRonld 12
26Mar88-6GG 1 1/16:464 1:104 1:423ft 10 117 75½ 64½ 812 812 Campbell B C 2 16000 74-15 Strelnikoff,CleverClayton,BlzeFlme 9
12Mar88-9GG 6f :211 :434 1:083ft 19 117 44 43 63½ 55½ SchvneveldtCP 5 25000 90-10 Tobn'sWsh,ShrpPrdcton,ShrSplndd 6
12Mar88—Bobbled start
28Feb88-5GG 6f :22 :443 1:092ft *2½ 119 87½ 85½ 108½ 108½ Doocy T T 10 c16000 84-12 Park Road, Witching, Walt 12
28Feb88—Broke in a tangle
11Feb88-7GG 6f :213 :44 1:091ft 8½ 117 22 32 33 3nk Doocy T T 7 20000 93-13 NorthwestTest,KenoKaptin,K.L'sPp 8
31Jan88-1SA 6f :22 :453 1:11 ft 9½ 117 63 63½ 96 77½ Pincay L Jr 12 20000 75-21 Melchip, Bum Bee Ray, Crack'n It 12
24Jan88-2SA 6½f:213 :442 1:164ft 9½ 114 46½ 69 612 912½ Hawley S 10 22500 74-18 GrowlerSndue,Ssebo,RedwoodBoy 12
24Jan88—Placed eighth through disqualification
17Jan88-3BM 6f :23 :461 1:121sy *2-3 119 2hd 1hd 13 1no Schacht R 4 c16000 78-32 K.L'sPapa,AgentTodd,StretchItOut 7
27Dec87-8BM 6f :22 :443 1:093ft 4½ 117 52¾ 42½ 32 2nk Schacht R 4 20000 91-22 Ack Ack's Joy,K.L'sPapa,ZarMoro 10

Happy Delaware
B. g. 4, by Happy Delegate—Delaware Dawn, by Delaware Chief
WARREN R J JR 117
Br.—Watson Sandra C (Ore) 1988 7 0 0 2 $2,160
Tr.—Glen James W $12,500 1987 9 1 3 1 $7,852
Own.—Watson Sandra Lifetime 21 4 5 3 $14,723 Turf 2 0 0 0 $450

28Apr88-9GG 1 :452 1:103 1:364ft 57 117 75 89 711 616½ Warren R J Jr4 20000 67-20 AlDeNskr,FrerJcqus,TkAGoodLook 8
3Apr88-8TuP a7½f ①:243 :4811:321fm 24 110 57 77 68½ 64 Iammarino MP5 17000 98 — Robert'sLuck,Rudy'sPrize,NtiveFell 8
20Mar88-9TuP 6½f:221 :442 1:153ft 15 114 21½ 43 75½ 74½ Iammarino MP6 16000 88-16 BlueGreene,SonoitBlue,SssyPrtner 7
12Mar88-9TuP 7f ①:223 :4521:242fm 14 114 35½ 38 46½ 44¾ IammrinoMP2 Aw7500 89-06 LifelongAmbition,Frezm,Rudy'sPriz 6
27Feb88-10TuP 5½f:213 :442 1:031ft 7 114 4nk 62½ 55½ 35 SteinbergPW4 Aw7000 87-17 Freezem,BoldCambro,HappyDelwre 7
6Feb88-8TuP 1 :46 1:104 1:361ft 19 112 23 31½ 34½ 34½ Iammarino MP2 12500 83-21 LotsOfWishes,SonoitBlu,HppyDlwr 7
23Jan88-10TuP 6f :213 :433 1:09 ft 23 114 58 58½ 48½ 48 Hadley R M7 Aw7500 81-18 PtoMundo,MinersvilleBluff,Grnspin 9
31Dec87-10TuP 6f :212 :44 1:091ft 38 114 44½ 44½ 58½ 58½ Hadley R M3 Aw7800 81-16 NturllyLucky,ToB.Noble,LtchKyKid 7
28Nov87-8TuP 1 :451 1:103 1:363ft 13 112 2hd 22 46½ 611½ Hadley R M8 Aw7400 75-16 TopJak,ThunderDuck,WeeWillieB. 10
11Nov87-11TuP 6f :212 :443 1:103ft 5 114 33 32 23 23 Hadley R M5 25000 78-23 ChrlieZee,HppyDelwre,BunnyBeter 7

Eldorado's Gold
Ch. g. 8, by Grey Eagle—Salty's Honey, by Deck Hand
SEGUNDO M A 117
Br.—Hanson Carol R (Cal) 1988 1 0 0 0
Tr.—Stewart Thomas J $12,500 1987 12 0 4 0 $9,124
Own.—The Stable of Oz Lifetime 62 7 10 9 $62,342

22Apr88-7GG 6f :213 :441 1:092ft 23 117 98¾ 814 813 814½ Segundo M A7 10000 77-14 Agent Todd, CuttingLine,K.L'sPapa 9
31Jly87-8SR 1⅛:462 1:104 1:494ft 4½ 116 1½ 11 11 1hd † Segundo M A8 A6250 88-15 ‡Eldorado'sGold,RpidAct,Schoenith 8
†31Jly87—Disqualified and placed second; Drifted out 1/16
21Jly87-10Sol 1⅛:471 1:111 1:503ft 4½ 115 1½ 1hd 1hd 2½ Segundo M A5 A6250 88-13 Rapid Act, Eldorado's Gold, Trajet 7
21Jly87—Drifted out into drive
6Jun87-3GG 1½:474 2:031 2:292ft 17 112 16 1hd 3nk 23 Segundo MA1 ⓈHcp0 97-07 Tbulr,Eldordo'sGold,SssfrsSummer 7
27May87-4GG 6f :22 :451 1:101ft 7½ 117 77½ 78 68½ 46½ Segundo M A3 8000 81-18 Transparent, What A Hoist,Secular 7
16May87-10GG 6f :21 :441 1:10 ft 25 117 1112 1012 85¾ 22½ Segundo M A11 6250 86-15 HustleUp,Eldordo'sGold,QueBuno 12
16May87—Wide turn
3May87-4GG 6f :214 :443 1:103ft 11 115 2hd 22 45½ 47 Segundo M A2 Ⓢ 7000 79-15 CallLeLulh,SirEdgrAlln,C.HowitFitz 7
22Apr87-9GG 1 1/16:464 1:112 1:441ft 16 116 78½ 813 818 719¾ Segundo M A6 8000 62-20 Snow Sioux, GueMerson,Siraluovat 9
27Mar87-3GG 1 :463 1:114 1:372ft 8 116 24 32½ 79 713½ Hummel C R3 12500 68-16 Manerly, Excess Profit, Miss A Bid 7
14Mar87-6GG 1 1/16:47 1:114 1:441m 16 116 1½ 21½ 36 414¾ Hummel C R4 12500 67-23 ScotT.NMe,Procurer,CptinPickring 8
Apr 15 GG 5f ft 1:013 h Apr 9 GG 3f ft :354 h Apr 2 GG 4f ft :49 h Mar 26 GG 4f ft :49 h

K. Gibran
Gr. h. 5, by Sure Fire—Real Money, by Real Luck
MAPLE S 117
Br.—Wakon Dr J (Cal) 1988 6 0 3 2 $7,875
Tr.—Offield Duane $12,500 1987 2 0 0 1 $1,875
Own.—Quinn J Lifetime 28 5 6 5 $84,970

14Apr88-3GG 6f :214 :443 1:093ft *8-5 117 54 21½ 21½ 34½ SchvneveldtCP5 c8000 86-16 AgentTodd,FelthorpeMrinr,K.Gibrn 7
14Apr88—Broke slowly, wide into stretch
1Apr88-7GG 6f :214 :443 1:093ft *2½ 117 51¾ 3½ 21½ 2¾ SchvaneveldtCP4 8000 90-15 Galnish, K. Gibran, Great Spirit 9
1Apr88—Bobbled start
22Mar88-3GG 6f :214 :444 1:103ft *8-5 117 2hd 1hd 1hd 2no SchvaneveldtCP1 8000 86-18 Galnish, K. Gibran, Irish Balcony 11
27Feb88-4GG 6f :214 :442 1:10 ft *2½ 117 31 1hd 1½ 32¾ SchvneveldtCP 1 10000 86-15 Perfect Fool, Say Man, K. Gibran 10
11Feb88-7GG 6f :213 :44 1:091ft *2½ 117 33½ 22 23 52½ SchvneveldtCP 1 20000 91-13 NorthwestTest,KenoKaptin,K.L'sPp 8
3Feb88-7GG 6f :22 :443 1:084ft 4½ 117 31½ 2½ 2hd 2hd SchvneveldtCP3 16000 95-12 Broad Jump, K. Gibran, Walt 10
27Dec87-8BM 6f :22 :443 1:093ft 10 117 78¾ 75¾ 88 107 Steiner J J8 c20000 84-22 Ack Ack's Joy,K.L'sPapa,ZarMoro 10
16Dec87-6BM 6f :221 :45 1:10 ft 5½ 117 33 21½ 31½ 34 Warren R J Jr2 25000 85-16 CordovaRed,GetUpAmerica,KGibrn 6
29Nov86-1Hol 6f :22 :453 1:104ft 14 117 78½ 77 78¾ 48½ Meza R Q 7 32000 83-12 AnotherBloom,Cbriome,GorgSlptHr 7
15Nov86-3Hol 6f :221 :452 1:10 ft 22 116 31 32½ 46½ 511 Kaenel J L 3 40000 82-14 Cracksman,RollANturl,PtriotGloves 6
Mar 18 GG 4f ft :50 h Mar 12 GG 4f ft :483 h

```
*Well Related                  Ch. g. 6, by Be My Guest—Second Bloom, by Double Jump
                               Br.—Shamrock Farms (Ire)              1988  7  0  0  2     $5,488
  HANSEN R D              117  Tr.—Jenda Charles J          $12,500  1987 11  1  0  1    $14,725
Own.—Goldstein S               Lifetime   40  3  5  6  $75,429      Turf 27  2  5  3    $57,241
16Apr88-7GG   6f :211 :434 1:092ft      11 117  814 812 69½ 54¼  Hansen R D 3      12500 88-13 FrOutPlsr,‡ScootrWfr,MnOfThHor 8
     16Apr88—Placed fourth through disqualification
31Mar88-7GG   1½(T):50 2:07 2:32 fm     4¼ 115  44½ 42½ 54½ 89   Baze R A 4       H12500 68-23 Secure II,LarryRoland,Abercrombie 9
26Mar88-9GG   1 1/16:453 1:103 1:424ft  5¼ 117  57½ 65 810 810¾  Castaneda M 3    16000 74-15 ITkeThFifth,Thquois,TkAGoodLook 9
12Mar88-10GG  1 1/16:461 1:101 1:412ft *3-2 117  711 64½ 65½ 45  Long B 8         c12500 87-10 GoSwiftly,Witin'ForBever,Bmidg 10
20Feb88-5GG   6f :22 :443 1:092ft       7½ 117  1011 97½ 75½ 52  Martinez O AJr 3 16000 90-12 Park Road, Witching, Walt       12
     20Feb88—Bumped start
6Feb88-7GG    1 1/16:453 1:10 1:411ft   7½ 117  913 77 44½ 33    Martinez O AJr 8 20000 90-09 BlondNtv,GoodThoghtWlly,WllRltd 9
10Jan88-11BM  1 1/16:472 1:121 1:454m   3½ 117  68 44½ 33 32¾   Warren R J Jr 8  20000 60-28 ExoticMotion,IronLeder,WellReltd 7
24Dec87-8BM   1 :471 1:112 1:354ft      7¾ 119  31 2hd 33½ 47    MrtinezOAJr 5Aw16000 82-22 Mean Cuisine, Art Of Dawn, Fly Up 5
5Dec87-6BM    1 :454 1:104 1:37 sy      9 114   711 67½ 49 38    Martinez O AJr 3 30000 75-22 AckLikeMe,SilverSurfer,WellRelted8
18Nov87-1BM   6f :221 :451 1:10 gd      6 117   56½ 54½ 41¾ 12½  Martinez O AJr 3 16000 89-19 WellRelated,NotbleHost,Numpkins 7
     May 2 GG 1ft 1:44 h
```

```
Dishonorable Guest             B. g. 5, by Grenfall—Table Flirt, by Round Table
                               Br.—Wygod M J (Ky)                    1988  7  0  0  1     $3,875
  BAZE R A                117  Tr.—Hellendorfer Jerry       $12,500  1987 22  3  2  2    $53,165
Own.—Hellendorfer-Tucker-Wong  Lifetime   34  5  2  4  $80,790      Turf  3  0  0  0
31Mar88-5SA   6f :214 :443 1:094ft      5 117   43 67 812 1114   Pincay L Jr 8    c16000 75-20 ClssicQuicki,RockEnSm,FirlyOmn 12
26Mar88-10SA  1 1/16:463 1:113 1:433ft  22 115  1½ 31½ 610 721¾  Gryder A T 5      25000 61-17 SiberinHero,HighRgrds,HighTouch 9
19Mar88-6SA   6f :211 :44 1:093ft       42 116  1013 912 78½ 58½ Velasquez J 3    25000 84-18 Fuzzy Bear, Bizeboy, Savio      11
     19Mar88—Pinched back, took up sharply start
5Mar88-2SA    6f :213 :444 1:092ft      24 115  85¾ 76½ 58 36½   Meza R Q 8       25000 84-14 ChynnTrpc,Pppy'sCnsl,DshnrblGst 12
28Feb88-5SA   6f :214 :443 1:094gd      42 116  72¾ 55 66 67¾   Velasquez J 7    32000 81-18 SundnceSqur,RulrOfFlts,NtivRlity 12
3Feb88-5SA    6½f:213 :442 1:163ft      22 115  74½ 74½ 54 911½  Velasquez J 2    32000 76-20 RoyalBlueEyes,Cliff'sPlace,Ssebo 10
     3Feb88—Broke in, bumped
27Jan88-9SA   6f :213 :443 1:094ft      22 116  96½ 99 89 87¾   Solis A 2        40000 81-19 Savio, Raise APound,SocietyRoad 11
31Dec87-5SA   6f :213 :443 1:112gd      19 116  44 44½ 44 96½   Velasquez J 1    c32000 75-19 LodTheWgon,IdelQulity,NtiveRlity 12
20Dec87-4Hol  6½f:221 :45 1:163ft       17 115  31½ 2hd 1hd 68¾  Meza R Q 4       35000 88-08 RisAPound,LuckyMsddo,MjstcIslnd 7
15Nov87-5SA   a6½f(T):21 :442 1:16 fm   70 115  66 63¾ 54½ 79½  Black C A 11     75000 69-26 BundleOfIron,HighHook,PrincSky 12
     May 6 GG 4f ft :481 hg     May 1 GG 5f ft 1:01 h     Apr 24 GG 5f gd 1:01 h     Apr 16 GG 4f ft :502 h
```

Golden Gate Fields Leading Jockeys and Trainers

(January 26 to May 7, Inclusive)

Jockey	Mts.	1st	2nd	3rd	Pct.
Baze R A	474	102	92	75	.22
Doocy T T	369	53	42	40	.14
Hansen R D	326	51	50	48	.16
Chapman T M	400	41	50	56	.10
Lambert J	286	38	42	31	.13
Castaneda M	264	35	26	32	.13
Warren R J Jr	274	31	31	34	.11
Kaenel J L	164	31	28	16	.19
Maple S	251	28	23	27	.11
Schvaneveldt C P	233	26	27	32	.11
Hummel C R	267	26	21	17	.10
*Camargo T	185	23	19	25	.12
Lamance C	201	22	19	21	.11
Diaz A L	205	19	34	21	.09
Tohill K S	290	19	30	34	.07

*Apprentice

(January 26 to May 7, Inclusive)

Trainer	Sts.	1st	2nd	3rd	Pct.
Hollendorfer Jerry	223	47	38	28	.21
Morey William J Jr	149	24	29	25	.16
Gilchrist Greg	85	22	21	14	.26
Arterburn Lonnie	86	20	14	13	.23
Utley Doug	122	17	14	13	.14
Fierce Fordell	91	17	11	18	.19
Dutton Jerry	132	16	22	19	.12
Knight Terry	52	16	9	5	.31
Greenman Walter	116	15	16	16	.13
Benedict Jim	82	15	15	5	.18
Martin R L	107	12	19	16	.11
Shoemaker Leonard	84	12	13	12	.14
Webb Bryan	81	11	17	3	.14
Hilling J M	81	11	11	14	.14
Sherman Art	98	10	13	15	.10

Approximate Odds, Post Time

Agent Todd	3–2
K. Gibran	5–1/6–1
Dishonorable Guest	6–1
Norway Bay	6–1/7–1
K.L's Papa	8–1

Well Related	9–1
Balmondancer	13–1
Mutown	16–1
El Dorado's Gold	40–1
Happy Delaware	50–1

Comments

Unlikely

1. Mutown, K.L's Papa, El Dorado's Gold, K. Gibran, and Well Related have all lost recent races at today's level and below. Double trouble in K. Gibran's last race suggests an improvement chance, but he hasn't won in two years.
2. Happy Delaware also lost at this level in a previous race, and since then has shown dull form against better.
3. Balmondancer's recent wins were at a minor-league track as an easy front runner, and his Golden Gate fraction (45.1) says he won't get the lead against the sharp riser, Agent Todd.
4. K.L's Papa's trouble against Agent Todd was self-inflicted, and he's a bad gate horse. His last and only win of 1988 was in the slop. He should move to Seattle.

Contenders

1. Agent Todd is a sharp horse now, *claimed while on the improve,* with a hot rider (Kaenel). His recent and improving speed figures outscore other horses who have races over the track.
2. Dishonorable Guest qualifies by our criteria for horses having three bad races in a row: *track switch/class drop.* Trainer Jerry Hollendorfer is fourth in percentage of winners, but none of the other trainers who make the standings, above him or below him, have horses in the race. He's the big fish in the small pond. The drop after the claim, usually a negative sign in the case of this trainer, will not be construed as negative; Hollendorfer spots his horses to win, and the horse's apparently dull form makes him virtually claim proof.

3. Norway Bay is only a possible contender; he has never beaten winners. But this is a weak field, and Norway Bay's sharp current form is partially eclipsed from the public for the following reasons:

   a. his April 16 race followed a layoff victory, so he was supposed to bounce, and he was on the wrong surface anyway

   b. his last race shows a sharp sprint within a route. Since routes are paced slower than sprints, this horse projects to shorten up to a speed figure that may rival that of Agent Todd

Of these three horses, Agent Todd is the only one without demerits, so he becomes the "most likely winner." The top two contenders are *five-year-old geldings*, as is Balmondancer, who has already reaped the benefits of the late-bloomer cycle.

	Our Line	Track Odds	Decision
Agent Todd	2–1	3–2	Under line, no bet
Dishonorable Guest	3–1	6–1	Over, *bet*
Norway Bay	4–1	6–1/7–1	Over, *bet*

Our line calls for bets on two horses, Dishonorable Guest and Norway Bay. In order to use two horses in the same race, the advantage must be greater than the "minimum acceptable odds," to compensate for the fact that at least one of the two horses will inevitably lose. Even when you win, the losing horse reduces the net return.

After the fact one could argue: if you've got two horses, why not just play the exacta? If the exacta is an overlay, by all means bet that too! Here, $290.50 was well above fair value. But you don't want to find yourself in the position, following a first-third finish, of saying, "I should've played 'em to win ... he paid $14.60." You don't want the big fish to get away while you are searching for Moby Dick.

FIFTH RACE
Golden Gate
MAY 8, 1988

6 FURLONGS. (1.07⅘) CLAIMING. Purse $10,000. 4-year-olds and upward. Weight, 122 lbs. Non-winners of two races since February 15 allowed 3 lbs.; a race since then, 5 lbs. Claiming price $12,500; if for $10,500 allowed 2 lbs. (Races when entered for $10,000 or less not considered.)

Value of race $10,000; value to winner $5,500; second $2,000; third $1,500; fourth $750; fifth $250. Mutuel pool $135,416. Exacta pool $179,714.

Last Raced	Horse	Eqt.	A.	Wt	PP	St	¼	½	Str	Fin	Jockey	Cl'g Pr	Odds $1
31Mar88 ^{5}SA^{11}	Dishonorable Guest	b	5	117	10	8	7½	4^2	2^{hd}	1^2	Baze R A	12500	6.30
28Apr88 ^{9}GG^5	Norway Bay		4	119	1	6	1½	1½	1^{hd}	2no	Chapman T M	12500	6.90
22Apr88 ^{7}GG^1	Agent Todd	b	5	117	4	4	3^2	3^3	3^4	3^4	Kaenel J L	12500	1.50
16Apr88 ^{7}GG^4	Well Related	b	6	117	9	10	10	10	8^2	4^2	Hansen R D	12500	9.00
22Apr88 ^{7}GG^3	K. L's Papa	b	6	117	5	2	5^{hd}	6^2	6½	5^{hd}	Nicolo P	12500	8.30
22Apr88 ^{7}GG^8	Eldorado's Gold		8	117	7	9	6^1	5^1	5^{hd}	6^1	Segundo M A	12500	39.90
28Apr88 ^{9}GG^6	Happy Delaware		4	117	6	1	$8^{1½}$	8½	7½	$7^{1½}$	Warren R J Jr	12500	49.90
16Apr88 ^{7}GG^6	Mutown	b	4	117	2	5	4^2	7^{hd}	9^2	8½	Diaz A L	12500	16.80
30Apr88 ^{6}GG^5	Balmondancer	b	5	112	3	3	2^1	2½	4^2	9^6	Camargo T^5	12500	13.00
14Apr88 ^{3}GG^3	K. Gibran		5	117	8	7	9^6	9^4	10	10	Maple S	12500	5.70

OFF AT 2:38. Start good. Won driving. Time, :21⅕, :44⅘, :57⅕, 1:10 Track fast.

$2 Mutuel Prices:

10–DISHONORABLE GUEST	14.60	7.60	4.60
1–NORWAY BAY		9.20	5.40
4–AGENT TODD			3.20

$5 EXACTA 10–1 PAID $290.50.

B. g, by Grenfall—Table Flirt, by Round Table. Trainer Hollendorfer Jerry. Bred by Wygod M J (Ky).

DISHONORABLE GUEST, reserved early, moved up outside on the turn, remained out into the stretch and rallied strongly to draw clear late. NORWAY BAY dueled for the lead from the outset, responded gamely in the drive and edged AGENT TODD for the place. The latter prompted the pace throughout and held on gamely in a long drive. WELL RELATED lagged far back early, came wide and found his best stride too late. K. L'S PAPA, reserved early, lacked the needed rally. MUTOWN was through early. BALMONDANCER pressed the pace for a half-mile and faltered. K. GIBRAN gave a dull effort.

Owners— 1, Hollendorfer-Tucker-Wong; 2, Plemmons J H ; 3, Boston Garden West; 4, Goldstein S; 5, Snodgress R; 6, The Stable of Oz; 7, Watson Sandra; 8, Rubin S; 9, Hjelm Susan; 10, Quinn J.

Trainers— 1, Hollendorfer Jerry; 2, Murphy G T; 3, Fuller Richard; 4, Jenda Charles J; 5, Yaka Roy; 6, Stewart Thomas J; 7, Glen James W; 8, McAnally Ronald; 9, Livingston Donald H; 10, Offield Duane.

Scratched—Summa Sol (24Apr88 ^{6}GG^3); Irish Balcony (24Apr88 ^{6}GG^1).

WORKSHOP TWO

May 12, 1988 (second day of meet, track *muddy*)

Even though Belmont is not a "short meet" (the type that most favors horses for courses), these are younger horses; in switching over to Belmont, many of these fillies may not have had the chance to become acclimated to *this particular track.* Which of these fillies may prefer this track? Which ones who are losers at other tracks may have Belmont victories that do not appear in the past performances?

5th Belmont

6 FURLONGS. (1.07⅘) CLAIMING. Purse $22,000. Fillies. 3-years-old. Weight, 121 lbs. Non-winners of two races since April 15 allowed 3 lbs. Of a race since then, 5 lbs. Claiming price $50,000; for each $2,500 to $45,000, 2 lbs. (Races when entered to be claimed for $40,000 or less not considered.)

Rajab's Tune

Ch. f. 3, by Rajab—Endless Tune, by Ever On
Own.—Rosbeck P Y — 111 5
Br.—Karutz Dr W S (Fla) — 1988 6 2 0 3 $35,880
Tr.—Lenzini John J Jr — $50,000 — 1987 0 M 0 0
Lifetime 6 2 0 3 $35,880

31Mar88-1Aqu	1	:472 1:124 1:384ft	9-5	112	61½	42	44	46¼	Santos J A5	Ⓕ 70000	65-30	SheldSyIt,Pggy'sProspct,Hlg'sHny	6
19Mar88-1Aqu	1	:472 1:124 1:39 ft	3½	116	62½	42	21	31¼	Kaenel J L6	Ⓕ 70000	69-23	Battlefront,ShouldSayIt,Rjb'sTune	7
5Mar88-3Aqu	1 1/16 ⊡	:4721:1221:45 gd	3	116	41½	31	1½	13½	Kaenel J L3	Ⓕ 35000	84-11	Rjb'sTune,Helg'sHoney,ByByBunny	7
18Feb88-3Aqu	6f ⊡	:223 :4641:122ft	12	115	31½	23	25	38	Kaenel J L1	Ⓕ 45000	74-23	LinksofGold,CraftyAlexs,Rjb'sTune	8
8Feb88-4Aqu	6f ⊡	:231 :4731:141ft	8½	117	2½	2½	12½	16	Kaenel J L3	ⒻM45000	73-24	Rajab's Tune, Dats Ruby, Senility	11
2Jan88-2Aqu	6f ⊡	:231 :4731:15 ft	2	117	2hd	2½	33½	33¾	Kaenel J L 8	ⒻM45000	65-30	Tatan Falls, Tagett, Rajab's Tune	12

May 9 Aqu 3f ft :36 h   May 1 Aqu 6f ft 1:153 h   Apr 25 Aqu 5f ft 1:01 h   Apr 18 Aqu 4f ft :491 b

Whisper Love

B. f. 3, by Baldski—Little Flutter, by Victoria Park
Own.—Maxwell Rita — 116
Br.—September Farm (Fla) — 1988 4 1 0 0 $8,185
Tr.—Domino Carl J — $50,000 — 1987 7 2 1 2 $17,428
Lifetime 11 3 1 2 $25,613 — Turf 1 0 0 0

8Apr88-6Aqu	6f	:222 :454 1:102m	11	116	616	69	612	617½	CordroAJr4	ⒻAw30000	78-17	NaturalElegance,Acquaint,Rocketai	6
8Apr88—Broke awkwardly													
13Mar88-9Crc	6f	:221 :461 1:131gd	14	112	108	610	59	46¾	Cruguet J11	ⒻAw12500	78-20	SturmndDrng,DoublePie,JoyAtLst	11
24Feb88-3GP	6f	:223 :463 1:13 ft	35	116	4½	21	2hd	11½	Romero R P8	Ⓕ 50000	74-25	WhisperLove,HiMaudie,SucyVoyge	9
19Jan88-7GP	6f	:22 :45 1:112ft	21	116	64	58	916	1118¼	Wade J T4	ⒻAw16000	63-26	Willing'NWiting,MissDlilh,Shrrign	12
26Dec87-8Hia	1 1/16 Ⓣ	1:45 fm	34	112	1214	1221	—	—	Wade J T7	ⒻSurfside	——	WshflNckl,AbovSpcl,Pnny'sGrowl	12
26Dec87—Eased													
13Dec87-3Hia	6f	:221 :453 1:112ft	56	113	41½	41½	21	12½	Wade J T 2	Ⓕ 40000	83-21	WhisprLov,RblFshion,MothrofEght	9
14Nov87-7Hia	6f	:221 :463 1:123ft	69	113	1hd	4½	1017	1823¼	Wade J T 1	ⒻAw12000	53-25	PlateQueen,MirnaM.,SaucyVoyage	11
8Oct87-9Bir	6f	:228 :463 1:132ft	*9-5	116	21½	32½	35	35	Luhr R D 5	ⒻAw7000	75-24	PowerTlks,SwiftAlexis,WhisperLov	8

May 9 Bel 4f ft :482 h

Koluctoo's Betty

Ch. f. 3, by Koluctoo Bay—Powerfully, by Jim J
Own.—Levine B — 116
Br.—Shirley Levine (Fla) — 1988 5 1 3 0 $26,820
Tr.—Levine Bruce — $50,000 — 1987 6 M 3 2 $10,335
Lifetime 11 1 6 2 $37,155

2May88-1Aqu	1	:46 1:113 1:372ft	8½	116	2½	1½	1½	21¾	Lovato F Jr 8	Ⓕ 50000	77-22	Yo'llbsrprsd,Klct'sBtty,CmpltAccrd	8
16Apr88-3Aqu	7f	:23 :464 1:25 ft	4½	116	52½	31½	33	42½	DesormuxKJ 8	Ⓕ 50000	73-21	Smrtn'Irish,HonysucklQun,Yllowtil	9
28Mar88-3Aqu	7f	:233 :472 1:26 ft	12	118	52	75½	43½	24	Lovato F Jr1	Ⓕ 50000	67-30	DustyDonn,Kolctoo'sBtty,ProdFlrt	9
10Mar88-9Aqu	6f ⊡	:231 :4821:15 ft	*4-5	121	77½	41½	1hd	11¾	Lovato F Jr4	ⒻM50000	69-34	Kolct'sBtty,HnyscklQn,Mttawrmrs	9
10Mar88—Bmpd, drew clear													
29Feb88-9Aqu	6f ⊡	:223 :4631:131ft	*7-5	121	75	68	34	21½	Santos J A8	ⒻM50000	77-25	Rocketi,Koluctoo'sBtty,TirofGold	12
5Dec87-3Med	6f	:221 :454 1:112ft	3-2	117	43	46	36½	35½	Vigliotti M J3	ⒻMdn	79-20	FrzngRn,ProdTrblnc,Kolctoo'sBtty	6
19Nov87-5Med	170	:474 1:133 1:443ft	2½	117	1hd	2½	33½	39¾	Vigliotti M J3	ⒻMdn	63-21	NoReviw,PrlofGold,Koluctoo'sBtty	8
10Nov87-7Med	6f	:223 :472 1:114sy	5½	117	32	25	34	22½	Vigliotti M J2	ⒻMdn	80-29	OntoRoylty,Kolctoo'sBtty,PrlofGld	8

Mar 22 Aqu 4f ft :501 b

Dancing Sal

Ch. f. 3, by Northern Jove—Quid Kit, by Quid Pro Quo
Own.—Austin Melissa — 112
Br.—Paxson Mrs H D (Ky) — 1988 1 0 0 0
Tr.—O'Brien Leo — $45,000 — 1987 6 1 0 1 $10,080
Lifetime 7 1 0 1 $10,080

25Apr88-3Aqu	6f	:23 :473 1:13 ft	20	116	1½	1hd	31½	55½	Goossens L1	Ⓕ 50000	69-24	Crafty Alexas, CuteMove,Yellowtail	6
24Oct87-6Med	6f	:223 :462 1:113ft	7½	113	42½	54½	58	513	EstradaJC1	ⒻAw15000	71-23	T.V.Countess,LsMnits,Prospectitut	8
8Oct87-1Bel	6f	:222 :461 1:121gd	*3½	114	53¾	34½	56½	57	Maple E1	Ⓕ 72500	71-23	Cute Move, Roleplay, Links ofGold	9
23Sep87-7Bel	6f	:223 :453 1:102ft	31	116	52½	22½	26	37½	Maple E6	ⒻAw28000	80-16	PrspctvBddr,HghlndPnny,DncngSl	11
24Aug87-1Sar	6f	:221 :461 1:12 ft	8½	116	32½	43	68	614¾	CordroAJr3	ⒻAw25000	65-19	GalwaySong,CuteMove,CraftyOrbit	6
18Jly87-8Pim	5½f	:222 :462 1:05 ft	14	110	42	31½	34½	48	Sarvis D A4	ⒻPlaypen	87-13	CrftyWif,SvdbyGrc,ArticEnchntrss	7
23Apr87-1Bir	4f	:23 :471ft	3½	118	1	2hd	2hd	1nk	Luhr R D1	ⒻMdn	98-02	DncingSl,MssGoldStg,Shnnon'sXod	8

Apr 22 Bel tr.t 3f ft :36 h   Apr 17 Bel 5f ft 1:00 h   Apr 11 Bel tr.t 4f ft :473 h   Mar 30 OTC 5f ft 1:03 b

*In Focus II

Ch. f. 3, by Cure the Blues—Clear Picture, by Polyfoto
Own.—Firestone Mrs B R — 116
Br.—Firestone B R & Mrs (Ire) — 1988 1 1 0 0 $8,400
Tr.—Mott William I — $50,000 — 1987 1 M 0 0
Lifetime 2 1 0 0 $8,400 — Turf 1 0 0 0

7Apr88-4Aqu	6f	:23 :471 1:12 sy	3	115	31½	2hd	12½	16	Krone J A 11	ⒻM35000	88-26	In FocusII,FestiveLady,FaciaBella	11
15Oct87♦1Punchestown(Ire)	6f	1:221sf	6	122	Ⓣ	58			KinnMJ	ⒻCarnalwayPlate		ToDiFor,SnsofRomnc,SuprmSunst	12

May 9 Bel 4f ft :483 h   May 1 Bel 4f ft :502 h   Apr 4 Bel 5f ft 1:003 hg   Mar 29 Bel tr.t 4f ft :481 hg

Lisa's Halo

B. f. 3, by Sunny's Halo—Gold Flee, by Mr Prospector
Own.—Mot Stable — 116
Br.—Mereworth Farm (Ky) — 1988 4 1 0 1 $20,160
Tr.—Myer Patrick — $50,000 — 1987 10 1 2 1 $19,130
Lifetime 14 2 2 2 $39,290

12Mar88-1Aqu	1 1/16 ⊡	:4941:1541:494ft	7	116	74	74½	77¾	69¾	Migliore R2	Ⓕ 50000	50-22	Helga's Honey, Outshine, Kim Cat	7
25Feb88-3Aqu	1 1/8 ⊡	:4741:1411:55 ft	7½	116	48	41½	38	314½	Migliore R6	Ⓕ 50000	52-25	Pggy'sProspct,GoldnSwthrt,Ls'sHl	7
11Feb88-6Aqu	1 1/16 ⊡	:49 1:1411:454ft	13	116	1011	915	924	931	Migliore R8	ⒻAw31000	49-30	FulbrightScholr,Ap'sPiv,Slwsbsqu	10
20Jan88-1Aqu	1 1/8 ⊡	:4831:1421:552sy	5½	114	412	42	2hd	1hd	Migliore R4	Ⓕ 47500	65-28	Lisa'sHalo,Outshine,HollywoodBarb	7
31Dec87-4Aqu	1 1/16 ⊡	:4831:1441:492ft	*8-5	113	48	31½	13½	13	Migliore R3	ⒻM45000	62-22	Lis'sHlo,TurntoSlew,Em'sMummy	11
5Dec87-4Aqu	1 1/16 ⊡	:49 1:1531:502ft	9½	117	62½	43	32	32¾	Migliore R12	ⒻM50000	54-27	Outshin,WirdCombintion,Lis'sHlo	12
19Nov87-6Aqu	1 1/8	:474 1:123 1:514ft	11	117	68½	57½	513	411½	Migliore R9	ⒻMdn	64-10	Fenimore,ArcticEvening,NskrFncy	12
30Oct87-4Aqu	1	:463 1:123 1:411ft	11	114	96½	98½	72¾	53	Velasquez J2	ⒻM45000	57-25	Dvsttd,WirdCombinton,FrndlyMst	12
30Oct87—Lacked room													

Apr 26 Bel 5f ft 1:002 h   Apr 10 Bel 4f ft :47 h

Cute Move

B. f. 3, by Cherokee Fellow—Lady Cliffe, by Norcliffe
Br.—Parkhurst Farm Inc (Fla) 1988 3 0 1 0 $6,720
Own.—Schaeffer Carol 112 Tr.—Schaeffer Stephen $45,000 1987 9 2 3 1 $49,860
Lifetime 12 2 4 1 $56,580

25Apr88-3Aqu 6f :23 :473 1:13 ft 8 112 2½ 2hd 2½ 23 Santagata N 2 Ⓕ 45000 72-24 Crafty Alexas, CuteMove,Yellowtail 6
6Apr88-1Aqu 6f :222 :461 1:121ft 11 112 55 44½ 54½ 46 Santagata N 5 Ⓕ 45000 73-25 SucyVoyg,HonysucklQun,CrftyAlxs 7
18Mar88-5Aqu 6f :214 :451 1:103ft 8½ 116 88½ 912 914 920 Cordero A Jr 5 Ⓕ 50000 67-22 Judy's Halo, DustyDonna,Rocketai 10
2Dec87-6Aqu 6f ⊡:223 :4711:131ft 6½ 113 85 76¾ 76 57¾ Migliore R 4 Ⓕ 70000 70-24 ‡BestNumber,StunchFlm,FrogLdy 10
2Dec87—Placed fourth through disqualification
11Nov87-3Aqu 1⅛ :484 1:144 1:544sy 4¾ 116 52½ 33 48½ 410¾ Migliore R 7 ⒻAw31000 50-36 TopPinchr,NtlyArrngd,SunnyRobrt 7
15Oct87-4Bel 7f :231 :471 1:261ft 9-5 114 11½ 12 11½ 2nk Migliore R 4 Ⓕ 70000 71-27 Roleplay, Cute Move, Bionaire 7
8Oct87-1Bel 6f :222 :461 1:121gd 5½ 113 64¾ 55 32½ 11 Migliore R 7 Ⓕ 70000 78-23 Cute Move, Roleplay, Links ofGold 9
23Sep87-7Bel 6f :223 :453 1:102ft 9½ 116 62¾ 65 511 611½ Migliore R 9 ⒻAw28000 76-16 PrspctvBddr,HghlndPnny,DncngSl 11
May 9 Bel tr.t 4f ft :50 b May 3 Bel tr.t 4f ft :49 b Apr 21 Bel tr.t 4f ft :49 b Apr 1 Bel tr.t 4f ft :483 h

Parasol

B. f. 3, by Star de Naskra—Mirasol, by Secretariat
Br.—Sixpence ThoroughbredGroup (Ky) 1988 6 1 1 2 $22,620
Own.—Peters Betty M 116 Tr.—Kelly Tim J $50,000 1987 0 M 0 0
Lifetime 6 1 1 2 $22,620

28Apr88-9Aqu 6f :223 :472 1:13 ft 5¾ 115 43½ 31½ 11 11 Antley C W3 ⒻM50000 75-26 Parsol,FestiveLdy,WellPersonified 11
21Mar88-2Aqu 6f :232 :48 1:14 ft *8-5e 121 41½ 31 65½ 65¾ Davis R G12 ⒻM50000 64-28 Wilton, Tagett, Imanair 12
13Mar88-5Aqu 6f ⊡:223 :46 1:123ft 3½ 121 76¾ 79½ 611 610½ Maple E 11 ⒻMdn 78-18 Pretiola,AmericnDnce,Lee'sTskus 12
15Feb88-6Aqu 6f ⊡:223 :4641:123ft 3½ 121 53¾ 32 33 35½ Antley C W7 ⒻMdn 75-22 ToweringSuccess,Levitation,Parsol 9
1Feb88-6Aqu 6f ⊡:231 :4721:124ft *4-5 121 2hd 2½ 2½ 31½ Antley C W5 ⒻMdn 78-23 DustyDonn,ToweringSuccess,Prsol 12
18Jan88-5Aqu 6f ⊡:222 :47 1:134sy *1 121 86¾ 57 33 22 Antley C W3 ⒻMdn 73-24 Say Geneva, Parasol, Top Turf 9
●May 9 Bel 4f ft :464 h May 2 Bel tr.t 4f ft :491 b Apr 15 Bel tr.t 5f ft 1:022 b Apr 7 Bel 4f ft :484 b

She's Freezing

Dk. b. or br. f. 3, by Quadratic—She's So Cold, by Hagley
Br.—GryhoundStsInc-SilvrsmthInv (Ky) 1988 2 0 0 0
Own.—Davis A 116 Tr.—Moschera Gasper S $50,000 1987 9 1 4 0 $24,865
Lifetime 11 1 4 0 $24,865

21Apr88-5Aqu 6f :224 :464 1:111ft 12 116 43½ 56 59 516½ RomeroRP1 ⒻAw30000 67-26 Redding Ridge,Judy'sHalo,Rocketai 8
6Apr88-1Aqu 6f :222 :461 1:121ft *8-5 116 1½ 21 24 58 Krone J A2 Ⓕ c50000 73-25 SucyVoyg,HonysucklQun,CrftyAlxs 7
27Oct87-3Kee 6f :222 :451 1:12 ft 4½ 115 11 11 2½ 21¾ MeIconL7 ⒻAw17300 80-12 MissThreesum,She'sFrzing,DrDusty 7
16Oct87-3Kee 7f :223 :45 1:234ft 2½ 115 2hd 2hd 33 57½ Day P1 ⒻAw17300 79-09 Loveswept, Strada, Dear Dusty 9
26Sep87-10TP 6½f :231 :462 1:182ft 14 112 64½ 1210 1014 1019 EspnozJC5 ⒻClipsetta 67-20 Sophi'sChoic,PrliGold,CushionCut 12
7Sep87-7AP 7f :23 :463 1:254gd *2-3 118 11½ 1½ 1½ 22 Day P4 ⒻAw13000 71-23 Gemell,She'sFreezing,Undrmythum 7
29Aug87-5AP 6½f :23 :47 1:194gd 3 118 74½ 74½ 44 23 Hawley S 3 ⒻAw13000 73-20 MdmQ.,She'sFreezing,MyMsseuse 10
12Aug87-8AP 6f :224 :471 1:123ft 9-5 115 11 1hd 45 68½ Day P 7 ⒻPolyana 68-26 Pearlie Gold,MadamQ.,MyMasseuse 8
12Aug87—Run in divisions
●May 5 Bel tr.t 3f ft :35 h Apr 1 Bel tr.t 4f ft :483 hg Mar 23 Bel tr.t 5f ft 1:014 b Mar 15 Bel tr.t 5f ft 1:014 b

Lyja

B. f. 3, by Lyphard's Wish—Inspiration Point, by Foolish Pleasure
Br.—Sandra Payson (Ky) 1988 5 1 0 1 $11,860
Own.—Manhasset Stable 114 Tr.—Zito Nicholas P $47,500 1987 0 M 0 0
Lifetime 5 1 0 1 $11,860

29Apr88-5Aqu 6f :22 :45 1:104ft 31 112 31½ 510 69½ 69 Pezua J M5 ⒻAw30000 78-17 Event Horizon,Rocketai,Judy'sHalo 8
8Apr88-6Aqu 6f :222 :454 1:102m 17 116 43 56 416 413 Pezua J M2 ⒻAw30000 75-17 NaturalElegance,Acquaint,Rocketai 6
26Mar88-9Aqu 6f :224 :464 1:123sy 3½ 121 21½ 21 21 11¾ Antley C W3 ⒻM35000 77-23 Lyja,SterlingFantasy,C'EstComplet 9
24Feb88-5GP 7f :232 :464 1:254ft 18 1147 41½ 54¾ 88½ 710¾ Munoz O R11 ⒻMdn 64-25 Wet Suit, Celtis,SaratogaWarning 12
29Jan88-2GP 6f :222 :471 1:133ft 12 1147 33 31 22½ 35¾ Munoz O R2 ⒻMdn 65-26 Double Pie, Strategic Issue, Lyja 12
Apr 23 Bel 4f ft :50 b Mar 17 Bel tr.t 3f ft :364 h Mar 13 Bel tr.t 3f ft :362 b

Her Way

B. f. 3, by Khartoum—Orange Sugar, by Jim J
Br.—Hackman William M (Va) 1988 4 1 0 1 $18,000
Own.—Hackman W 112 Tr.—DiMauro Stephen L $45,000 1987 4 1 1 0 $11,860
Lifetime 8 2 1 1 $29,860

6Apr88-1Aqu 6f :222 :461 1:121ft 8¾ 116 44½ 55½ 69½ 67 Migliore R7 Ⓕ 50000 72-25 SucyVoyg,HonysucklQun,CrftyAlxs 7
17Mar88-7Aqu 7f :23 :462 1:242ft 38 116 105½ 119¾ 1115 1121½ SantagatN2 ⒻAw30000 58-27 OurGllmr,EmpressofLov,MyCrvnn 11
29Feb88-8Aqu 6f ⊡:221 :4521:112ft 22 116 67 56½ 55 46½ Davis R G5 ⒻAw30000 81-25 Avie'sGal,MyCarvnn,‡NturlElegnce 7
29Feb88—Placed third through disqualification
27Jan88-1Aqu 6f ⊡:231 :4711:142ft 29 112 72¾ 63½ 31½ 11½ Davis R G3 Ⓕ 45000 72-27 HerWy,LinksofGold,GoldenSwethrt 9
28Nov87-1Aqu 6f :223 :471 1:114ft 15 116 98 96¾ 77 616½ Krone J A3 Ⓕ 50000 71-23 Best Number, Clara Drive, Kim Cat 9
2Nov87-1Aqu 1 :472 1:124 1:384ft 6½ 116 42½ 46½ 611 616 Davis R G5 Ⓕ 50000 56-21 Battlefront, Air Star, TrendyWendy 7
14Oct87-2Bel 7f :23 :47 1:27 ft *2½ 113 62¾ 63 42½ 1nk Davis R G4 ⒻM45000 67-28 Her Way, Syllogy, Cool Embrace 10
24Sep87-4Bel 6f :23 :47 1:122ft 14 117 97½ 78½ 45½ 24 Davis R G5 ⒻM35000 73-20 Joanie'sNative,HerWay,DncingElf 13
May 9 Bel 4f ft :481 b May 2 Bel tr.t 3f ft :363 b Apr 1 Bel tr.t 4f ft :48 h

Ap's Piv

B. f. 3, by Quadratic—Big Apple Baby, by Tumiga
Br.—Ryehill Farm (Md) 1988 6 1 1 1 $31,780
Own.—Ryan J P Jr 116 Tr.—Badgett William Jr $50,000 1987 14 3 2 3 $51,545
Lifetime 20 4 3 4 $83,325 Turf 1 0 0 0

1May88-7Aqu 1⅛ Ⓣ:5021:16 1:542gd 9½ 113 11 1hd 74¾ 713½ VelsquezJ1 ⒻAw31000 49-33 LadyTalc,Reasonble,NoblePreview 10
31Mar88-1Aqu 1 :472 1:124 1:384ft 11 116 41½ 65 68½ 613½ Baird E T3 Ⓕ 75000 58-30 SholdSylt,Pggy'sProspct,Hlg'sHny 6
19Mar88-1Aqu 1 :472 1:124 1:39 ft 2¾ 116 2hd 21½ 41½ 43 Baird E T4 Ⓕ 75000 68-23 Battlefront,ShouldSayIt,Rjb'sTune 7
21Feb88-3Aqu 170 ⊡:4831:15 1:461ft 4 116 2hd 2hd 1hd 11 Baird E T3 Ⓕ 75000 69-21 Ap's Piv, Battlefront, Proud Flirt 7
11Feb88-6Aqu 1¹⁄₁₆ ⊡:49 1:1411:454ft 11 116 21½ 22½ 28 214 Baird E T6 ⒻAw31000 66-30 FulbrightScholr,Ap'sPiv,Slwsbsqu 10
29Jan88-5Aqu 170 ⊡:4731:1311:46 ft 6½ 116 42½ 32 36 36½ Maple E2 Ⓕ 75000 64-26 Proud Flirt, Battlefront, Ap's Piv 9
21Dec87-5Aqu 1¹⁄₁₆ ⊡:4731:13 1:471ft 14 114 42 32 2½ 1nk Velasquez J3 Ⓕ 70000 73-15 Ap'sPiv,ShouldSayIt,CourtObserver 7
30Nov87-7Aqu 7f :231 :47 1:26 sy 9½ 116 62½ 52½ 611 614¾ Antley CW7 ⒻAw30000 56-30 DangerousType,OntoRoylty,TollFee 7
Apr 24 Bel 4f ft :48 h Apr 20 Bel 5f ft 1:013 b Apr 15 Bel tr.t 4f ft :50 b Mar 28 Bel tr.t 4f ft :492 h

The past performances we must look up are those of Cute Move. Her first victory does not show in the ten races listed. Since her second win was *at Belmont*, we must check back:

Cute Move

B. f. 2, by Cherokee Fellow—Lady Cliffe, by Norcliffe
Br.—Parkhurst Farm, Inc. (Fla)　　　1987　1 1 0 0　　$10,200

Own.—Schaeffer Carol　　**116**　Tr.—Schaeffer Stephen

Lifetime　1 1 0 0　$10,200

1Jly87-3Bel　5½f :22⁴ :47³ 1:08³ft　5 115　11　2ʰᵈ 1ʰᵈ 11¼　CorderoAJr ² ⑦M70000 72-22　CuteMove,FlighttoNowhr,Ap'sPiv 1⅌
1Jly87—Bumped, driving
Aug 5 Sar tr.t 4f ft :58² b　　Jly 29 Bel 4f ft :47³ h　　Jly 23 Bel 4f ft :47⁴ h　　Jly 17 Bel 4f ft :48³ b

Following Cute Move's maiden victory at Belmont, she lost two races at Saratoga and one at Belmont prior to the current past performances.

Approximate Odds, Post Time

In Focus II	9–5	(Day, P.)
Koluctoo's Betty	4–1	(Santos)
She's Freezing	5–1	(Cordero)
Rajab's Tune	5–1	(Peck)
Cute Move	10–1	(Santagata)
Whisper Love	22–1	(Velasquez)
Ap's Piv	25–1	(Bailey)
Her Way	25–1	(Davis)
Lisa's Halo	25–1	(Migliore)
Lyja	25–1	(Romero)
Parasol	25–1	(Antley)
Dancing Sal	30–1	(Pezua)

Comments

Unlikely

1 Horses with dull current form who have never beaten winners, two serious negatives: She's Freezing and Lyja.
2 Horses that have never beaten winners and are recent losers at today's level: Dancing Sal and Koluctoo's Betty (a seconditis horse)
3. Just won maiden-claiming race after many tries, probably will need many tries for first win vs. winners: Parasol.
4. Recent losses this level coupled with dull current form: Lisa's Halo (never won a sprint) and Her Way. Her Way shows a victory on this track and could surprise, but that

is only a one-dimensional positive factor; she has also won at a different track, so there is little evidence of a preference for Belmont.

5. Negative drops off dull current form: Whisper Love and Ap's Piv (who is a router).
6. None of these eliminations show any kind of preference for a wet track which would have implied the potential for a form reversal.

Contenders

"Muddy" means somewhere between sloppy and good, probably nearer to sloppy. That will favor In Focus II, who has won over a sloppy surface. Since "muddy" can also be in transition toward "good," Cute Move and Rajab's Tune both get a possible plus. Their "good" track wins would mean nothing had today's surface been a sloppy one. There is a distinct difference between wet/sloppy and good/drying out. Surface, though, is not the only factor in this race; all factors included, Cute Move becomes the most likely winner.

1. Cute Move's "good" track win was *at Belmont*, so her *good-Belmont* surface combination may be closer to today's strip than In Focus II's *sloppy-Aqueduct* win. Horse for course? Cute Move is not only 2 for 4 *at this track*, but she is 0 for 8 at other tracks. She is the only horse in the field to have handled successfully a Belmont off-track surface. She is a multiple winner in a field with many horses that have beaten only maidens. Her form cycle says "pop-up" victories at Belmont. But it also shows the pattern of an *improving horse*:

	Finish Position	Lengths Behind
3 races back	9	20
2 races back	4	6
1 race back	2	3

Her early fractions show the same pattern of improvement.
2. In Focus II is nearly a bounce candidate, having just won after a layoff. However, the filly has been freshened for more than a month following that victory. Usually maiden-

claiming winners have no chance in their next race,which is their first against winners. But In Focus II is a *lightly-raced* filly (in other words, not a proven loser) who has *never lost a maiden race*, and looked good in winning over a wet track.

3. Rajab's Tune finished out of the money for the first time in her career in her last race and has been freshened for today's race. Win or lose, this horse always runs well. Rajab's Tune has the rail, usually a negative in the mud; but today, after four races, two rail horses have won, with the other two winners coming from post three.

	Our Line	*Track Odds*	*Decision*
Cute Move	2–1	10–1	Way over. *Bet.*
In Focus II	3–1	9–5	Under. No bet.
Rajab's Tune	4–1	5–1	Under the 6–1 minimum. Would need more than 6–1 in any case, since we already have another bet.

FIFTH RACE
Belmont
MAY 12, 1988

6 FURLONGS. (1.07⅗) CLAIMING. Purse $22,000. Fillies. 3-years-old. Weight, 121 lbs. Non-winners of two races since April 15 allowed 3 lbs. Of a race since then, 5 lbs. Claiming price $50,000; for each $2,500 to $45,000, 2 lbs. (Races when entered to be claimed for $40,000 or less not considered.)

Value of race $22,000; value to winner $13,200; second $4,840; third $2,640; fourth $1,320. Mutuel pool $251,030. Exacta Pool $478,069.

Last Raced	Horse	Eqt.A.Wt	PP	St	¼	½	Str	Fin	Jockey	Cl'g Pr	Odds $1
25Apr88 ^{3}Aqu^{2}	Cute Move	b 3 112	7	9	2½	2^{2½}	1^{hd}	1½	Santagata N	45000	10.00
21Apr88 ^{5}Aqu^{5}	She's Freezing	3 116	9	1	1^{2}	1½	2^{3}	2^{nk}	Cordero A Jr	50000	5.10
31Mar88 ^{1}Aqu^{4}	Rajab's Tune	3 111	1	5	9½	7^{hd}	4^{1½}	3^{2}	Peck B D^{5}	50000	5.60
20Apr88 ^{9}Aqu^{1}	Parasol	3 116	8	6	4½	4^{1}	3^{1½}	4^{2¾}	Antley C W	50000	24.40
7Apr88 ^{4}Aqu^{1}	In Focus II	b 3 116	5	11	7½	8½	5^{2}	5^{1¼}	Day P	50000	1.90
6Apr88 ^{1}Aqu^{6}	Her Way	3 112	11	12	10^{1½}	10½	6½	6^{1¼}	Davis R G	45000	25.80
12Mar88 ^{1}Aqu^{6}	Lisa's Halo	3 116	6	2	12	11½	8^{hd}	7¾	Migliore R	50000	25.50
29Apr88 ^{5}Aqu^{6}	Lyja	3 114	10	7	6^{1}	6½	9^{1}	8^{hd}	Romero R P	47500	26.30
2May88 ^{1}Aqu^{2}	Koluctoo's Betty	b 3 116	3	10	11^{hd}	12	10^{2}	9^{1¾}	Santos J A	50000	4.00
25Apr88 ^{3}Aqu^{5}	Dancing Sal	3 112	4	3	3^{4}	3^{1½}	7½	10^{3¼}	Pezua J M	45000	31.40
1May88 ^{7}Aqu^{7}	Ap's Piv	3 116	12	8	8½	9½	11^{hd}	11^{1¼}	Bailey J D	50000	24.50
8Apr88 ^{6}Aqu^{6}	Whisper Love	3 116	2	4	5^{hd}	5½	12	12	Velasquez J	50000	22.40

OFF AT 2:50 Start good, Won driving. Time, :22, :45⅗, 1:10⅘ Track muddy.

$2 Mutuel Prices:			
7–(G)–CUTE MOVE	22.00	10.80	6.20
9–(I)–SHE'S FREEZING		7.20	4.60
1–(A)–RAJAB'S TUNE			4.20

$2 EXACTA 7–9 PAID $151.40.

B. f, by Cherokee Fellow—Lady Cliffe, by Norcliffe. Trainer Schaeffer Stephen. Bred by Parkhurst Farm Inc (Fla).

CUTE MOVE pressed the pace outside SHE'S FREEZING into the stretch then drew clear under brisk urging. SHE'S FREEZING sprinted clear at once, continued on the front for five furlongs and held on well after relinquishing the lead to gain the place. RAJAB'S TURN far back while saving ground, rallied belatedly along the inside. PARASOL lodged a mild bid from outside on the turn then finished evenly. IN FOCUS failed to threaten after steading between horses on the far turn. KOLUCTOO'S BETTY, sluggish early, checked and altered course to the middle of the track when blocked behind a wall of horses entering the stretch. DANCING SAL was used up after going a half. WHISPER LOVE checked while trying to drift out on the far turn.

Owners— 1, Schaeffer Carol; 2, Davis A; 3, Rosbeck P Y; 4, Peters Betty M; 5, Firestone Mrs B R; 6, Hackman W; 7, Mot Stable; 8, Manhasset Stable; 9, Levine B; 10, Austin Melissa; 11, Ryan J P Jr; 12, Maxwell Rita.

Trainers— 1, Schaeffer Stephen; 2, Moschera Gasper S; 3, Lenzini John J Jr; 4, Kelly Tim J; 5, Mott William I; 6, DiMauro Stephen L; 7, Myer Patrick; 8, Zito Nicholas P; 9, Levine Bruce; 10, O'Brien Leo; 11, Badgett William Jr; 12, Domino Carl J.

Corrected weight: Parasol 116 pounds.

On several occasions students of mine have related that when a tremendous advantage arises (such as that of Cute Move), they begin to doubt themselves and the whole process of line making. The crowd is supposed to be relatively accurate, "so I must be wrong," they say. Yes, the crowd is indeed accurate, *in the long run*. But in the short run one need only see the tremendous variations in odds on the same horse for races simulcast at different tracks. There have been occasions when the horse at 2–1 on one track is 10–1 at another. This has been amply documented in many books and articles. Public action is unstable and subject to incredible fluctuations.

In front of a different betting public, Cute Move might have been 2–1 or 3–1. The crowd is capable of major errors. You've just read all the arguments I had in favor of Cute Move. Judge for yourself. Most likely the crowd overestimated the sloppy track win of In Focus II. Modern racetracks now tend to go from sloppy to muddy to good without passing through the "slow" phase: modern drainage systems. That means that some muddy tracks are closer to sloppy and others are closer to good. The crowd should have given more weight to the "good" track victory of Cute Move, at least for the reason that it took place at Belmont. Which leads me to suspect that now, like so often, the betting public underestimated the horse-for-course factor, either because they failed to see that many of the entrants were *racing on the Belmont track for the first time* or because they failed to look up or remember Cute Move's first win. Cute Move had beaten winners; In Focus II had not. And Cute Move had done so *at Belmont.*

It's hard for me to believe that the crowd didn't notice Cute Move's form-cycle improvement, but that's another possible reason why they let her get to post at 10–1.

Suppose you'd have made Cute Move your third choice at 4–1, or even 5–1. The line-making strategy of betting any contender that offers an advantage would have allowed you to collect anyway.

Cute Move's victory occurred only eight days after Showerstime won in a similar context on the opposite coast (see Chapter 10). Although this particular racing cycle will not produce enough betting opportunities for it to be a major part of your investment portfolio, it deserves a special mention because it is overlooked by the betting public.

Scenario

1. Winter meet is just over, summer meet begins. In many parts of the country, this shift will occur in mid-April.
2. Fields limited to three-year-olds.
3. Look for horses that, as late-year two-year-olds, won at the *same track* as today's race.
4. Look for horses that show indications of improving form.

Within the pure parameters, this is not a horse-for-course situation, since we are not dealing with a shorter meet, nor do we have a "track record" for all the horses in the field. Perhaps we might better call this the "track experience" factor since the type of field we have isolated will contain many horses with no experience at the particular racetrack. Horses that began racing as three-year-olds have never even had the opportunity to race on today's track. Those who began as two-year-olds may have never had the chance to get acclimated to the present venue.

We look for horses, then, who have an experiential head start. In the long run, the whole three-year-old colony gains experience over the particular track, nullifying the head start of our target horses.

That means the cycle is *seasonal*, appearing only in the month of April or May, depending on when the spring-summer meet begins in your part of the country. Since this is not a strict horse-for-course form reversal, we look for form improvement signs to go along with the track switch. Showerstime had the freshening, Cute Move had ascending numbers.

WORKSHOP THREE

May 8, 1988 (course firm)

9th Hollywood

1 ¼ MILES. (Turf). (1.45¾) ALLOWANCE (Chute Start). Purse $40,000. 4-year-olds and upward which have not won $3,000 twice other than maiden, claiming or starter. Weight, 120 lbs. Non-winners of such a race at a mile or over since March 15 allowed 3 lbs.; such a race since February 15, 6 lbs.

Dennis D. *

SHERMAN A B	120	Gr. g. 5, by Hawkin's Special—Wink an Eye, by Stop the Music		
Own.—Burke G W		Br.—Malmuth Mr-Mrs M (Ky)	1988 7 1 1 2	$33,050
		Tr.—Lage Armando	1987 12 3 2 1	$47,155
		Lifetime 29 5 4 5 $94,630	Turf 5 1 2 2	$40,050

27Apr88-7Hol 1⅛①:46¹1:10²1:47²fm 7½ 1095 5⁴ 2½ 2½ 1½ Sherman AB⁷ Aw34000 91-09 DennisD.,HowVryTouching,Crmntl 12
3Mar88-8SA 1⅛①:46³1:11¹1:36 fm 7 1115 65½ 4³ 22½ 22½ Sherman AB¹ Aw36000 92-05 Daloma, Dennis D., Don Bruce 10
22Mar88-8GG 1⅛①:47¹1:11³1:43³fm 2 1106 2¹ 1hd 31½ 33½ Sherman A B Z 45000 88-16 Pair Of Aces, Open Hero, Dennis D. 8
25Feb88-9SA 1⅛①:46¹1:10⁴1:50⁴fm 27 1125 55½ 4³ 4½ 3² Sherman AB Z Aw34000 71-27 All Cat, Sharp Choice, Dernis D. 12
17Feb88-9SA 1⅛:46²1:11⁴1:44⁴ft 18 116 7⁰ 77½10¹410¹4½ Cordero A Jr Z 20000 62-23 MischivousMtt,SbrnHro,HghRgrds 11
    17Feb88—Wide into stretch
7Feb88-9SA 1½:47 1:11³ 1:43⁴ft 27 1096 7⁷ 106½ 6⁵ 67½ Valenzuela F H ½ 20000 74-16 OnoGummo,SavorFire,SuperPunk 12
31Jan88-4SA 1¹:46² 1:11 1:37²ft 19 1086 3¹ 86½ 9¹5 9²¹ Sherman A B Z 45000 60-21 MoveFree,LastCommnd,QuickTwist 9
5Dec87-10Hol 1½:47⁴1:13 1:41¹m 2½ 1115 31½ 31½ 43½ 64½ Gryder A T Z Aw31000 76-17 Jonleat, Everso, Bronze Tudor 7
28Nov87-9Hol 1⅛:47²1:11 1:48¹fm 36 1115 1½ 11 12 2hd Sherman AB ½Aw31000 87-13 Point D'Artois, DennisD.,Unicopia 11
15Nov87-9SA 1¹:47 1:11³ 1:43¹ft 6 115 8½³ 96½ 8⁸ 79½ McCarron C J 10 32000 76-16 Bedouin, Shigamba, Air A'ert 10
  Apr 18 SA 1R 1:41¹ h   ●Mar 15 SA 3f R :36³ h   Mar 8 SA 4f R :48³ h

Lonesome Dancer

SOLIS A	114	B. g. 5, by Green Dancer—Belle Foulee, by Tom Fool		
Own.—4-Fun Stable & Murphy		Br.—Stratford Farms (Ky)	1988 4 0 0 2	$6,450
		Tr.—Murphy Chuck	1987 15 1 1 1	$22,387
		Lifetime 24 2 1 3 $33,190	Turf 15 1 1 3	$25,275

23Apr88-10GG 1⅛①:47³1:11¹2:19⁴yl 9½ 115 51⁵ 32½ 3² 31½ Warren R J Jr ½ 35000 65-38 KentuckyLurel,Enbrr,LonesomDncr 8
2Apr88-7CG 1⅛①:49⁴1:13³1:51 fm 26 115 21½ 3⁴ 35 33½ Warren R J Jr ½ 45000 — — — MinutesAwy,Enbrr,LonesomeDncer 7
22Mar88-8GG 1⅛①:48³1:13 1:50¹fm 29 119 4² 5⁵ 6⁸ 5⁹ Hummel C R ½Aw18000 — — SuperPunk,Nikambar,ButterflyBoy 10
    23Mar88—Wide
26Jan88-6GG 1¹:45³1:10⁴1:43⁴ft 12 119 51⁸ 61³ 51¹ 51⁴½ Castaneda M⁴ Aw16000 67-15 Fly Up, Salty Shoes, Bold Bargain 6
    26Jan88—Bumped start
20Dec87-4BM 1¹:45⁴ 1:10¹ 1:43 ft 17 117 6¹³ 61⁰ 66½ 4⁹ Castaneda M ½ Aw18000 68-18 GallantHawk,DustyOkie,RrgerRoni 6
29Nov87-4BM 1⅜①:49¹1:39²1:101fm 7½ 113 43½ 53½ 5⁷ 94½ Warren R J Jr ½ HcpO 04-09 ⅟₂FlindsRlr,WidrnssBnd,GrrdEchng 6
    29Nov87—Placed fourth through disqualification
8Nov87-7BM 1⅛:50¹1:40 2:10³m 11 119 2¹ 2½ 21 21½ Castaneda M ½ 38000 87-11 Rajhan,LonesomeDncer,JetAwyBill 6
11Oct87-5BM 1⅛①:46 1:12¹1:44³ft 12 122 86½ 7⁵ 8⁵ 58½ McHrgueOG ½ Aw20000 74-16 MckiBnd,MnCsn,GoodThoghtWlly 10
26Sep87-3BM 1⅛①:47³1:12⁴1:44½fm 27 119 33½ 3hd 11 Castaneda M Z Aw19000 82-13 LonesomeDncer,ChiefPl,MenCuisin 8
7Sep87-9Bmf 1 :46² 1:09³ 1:34⁴ft 34 116 7⁰ 66½ 7½ 48½ Yammoto TJ ½ Aw15000 90-16 Majashed, Mean Cuisine, Finalized 8
  Apr 17 GG 5f R 1:02³ b   Mar 22 GG 3f R :36³ h   Mar 15 GG 5f R 1:02³ h

*Millero Y Medio *

SIBILLE R	114	B. h. 7, by Mr Long—Maria Blanca, by Blakemore		
Own.—Pullman C H		Br.—Haras Santa Amelia (Chile)	1988 7 0 1 1	$16,150
		Tr.—Pullman Vivian M	1987 15 1 1 2	$42,200
		Lifetime 56 11 11 8 $901,747	Turf 24 2 2 3	$26,727

25Apr88-8SA 1⅛①:46³1:37¹2:03²ft 19 116 86 1⁰7½ 96½ 6³½ Sibille R ½ 62500 66-24 Danielli, Point D'Artois, Ataghan 12
9Apr88-2SA 1⅛①:47³1:11³1:49³fm 35 115 11 2hd 7½½ 7½½ Sibille R ½ 62500 78-08 RomanticPrince,BrekfstTbl,SlrtPrty 9
25Mar88-8SA 1⅛①:46³1:11³1:48²fm 5 116 4¹ 4½½ 9⁰ 91⁰½ Sibille R⁰ Aw42000 75-15 RoiNormnd,Eliminnte,DfinitSigns 10
12Mar88-8SA 1⅛①:46²1:11⁴2:01⁴fm 20 113 53½ 7³² 8¹²⁹1³½ Hawley S² ☒ Sn Mrno H 70-11 Putting, Fiction, Chinoiserie 11
27Feb88-5SA 1⅛:46³ 1:11² 1:50⁴ft 13 116 5⁰ 3⁵ 2¹ Sibille R⁰ Aw42000 74-17 Reland, Miller Y Medio, ProudCat 10
25Jan88-8SA 1⅛:46¹ 1:11 1:50⁴sy 5½ 116 5⁴ 5³ 4⅜ Sibille R² Aw30000 65-29 Fiction, Be Scenic, L'Empire 12
17Jan88-7SA 1⅛:46¹ 1:11 1:50⁴sy 5½ 116 2¹½ 21½ 3⁵ 30½ Stevens S A⁹ Aw30000 73-17 Rupperto,Shigamba,MilleroYMedio 9
    17Jan88—Wide into stretch
19Dec87-9Hol 1⅛:47 1:10³ 1:47³gd 64 112 7⁵½ 81³ 86½ 7⁵½ StvnsSA⁷ Ntv Dvr H 80-10 Epidaurus,MidwestKing,He'sASros 8
    19Dec87—Grade III
29Nov87-8Hol 1⅛①:47³1:11 1:47²fm 19e 113 12¹¹12¹²12¹¹9½11⁹½ BlackCA¹² Citation H 81-11 Forlitano, Conquering Hero, Ifrad 12
    29Nov87—Grade II; Wide into stretch
16Nov87-5SA 1⅛①:47²1:12 2:00⁴fm 9 116 7⁵¹11⁶³10⁰½ 91²½ Pedroza MA¹² Aw33000 68-34 Chess Set, L'Empire, Feraud 12
  May 4 Hol 4f R :49³ h   Apr 17 SA 6f R 1:14² h   Apr 4 SA 6f R 1:13¹ h   Mar 28 SA 4f R :46⁴ h

Table Glow

PINCAY L JR	114	B. g. 4, by Never Tabled—Radiant Glow, by Northern Dancer		
Own.—Sarkowsky H		Br.—Sarkowsky S H (Cal)	1988 4 0 1 0	$4,400
		Tr.—Mandella Richard	1987 8 2 2 2	$34,100
		Lifetime 13 2 3 2 $38,500	Turf 9 1 3 1	$38,050

17Apr88-7GG 1⅛①:48 1:12 1:48²fm 3½ 117 44½ 4⁴ 32 2² Castaneda M ½ 62500 82-20 QuickTwist, TbleGlow, Position'sBst 8
25Mar88-8SA 1⅛①:46³1:11³1:48²fm 6 115 4½ 2hd 42½ 64½ Hawley S ½ Aw42000 70-15 RoiNormnd,Eliminnte,DfinitSigns 10
18Mar88-7SA 1⅛①:21³ :44 1:14³fm 6½ 116 74½ 66½ 9⁰ 10½½ Stevens L ½ Aw30000 74-14 MidnghtLC,RmntcPrnc,ChrlThStrs 10
    18Mar88—Lugged in badly throughout
21Feb88-7SA a6½①:21¹ :43⁴1:14¹fm 12 116 7⁶ 86½ 86½ 86½ DelahoussayeE⁷ 60000 82-13 BrghtAndRght,HppyInSpc,Illumnux 9
    21Feb88—Broke slowly; wide in stretch
12Sep87-7Dmr 1①:47 1:11⁴1:37⁹fm 3 116 74½ 1¹⁴ 7³⁹ 7¹⁰ McCavronCJ¹ Aw20000 64-16 OnTheCrpet,DerDiogwrl,UrtothhiM 8
    12Sep87—Bumped start
30Aug87-5Dmr 1⅛①:47¹1:12³1:49⁰fm 14 114 5⁵ 2hd 1½ 1½ Stevens G L⁰ Aw20000 77-21 Table Glow, Jonleat, Visible Asset 10
25Jly87-9Dmr 1⅛①:47⁴1:12²1:43¹fm ⁵−5 114 1hd 1hd 3½ 3⅛ Stevens G L³ Aw23000 86-13 Quietly Bold, L'Empire, Table Glow 9
3Jly87-8Hol 1⅛①:46³1:10³1:41⁴fm 2½ 114 11½ 11½ 11½ 2hd Stevens G L ½ Aw20000 65-11 BooBoo'sBuckroo,TblGlow,Pondrbl 9
19Jun87-5Hol 1⅛①:05⁴1:40¹ fm 2½ 114 1½ 1¹ 1½ 2hd Stevens G L ½ Aw20000 91-09 Forlaway,TableGlow,ContactGame 10
12Jun87-6Hol 6f :22¹ :45³ 1:11²ft 2½ 115 2¹ 2hd 1½ 11½ Stevens GL ½ ☒M32000 86-16 TbleGlow,BrothersSteve,L W.Kidd 11
  ●Apr 18 SA 7f R 1:25 h   Apr 4 SA 5f R 1:00¹ h   Mar 13 SA 6f R 1:14 h

***Nilambar** — Dk. b. or br. h. 5, by Shergar—Noureen, by Astec

MCCARRON C J — 114 — Br.—H H Aga Khan (Ire) — 1988 5 0 3 0 $19,600

Own.—Red Baron's Barn — Tr.—Vienna Darrell — 1987 2 1 0 0 $17,050

Lifetime 16 3 5 2 $44,331 — Turf 16 3 5 2 $44,331

24Apr88-9SA 1⅛ⓣ:4821:1231:501gd 4 116 11 1½ 1hd 21½ Toro F2 Aw42000 75-25 Eliminante, Nilambar, All Cat 8

24Apr88—Bumped start

23Mar88-8GG 1⅛ⓣ:4831:13 1:501fm*4-5 119 11 1hd 21½ 25 Baze R A9 Aw18000 — — SuperPunk,Nilambar,ButterflyBoy 10

11Mar88-5SA 1⅛ⓣ:4611:1041:482fm 3 116 34½ 53½ 55½ 69½ DelhoussyeE9 Aw38000 75-15 PleasantVriety,Eliminnte,ProudCt 10

14Feb88-7SA 1¼ⓣ:4641:3712:024fm 4½ 1115 17 12½ 11½ 21¾ Gryder A T10 Aw38000 71-23 Uptothehilt, Nilambar, Feraud 10

23Jan88-8SA 1⅛ⓣ:4731:1221:511fm 10 1125 1½ 1½ 21½1110½ Gryder A T4 Aw38000 61-29 Fiction, Be Scenic, L'Empire 12

9May87-6Bel 1 1/16ⓣ:4831:13 1:45 gd 7½ 110 31½ 54 614 614½ AntlCW1 Fort Mrcy H 56-33 Dance of Life, Regal Flier, Iroko 7

9May87—Grade III; Run in divisions

18Apr87-3SA 1⅛ⓣ:4841:1221:492fm 2¾ 117 11 11½ 12 12 Toro F4 Aw31000 88-16 Nilambr,Dhleem,WutheringHeights 7

11Aug86♦5Windsor(Eng) a1⅛ 2:093gd*1-2 135 ⓣ 35 Cauthen S Skyport Boon Point, Prince Orac, Nilambar 9

1Aug86♦3Goodwood(Eng) 1¼ 2:062fm 8 117 ⓣ 45½ ThomsonB Extel H Chinoiserie,SwetMovr,ClstilStorm 13

21Jly86♦6Windsor(Eng) a1⅛ 2:08 gd*1-5 132 ⓣ 112 Cauthen S July Nilambar, Benarosa, ShajarAdDurr 6

May 6 Hol 3f ft :374 h — Apr 18 SA 3f ft :37 h — Apr 13 SA 3f ft :361 b — Mar 19 SA 5f ft 1:002 h

Street Party — B. c. 4, by Val de l'Orne—Eastern Prancer, by Northern Dancer

SHOEMAKER W — 114 — Br.—Taylor E P (Ont-C) — 1988 5 0 1 1 $13,920

Own.—Kinghaven Farms — Tr.—Attfield Roger — 1987 12 2 1 3 $69,490

Lifetime 20 2 3 4 $87,160 — Turf 10 1 2 3 $62,525

24Apr88-9SA 1⅛ⓣ:4821:1231:501gd 6¾ 116 21 2½ 32 57½ Seymour D J 4 Aw42000 69-25 Eliminante, Nilambar, All Cat 8

9Apr88-2SA 1⅛ⓣ:4731:1131:483fm 7 115 33 3½ 21½ 32½ Toro F 4 Aw42000 81-08 RomaticPrince,BrekfstTbl,StrtPrty 9

25Mar88-8SA 1⅛ⓣ:4631:1131:482fm 5½ 116 72½ 73½ 65 46 Toro F 4 Aw42000 79-15 RoiNormnd,Eliminnte,DfintSigns 10

15Feb88-9GP a1 1/16ⓣ 1:46 fm 6½ 117 43 41½ 22½ 21½ Seymour D J 3 Aw18000 74-21 SetaRecord,StreetParty,LordLser 10

7Jan88-8Hia 1⅛ⓣ 1:502gd 5 116 57 52½ 57½ 89 Santos J A 2 Aw18000 71-23 BrightBalloon,Hendeka,JusAileron 12

28Nov87-7Grd 1 3/16:482 1:133 2:002gd *2 114 47½ 37 412 412 Seymour D J 4 Aw24600 71-25 Interrex,BoldPresence,RoylTresurr 7

25Oct87-4WO 1 1/16:484 1:132 1:462gd *7-5 114 32½ 32½ 49 511 Seymour D J 6 Aw24600 66-24 ThroneSpech,ModrnLov,LmrSctBlu6

10Oct87-9WO 1 3/16:481 1:13 1:592ft 2½ 118 31½ 42 32½ 34 SmrDJ 5 Col Mclaun H 78-23 Duckpower,Chteud'Irlnde,StretPrty 7

13Sep87-9WO 1 1/16ⓣ:5141:1741:504sf *9-5 118 21 2½ 2½ 21½ SymrDJ 2 Trnto Cuph 48-36 Duckpower, Street Party, TimeLap 7

13Sep87—Grade III-C

30Aug87-8WO 1½ⓣ:4822:0432:30 fm*9-5e126 68½ 21½ 1½ 3nk DsRsRA 2 ⓢBreeders 90-10 HanginOnStr,Coryphee,StreetPrty 15

30Aug87—Grade I-C

May 5 Hol 5f ft 1:011 h — Apr 30 Hol 3f ft :372 b — Apr 21 SA 5f sy 1:051 h (d) — Apr 5 SA 6f ft 1:133 h

Rafael's Dancer — B. h. 5, by Northern Baby—Bannockburn, by Count Brook

OLIVARES F — 120 — Br.—Adger-Mandato-Lombardi (Ky) — 1988 2 1 0 0 $20,650

Own.—Lombardi & Mandato — Tr.—Whittingham Michael — 1987 3 0 1 0 $8,100

Lifetime 18 2 4 2 $93,525 — Turf 3 0 0 0 $5,625

13Apr88-7SA 1 :452 1:111 1:373ft 2½ 116 45½ 21 1hd 12½ Olivares F 6 Aw36000 80-22 Rfel'sDncer,NorthrnVlor,DsrtClssic 7

6Apr88-7SA 6f :214 :45 1:094ft 9 118 63¾ 73½ 73½ 52¾ Olivares F 7 Aw34000 86-17 PowrflNtv,FlyngNwsboy,PrmCncrd 7

17Mar87-7SA 1 1/16:46 1:102 1:423ft *9-5 117 54½ 55½ 710 614¾ Pincay L Jr 6 Aw31000 73-16 PrinceO'Fire,It'sNotMyJob,Athlone 9

17Mar87—Bumped start; wide

4Mar87-5SA 1 1/16:453 1:101 1:432ft *2 117 42 32½ 2½ 2¾ Pincay L Jr 2 Aw30000 83-16 RidgeReview,Rafel'sDncer,Athlone 12

4Mar87—Lugged in late

5Feb87-5SA 1 1/16:462 1:11 1:434ft *1 117 55½ 64½ 64½ 58½ Pincay L Jr 9 Aw28000 76-22 Centenary, Trump Up, Sun Man 12

5Feb87—Awarded fourth purse money; Wide into stretch

16Nov86-8Hol 1⅛ⓣ:4631:1021:464fm 104 122 1110121112121114½ OlivaresF 2 Hol Dby 79-07 Spellbound, Double Feint, Bruiser 12

16Nov86—Grade I; Run in divisions; Wide 7/8

31Oct86-5SA 1⅛:461 1:103 1:492ft *2½ 113 42 31½ 22½ 32½ Olivares F 1 Aw27000 80-16 Mr. Media, Jota, Rafael's Dancer 9

27Sep86-9Pom a1⅛:462 1:12 1:503ft 3 114 74 84½ 54½ 2½ Olivares F 2 Pom Dby 93-10 LghtnngToch,Rfl'sDncr,BoldBrvII 10

27Sep86—Run in divisions

20Sep86-11Pom 1 1/16:451 1:103 1:44 ft 2½ 114 36 35 2hd 2½ OlivaresF 1 ⓡDerby Trl 90-09 BoldBrvoII,Rfl'sDncr,J.R.Johnson 10

3Aug86-8Dmr 1 ⓣ:46 1:11 1:351fm 42 113 84½114½ 86¾ 78½ Solis A 2 La Jla Mi H 87-08 VrnonCstl,TrpolShors,Mrvn'sPlcy 12

3Aug86—Grade III

May 4 Hol 5f ft 1:02 h — ●Apr 29 Hol 6f ft 1:123 h — Apr 24 SA 5f m 1:003 h — Apr 19 SA 3f ft :363 h

All Cat — B. g. 4, by Cougar II—Almira, by Sheet Anchor

STEVENS G L — 117 — Br.—Bradley-Whittingham-Chandler (Ky) — 1988 5 2 0 1 $40,700

Own.—Bradley & Chandler Mmes — Tr.—Whittingham Charles — 1987 14 M 4 4 $36,125

Lifetime 20 2 4 5 $78,250 — Turf 6 1 0 1 $27,350

24Apr88-9SA 1⅛ⓣ:4821:1231:501gd 4½ 118 86½ 85 74¾ 34¾ Stevens G L 6 Aw42000 71-25 Eliminante, Nilambar, All Cat 8

12Mar88-8SA 1½ⓣ:4642:0142:261fm 6½ 115 1011118 1014 713 Toro F 8 ⓡSn Mrno H 71-11 Putting, Fiction, Chinoiserie 11

12Mar88—Broke slowly

25Feb88-5SA 1⅛ⓣ:4611:1041:504fm 4½ 119 1011119½ 96 11¾ ValenzuelPA 6 Aw34000 73-27 All Cat, Sharp Choice, Dennis D. 12

25Feb88—Bumped, steadied sharply 3/8, extremely wide into stretch

13Feb88-3SA 1¼ⓣ:4911:3912:04 fm *1e117 52½ 75½ 75½ 55 Velasquez J 2 Aw34000 62-24 DefiniteSigns,SpruceSkipper,Deput 8

13Feb88—Rank early

30Jan88-2SA 1 1/16:47 1:121 1:452ft 2½ 119 68½ 64½ 62½ 12½ Valenzuela P A 1 Mdn 74-20 All Cat, Eagle Dive, ParadeLeader 12

28Nov87-7Hol 1 1/16:47 1:113 1:433ft 2½e118 84½ 63½ 43½ 22½ Valenzuela P A 8 Mdn 83-12 Silver Dude, All Cat, Vysotsky 10

28Nov87—Wide into stretch

14Nov87-4SA 1 1/16:48 1:124 1:452ft 3½ 117 68½ 68½ 67 44½ Valenzuela P A 6 Mdn 70-22 Syrian Wind, Silver Dude, Vysotsky 9

14Nov87—Bumped start; wide into stretch

13Sep87-4Dmr 1 1/16:462 1:112 1:433ft 6½e1115 67 58½ 34½ 2nk Patton D B 7 Mdn 82-18 Unicopia, All Cat, Ma GrandVitesse 8

31Aug87-6Dmr 1 1/16:452 1:113 1:43 ft *2½e1115 1013 75½ 45½ 44¾ Patton D B 9 Mdn 88-14 Chess Set, Unicopia, Darabi 12

15Aug87-6Dmr 1 1/16:461 1:113 1:433ft 7½ 1115 56½ 42½ 32 23 Patton D B 4 Mdn 79-14 BreakfastTable,AllCt,DefiniteSigns 8

15Aug87—Pinched at start

May 5 Hol 5f ft 1:014 h — May 1 Hol 3f ft :383 h — Apr 19 SA 5f ft 1:012 h — Apr 14 SA 7f ft 1:263 h

Definite Signs 9
DELAHOUSSAYE E 114
Own.—Summa Stable
Ch. c. 4, by Affirmed—Sign of the Times, by Francis S
Br.—Mabee Mr-Mrs J C (Ky) 1988 8 2 2 1 $40,450
Tr.—Frankel Robert 1987 4 M 0 2 $5,700
Lifetime 12 2 2 3 $46,150 Turf 5 1 0 2 $31,150

24Apr88-9SA 1⅛Ⓣ:4821:1231:581gd 7¾ 120 63½ 63 44 44¾ DelhoussyeE3 Aw42000 71-25 Eliminante, Nilambar, All Cat 8
9Apr88-2SA 1⅛Ⓣ:4731:1131:483fm 8¾ 120 45½ 52¾ 33½ 63¾ DelhoussyeE6 Aw42000 88-08 RomnticPrince,BrekfstTbl,StrtPrty 9
25Mar88-8SA 1⅛Ⓣ:4631:1131:482fm 4¾ 121 51 51½ 53½ 34½ DelhoussyeE7 Aw42000 81-15 RoiNormnd,Eliminnte,DfintSigns 10
13Feb88-3SA 1⅜Ⓣ:4911:3912:04 fm 5¾ 117 1hd 2½ 2½ 1no DelhoussyeE1 Aw34000 67-24 DefiniteSigns,SpruceSkipper,Deput 8
13Feb88—Steadied early drive
4Feb88-1GG 1 :463 1:103 1:35 ft *3-5 120 31½ 2hd 2hd 1no Maple S3 Mdn 93-10 DfntSgns,KnndyExchng,CrystoMon 5
15Jan88-7BM 1 :464 1:113 1:374m *6-5e 120 21½ 2hd 21 22 Maple S7 Mdn 77-25 GoldnQuivr,DfntSgns,KnndyExchng 7
7Jan88-5BM 6f :221 :453 1:11 m 6 122 52½ 22 25 28 Maple S 2 Mdn 75-20 InhrntBttl,DfinitSigns,Zngr'sTowr 11
2Jan88-4SA 1 1/16:462 1:112 1:441ft 7¾ 119 56 65½ 811 822¾ Shoemaker W 8 Mdn 57-15 ProudCt,RoylTroubdor,BuMondII 11
2Jan88—Lugged out
18Oct87-6SA 1 1/16:461 1:111 1:433ft *4½ 117 44 43 58½ 611¾ Valenzuela P A4 Mdn 71-15 Bold Mistral, Silver Dude, Daraki 12
18Oct87—Bobbled start
15Aug87-6Dmr 1 1/16:461 1:113 1:433ft *3-2 116 32 21 22 35½ Delahoussaye E8 Mdn 76-14 BreakfastTable,AllCt,DefiniteSigns 8
May 3 Hol 5f ft 1:013 h Apr 3 Hol 4f ft :483 h Mar 21 Hol 5f ft 1:00 h Mar 15 Hol 7f ft 1:28 h

Wishful Thinker 10
BLACK C A 114
Own.—Nor Joanne H
B. c. 4, by Lyphard's Wish—Malaysia II, by Val de Loir
Br.—Nor Joanne H (Ky) 1987 8 2 0 0 $19,000
Tr.—Nor Fabio Turf 4 1 0 0 $13,200
Lifetime 8 2 0 0 $19,000

7Oct87-5SA 1⅛Ⓣ:4731:1211:49 fm 29 118 86¾ 96 109½ 88 DelhoussyeE 2Aw33000 74-16 MgnPlus,QuietlyBold,BstSolution 10
9Sep87-7Dmr 1 1/16Ⓣ:48 1:1231:441fm 14 117 53 41¾ 1½ 1¾ Black C A 5 Aw24000 79-21 WishfulThinkr,JohnVgors,BrdDncr 10
9Sep87—Lugged in
30Aug87-5Dmr 1 1/16Ⓣ:4711:1231:443fm 49 113 1014 94½ 86½ 87½ Black C A 2 Aw24000 69-21 Table Glow, Jonleat, Visible Asset 10
30Aug87—Broke in air; lugged in, unmanageable final 1/8
12Aug87-7Dmr 1⅛Ⓣ:4741:1221:50 fm 63 116 11 11 2½ 64½ McHrgueDG 1 Aw23000 78-17 PoltclAmbtn,CntctGm,LckyHrldH. 10
22Jly87-6Hol 1⅛:47 1:113 1:512ft 6 116 21 2hd 1hd 11½ McHargue DG 2 M32000 80-15 WishfulThinkr,HndiRon,KingTung 10
22Jly87—Raced wide 7/8 turn
24Jun87-6Hol 7f :22 :451 1:24 ft 24 116 53¾ 31½ 44½ 913 McHargue DG 4 M50000 71-13 MonLgonnr,ExplosvDrm,CrystlFx 12
14Jun87-6Hol 7f :222 :452 1:23 ft 63 115 3½ 52 108¾ 1017½ Castanon A L 4 Mdn 71-14 PolitclAmbtn,BstOfDnzg,Amrcno 10
29May87-6Hol 6½f :221 :45 1:162ft 18 116 31½ 55 916 1222½ McHargue D G 9 Mdn 76-16 MajesticMission,Fnticol,Acquired 12
May 5 Hol 4f ft :484 h ●Apr 28 Hol 6f ft 1:111 h Apr 22 Hol 3f ft :36 hg ●Apr 16 Hol 5f ft 1:012 h

Be Scenic 11
CASTANON A L 114
Own.—Hooper F W
Ch. c. 4, by If This Be So—Scenic Flight, by Crozier
Br.—Hooper F W (Fla) 1988 5 0 1 0 $13,450
Tr.—Russell John W 1987 12 2 3 1 $51,625
Lifetime 24 2 5 4 $78,780 Turf 5 0 2 0 $18,775

28Apr88-8Hol 1 :443 1:10 1:361ft 36 115 98¾ 95¾ 53 43¾ Castanon AL 2 Aw40000 78-18 OnceForLee,PrinceSssfrs,DryRidge 9
28Apr88—Bumped late
11Mar88-5SA 1⅛Ⓣ:4611:1041:482fm 9½ 117 911 88¾ 87 45½ Pincay L Jr 2 Aw38000 80-15 PleasantVriety,Eliminnte,ProudCt 10
14Feb88-7SA 1¼Ⓣ:4641:3712:024fm *4 115 914 99 77 64 Castanon AL 8 Aw38000 63-23 Uptothehilt, Nilambar, Feraud 10
29Jan88-8SA 1⅛Ⓣ:4731:1221:511fm 18 116 1211 1117 63½ 23½ Castanon AL 6 Aw38000 67-29 Fiction, Be Scenic, L'Empire 12
29Jan88—Wide; lugged in stretch
10Jan88-5SA 7f :222 :444 1:221ft 9½ 115 99¾ 911 98 95½ McHrgueDG 4 Aw35000 84-15 ReEnter,Fanticola,Buckland'sHalo 10
28Nov87-8Hol 1 1/16:47 1:112 1:432ft 5½ 114 44 54 34 21½ Castanon AL 3 Aw35000 85-12 Captain Valid, Be Scenic, Rupperto 7
21Nov87-9Hol 1 :451 1:093 1:343ft 13f 113 107½ 1011 910 812½ HwleyS 11 Affirmed H 78-12 W.D.Jcks,Wyn'sCrn,ErnYourStrips 12
21Nov87—Grade III
7Oct87-5SA 1⅛Ⓣ:4731:1211:49 fm 7½ 116 1011 85¾ 87½ 56½ ShoemkerW 8 Aw33000 75-16 MgnPlus,QuietlyBold,BstSolution 10
4Sep87-7Dmr 1 :46 1:103 1:362ft *3-2 114 63¾ 65¾ 54 53¾ McCarronCJ 1 Aw26000 82-16 Mark Chip, NoMarker,CaptainValid 6
4Sep87—Bumped hard start
29Jly87-8Dmr 1 Ⓣ:4631:1111:362fm 11 118 74¾ 53½ 43½ 21 McCrrCJ 6 ⓇOceanside 88-13 SavonaTower,BeScenic,CelticRelity 9
29Jly87—Run in divisions
Apr 22 Hol 6f ft 1:152 h Apr 14 Hol 6f ft 1:153 h Apr 9 Hol 5f ft 1:05 h Apr 2 Hol 5f ft 1:004 h

***Falcon Eye** 12
TORO F 120
Own.—ShkhMktmBnRshdAlMktoum
Dk. b. or br. c. 4, by Touching Wood—Greenland Park, by Red God
Br.—Gainsborough StudMgmtLtd (Eng) 1988 2 1 0 0 $20,675
Tr.—Drysdale Neil 1987 7 1 2 0 $24,007
Lifetime 12 2 4 1 $55,354 Turf 12 2 4 1 $55,354

17Apr88-9SA 1 Ⓣ:4641:1041:353fm 4 118 64½ 84½ 4nk 13 Toro F10 Aw36000 97-17 Falcon Eye, Vysotsky, L. A. Fire 10
17Apr88—Wide into stretch
13Feb88-7SA a6½f Ⓣ:214 :4441:15 fm 4½ 116 44 44 55 57½ DelhoussyE10 Aw35000 77-24 The Scout,IHumineux,MidnightIce 10
17Oct87♦4CrLaroche(Fra) a1⅛ : yl — 123 Ⓣ 2hd GuignrdG G P d Nord FabulousMorn,FlconEye,AymZmn 13
17Oct87—No time taken
5Sep87♦3Evry(Fra) a1⅛ 1:534gd 12 124 Ⓣ 72 MorGW Px d Lion d'Agrs SuprArnn,Fruhlingschochzt,RchMn 11
7Aug87♦3Clairefont'e(Fra a1⅛ 1:51 yl 9½ 123 Ⓣ 2½ MooreGW Px d Cls Flri FbulousMorn,FlconEye,RttlAlong 13
25Jun87♦4Chantilly(Fra) a1 1:43 gd 20 123 Ⓣ 11 GugnrdG Px d Pntrm Solido, GreatBooby, Boquen 11
2Jun87♦7StCloud(Fra) a1 1:453gd 3 123 Ⓣ 11 MrGW Px Fauchr(Mdn) FalconEye,PremierPrix,Tboushkn 16
21Apr87♦7MLaffitte(Fra) a1 1:364gd 9-5 123 Ⓣ 44½ MrGW Px Flyng Fx(Mdn) SoftCurrncy,BrightBloon,OnThHill 16
31Mar87♦7StCloud(Fra) a7½f 1:483sf *3-2 123 Ⓣ 53¼ MooreGW Px Bosilino Mallypha, Banc d'Or, Lancret 17
May 3 Hol 5f ft 1:004 h Apr 28 Hol 7f ft 1:253 h ●Apr 11 Hol 6f ft 1:143 h Apr 6 Hol 7f ft 1:273 h

Selected Support Information

```
Rafael's Dancer                  B. c. 4, by Northern Baby—Bannockburn, by Count Brook
  PINCAY L JR            116     Br.—Adger-Mandate-Lombardi (Ky)       1986 13 1 3 2      $64,775
                                 Tr.—Whittingham Michael               Turf  3 0 0 0       $5,625
Own.—Adger-Lombardi-Mandate      Lifetime   13 1 3 2   $64,775
10Nov86-8Hol   1⅛ Ⓣ:463 1:102 1:464fm 104 122  1110 1211 1212 1114¼ OlivaresF9   Hol Dby   79-07 Spellbound, Double Feint, Bruiser 12
     10Nov86—Grade I; Run in divisions; Wide 7/8
31Oct86-5SA    1⅛ :461 1:103 1:492ft   *2¼ 113  42  31½ 22½ 32½  Olivares F1  Aw27000   80-16 Mr. Media, Jota, Rafael's Dancer 9
27Sep86-9Pom   a1⅛ :462 1:12 1:503ft    3 114   74  84¾ 54¾ 2½   Olivares F2  Pom Dby   93-10 LghtnngToch,Rfl'sDncr,BoldBrvII 10
     27Sep86—Run in divisions
20Sep86-11Pom  1 1/16 :451 1:103 1:44 ft  2½ 114  36  35  2hd 2½  OlivaresF1 ⓇDerby Trl  90-09 BoldBrvoII,Rfl'sDncr,J.R.Johnson 10
3Aug86-8Dmr   1 Ⓣ:46 1:11 1:351fm      42 113   84½ 114½ 86¾ 78¼ Solis A3     La Jla Mi H 87-08 VrnonCstl,TrpolShors,Mrvn'sPlcy 12
     3Aug86—Grade III
21Jly86-8Hol   1¼ :471 1:363 2:033ft    24 114   41½ 54½ 54  41¾  Solis A8     Swaps     72-16 Clear Choice, Southern Halo, Jota 9
     21Jly86—Grade I; Wide 3/8 turn
22Jun86-9Hol   1 :444 1:093 1:343ft    *9-5 108  43  55½ 57¾ 310  ShoemkerW1   Aw21000   80-08 Enviro, T. V. Oil, Rafael's Dancer 8
8Jun86-7Hol    1 :452 1:10 1:353ft      6¼ 108  21  24  31  21¾  ShoemkerW7   Aw21000   83-11 Mastery, Rafael's Dancer, Arcadius 7
24May86-8Hol   1 1/16 Ⓣ:481 1:12 1:422fm 41 112  1hd 2hd 5¾  54¼  OlivresF3    W Rgrs H  88-09 ‡Sovereign Don, Mazaad, Autobot 7
     24May86—Grade III; Took up late; Placed fourth through disqualification
4May86-3Hol    7f :224 :461 1:24 ft    *2 115   21½ 2½  1½  12½  Olivares F1  Mdn       84-18 Rfel'sDncer,BrndImge,FifteenGrnd 8
 ●Feb 1 SA 6f ft 1:114 h    ●Jan 26 SA 1 ft 1:382 h    ●Jan 21 SA 7f ft 1:262 h    ●Jan 15 SA 6f ft 1:113 h
```

NINTH RACE
Santa Anita
APRIL 24, 1988

1 ⅛ MILES.(Turf). (1.45⅘) ALLOWANCE. Purse $42,000. 4-year-olds and upward, which are non-winners of $3,000 twice other than maiden, claiming or starter. Weight, 120 lbs. Non-winners of two races other than claiming at one mile or over since February 1, allowed 2 lbs.; a race other than maiden or claiming since then, 4 lbs.

Value of race $42,000; value to winner $23,100; second $8,400; third $6,300; fourth $3,150; fifth $1,050. Mutuel pool $483,439. Exacta pool $822,816.

Last Raced	Horse	Eqt.A.Wt	PP	St	¼	½	¾	Str	Fin	Jockey	Odds $1
9Apr88 2SA5	Eliminante	7 116	7	6	8	71	51	22	11½	Pedroza M A	6.00
23Mar88 8GG2	Nilambar	5 116	2	1	1½	11	1½	1hd	23½	Toro F	3.90
12Mar88 8SA7	All Cat	b 4 118	6	7	71½	8	8	73½	3hd	Stevens G L	4.40
9Apr88 2SA6	Definite Signs	4 120	3	4	61½	62	6½	4hd	42½	Delahoussaye E	7.80
9Apr88 2SA3	Street Party	b 4 116	4	3	21	21	21	32	51	Seymour D J	6.70
17Apr88 3SA7	His Highness	4 116	5	5	3½	41	4½	5hd	6¾	Gryder A T	70.50
9Apr88 2SA2	Breakfast Table	b 4 118	8	8	5hd	5hd	71½	6½	74½	McCarron C J	1.80
17Apr88 3SA6	Bold Crusader	b 4 116	1	2	41	3½	3hd	8	8	Olivares F	20.70

OFF AT 5:41. Start good. Won driving. Time, :23⅗, :48⅖, 1:12⅗, 1:37⅗, 1:50⅕ Course good.

$2 Mutuel Prices:			
7-ELIMINANTE	14.00	6.20	4.00
2-NILAMBAR		5.40	4.00
6-ALL CAT			3.40

$5 EXACTA 7–2 PAID $203.50

Ch. g, by Practicante—Elevacion, by Aristophanes. Trainer Borick Robert. Bred by Haras La Biznaga (Arg).

ELIMINANTE, devoid of early speed, rallied to engage for the lead while outside NILAMBAR with a little more than a furlong remaining, battled for command with that rival in the final furlong and had the needed late response to edge clear. NILAMBAR went to the front at once, resisted well when engaged by ELIMINANTE early in the drive to battle for command with that rival in the last furlong but had to settle for the place. ALL CAT, devoid of early foot, found his best stride too late. DEFINITE SIGNS, outrun early, came into the stretch four wide and could not gain the needed ground in the drive. STREET PARTY forced the early pace and weakened in the drive. BREAKFAST TABLE, outrun early, lacked the necessary response in the last quarter. BOLD CRUSADER, close up early, faltered.

Owners— 1, Four Four Forty Farms; 2, Red Baron's Barn; 3, Bradley & Chandler Mmes; 4, Summa Stable; 5, Kinghaven Farms; 6, Hoffman-Kruse-Sweeney; 7, Taub S; 8, La Torre-Rubnstein-Rubnstein.

Trainers— 1, Borick Robert; 2, Vienna Darrell; 3, Whittingham Charles; 4, Frankel Robert; 5, Attfield Roger; 6, Sweeney Brian; 7, Gosden John H M; 8, Palma Hector O.

Approximate Odds, Post Time

Falcon Eye	3–2
Nilambar	5–1
All Cat	6–1
Dennis D.	8–1
Definite Signs	10–1
Table Glow	12–1
Street Party	15–1

Be Scenic	15–1
Rafael's Dancer	18–1
Millero Y Medio	35–1
Wishful Thinker	50–1
Lonesome Dancer	85–1

Comments

Unlikely

If there can be a *Rocky III* and an *Animal House 2*, then there can also be an Eliminante 2. Eliminante has returned on April 24, to win a race! Will he continue his role as The Eliminator?

Eliminante has won not because he has suddenly changed his spirit, but because this antihero has remained the same while around him the southern California colony of turf horses has suffered a decline that rivals the stock-market crash of October 1987. Eliminante has won a race the way he knows best: by default. Let his infamous victory serve as one more lesson in thoroughbred cycles that whole "crops" of horses can come up strong or weak, that the rise and fall of particular horse groupings is a periodic occurrence.

This phenomenon will have a tremendous effect on today's race and most others to be run at allowance level on the grass during this period. This will set the stage for a low percentage of winning favorites within the category, and a better-than-average performance for the outsiders that do not belong to this mediocre community.

Not only can we eliminate all the horses that lost to Eliminante, a *standard procedure*, but we can demote the value of turf victories by other horses in today's field, especially the favorite, Falcon Eye, who beat Vysotsky, a horse from the same club as Eliminante.

1. Losing to Eliminante on April 24, and therefore functioning as mirages in today's field, are: Nilambar (a seconditis horse), All Cat (who only wins when everyone else backs up in the stretch), Definite Signs, Street Party, and Breakfast Table.
2. Tossouts due to dull current form are Be Scenic (with a

cold trainer and a 0 for 5 turf record) and Millero Y Medio (whose turf wins were in South America and whose only U.S. win was a lone front-running trip in the slop vs. grass horses who ended up on the dirt when it rained).

3. The layoff horse, Wishful Thinker, is expected to lose because he shows no signs of doing well after a layoff, running terribly as a first-time starter and showing both wins with recency.

4. Lonesome Dancer is a claimer from a track that is one notch below today's racing circuit. Shippers from "lesser" tracks tend to do surprisingly well when confronting fields such as this one, which don't measure up to their denoted class level. However, his poor win record gives no arguments in his favor, especially since he must defeat three horses that just won their last races.

Contenders

If the current crop of turf horses is as poor as we think, then it stands to reason that horses that were raced against superior fields during better harvests would be highly valued in today's field. Rafael's Dancer is 0 for 3 on the grass, but the two turf races appearing in today's past performances were against graded-stakes fields in a period of rich abundance in the turf colony.

More Memories. In order to remember the history of southern California, I've had to exercise selective exclusion of unnecessary information, such as mayors, governors, and earthquakes. In this way, I can remember things that are truly important, such as Rafael's Dancer's first turf race, which does not appear in today's past performances. Significantly, his first turf race followed a dirt victory, as today's turf race does. That grass debut of Rafael's Dancer saw him pressing the pace against Sovereign Don, Mazaad, and Autobot, each of whom would be 1–5 in today's field. To assure myself that my memory was correct, I looked up the past performances from that period, which were included with today's pps. Now we can situate Rafael's Dancer objectively in relationship to the horses he will meet.

Rafael's Dancer has four factors in his favor:

1. Sharp current form.
2. A losing turf race (following his last win) that is superior to the winning races of today's rivals.

3. A *pattern match* in that his peak turf effort followed his last peak dirt race.
4. A long-shot turf trainer, one who believes in the grass capabilities of this horse, because he thought nothing of entering him in three graded-stakes turf events. (And when it says that Rafael's Dancer was wide at the ⅞ on November 16, 1986, it doesn't tell *Racing Form* readers the whole story. I was there, and I remember that he was forced so wide that pedestrians over on Century Boulevard could smell him.)

Pact with the Devil. Ultimately, the positive features of Rafael's Dancer coalesce into a picture of the proven loser who wins a cluster of races because the right situation is created for him, as if the Devil had moved in and set it up. Recall the different types of proven losers; Rafael's Dancer appears to be the type that has been forced to labor at the wrong level. He was clearly overmatched in his grass races, and he is just the type of allowance horse to win when the rest of the field comes down to his level.

Today's spot is ideal. And if he should win, it may represent the culmination of a brief winning interlude and a return to a life of knocking at the door and not entering, à la Willy Loman. A win today would force him into tougher allowance conditions. In southern California there will be few turf claiming races and none that offer weak fields like today's. This trainer is not willing to part with horses, so don't expect to see him in claiming events. If he wins today, he'd better enjoy it.

In Chapter 3 we wrote that the brief-interlude win period of the chronic loser is frequently accompanied by a class drop. Appearances in past performances frequently cover up reality rather than expressing it; Rafael's Dancer is going up in class from his previous race but dropping in class *from his previous turf races.* We also wrote that the second win of the brief interlude cluster usually adhered to the same conditions of the first win. In the letter of the law, Rafael's Dancer does not comply, but in the spirit of the law, he is indeed repeating a pattern with which he was successful in the past.

Why is it when I have enough reasons to fill a doctoral thesis for a particular horse, there is another contender in the same race? Dennis D. deserves the label of contender. Granted he beat a poor field in his last race. But he seems to be developing into a master of a trade, a turf specialist (never off the board on the grass, runs much better than his odds). He's also a five-year-old gelding, which implies the possibility of prolonged success as a late bloomer. He's got the rail in a race that begins on a turn (big advantage).

And there's Falcon Eye. You just can't throw him out. He is sharp right now. But he draws way outside in a race that begins on a turn.

	Our Line	Track Odds	Decision
Rafael's Dancer	2–1	18–1	Way over. *Bet.*
Dennis D.	3–1	8–1	Clearly over. *Bet.*
Falcon Eye	4–1	3–2	Way under. No bet.

With the advantage so much greater on the top choice, more money goes on that one, less on Dennis D. Anderson, Meadow, Mitchell, and Ziemba have made it clear that in money management you bet more when you have a greater advantage and you don't bet at all when there is no advantage.

NINTH RACE
Hollywood
MAY 8, 1988

1 1/8 MILES.(Turf). (1.45$\frac{3}{5}$) ALLOWANCE (Chute Start). Purse $40,000. 4-year-olds and upward which have not won $3,000 twice other than maiden, claiming or starter. Weight, 120 lbs. Non-winners of such a race at a mile or over since March 15 allowed 3 lbs.; such a race since February 15, 6 lbs.

Value of race $40,000; value to winner $22,000; second $8,000; third $6,000; fourth $3,000; fifth $1,000. Mutuel pool $348,728. Exacta pool $539,444.

Last Raced	Horse	Eqt.	A.	Wt	PP	St	1/4	1/2	3/4	Str	Fin	Jockey	Odds $1
13Apr88 ^{7}SA^{1}	Rafael's Dancer	b	5	120	7	4	4^{1}	2^{1}	2^{1}	1^{hd}	$1^{\frac{1}{2}}$	Olivares F	18.80
23Apr88 ^{10}GG^{3}	Lonesome Dancer	b	5	114	2	3	3^{hd}	4^{hd}	$5^{1\frac{1}{2}}$	$4^{\frac{1}{2}}$	2^{hd}	Solis A	87.30
24Apr88 ^{9}SA^{5}	Street Party	b	4	114	6	8	8^{1}	8^{hd}	7^{hd}	$5^{1\frac{1}{2}}$	$3^{1\frac{1}{2}}$	Shoemaker W	15.50
24Apr88 ^{9}SA^{2}	Nilambar		5	115	5	2	1^{hd}	1^{1}	$1^{\frac{1}{2}}$	$2^{1\frac{1}{2}}$	4^{hd}	McCarron C J	5.20
24Apr88 ^{9}SA^{4}	Definite Signs		4	116	9	5	$9^{1\frac{1}{2}}$	$9^{1\frac{1}{2}}$	9^{hd}	$8^{1\frac{1}{2}}$	$5^{\frac{3}{4}}$	Delahoussaye E	9.80
25Apr88 ^{9}SA^{6}	Millero Y Medio	b	7	115	3	7	$5^{\frac{1}{2}}$	$6^{1\frac{1}{2}}$	6^{hd}	$7^{\frac{1}{2}}$	$6^{1\frac{1}{2}}$	Sibille R	34.40
17Apr88 ^{7}GG^{2}	Table Glow	b	4	117	4	6	6^{hd}	5^{hd}	4^{hd}	3^{hd}	7^{hd}	Pincay L Jr	12.00
7Oct87 ^{5}SA^{8}	Wishful Thinker		4	114	10	10	$10^{\frac{1}{2}}$	7^{hd}	8^{1}	$9^{1\frac{1}{2}}$	8^{hd}	Black C A	50.80
24Apr88 ^{9}SA^{3}	All Cat	b	4	117	8	12	12	12	12	$10^{\frac{1}{2}}$	9^{2}	Stevens G L	6.10
28Apr88 ^{8}Hol^{4}	Be Scenic	b	4	114	11	9	$7^{1\frac{1}{2}}$	$10^{1\frac{1}{2}}$	$11^{1\frac{1}{2}}$	12	$10^{1\frac{1}{2}}$	Castanon A L	15.80
27Apr88 ^{7}Hol^{1}	Dennis D.		5	120	1	1	$2^{1\frac{1}{2}}$	$3^{\frac{1}{2}}$	3^{hd}	6^{hd}	$11^{\frac{1}{2}}$	Sherman A B	8.20
17Apr88 ^{9}SA^{1}	Falcon Eye		4	120	12	11	11^{hd}	$11^{1\frac{1}{2}}$	$10^{\frac{1}{2}}$	$11^{\frac{1}{2}}$	12	Toro F	1.60

OFF AT 5:51. Start good. Won driving. Time, :23$\frac{4}{5}$, :47$\frac{4}{5}$, 1:10$\frac{4}{5}$, 1:35, 1:47$\frac{3}{5}$ Course firm.

$2 Mutuel Prices:			
7–RAFAEL'S DANCER	39.60	21.00	15.40
2–LONESOME DANCER		50.20	21.20
6–STREET PARTY			12.60

$2 EXACTA 7–2 PAID $1,324.40.

B. h, by Northern Baby—Bannockburn, by Count Brook. Trainer Whittingham Michael. Bred by Adger–Mandato–Lombardi (Ky).

RAFAEL'S DANCER, close up early, battled for command around the far turn and through the drive and had the needed late response to prevail. LONESOME DANCER, never far back, kept to his task in the drive and gct up for the place. STREET PARTY, outrun early, rallied in the last quarter but could not get up. NILAMBAR vied for the lead all the way to the final yards and weakened slightly. DEFINITE SIGNS, outrun early, was full of run late. TABLE GLOW, in contention early, menaced on the far turn and in the upper stretch but weakened a bit from midstretch to the finish. ALL CAT, devoid of early speed, lacked the needed rally. DENNIS D., close up or the backstretch after vying for the early advantage, gave way in the final three furlongs. FALCON EYE had no visible mishap.

Owners— 1, Lombardi & Mandato; 2, 4-Fun Stable & Maybury; 3, Kinghaven Farms; 4, Red Baron's Barn; 5, Summa Stable; 6, Pulliam C N; 7, Sarkowsky H; 8, Nor Joanne H; 9, Bradley & Chandler Mmes; 10, Hooper F W; 11, Burke G W; 12, Sheikh Mktm Bn Rshid Al Mktoum.

Trainers— 1, Whittingham Michael; 2, Murphy Chuck; 3, Whittingham Michael; 4, Vienna Darrell; 5, Frankel Robert; 6, Pulliam Vivian M; 7, Mandella Richard; 8, Nor Fabio; 9, Whittingnam Charles; 10, Russell John W; 11, Lage Armando; 12, Drysdale Neil.

Overweight: Nilambar 1 pound; Definite Signs 2; Millero Y Medio 1; Table Glow 3.

Scratched—Creative Financing (25Mar88 ^{8}SA^{10}).

Lonesome Dancer, second in the "Dancer's Exacta," was the horse that nearly became a contender by default. When he got up for second, the $2 exacta paid $1324.40. He did not have the profile of a winning horse, but *the second horse in exactas is usually not the second-most-likely winner*. Lonesome Dancer's recent form was that of a come-close horse.

The secondary plot of the Rafael's Dancer's race unfolded as expected. Eliminante had done it again. As usual, he was not present to observe the outcome of his labors. He was hiding in his stable, where no one would associate him with the mysterious factor that undermined the future of certain horses. All five horses that had lost to Eliminante finished out of the money.

Epilogue: Insight vs. Objectivity

I've always believed that the more insight needed to discover a contender, the more money I should bet. But how do you define insight, and when does insight become so esoteric that it leads to a pie in the sky? After the fact, I suffered a moment of regret that instead of betting all three units on Rafael's Dancer, I had made it two units on him and one on Dennis D. I considered that, after all, Dennis D. was much more *obvious* than Rafael's Dancer and therefore should not have intervened in my betting decision.

But it often works both ways. In Workshop One, Norway Bay required more insight than Dishonorable Guest. If insight is over-emphasized, creative handicappers will outfinesse themselves and pass by too many winners whose only attributes are based on clear reasoning and ascending numbers. The betting-line strategy allows for the balanced coexistence of insight and objectivity, as well as the overlapping of these two forces.

One looks at race results as if they are the culmination of a deterministic process. In reality, a race result means that one of several possible scenarios happened to materialize. By balancing insight with objectivity, handicappers will be liberated from one-dimensionalism. In this way, mechanically-oriented handicappers will not be victims of dogmatism, and the more creative players will not go off the deep end.

WORKSHOP FOUR

April 14, 1988

8th Pimlico

1 ⅜ MILES. (1.53¾) 22rd Running THE PIMLICO SPECIAL. Purse $500,000 Guaranteed (Additional $100,000 Bonus to the Winner if previously nominated to the Triple Crown Races.) A handicap for 4-year-olds and upward. By subscription of $600 each on or before Monday, February 1, 1988, which should accompany the nomination. a sustaining payment of $1,200 each is due on or before Friday, April 1, 1988. Late nominations may be made on or before Tuesday, April 26, 1988, by payment of $15,000 each, which should accompany the nomination and is refundable is the nominee does not draw into the body of the race. There will be no supplement nominations. A fee of $4,000 should be paid at the time of pre-entry by 12 noon Thursday, May 5, 1988, with an additional $3,000 to pass the entry box on Thursday, May 12, 1988 and an additional $3,000 to start, with $500,000 guaranteed, to be divided 65% to first, 20% to second, 10% to third, 5% to fourth, with an added $100,000 bonus to the winner if previously nominated to the Triple Crown races. Weights to be released on Tuesday, May 3, 1988. The field will be limited to 14 starters. In the event that more than 14 horses should pass the entry box, preference shall be given to the high weights based upon the weight assignments adjusted for the sex allowance. Total earnings from January 1, 1988 will be used in determining the preference of horses with equally assigned weights. Horses not drawn into the race will be placed on an Also Eligible list in order of preference as specified herein. In the event of a scratch in the body of the race prior to the official scratch time, horses on the Also Eligible list will be moved into the body of the race based upon their order of preference. Any nominees excluded from running as a result of the aforementioned rule shall be refunded all payments. Trophies will be presented to the winning owner, trainer and jockey. Closed Monday, February 1, 1988 with 82 nominations.

Little Bold John *
B. g. 6, by John Alden—Little Bold Sphinx, by Bold Ambition
MILLER D A JR 117
Br.—Clagett Hal C B (Md) 1988 4 4 0 0 $138,221
Tr.—Robb John J 1987 10 8 3 3 $580,041
Own.—Owens J E III
Lifetime 50 24 11 6 $1,102,313 Turf 7 1 3 0 $85,358

7May88-9Pim 1 1/16 :472 1:112 1:431gd *4-5 123 31 2hd 2hd 1 1/2 MillrDAJr 4 Riggs H 88-24 LittlBoldJohn,AlongCmJons,Entrtn 6
7May88—Grade III
23Apr88-10Pim 1 1/8 :472 1:113 1:502ft *2-3 124 22 1/2 22 1/2 31 1/2 1 1/2 MllrDAJr 2 NeverBndH 98-22 LittlBoldJohn,AlongCmJons,Entrtn 7
1Apr88-9Pim 1 1/8 :473 1:114 1:504ft *1-2 123 44 44 21 1nk MllrDAJr 2 JeningsH 88-23 LittlBoldJohn,Silno,InfirmtivAction 7
20Mar88-8Pim 6f :224 :462 1:114ft *1 122 35 1/2 33 1/2 23 11 Miller D AJr 3 Aw27000 87-26 LttlBoldJohn,GlGoldDst,WlrdScott 5
19Sep87-7Pim 1 1/4 :481 1:383 2:034ft 9-5 126 21 12 13 14 MllrDAJr 5 BudClssic 96-12 Little BoldJohn,Bagetelle,Castelets 6
12Sep87-9Pim 1 1/16 :461 1:113 1:424gd *1-2 122 31 1/2 63 77 710 MllrDAJr 5 PolynesinH 80-15 SouthrnAppl,MortggMn,BgEydBtty 7
15Aug87-10Tdn 1 1/8 :463 1:112 1:501ft *3-5 122 21 1/2 21 1/2 22 21 MllrDAJr 4 BudBdCpH 85-22 Savings,LittleBoldJohn,FullCourge 9
1Aug87-9Pim 1 1/8 :48 1:114 1:484ft *3-5 121 1 1/2 1hd 1 1/2 1 1/2 MllrDAJr 4 MrylndHcp 98-16 LittleBoldJohn,EntitledTo,Cstelets 5
15Jly87-4Atl 1 3/16 (T):5121:1611:584sf 8 116 1 1/2 2 1/2 54 1/2 514 1/2 MllrDAJr 4 U NationsH 54-33 Manila, Racing Star, Air Display 5
15Jly87—Grade I
4Jly87-10Pim 1 1/16 :46 1:103 1:432ft *2-5 119 1 1/2 1hd 11 1/2 11 1/2 MllrDAJr 3 FtMchnryH 87-19 LittleBoldJohn,Bgetll,BrillintStppr 5
May 3 Bow 5f ft 1:014 b ●Mar 26 Bow 1 sy 1:413 b ●Mar 15 Bow 3f ft :351 hg

Alysheba
B. c. 4, by Alydar—Bel Sheba, by Lt Stevens
MCCARRON C 127
Br.—Madden Preston (Ky) 1988 3 3 0 0 $1,175,000
Tr.—Van Berg Jack C 1987 10 3 3 1 $2,511,156
Own.—Scharbauer Dorothy&Pamela
Lifetime 20 7 7 2 $4,045,642

17Apr88-8SA 1 1/8 :462 1:094 1:471ft *4-5 127 21 1/2 1hd 2hd 1no McCrrCJ 1 S BrndinoH 93-17 Alysheba, Ferdinand, Good Taste 5
17Apr88—Grade II
6Mar88-8SA 1 1/4 :463 1:343 1:594ft *1 126 33 1 1/2 11 1 1/2 McCrrCJ 2 S Anita H 98-13 Alysheba, Ferdinand,SuperDiamond 4
6Mar88—Grade I
7Feb88-8SA 1 1/4 :453 1:351 2:002ft *4-5 126 58 1/2 1hd 1hd 13 McCrrCJ 3 C H Strub 87-16 Alysheba, Candi's Gold, OnTheLine 6
7Feb88—Grade I
21Nov87-7Hol 1 1/4 :462 1:352 2:012ft 3 1/2 122 98 1/2 54 41 2no McCrrCJ 2 Br Cp Class 85-12 Ferdinnd,Alysheb,JudgeAngelucci 12
21Nov87—Grade I
27Sep87-10LaD 1 1/4 :47 1:362 2:031ft *1-2 126 78 1/2 32 1/2 21 1 1/2 McCrrCJ 2 Super Dby 85-19 Alysheba, Candi's Gold, Parochial 8
27Sep87—Grade I; Brushed rival
22Aug87-8Sar 1 1/4 :461 1:362 2:02 sy *2 1/2 126 712 78 1/2 69 620 1/2 McCrrnCJ 8 Travers 70-16 JavaGold,Cryptoclearnce,PolishNvy 9
22Aug87—Grade I
1Aug87-9Mth 1 1/8 :463 1:093 1:47 ft 3-2 126 32 1/2 21 32 1/2 2nk McCrrCJ 4 Haskell H 99-07 Bet Twice, Alysheba, Lost Code 5
1Aug87—Grade I; In close on turn
6Jun87-8Bel 1 1/2 :492 2:03 2:281ft *4-5 126 47 47 39 414 1/2 McCrrCJ 2 Belmont 65-15 Bet Twice, Cryptoclearance, Gulch 9
6Jun87—Grade I; Rough trip
16May87-9Pim 1 3/16 :471 1:113 1:554ft *2 126 58 1/2 43 2hd 1 1/2 McCrrCJ 8 Preakness 88-18 Alysheba,BetTwice,Cryptoclearnce 9
16May87—Grade I
2May87-8CD 1 1/4 :462 1:364 2:032ft 8 1/2 126 1312 31 1/2 21 1 3/4 McCrrCJ 3 Ky Dby 80-08 Alysheba, Bet Twice, Avies Copy 17
2May87—Grade I; Stumbled mid-str
●May 11 Pim 5f gd 1:013 h Apr 14 SA 5f ft :594 h ●Apr 7 Hol 1 ft 1:381 h ●Apr 2 Hol 7f ft 1:283 h

Lac Ouimet *
B. h. 5, by Pleasant Colony—Northern Sunset, by Northfields
BAILEY J D 117
Br.—Payson Virginia Kraft (Ky) 1988 2 1 1 0 $152,980
Tr.—Lundy Richard J 1987 10 3 1 0 $271,978
Own.—Payson Virginia Kraft
Lifetime 24 8 3 2 $576,988 Turf 1 0 0 0 $220

24Apr88-8Aqu 1 1/4 :481 1:361 2:001ft 3 1/2 116 11 1/2 11 1hd 1hd BaileyJD 5 Excelsior H 95-17 Lac Ouimet, Personal Flag,Talinum 9
24Apr88—Grade II; Drifted,drvng
14Apr88-8Aqu 1 :452 1:092 1:344ft 8 1/2 122 3 1/2 1hd 2hd 2hd Bailey J D 3 HcpO 92-21 RoylPnnnt,LcOuimt,CountOnRomo 9
12Sep87-8Med 1 1/16 :47 1:104 1:412sy *3-2 117 3 1/2 44 1/2 510 512 3/4 BaileyJD 4 Clif Hngr H 83-15 Foligno, Cost Conscious,AirDisplay 7
12Sep87—Grade III; Run in Divisions
22Aug87-7Mth 1 1/8 :454 1:09 1:481ft 19 116 58 1/2 719 728 — Bailey J D 6 Iselin H — — BordeuxBob,SilverComet,LostCode 7
22Aug87—Grade I; Eased
8Aug87-8Sar 1 1/8 :462 1:102 1:482ft 19 117 44 31 57 1/2 510 BaileyJD 5 Whitney H 85-13 Java Gold, Gulch, Broad Brush 7
8Aug87—Grade I
30Jly87-8Bel 1 1/8 :462 1:104 1:503ft *1 122 43 1/2 31 11 13 Bailey J D 1 HcpO 74-24 Lac Ouimet, I Rejoice, Carjack 6
30Jly87—Bobbld;ridden out
4Jly87-8Bel 1 1/4 :481 1:371 2:03 ft 3 1/2 117 12 32 44 44 Maple E 5 Suburban H 79-23 Broad Brush,SetStyle,BordeauxBob 5
4Jly87—Grade I
7Jun87-8Bel 1 1/8 :47 1:11 1:481ft 3 1/2 116 11 1/2 1 1/2 12 1/2 12 1/2 Maple E 4 Nssu Cty H 86-22 LcOuimet,FobbyForbes,JohnsTrsur 6
7Jun87—Grade II
16May87-7Pim 1 1/16 :463 1:103 1:432ft 6 118 54 41 1/2 52 1/2 43 1/2 BrccIVJr 9 Bud BrdrsH 84-18 Bgetelle,FobbyForbs,LittlBoldJohn 9
17Apr87-8Aqu 1 1/4 :463 1:36 2:02 sy 7 1/2 114 2 1/2 11 1/2 12 1/2 13 1/2 Maple E 4 Excelsior H 86-22 Lac Ouimet, Alioth, ProudDebonair 9
17Apr87—Grade II
●May 11 Pim 4f gd :483 h May 6 Bel 1 sy 1:402 h May 1 Bel 3f ft :37 b Apr 21 Bel 4f ft :471 h

Cryptoclearance *
CORDERO A JR — 121
Own.—Teinowitz P
Dk. b. or br. c. 4, by Fappiano—Naval Orange, by Hoist the Flag
Br.—George S Farm Inc (Ky) — 1988 5 1 4 0 $250,520
Tr.—Schulhofer Flint S — 1987 15 4 4 3 $1,357,150
Lifetime 25 7 8 4 $1,880,670

16Apr88-9OP 1⅛ :463 1:103 1:47 gd 2½ 122 89¾ 76½ 43 2¾ CrdrAJr4 Oaklawn H 97-12 Lost Code, Cryptoclearance, Gulch 8
16Apr88—Grade I
26Mar88-10Crc 1¼ :49 1:391 2:054ft *3-5 122 811 33½ 2hd 2no VsquezJ2 Trop Park H 106-12 CremeFrich,Cryptoclrnc,AllSincrity 8
21Feb88-10GP 1¼ :482 1:38 2:013sy *6-5 122 46 44 22 2no Day P5 Gulf Park H 87-22 JdeHunter,Cryptoclernce,CrmFrich 6
21Feb88—Grade I
30Jan88-10GP 1⅛ :473 1:114 1:484ft *6-5 123 88 87 34½ 21 Day P5 Donn H 87-25 JdeHunter,Cryptoclernce,PrsonlFlg 8
30Jan88—Grade I
21Jan88-9GP 1 1/16 :472 1:114 1:43 ft *1-3 119 78¾ 33 11½ 18½ Day P1 Aw26000 86-22 Cryptoclernce,FullCourg,SilvrComt 9
21Nov87-7Hol 1¼ :462 1:352 2:012ft 24 122 1113 98¾ 66 55¾ Day P5 Br Cp Class 79-12 Ferdinand,Alysheb,JudgeAngelucci 12
21Nov87—Grade I
23Oct87-9Med 1¼ :47 1:361 2:014ft 9-5 120 54 41½ 33 36 SntsJA2 Med Cup H 87-16 CremeFraiche,Afleet,Cryptoclernce 7
23Oct87—Grade I
19Sep87-9Med 1⅛ :464 1:103 1:483ft 9-5 122 68½ 63¾ 1hd 13½ SntosJA3 Pegasus H 90-12 Cryptoclernce,LostCode,TemplrHill 8
19Sep87—Grade I
5Sep87-8Bel 1⅛ :46 1:091 1:47 ft 5¾ 118 914 811 65½ 43¾ CrdrAJr6 Woodward 88-15 Polish Navy, Gulch, Creme Fraiche 9
5Sep87—Grade I
22Aug87-8Sar 1¼ :461 1:362 2:02 sy 8 126 919 32 11½ 22 CordroAJr2 Travers 88-16 JavaGold,Cryptoclearnce,PolishNvy 9
22Aug87—Grade I; Drifted out
May 10 Bel 5f ft :59 h   May 5 Bel 5f ft 1:004 h   Apr 29 Kee 4f ft :481 b   Apr 24 Kee 4f ft :501 b

Bet Twice
PERRET C — 124
Own.—Cisley Stable&LevyBlancheP
B. c. 4, by Sportin' Life—Golden Dust, by Dusty Canyon
Br.—Farish W S & Hudson E J (Ky) — 1988 2 1 1 0 $31,820
Tr.—Croll Warren A Jr — 1987 9 3 3 0 $1,922,642
Lifetime 18 9 4 1 $2,645,827

27Apr88-8Kee 1⅛ :49 1:132 1:512ft *1-5 126 34½ 2½ 1hd 2hd Perret C4 Ben Ali H 77-22 Homebuilder,BetTwice,BluBuckroo 4
27Apr88—Grade III
13Apr88-6Kee 7f :24 :463 1:231ft *1-9 121 31 1hd 12 13½ Perret C1 Aw24200 90-15 Bet Twice,IrishFreeze,PassingShips 4
5Sep87-8Bel 1⅛ :46 1:091 1:47 ft *3-2 121 42½ 33 43½ 64¾ PerretC6 Woodward 87-15 Polish Navy, Gulch, Creme Fraiche 9
5Sep87—Grade I
22Aug87-8Sar 1¼ :461 1:362 2:02 sy 4½ 126 49½ 2hd 44 512½ Perret C8 Travers 78-16 JavaGold,Cryptoclearnce,PolishNvy 9
22Aug87—Grade I
1Aug87-9Mth 1⅛ :463 1:093 1:47 ft *6-5 126 22 31 1hd 1nk Perret C5 Haskell H 99-07 Bet Twice, Alysheba, Lost Code 5
1Aug87—Grade I
6Jun87-8Bel 1½ :492 2:03 2:281ft 8 126 34 16 17 114 Perret C4 Belmont 79-15 Bet Twice, Cryptoclearance, Gulch 9
6Jun87—Grade I
16May87-9Pim 1 3/16 :471 1:113 1:554ft 5 126 32 31½ 1hd 2½ Perret C1 Preakness 87-18 Alysheba,BetTwice,Cryptoclearnce 9
16May87—Grade I
2May87-8CD 1¼ :462 1:364 2:032ft 10 126 65 1hd 11 2¾ Perret C14 Ky Dby 79-08 Alysheba, Bet Twice, Avies Copy 17
2May87—Grade I; Drifted late
4Apr87-10GP 1⅛ :472 1:114 1:493ft *2-3 122 48 42 51¾ 54 Perret C7 Fla Derby 80-23 Cryptoclernc,NoMorFlowrs,Tlinum 9
4Apr87—Grade I; Blockd,lckd room
22Mar87-10GP 1 1/16 :47 1:114 1:432ft *1 122 31½ 11½ 12½ 12½ Perret C5 Fountin Yth 84-24 BetTwice,NoMoreFlowers,GoneWst 9
22Mar87—Grade II
May 10 Mth 5f ft :594 b   May 6 Mth 5f sy 1:01 b   Apr 26 Kee 3f ft :37 b   ●Apr 20 Kee 1 ft 1:38 b

Lost Code ×
BAY P — 126
Own.—Wendover Stable
Dk. b. or br. c. 4, by Codex—Loss Or Gain, by Ack Ack
Br.—Marablvest-83 Ltd (Fla) — 1988 3 3 0 0 $391,580
Tr.—Donovan L William — 1987 14 7 3 2 $1,115,218
Lifetime 23 12 4 2 $1,525,648

16Apr88-9OP 1⅛ :463 1:103 1:47 gd *4-5 126 11½ 12 12 1¾ Perret C2 Oaklawn H 98-12 Lost Code, Cryptoclearance, Gulch 8
16Apr88—Grade I
26Mar88-9OP 1 1/16 :464 1:101 1:402ft *1-2 123 11½ 13 13½ 13½ PerretC5 Razorback H 99-18 LostCode,RedAttck,DemonsBegone 7
26Mar88—Grade II
5Mar88-9GP 7f :221 :443 1:211ft *1-2 122 1½ 11½ 17 115½ Perret C2 Aw30000 98-16 LostCod,Crborundum,I'llRisYouOn 8
4Oct87-9Pha 1⅛ :47 1:102 1:481ft 3-2 122 2hd 1½ 12½ 22½ St LeonG2 Pa. Derby 92-17 Afleet, Lost Code, Homebuilder 8
4Oct87—Grade II
19Sep87-9Med 1⅛ :464 1:103 1:483ft *7-5 122 2hd 12 2hd 23½ StLeonG6 Pegasus H 86-12 Cryptoclernce,LostCode,TemplrHill 8
19Sep87—Grade I; Brk in start
22Aug87-7Mth 1⅛ :454 1:09 1:481ft *1 117 13 14 13 33 St Leon G7 Iselin H 90-15 BordeuxBob,SilverComet,LostCode 7
22Aug87—Grade I
1Aug87-9Mth 1⅛ :463 1:093 1:47 ft 2½ 124 12 11 2hd 3½ St LeonG3 Haskell H 98-07 Bet Twice, Alysheba, Lost Code 5
1Aug87—Grade I
11Jly87-8AP 1⅛ :454 1:093 1:493ft *1-2 123 11½ 12½ 16 12¾ St Leon G2 Classic 83-25 Lost Code, Gem Master, AviesCopy 7
11Jly87—Grade I
28Jun87-9Cby 1⅛ :47 1:103 1:492ft *6-5 124 11½ 12 13 11½ StLeonG3 St Paul Dby 93-10 Lost Code,ProudestDuke,StaffRiot 8
28Jun87—Grade III
13Jun87-9Tdn 1⅛ :462 1:104 1:503ft 3 126 14 14 16 13½ St LeonG3 Ohio Dby 84-23 LostCode,ProudestDuke,Hombuildr 9
13Jun87—Grade II
May 8 Pim 1 ft 1:394 b   ●Apr 29 Lrl 6f ft 1:13 b   ●Apr 10 OP 1 ft 1:382 b   ●Mar 20 OP 6f ft 1:122 b

The contenders in this race have taken turns defeating each other, so pace, speed, and class are superseded by current form as the dominant factor. Of course, current form does not mean which horse ran best in its last race, but rather, which horse projects to run best today. The model for solving this race resembles the scenario of Rivlia–Great Communicator, et al: stakes horses who take turns.

Approximate Odds, Post Time

Alysheba	3–5
Lost Code	3–1
Cryptoclearance	6–1 (more money wagered than Bet Twice)
Bet Twice	6–1 (less money wagered than Cryptoclearance)
Little Bold John	13–1
Lac Ouimet	30–1

Comments

Unlikely

Both Little Bold John and Lac Ouimet do not show Grade 1 wins, and they face four Grade 1 winners. At least one of those four should beat these two, as it is highly unlikely that all four of the contenders would be off form at the same moment in time.

Contenders

Who beat whom, when and why? Which of these four lose to their peers only during a down part of their cycle? Which of these four were running in top form when beaten by their colleagues? Which of these won Grade 1 races against sharp horses, and which ones inherited victories by facing horses on the skids? Which horses are now rounding into form, and which ones may have peaked prior to today's race?

I selected this particular race precisely because all of the significant handicapping questions relate to form cycle. In other words, *whichever horse wins this race will most certainly lose to the same rivals in future races.* Let's liberate the bureaucracy of the mind from inhibiting our potential for logical thinking by considering our contenders from bottom to top.

4. The least likely of the big four is Cryptoclearance. When he beat Lost Code (19Sep87), Lost Code was in the midst of a losing period. (Wouldn't you love to own a horse that bottoms out near the top?) Cryptoclearance defeated Bet Twice (4Apr87) during a period of prep races prior to the Derby, when Bet Twice had no room to make his move. Bet Twice was also victimized by Cryptoclearance on a sloppy track that favored Cryptoclearance, just a race before Bet Twice needed a long layoff. Cryptoclearance lost to Bet Twice in all three Triple Crown races, when the money was on the line.

   Cryptoclearance is an opportunistic horse who will beat you when you're down. He can win today's race, but he'll need a pace duel in front with the help of noncontender Little Bold John to soften up Lost Code. This is possible but not probable.

3. Lost Code is a sharp and consistent horse. He is a craftsman in big stakes with weak fields. His opportunism differs from that of Cryptoclearance in that, instead of catching the top horses in their moments of weakness, he goes down one notch to confront fields that don't quite measure up to the best. Now he must face the best, at a time when the margin of his victories has been diminishing (from 15 ½ lengths to 3 ¼ to ¾).

   Lost Code was beaten fair and square (1Aug87) by both Bet Twice and Alysheba, notably coming off the heels of a winning streak similar to the one that leads him into today's race.

2. Two consecutive efforts in high gear plus a long trip may take something out of Alysheba. After two hard-fought battles in the Derby and Preakness, the tables turned and Alysheba was beaten twice by Bet Twice. The pair of all-out heart throbbers against Ferdinand may be a prelude to another brief decline. The high-pitched din that shook the grandstand during those two stretch duels seemed like a metaphor for a peak experience, the kind that leads to a letdown. Alysheba and Bet Twice have beaten each other regularly, and there is no evidence that either one of these will dominate the other. They figure to continue their rivalry.

1. Bet Twice is the fresh horse. Throw out his last race. First, that race followed a comeback victory, so there might have been a mild bounce. Second, his defeat was an obvious prep for today's race (Grade 3 to Grade 1). Of today's big four, Bet Twice is most likely to be on the way up in his form cycle. On the other hand, we have no proof that he's the same horse this year as he was last year.

   For this reason, it is nearly impossible to separate the two likely rivals in our betting line, Bet Twice and Alysheba. Two form-cycle considerations virtually negate each other.

   a. Bet Twice is the fresh horse vs. the hard campaigners, the most likely to improve.
   b. but Alysheba has benefited from a maturing process from races against the older Ferdinand. He is a superior horse now than when he competed with Bet Twice last year.

In a four-horse contention situation, top choice is 5–2 and second choice is 7–2. Let's try two simultaneous lines, one with Bet Twice as "most likely winner" and one with Alysheba in the top spot.

	Our Line	Track Odds	Decision
Bet Twice	5–2/7–2	6–1	Over. *Bet.*
Alysheba	5–2/7–2	3–5	Under. No bet.
Lost Code	5–1	3–1	Under. No bet.
Cryptoclearance	6–1	5–1/6–1	No advantage. No bet.

The tote board resolves the problem, and hairsplitting becomes a wasted exercise. Bet Twice qualifies as a wager whether first or second choice in our line. Alysheba doesn't qualify for a wager regardless of whether he is top choice or not. And if you had made them co-favorites, you'd still bet the one with the highest odds, so there is never a need to split hairs when two horses qualify for equal ratings on a betting line.

Pimlico Special Handicap

EIGHTH RACE
Pimlico
MAY 14, 1988

1 3/16 MILES. (1.53⅗) 23rd Running THE PIMLICO SPECIAL HANDICAP. Purse $500,000 Guaranteed (Additional $100,000 Bonus to the Winner if previously nominated to the Triple Crown Races.) A handicap for 4-year-olds and upward. By subscription of $600 each on or before Monday, February 1, 1988, which should accompany the nomination, a sustaining payment of $1,200 each is due on or before Friday, April 1, 1988. Late nominations may be made on or before Tuesday, April 26, 1988, by payment of $15,000 each, which should accompany the nomination and is refundable is the nominee does not draw into the body of the race. There will be no supplement nominations. A fee of $4,000 should be paid at the time of pre-entry by 12 noon Thursday, May 5, 1988, with an additional $3,000 to pass the entry box on Thursday, May 12, 1988 and an additional $3,000 to start, with $500,000 guaranteed, to be divided 65% to first, 20% to second, 10% to third, 5% to fourth, with an added $100,000 bonus to the winner if previously nominated to the Triple Crown races. Weights to be released on Tuesday, May 3, 1988. The field will be limited to 14 starters. In the event that more than 14 horses should pass the entry box, preference shall be given to the high weights based upon the weight assignments adjusted for the sex allowance. Total earnings from January 1, 1988 will be used in determining the preference of horses with equally assigned weights. Horses not drawn into the race will be placed on an Also Eligible list in order of preference as specified herein. In the event of a scratch in the body of the race prior to the official scratch time, horses on the Also Eligible list will be moved into the body of the race based upon their order of preference. Any nominees excluded from running as a result of the aforementioned rule shall be refunded all payments. Trophies will be presented to the winning owner, trainer and jockey. Closed Monday, February 1, 1988 with 82 nominations.
Value of race $600,000; value to winner $425,000; second $100,000; third $50,000; fourth $25,000. Mutuel pool $309,913. Exacta Pool $343,993.

Last Raced	Horse	Eqt.A.Wt	PP	St	¼	½	¾	Str	Fin	Jockey	Odds $1
27Apr88 8Kee2	Bet Twice	4 124	5	6	5^{8}	5^{6}	5^{5}	1^{hd}	$1^{\frac{3}{4}}$	Perret C	6.50
16Apr88 9OP1	Lost Code	4 126	6	1	$2^{1\frac{1}{2}}$	1^{hd}	$1^{\frac{1}{2}}$	2^{4}	2^{1}	Day P	3.10
16Apr88 9OP2	Cryptoclearance	4 121	4	5	6	6	6	$3^{\frac{1}{2}}$	$3^{2\frac{1}{2}}$	Cordero A Jr	5.90
17Apr88 8SA1	Alysheba	b 4 127	2	4	3^{1}	$3^{\frac{1}{2}}$	$2^{\frac{1}{2}}$	4^{5}	$4^{8\frac{1}{2}}$	McCarron C J	.60
7May88 9Pim1	Little Bold John	b 6 117	1	2	1^{hd}	2^{2}	$4^{\frac{1}{2}}$	5^{1}	$5^{8\frac{1}{2}}$	Miller D A Jr	13.50
24Apr88 8Aqu1	Lac Ouimet	5 117	3	3	4^{2}	4^{2}	3^{1}	6	6	Bailey J D	33.40

OFF AT 5:07. Start good, Won driving. Time, :23, :46⅖, 1:10⅖, 1:35⅘, 1:54⅕ Track fast.

$2 Mutuel Prices:				
	5–BET TWICE	**15.00**	**5.60**	**3.80**
	6–LOST CODE		**4.80**	**3.20**
	4–CRYPTOCLEARANCE			**3.80**
	$2 EXACTA 5–6 PAID $80.80.			

B. c, by Sportin' Life—Golden Dust, by Dusty Canyon. Trainer Croll Warren A Jr. Bred by Farish W S & Hudson E J (Ky).

BET TWICE, never far back, moved up between horses on the far turn, came inside LOST CODE when challenging in the upper stretch, drifted out inside the eighth pole, drifted out and brushed LOST CODE inside the sixteenth pole and was drawing off at the wire. LOST CODE disputed the early pace outside LITTLE BOLD JOHN, drifted out in midstretch and finished gamely. An objection by the rider of LOST CODE against the winner for alleged interference the final furlong was not allowed. CRYPTOCLEARANCE swung out entering the stretch, angled inside in midstretch and closed strongly. ALYSHEBA advanced on the far turn, drifted out near the three-sixteenths pole and lugged in near the eighth pole while weakening. LITTLE BOLD JOHN had speed along the rail and dropped back. LAC OUIMET fanned wide entering the stretch and fell back.

Owners— 1, Cisley Stable & Levy Blanche P; 2, Wendover Stable; 3, Teinowitz P; 4, Scharbauer Dorothy & Pamela; 5, Owens J E III; 6, Payson Virginia Kraft.

Trainers— 1, Croll Warren A Jr; 2, Donovan L William; 3, Schulhofer Flint S; 4, Van Berg Jack C; 5, Robb John J; 6, Lundy Richard J.

Pace handicappers may argue convincingly that the best horse in the race was Lost Code, who was softened up by his class inferior, Little Bold John (46.2 half-mile fraction) and then forced to fight off Alysheba (1:10.2 6F fraction). But Lost Code had successfully handled those fractions in previous races. If Lost Code were to have "backed up," then why did he maintain a similar margin over Cryptoclearance from their previous race? If Lost code had been "backing up," he'd have been caught by his opportunistic rival.

Several post-race developments further highlighted the fact that these horses were capable of beating each other and that race results are not deterministic phenomena which are derived from the fixed equations of relative horse abilities. First, Donald Levinson, owner of Lost Code and former member of the Maryland Racing Commission, saw fit to appeal the stewards' ruling regarding a foul claim against Bet Twice. Bet Twice and Lost Code brushed several times as they both drifted out through the final furlong.

Jack Van Berg made some statements regarding Alysheba which suggested that his horse would run better later in the summer. Van Berg blamed himself for allowing only a week to take Alysheba from California (fast-track territory) to a deeper Eastern track. He added that he should have shipped Alysheba earlier to give the colt enough time to acclimate.

Later in the summer Cryptoclearance went to Hawthorne to win the Hawthorne Gold Cup by ten lengths over Cutlass Reality, a horse that had beaten Alysheba by 6½ lengths in June at Hollywood Park. Meanwhile, at Monmouth Park, Alysheba changed her style and stormed from far back to run down Bet Twice in the Iselin Handicap. Alysheba broke a string of two defeats, as well as a string of four losses in a row to Bet Twice. At this point in their careers these two rivals had now split their eight meetings, four/four.

I do not enumerate the results of these races as a historian goes over the battles of the Civil War, but simply to make the point that *change* in its form-cycle vehicle outdoes *continuity* as a force in horse-race handicapping. How else to explain a horse like Cutlass Reality, entering the most exclusive club of thoroughbreds as a late bloomer? And when the mechanisms of change are too complex for the mechanics of handicapping, let the tote board do the fine tuning.

Alysheba did not look like the future Breeders' Classic winner in his Pimlico appearance. But with an ascending performance record each year, he had the appearance of the ultimate of late bloomers. He did not reach his first peak until the Kentucky Derby, as a three-year-old. His second peak involved his double-header wins over Ferdinand. His third peak followed his most sustained string of races; but his 1988 Breeders' Cup triumph may be his last. At this writing, it appears that he will be retired to stud.

WORKSHOP FIVE

May 19, 1988 (course firm)

5th Hollywood

1 1/16 MILES. (Turf). (1.39⅘) ALLOWANCE (Stretch Start). Purse $46,000. 4-year-olds and upward which have not won $3,000 three times other than maiden, claiming or starter. Weight, 120 lbs. Non-winners of two such races at a mile or over since March 15, allowed 2 lbs.; two such races since February 15, 4 lbs.; such a race since March 1, 6 lbs.

***King Hill** — B. h. 5, by King's Archer—Horris Hill, by Vervain
DELAHOUSSAYE E — 114
Br.—Fazenda Agro (Brz) — 1988 5 1 3 0 $44,650
Tr.—Pulliam Vivian M — 1987 2 0 1 0 $816
Own.—Pulliam C N — Lifetime 22 3 6 5 $66,610 — Turf 16 2 5 4 $62,939

2Apr88-8SA 1⅛ Ⓣ:452 1:352 2:004fm 2½ 117 11½ 42 99½ 916¾ PncLJr1 Ⓡ Sta Grts H 66-17 Fiction, Proud Cat, Five DaddyFive 9
20Mar88-5SA 1 Ⓣ:46 1:101 1:354fm 3½ 116 64½ 53½ 22½ 2hd DelhoussyeE8 Aw40000 96-06 Art Francais, King Hill, Kadial 9
26Feb88-7SA 1 Ⓣ:47 1:113 1:364fm 8½ 117 1½ 2hd 2hd 2nk DelhoussyeE2 Aw44000 91-09 Gorky, King Hill, Fiction 10
23Jan88-7SA a6½f Ⓣ:214 :444 1:163fm 8½ 117 32 31½ 3nk 1nk McCarronCJ7 Aw35000 76-28 King Hill, Illumineux, JazzMusician 12
3Jan88-5SA a6½f Ⓣ:22 :45 1:154fm 48 1125 74¾ 53½ 44½ 26 Banderas AL6 Aw35000 74-23 Crystal Run, KingHill, GloryForever 12
3Jan88—Bumped start, 5/8
24Jun87♦4CidJardim(Brazil a1 1:372hy — 117 610 Penachio R Alw Georgia Peach, Kill Me, Dororic 7
4Jun87♦5CidJardim(Brazil a7f 1:263fm — 117 Ⓣ 26 Penachio R Alw Gioviale, King Hill, Pratum Boy 8
28Dec86♦7CidJardim(Brazil a1⅛ 1:534fm — 117 Ⓣ 16¾ PnchioR PrvNrdstSgrdr King Hill, Inferno, Amigo 9
4Dec86♦9CidJardim(Brazil a1⅛ 1:534sy — 123 22½ Matias A Alw Hijo, King Hill, Nasamu 7
16Nov86♦7CidJardim(Brazil a1½ 2:30 fm — 123 Ⓣ 1813 Matias A Dby Plsta(Gr1) Jabble, Ken Graf, New Orleans 22
May 16 Hol 4f ft :474 h May 11 Hol 4f ft :47 h May 6 Hol 1 ft 1:433 h May 1 Hol 6f ft 1:134 h

Chess Set — Gr. c. 4, by Ack Ack—Be Cle, by Tom Rolfe
GRYDER A T — 114
Br.—Keck H B (Ky) — 1987 8 3 0 0 $44,050
Tr.—Whittingham Charles — 1986 6 M 1 2 $10,850
Own.—Keck H B — Lifetime 14 3 1 2 $54,900 — Turf 4 1 0 0 $19,125

29Nov87-9Hol 1 1/16 Ⓣ:471 1:11 1:412fm 3½ 1105 75½ 65 54 51½ Gryder A T7 Aw39000 85-11 Samarid, Il Miracolo, Dark Promise 8
16Nov87-5SA 1⅛ Ⓣ:472 1:12 1:504fm 26 1105 86½ 76 42½ 1¾ Gryder A T11 Aw33000 73-34 Chess Set, L'Empire, Ferand 12
7Oct87-5SA 1⅛ Ⓣ:473 1:121 1:49 fm 11 120 99½ 107½ 97¾ 64½ Black C A10 Aw33000 75-16 MgnPlus, QuietlyBold, BstSolution 10
13Sep87-3Dmr 1 1/16 :46 1:112 1:434ft 6½ 116 510 44½ 41 1¾ Black C A4 Aw24000 81-18 ChessSet, CircleViewDrive, Mondnit 6
31Aug87-6Dmr 1 1/16 :452 1:113 1:43 ft *2½e116 610 51¾ 21½ 1½ Black C A5 Mdn 85-14 Chess Set, Unicopia, Daraki 12
24Jly87-4Hol 1 1/16 Ⓣ:464 1:112 1:433fm 3½e115 64¾ 85¾ 77½ 77½ Shoemaker W11 Mdn 69-20 ‡DefiniteSigns, Fnticol, BstOBunch 11
24Jly87—Steadied 3/8 turn
11Jly87-4Hol 1 1/16 :471 1:114 1:433ft 7¾ 115 64½ 54½ 54½ 48½ Shoemaker W6 Mdn 83-12 Sobek, Fanticola, Best Of Danzig 8
3Jun87-6SA 1 1/16 :472 1:113 1:442ft 7½e117 89 79½ 59¾ 510 Shoemaker W2 Mdn 69-16 SvorFire, NstyNskr, FmousForever 11
18Dec86-5Hol 1 :461 1:111 1:37 ft 8½ 118 68 510 513 519¾ Shoemaker W5 Mdn 58-20 LightSabre, Brb'sRelic, S'Mximillion 7
8Nov86-5Hol 1 :451 1:101 1:36 ft 4 118 914 811 711 613½ Shoemaker W5 Mdn 69-13 ThunderCat, Barb'sRelic, LightSabre 9
8Nov86—Pinched at break
May 15 Hol 5f ft 1:011 h ●May 10 Hol 1 ft 1:384 h May 5 Hol 1 ft 1:402 h Apr 30 Hol 7f ft 1:281 h

Gallant Sailor — B. g. 5, by Gallant Best—Sailing Joy, by Sailing Along
SHOEMAKER W — 114
Br.—Jones K & Sheryl (Wash) — 1988 7 0 3 1 $42,850
Tr.—Jones Kenneth G — 1987 16 0 2 3 $35,900
Own.—Jones K G — Lifetime 42 3 8 5 $107,150 — Turf 10 0 0 2 $19,100

7May88-8Hol 7f :214 :44 1:221ft 26 112 96½ 97½ 98½ 816¾ OlivresF6 Trpl Bnd H 83-14 PrfcTrvl, Rconnotrng, Dn'sIrshMldy 9
7May88—Grade III
23Apr88-5SA 6½f :221 :45 1:152m 4½ 112 43½ 42½ 43 21½ ShmrW5 Sn Smn H 92-15 CblloDeOro, GllntSilor, SylvnExpress 5
23Apr88—Grade III
30Mar88-8SA 6½f :214 :442 1:15 ft 8½ 111 34½ 34 33½ 33½ OlivresF2 Ptro Grnd H 91-18 Gulch, Very Subtle, Gallant Sailor 3
23Mar88-7SA 6½f :212 :434 1:152ft 6 1105 510 53½ 34½ 2no Banderas AL1 Aw43000 93-18 Fracoza, GallantSailor, RightRudder 5
23Mar88—Broke slowly
4Feb88-8SA 6½f :212 :44 1:152ft 55 1105 67½ 67 55½ 23 Gryder A T1 Aw40000 90-20 Sebrof, Gallant Sailor, RightRudder 7
4Feb88—Wide into stretch
23Jan88-6SA 1 1/16 :461 1:102 1:421ft 30 116 74¾ 88½ 913 817½ McHrgueDG5 Aw44000 72-14 Crimson Slew, CaptainValid, HillsBid 9
23Jan88—Lugged out 3/8
14Jan88-8SA 1⅛ Ⓣ:471 1:114 1:492fm 34 115 42 74 1010 912½ Sibille R10 Aw44000 68-20 Light Sabre, Mazilier, Gorky 10
23Dec87-8Hol 1 1/16 Ⓣ:484 1:13 1:433fm 26 1115 42 52 3½ 32½ Banderas AL5 Aw45000 73-24 FiveDddyFive, RufusDwes, GllntSilor 8
12Dec87-10Hol 1 Ⓣ:47 1:114 1:363fm 15 1115 57½ 53 41¾ 31 Banderas AL7 Aw45000 83-14 KingBlldeer, Uptothehilt, GllntSilor 10
29Nov87-9Hol 1 1/16 Ⓣ:471 1:11 1:412fm 15 1115 31 43½ 64½ 63 Banderas AL4 Aw39000 84-11 Samarid, Il Miracolo, Dark Promise 8
May 3 Hol 3f ft :353 h Apr 19 Hol 3f ft :364 h Apr 15 Hol 6f gd 1:152 h Apr 9 Hol 5f ft 1:011 h

Little Red Cloud — Ch. g. 5, by Nostoques—Rosy Cloud, by Racing Room
SOLIS A — 114
Br.—The Hat Ranch West (Cal) — 1988 3 1 1 0 $25,900
Tr.—Stute Melvin F — 1987 12 1 3 1 $33,750
Own.—The Hat Ranch — Lifetime 24 3 8 2 $136,700 — Turf 2 1 1 0 $25,900

29Apr88-8GG 1 Ⓣ:473 1:121 1:364fm 5 116 42½ 21½ 1hd 2½ CstnedM 8 Ⓡ Dandln H 82-17 QuckTwst, LttlRdCloud, Poston'sBst 8
17Apr88-3SA a6½f Ⓣ:221 :45 1:153fm 14 116 63 62½ 32 1nk Solis A 4 Aw38000 81-17 LittleRedCloud, DryRidge, FltSudn 10
9Apr88-7SA 6f :211 :43 1:08 ft 15 117 89½ 814 816 818 Castanon AL 1 Aw38000 80-13 OlympicProspct, DncForL, 'nsMnus 9
9Apr88—Steadied early
14Nov87-6SA 6f :213 :45 1:11 ft 17 120 99½ 86¾ 85½ 75¾ Castanon AL 2 Aw31000 77-22 HppyInSpc, HlCmmndr, SprbMmnt 12
1Nov87-5SA 6½f :213 :442 1:16 m 7 119 2½ 2hd 22½ 78 Castanon AL 5 Aw38000 84-12 BoldArchon, WindwoodLne, MiBeso 8

21Oct87-5SA 6f :21⁴ :44⁴ 1:09⁴ft 8½ 119 11¹³10¹⁰ 79¼ 87¾ Castanon AL 5 Aw30000 81-20 Pialor, Mi Beso, Happy In Space 11
21Oct87—Bobbied, bumped start
11Oct87-7SA 1⅛ :45¹ 1:09³ 1:42²ft *3½ 117 45 43½ 44½ 810½ Castanon AL 5 Aw33000 78-14 No Marker, Valiant Cougar, Fracoza 9
3Oct87-8Fpx 6½f :21³ :45¹ 1:15³ft 3½ 115 53½ 22 1hd 14½ Castanon AL 2 Aw28000 90-10 Little Red Cloud, MiBeso, TokyoBoy 7
21Sep87-10Fpx 6½f :21³ :45² 1:17¹ft 2¾ 120 74½ 64½ 42½ 21½ Castanon AL 7 Aw25000 89-15 NorthYrd, LittleRedCloud, DryRidg 10
21Sep87—Wide 1st turn
4Sep87-5Dmr 7f :22 :44⁴ 1:22¹ft 4½ 113⁵ 42½ 31½ 21 65¾ Patton D B 8 Aw22000 85-16 KingOfBazar, Athlone, Bride'sAdvice 8
4Sep87—Broke in, bumped
●May 13 Hol 5f ft :59² h May 7 Hol 5f ft 1:01¹ h Apr 24 SA 5f m 1:00³ h Apr 7 SA 4f ft :46² h

Rai Den . g. 5, by Big Spruce—Splendid Spree, by Damascus
STEVENS G 114 Br.—Webb Mrs Lillie F (Ky) 1988 3 0 1 1 $16,850
Own.—Yasuda G Tr.—Palma Hector O 1987 8 0 2 2 $22,925
Lifetime 21 3 5 4 $96,160 Turf 14 2 2 4 $71,050
30Apr88-7Hol 1⅛ Ⓣ:47⁴1:11²1:48 fm 4 116 32½ 32 21½ 22½ DelhoussyeE 5 Aw45000 85-14 Kadial, Rai Den, Motley
1Apr88-5SA a6½f Ⓣ:21² :44 1:15 fm 6½ 116 32 62¾ 63 31 DelahoussayeE 4 90000 83-11 Hermes, Bright And Right, Rai Den
1Apr88—Crowded 1/16
5Mar88-3SA 1 :46² 1:10³ 1:35 ft 5 116 32½ 44½ 48 512¼ DelhoussyeE 3 Aw44000 80-14 Good Taste, Talinum, Fancy Oats 6
2Aug87-7Dmr 1⅛ Ⓣ:48 1:12¹1:42⁴fm 4 116 1hd 21 32 77 DelhoussyeE 2 Aw28000 79-13 Santella Mac, A New Era, Sanctarid 10
1Jly87-8Hol 1⅛ Ⓣ:46⁴1:10²1:40²fm 8½ 118 2hd 3½ 2hd 2hd DelhoussyeE 2 Aw30000 92-08 Rufjan, Rai Den, Centenary 7
13Jun87-7Hol 1⅛ Ⓣ:46⁴1:10²1:40²fm 13 113⁵ 32 52 77½ 810¾ Gryder A T 6 Aw30000 81-08 Castlemartin King, Swink, Kadial 8
5Jun87-8Hol 1⅛ Ⓣ:48²1:12 1:41²fm 3 117 1½ 2hd 2½ 32 Pincay L Jr 3 Aw30000 85-13 StopTheFighting, ArcticBlstII, RiDn 6
23May87-7Hol 1 :45¹ 1:09⁴ 1:35¹ft 5½ 117 42 31½ 23 24½ Pincay L Jr 2 Aw30000 82-15 Sperry, Rai Den, High Hook 7
26Mar87-8SA a6½f Ⓣ:21³ :43²1:15¹fm 7 116 77½ 57½ 55 3nk DelhoussyeE 5 Aw37000 83-17 Hydrostatic, SpeedyShannon, RiDen 8
26Mar87—Broke in a tangle
27Feb87-8SA a6½f Ⓣ:21³ :44 1:15²fm 14 116 75¾ 98 79 55¾ DelhoussyeE 2 Aw35000 76-18 LeBelvedere, ‡Mr.Media, HardRound 9
●May 8 Hol 5f ft :59² h Apr 25 SA tr.t 6f ft 1:13³ h Apr 17 SA tr.t 6f ft 1:13¹ h Apr 10 SA tr.t 5f ft 1:00² h

***Milouin** B. h. 5, by Arctic Tern—Milabellele, by White Label
CASTANON A L 114 Br.—Societe R & M (Fra) 1988 1 0 0 0
Own.—Prince Kais Al Said Tr.—Russell John W 1987 11 1 5 0 $60,377
Lifetime 23 3 6 1 $88,160 Turf 23 3 6 1 $88,160
14Jan88-8SA 1⅛ Ⓣ:47⁴1:11⁴1:49²fm 6½ 115 64½ 85½ 99 810¾ Castanon AL 5 Aw44000 63-20 Light Sabre, Mazilier, Gorky 10
14Jan88—Steadied start, rank
12Dec87-8Hol 1 Ⓣ:46¹1:10⁴1:35⁴fm 5½ 116 67 41½ 53 52¾ Cordero AJr 5 Aw45000 86-14 DrkPromise, Digger'sRst, HppyInSpc 9
12Dec87—Lacked room 3/8
27Nov87-9Hol 1⅛ Ⓣ:48⁴1:13¹1:49 fm 10 114 87½ 85 75 73½ ShoemkerW 2 Aw52000 78-14 Havildar, Narghile, Bello Horizonte 8
23Aug87♦5Deauville(Fra) a1⅛ 2:07⁴yl 4 126 Ⓣ 22 StMrtinY GP Fds l'Elvg Street Line, Milouin, Great Booby 11
15Aug87♦3Deauville(Fra) a1 1:36²gd 8½ 127 Ⓣ 2hd MorGW G Hcp d Deauvl Lake Success, Milouin, ‡Pitchnet 17
15Aug87—Impeded
23Jun87♦6Chantilly(Fra) a1 1:46 sf *2 130 Ⓣ 2¾ StMrtnE Px d Chmnt Bestebreuje, Milouin, Vagadancer 10
7Jun87♦3Chantilly(Fra) a1 1:39³sf 8 129 Ⓣ 2hd STMrtY Px Lncia Thma H AmeliePleasures, Milouin, OrdeMre 10
28May87♦2Longchamp(Fra) a1 1:45 sf *1 121 Ⓣ 1hd StMrtinY Px D'Argntuil Milouin, Cornish Kiss, Vagadancer 7
3May87♦5Longchamp(Fra) a1⅜ 2:15 gd 7e128 Ⓣ 10²⁴ Prou S Px Ganay (Gr1) Triptych, TkfYhmed, HighestHonor 10
14Apr87♦5StCloud(Fra) a1⅛ 2:16⁴yl 4½ 126 Ⓣ 47¾ StMartinE Px Altipan Trokhos, Star Rose, Roi Normand 10
May 10 Hol 5f ft 1:02² h May 3 Hol 7f ft 1:29² h Apr 26 Hol 1 ft 1:42² h Apr 19 Hol 7f ft 1:27¹ h

Star Cutter Gr. h. 5, by Star de Naskra—Axes, by Al Hattab
PINCAY L JR 114 Br.—Pillar Stud Inc (Ky) 1988 1 0 0 0 $1,250
Own.—ShkhMhmdBnRshdAlMktom Tr.—Gosden John H M 1987 4 0 2 1 $110,607
Lifetime 9 3 3 1 $155,501 Turf 9 3 3 1 $155,501
29Apr88-8Hol 1⅛ Ⓣ:45⁴1:09 1:40²fm *6-5 117 68 75½ 56 57½ Pincay L Jr 4 Aw50000 84-08 SkpOtFront, ForThExprts, ArtFrnc 8
29Aug87♦3Goodwood(Eng) 1 1:36⁴gd *6-5 126 Ⓣ 31½ CthnS WtrfrdCrystlMl(Gr2) Milligram, Waajib, Star Cutter 4
29Jly87♦4Goodwood(Eng) 1 1:38⁴gd 6 133 Ⓣ 2½ CauthenS Sussex (Gr1) Soviet Star, Star Cutter, Hadeer 7
11Jly87♦2Lingfield(Eng) a7½f 1:26³gd 12 138 Ⓣ 2hd EddrPA BetWthThToteS Hiaam, Star Cutter, HomoSapien 9
16Jun87♦2Ascot(Eng) 1¼ 2:07¹gd 5 132 Ⓣ 9 CuthnS Prnce oWles(Gr2) Mtoto, Amerigo Vespcci, Gesedeh 10
19Oct86♦5Milan(Italy) a1 1:37⁴gd 3-2 121 Ⓣ 11 RyanW PrVtroDCpu(Gr2) StrCutter, Kibiyl, SplendidMoment 11
29Jly86♦5Goodwood(Eng) 1 1:39²gd 3½ 132 Ⓣ 12½ CuthnS Paul Masson H StarCutter, MeetTheGreek, Ininsky 12
27Jun86♦4Newcastle(Eng) 1 1:44¹fm *1-5 126 Ⓣ 1¾ CuthnS StOswld(Mdn) Star Cutter, Ortica, North Ocean 5
14Jun86♦1Sandown(Eng) 7f 1:26¹gd *8-5 126 Ⓣ 2no RyanW BkerLrnz(Mdn) Mawsuff, StarCutter, RueStJcques 10
●May 12 Hol 6f ft 1:14¹ h May 6 Hol 4f ft :47 h Apr 25 Hol 6f ft 1:13³ h ●Apr 17 Hol 6f ft 1:14¹ h

Cannon Bar B. h. 5, by Cannonade—Miss Ocean Bar, by Ocean Bar
BLACK C A 114 Br.—Cowan Marjorie (Fla) 1988 1 0 0 1 $3,150
Own.—Cowan I Tr.—Gosden John H M 1987 6 3 0 0 $38,375
Lifetime 12 3 1 4 $47,055 Turf 5 2 0 1 $33,450
1May88-5GG 1 Ⓣ:48¹1:13 1:37⁴fm 7¾ 117 31 3½ 2½ 3nk Tohill K S 5 Aw21000 78-18 JustTooMuch, Sunstorm, CannonBar 7
25Jly87-9AP 1½ Ⓣ:49²2:05 2:30²fm 4e115 12½ 2hd 79 915½ HwleyS 2 L Armour H 72-18 ComplcII, AtmnGlttr, ExplosvDrlng 10
25Jly87—Grade II
1Jly87-8Hol 1⅛ Ⓣ:46⁴1:10²1:40²fm 2½ 120 51¾ 52½ 42 41 McCarronCJ 1 Aw30000 91-08 Rufjan, Rai Den, Centenary 7
18Jun87-8Hol 1⅛ Ⓣ:47²1:11 1:41 fm 2¾ 118 2½ 2½ 1½ 12 McCarronCJ 2 Aw27000 89-11 CannonBar, FbulousSound, Euphrtes 6
25May87-9Hol 1⅛ :46¹ 1:10⁴ 1:42⁴ft 3½ 121 33 44 48½ 413½ McCarronCJ 1 Aw27000 81-15 Recognized, EightyBlowZro, Extrnix 6
25Apr87-9Hol 1⅛ Ⓣ:46³1:11 1:42²fm 7½ 115 1½ 2hd 2hd 11½ McCarronCJ 2 Aw24000 82-14 Cannon Bar, Danski, First Dibs 7
7Apr87-4GG 6f :21⁴ :44² 1:09²ft 8¾ 120 57 56 32½ 1hd Tohill K S 3 M32000 92-14 Cannon Bar, Winter Tan, Bledsoe 8
7Apr87—Poor start
12Aug85-8Crc 6f :22³ :46¹ 1:13¹ft 6 117 87 54½ 54 43 Soto S B 7 ⓈMdn 82-15 LegalLegacy, BetABuck, FstPhillip 11
3Aug85-5Crc 6f :22¹ :46² 1:13¹sy *1 117 53 47 37 37 Smith A Jr 7 Mdn 78-17 GreekRunner, BrightCopy, CannonBr 9
27Jly85-2Crc 6f :22² :46¹ 1:12⁴ft *2 116 53½ 67¾ 43 33 Smith A Jr 4 Mdn 84-13 MedievalWorld, TuriBoy, CannonBr 10
May 15 Hol 5f ft 1:01 h May 10 Hol 4f ft :48³ h Apr 25 Hol 6f ft 1:14² h Apr 17 SA 6f ft 1:14² h

Pleasant Variety — by Pleasant Colony—Variety Show, by T V Lark
TORO | | 116 | Br.—Evans T M (Ky) | 1988 6 1 1 0 $43,700
Own.—Buckland Farm | | Tr.—Speckert Christopher | 1987 7 1 1 1 $14,900
| | | Turf 5 1 1 0 $34,450
| | | Lifetime 15 3 3 1 $76,707

25Apr88-8SA 1¼①:46 1:36 2:01⁴gd 10 114 67½ 64½ 64½ 41½ GrydrA⁷³ ■Sn Jcnt H 76-24 The Medic, Trokhos, Uptothehilt 10
14Apr88-8SA 1½ :45³ 1:10⁴ 1:50³sy 5½ 118 51½ 54½ 33 21½ Toro F⁵ Aw40000 75-27 KnightsLegend,PleasantVriety,Kgll 6
11Mar88-8SA 1½①:46 1:10⁴ 1:48²fm 12 116 67 32 13½ 13 Toro F¹ Aw30000 85-15 PleasantVriety,Eliminnte,Prowict 10
27Feb88-5SA 1½ :46 1:11² 1:50⁴ft 30 115 1018 912 57¼ 42⅜ Velasquez J⁷ Aw30000 72-17 Reland, Millero YMedio,Prowict 10
14Feb88-7SA 1¼①:46 1:37 2:02⁴fm 99 114 36½ 44 44 43 Black C A⁵ Aw30000 78-23 Uptothehilt, Nilambr, Periud 10
14Feb88—Veered in start; wide into stretch
23Jan88-8SA 1¼①:47³ 1:22 1:51¹fm 50 118 108½ 96½ 117½ 109½ VienzuelPA¹¹ Aw30000 62-29 Fiction, Be Scenic, L'Empire 12
23Jan88—Erratic early, wide
19Dec87-8Pha 1 :47² 1:11³ 1:37¹ft 4½ 115 42½ 66½ 58½ 511 Vigliotti MJ² Flintlock 77-26 Eclipso,NeverForgottn,DvidL.'sRib 8
5Dec87-3Pha 1 :48² 1:13² 1:39 ft ∗0-5 113 31 1hd 11½ 13 Vigliotti M J⁵ Aw12500 79-29 PlesntVrity,DtrmmdRun,RrWishBit 8
10Nov87-9Lrl 1½ :46 1:39⁴ 2:06²sy ∗6-5 114 43½ 610 615 613½ Lloyd J S² Aw15000 78-27 QuailRidgeSwap,Bounden,FtherHill 9
23Oct87-5Med 1¼①:46 1:10³ 1:42²fm 6½ 110 67 54½ 52½ 21½ Kroae J A⁹ Aw16000 90-09 FirsidDriv,PlsntVrity,Elmr'sAPrnc 11
23Oct87—Fractious gate
May 13 SA 5f ft :59³ h   May 8 SA 5f R 1:02² h   May 3 SA 4f R :50³ h   Apr 22 SA 4f gd :47¹ h

War Debt — Gr. g. 5, by Ack Ack—Debt, by Warfare
MCCARRON C J | | | Br.—Lasker E (Ky) | 1988 1 0 0 0 $3,750
Own.—Lasker Mrs E | | Tr.—Drysdale Neil | 1987 3 1 1 0 $19,350
| | | Turf 2 1 1 0 $19,350
| | | Lifetime 9 3 2 1 $53,900

4May88-7Hol 1 :45³ 1:10⁴ 1:36²ft 17 115 42½ 41½ 31½ 45½ Toro F¹ 95000 75-19 Rich Earth, BoldArchon,FancyOats 7
27Sep87-9Cby 1 :46 1:09¹ 1:35²ft 7½ 115 710 914 917 918 Toro F⁷ 8d Br Cp H 87-09 Minneapple,OnTheLine,ArcticDrem 9
25Aug87-7Dmr 1½①:48¹1:13 1:44 fm 4½ 120 21 32 32½ 21½ DelhoussyeE³ Aw28000 78-14 Bestebreuje, War Debt, Aviator II 10
6Aug87-5Dmr 1½①:48 11:11⁴1:43¹fm ∗8-5 117 3½ 31½ 2hd 1½ DelhoussyeE¹ Aw25000 84-16 WrDbt,MdnghtIc,BooBoo'sBuckroo 9
4Aug87-8Dmr 1½ :45 1:10¹ 1:41⁴ft ∗3-2 116 32½ 2½ 2hd 21½ DelhoussyeE⁷ Aw23000 90-13 RobertoReason,WarDebt,FullOfStrs 9
28Jly87-10Hol 1 :46 1:10² 1:35³ft 4½ 116 3½ 31½ 1½ 12½ DelhoussyeE⁴ Aw25000 85-10 WrDbt,‡MidnightCocktil,GnunJohn 6
6Jly87-6Hol 1 :44³ 1:09³ 1:35⁴ft 5 113 43½ 42½ 21½ 1½ DelahoussyeE¹⁰ Mdn 94-09 WarDebt,Extranix,Cro'sHollywood 10
22Jun87-6Hol 7f :22¹ :45¹ 1:22²ft 66 116 52 97½ 79½ 35½ Delahoussaye E¹ Mdn 86-08 MidnightCocktail,Norquin,WrDebt 12
8Jun87-6Hol 6f :22³ :46³ 1:11¹ft 29 116 94½ 87½ 87½ 79 McHargue D G² Mdn 79-11 NorthrnVlor,Mondnt,MdnghtCcktl 11
8Jun87—Bumped start
May 15 Hol 4f ft :49¹ h   May 10 Hol 3f ft :36⁴ h   Apr 28 Hol 7f R 1:26³ h   Apr 23 Hol 6f R 1:15² h

Along with the past performances, trainer and bias trends that become factors in today's race are:

a. Ice cold trainers, Jumps and Russell
b. Mild double bias on turf course in favor of early and tactical speed as well as inside post positions

Approximate Odds, Post Time

Star Cutter	even
Pleasant Variety	5–1
King Hill	5–1
Rai Den	8–1
Chess Set	17–1
Little Red Cloud	17–1
Gallant Sailor	17–1
War Debt	20–1
Cannon Bar	28–1
Milouin	95–1

Comments

Unlikely

1. With an 0 for 10 turf record, Gallant Sailor has proven he can't win on the grass; his trainer is cold. Also on an "0

for" streak is Rai Den, with no wins in the last two calendar years.

2. Milouin's trainer is in a prolonged slump. The horse itself shows no evidence of ability to race sharply after a layoff. The same layoff factor works against Chess Set, whose three wins all came with recency.

3. Pleasant Variety will battle against a double bias: outside post plus no tactical speed. He has recently beaten the now infamous Eliminante, which may mean a long winless period in the months to come.

4. War Debt is hung out on the extreme outside. His first career win came in his third try; today represents the second try after a long layoff, so he'll probably need one more race.

Contenders

4. A month and a half freshening period follows a tough campaign in which King Hill appeared sharpest when running at distances shorter than today's. With one win and three seconds in the U.S., King Hill may be a "hanger," which makes the extra sixteenth of a mile seem like a potential eternity for a King Hill, who figures to be in a good position in the stretch. Nevertheless, with early speed plus an inside post, he figures to be among the contenders.

3. Little Red Cloud has shown a radical form improvement that coincides with his switch to the grass. Two possible cycles come to mind: potential master of a trade-steady performer, and potential brief-interlude win period for a former proven loser (he stays on the grass, which seems to have been the primary factor-setting for his positive form reversal). His mile time at Golden Gate is four ticks better than rival Cannon Bar's (both recent races). Little Red Cloud is also a five-year-old gelding, which adds another dimension to the hypothesis that this may be a late bloomer. He gets the chance to prove the hypothesis against horses that all have more reason to lose than to win.

2. Cannon Bar. His Golden Gate turf-mile time is slower than Little Red Cloud's, but that race followed a layoff and may have been a prep. Two factors give Cannon Bar an edge over Little Red Cloud.

a. Trainer/horse partnership. This is the pattern match that nostalgically recalls the All In Tune cycle, the one I thought was so unique it would never appear again. The last time Cannon Bar followed a layoff with a sharp Golden Gate race, he followed it up with a move south to Hollywood Park where he won a turf race at $1\frac{1}{16}$ miles, at over 7–1. Today the same pattern repeats:

> *Layoff*—sharp Golden Gate race—*Hollywood Park turf victory at $1\frac{1}{16}$ miles*

b. Cannon Bar is a horse for course. With the exception of Rai Den (two years ago), no other horse in this field has won on the Hollywood Park turf course. Cannon Bar has done it twice in three attempts, his only loss finding him only one length back.

Cannon Bar has the early or tactical speed that will allow him to overcome an outside post position; the plus and minus biases negate each other.

1. Star Cutter. Trainer John Gosden is currently in the midst of a hot streak with European imports. This race represents a significant class drop for Star Cutter, his last race being a classified-allowance event. In Europe he was competitive against two of the highest-rated horses (Milligram and Soviet Star). Star Cutter has finished second in a Grade 2 race.

Once more we are confronted with the contradiction between insight and objectivity. Objectively, Star Cutter is simply superior to Cannon Bar, as a proven graded stakes runner. On the other hand, the reasons in favor of Cannon Bar are more esoteric and less obvious to the crowd. We do the best we can to establish a fair hierarchy of contenders and let the tote board intervene in the betting decision. Even if we reverse the order of preference between the top two contenders, the betting decision remains the same:

	Our Line	*Track Odds*	*Decision*
Star Cutter	5–2	even	Under. No bet.
Cannon Bar	7–2	28–1	Way over. *Bet.*
Little Red Cloud	5–1	17–1	Way over. *Bet.*
King Hill	6–1	5–1	Under No bet.

FIFTH RACE
Hollywood
MAY 19, 1988

1 1/16 MILES.(Turf). (1.39⅗) ALLOWANCE (Stretch Start). Purse $46,000. 4-year-olds and upward which have not won $3,000 three times other than maiden, claiming or starter. Weight, 120 lbs. Non-winners of two such races at a mile or over since March 15, allowed 2 lbs.; two such races since February 15, 4 lbs.; such a race since March 1, 6 lbs.
Value of race $46,000; value to winner $25,300; second $9,200; third $6,900; fourth $3,450; fifth $1,150. Mutuel pool $275,815. Exacta pool $290,057.

Last Raced	Horse	Eqt.	A.	Wt	PP	St	¼	½	¾	Str	Fin	Jockey	Odds $1
1May88 5GG3	Cannon Bar		5	114	8	6	6½	6hd	61	5½	1nk	Black C A	28.50
23Apr88 8Hol5	Star Cutter		5	117	7	4	51½	51	5hd	61½	21½	Pincay L Jr	1.10
25Apr88 8SA4	Pleasant Variety		4	116	9	9	10	10	8½	9½	3hd	Toro F	4.80
2Apr88 8SA9	King Hill		5	116	1	2	4½	31	1hd	1½	4½	Delahoussaye E	4.70
29Nov87 9Hol5	Chess Set		4	114	2	7	8½	71	7½	4½	5nk	Gryder A T	17.80
4May88 7Hol4	War Debt		5	115	10	10	3½	4½	41½	2hd	61½	McCarron C J	20.70
29Apr88 8GG2	Little Red Cloud	b	5	114	4	5	71	91½	91½	7½	7hd	Solis A	17.90
7May88 8Hol8	Gallant Sailor		5	114	3	8	92½	8hd	10	10	81½	Shoemaker W	17.40
30Apr88 7Hol2	Rai Den	b	5	114	5	1	21	1hd	2hd	3½	95	Stevens G L	7.90
14Jan88 8SA8	Milouin		5	115	6	3	1hd	2½	3½	81½	10	Castanon A L	95.80

OFF AT 3:45. Start good. Won driving. Time, :23⅗, :47⅗, 1:11, 1:34⅘, 1:41⅕ Course firm.

$2 Mutuel Prices:			
8-CANNON BAR	59.00	15.20	7.00
7-STAR CUTTER		3.20	3.00
9-PLEASANT VARIETY			3.40

$2 EXACTA 8-7 PAID $169.80.

B. h, by Cannonade—Miss Ocean Bar, by Ocean Bar. Trainer Gosden John H M. Bred by Cowan Marjorie (Fla).

CANNON BAR, allowed to settle into stride early, entered the stretch four wide, came on to get the lead in the final sixteenth and prevailed by a narrow margin in a stiff drive. STAR CUTTER, within easy striking distance early after being bumped in the initial strides, found himself having to await a clear path when blocked behind a wall of rivals turning into the stretch and in the upper stretch, came on strongly in the last furlong once getting through between rivals and lost a close decision. PLEASANT VARIETY, devoid of early speed, came into the stretch five wide, closed with a rush and was up for the show. KING HILL, close up early, vied for the lead around the far turn and in the drive to the last sixteenth, then weakened slightly. CHESS SET, outrun early, rallied to look dangerous from along the inner rail a furlong out but hung. WAR DEBT, prominent early and four wide into the far turn, vied for the lead around the far turn, came into the stretch four wide, continued vying for the lead in the upper stretch but weakened in the last furlong. GALLANT SAILOR, wide down the backstretch, was five wide into the stretch. RAI DEN, a pace factor to the furlong marker, gave way. MILOUIN, bumped in the opening strides, and a bit rank to place early when full of run, vied for the lead on the backstretch and around the far turn, then gave way in the drive.

Owners— 1, Cowan I; 2, ShkhMhmdBnRshd Al Maktoum; 3, Buckland Farm; 4, Pulliam C N; 5, Keck H B; 6, Lasker Mrs E; 7, The Hat Ranch; 8, Jones K G; 9, Yasuda G; 10, Prince Kais Al Said.

Trainers— 1, Gosden John H M; 2, Gosden John H M; 3, Speckert Christopher; 4, Pulliam Vivian M; 5, Whittingham Charles; 6, Drysdale Neil; 7, Stute Melvin F; 8, Jones Kenneth G; 9, Palma Hector O; 10, Russell John W.

Overweight: Star Cutter 3 pounds; King Hill 2; War Debt 1; Milouin 1.

The results of this event call for some observations. Although Cannon Bar earned his victory, having gone four wide while on the move, the best horse, in a losing effort, was Star Cutter. Bumped at the outset, Star Cutter had nowhere to go for what must have seemed like an eternity to his rider and the majority of the crowd, which had invested in his fortunes. As expected, King Hill had the lead in the stretch and didn't know what to do with it. The fastest closer was Pleasant Variety, who came close, as many horses do when they run against a bias.

What If?

Assume for one moment that Cannon Bar had run into the traffic and Star Cutter had avoided the delay by going four wide. Now the tables have turned and the best horse, Star Cutter, has won the race. Put yourself in the situation in which you have just bet on your second and third choices, only to see your first choice, Star Cutter, win and pay $4.20. You have just lost two bets in a race where your top choice has won! Consider, too, that in the long run this type of situation will recur with some frequency; if your betting lines are relatively accurate, your first choices will win more often than your second choices, second picks will come in more regularly than third choices. In other words, you will watch your first choices win (with no investment) as regularly as you will see your second or third choices win (with investment). While you will have many a wager on your top choice when the odds dictate, the total picture of this strategy will result in a lower percentage of winning bets, more than compensated for by a much higher average mutuel.

Just how you react psychologically to watching 'em win and not collecting will be crucial to your long-term success in the fundamental department of return on investment. If you feel stung and hurt by not collecting on $4.20 payoffs, it will affect your willingness to invest properly on overlays in subsequent races. It will also have an impact on your ability to be judgmental as a handicapper.

In the spirit of this vital question, it might have been better for this workshop if Star Cutter had won the race. A psychological test. Whenever I have a 27–1 investment run second, beaten by my most likely winner, I give myself a pat on the back for a job well done. I use that type of experience to build confidence rather than to tear myself apart. I know beyond a doubt that my strategy will lead to an average mutuel considerably higher than a top-choice betting method.

The average mutuel in our short run of workshops is not a mathematical representation of an average mutuel for this particular approach, which will vary from one good handicapper to another. On the other hand, the combination of a cycle-oriented handicapping approach and a betting-line money management strategy will lead to a high average mutuel. I have already emphasized with considerable inspiration that a high percentage of winners is of little relevance to profitable horse-race investment. Quantitatively, we need to win a greater than fair percentage *in relation to the odds.* For example, for 20–1 investments, we need only win 10 percent of the time for a 100 percent profit. For Cannon Bar–type wagers, then, below 10 percent winners still leads to a substantial profit. On the other hand, 33 percent wins with an average mutuel of $5.00 will demolish your bankroll in short order. And if you want to earn a profit with the Star Cutters of horse racing, you'll need to win more than 50 percent of the time.

In this context, if Cannon Bar had lost by a nose, he still would have been a perfect illustration of how thoroughbred cycle handicapping leads to great bets.

There is one way to minimize the effects of not having win money on one's top choice when that horse has a high percentage chance of winning. Put that top choice on top of exacta combinations that offer overlay payoffs. Usually when a contender is overlayed in the win hole, it will also offer better than fair value in second spot of an exacta combo with the most likely winner on top. That way, if Cannon Bar gets nailed at the wire, you collect at more than consolation payoffs.

In the meantime, Little Red Cloud is still running. But at these high odds you can afford to invest in two separate logics within the same race.

WORKSHOP SIX

May 14, 1988 (course *firm*)

6th Belmont

1 ¼ MILES. (InnerTurf). (1.58⅘) ALLOWANCE. Purse $29,000. Fillies and mares. 3-year-olds and upward, which have never won a race other than Maiden, Claiming or Starter. Weight, 3-year-olds, 115 lbs., Older, 124 lbs., Non-winners of a race other than claiming over a mile since April 15, allowed 3 lbs.

Coupled—Pleasent Ring and Rain Date.

Reasonable
Own.—Fertile Acres Farm **121**

Dk. b. or br. f. 4, by Far North—Mucchina, by Limit to Reason
Br.—Newman Don (Ky) 1988 5 0 2 0 $19,220
Tr.—DiMauro Stephen L. 1987 14 2 4 4 $60,920
Lifetime 19 2 6 4 $80,140 Turf 7 1 5 0 $43,600

1May88-7Aqu 1⅛Ⓣ:5021:16 1:542gd *8-5 121 53½ 41½ 2hd 22¼ Migliore R6 ⒻAw31000 61-33 LadyTalc,Reasonble,NoblePreview 10
10Apr88-7Aqu 1 :472 1:124 1:381ft 16 121 75 44½ 45½ 49 Migliore R7 ⒻAw31000 66-26 EmprssofLv,BMyCnqstdr,TkThOffr 7
20Mar88-7Aqu 1⅛ :483 1:143 1:531ft 3½ 1125 43 76½ 510 49½ Peck B D3 ⒻAw31000 60-27 PreciousTiffini,Fontine,TkeTheOffr 9
17Feb88-7Aqu 1⅛⊡:4911:1411:55 ft 3½ 117 85½ 54 21½ 21¾ Davis R G8 ⒻAw31000 65-21 NativeCandy,Resonble,BrvestAngel 9
17Feb88—Lagged early
17Jan88-6Aqu 1 1/16⊡:4841:1341:471ft 17 1125 54 43½ 43½ 44½ Peck B D10 ⒻAw31000 69-23 TrnshdGold,AdrblAngl,StckngFnd 11
27Dec87-7Aqu 1 1/16⊡:4731:1221:45 ft 5½ 1105 812 711 514 314½ Peck B D7 ⒻAw31000 69-18 BuckMgic,TrnishedGold,Resonble 11
7Dec87-7Aqu 1 1/16⊡:5021:1521:47 ft 3½ 1087 84½ 65½ 67¾ 411½ Peck B D10 ⒻAw31000 62-24 SallySaysSo,HolidyPond,FirstShot 10
7Dec87—L'ckd rm. str.
25Nov87-6Aqu 1⅛ :494 1:152 1:552ft 2 1087 53 43 35 34 Peck B D7 ⒻAw31000 54-35 RunComeSee,LotusSpring,Resonbl 7
May 9 Bel 4f ft :483 h Apr 26 Bel tr.t 4f ft :483 h Apr 20 Bel tr.t 4f ft :483 h Mar 31 Bel tr.t 4f ft :481 b

Sunny Roberta
B. f. 3, by Robellino—Tsaritsyna, by Filiberto
Own.—Ol' Silverbell Farm 112
Br.—Hidden Lane Stable (Md) 1988 3 0 0 1 $6,000
Tr.—Minton Jeffrey T 1987 12 1 0 2 $25,590
Lifetime 15 1 0 3 $31,590 Turf 3 1 0 0 $18,360
1May88-9Pim 1 1/16 Ⓣ:472 1:112 1:431fm 19 105 31 75¼ 713 722¼ MnoDR4 ⒻⓈGeisha H 64-13 ThirtyEghtGoGo,Smrt'nQuck,Lndur 7
1May88—Dwelt st.
4Apr88-9Pim 1 1/16 :48 1:123 1:44 ft 28 114 68½ 34½ 38½ 319½ PMG4 ⒻⓈCaesr'sWsh 65-22 WillonthMov,FtndFoxy,SunnyRobrt 6
28Mar88-7Aqu 6f :222 :462 1:11 ft 68 116 77½ 911 1024 1027½ Migliore R9 ⒻAw30000 57-30 MyCrvnn,NturlElegnce,JckieMcGe 10
12Dec87-8Pha 1 1/16 :472 1:123 1:47 ft 13 114 63½ 811 817 832¼ Verge M E 7 ⒻVillager 36-23 EmprssTigr,SovrignSign,Topicount 9
5Dec87-9Lrl 1 1/16 :47 1:124 1:433gd 61 119 34 47 517 525¾ PMG5 ⒻⓈMarylndJuv 64-23 ShmSy,ThirtyEightGoGo,BttyLobli 7
11Nov87-3Aqu 1 1/8 :484 1:144 1:544sy 10 118 79½ 58 38 38½ Maple E6 ⒻAw31000 52-36 TopPinchr,NtlyArrngd,SunnyRobrt 7
31Oct87-2Aqu 1 1/16 Ⓣ:482 1:144 1:47 gd 5½ 117 21½ 2hd 1hd 17¾ Maple E9 ⒻMdn 70-32 SunnyRoberta,Suedemark,Ribldry 10
15Oct87-2Bel 1 1/16 Ⓣ:474 1:133 1:462gd 35 117 22 1hd 21½ 412¼ Maple E12 ⒻMdn 52-33 BettyLobelia,NetlyArrnged,Bippus 12
May 11 Sar tr.t 3f ft :372 b ●May 8 Sar tr.t 3f ft :37 h Apr 20 Sar 5f ft 1:03 h Mar 18 Fai tr.t 5f gd 1:00 b

Plum Suite
Dk. b. or br. f. 4, by Plum Bold—Our Suiti Pie, by Cougar II
Own.—Bradley & Lundy Mmes 121
Br.—Bradley Mary (Ky) 1988 3 1 0 0 $17,440
Tr.—Lundy Richard J 1987 9 M 3 0 $16,750
Lifetime 12 1 3 0 $34,190 Turf 4 0 1 0 $4,950
15Apr88-3Aqu 1 1/8 :48 1:13 1:544ft 3½e 124 77¾ 67¾ 34 1¾ Davis R G3 ⒻMdn 61-23 PlumSuite,MenddHrt,ArcticEvning 8
15Apr88—Bumped st., drvg
1Apr88-3Aqu 1 1/8 :493 1:141 1:522ft 4½e 124 914 711 517 518¾ Davis R G10 ⒻMdn 54-24 BMyConqustdor,JolScot,DwnOnM 10
1Apr88—Checked
11Feb88-5GP 1 1/16 :473 1:132 1:48 ft *2½ 122 1120 917 712 411½ St Leon G1 ⒻMdn 49-27 ReassertYourself,Bandids,LdyBlyn 12
29Oct87-5Aqu 1 1/8 :492 1:142 1:55 ft 2¾ 119 64¾ 44 32½ 21½ Antley C W3 ⒻMdn 58-28 Prince of aLady,PlumSuite,Hassam 8
13Sep87-1Bel 1 1/4 :47 1:391 2:054sy *2 118 811 48 411 414¾ Bailey J D3 ⒻMdn 54-23 DviousDutchss,PrncofLdy,GltzyLdy 8
28Aug87-4Mth 1 :481 1:131 1:40 sy 4 115 513 36½ 35½ 27 St Leon G2 ⒻMdn 66-29 AwesomSuzy,PlumSuit,ModrnGrcin 7
8Aug87-11Mth 1 1/8 Ⓣ:483 1:131 1:513fm 4 116 118½ 75½ 54 23 St Leon G2 ⒻMdn 86-10 Bodecia, Plum Suite, Overnight 11
22Jly87-10Mth 1 1/16 Ⓣ:464 1:112 1:451fm 10 115 1217 1015 79 41¾ St Leon G5 ⒻMdn 73-21 She's So Hot, Veronica, Atlatl 12
May 10 Bel 6f ft 1:144 h May 1 Bel 6f ft 1:20 b Apr 25 Bel 4f ft :492 b Apr 14 Bel 3f ft :381 hg

Premier Ballerina
B. f. 4, by Sovereign Dancer—Silver Rain, by Roan Rocket
Own.—Wootten Mary L 121
Br.—Maxwell Russell (Fla) 1988 8 1 3 1 $14,705
Tr.—Dutrow Anthony W 1987 5 M 2 2 $4,472
Lifetime 13 1 5 3 $19,177 Turf 5 1 2 1 $12,700
27Apr88-2Crc a1 Ⓣ:491 1:141 1:392fm *2-3 116 4¾ 1hd 12½ 13¾ Velez J A Jr 5 Ⓕ 25000 76-21 PrmrBllrn,Cucu-Ru-Cc,LttlEmoton 8
19Apr88-8Crc a1 1/8 Ⓣ 1:484fm 12 116 53½ 43 34 23¾ Velez J A Jr 3 Ⓕ 30000 72-25 Dawandeh,PremierBllerin,Cremos 10
13Apr88-1Crc 7f :23 :48 1:291ft *7-5 1157 54½ 45 22½ 23 Vives J C 4 ⒻM32500 67-22 AllArts,PremierBallerin,Vite'Victori 8
31Mar88-10Crc 1 1/16 :494 1:16 1:51 ft 3½ 1137 33 34 25 36¾ Vives J C 2 ⒻMdn 57-27 Dixie Gray,Sendia,PremierBallerina 9
13Mar88-6Crc 1 Ⓣ:48 1:13 1:384gd 11 114 21 31½ 79½ 89¾ Lester R N 6 Ⓕ 45000 78-17 BellMountain,Dwndeh,Pete'sTrick 12
26Feb88-9GP a1 1/16 Ⓣ 1:45 fm 45 117 87½ 64½ 21½ 2½ Fires E 2 ⒻAw18000 80-18 DncingAllNight,PremierBllrin,Llul 11
12Jan88-3GP 7f :224 :463 1:241ft 6 122 97½ 79¾ 514 514 Fires E 10 ⒻMdn 69-25 DmeDusty,SenseofUnity,RedGrdni 12
1Jan88-11Hia 7f :231 :463 1:26 ft 2½ 122 85½ 66½ 64½ 65 Valiente D 8 ⒻMdn 68-25 FirstVenture,Forlvich,Juli'sDouble 12
Apr 11 Crc 3f ft :37 b Mar 26 Crc 3f ft :353 b

Timely Business
B. f. 3, by Diesis—Amatiña, by In Reality
Own.—Matczak J F 112
Br.—Pennfield Farms Inc (Fla) 1988 5 1 1 0 $17,820
Tr.—Hertler John O 1987 4 M 0 0
Lifetime 9 1 1 0 $17,820 Turf 1 0 1 0 $6,820
27Apr88-4Aqu 1 1/16 Ⓣ:473 1:122 1:442fm 22 114 57 75½ 32 22 VelsquezJ 7 ⒻAw31000 81-16 GtherTheCln,TimlyBusinss,Strofnr 10
28Mar88-3Aqu 7f :233 :472 1:26 ft 25 116 83½ 43½ 86¾ 811½ Romero R P 2 Ⓕ 50000 59-30 DustyDonn,Kolctoo'sBtty,ProdFlrt 9
28Mar88—Steadied str.
29Feb88-8Aqu 6f ⊡:221 :452 1:112ft 39 1115 710 78½ 69 611 BoulngerG 2 ⒻAw30000 76-25 Avie'sGal,MyCarvnn,‡NturlElegnce 7
22Feb88-3Aqu 6f ⊡:231 :464 1:141ft 14 1165 93½ 75 2hd 13 BoulangerG 2 ⒻM50000 73-32 TimlyBusnss,TrofGold,WllRomncd 12
22Feb88—Bore in,clear
25Jan88-4Aqu 6f ⊡:23 :464 1:123ft 70 121 82½ 54¾ 59½ 510½ Skinner K 8 ⒻM50000 70-23 Smrtn'Irish,Mymotherwndm,Tgtt 10
31Dec87-4Aqu 1 1/16 ⊡:483 1:144 1:492ft 11 117 911 1118 821 817¼ Skinner K6 ⒻM50000 44-22 Lis'sHlo,TurntoSlew,Em'sMummy 11
10Dec87-2Aqu 1 70 ⊡:49 1:153 1:462ft 25 117 23 32½ 715 713½ Skinner K3 ⒻMdn 53-24 Stonigh'sHp,MssEmbssy,CmInAgn 10
3Dec87-6Aqu 6f ⊡:221 :461 1:123ft 89 117 911 811 810 610¼ Skinner K8 ⒻMdn 71-19 To Excel, Private Micki, Tagett 10
May 9 Bel 6f ft 1:15 b Apr 25 Bel 3f ft :35 h Apr 18 Bel 5f ft 1:014 h Apr 10 Bel 4f ft :50 b

Tango Tune
B. m. 5, by Dance Bid—Satan's Cheer, by Crimson Satan
Own.—Roslyn Farm 112
Br.—Crimson King Farm (Ky) 1988 3 0 0 1 $2,250
Tr.—Kelly Thomas J 1987 8 1 1 1 $21,635
Lifetime 23 2 2 5 $38,046 Turf 14 1 2 4 $38,777
31Mar88-9Crc 1 70 :494 1:154 1:493ft 3½ 112 52½ 56½ 65 54½ Valiente D 5 ⒻAw15500 58-27 AlwaysBeutiful,TokyoStutz,Strictly 6
23Feb88-9GP a1½ Ⓣ 2:331fm 6½ 117 55 22 31 33½ ValienteD 10 ⒻAw18000 75-22 JackyMax,StallSociety,TangoTune 10
20Jan88-10GP a1 Ⓣ 1:382fm *2½ 117 911 77 65½ 54½ Cruguet J 5 Ⓕ 50000 84-13 CltchPrfrmnc,FlngP.J.,Tht'sMMrg 11
15Dec87-8Hia a1 1/8 Ⓣ 1:532fm 7½ 112 52½ 52¾ 2hd 2nk Cruguet J 3 Ⓕ 55000 64-36 HeatWave,TngoTune,Erin'sDunloe 10
15Dec87—Lacked room
30Oct87-8Crc a1 1/16 Ⓣ:483 1:124 1:431fm 3½ 119 65½ 54 67½ 49¾ Lester R N 4 ⒻAw11500 81-09 MissGybddrd,HtWv,BbyDuckFoot 10
21Oct87-6Crc a1 1/16 Ⓣ:482 1:132 1:454fm 4 119 53¾ 21 1hd 32½ Lester R N 7 ⒻAw12500 75-20 Codessa, Regular Miss, TangoTune 8
6Sep87-1Bel 1 1/4 Ⓣ:502 1:394 2:05 fm 15 113 42½ 32½ 32 1hd Cruguet J 7 Ⓕ 45000 69-20 TngoTun,HightOfPlsur,FrAndAbov 7
1Aug87-3Bel 1 1/16 Ⓣ:453 1:11 1:43 fm 10 117 1010 109¾ 813 713½ Bailey J D 5 ⒻAw27000 67-10 MissUnnmebl,TimForEmrlds,Strit 10
May 8 Bel 7f ft 1:273 b Apr 19 Bel 5f ft 1:02 b Apr 13 Bel 4f ft :52 b

Pleasent Ring

B. f. 4, by Ieasant Colony—Distinctive Ring, by Distinctive
Br.—Evans Robert S (NJ) 1987 11 1 2 0 $18,336
Own.—Evans R S 112 Tr.—Schulhofer Flint S 1986 1 M 0 0
Lifetime 12 1 2 0 $18,336 Turf 1 0 0 0
31Oct87-5Med 6f :23 :46² 1:12²ft 4 106⁷ 62¾ 56½ 59 58½ Carr D² ⒻⓈAw18700 71-21 MintedLady,TijenDoll,PrincessLuis 6
13Oct87-8Med 6f :22⁴ :46² 1:12¹ft *4-5e 113 31½ 34½ 57 77¼ Terry J⁴ ⒻⓈAw18700 74-22 Procuratrix, Jitters,DegreeinReality 8
24Sep87-9Med 1⅟₁₆ :47¹ 1:12² 1:45²ft 10 113 32½ 44½ 66½ 615¼ SntosJA² ⒻⓈAw18700 60-22 LittleCommie,SpeedyJn,TrgrinDrm 9
7Sep87-7Med 6f :22¹ :45² 1:10⁴ft 16 111 85½ 63¾ 86½ 77½ SantgtN¹ ⒻⓈAw18700 81-12 M. D. Duchess, Ida Good Girl,Supai 9
29Aug87-5Mth 6f :22⁴ :46¹ 1:12²gd 11 113 31½ 63½ 43½ 53 Terry J⁴ ⒻⓈAw17500 75-17 ‡TijnDoll,ChicgoPrncss,M.D.Duchss 7
29Aug87—Placed fourth through disqualification
19Aug87-4Mth 1 :47² 1:11⁴ 1:38²ft 8 112 86½ 918 823 930 Terry J⁹ ⒻⓈAw17500 51-18 WltzngEmprss,ChckBomBm,TjnDll 9
7Aug87-9Mth 1⅛Ⓣ:49 1:13²1:51¹fm 26 109⁵ 43 64 816 821½ RomeroJA¹ ⒻAw15000 63-18 Dons Beauty,OneForBess,Horsafire 8
7Aug87—Bobbled
22Jly87-8Mth 6f :22¹ :45² 1:11²ft 12 107⁷ 53½ 65½ 66½ 59½ HethMJ⁹ ⒻⓈAw17500 74-21 IronAnni,DgrinRlty,WltzngEmprss 10
May 8 Bel 4f ft :47⁴ h Apr 26 Bel 5f ft 1:03 b Apr 21 Bel 4f ft :49⁴ h Apr 11 Bel 4f ft :50² b

Terri Nivas

Ch. f. 3, by Assert—Four Bells, by Quadrangle
Br.—Pillar Stud Inc (Ky) 1988 1 1 0 0 $9,600
Own.—Petelain Stable 112 Tr.—Byrne Patrick B 1987 1 M 0 0
Lifetime 2 1 0 0 $9,600 Turf 1 1 0 0 $9,600
5Feb88-6GP 1⅟₁₆Ⓣ:48³1:13²1:44³fm 4½ 122 64½ 64½ 76½ 1no Romero R P ⁹ ⒻMdn 77-15 Terri Nivas, So Rarely, OrchidLeaf 12
18Oct87-4Bel 6f :22⁴ :46¹ 1:11⁴ft 29 117 66 69 58½ 513½ Santagata N ⁶ ⒻMdn 67-23 OurMri,Judy'sHlo,BlossomingButy 14
May 8 Bel 6f ft 1:15 h May 2 Bel 5f ft 1:01 h Apr 22 Bel 3f ft :36 h

Perjurer

B. f. 3, by Clev Er Tell—Juress, by Advocator
Br.—Ralph G. Kercheval (Ky) 1988 6 1 0 1 $10,620
Own.—Watral M 112 Tr.—Brida Dennis J 1987 3 M 0 0 $840
Lifetime 9 1 0 1 $11,460
30Apr88-3Aqu 1⅛ :48³ 1:13² 1:52³ft 8½ 114 44 45 44½ 33½ Belmonte JF³ Ⓕ 16500 69-13 Crystalero, Ballet Birdie, Perjurer 5
20Apr88-3Aqu 6f :23 :47² 1:12⁴ft 19 118 76½ 77 68½ 69 Migliore R² Ⓕ 17500 67-26 MnShe'sSwt,Int'lGust,DncingSocks 8
8Apr88-3Aqu 7f :22⁴ :46² 1:24²m 27 116 76½ 52½ 57½ 511¾ Pezua J M² Ⓕ 22500 67-17 Roleplay, Split Moment, Fencible 7
17Mar88-3Aqu 7f :23³ :48² 1:27⁴ft 40 117 105½ 106½ 42 11¾ SantagatN¹² ⒻM30000 62-27 Perjurer, Freed, Num Num 14
11Feb88-3Aqu 1⅛⊡:51²1:18¹1:59³ft 21 110⁷ 105½ 88½ 711 714 Carr D ⁵ ⒻM30000 30-30 Argnt'sPrncss,InDn'sLght,DmSmr 12
29Jan88-3Aqu 6f ⊡:23¹ :47²1:13⁴ft 19 110⁷ 52½ 53½ 69½ 812¾ Carr D ² ⒻM30000 62-26 CompleteAccord,SexysHll,JntPlnt 12
30Nov87-3Aqu 7f :23¹ :47² 1:28¹sy 11 117 95¾ 96½ 79½ 817¾ Davis R G⁵ ⒻM35000 42-30 Pggy'sProspct,CtsndTigrs,Brvolly 14
3Nov87-3Aqu 7f :23 :46³ 1:27²ft 21 117 137½ 119¾ 59 47 Samyn J L¹⁰ ⒻM35000 57-23 Should Say It, Senility, Sexy Lady 14
May 9 Bel 3f ft :37 b Apr 27 Bel tr.t 3f ft :36² h Apr 16 Bel 5f ft 1:03² b Apr 6 Bel tr.t 4f ft :50 b

Rain Date

B. f. 4, by Blushing Groom—Miss Mazepah, by Nijinsky II
Br.—King Ranch Inc (Ky) 1988 3 1 0 1 $13,350
Own.—King Ranch 121 Tr.—Schulhofer Flint S 1987 3 M 1 0 $5,720
Lifetime 6 1 1 1 $19,070 Turf 2 0 1 0 $5,720
27Apr88-2Kee 6f :22 :45⁴ 1:12⁴ft *4-5 126 86½ 44 2hd 12½ McCauleyWH¹¹ ⒻMdn 78-22 RainDate,It'sSharp,MistyBluebelle 11
19Apr88-1Kee 6f :22² :46¹ 1:12⁴gd *6-5 120 98½ 86 54½ 32½ McCauleyWH ¹¹ ⒻMdn 76-22 ReasontoBab,PreciousLdy,RinDte 12
19Apr88—Stumbled start
16Feb88-6GP 7f :22⁴ :46³ 1:25⁴ft *2½ 122 73½ 42 12½ 14½ † McCauleyWH¹⁰ ⒻMdn 75-27 ‡RainDte,Norrsken,GildedMoment 12
†16Feb88—Disqualified and placed eleventh; Bore out
6Nov87-4Aqu 1⅛Ⓣ:49¹1:14³1:53¹fm 3½ 120 52 42½ 915 917½ Cruguet J⁷ ⒻMdn 51-28 Majeboo, Pot o' Jam,PekaboBaby 12
6Nov87—Unruly pre-st.
4Sep87-6Bel 1⅟₁₆Ⓣ:46¹1:11⁴1:45 gd 23 118 77½ 64½ 31 25¾ Maple E⁸ ⒻMdn 65-23 OneForest,RainDte,RellyWelcome 11
16Aug87-9Sar 6f :21³ :44³ 1:10¹ft 20 117 88½ 713 68½ 66¾ Cruguet J⁸ ⒻMdn 82-12 Crystal Blaze,MissCzara,Wakonda 12
16Aug87—Broke slowly
May 9 Bel 4f ft :52² b Apr 14 Kee 4f ft :48³ b Apr 9 Kee 4f ft :49⁴ b

Anorada

B. f. 4, by His Majesty—Southern Melody, by Bold Lad
Br.—Wimborne Farm Inc (Ky) 1988 2 0 0 1 $3,720
Own.—Egide J A 121 Tr.—Sedlacek Michael C 1987 12 1 4 1 $23,510
Lifetime 14 1 4 2 $27,230 Turf 6 1 2 2 $20,250
8May88-7Aqu 1⅛Ⓣ:50⁴1:16²1:53³gd 4¾ 121 53 41½ 34 310½ Davis R G¹⁰ ⒻAw31000 57-33 BlossomngBty,CompltAccrd,Anrd 10
18Apr88-7Aqu 7f :22³ :46 1:24³ft 35 121 611 67¼ 77 710 Pezua J M⁶ ⒻAw30000 68-20 RobertBbe,CrystlBlze,EvntHorizon 7
18Oct87-6Bel 1⅜Ⓣ:51 1:40²2:18¹fm 24 114 63 55 411 314½ Antley CW⁶ ⒻAw29000 57-23 Latin Lyric, DancingRags,Anorada 11
8Oct87-7Bel 1⅟₁₆ :48 1:12³ 1:44³gd 11 114 912 812 711 714¾ Santos J A⁷ ⒻAw29000 64-23 Sunset Cloud, Magical, Latin Lyric 9
16Sep87-8Pha 1⅟₁₆Ⓣ:48²1:13 1:45³yl *3-2 113 64½ 42 2½ 4¾ Ayarza I⁹ ⒻAw12500 73-29 Smiling Fay, Chervil, Phinques 11
2Sep87-9Mth a1⅟₁₆Ⓣ 1:45³fm*9-5 111 55½ 42½ 2½ 23 Jimenez IJ⁵ ⒻAw15000 — — Reassert, Anorada, Dissembler 6
25Aug87-7Mth 1⅛Ⓣ:48³1:12⁴1:51 fm 4¾ 112 77½ 87 64 22 Jimenez IJ⁷ ⒻAw15000 83-14 Cream Sauce, Anorada, Chervil 9
5Aug87-8Pha 1 :47 1:11³ 1:38⁴sy 5½ 114 310 310 39 25½ CastanedK⁴ ⒻAw12500 74-29 Lady Lake, Anorada, BlancheNeige 6
May 3 Aqu 4f ft :49² b Apr 27 Aqu 4f ft :49⁴ b Apr 14 Aqu 3f ft :35³ h ●Apr 9 Aqu 5f gd 1:01¹ h

```
Ridgedale Ave.                  B. f. 4, by Apalachee—Show Gal, by Gallant Man
                                Br.—September Farm (Fla)          1988 7 M 0 0      $900
Own.—Suss Five Stable      121  Tr.—Horn Philip J Jr              1986 2 M 0 0      $660
                           Lifetime   9 0 0 0   $1,560            Turf 1 0 0 0
27Apr88-4Aqu  1 1/16 (T):47 3 1:12 2 1:44 2 fm 68 121  9 14 10 15 10 18 10 22 1/2  ThibeauRJ 5 (F)Aw31000 60-16 GtherTheCln,TimlyBusinss,Strofnr 10
     27Apr88—Steadied start
22Apr88-2Aqu  1 :47 3 1:14 1:41 1 ft  46 120  10 12 9 14 9 20 9 21 1/2  Thibeau R J 5 (F)M30000 38-28 Traveat, D'or Etoile, Shmenge 11
     22Apr88—Broke awkwardly
6Apr88-2Aqu  1 1/8 :50 1:15 2 1:55 3 ft  25 120  9 7 7 6 1/2 6 11 6 14 1/2  Thibeau R J 5 (F)M30000 43-25 Vtod,Dontylovhrmdly,NoWyThrgh 11
     6Apr88—Pinched start
25Mar88-3Aqu  1 1/8 :49 1:14 4 1:55 2 ft  14 118  5 13 5 9 1/2 4 12 4 15 3/4  Thibeau R J 7 (F)M30000 42-27 Flcon'sFrdy,DlghtflNsh,MyGntlRos 7
10Mar88-2Aqu  6f [•]:24 :49 2 1:15 2 ft  22 122  12 13 11 8 3/4 9 15 7 15 1/2  Maple E 3  (F)M35000 51-34 Never There, Zolotaya,Rexi'sHour 12
25Feb88-9Aqu  6f [•]:23 1 :47 4 1:14 4 ft  12 122  11 12 10 14 10 9 3/4 10 9 1/2  Maple E 12  (F)M35000 61-25 I'mHome,TokyoBound,Cntkepscrt 12
21Jan88-5Aqu  6f [•]:22 3 :47 1 1:13 2 m  9 118  9 13 10 14 11 20 10 24 1/2  Santos J A 6 (F)M45000 53-21 WllflWndy,Flcn'sFrdy,ChrrpgnDbl 11
     21Jan88—Slow start
22Nov86-3Aqu  6f :22 2 :46 3 1:12 4 ft  3 3/4 114  11 4 1/2 10 4 1/2 9 7 3/4 8 7 3/4  Romero RP 5 (F)M45000 69-18 CzrTrek,GotTheGreenlight,HlfScrt 12
     22Nov86—Bled mouth
  ● May 5 Bel tr.t 5f ft 1:02 b       Apr 15 Bel 4f ft :49 2 h
```

We are looking at a field of entry-level allowance horses with a serious built-in contradiction. Generally at this class level horses are preferred by the handicapper because they have not already proven to be chronic losers. The more attempts a horse makes at this condition level, the more likely it will never pass the test and will have to drop into claimers to find its win level.

That means lightly-raced horses should be favored because they are not proven failures. But today's field only has two lightly-raced entrants, both of which earned their victory at a minor-league circuit; on the other hand, many of the chronic losers won their maiden race at major-league tracks. In theory, none of these horses will win. Now, we are required to rewrite the textbook and find some other basis of comparison.

In this setting, the proven failures now deserve serious consideration. They will be racing on the grass. What happens if we throw out all dirt races from the past performances and search for a potential master of the turf trade?

Approximate Odds, Post Time

Rain Date	2–1/5–2	(Cruguet)
Pleasent Ring	2–1/5–2	(Vasquez)
Timely Business	4–1	(Velasquez)
Reasonable	4–1	(Migliore)
Tango Tune	6–1/7–1	(Valiente)

Terri Nivas	7–1/8–1	(Samyn)
Premier Ballerina	11–1	(Antley)
Plum Suite	14–1	(Davis)
Anorada	16–1	(Romero)
Sunny Roberta	19–1	(Santos)
Perjurer	62–1	(Belmonte)
Ridgedale Ave.	99–1	(Thibeau)

Comments

Unlikely

1. So near and yet so far. Reasonable, Anorada, and Premier Ballerina come close often but rarely win. Reasonable runs like her name, while Anorada's in-the-money record is suspect because two of her "good" races on a major circuit were well-beaten thirds, more than ten lengths back. Both Anorada and Premier Ballerina have no credentials on this racing circuit. Premier Ballerina had to wait for a field so poor that she was 2–3 when she finally won. These three have all shown enough grass racing to assure us there will be no surprises in that "terrain."
2. Horses that have proven they dislike the grass are Plum Suite, Pleasant Ring, and Ridgedale Ave., who is still a maiden.
3. Even for people, it's tough to do new things right the first time. Perjurer, who has never tried the turf and never won a route, must be successful in two new areas for the first time.
4. Of the two lightly-raced horses, Rain Date is the most vulnerable. This filly has never won a route race, nor has she won on the grass. Her turf breeding is a plus, but she's already tried twice on the grass and disappointed her backers both times. She's the type of publicity horse that always gets bet. She won going from turf to dirt, route to sprint, New York to Florida, only to be disqualified; now she makes the symmetrically opposite changes into today's race. Her record as it relates to her breeding is like baked beans with hot dogs served on expensive china.

Contenders

Three contenders show the potential to become masters of their trade (turf) while the other contender may have a more specialized trade, that of horse for course.

4. Timely Business is the only one of our four contenders to have never won on the turf and never won a route. Signs of the future are present, though, in her last race, for she improved nine lengths going from sprint to route *and* dirt to turf, finishing second on the grass at 22–1. She projects well against this field.

3. Of the three remaining contenders, Tango Tune is the only horse with but a one-dimensional reason for being labeled a contender. Her 1 turf victory in 14 tries was right here: *Belmont Inner Turf Course* at today's distance: 1¼ miles. That's a very powerful reason, but it's still only one dimension. A switch to Cruguet, for example, would have added a second dimension, since that rider was aboard for her victory, as well as for her second by a neck at 7–1.

2. Sunny Roberta is 0 for 12 on dirt and 1 for 3 on the grass. That fact is the cover of the book that talks about a future turf specialist. Inside the cover are two important details.
   a. Her first turf victory (at 5–1!) was the second in a series of two races, both on the grass. Today's race is also the second of a pair on that surface. Could this pattern match refer to a trainer who has his filly retrace the steps that led to her last victory?
   b. Her last race against superior horses displays a hidden form revival: *early speed for the first time* since her last turf win. After having dwelt at the start, Sunny Roberta's third by one length at the half-mile call represents some "better than looks" racing. True, she dropped back afterwards, but she also dropped back in the race prior to her last victory. Had the trainer advised the rider to put some pace into the horse early? Or had the horse felt more like running with the switch to turf? The potential repetition of a cycle appears as follows:
      dirt to turf—early speed/drop back—win second turf race

One more plus, which does not relate to the above—for today's race Sunny Roberta gets Santos.

1. Terri Nivas is undefeated on the turf. Granted that's only one for one, but she did it at 9–1 odds, and she's the only horse in this field without a "proven loser" stigma. This future turf specialist may also be a layoff specialist. Defying the Myth of Tamtulia, her first win came after a

3½-month layoff. Is the trainer in tune with a secret horse cycle? Today's race also follows a 3½-month layoff!

	Our Line	Track Odds	Decision
Terri Nivas	5–2	7–1/8–1	Over. Bet.
Sunny Roberta	7–2	19–1	Over. Bet.
Tango Tune	5–1	6–1/7–1	Too close. No bet, especially with two other bets in same race.
Timely Business	6–1	4–1	Under. No bet.

At this moment it will be proper to raise two theoretical questions while we have available a practical context. Can we bet a third horse in the same race? What if Tango Tune had gone off at higher odds?

Normally, 5–1 line odds demand at least 7½–1 tote odds for a bet. The theory is that you bet if you have an advantage, and you ask for more of an advantage if you are betting more than one horse per race. If Tango Tune had been a second bet, we'd have demanded an 8–1 minimum. And under today's conditions, as a third bet, we would have required a minimum of 9–1. By requiring more in multiple-bet situations, you demand to collect enough in order to pay for the inevitable loser(s) in the same race. In other words, losers must be paid for from funds of *surplus value* and not of *principal*.

The next question, I expect, has already been asked several times by the reader. How is it that, in these workshops, our line odds are so different from tote-board odds? Perhaps some readers feel anxiety when so far away from the public. The answer is simple. To win at the races, we need to feel lonely and apart from the crowd because we need to do things differently. Not because the public is dumb; simply because the handicapping techniques employed by the public are highly taxed by the pari-mutuel system. The thoroughbred-cycles methodology comes up with distinct odds because its primary handicapping tool, form cycle, is but a secondary tool for the majority of handicappers.

SIXTH RACE **1 ¼ MILES.(InnerTurf). (1.58⅘) ALLOWANCE. Purse $29,000. Fillies and mares. 3-year-olds and upward, which have never won a race other than Maiden, Claiming or Starter. Weight, 3-year-olds, 115 lbs., Older, 124 lbs., Non-winners of a race other than claiming over a mile since April 15, allowed 3 lbs.**

Belmont

MAY 14, 1988

Value of race $29,000; value to winner $17,400; second $6,380; third $3,480; fourth $1,740. Mutuel pool $231,272. Exacta Pool $611,503.

Last Raced	Horse	Eqt.	A.	Wt	PP	¼	½	¾	1	Str	Fin	Jockey	Odds $1
1May88 ^{9}Pim^{7}	Sunny Roberta		3	112	2	$1^{1\frac{1}{2}}$	1^{1}	1^{2}	$1^{\frac{1}{2}}$	1^{4}	1^{7}	Santos J A	19.80
31Mar88 ^{9}Crc^{5}	Tango Tune	b	5	121	6	9^{3}	$7^{\frac{1}{2}}$	6^{hd}	7^{hd}	3^{1}	$2^{\frac{3}{4}}$	Valiente D	6.70
1May88 ^{7}Aqu^{2}	Reasonable		4	121	1	11^{2}	9^{hd}	8^{hd}	$5^{\frac{1}{2}}$	$5^{2\frac{1}{2}}$	3^{hd}	Migliore R	4.20
5Feb88 ^{6}GP^{1}	Terri Nivas	b	3	112	8	$6^{\frac{1}{2}}$	$4^{\frac{1}{2}}$	$3^{\frac{1}{2}}$	2^{2}	2^{1}	$4^{1\frac{1}{2}}$	Samyn J L	7.80
27Apr88 ^{4}Aqu^{2}	Timely Business	b	3	112	5	$4^{\frac{1}{2}}$	$6^{\frac{1}{2}}$	7^{1}	$4^{1\frac{1}{2}}$	6^{1}	5^{2}	Velasquez J	4.00
8May88 ^{7}Aqu^{3}	Anorada		4	121	12	3^{hd}	$5^{1\frac{1}{2}}$	$5^{\frac{1}{2}}$	3^{hd}	4^{1}	$6^{5\frac{1}{4}}$	Romero R P	16.60
15Apr88 ^{3}Aqu^{1}	Plum Suite	b	4	121	3	12	12	12	10^{1}	$8^{2\frac{1}{2}}$	7^{hd}	Davis R G	14.10
27Apr88 ^{2}Kee^{1}	Rain Date		4	121	10	8^{hd}	10^{1}	$9^{\frac{1}{2}}$	6^{1}	$7^{1\frac{1}{2}}$	8^{5}	Cruguet J	a-2.30
27Apr88 ^{2}Crc^{1}	Premier Ballerina	b	4	121	4	$10^{\frac{1}{2}}$	$11^{2\frac{1}{2}}$	10^{1}	8^{1}	$9^{\frac{1}{2}}$	$9^{2\frac{1}{4}}$	Antley C W	11.00
27Apr88 ^{4}Aqu^{10}	Ridgedale Ave.		4	121	11	$5^{\frac{1}{2}}$	2^{1}	$2^{\frac{1}{2}}$	$9^{\frac{1}{2}}$	$10^{1\frac{1}{2}}$	$10^{1\frac{1}{4}}$	Thibeau R J	117:40
31Oct87 ^{5}Med^{5}	Pleasent Ring		4	121	7	$2^{\frac{1}{2}}$	$3^{\frac{1}{2}}$	4^{1}	$11^{2\frac{1}{2}}$	11^{3}	11^{5}	Vasquez J	a-2.30
30Apr88 ^{3}Aqu^{3}	Perjurer		3	112	9	$7^{1\frac{1}{2}}$	8^{2}	11^{1}	12	12	12	Belmonte J F	62.60

a–Coupled: Rain Date and Pleasent Ring.

OFF AT 3:32. Start good, Won driving. Time, :25, :50, 1:15⅘, 1:41, 2:05⅘ Course firm.

$2 Mutuel Prices:				
	3–(B)–SUNNY ROBERTA	**41.60**	**22.60**	**11.20**
	7–(F)–TANGO TUNE		**10.60**	**6.20**
	2–(A)–REASONABLE			**3.60**
	$2 EXACTA 3–7 PAID $446.60.			

B. f, by Robellino—Tsaritsyna, by Filiberto. Trainer Minton Jeffrey T. Bred by Hidden Lane Stable (Md).

SUNNY ROBERTA sprinted clear at once was rated on the lead while saving ground to the top of the stretch then drew off under strong handling. TANGO TURN, angled to the outside while advancing on the far turn, steadily closed ground between horses entering the stretch and finished willingly for the place. REASONABLE, raced in traffic along the backstretch, split horses to get clear in upper stretch and was going well at the finish. TERRI NIVAS, steadied along while caught in tight quarters on the first turn, moved to the outside to work his way forward on the backstretch, remained a factor into the stretch and lacked the needed response when called upon. TIMELY BUSINESS steadied along the inside on the first turn, moved within striking distance while saving ground on the far turn then took up sharply when blocked and was no threat thereafter. RAIN DATE was never a serious threat. RIDGEDALE AVE. was finished after going five furlongs. PLEASANT RING showed only brief speed.

Owners— 1, Ol' Silverbell Farm; 2, Roslyn Farm; 3, Fertile Acres Farm; 4, Petelain Stable; 5, Matczak J F; 6, Egide J A; 7, Bradley & Lundy Mmes; 8, King Ranch; 9, Wootton Mary L; 10, Suss Five Stable ; 11, Evans R S; 12, Watral M .

Trainers— 1, Minton Jeffrey T; 2, Kelly Thomas J; 3, DiMauro Stephen L; 4, Byrne Patrick B; 5, Hertler John O; 6, Sedlacek Michael C; 7, Lundy Richard J; 8, Schulhofer Flint S; 9, Dutrow Anthony W; 10, Horn Philip J Jr; 11, Schulhofer Flint S; 12, Brida Dennis J.

Scratched—Classic Index (7May88 ^{8}GS^{7}).

And the exacta? That's the kind of big fish that gets away from me too often. In the long run, boxing four contenders is a folly. Boxing three contenders? Maybe. Only if they are all leading to big payoffs. The correct strategy is to check the payoffs on all combinations involving contenders and bet those that are better than fair value. Dick Mitchell would have advised to key the longest-priced contender, boxing it with the others. I saw the presence of seconditis horses with a potential for causing my combo to run first-third. Had Reasonable not been held up in traffic, she might have done just that, nearly getting up for second. As it was, our second and third choices combined for a $446.60 payoff on a $2 minimum exacta investment. Of course, without going into the exacta, you would have collected "only" $41.60 for each $2 invested on a simple win bet.

Sunny Roberta had qualified within the parameters of two types of cycle. First, the horse/trainer partnership, which retraces the same path that led to a previous victory. Second, the potential master-of-trade consistency *within* inconsistency, where a horse that is unsuccessful at most endeavors is highly dependable, steady, within one particular specialty.

Tango Tune represented the cycle that peaks because of place and not necessarily time, the horse for course. The fact that the scene of her last 15–1 robbery was also the identical specialty distance of today's race, suggested that the trainer was a knowing accomplice in Tango Tune's attempt to pilfer another one.

Wouldn't it be wonderful if we could find races with only one clear scenario, like in Pittsburgh Phil, rather than this Marx Brothers situation of confusion and contradicting alternatives; but isn't this why so many good horseplayers miss out on long shots they should have had, precisely because they don't attack as boldly when the situation is more complex? As you can see, a betting line with only reasonable accuracy resolves the problem of complicated races, allowing the handicapper to more fully exploit the insights found in a successful handicapping methodology.

WORKSHOP SEVEN

April 26, 1988

Here is a stakes race for younger colts. We are approaching Kentucky Derby day, but none of these runners will make an appearance at Churchill Downs. This type of race includes horses within three categories:

a. Good enough for the Kentucky Derby, but peaked too early and are on the way down (child prodigy)
b. Never going to be of Derby caliber, but potentially competitive at this level
c. At a later time may defeat Triple Crown horses, but were allowed to mature later, at a slower pace

8th Hollywood

7 FURLONGS. (1.20⅘) 37th Running of THE DEBONAIR STAKES. $75,000 added. 3-year-olds. By subscription of $100 each, which shall accompany the nomination, $750 additional to start, with $75,000 added, of which $15,000 to second, $11,250 to third, $5,625 to fourth and $1,875 to fifth. Weight, 122 lbs. Non-winners of $25,000 twice since December 25 or $50,000 at any time allowed 3 lbs.; a race of $25,000 or two races of $18,000 at any time, 5 lbs.; a race of $18,000 or two races other than maiden or claiming, 8 lbs. Starters to be named through the entry box by closing time of entries. A trophy will be presented to the owner of the winner. Closed Wednesday, April 20, with 31 nominations.

START — 7 FURLONGS — HOLLYWOOD PARK — FINISH

Success Express

STEVENS G L — 122
Own.—Klein E V
B. c. 3, by Hold Your Peace—Au Printemps, by Dancing Champ
Br.—Tri Star Stable (Ky)
Tr.—Lukas D Wayne
1988 4 0 1 2 $84,252
1987 8 4 1 1 $737,207
Lifetime 12 4 2 3 $821,459

9Apr88-7Aqu 1 :45 1:10 1:34⅘ft 3½ 123 12½ 11 44 48¾ SantosJA5 Gotham 83-19 PrivteTerms,SkingthGold,PrfctSpy 8
9Apr88—Grade II
26Mar88-8Aqu 7f :22⅗ :45 1:22⅗sy *1 123 2½ 21 2½ 2¾ SntosJA2 Bay Shore 87-23 PrfctSpy,SuccssExprss,ProudndVld 5
26Mar88—Grade II
27Feb88-8SA 1 :45⅕ 1:10⅖ 1:38 ft 8½ 121 12½ 11 11½ 3nk PincayLJr3 Sn Rafl 78-17 WhtADplmt,FlyngVctr,SccssExprss 9
27Feb88—Grade II
27Jan88-8SA 7f :22 :44⅕ 1:22⅘ft *6-5 123 31 32 33 39½ SantosJA2 Sn Vcnt 77-19 MPrfrdo,NoCmmtmnt,SccssExprss 5
27Jan88—Grade III
20Dec87-8Hol 1 :45 1:09⅕ 1:34⅘ft 9-5 121 43 53 57½ 611 Santos JA4 Hol Fut 79-08 Tejano, Purdue King, Regal Classic 8
20Dec87—Grade I
21Nov87-5Hol 1 :44⅘ 1:09⅖ 1:35⅕ft 4e122 11½ 11½ 13 11¾ SntosJA11 Br Cp Juv 87-12 SuccessExpress,RegalClssic,Tejno 13
21Nov87—Grade I
31Oct87-8SA 11/16 :46⅗ 1:11⅖ 1:45 sy *3-2 118 1hd 1hd 2½ 48½ Santos J A4 Nrflk 68-25 SrtogPssge,PurdueKing,BoldScond 7
31Oct87—Grade I
11Oct87-10LaD 7f :23⅕ :46⅖ 1:22⅘ft *1-2 121 1hd 1½ 16 115 SntsJA6 Spt O Kng Ft 95-21 Success Express,RisenStar,BigSnoz 6
27Sep87-10Cby 170 :47 1:10⅗ 1:42⅕ft *1-2 120 1½ 11½ 11 1nk Perret C4 Cby Juv 90-09 SuccssExprss,HousAccount,BgSnoz 8
14Sep87-5Bel 6f :22⅕ :45⅖ 1:08⅘gd *1-2 118 1½ 12 15 16¾ Santos J A5 Mdn 95-13 SuccssExprss,SunrsShowr,ZWorld 10
Apr 23 Hol 4f ft :50 h Apr 5 Bel 4f ft :50⅗ b Mar 21 Aqu 5f ft 1:01⅗ h Mar 15 Bel tr.t 5f ft 1:01⅗ h

Dr. Brent

SOLIS A — 119
Own.—Braverman & Colvin
Dk. b. or br. g. 3, by Naevus—Renata's Love, by Nantequos
Br.—Colvin R (Cal)
Tr.—Soriano Morris
1988 5 3 0 1 $76,262
1987 8 1 3 0 $18,085
Lifetime 13 4 3 1 $94,347 Turf 1 1 0 0 $38,262

6Apr88-8SA a6½f ⓣ:21 :43⅗1:15 fm 7¾ 117 43½ 31½ 1hd 11½ Solis A8 Baldwin 84-13 Dr.Brent,AccomplishRidg,GldMusic 9
6Apr88—Run in divisions
17Mar88-7SA 6½f :21⅘ :45⅕ 1:16⅘ft *9-5 116 54½ 31 11½ 12¾ DlhoussyE3 Aw34000 86-20 Dr.Brent,GoForBroadway,Vancealot 8
17Mar88—Bumped hard start
4Mar88-5SA 6f :21⅗ :44⅗ 1:10 ft 6 116 41½ 43 31 12¾ DelahoussayeE5 50000 88-19 Dr. Brent, Hard To Miss, Ekahi 10
5Feb88-5SA 6f :22 :45⅕ 1:11⅗ft 7½ 116 1hd 2hd 11½ 3¾ Shoemaker W3 50000 79-20 Temper T., Hard To Miss,Dr.Brent 12
5Feb88—Bumped twice start
24Jan88-8SA 6f :21⅖ :44⅖ 1:09⅗ft 30 116 54½ 69 69 511½ ShoemkerW7 Aw32000 79-18 PrspctrsGmbl,SmWh,GryLnExprss 10
24Jan88—Wide 3/8 turn
11Nov87-3SA 6½f :22 :45⅗ 1:17⅘ft 3½ 117 42 2½ 11 22½ Pincay L Jr2 40000 79-18 Rullah's Sky, Dr. Brent, Alandvon 7
11Nov87—Broke in a tangle
29Oct87-1SA 6f :21⅗ :45 1:11 gd 5½ 118 52½ 2½ 21½ 2¾ DelahoussyeE10 32000 82-16 Dear John, Dr. Brent, Gaelic Bid 10
8Oct87-4SA 6f :21⅘ :45⅗ 1:12⅕ft 3½ 118 31 31½ 21 13½ DelahoussyeE9 M32000 77-19 Dr. Brent,LuckyTryst,ParOfCourse 11
3Oct87-6Fpx 6f :22⅗ :46⅕ 1:12⅕ft 2½ 118 813 816 716 716 Solis A9 M32000 70-18 Bttrynotincludd,Flpr,SnoritDmond 10
3Oct87—Lugged out
3Sep87-4Dmr 6f :22⅕ :46 1:11⅘ft 6½ 118 2½ 1hd 2hd 2½ DelahoussyeE4 M32000 78-18 Desecrator,Dr.Brent,Corie'sPrince 12
●Apr 17 SA 6f ft 1:13 h Apr 1 SA HC 5f fm :59⅖ h (d) Mar 27 SA 4f ft :48⅖ h Mar 15 SA 4f ft :46⅗ h

Secret Meeting

PINCAY L JR — 114
Own.—Hubbard R D
Dk. b. or br. c. 3, by Buckfinder—Windrush Lady, by Unconscious
Br.—Jones R D Jr (Pa)
Tr.—Mandella Richard
1988 1 0 1 0 $6,000
1987 2 1 1 0 $13,900
Lifetime 3 1 2 0 $20,300

7Apr88-3SA 6f :21⅕ :44 1:10 ft 2½ 117 53½ 34½ 32½ 21 Pincay L Jr1 Aw34000 87-17 MichelD.Mn,SecretMeeting,BsicRte 7
7Apr88—Broke in a tangle, bumped, steadied and altered course 1/16
7Sep87-4Dmr 6f :22 :45⅕ 1:10 ft *8-5 117 32½ 1hd 11½ 13½ Pincay L Jr10 Mdn 88-14 ScrtMtng,SwtchCods,MonMdnssI 11
7Sep87—Bobbled start
22Aug87-6Dmr 6f :21⅘ :45⅖ 1:11 ft *4-5 117 79 56 36 23 Pincay L Jr2 Mdn 89-15 Skr'sJorny,ScrtMtng,ClssInvstmnt 8
Apr 23 SA 5f ft :59⅘ h Apr 16 SA 4f gd :49⅗ h Apr 3 SA 4f ft :47⅕ hg Mar 29 SA 7f ft 1:26⅖ h

Accomplish Ridge

MEZA R Q — 114
Own.—Tsurumaki T
B. c. 3, by Cox's Ridge—Empress of Canada, by Accomplish
Br.—Tenney E W & Indian Creek (Ky)
Tr.—Palma Hector O
1988 2 1 1 0 $28,850
1987 4 1 2 0 $26,450
Lifetime 6 2 3 0 $55,300 Turf 1 0 1 0 $11,250

6Apr88-8SA a6½f ⓣ:21 :43⅗1:15 fm*6-5 117 54½ 43 31½ 21½ DlhoussyeE9 Baldwin 83-13 Dr.Brent,AccomplishRidg,GldMusic 9
6Apr88—Run in divisions
10Mar88-3SA 6f :21⅘ :45⅕ 1:10⅗ft *8-5 117 3nk 2hd 1hd 1½ DelhoussyeE6 Aw32000 85-19 AccomplishRdg,EstrnEgl,ChmALot 8
10Mar88—Bumped at 1/2
16Sep87-8Dmr 1 :46⅖ 1:11⅕ 1:36⅕ft 7 116 41½ 42½ 52¾ 68 DlhossyE1 Dmr Fut 81-15 Lost Kitty,BoldSecond,PurdueKing 9
16Sep87—Grade I
2Sep87-8Dmr 7f :22⅕ :44⅘ 1:23⅕ft 2½ 117 2hd 2½ 11 2no DlhoussyE8 Balboa 86-17 PurduKng,AccomplshRdg,MxdPlsr 8
2Sep87—Grade III
7Aug87-7Dmr 5½f :21⅕ :44⅘ 1:03⅕ft 4 118 2½ 32½ 32½ 2¾ Solis A3 Aw20000 94-15 Bold Second,AccomplishRidge,Pain 7
26Jly87-7Hol 5½f :22⅗ :46⅕ 1:04⅖ft 12 117 11 1½ 11 11¾ Solis A8 Mdn 92-12 AccomplshRdg,Scntfc,MnstrlShw 11
Apr 25 Hol 4f ft :48 h ●Apr 16 SA 4f gd :46⅘ h ●Apr 1 SA HC 5f fm :58⅖ h (d) ●Mar 26 SA 7f ft 1:25⅗ h

```
Prospectors Gamble                    Ro. c. 3, by Crafty Prospector—Fannie C, by Sunny South
MCCARRON C J                          Br.—Happy Valley Farm (Fla)              1988 5 2 2 0   $49,850
                                117   Tr.—Mayberry Brian A                     1987 5 1 2 0   $22,925
Own.—Siegel Jan-M-Samantha            Lifetime  10 3 4 0  $72,775              Turf 1 0 1 0   $11,250
6Apr88-5SA   a6½f (T):21^2 :43^4 1:14^2fm *8-5 117  1hd 2hd 1hd 21¾  Solis A^9     Baldwin  85-13 ExclsvNryv,ProspctrsGmbl,Mhmtsk 9
     6Apr88—Run in divisions
16Mar88-8GG   6f :21^2 :43^3 1:08^2ft  *4-5 120  32½ 32 2hd 14  Castaneda M^6  HcpO     97-13 ProspctrsGmbl,LckySn'S,HrdTMss 6
15Feb88-8GG   6f :21^3 :43^4 1:07^4ft  23 119  12 1½ 2hd 2½  Solis A^5       Gldn Bear 98-10 Chrl'sNots,PrspctrsGmbl,HstyPsty 5
24Jan88-8SA   6f :21^2 :44^2 1:09^3ft  14 118  2hd 1½ 12½ 1½  Solis A^10     Aw32000  90-18 PrspctrsGmbl,SmWh,GryLnExprss 10
8Jan88-5SA    6f :21^2 :44^1 1:09^4ft  7 118  63¼ 78½ 67½ 6¾  ShoemkerW^6    Aw32000  79-19 Overbrook, Gran Musico,TemperT. 10
18Nov87-7Hol  6½f :21^4 :44^2 1:16^4ft  3½ 119  2½ 2^2 2^4 24½  Vasquez J^1   Aw25000  89-12 Bolsure, Prospectors Gamble, Pain 9
28Oct87-7SA   6f :21^4 :44^4 1:10 ft  24 120  63½ 66 54½ 57½  Espino G G^6     Aw27000  80-16 Mr.GamePlayer,HardToMiss.Blote 10
     28Oct87—Broke slowly; lugged in stretch
17Oct87-6SA   6f :22^1 :45^3 1:10^2ft  12 117  1^1 12½ 1^3 14½  Espino G G^8     Mdn  85-16 ProspctorsGmbl,Ovrbrok,BlArDncr 9
     17Oct87—Hopped in air
7Sep87-4Dmr   6f :22 :45^1 1:10 ft  3 117  11½ 3½ 31½ 48½  McHargue D G^8    Mdn  79-14 ScrtMtng,SwtchCods,MonMdnssl 11
     7Sep87—Lugged out 1/4
27May87-6Hol  5f :22^3 :46 :58^3ft  4¾ 116  1½ 1hd 2½ 24½  McHargue D G^2    Mdn  88-16 MxdPlsr,ProspctorsGmbl,GrtForm 10
     27May87—Bumped start
  Apr 17 SA 5f ft 1:00^4 h     Mar 31 SA (T) 4f fm :51^3 h     Mar 12 SA 4f ft :48^2 h

Claim        Right to improve         B. c. 3, by Mr Prospector—Santiago Lassie, by Vertex
GRYDER A T                            Br.—Claiborne Farm (Ky)                  1988 2 2 0 0   $31,350
                                114   Tr.—Proctor Willard L                    1987 0 M 0 0
Own.—Claiborne Farm                   Lifetime  2 2 0 0  $31,350
7Feb88-3SA    6f :21^1 :44^1 1:10 ft  4 113^5  3^2 3nk 1½ 1nk  Gryder A T^7   Aw32000  88-16 Claim, Sam Who, Aloha Prospector 8
     7Feb88—Bumped late
24Jan88-6SA   6½f :22 :45^2 1:16^4ft  2½ 113^5  2½ 1½ 1^2 12½  Gryder A T^9   Mdn  86-18 Claim, Freeskate, Our NativeWish 12
  Apr 25 SA 5f ft 1:00^2 h     Apr 17 SA 7f ft 1:28^1 h     Apr 9 SA 6f ft 1:14 h     ●Apr 3 SA 6f ft 1:13^2 h

Mr. Game Player                       B. g. 3, by Fleet Twist—Playing the Game, by Windy Sea
DELAHOUSSAYE E                        Br.—Hemming Brothers (Cal)               1987 6 2 3 0   $95,000
                                114   Tr.—Luby Donn
Own.—HemmingJr-Jhnstn-JhnstnEtl       Lifetime  6 2 3 0  $95,000
29Dec87-8SA   6f :21^3 :44^2 1:09^4sy  3½ 114  65½ 43¾ 5^6 2^6  ShmkrW^4  Sn Miguel  84-24 Drouilly'sBoy,Mr.GmePlyer,SmWho 6
     29Dec87—Wide into stretch
14Nov87-8SA   1 :46^4 1:12^1 1:38^2ft  3 118  5^3 31½ 31½ 29¾  ShmkrW^2 (G)B J Rddr  72-22 PurdueKing,Mr.GmePlyr,Winnrwld 8
28Oct87-7SA   6f :21^4 :44^4 1:10 ft  3½ 120  52¼ 42½ 32½ 11  ShoemkerW^8  Aw27000  88-16 Mr.GamePlayer,HardToMiss.Blote 10
16Sep87-8Dmr  1 :46^2 1:11^1 1:36^1ft  8 114  1hd 3nk 4¾ 46¾  ShmkrW^4  Dmr Fut  81-15 Lost Kitty,BoldSecond,PurdueKing 9
     16Sep87—Grade I
29Aug87-6Dmr  6f :22^1 :45^2 1:09^3ft  *1-2 117  2^1 2hd 1½ 1½  Shoemaker W^5 (S)Mdn  90-12 Mr.GamePlyer,HrdToMiss,TrickyLd 7
5Aug87-8Dmr   6f :21^4 :45^1 1:10^2ft  22 114  4^2 31½ 22½ 29½  ShmrW^8 (S)Graduation  80-20 PurduKng,Mr.GmPlyr,WhtADplomt 9
  ●Apr 19 SA 6f ft 1:12 h     ●Apr 13 SA 7f ft 1:25 hg     Apr 7 SA 6f ft 1:13^4 h     Apr 1 SA 6f ft 1:12^2 h
```

Child prodigies win this type of race occasionally; but when they do, you'll have to put down your binoculars and find a microscope in order to distinguish the minute payoff. Type b will sometimes win this type of race, always in an opportunistic fashion, when it can catch a field of horses on a downward turn in their performance cycles. Type c is preferred but not always easy to identify. In races for younger horses, "current form" quickly becomes past form; just to maintain their current levels of productivity, horses need to be on the improve. Handicappers proficient with maiden races will do well to apply similar methods at this level, where the most likely improver will be the most likely winner.

Approximate Odds, Post Time

Success Express	even
Prospectors Gamble	7–2
Mt. Game Player	5–1
Secret Meeting	6–1
Claim	9–1
Dr. Brent	11–1
Accomplish Ridge	28–1

Comments

Unlikely

1. Success Express is clearly the child prodigy on the decline. Winner of the Breeders' Cup Juvenile, nearly a millionaire after hardly becoming three years old, Success Express won't even make it to the Derby as an outsider. Winner of four of his first five races as a two-year-old, he has lost all four of his races as a three-year-old, twice as a beaten favorite.

   Success Express is the reason for investing in this race. If there were no up-and-coming horses, he might win by default, but several of his rivals figure to have a bright future. By eliminating a Success Express, we eliminate between 40 and 50 percent of the win pool! Let's call it 40 percent in order to take the worst case scenario:

Gross Advantage	40%	(amount of pool eliminated)
Disadvantage (take)	– 16%	(varies from state to state)
Net Advantage	24%	

   With a net advantage of 24 percent, in a long series of equal races, we could employ any random-selection method (excluding Success Express, of course), to extract a flat-bet profit. No handicapping necessary; get your kid to pick a number before he goes to school in the morning.

2. Secret Meeting. Although his last race was a troubled event, it was an extremely poor field that he was unable to defeat. Most important, Secret Meeting is the only horse in this field that has never beaten winners.

3. Accomplish Ridge and Dr. Brent come out of the same race. Relatively between the two, Dr. Brent is the late bloomer and Accomplish Ridge is the child prodigy. While it is true that Accomplish Ridge was in a bounce situation when just losing to Dr. Brent, it is also true that his layoff win as the favorite came against a rather poor bunch of runners. He now plays the role of beaten favorite, one which often leads to decline in form. And it is not that Dr. Brent makes Accomplish Ridge look good, but rather, that Accomplish Ridge makes Dr. Brent look bad. Dr. Brent has had the fortune to string three wins together, all of them against horses that would not have a prayer in today's race.

Contenders

Prospectors Gamble, Claim, and Mr. Game Player have competed against similar fields. In fact, they have all beaten the same horse, Sam Who, at different times.

1. Of the three horses who've made a living beating Sam Who, Claim is the most likely to improve. Look at the improvement in his fractions from race one to race two. Especially note the "turn time" (second quarter) improvement, from 23.2 to 22.4. Also note that he beat a horse named Aloha Prospector, a name recognized on both coasts for stakes-winning performances around the time of this workshop race. The public should have seen Claim as the lightly-raced horse that had not reached its peak. And if the crowd did not calculate turn time, they shouldn't have missed the half-mile fractional improvement from 45.2 to 44.1. A horse with lesser competitive spirit would not have survived a 44.1. The spacing of his races represents a superb training job; he is being nurtured toward the highest peak that his natural ability will allow him to reach.
2. Prospectors Gamble has had his moments of brilliance, but he has also padded his record by opportunistically shipping to a place where he could be the big fish in the small pond. One can find reasons for liking Prospectors Gamble just as much as Claim, depending on which of his races you choose to highlight. However, he has had enough races

to let us all know what his potential is; while his rival, Claim, has not shown any evidence of leveling off at a particular plateau.

3. Mr. Game Player is the layoff horse with no layoff credentials but for a second-place finish as a first-time starter. He must face sharp horses for his comeback race. Both our second and third choices here are second-place types, placing more than they win; Claim is obviously a win type.

In summary, the three contenders have very similar credentials, but they find themselves at different points in their form cycle. Claim is on the way up, until otherwise evidenced; Prospector's Gamble seems to have settled at a plateau; and Mr. Game Player will need some tuning following the layoff.

	Our Line	Track Odds	Decision
Claim	2–1	9–1	Way over. *Bet.*
Prospectors Gamble	3–1	3–1/7–2	No advantage. Pass.
Mr. Game Player	4–1	5–1	Negligible advantage, under required 6–1. No bet.

With Success Express out of our line, the whole field is on the verge of being an overlay. The advantage of Claim is so clearly superior to the apparent slight edge for the other two contenders that we need no splitting of hairs to make this decision.

EIGHTH RACE
Hollywood
APRIL 27, 1988

7 FURLONGS. (1.20⅗) 37th Running of THE DEBONAIR STAKES. $75,000 added. 3-year-olds. By subscription of $100 each, which shall accompany the nomination, $750 additional to start, with $75,000 added, of which $15,000 to second, $11,250 to third, $5,625 to fourth and $1,875 to fifth. Weight, 122 lbs. Non-winners of $25,000 twice since December 25 or $50,000 at any time allowed 3 lbs.; a race of $25,000 or two races of $18,000 at any time, 5 lbs.; a race of $18,000 or two races other than maiden or claiming, 8 lbs. Starters to be named through the entry box by closing time of entries. A trophy will be presented to the owner of the winner. Closed Wednesday, April 20, with 31 nominations.
Value of race $82,850; value to winner $48,300; second $15,000; third $11,250; fourth $5,625; fifths $937.50 each. Mutuel pool $354,694. Exacta pool $300,947.

Last Raced	Horse	Eqt.A.Wt	PP	St	¼	½	Str	Fin	Jockey	Odds $1
7Feb88 3SA1	Claim	3 114	6	1	6$1\frac{1}{2}$	4$\frac{1}{2}$	1$\frac{1}{2}$	1^3	Gryder A T	9.40
6Apr88 5SA2	Prospectors Gamble	3 117	5	6	5^{hd}	5^{hd}	4^{hd}	2^5	McCarron C J	3.40
6Apr88 8SA1	Dr. Brent	3 119	2	5	4^{hd}	6^2	3$1\frac{1}{2}$	3$\frac{1}{2}$	Solis A	11.80
9Apr88 7Aqu4	Success Express	b 3 122	1	7	2^1	1^{hd}	2^{hd}	4$1\frac{3}{4}$	Stevens G L	1.20
6Apr88 8SA2	DH Accomplish Ridge	3 114	4	4	3^1	3^1	5$1\frac{1}{2}$	5	Meza R Q	28.20
29Dec87 8SA2	DH Mr. Game Player	3 116	7	2	7	7	6^5	5^{15}	Delahoussaye E	5.10
7Apr88 3SA2	Secret Meeting	3 117	3	3	1^{hd}	2$\frac{1}{2}$	7	7	Pincay L Jr	6.50

DH—Dead heat.

OFF AT 5:14 Start good. Won driving. Time, :21⅗, :44⅘, 1:09⅘, 1:22⅕ Track fast.

$2 Mutuel Prices:

6–CLAIM	20.80	7.40	4.20
5–PROSPECTORS GAMBLE		4.80	3.20
2–DR. BRENT			4.20

$2 EXACTA 6–5 PAID $70.80.

B. c, by Mr Prospector—Santiago Lassie, by Vertex. Trainer Proctor Willard L. Bred by Claiborne Farm (Ky).

CLAIM, within easy striking distance early while being rated, took command in the upper stretch and drew away. PROSPECTORS GAMBLE, never far back after being crowded and jostled a bit in the initial strides, could not catch CLAIM in the final furlong but finished willingly to prove clearly best of the others. DR. BRENT, close up early, was shuffled back a bit on the far turn when boxed in, moved up along the inner rail to bid for command at the furlong marker, then weakened. SUCCESS EXPRESS, a bit slow to begin, advanced along the inside early to engage for the lead before going a quarter, continued as a pace factor on the far turn and in the upper stretch, then weakened in the last furlong. ACCOMPLISH RIDGE pressed the early pace after being crowded and jostled a bit in the opening strides, gave way in the drive and finished on even terms with MR. GAME PLAYER for fifth. MR. GAME PLAYER, the early trailer and wide down the backstretch, came into the stretch four wide and lacked the necessary rally. SECRET MEETING, a pace factor for a half, faltered badly and was not persevered with late after dropping far behind.

Owners— 1, Claiborne Farm; 2, Siegel Jan-M-Samantha; 3, Braverman & Colvin; 4, Klein E V; 5, Tsurumaki T; 6, Hemming Jr-Jhnstn-Jhnstn Et al; 7, Hubbard R D.

Trainers— 1, Proctor Willard L; 2, Mayberry Brian A; 3, Soriano Morris; 4, Lukas D Wayne; 5, Palma Hector O; 6, Luby Donn; 7, Mandella Richard.

Overweight: Mr. Game Player 2 pounds; Secret Meeting 3. **Scratched**—Balote (15Apr88 8GG1).

As it turned out, not only was Success Express overbet, but for some weird reason Secret Meeting, a horse that had never beaten winners, received more than his fair chunk of action. With horses like those being overbet, the public proved once again that it could be amazingly inefficient in the win pool, making it inevitable that some contender would be underbet. Fortunately, that contender was Claim. Meanwhile, Prospectors Gamble continued to race on a consistent plateau. And Success Express looked like the overworked child prodigy, flashing talent and then losing interest.

WORKSHOP EIGHT

May 26, 1988 (course *firm*)

3rd Santa Anita

1 ⅛ MILES. (Turf). (1.45⅘) CLAIMING. Purse $52,000. 4-year-olds and upward. Weight, 121 lbs. Non-winners of two races at one mile or over since February 1, allowed 2 lbs.; of such a race since then, 4 lbs. Claiming price $150,000; for each $5,000 to $125,000, allowed 2 lbs. (Claiming and starter races for $100,000 or less not considered).

THIS PAGE SHORT ...GL

***In Focus** Beat bad field
STEVENS G L 112
Own.—Moss J S
B. h. 7, by Sharpman—Model Girl, by Lyphard
Br.—Ballymacoll Stud Farm Ltd (Fra) 1988 2 1 0 0 $23,100
Tr.—Frankel Robert $125,000 1986 8 0 2 5 $21,812
Lifetime 24 6 3 8 $94,963 Turf 24 6 3 8 $94,963
6Mar88-7SA 1¼Ⓣ:4821:3812:042fm 10 116 66 42 21½ 1¾ Stevens G L6 75000 65-30 InFocs,HowVryTochng,RndomRvr 12
21Jan88-8SA 1⅛Ⓣ:4731:12 1:503fm 24 115 96½ 86¾ 8101013 Toro F8 Aw55000 61-26 TemperateSil,Ivor'sImge,Steinlen 12
22Aug86♦4Clairefont'e(Fra a1⅛ 1:544gd 2 130 Ⓣ 34¾ LquuxA Px Csno d Deavlle ChildresCorner,QuillRomnc,InFocus 7
16Aug86♦4Deauville(Fra) a1¼ 2:062gd 13 120 Ⓣ 53¾ LqxA Px Gontau Biron(Gr3) Over The Ocean, Iades, Baby Turk 10
20Jly86♦6MLaffitte(Fra) a1⅜ 2:162gd *1 123 Ⓣ 32 LequeuxA Px Hermit Akdar, Letkiss, InFocus 5
6Jly86♦2StCloud(Fra) a1⅜ 2:182gd 3½ 128 Ⓣ 3hd LequeuxA Px Fourire Merzak, AfterParty, InFocus 8
21Jun86♦6StCloud(Fra) a1 1:42 gd 9-5 123 Ⓣ 2no LequeuxA Px Trtulien Kensof, In Focus, Brownstone 6
9Jun86♦5StCloud(Fra) a1⅜ 2:134gd *6-5 121 Ⓣ 32½ LequeuxA Px Durbar Antheus, Grundyssime, InFocus 8
24May86♦5StCloud(Fra) a1⅜ 2:183gd 5½ 126 Ⓣ 31 Lequeux A Px Edellic King Luthier, Grundyssime,InFocus 7
6May86♦5StCloud(Fra) a1¼ 2:17 gd 5½ 126 Ⓣ 21½ LequuxA Px Sea Sick Tilt, InFocus, SiriusSymboli 5
Mar 20 Hol 5f ft 1:011 h Mar 14 Hol 4f ft :492 h Mar 4 Hol 6f gd 1:172 h Feb 26 Hol 5f ft 1:021 h

Telephone Canyon May prefer shorter
SOLIS A 112
Own.—Dolan J F & Clara
Dk. b. or br. g. 4, by Assagai Jr—Determining, by Decidedly
Br.—Van Berg J C (Ky) 1988 3 0 1 0 $11,500
Tr.—Hutchinson Kathy $125,000 1987 14 4 4 1 $86,499
Lifetime 20 5 5 1 $110,524 Turf 8 2 1 1 $40,714
10Mar88-8SA 1⅛Ⓣ:4611:1041:473fm 14 115 47½ 58½ 57 58½ McCarronCJ 5 Aw60000 80-11 AviatorII,CaptinVigors,LordGrundy 6
11Feb88-8SA 1⅛Ⓣ:4611:1121:501fm 61 117 65 63¾ 51¾ 2no Pedroza M A 5 150000 76-24 AvitorII,TelephoneCnyon,RichErth 8
21Jan88-8SA 1⅛Ⓣ:4731:12 1:503fm 75 116 52¾121012 13 912 McHrgueDG 7 Aw55000 62-26 TemperateSil,Ivor'sImge,Steinlen 12
31Dec87-7SA 6½f :22 :443 1:154gd 38 116 69 64½ 57 410½ Hawley S 11 Aw55000 81-19 SylvnExprss,BndlOfIron,CptnVgors 7
27Sep87-8LaD 1⅟₁₆Ⓣ:47 1:1111:42 fm 7½ 115 51¾ 31 68½ 69½ HwrdDL 5 Temp Hill H 81-08 CrosLove,GoodSm,SoverignDignity 9
13Sep87-10LaD a1 Ⓣ 1:353fm*2-3 116 54 41½ 43 34½ Howard D L 6 Aw17000 85-10 Jody'sHro,CmmndrDsty,TlphnCnyn 7
13Sep87—Hand Timed
22Aug87-9AP 1⅛Ⓣ:5041:1621:552sf 88 115 54½ 64½ 48 413¾ MrtnzFIII 8 R Table 46-40 BluFinn,DysGonBy,Spctculrphntom 9
22Aug87—Grade II
9Aug87-10Cby 1 Ⓣ:47 1:1121:362fm*6-5 120 32 2½ 1½ 11½ MrtnFIII 2 New Ulm H 94-06 TelephoneCnyon,ButterflyBoy,Fudl 9
12Jly87-9Cby 1 :463 1:113 1:391gd *6-5 120 43¾ 4½ 2hd 11½ KtzD 2 Ⓢ Minn Brd Dby 85-17 TelephonCnyon,Momsfurrri,SvorFir 5
20Jun87-9Cby 7½f Ⓣ:241 :4721:29 fm 4½ 114 64½ 52½ 11½ 1nk MrtinzFIII 3 Chanhssn 100-06 TelephoneCnyon,Fudl,ArrowSport 10
Mar 21 SA 5f ft 1:011 h Mar 6 SA 5f ft :591 h Feb 25 SA 5f ft :593 h Feb 8 SA 4f ft :473 h

Keyala Dull recent form
CASTANON A L 114
Own.—Vicki Beth Stables Inc
Dk. b. or br. h. 7, by Key to the Kingdom—Alathea, by Lorenzaccio
Br.—de Briones G B (Ky) 1988 2 0 0 0 $1,850
Tr.—Palma Hector O $135,000 1987 10 5 3 1 $127,075
Lifetime 58 10 7 10 $223,290 Turf 53 10 7 10 $220,590
6Mar88-7SA 1¼Ⓣ:4821:3812:042fm 10 115 32½ 31½ 46 58 Castanon A L8 70000 57-30 InFocs,HowVryTochng,RndomRvr 12
20Feb88-7SA 1 Ⓣ:4641:1021:354fm 9 114 63½ 75 911 815½ Velasquez J2 85000 81-05 Rufjan, Narghile, Peter Moon 10
20Feb88—Rank backstretch, 3/8 turn
13Dec87-9Hol 1⅟₁₆Ⓣ:4711:1111:422fm 3 116 21 2hd 1½ 44½ Valenzuela P A6 62500 78-16 Pinstripe II, Kensof, Centenary 12
28Nov87-10Hol 1⅟₁₆Ⓣ:4641:1031:412fm*7-5 116 1011 99½ 96½ 73¾ DelahoussayeE8 80000 83-08 PatchyGroundfog,AvitorII,Kensof 12
14Nov87-7SA 1 Ⓣ:4741:1221:374fm 3½ 116 75¾ 52 43½ 23½ DelahoussayeE7 90000 82-25 Samarid, Keyala, Rufjan 10
10Oct87-5SA 1¼Ⓣ:4711:3722:022fm 3½ 116 42½ 32 21 2hd DelahoussayeE5 80000 75-25 Clanrallier, Keyala, Migrator 9
10Oct87—Bumped start
4Oct87-11Fpx a1⅛ :454 1:104 1:493ft 22 114 63¾ 74¾1013 1020½ Sibille R3 Pom Inv H 75-12 He'sASaros,QuickTwist,Emperdori 11
31Aug87-8Dmr 1 Ⓣ:4711:1121:363fm*6-5 119 711 87½ 65 65¾ DelahoussayeE8 95000 82-16 Pokare, Fabulous Sound,Emperdori 8
3Aug87-8Dmr 1⅟₁₆Ⓣ:4841:1241:422fm 11 116 66 65½ 58 56 DelhoussyeE1 Aw40000 82-14 ExclusvPrtnr,RchErth,SkpOutFront 6
17Jly87-5Hol 1⅟₁₆Ⓣ:47 1:1041:403fm*6-5 116 55½ 52½ 31½ 1½ DelhoussyeE1 Aw34000 91-12 Keyala, Varick, Noble Fighter 5
Mar 21 SA tr.t 5f ft 1:001 h Mar 14 SA tr.t 5f ft 1:001 h Feb 29 SA 4f m :503 h (d) Feb 12 SA 6f ft 1:143 h

***Aviator II**
PINCAY L JR 119
Own.—Green Thumb Farm Stable
Ch. h. 8, by Locris—Bright Penny, by Skymaster
Br.—Agro Pecria Inshalla Ltd (Brz) 1988 4 3 0 0 $87,725
Tr.—Ippolito Steve $150,000 1987 14 2 3 4 $67,150
Lifetime 54 15 9 9 $293,537 Turf 48 14 8 8 $291,582
10Mar88-8SA 1⅛Ⓣ:4611:1041:473fm 8 117 21½ 21 2½ 11½ Pincay L Jr1 Aw60000 89-11 AviatorII,CaptinVigors,LordGrundy 6
11Feb88-8SA 1⅛Ⓣ:4611:1121:501fm 5½ 117 33 32½ 41½ 1no Pincay L Jr2 100000 76-24 AvitorII,TelephoneCnyon,RichErth 8
11Feb88—Crowded 3/8-1/8
21Jan88-8SA 1⅛Ⓣ:4731:12 1:503fm 18 114 41½ 32 42¾ 45 Meza R Q1 Aw55000 69-26 TemperateSil,Ivor'sImge,Steinlen 12
1Jan88-7SA 1⅛Ⓣ:4741:1241:503gd 2¾ 1075 21 2½ 11 1¾ Gryder A T4 70000 74-26 AvtorII,PtchyGrondfog,RoghPssg 10
28Nov87-10Hol 1⅟₁₆Ⓣ:4641:1031:412fm 4½ 1075 32½ 31½ 2½ 2no Gryder A T5 70000 87-08 PatchyGroundfog,AvitorII,Kensof 12
28Nov87—Bumped start
27Sep87-10Fpx 1⅟₁₆ :46 1:103 1:43 ft 8½ 122 54 88½ 912 915½ BlckCA1 Ⓢ C B Aflbgh 81-13 ForignLgion,Rcognizd,LstCommnd 9
13Sep87-5Dmr 1⅟₁₆Ⓣ:4741:1221:431fm 5¾ 116 1hd 1½ 1hd 32½ DelahoussayeE6 70000 82-17 Clanrallier,CoastingCougar,AvitorII 8
29Aug87-7Dmr 1⅟₁₆Ⓣ:4841:13 1:44 fm 11 1115 31½ 2½ 21 32½ Gryder A T8 Aw20000 78-18 Bestebreuje, War Debt, Aviator II 10
29Aug87—Rank 3/4
8Aug87-5Dmr 1⅛Ⓣ:4731:1141:49 fm 8½ 1125 42½ 3½ 1hd 1hd Gryder A T7 62500 88-13 Aviator II, Solidified, Jet Away Bill 7
27Jly87-9Hol 1⅟₁₆Ⓣ:47 1:1021:413fm 4 116 2½ 21½ 23½ 32¾ Valenzuela P A1 62500 83-08 Sherkin, Kingsbury, Aviator II 7
27Jly87—Lugged out backstretch, 3/8 turn
Mar 28 SA 5f ft 1:013 h Mar 6 SA 7f ft 1:281 h Feb 28 SA 6f m 1:17 h (d) Feb 22 SA 5f ft 1:024 h

Knights Legend
GRYDER A T — 117
Own.—LTerra-Rubenstein-Rubmolin
B. h. 5, by Sir Ivor—Gimme Love, by Dr. Fager
Br.—Leigh G (Ky)
Tr.—Palma Hector 0 — $150,000
Lifetime 9 3 3 1 $23,523
1987 4 1 1 0 $7,295
1986 5 2 2 0 $16,228
Turf 9 3 3 1 $23,523

29Sep87♦3Goodwood(Eng) 2⅝ 4:17⁴gd *2¼ 132 ① 2¹ StrkyG Ajax Engnrng Ins H JohnDory,KnightsLgnd,HrlstonLk 10
29Jly87♦3Goodwood(Eng) 2⅝ 4:14³gd *2¼ 136 ① 5¹⁴ StrkyG Pmm's Gdwd H Actinium,HarlestoneLke,WhiteMill 7
8Jun87♦1Goodwood(Eng) 2⅝ 4:20⁴gd*4-5 140 ① 1¾ EddryP BBC Rdo Ssx H KnightsLegend, Janus, Laxdaela 5
30Apr87♦6Newmarket(Eng) 2 3:26⁴gd 4¼ 131 ① 3³ Starkey G March H CesrImpertor,InDrms,KnightsLgnd 8
21Sep86♦2Longchamp(Eng) a1⅞ 3:28³gd 4 119 ① 6¹⁴ StrkyG Px de Lutece(Gr3) Anazid, Alesso, Mister Big Louie 8
15Jly86♦2Folkestone(Eng) a1⅞ 3:23¹gd*1-3 124 ① 1¹ StarkeyG D Undrwd KnightsLegend, Debco, DryGin 8
18Jun86♦5Ascot(Eng) 2 3:28¹fm 6 112 ① 2³ Clark A Queen's Vase Stverdle,KnightsLegend,RsonToB 13
14Jun86♦5Sandown(Eng) 1⅝ 2:55³fm*8-5 123 ① 1½ Starkey G Valuation KnightsLegend, Actinium, Zaajer 4
3Jun86♦5Salisbury(Eng) 1½ 2:35⁴gd 5 126 ① 2³ StrkeyG Lvrstck(Mdn) Almaarad, KnightsLegend,Sadeem 20
●Mar 28 SA 6f ft 1:11⁴ h ●Mar 13 SA 6f ft 1:12³ h Mar 7 SA 5f ft 1:00 h Feb 29 SA 5f m 1:03² h (d)

Hawaiian Spring
DELAHOUSSAYE E — 115
Own.—Bann E A
Dk. b. or br. h. 6, by Spring Double—Twice Hawaiian, by Twice Worthy
Br.—Kaye Mr-Mrs C F (Md)
Tr.—Frankel Robert — $140,000
Lifetime 20 3 4 2 $80,632
1988 1 0 0 0 $3,300
1987 9 3 2 1 $45,474
Turf 20 3 4 2 $80,632

14Jan88-8SA 1⅛①:47¹1:11⁴1:49²fm 7¾ 115 8⁶½ 5¹½ 4²½ 4⁴¾ Hawley S¹ Aw46000 75-20 Light Sabre, Mazilier, Gorky 10
14Jan88—Wide 3/8 turn
23Dec87-8Hol 1⅟₁₆①:48⁴1:13 1:43³fm 4 116 7⁴½ 7³½ 8³¾ 4²¾ ValenzuelPA⁴ Aw45000 73-24 FiveDddyFive,RufusDwes,GlintSilor 8
12Dec87-8Hol 1 ①:46¹1:10⁴1:35⁴fm 30 116 8⁴½ 3½ 3² 4² Hawley S⁹ Aw45000 86-14 DrkPromise,Digger'sRst,HppyInSpc 9
12Dec87—Wide backstretch
14Aug87♦6Clairefonte(Fra) a1½ 2:35²yl 7¾ 118 ① 3¾ LequeuxA G P d Clrfnt Ordinance,Shimbori,HawiinSpring 12
1Aug87♦3Deauville(Fra) a1⅝ 2:46 sf 13 128 ① 2¹ LequeuxA Px d Ssy H Bullseye,HawiinSpring,PuyVlence 16
27Jun87♦3Longchamp(Fra) a1½ 2:33⁴yl 8 127 ① 12 LequeuxA Px Cstrs H Hardelot, Limbo Dance, Tongan 18
7Jun87♦7Chantilly(Fra) a1⅜ 2:15⁴gd 6¼ 127 ① 1¾ LequuxA Px d Etngs H HwiinSpring,Bmwhite,SunnyHunt 12
20May87♦7Evry(Fra) a1½ 2:40²yl 9 116 ① 1½ Camus E Px d St Chrn HwiinSpring,LimboDnc,HilingShip 13
6May87♦7Evry(Fra) a1⅝ 2:08 gd 14 116 ① 2³ Camus E Px d Smos WlerlooRevng,HwiinSpring,Highld 12
19Apr87♦7Lisieux(Fra) a1⅜ : yl 4¼ 128 ① 1⁶ CoursM Px d'Hrmvl L Vx HawaiianSpring,Trajana,LordHrry 10
19Apr87—No time taken. For lady riders
Mar 22 Hol 6f ft 1:14 h Mar 17 Hol 4f ft :48² h Mar 11 Hol 6f ft 1:13³ h Mar 5 Hol 7f ft 1:29³ h

***Super Dupont**
HAWLEY S — 112
Own.—Rosenblum H
B. h. 7, by Bay Express—Be Self, by Derring-Do
Br.—J R S Coggan (Eng)
Tr.—Van Berg Jack C — $125,000
Lifetime 29 5 2 4 $91,555
1988 3 1 0 0 $26,550
1987 3 1 0 0 $13,500
Turf 29 5 2 4 $91,555

17Mar88-8SA a6½f①:21⁴ :43⁴1:13⁴fm 9 115 9⁸ 5⁶½ 7⁴½ 8⁴½ Toro F³ Sra Mdre H 85-06 HppyInSpce,CblloDeOro,WillDncer 9
17Mar88—Grade III
6Feb88-7SA a6½f①:21⁴ :44³1:15¹fm 17 116 4⁵½ 3⁴½ 3³ 1hd Toro F² 90000 83-26 SprDpont,MyGlintGm,Mrvn'sPolcy 9
10Jan88-7SA 1 ①:46³1:11¹1:36⁴fm 5¾ 114 4³ 3² 4² 4²¾ Velasquez J⁶ 90000 80-09 Neferou, Crimson Slew, Arcadius 10
10Jan88—Floated out, bumped 5/16; bumped again at 1/8
4Dec87-8Hol 1 ①:46³1:10³1:34⁴fm 30 115 5⁵½ 5³ 3²½ 4⁵½ Velasquez J⁶ Aw44000 87-07 Santella Mac, Sperry, Rufjan 9
4Sep87-8AP 1 ①:50 1:14⁴1:37²gd 6½e 114 1½ 1½ 1½ 6⁹ BrfldD² Bud Brd Cup 79-23 PersianMews,MisterC.,VernonCstle 7
7Aug87-8AP 1⅟₁₆Ⓣ:48²1:15 1:45³fm 6¼ 114 3⁶ 3² 3¹½ 1nk Brumfield D¹ Aw17000 75-32 SuprDupont,NudistColony,JckClim 6
27Mar86-8SA 1⅛①:46⁴1:11³1:48 fm 11 117 7⁷¾ 6⁴ 5²¾ 4²¾ McCarron C J⁸ 125000 84-12 EvnngM'Lord,RvrOfKngs,PlAndDc 8
27Mar86—Lugged in late
1Mar86-5SA 1⅛①:45³1:10¹1:49¹fm 17 118 4⁷ 2³½ 3³½ 5⁸½ Meza R Q⁶ 150000 74-16 Clanrallier,Vulnerability,Steepbnk 10
24Jan86-5SA 1⅛①:46³1:11³1:49³fm 3 115 7⁴½ 3² 2² 5¹¾ Stevens G L² Aw35000 77-19 AllHandsOnDeck,CptinVigors,Fuzzy 8
16Jan86-8SA 1⅛①:46 1:10¹1:47³fm 15 115 7⁷ 7⁹½ 6⁸ 7⁴¾ DelhoussyeE⁴ Aw45000 84-11 Trucalat,DoublQckTm,TppngWood 9
16Jan86—Crowded stretch
Mar 15 Hol 3f ft :38¹ h Mar 3 Hol 7f gd 1:28³ h Feb 23 Hol 5f ft 1:01³ h Jan 27 Hol 5f ft 1:01⁴ h

I've selected this particular race because it represents the classic contradictions of form-cycle analysis.

a. Aviator II. How long can a horse remain in peak form?
b. Knights Legend. When do horses win following a layoff, without needing to race into form?
c. In Focus, Super Dupont. When can infrequent winners put together clusters of victories?
d. Telephone Canyon, Keyala, and Hawaiian Spring. When do horses racing in dull form suddenly wake up?

In previous chapters we have approached these issues from top to bottom, by way of survey and overview of many horses;

now we look from the bottom up, through the case of particular horses. In order to present this microcosmic view, pertinent information from before and beyond the ten listed past performance races must be considered. That information includes trainer tactics as they relate to horse cycles.

Aviator II is the horse to beat. His past record allows us to project how long this horse can maintain his high plateau.

```
*Aviator II                      Ch. h. 7, by Locris—Bright Penny, by Skymaster
 GRYDER A T                      Br.—Agro Pecria Inshalla Ltd (Brz)            1987 13  2  2  4     $50,350
                          1075   Tr.—Ippolito Steve                  $70,000   1986  8  2  1  3     $44,300
Own.—Green Thumb Farm Stable     Lifetime   49 12  8  9   $198,012             Turf 43 11  7  8    $196,857
27Sep87-10Fpx 1 1/16 :46 1:103 1:43 ft  8 1/4 122   54 88 1/4 912 915 1/4 BlckCA1 (R)C B Aflbgh 81-13 ForignLgion,Rcognizd,LstCommnd 9
13Sep87-5Dmr 1 1/16 (T):4741:1221:431fm 5 3/4 116  1hd 1 1/2 1hd 32 1/4 DelahoussayeE6 70000 82-17 Clanrallier,CoastingCougar,AvitorII 8
29Aug87-7Dmr 1 1/16 (T):4841:13 1:44 fm 11 1115  31 1/2 2 1/2 21 32 1/4 Gryder A T8 Aw28000 78-18 Bestebreuje, War Debt, Aviator II 10
     29Aug87—Rank 3/4
 8Aug87-5Dmr 1 1/8 (T):4731:1141:49 fm 8 1/4 1125  42 1/2 3 1/2 1hd 1hd Gryder A T7 62500 88-13 Aviator II, Solidified, Jet Away Bill 7
27Jly87-9Hol 1 1/16 (T):47 1:1021:413fm 4 116    2 1/2 21 1/2 23 1/2 32 3/4 Valenzuela P A1 62500 83-08 Sherkin, Kingsbury, Aviator II 7
     27Jly87—Lugged out backstretch, 3/8 turn
18Jly87-10Hol 1 1/16 (T):4711:1031:412fm 6 1/2 116  2 1/2 2hd 11 1/2 11 1/2 Valenzuela P A2 50000 87-13 Aviator II, DarkAccent,WillSpring 10
26Apr87-9Hol 1 (T):4621:1041:353fm *3 116  42 1/2 52 1/4 75 1/4 77 1/4 Valenzuela P A4 62500 82-13 Cracksman,RisingChum,DrkAccent 8
19Apr87-9SA 1 (T):46 1:10 1:352fm 4e114  63 1/2 61 1/2 31 1/2 2 1/2 Meza R Q6 62500 97-11 Millbow, Aviator II, Bugarian 10
     19Apr87—Crowded 3/8 turn
 4Apr87-6SA a6 1/2f (T):213 :4411:154fm 3 3/4 116  105 74 1/2 77 95 1/2 ValenzuelaPA10 70000 74-16 PolyTest,PrincPcdillo,PrAuxClrcs 12
     4Apr87—Took up start, 3 1/2
13Mar87-5SA a6 1/2f (T):22 :4421:16 fm 9 3/4 116  42 42 31 2hd Valenzuela P A1 70000 79-21 Amnothrbrothr,AvitorII,Hydrosttc 10
     13Mar87—Broke slowly
  Nov 24 Hol 7f ft 1:301 h    Nov 18 Hol 7f ft 1:274 h    Nov 6 SA 5f sy 1:04 h    Oct 28 SA 6f ft 1:152 h
```

```
*Aviator II                      Ch. h. 7, by Locris—Bright Penny, by Skymaster
 VALENZUELA P A                  Br.—Agro Pecria Inshalla Ltd (Brz)            1987  6  0  2  1     $19,950
                          116    Tr.—Ippolito Steve                  $62,500   1986  8  2  1  3     $44,300
Own.—Green Thumb Farm Stable     Lifetime   42 10  8  6   $158,612             Turf 37  9  7  5    $156,657
19Apr87-9SA 1 (T):46 1:10 1:352fm 4e114  63 1/2 61 1/2 31 1/2 2 1/2 Meza R Q6 62500 97-11 Millbow, Aviator II, Bugarian 10
     19Apr87—Crowded 3/8 turn
 4Apr87-6SA a6 1/2f (T):213 :4411:154fm 3 3/4 116  106 74 1/2 77 95 1/2 ValenzuelaPA10 70000 74-16 PolyTest,PrincPcdillo,PrAuxClrcs 12
     4Apr87—Took up start, 3 1/2
13Mar87-5SA a6 1/2f (T):22 :4421:16 fm 9 3/4 116  42 42 31 2hd Valenzuela P A1 70000 79-21 Amnothrbrothr,AvitorII,Hydrosttc 10
     13Mar87—Broke slowly; bumped 1/8
 4Feb87-5SA 1 1/8 (T):4541:1031:483fm 6 1/2 116  21 1/2 2 1/2 21 1/2 44 3/4 Valenzuela P A2 62500 79-16 Kingsbury, Dark Accent, Straw 10
     4Feb87—Took up 1/8
29Jan87-8SA a6 1/2f (T):212 :44 1:15 fm 15 116  76 77 88 3/4 88 McHrgueDG3 Aw34000 76-16 PrincBobbyB.,Mr.Mdi,ThlssnoAstr 10
10Jan87-5SA 1 1/8 (T):4721:1221:50 gd *3 1/2 118  2hd 2hd 2 1/2 32 Valenzuela P A7 62500 75-23 Kingsbury,BoardMeeting,AvitorII 10
13Dec86-9Hol 1 (T):4631:1021:342fm *2 1/2 119  32 41 1/2 53 1/4 64 3/4 Stevens G L4 62500 90-08 AutoCommander,DrkAccent,Dr.Dly 9
23Nov86-9Hol 1 1/8 (T):4811:3642:021fm*3-2 119  31 1/2 3 1/2 3 1/2 3 1/2 Valenzuela P A5 62500 83-13 Rampour, Travet, Aviator II 11
     23Nov86—Rank early
11Nov86-9Hol 1 1/8 (T):4721:1121:472fm*9-5 119  21 2hd 2hd 1 3/4 Valenzuela P A1 62500 91-09 Aviator II, Auto Commander,Crony 8
     11Nov86—Lugged in late
15Oct86-5SA 1 1/8 (T):47 1:1041:471fm 6 114  21 2 1/2 33 35 Cordero A Jr1 75000 86-09 River Of Kings, Keyala, Aviator II 10
  Apr 14 SA 6f ft 1:153 h    Apr 3 SA 3f ft :352 h    Mar 26 SA 5f ft 1:011 h    Mar 21 SA 4f ft :483 h
```

Knights Legend's whole career is before us in the pps of today's *Racing Form*. But with layoff horses the trainer factor is often of primary importance. What we need to look for are other Hector Palma European horses, first time in U.S., racing after a layoff. I found only two. One of them, below, was successful. Coincidentally, Pen Bal Lady had the same owners as Knights Legend, similar period and time of layoff. Possible short cycle (see Chapter 9).

```
*Pen Bal Lady                  Ch. f. 4, by Mummy's Game—Northern Queen, by Northfields
  VELASQUEZ J                  Br.—Highfield Stud Ltd (Eng)          1987  4 2 0 1   $164,150
                         118   Tr.—Palma Hector O                    1986  7 3 1 2    $12,137
Own.—DeCarlo-LaTorre-Rbnstn Etl   Lifetime  11 5 1 3  $176,287       Turf 10 5 1 2   $153,787
 9Aug87-8Dmr  1⅟₁₆Ⓣ:4721:1111:421fm 10 115  73¾ 84½ 99¼ 99½  Solis A7  La Jolla H 79-12 ThMdic,SomthingLucky,SvonTowr 11
     9Aug87—Grade III; Lugged out
12Jly87-8Hol  1⅛:461 1:101 1:483ft  3½ 121  66 65 44 35½  DlhssE5  ⒻHol Oaks 88-09 PerchnceToDrem,Schuist,PenBlLdy 6
     12Jly87—Grade I
17May87-8Hol  1⅟₁₆Ⓣ:4621:1031:411fm*2-3 119  94¾ 2hd 1½ 11¾  DlssE8  ⒻHnymn H 88-09 PenBlLdy,SomeSenstion,Dvi'sLmb 10
     17May87—Grade III. Wide 3/8 turn
25Apr87-8Hol  1 Ⓣ:47 1:1111:352fm  5 117  66½ 53½ 41¾ 11½  DlhoussyE5 ⒻSenorita 90-14 PenBalLady,Sweettuc,Davie'sLamb 6
20Sep86♦4Ayr(Scot)  6f      1:104fm  16 120  Ⓣ 64½  WldronP   ⒻFrth of Clyd  LindasMagic,Attempting,Kyverdle  13
30Aug86♦3Chester(Eng) 7f    1:313sf  *3 126  Ⓣ 37   RchrdsA   Mtchls Nsy H   BrewinTime,ShadeofPle,PenBlLdy  10
19Aug86♦1York(Eng) 7f       1:264gd  12 120  Ⓣ 3½   RichrdsA  Eglntn Nsy H   Gulf King,JaysSpecial,PenBalLady  14
 1Aug86♦4Thirsk(Eng) 7f     1:28 gd  *3 121  Ⓣ 12   RichrdsA  Sessay Auctn   PenBalLady,BothyBallad,GrecinJos  6
 2Jly86♦3Warwick(Eng) 7f    1:26 gd  2¼ 123  Ⓣ 12½  CauthenS  ⒻStrt & Prkr   PenBlLdy,FreshThoughts,BsicBliss  6
18Jun86♦6Beverley(Eng) a7½f 1:324hd   5 122  Ⓣ 2hd  DuffildG  Snngtn Auctn   Sparsholt, Pen BalLady,LastStand  17
   Feb 10 SA 6f ft 1:15 h     Feb 4 SA 5f ft 1:00 h     Jan 27 SA 5f ft 1:003 h     Jan 20 SA 4f ft :472 h
```

Additional pps below will allow us to see Super Dupont's total U.S. record:

```
*Super Dupont                  B. h. 6, by Bay Express—De Seill, by Derring-Do
  VELASQUEZ J                  Br.—J R S Coggan (Eng)                1987  2 1 0 0    $10,200
                         115   Tr.—Van Berg Jack C                   1986  4 0 0 0     $4,525
Own.—Rosenblum H T               Lifetime  25 4 2 4  $61,785         Turf 25 4 2 4    $61,785
 4Sep87-8AP   1 Ⓣ:58 1:1441:372gd 6½e114  1½ 1½ 1½ 69  BrfldD2  Bud Brd Cup 79-23 PersianNews,MisterC.,VernonCstle 7
 7Aug87-8AP   1⅟₁₆Ⓣ:4821:15 1:453fm 6½ 114  35 32 31½ 1nk  Brumfield D1 Aw17000 75-32 SuprDupont,NudistColony,JckClim 6
27Mar86-8SA   1⅛Ⓣ:4541:1131:48 fm 11 117  77¾ 64 52¾ 42¾  McCarron C J8 125000 84-12 Evngld'Lord,RvrOfKngs,PlAndDc 8
     27Mar86—Lugged in badly final 3/8; bumped 1/16
 9Mar86-5SA   1⅝Ⓣ:4531:1011:491fm 17 118  47 23½ 33½ 56½  Meza R Q5  150000 74-16 Clanraltier,Vulnerability,Steepbnk 10
24Jan86-5SA   1⅝Ⓣ:4531:1131:493fm  3 115  74¾ 32 22 51¾  Stevens G L2 Aw35000 77-19 AllHandsOnDeck,CptinVigors,Fuzzy 8
16Jan86-8SA   1⅛Ⓣ:46 1:1011:473fm 15 115  77 75½ 65 74¾  DelhoussyeE4 Aw45000 84-11 Truculnt,DoublQckTm,TppngWood 9
     16Jan86—Bumped, jostled at start, lacked room through stretch
29Dec85-8Hol  1¼Ⓣ:4931:38 2:012fm 7½ 116  43 64½ 73¾ 65½  McHrgueDG7 600000 S  — —  El Asesor, Foscarini, Palestiglio 8
     29Dec85—Wide into stretch
 8Dec85-9Hol  1⅟₁₆Ⓣ:4741:1211:43 fm 27 119  74¾105½ 43 2no  McCarron C J1 150000  — —  ‡Steepbnk,SuperDupont,Plestiglio 12
     8Dec85—Placed first through disqualification; Took up at 1/16
18Jun85♦5StCloud(Fra) a1⅛  2:181yl  7 121  Ⓣ 32  Badel A      Px Durbar  Olindo, Abdali, SuperDupont  6
   Nov 27 Hol Ⓣ 7f fm 1:282 h (d)     Oct 14 SA Ⓣ 5f fm 1:024 h (d)
```

In Focus, however, calls for a trainer analysis. The Frankel pattern is to win early with European immigrants. But rarely do those winners follow up a victory with another sharp effort.

```
*Point D'Artois                Dk. b. or br. g. 5, by Fabulous Dancer—Pointe Alezane, by Bon Mot
  STEVENS G L                  Br.—Wattinne R & M (Fra)               1987  3 1 0 0   $17,800
                         120   Tr.—Frankel Robert        $80,000      1986  5 0 2 0   $31,652
Own.—Moss Mr-Mrs J S             Lifetime  10 2 2 1  $59,972          Turf 10 2 2 1   $59,972
 6Dec87-9Hol  1⅛Ⓣ:4911:1321:52 yl  3¾ 122  119¾ 86 68 65¾  VlenzuelPA12 Aw40000 62-29 FivDddyFiv,L'Empir,CrtivFinncing 12
26Nov87-9Hol  1⅛Ⓣ:4721:11 1:481fm  3 116  85½ 84½ 33 1no  ValenzuelPA8 Aw31000 87-13 Point D'Artois, DennisD.,Unicopia 11
12Nov87-7SA   1¼Ⓣ:4811:3832:041fm *2½ 117  54 41¾ 42 56  ValenzuelPA6 Aw30000 60-34 Convincing, Proud Cat, Unicopia 8
     12Nov87—Broke slowly; checked 1/16
14Sep86♦4Longchamp(Fra)  a1½ 2:364yl   7½ 123  Ⓣ 55¾  LequuxA     Px Niel(Gr3)      Bering, Malakim, ArcticBlast  5
30Aug86♦4Deauville(Fra)  a1¼ 2:162sf *4-5 119  Ⓣ 64½  LequuxA     Px Ridgway        NewBruce, Malakim, SoirdeNoces  12
 8Jun86♦4Chantilly(Fra)  a1½ 2:24 gd   12 128  Ⓣ 57¾  Head F      Px d Jky Clb(Gr1) Bering, Altayan, Bakharoff  13
11May86♦5Longchamp(Fra)  a1½ 2:36 gd    6 128  Ⓣ 22   KsssJL      Px Hocquart(Gr2)  Bering, Point d'Artois, Silver Band  7
20Apr86♦5Longchamp(Fra)  a1⅜ 2:44 sf   5¼ 128  Ⓣ 28   KesssJL     Px Noaills(Gr2)   Bering, Point d'Artois, PortEtienne  9
11Nov85♦2StCloud(Fra)    a1¼ 2:18 yl   4½ 123  Ⓣ 16   KsssJL      Rx d Vrdun(Mdn)   Point d'Artois,Solberg,SilverWord  21
29Oct85♦8StCloud(Fra)    a1  1:453gd    5 118  Ⓣ 33½  KsssJL      Px duVallon(Mdn)  TimeWillTll,Arcdius,Pointd'Artois  16
   Dec 28 Hol 5f ft 1:003 h     Dec 22 Hol 5f ft 1:02 h     Dec 15 Hol 5f ft 1:012 h     Nov 20 Hol 5f ft 1:012 h
```

Point D'Artois, for example, lost on December 6 while being bet fairly heavily. Beyond his past performances listed here, he continued losing throughout the Santa Anita meet (1Jan, 14Feb,

9Apr, and 25Apr). Even those Frankel foreign horses that eventually win U.S. stakes races always seem to follow up an initial victory with a loss (most recently, Roi Normand, who won on March 25 following a year-plus layoff and then finished out of the money on April 24 at Aqueduct). Roi Normand was to eventually become a stakes winner. And during this same period, another Frankel import, Solany, won first time in U.S. after a layoff, only to come back and lose. This is the total trainer context, within which In Focus must participate. (The Frankel story continues in Chapter 13.)

Dull horses in this field are Telephone Canyon, Hawaiian Spring, and Keyala. Telephone Canyon's record in his last ten races speaks for itself. Hawaiian Spring is one of those rare Frankel imports that did not win early in the United States. Keyala's previous winning periods are here set forth so that the reader may judge whether this horse is capable of radical form reversals, which he'd need today, or if he needs to race himself into peak condition. The following past performances will cover a span that includes Keyala's last two peak periods:

5th Hollywood

1 1/16 MILES. (Turf). (1.39⅗) ALLOWANCE. (Stretch start) Purse $34,000. 4-year-olds and upward. Non-winners of $3,000 four times other than maiden, claiming or starter. Weight, 122 lbs. Non-winners of two such races at a mile or over since March 1 allowed 3 lbs.; such a race since April 22, 6 lbs.

Keyala — Dk. b. or br. h. 6, by Key to the Kingdom—Alathea, by Lorenzaccio

DELAHOUSSAYE E — **116**

Own.—Vicki Beth Stables Inc	Br.—de Briones G D (Ky)	1987	10	4 1 1		$89,175
	Tr.—Palma Hector O	1986	15	1 2 6		$35,351
	Lifetime 40 9 5 10 $184,340	Turf	44	9 5 10		$181,640

10Jly87-8Hol	1 1/16 Ⓣ:46^{1}1:09^{3}1:40^{3}fm	9-5	116	2^{hd} 2^{hd} 1^{hd} 2^{1½}	DelhoussyeE^1 Aw40000	90-09	Rich Earth, Keyala, Willingness	6
28Jun87-7Hol	1½ Ⓣ:47 2:00^{3}2:26^{2}fm	2¼	118	4^{6½} 3^1 3^1 5^{5¾}	ValenzuelPA^5 ⓈHcp0	85-11	Circus Prince,Truth,MilleroYMedio	9
14Jun87-3Hol	1 1/16 Ⓣ:46^{2}1:10 1:40^{1}fm	9-5	119	3^2 1^{hd} 1^{2½} 1^{5½}	DelahoussyeE^4 100000	93-03	Keyala, Lucky NGreen,PlumCertain	6
16May87-8Hol	1½ Ⓣ:48^{3}2:01^{2}2:26^{3}fm	9½	117	5^{3½} 4^2 4^3 5^{1½}	PincyLJr^3 ⓈCbllero H	88-12	LordGrndy,GrtCmmnctr,CrcsPrnc	12
23Apr87-5Hol	1 1/16 Ⓣ:48 1:11^{4}1:41^{4}fm	5¼	116	7^{7½} 7^5 4^3 1^1	DelahoussyeE^7 100000	85-14	Keyala, Emperdori, Siberian Hero	7
23Apr87—Broke in a tangle								
20Apr87-8SA	1¼ Ⓣ:46 1:34^{1}1:59^{1}fm	25	114	10^{12} 7^{3¾} 7^5 8^6	OlvrsF^{11} ⓈSn Jcnto H	85-06	Forlitano, Bello Horizonte, Reco	11
14Mar87-8SA	1½ Ⓣ:47^{4}2:03 2:28^{1}fm	9½	116	3^{2½} 2^{hd} 3^1 7^5	DlhssyE^2 ⓈSn Mrno H	69-22	Rosedale, Forlitano, Bob Back	10
14Mar87—Lugged out drive								
31Jan87-5SA	1⅛ Ⓣ:46^{4}1:10^{3}1:47^{2}fm	2¾	119	2^1 2^{hd} 1^{hd} 1^{nk}	DelahoussayeE^4 80000	90-09	Keyala, River Of Kings, Sherkin	8
10Jan87-5SA	1¼ Ⓣ:46^{3}1:36 2:00^{4}fm	*2¾	116	2^2 1^2 1^5 1^7	Valenzuela P A^1 80000	83-15	Keyala, Manzotti, Pas De Choix	8
1Jan87-5SA	1⅛ Ⓣ:47^{1}1:11^{2}1:48^{1}fm	16	116	7^{3½} 6^{2¾} 5^3 3^{2¾}	Valenzuela P A^9 95000	83-14	Steepbank, River Of Kings, Keyala	9
1Jan87—Wide into stretch								

●Jly 7 Hol 5f ft :59^2 h   Jun 24 Hol 5f ft :59^3 h   Jun 7 Hol 5f ft 1:01^4 h   May 31 Hol 5f ft 1:01 h

9th Del Mar

1 1/16 MILES. (Turf). (1.41⅗) CLAIMING. Purse $30,000. 3-year-olds and upward. Weights, 3-year-olds, 116 lbs.; older, 122 lbs. Non-winners of two races at one mile or over since April 21 allowed 2 lbs.; such a race since then, 4 lbs. Claiming price $100,000; for each $5,000 to $85,000 allowed 1 lb. (Claiming and starter races for $80,000 or less not considered.)

Keyala — Dk. b. or br. h. 5, by Key to the Kingdom—Alathea, by Lorenzaccio
TORO F — 118 — Br.—de Briones G D (Ky) — 1986 8 1 0 4 $12,483
Tr.—Brothers Frank L. $100,000 — 1985 14 2 1 1 $31,265
Own.—Oak Cliff Stable — Lifetime 32 5 2 7 $72,277 — Turf 27 5 2 7 $68,577

21Jun86-9LaD	a1 1/16 ⓣ		1:41³fm	22	116	76½	4¾	51¾	51½	SimngtonDE⁴	Aw17000	92-06	TrickyBond,Mimir,Don'tFoolWithM	8
21Jun86—Hand Timed														
7Jun86-10LaD	a7½f ⓣ		1:29 fm	6½	116	64¾	6⁴	4³	32½	SimngtonDE³	Aw16000	92-10	Jamie Joe, Bold Run, Keyala	7
26May86-9LaD	170	:47³ 1:12¹	1:42 ft	3¾	118	5³	54½	6¹⁴	624½	Snyder L⁶	Aw16000	62-19	Under Orders, Dr. Spanky, Sway	6
13Apr86-10FG	a1⅛ ⓣ	:49¹1:13²	1:52²fm	*1e	114	53½	2hd	2hd	3²	Melancon G¹	Aw15000	78-22	LordOfTheWind,StarTopper,Keyala	9
16Mar86-11FG	1¼	:47⁴ 1:36⁴	2:01⁴ft	120	106	9¹⁶	11¹⁹	10²³	1018½	MontyD⁴	Nw Orln H	82-18	Heral, Hopeful Word, Kamakura	11
16Mar86—Grade II														
15Feb86-7FG	a7½f ⓣ:25	:48²1:34¹	fm	3½	114	4⁷	45½	3²	1¹	Melancon G⁴	Aw10500	78-27	Keyala, Career Kid, Little Fleet	7
1Feb86-9FG	a1	ⓣ:46⁴1:13	1:40²fm	*6-5	115	47½	2⁷	22½	3³	Perrodin E J⁸	Aw9000	74-23	Young Turk II, Little Fleet,Keyala	12
5Jan86-9FG	a1 1/16	ⓣ:49²1:14³	1:47 yl	2½	114	63½	6⁶	41¾	3hd	Faul J H⁷	Aw10500	77-23	Zuppardo'sLove,UnderOrders,Keyl	11
26Dec85-9FG	a1 1/16	ⓣ:48¹1:13¹	1:45 fm	5¾	116	3²	2½	12½	1⁴	Perrodin E J²	65000	87-13	Keyl,LordOfTheWind,SilverDiplomt	7
23Nov85-9FG	a7½f ⓣ:24	:47⁴1:31³	fm	*3-2e	115	3⁶	31½	3nk	4¹	Perrodin E J¹	Aw11000	90-10	JetAwayBill,SolitaryPlayer,MoroBy	9

●Jly 18 Dmr 6f ft 1:10⁴ h   Jly 12 SA 6f ft 1:13¹ h   Jly 5 SA 4f ft :47² h

Approximate Odds, Post Time

Aviator II	3–5
Hawaiian Spring	5–1
Knights Legend	5–1
Super Dupont	9–1
In Focus	10–1
Telephone Canyon	17–1
Keyala	34–1

Comments

Unlikely

Keyala's victories have never come with the type of form reversal he'd need today. Even his 29Apr87 win was not an "awakening" since he was severely overmatched in the two losses that preceded that victory.

Horses that finish second at 61–1 often come back to win at big odds. However, Telephone Canyon's second-place finish was slow, and in that same race, Aviator II encountered severe racing traffic and still won. Telephone Canyon's most recent high period corresponds to a trip to the minor leagues.

Hawaiian Spring proves that not all of Robert Frankel's European immigrants are destined to find the American Dream.

The short-cycle trainer pattern says that In Focus will follow up his win with a loss. He will be rudely awakened to the fact that not all fields in his new country are as mediocre as the one he was lucky enough to encounter on March 6.

Super Dupont nearly becomes a contender. But since he's been in the U.S., he's never put victories back to back. His physical condition has not even allowed him to run too many races back to back before he needs a layoff. He is now going for his fifth race since his most recent layoff. Prior to that, he was good for a period of only two races (AP). Before that he put together a string of six races, run, not won. He has discovered how to live very well on disability insurance.

On the other hand, perhaps he has begun to enjoy his trade. His latest U.S. victory was the only one of three that did not come on the heels of a layoff. This means that the current series of races may differ from the previous sets. He is not a total tossout, but 60 percent says he'll decline while 40 percent says he'll want to run today. Sounds like hedging, like the weather reporter, but we're dealing with a game of percentages.

Contenders

2. It's a close call. Aviator II has never sustained a winning streak for such a long period. On the other hand, he's a remarkably consistent horse and a win today would be no surprise. Even though a decline in his form cycle is likely,

he still may inherit the win. Everything else in this field seems to be going down or going nowhere. Except the lay-off horse.

1. Knights Legend sends us contradictory messages. How will he do first time back after a layoff? While he did not win as a first-time starter, he did finish *second* in a *field of twenty.* He beat more horses as a first-timer in a defeat than every winning first-time starter in the U.S. By the letter of the law, he does not qualify, but by the spirit of the law, he fits the pattern of first-time-starter winners doing well after layoffs later in their career. His one European layoff race was a competitive third at 4½–1. He projects to run well after his present layoff but not necessarily to win.

A second contradiction resides in the fact that in Europe he has been accustomed to running at marathon distances which make today's race seem like a sprint. The opposite pole of logic says that the distance question has been neutralized by two six-furlong bullet workouts which imply that he will like the shorter route even better than he liked the marathons.

The trainer short cycle, while not offering an abundance of evidence, implies that today is the day for Knights Legend. Approximately one year ago trainer Hector Palma brought over a European horse with a layoff similar to that of Knights Legend, for the same owners. Pen Bal Lady won her first new-world race, and Knights Legend, under the same tutelage, can do the same thing.

Aviator II and Knights Legend are contenders for completely different reasons. With no "comparables," they can't be measured against each other. Knights Legend becomes our top choice only because the information we have used to judge him is less accessible to the betting public than the data on Aviator II.

The match-up is a good one; one horse that may have had too little racing against another that may have had too much.

	Our Line	*Track Odds*	*Decision*
Knights Legend	3–2	5–1	Over. *Bet.*
Aviator II	9–5	3–5	Under. No bet.

THIRD RACE
Santa Anita
MARCH 26, 1988

1 ⅛ MILES.(Turf). (1.45⅗) CLAIMING. Purse $52,000. 4-year-olds and upward. Weight, 121 lbs. Non-winners of two races at one mile or over since February 1, allowed 2 lbs.; of such a race since then, 4 lbs. Claiming price $150,000; for each $5,000 to $125,000, allowed 2 lbs. (Claiming and starter races for $100,000 or less not considered).
Value of race $52,000; value to winner $28,600; second $10,400; third $7,800; fourth $3,900; fifth $1,300. Mutuel pool $408,113. Exacta pool $578,678.

Last Raced	Horse	Eqt.A.Wt	PP	St	¼	½	¾	Str	Fin	Jockey	Cl'g Pr	Odds $1
29Sep87 ^{3}Eng^{2}	Knights Legend	5 117	5	4	$1^{1/2}$	1^{1}	1^{1}	$1^{1/2}$	$1^{1\,1/2}$	Shoemaker W	150000	5.30
17Mar88 ^{8}SA^{8}	Super Dupont	7 112	7	6	4^{1}	$3^{1/2}$	$2^{1/2}$	2^{1}	2^{2}	Hawley S	125000	9.40
10Mar88 ^{8}SA^{1}	Aviator II	8 119	4	2	3^{hd}	$4^{1\,1/2}$	$6^{1/2}$	$4^{1\,1/2}$	$3^{1\,1/2}$	Pincay L Jr	150000	.60
6Mar88 ^{7}SA^{1}	In Focus	7 114	1	7	$5^{1/2}$	5^{hd}	4^{hd}	3^{hd}	$4^{1\,1/2}$	Stevens G L	125000	10.10
14Jan88 ^{8}SA^{4}	Hawaiian Spring	6 116	6	5	2^{1}	2^{1}	$3^{1/2}$	5^{4}	5^{4}	DelahoussyeE	140000	5.20
16Mar88 ^{8}SA^{5}	Telephone Canyon	b 4 113	2	1	6^{1}	7	7	6^{hd}	$6^{2\,3/4}$	Solis A	125000	17.90
6Mar88 ^{7}SA^{5}	Keyala	7 115	3	3	7	$6^{1/2}$	5^{1}	7	7	Castanon A L	135000	34.50

OFF AT 2:07. Start good. Won ridden out. Time, :23⅕, :47⅘, 1:12⅕, 1:36⅘, 1:49⅘ Course firm.

$2 Mutuel Prices:			
5-KNIGHTS LEGEND	12.60	6.60	3.40
7-SUPER DUPONT		9.40	4.80
4-AVIATOR II			2.40

$2 EXACTA 5–7 PAID $103.60.

B. h, by Sir Ivor—Gimme Love, by Dr Fager. Trainer Palma Hector O. Bred by Leigh G (Ky).

KNIGHTS LEGEND, a pace factor from the start, had plenty left when hooked by SUPER DUPONT turning into the stretch to draw clear in midstretch when roused with the whip once right handed, then maintained a clear lead in the last sixteenth while under a brisk hand ride. SUPER DUPONT, never far back, moved up to reach equal terms for the lead outside KNIGHTS LEGEND between calls turning into the stretch but did not have the same response as that opponent in the final furlong. AVIATOR II, close up early, was shuffled back a bit approaching the far turn while in traffic, came into the stretch four wide, came back on to menace in the upper stretch but lacked the needed continued response in the last furlong. IN FOCUS, within easy striking distance early after bobbling at the break and being bumped in the initial strides, moved up to menace along the inside rail in the upper stretch but lacked the necessary response in the last furlong. HAWAIIAN SPRING forced the issue early and gave way in the final quarter. TELEPHONE CANYON, bumped in the opening strides, was five wide into the stretch. KEYALA, wide down the backstretch, was six wide into the stretch.

Owners— 1, LaTerre-Rubenstein-Rubenstein; 2, Rosenblum H; 3, Green Thumb Farm Stable; 4, Moss J S; 5, Gann E A; 6, Dolan J F & Clara; 7, Vicki Beth Stables Inc.

Trainers— 1, Palma Hector O; 2, Van Berg Jack C; 3, Ippolito Steve; 4, Frankel Robert; 5, Frankel Robert; 6, Hutchinson Kathy; 7, Palma Hector O.

Overweight: In Focus 2 pounds; Hawaiian Spring 1; Telephone Canyon 1; Keyala 1.

Even if we had reversed the order of preference of the two contenders, the tote board calls for a bet on Knights Legend. When this Hector Palma horse wins the race, a new message materializes. If Pen Bal Lady was the model for Knights Legend, then the short cycle is only half complete. Recall that after Pen Bal Lady's layoff victory, she defied the bounce theory and came right back for a second win.

Knights Legend would have the opportunity to duplicate the pattern of his stablemate. Futures investors who follow patterns of events could make an automatic bet on Knights Legend, even before seeing the field of the past performances! But wait. When Knights Legend comes on to the track, April 14, to finish weaving a new quilt in the exact image of the old one, the rains come down. The race is put off the grass and on the sloppy dirt. Which force is stronger, the Hector Palma trainer pattern or its opposite, which says that Knights Legend has never raced on the dirt, no less in the slop?

Evidently, in the nature of things, phenomena such as rain and sleet are not as powerful as the force of trainer orbits. Knights

Legend will complete the short cycle as surely as the earth will travel around the sun.

8th Hollywood

Knights Legend *

1 ⅛ MILES. (Turf). (1.45⅜) ALLOWANCE. (Stretch Start). Purse $52,500. 4-year-olds and upward. Non-winners of $19,500 twice other than closed or claiming at a mile or over since July 27. Weight, 122 lbs. Non-winners of two such races of $22,500 since July 15 allowed 3 lbs.; two such races of $19,000 since September 1, 5 lbs.; one such race of $22,000 since then, 7 lbs.

WORKSHOPS NINE/TEN

Maiden Races

As a special feature, the last two races on our workshop card combine to make up our very own "late daily double": both maiden races.

Handicappers who choose to bypass the form factor will always feel uncomfortable with maiden races. Most maidens have established no *routine* in their past performances, so it is in this type of race where form cycle is most obviously the primary handicapping factor. The ability to *project* future performances, completely replaces the skill of identifying consistency and continuity. In fields of maiden races, the only horses who abide by a routine are the proven losers!

Ironically, some of those horses who have found their routine (read "rut") attract more than their fair share of betting action. Their fatal routine can be described as a tendency to come close often, displaying talent but lacking competitive spirit. When facing this type of horse-in-a-rut, up-and-coming competitors, who are likely to be lightly raced, are highly preferred by the form-oriented handicapper; they will yield more than their fair share of pari-mutuel returns.

Most of the patterns that have been examined in expository

chapters of *Thoroughbred Cycles* will play a major role in the maiden race. The projection of change eclipses factors of "routine" (Preface). Ascending numbers are more significant than high numbers (Chapter 1). Recency is no great asset (Chapter 2), in most cases, with first-time starters (Chapters 9, 10) and layoff horses (Chapter 11) often finding themselves in advantageous spots. Radical but predictable change is commonplace (Chapter 6). Awareness of which stables specialize in child prodigies, as opposed to late bloomers, is crucial to establishing the significance of the *moment in time* of a maiden race in a horse's career.

In some ways the maiden race is a display, in microcosm, of the whole form-cycle approach. Even the horse-for-course factor may surface, in cases when, with a change of track, a maiden's workouts show radical improvement.

Above all, in maiden races handicappers sensitive to form-cycle considerations encounter their best advantage; as routine-oriented horseplayers complain, with much anxiety, that there is insufficient data. These players deserve a free vacation to Europe, in order to see maidens compete regularly against winners, often successfully.

A by-product of maiden races is a wealth of information that is valuable for future projections. First-time starter winners have a better than fair chance to win as layoff comebackers. Maiden winners that pay big pari-mutuel returns are more likely to pay long-shot prices later in their careers. Already in maiden races the class factor has surfaced, with the class drop becoming a major contributor to maiden victories.

Remember that maidens display certain "personality" traits that are significant influences on career performance cycles. It was in a maiden race that I identified a behavior trait that years later was to lead to a big payoff. Maiden races provide the handicapper/child psychologist with valuable leads about expected performance phases.

It is a rare Pick 6 that will be without at least one maiden race. Trifectas and daily doubles will frequently include this type of race. There is a very practical reason for mastering one's understanding of the newcomers. Handicappers with serious problems in dealing with maiden races will probably find the exact same problems, more camouflaged, in all other types of races.

But let's look at our maiden daily double on a more positive note. There is lots of money to be won in this type of race.

WORKSHOP NINE

February 20, 1988

4th Santa Anita

OUT OF CHUTE
7 FURLONGS
SANTA ANITA
FINISH

7 FURLONGS. (1.20) MAIDEN. Purse $25,000. 3-year-olds. Weight, 118 lbs. (Non-starters for a claiming price of $32,000 or less preferred.)

Elite Regent 15
TORO F 118
Own.—Saud Bin Khaled
Ch. c. 3, by Vice Regent—Elite, by Exclusive Native
Br.—Bittersweet (Pa) 1988 1 M 0 0
Tr.—Van Berg Jack C 1987 1 M 0 0
Lifetime 2 0 0 0
14Feb88-4SA 6f :22³ :46³ 1:11³ft 13 118 84¼ 87½ 108¼ 79 Toro F6 Mdn 71-20 OurNtivWsh,J.B.Tpton,ClpprtonIsl 12
14Feb88—Bumped start; wide into stretch
10Dec87-4Aqu 6f ⊡:22³ :46⁴1:13 ft 10 118 1010 109¾ 97½ 64¾ Romero R P7 Mdn 74-24 IntrpdVoygr,PrftbyEntry,FlrscntL 11
10Dec87—Slow start
Feb 8 Hol 5f ft 1:00³ h Feb 5 Hol 3f gd :38³ h Jan 28 Hol 5f ft 1:01³ h Jan 22 Hol 5f ft 1:01³ hg

Cajun Gardens 7-2
PINCAY L JR 118
Own.—Slusher & Towle
Dk. b. or br. g. 3, by Cajun Prince—Erin's Sham, by The Irish Lord
Br.—Erin's Sham Joint Venture (Cal) 1988 1 M 0 0 $1,875
Tr.—Manzi Joseph 1987 0 M 0 0
Lifetime 1 0 0 0 $1,875
7Feb88-4SA 6f :21⁴ :45¹ 1:10⁴ft 7½ 118 76½ 65½ 64¾ 47¾ Hawley S7 ⓈMdn 76-16 WhtADplomt,MjrMn,Knndy'sKnckt 9
7Feb88—Wide 3/8 turn; checked 1/8
●Feb 15 SA 3f ft :34³ h Feb 4 SA 4f ft :47² hg Jan 30 SA 5f ft 1:01¹ h Jan 25 SA 4f ft :48² h

Freeskate 2
DELAHOUSSAYE E 118
Own.—Triple Dot Dash Stable
Ch. c. 3, by Overskate—Kimberly June, by Good Old Mort
Br.—deCstlla deDlly-Hayes-Bnkrd (NY) 1988 3 M 2 0 $12,025
Tr.—Vienna Darrell 1987 6 M 1 3 $17,807
Lifetime 9 0 3 3 $29,832
6Feb88-4SA 6½f :21³ :44¹ 1:16⁴ft 5 118 77 57¾ 45 21¾ Delahoussaye E 2 Mdn 84-18 Sutter'sProspect,Freskt,Art'sAngl 12
6Feb88—Veered out start; checked 3/8
24Jan88-6SA 6½f :22 :45² 1:16⁴ft 6½ 118 64 53 22 22½ DelahoussayeE 11 Mdn 83-18 Claim, Freeskate, Our NativeWish 12
10Jan88-6SA 1 1/16 :46⁴ 1:11¹ 1:43²ft 20 117 51¾ 42½ 44½ 49½ Delahoussaye E 9 Mdn 74-15 Stalwars, Sky High, Major Man 9
27Dec87-6SA 1 1/16 :46⁴ 1:12¹ 1:44⁴ft 4½ 112⁵ 42 2hd 1hd 26 Gryder A T 6 Mdn 71-17 GladMusic,Freeskate,RecitlionSpin 9
22Nov87-9AC 1 1/16 :47¹ 1:12² 1:46³ft 3½ 117 53 52 62½ 35½ Martinez J C 4 A C Fut 66-25 Patron C., DelMarRuler,Freeskate 10
8Nov87-4SA 1 :47³ 1:13 1:41 gd 4½ 117 1hd 2hd 54 811½ Stevens G L 5 Mdn 51-25 KingAlobar,PureExpense,GldMusic 8
24Oct87-6SA 1 1/16 :46² 1:11⁴ 1:45³gd 3 117 21 11 12½ 33¾ Stevens G L 7 Mdn 69-17 Propost, Winnerwald, Freeskate 8
16Sep87-4Dmr 6f :21⁴ :44³ 1:09²ft 19 117 21½ 23½ 25 38 Meza R Q4 Mdn 83-15 Speedratic,GrndAvenger,Freeskte 12
15Aug87-4Dmr 6f :22 :45³ 1:11 ft 14 117 52½ 41½ 45 56 McCarron C J10 Mdn 77-14 Doctr'sTrbt,CrstngWtr,OrNtvWsh 10
Feb 18 SA 3f ft :36¹ h Feb 13 SA 3f ft :36⁴ h Jan 31 SA 3f ft :37³ h Jan 19 SA 3f gd :37¹ h

Valance 10
SOLIS A 118
Own.—Summa Stable
Ch. g. 3, by Jaklin Klugman—Ballrina, by Dewan
Br.—Summa Stable (Ky) 1988 3 M 0 1 $3,750
Tr.—Corin Vladimir 1987 0 M 0 0
Lifetime 3 0 0 1 $3,750
6Feb88-4SA 6½f :21³ :44¹ 1:16⁴ft 11 118 68½ 78½ 712 711 Solis A10 Mdn 75-18 Sutter'sProspect,Freskt,Art'sAngl 12
16Jan88-6SA 6f :21³ :44⁴ 1:11¹ft 18 118 63½ 54 55 33 Solis A12 Mdn 79-20 FrontlineFble,Suttr'sProspct,Vlnc 12
16Jan88—Wide into stretch
2Jan88-6SA 6f :21² :44³ 1:11¹ft 37 118 98½ 67½ 44½ 62¾ Solis A11 Mdn 79-15 SrRobrto,MoonMdnssI,OrNtvWsh 12
2Jan88—Broke slowly
Feb 15 SA 5f ft 1:01¹ hg Jan 29 SA 5f ft 1:03³ h Jan 12 SA 4f ft :47¹ h Dec 29 SA 3f ft :36 h

Combat Pilot 30
CISNEROS J E 118
Own.—Delaplane E E
Dk. b. or br. c. 3, by Ack Ack—Hail to Boldness, by Bold Reason
Br.—Chillingwrth-Capehart-Lieban (Ky) 1988 3 M 0 0 $475
Tr.—Dunn Larry 1987 1 M 0 0
Lifetime 4 0 0 0 $475
7Feb88-6SA 1 1/16 :46¹ 1:11² 1:44²ft 133 117 1220 1213 1015 919 Cisneros J E8 Mdn 60-16 Slewbop, Royal Lyphard, Peace 12
24Jan88-4SA 1 1/16 :47² 1:12⁴ 1:44³ft 110 117 1112 1210 1219 1223½ Olivares F 7 Mdn 54-18 Bel AirDancer,Addie'sBro,SkyHigh 12
24Jan88—Wide
7Jan88-6SA 7f :22³ :46 1:24⁴ft 33 118 1112 89¾ 69 58½ Patton D B 10 M50000 67-23 Mehmetski,Ship'sLog,FineHostge 12
30Dec87-6SA 6f :22 :45³ 1:11³m 19 118 1213 1110 810 79¾ DelahoussyeE 5 M50000 70-23 Davy'sMarket,Natnlive,MnO'Glory 12
30Dec87—Very wide stretch
Feb 10 SA 3f ft :35³ hg Feb 3 SA 4f gd :48² hg Jan 20 SA 5f ft 1:03³ h Dec 26 SA 4f ft :52 h

Mikeylikeshim 30
BRUMFIELD D 118
Own.—Straub-Rubens Cecilia P
B. c. 3, by Raise A Man—Flashy Fleet, by Prolesse
Br.—Northwest Farms (Ky) 1988 1 M 0 0
Tr.—Fulton John W 1987 0 M 0 0
Lifetime 1 0 0 0
6Feb88-4SA 6½f :21³ :44¹ 1:16⁴ft 87 118 1014 1015 1014 812¾ Toro F1 Mdn 74-18 Sutter'sProspect,Freskt,Art'sAngl 12
Feb 5 SA 3f ft :36¹ h Jan 6 SA 6f ft 1:15⁴ h Dec 31 SA 6f m 1:16³ h Dec 26 SA 6f ft 1:17² h

Big Mukora 8
B. c. 3, by Mr Prospector—Jameela, by Rambunctious
CORDERO A JR 118 Br.—Brant P M (Ky) 1988 1 M 0 0 $625
Tr.—Lukas D Wayne 1987 4 M 0 0
Own.—Brant P M Lifetime 5 0 0 0 $625
6Feb88-4SA 6½f :21³ :44¹ 1:16⁴ft 32 118 56 47½ 58½ 55 Pincay L Jr7 Mdn 81-18 Sutter'sProspect,Freskt,Art'sAngl 12
10Dec87-4Hol 6f :22² :46¹ 1:10⁴sy 6½ 117 42½ 23 46½ 617½ Cordero A Jr4 Mdn 71-21 Brave Capade,Script,MajesticSight 9
8Nov87-6SA 6f :22¹ :45¹ 1:11²gd 9½ 117 42½ 46½ 46½ 816½ Meza R Q3 Mdn 65-25 SweetNGo,SelfContined,LivelyOne 10
8Nov87—Broke in, bumped
21Oct87-6Aqu 6f :22² :45⁴ 1:11³ft 4½ 118 41½ 54½ 810 910 Santos J A12 Mdn 73-19 Estes,GrumpyMiller,SuprNutcrckr 14
10Oct87-2Bel 6f :23 :47¹ 1:12²ft *4-5e118 11 1hd 1hd 57 Santos J A1 Mdn 78-22 IntnsivCommnd,InLgu,DimondDog 9
Feb 14 SA 4f ft :48² h Jan 21 Hol 5f ft 1:02⁴ h Jan 8 Hol 1 ft 1:43² h ●Dec 29 Hol 7f ft 1:28 h

Art's Angel 5-2
B. c. 3, by Czaravich—Laura's Star, by Key to the Kingdom
MEZA R Q 118 Br.—Mabee Mr-Mrs J C (Ky) 1988 2 M 0 1 $3,750
Tr.—French Neil 1987 0 M 0 0
Own.—Walker R & Bonnie J Lifetime 2 0 0 1 $3,750
6Feb88-4SA 6½f :21³ :44¹ 1:16⁴ft 17 118 11 11½ 2hd 33 Meza R Q11 Mdn 83-18 Sutter'sProspect,Freskt,Art'sAngl 12
16Jan88-6SA 6f :21³ :44⁴ 1:11¹ft 54 118 75¾ 78 88½ 76¾ Meza R Q4 Mdn 75-20 FrontlineFble,Suttr'sProspct,Vlnc 12
Feb 15 SA 4f ft :48² h ●Feb 3 SA 4f gd :46³ h ●Jan 27 SA 4f ft :47¹ h Jan 12 SA 4f ft :48 h

Gràn Judgement 8
Gr. g. 3, by Gran Zar—Just Judgment, by Hail to Reason
SHOEMAKER W 118 Br.—Hagopian R R (Ky) 1988 2 M 0 0
Tr.—Greenman Dean 1987 2 M 0 0 $1,650
Own.—Greenman & Murison Lifetime 4 0 0 0 $1,650
7Feb88-6SA 1 1/16 :46¹ 1:11² 1:44²ft 3 117 810 78½ 712 713¾ DelahoussayeE 10 Mdn 65-16 Slewbop, Royal Lyphard, Peace 12
2Jan88-6SA 6f :21² :44³ 1:11¹ft 18 118 1215 1216 97½ 73¾ Shoemaker W 1 Mdn 78-15 SrRobrto,MoonMdnssI,OrNtvWsh 12
15Nov87-6SA 7f :22³ :46 1:23⁴ft 7 117 511 41½ 43 44½ Shoemaker W 1 Mdn 77-18 AbbyB.Runnr,BlArDncr,OurNtvWsh 8
1Nov87-6SA 6f :21³ :45 1:11 m 13 119 79 78½ 57 65½ Cordero A Jr 1 Mdn 77-12 GrnMusico,SweetNGo,BelAirDncr 10
Feb 6 SA 3f ft :37³ h Jan 31 SA 7f ft 1:27⁴ h Jan 23 SA 6f ft 1:13⁴ h Jan 17 SA 4f sy :50² h (d)

Workshop Nine departs from the standard format to ask one question: What are the reasons why Art's Angel should win this race and beat the horse he just lost to, Freeskate? I have penciled-in the program morning line as well as some circles which represent the pace outlook for the race.

Stop here for your analysis before resuming with the text.

A static analysis frozen in time—as if yesterday's results should translate into tomorrow's outcomes—will argue that Freeskate beat Art's Angel by a length and a quarter, catching him from behind at 6½ furlongs. As they stretch out today an extra half-furlong, it should be easier for the closer to catch the front runner. Pardon me if I have insulted your intelligence with this argument, but there are many seasoned handicappers who abide by such logic. Before I can contradict them, they will add that Freeskate accomplished a second-place finish in spite of a severely troubled trip. Factor in the trouble and he should sweep past Art's Angel effortlessly.

Now turn the above argument on its opposite side and you'll have the only solution to this race. We have been insisting that most races have several possible scenarios. We are now obligated to present here the 10 percent of races that are determined by only one logic. This, my friends, is a one-horse race.

With absolutely no early pressure, Art's Angel will be able to travel as slowly as he likes in the early going and have plenty of gas left for the extra half-furlong. Going from six to 6½ furlongs, he has run an improved race, so he projects to continue improving with an extra half-furlong. He won't have to run a 44.1 or even near that figure to monopolize the pace of the race.

And while Art's Angel's performance cycle is on the improve, Freeskate is going absolutely nowhere. After nine races he is no more competitive than he was after his second and third races. Although his finish positions remain deceptively close, he has actually lost much of his early speed; observe the descending early fractions.

The oddsmaker has correctly made Cajun Gardens the third choice. With only one career race, he is more likely to improve than horses that have already run several times. He had double trouble in his first race and still ran evenly. A subsequent workout implies that he may have the sort of early speed that will allow him to stay close enough to Art's Angel to see his tail.

The morning linemaker has done an admirable job in predicting the betting public's behavior at the window. That is his job. You'll never make me believe that in his heart and his head he didn't favor Art's Angel. I'll bet it was a painful experience for him to have to write in lower odds for an inferior horse. But he knows that the public ranks continuity over change and finish position over pace-improvement factors. Now let's observe how admirably close he was in judging the mass psychology of the betting public (top seven public choices):

	Program Odds	Track Odds
Freeskate	2–1	1.7–1
Art's Angel	5–2	4.8–2
Cajun Garden	7–2	9–2
Big Mukora	8–1	7.8–1
Gran Judgement	8–1	8.6–1
Valance	10–1	13–1
Elite Regent	15–1	21.9–1

This guy should be hired to calculate how we are going to vote in congressional and presidential elections. The government would save millions of dollars in expenses of running voting machines and printing ballots. Of course, our probability line is a distinct task which relates to horses' chances of winning rather than mass psychology.

Handicappers who saw the extra half-furlong as an asset rather than a liability for Art's Angel would be obligated to rank him as an only contender. In doing so, he qualifies for a 67 percent chance of winning. You can't give him a 100 percent because he's eligible to bobble at the start and Cajun Gardens is eligible to improve, as are the other light-raced horses. Sixty-seven percent translates into 1–2, which means that if Art's Angel had gone off at even money, you would still have a bet. This makes his track odds of nearly 5–2 as one of the biggest bargains of the meet.

The race was run with such leisurely fractions that none of the early runners lost positions in the stretch. That made it impossible for Freeskate to opportunistically pass tiring horses. Thanks to tiring horses, Freeskate has been able to make a living finishing second and third, without needing to be truly competitive.

Once more, who beat whom last time becomes a distracting nonfactor, as the universe of thoroughbred racing is composed of the orbits of improving and retrogressing horses.

FOURTH RACE
Santa Anita
FEBRUARY 28, 1988

7 FURLONGS. (1.20) MAIDEN. Purse $25,000. 3-year-olds. Weight, 118 lbs. (Non-starters for a claiming price of $32,000 or less preferred.)

Value of race $25,000; value to winner $13,750; second $5,000; third $3,750; fourth $1,875; fifth $625. Mutuel pool $745,644.

Last Raced	Horse	Eqt.	A.	Wt	PP	St	¼	½	Str	Fin	Jockey	Odds $1
6Feb88 ^{4}SA^{3}	Art's Angel		3	118	8	2	$1^{1/2}$	$1^{1/2}$	1^{3}	1^{2}	Meza R Q	2.40
14Feb88 ^{4}SA^{7}	Elite Regent	b	3	118	1	6	2^{hd}	2^{2}	2^{1}	$2^{2\frac{3}{4}}$	Toro F	21.90
7Feb88 ^{4}SA^{4}	Cajun Gardens		3	118	2	4	$3^{1\frac{1}{2}}$	$3^{1/2}$	3^{hd}	$3^{1\frac{3}{4}}$	Pincay L Jr	4.60
7Feb88 ^{6}SA^{7}	Gran Judgement	b	3	118	9	3	4^{hd}	4^{hd}	$5^{2\frac{1}{2}}$	$4^{1/2}$	Shoemaker W	8.60
6Feb88 ^{4}SA^{2}	Freeskate	b	3	118	3	5	6^{4}	5^{2}	$4^{1\frac{1}{2}}$	$5^{2\frac{1}{4}}$	Delahoussaye E	1.70
6Feb88 ^{4}SA^{5}	Big Mukora		3	118	7	1	$5^{1/2}$	6^{4}	6^{3}	$6^{2\frac{1}{2}}$	Cordero A Jr	7.80
6Feb88 ^{4}SA^{8}	Mikeylikeshim		3	118	6	7	$7^{1/2}$	$8^{1\frac{1}{2}}$	$7^{1\frac{1}{2}}$	7^{2}	Brumfield D	57.80
6Feb88 ^{4}SA^{7}	Valance	b	3	118	4	9	9	$7^{1\frac{1}{2}}$	8^{5}	$8^{5\frac{1}{4}}$	Solis A	13.30
7Feb88 ^{6}SA^{9}	Combat Pilot		3	118	5	8	$8^{1\frac{1}{2}}$	9	9	9	Cisneros J E	130.40

OFF AT 2:38. Start good. Won driving. Time, :22⅗, :45⅘, 1:11⅕, 1:24⅘ Track fast.

$2 Mutuel Prices:			
8–ART'S ANGEL	6.80	5.00	4.60
1–ELITE REGENT		15.20	9.60
2–CAJUN GARDENS			4.80

B. c, by Czaravich—Laura's Star, by Key to the Kingdom. Trainer French Neil. Bred by Mabee Mr–Mrs J C (Ky).

ART'S ANGEL, a pace factor from the start, drew well clear in the upper stretch and retained a clear advantage in the final sixteenth while being hard ridden. ELITE REGENT moved up early to get near the lead from the inside before going a quarter, pressed the pace to the three-eighths pole, continued close up thereafter but had to settle for the place. CAJUN GARDENS, close up early, lacked the needed response in the final quarter. GRAN JUDGEMENT, also close up, lacked the needed response in the final quarter and was four wide into the stretch. FREESKATE had no visible mishap. BIG MUKORA, close up early, gave way. MIKEYLIKESHIM was wide down the backstretch. VALANCE, wide down the backstretch after breaking slowly, was five wide into the stretch. COMBAT PILOT brushed the side of the gate at the break.

Owners— 1, Walker R & Bonnie J; 2, Saud Bin Khaled; 3, Slusher & Towle; 4, Greenman & Murison; 5, Triple Dot Dash Stable; 6, Brant P M; 7, Straub-Rubens Cecilia P; 8, Summa Stable; 9, Delaplane E E.

Trainers— 1, French Neil; 2, Van Berg Jack C; 3, Manzi Joseph; 4, Greenman Dean; 5, Vienna Darrell; 6, Lukas D Wayne; 7, Fulton John W; 8, Cerin Vladimir; 9, Dunn Larry.

WORKSHOP TEN

May 19, 1988

2nd Golden Gate

6 FURLONGS
GOLDEN GATE

6 FURLONGS. (1.07⅘) MAIDEN CLAIMING. Purse $6,500. 3-year-olds. Bred in California. Weight, 118 lbs. Claiming price $12,500.

Ewok Wickett — Dk. b. or br. c. 3, by Tell—Ick's Exotic, by Ruken
LAMBERT J — 118 — Br.—Jen-Don Farms (Cal) — 1988 5 M 0 0 $488
Tr.—Cotton Perry — $12,500 — 1987 3 M 0 1 $2,375
Own.—Jen-Don Farm — Lifetime 8 0 0 1 $2,863

8Apr88-2GG 6f :222 :46 1:11 ft 16 118 52½ 52½ 44 45½ SchvnevldtCP9 M12500 78-13 Me'NJ.B.,ChangosLst,Whydididoit 11
18Mar88-1GG 6f :221 :453 1:112ft 5½ 118 52½ 75¾ 911 913½ ChpmnTM10 [S]M12500 68-23 Sndi'sTresure,Jim'sDiffrnt,KuKini 11
4Feb88-2GG 6f :22 :452 1:11 ft 16 118 109¾ 910 74¾ 63½ Lambert J4 [S]M12500 80-10 Pushin'Fte,MnInChrge,VlntinoMio 12
15Jan88-2BM 6f :223 :462 1:132m 11 120 43 54 78½ 79 SchvnldtCP9 [S]M12500 63-25 Dck'sSprStr,VlntnoMo,Mn'nChrg 11
3Jan88-2BM 6f :222 :461 1:122sy 21 118 88 812 615 613 SchvnevldtCP7 M16000 64-28 Swez, Prince Wellred, Pure Fali 9
18Dec87-4BM 6f :223 :454 1:121gd 19 118 97¾ 1113 1219 1214½ SchvnevldtCP1 M32000 64-25 QuickSketch,APerfectShm,SoSuM 12
1Jly87-6Pln 5½f :222 :46 1:05 ft 5 118 45 35 47 57 Hummel C R5 Mdn 78-15 Gampord,FlgCommndnt,Reb'sNturl 7
1Jly87—Broke in a tangle
22May87-3GG 4½f :214 :452 :514ft 15 118 7 78½ 48 311 SchvaneveldtCP3 Mdn 86-03 WuzWndr,PrncMtthw,EwokWcktt 10
May 2 Pln 5f ft 1:003 h — Apr 25 Pln 4f ft :481 h — Apr 4 Pln 4f ft :474 h — Mar 31 Pln 5f ft 1:001 h

Jessa Steele — Ch. g. 3, by Fort Ruler—Jess Sandy, by Big Jess
CAMPBELL B C — 118 — Br.—Steele Eileen (Cal) — 1988 4 M 1 0 $1,838
Tr.—Steele Eileen — $12,500 — 1987 0 M 0 0
Own.—Steele Eileen — Lifetime 4 0 1 0 $1,838

17Apr88-1GG 1 :47 1:112 1:371ft 23 118 42½ 21½ 55½ 610 Campbell B C7 M20000 72-11 Raw Force, Mr.Rusty,ClearViewBoy 9
9Apr88-2GG 6f :214 :443 1:091ft 57 118 52½ 44½ 57½ 413½ Campbell B C7 M20000 79-09 Don Mario, J. Zac, Now It's Kris 12
9Apr88—Bumped start, lugged out
18Mar88-2GG 6f :22 :451 1:103ft 22 118 21 21½ 24 28 CmpbellBC4 [S]M12500 78-23 I Got Lucky,JessaSteele,FastHoop 12
11Feb88-2GG 6f :214 :442 1:094ft 44 118 1110 910 1118 1220½ SchvnevldtCP 5 M12500 69-13 MrktThFortn,TzzyDt,OrbtsJstRght 12
11Feb88—Bumped start; wide on turn
May 14 Sol 5f ft 1:04 h — Mar 29 GG 5f ft 1:044 h

Rhythm Of Silk — B. g. 3, by Fleet Tempo—Unspun Silk, by Cari County
HUMMEL C R — 118 — Br.—Beal-Burns-Frisby (Cal) — 1988 3 M 0 0
Tr.—Lonnberg Fred — $12,500 — 1987 0 M 0 0
Own.—Beal & Burns — Lifetime 3 0 0 0

13Apr88-4GG 6f :213 :444 1:104ft 58 118 105½ 1114 — — Lamance C 8 [S]M12500 — — BlckFir,GoodOl'Murry,ImpccblSth 12
13Apr88—Eased
4Mar88-2GG 6f :222 :461 1:131ft 47 118 42½ 41½ 44 610¾ ChapmanTM 10 M12500 62-26 IrishGiant,AppleVerde,NobleVlley 12
4Mar88—Bobbled start
6Jan88-2BM 6f :224 :463 1:14 m 17 118 68½ 611 1018 1021½ ChapmnTM 7 [S]M12500 46-26 Solar Flare, Me 'n J. B.,InTheBuff 11
6Jan88—Ducked in start
May 16 GG 3f gd :352 h — May 5 GG 5f ft 1:012 h — Apr 25 GG 6f ft 1:132 h — Apr 8 GG 5f ft 1:011 h

Don's Penny — Dk. b. or br. g. 3, by Don Victor—Penny Who, by Catchpenny II
THOMAS D S — 118 — Br.—Maniar Dinesh (Cal) — 1988 2 M 0 0
Tr.—Morgan Doug — $12,500 — 1987 0 M 0 0
Own.—Maniar Dinesh — Lifetime 2 0 0 0

24Apr88-4GG 6f :214 :451 1:104ft 65 116 1hd 2hd 910 1217½ Garcia K M1 M14000 68-14 Desert Road,BigDaveAllison,FaliHi 12
24Apr88—Lugged out
2Apr88-2GG 6f :213 :441 1:094ft 58 118 109½ 1116 1118 1117½ Garcia K M8 [S]M20000 72-10 RiseCotton,ArYouMyCsy,Mgnifico 11
2Apr88—Stumbled break
May 6 GG 5f ft 1:004 hg — Apr 13 GG 5f ft 1:00 h — Mar 28 Pln 6f ft 1:132 hg — Mar 21 Pln 5f ft 1:011 h

Peterkin — B. g. 3, by Petrone—Cute Piece, by Pretense
MAPLE S — 118 — Br.—The Hat Ranch West (Cal) — 1988 3 M 0 0 $1,200
Tr.—Tate Richard — $12,500 — 1987 0 M 0 0
Own.—The Hat Ranch — Lifetime 3 0 0 0 $1,200

7Apr88-2SA 1 1/16 :47 1:124 1:463ft 6½ 117 73¾ 109¾ 1018 1028 CastnonAL 7 [S]M32000 42-17 CutiousEgle,WickerBsket,FireGlss 12
7Apr88—Veered out start
10Mar88-4SA 1 1/16 :472 1:131 1:46 ft 5 117 88½ 69 916 918½ CastnonAL2 [S]M32000 52-19 TimothyA.,NothingLft,AdiosPowr 11
10Mar88—Bumped hard start; lugged out 7/8; returned bleeding from nostrils
13Jan88-4SA 6f :22 :453 1:112ft 13 118 107½ 97¾ 67½ 47¾ CastnonAL9 [S]M32000 73-20 Emigrant Gap,Dandyroo,Ir'shJohn 12
May 11 GG 4f ft :481 hg — Apr 30 GG 4f ft :582 h — Apr 24 GG 4f gd :48 h — Mar 31 SA 4f ft :48 hg

He's Beautiful
Dk. b. or br. g. 3, by Erins Isle—Rihuana, by Rigel II
BOULANGER G 118 Br.—Rancho Jonata (Cal) 1988 2 M 0 0
Own.—Schleiger D Tr.—Lippmann Mary $12,500 1987 0 M 0 0
Lifetime 2 0 0 0
26Mar88-2GG 1 1/16 :47 1:11³ 1:44²ft 68 118 12¹⁹ 12²⁸ — — Tohill K S³ [S]M12500 — — Kua Kini, Stand Up Guy, Hey Bob 12
26Mar88—Eased
5Mar88-2GG 6f :21⁴ :45² 1:11³ft 49 116 12¹³ 12¹⁶ 12²⁰ 12²²¾ Tohill K S³ M14000 58-16 L'Cottontail,RaiseCotton,CityBred 12
5Mar88—Bumped hard start
May 14 GG Tr. 5f ft 1:01³ hg May 8 GG 5f gd 1:05⁴ h Apr 30 GG 3f ft :36 h Apr 8 GG 4f ft :51² h

B. J.'s Day
B. c. 3, by Bargain Day—Maud Piggott, by Pampered King II
DIAZ A L 118 Br.—DeMeo Mr–Mrs J F (Cal) 1987 0 M 0 0
Own.—DeMeo Mr–Mrs J F Tr.—Hess R B $12,500
Lifetime 0 0 0 0
May 13 GG 6f ft 1:14⁴ h May 7 GG 5f sy 1:05 h (d) Apr 30 GG 5f ft 1:0?⁴ hg Apr 22 GG 4f ft :47² h

Hey Del
B. c. 3, by Hey Rob—Delicious Pinkie, by Donut King
BAZE R A 118 Br.—Dutton J (Cal) 1987 4 M 1 0 $2,550
Own.—Dutton & Eaton Tr.—Dutton Jerry $12,500
Lifetime 4 0 1 0 $2,550
28Oct87-6BM 6f :22¹ :45³ 1:10⁴sy 6 118 3³ 4⁸ 6¹⁰ 8²⁶¾ Baze R A 2 M32000 58-26 Greager, First David, Co Ack 8
12Oct87-6BM 6f :22² :45² 1:09⁴ft 4 118 31½ 3⁴ 47½ 511½ Lambert J⁶ Mdn 78-18 Clssino,TuneInNextWk,Stt'ltbltdwn 7
27Sep87-9BM 6f :22³ :45² 1:10³ft 2¾ 118 53½ 55½ 99½ 10¹⁰ McHargue D G¹⁰ Mdn 76-10 HndsomHsIt,OvrDuPlsur,S'fTught 12
12Sep87-6Bmf 6f :22² :45³ 1:11²ft *4-5 118 41½ 2¹ 1hd 2¾ Baze R A⁸ Mdn 81-16 Silver Sass, Hey Del, Wonder How 8
May 16 GG 4f gd :50¹ h May 10 GG 6f ft 1:14³ h May 4 GG 5f ft 1:02⁴ h Apr 27 GG 5f ft 1:00¹ hg

Go Gill
Dk. b. or br. g. 3, by To B Or Not—Windy Gill, by Torsion
WALES H 118 Br.—Lefort D G (Cal) 1987 1 M 0 0
Own.—Lefort D G Tr.—Lefort Michel $12,500
Lifetime 1 0 0 0
23Dec87-1BM 6f :23 :46³ 1:11⁴ft 88 118 10⁹½ 10⁹½ 8¹¹ 6¹⁰ Lozoya D A⁴ M12500 70-20 RulrOfMrit,Don'sPrk,Whydididoit 11
May 16 Pln 3f ft :36² h May 9 Pln 5f ft 1:02⁴ hg May 2 Pln 5f ft 1:01⁴ h

Franbo
Dk. b. or br. g. 3, by Loma Malad—Tuderulla, by Orbit Ruler
CHAPMAN T M 118 Br.—Rose R R (Cal) 1988 2 M 0 0 $562
Own.—Capehart & Liebau Tr.—Offield Duane $12,500 1987 0 M 0 0
Lifetime 2 0 0 0 $562
24Apr88-4GG 6f :21⁴ :45¹ 1:10⁴ft 28 118 3¹ 3¹ 3½ 42½ ChapmanTM¹⁰ M16000 82-14 Desert Road,BigDaveAllison,FaliHi 12
17Mar88-4SA 6f :21⁴ :45⁴ 1:11²ft 31 117 3¹ 76½ 9¹⁴ 11¹⁸ CastnonAL¹⁰ [S]M32000 62-20 MowshkDncr,MyB.Tim,MikgrfBrnl 12
May 5 GG 4f ft :48¹ h Apr 19 GG 4f m :50⁴ h Apr 9 SLR tr.t 3f ft :36⁴ h

Exact Image
Dk. b. or br. g. 3, by Exact Duplicate—Be Queenly, by Berseem
MARTINEZ O A JR 118 Br.—Probert Mr–Mrs D (Cal) 1988 4 M 1 1 $2,325
Own.—Lanning C or Lila Tr.—Aubuchon Bill $12,500 1987 2 M 1 0 $880
Lifetime 6 0 2 1 $3,205
24Apr88-4GG 6f :21⁴ :45¹ 1:10⁴ft 3¾ 116 5³ 51½ 10¹¹ 10⁹¾ MartinezOAJr⁶ M14000 75-14 Desert Road,BigDaveAllison,FaliHi 12
24Apr88—Steadied 1/4
7Apr88-6GG 6f :22¹ :45² 1:11¹ft 12 116 7⁶ 57½ 56½ 3³ MartinezOAJr¹ M14000 80-19 Pssino,HurriedPrediction,ExctImg 10
7Apr88—Stumbled start
30Mar88-2GG 6f :22² :46¹ 1:11³ft 6¾ 118 2³ 21½ 11½ 2⁵ MartinezOAJr⁷ M12500 76-16 YankeeDon,ExctImge,MnInChrge 12
5Mar88-2GG 6f :21⁴ :45² 1:11³ft 23 116 2hd 2¹ 9¹² 11²¹½ MrtinezOAJr 12 M14000 60-16 L'Cottontail,RaiseCotton,CityBred 12
11Aug87-3Stk 5½f :22² :46³ 1:05²ft 2½ 118 1¹ 1½ 2½ 2¹ Lozoya D A 7 [S]M16000 89-10 MyMySue,ExactImage,Rito'sBndito 8
11Aug87—Drifted out, brushed at 1/8
22Jly87-3Sol 5½f :22¹ :46 1:04⁴ft 12 118 3¹ 2hd 2² 78½ Judice J C 10 M16000 78-13 StPtrick'sCt,CullnLn,Bloopr'sDrm 10
May 16 GG 3f gd :37² h May 11 GG 5f ft 1:01⁴ h May 4 GG 5f ft 1:03 h ●Apr 22 GG 3f ft :35³ h

Man In Charge
Dk. b. or br. g. 3, by Maui No Ka Oi—Maui Hula, by Distinctive
HANSEN R D 118 Br.—Takitani Mr–Mrs M (Cal) 1988 7 M 2 3 $5,725
Own.—Bongi & Delima Tr.—DeLima Clifford $12,500 1987 3 M 0 0
Lifetime 10 0 2 3 $5,725
27Apr88-4GG 6f :22¹ :45⁴ 1:11 ft 8¾ 118 7⁵ 6⁴ 4⁷ 3¹¹ Tohill K S 12 M12500 73-21 ChangosLst,TizzyDuet,MnInChrge 12
30Mar88-2GG 6f :22² :46¹ 1:11³ft 4¾ 118 67½ 45½ 34½ 3⁹ Tohill K S 8 M12500 72-16 YankeeDon,ExctImge,MnInChrge 12
11Mar88-2GG 1 1/16 :46¹ 1:11 1:43⁴ft 4 118 6⁵ 86½ 68½ 712½ Tohill K S 8 M12500 67-13 GoldenFir,Fiddle'sPlesure,HeyBob 12
11Mar88—Stumbled start
23Feb88-2GG 1 1/16 :46⁴ 1:12 1:47 ft 3¾ 118 3³ 2² 2½ 24½ Tohill K S 2 M12500 59-21 WveToMe,MnInChrg,Ruthl'ssDncr 12
23Feb88—Ducked out start
4Feb88-2GG 6f :22 :45² 1:11 ft 9¾ 118 41¾ 2hd 1hd 2nk Tohill K S 7 [S]M12500 84-10 Pushin'Fte,MnInChrge,VlntinoMio 12
15Jan88-2BM 6f :22³ :46² 1:13²m 2¾ 120 21½ 21½ 2¹ 32¾ Baze R A 8 [S]M12500 69-25 Dck'sSprStr,VlntnoMo,MnInChrg 11
2Jan88-1BM 6f :22² :46² 1:13³sy 17 120 3⁴ 3³ 2hd 41½ Tohill K S 1 M12500 70-26 FrwyChmp,GroussRn,J.W.Woodly 12
2Dec87-2BM 6f :22¹ :45⁴ 1:11⁴sy 42 118 95½ 11¹⁰ 10¹³ 10¹⁵½ ChapmanTM 10 M20000 65-21 Dispeller, Coul Trip,Halley'sStreak 12
2Dec87—Ducked in start
28Nov87-1BM 6f :22² :45³ 1:12 sy 27 118 78¾ 4⁷ 4⁷ 77½ ChapmnTM⁶ [S]M16000 71-33 FrlssDys,MrktThFortn,WthtDrctn 12
28Nov87—Ducked out start
24Oct87-2BM 6f :22³ :46² 1:12 gd 23 118 87½ 8¹⁰ 9¹⁰ 8¹³ Diaz A L⁶ M20000 66-28 DelMrRuler,TwiceTm,TidesOfSinn 12
24Oct87—Bumped start; steadied
May 10 Pln 4f ft :48² h Apr 18 Pln 4f ft :50 h Apr 11 Pln 3f ft :37² h

Please recall, before analyzing, that the more races a maiden has lost at today's level, the more it qualifies for the distinction of "proven loser." Maidens who chronically finish second or third are no closer to the winners' circle than those who run in back of the pack.

Approximate Odds, Post Time

Franbo	3–1
Hey Del	4–1
Exact Image	5–1
B.J.'s Day	7–1
Jessa Steele	9–1
Man In Charge	10–1
Don's Penny	10–1
Peterkin	11–1
Ewok Wickett	15–1
Rhythm Of Silk	50–1
He's Beautiful	70–1
Go Gill	80–1

Comments

Unlikely

1. Proven losers. Ewok Wickett, Rhythm Of Silk, and He's Beautiful have announced clearly that they can't run, having been trounced more than once at today's level.
2. Teasers. Exact Image and Man In Charge are also proven losers, but they have come close often. But being near the lead does not mean being near to a win. After several chances within striking distance close to the wire, these horses have paraded skillfully but uncompetitively in front of the grandstand.
3. No signs. First-time starter B.J.'s Day has only moderate workouts. Go Gill lost only once at today's level, but he ran like a horse that was 88–1.
4. Nearly qualifies. Jessa Steele ran well for six furlongs in his last route, but this horse is a two-time loser at today's level, and other competitors in the same field show stronger signs of improvement.

Many of these horses represent the hopes and dreams of owners who could not afford more expensive animals. Soon, some will be gone forever, never to have won a race. Others will move to pastures where maidens can be entered at three or six thousand dollars. They will win a few small purses, and they will eat just as much as John Henry and Spectacular Bid, and will probably require higher vet bills than their famous and wealthy peers.

Contenders

The four contenders are the only horses in this field that have never lost a race at today's level.

Improvers. Franbo, as a track switch/class drop his last race, showed improved early fractions and improved finish position. He drops another notch today. Don's Penny showed wake-up early fractions when dropping slightly in class. He goes down another step today and adds blinkers.

Layoff pattern match. Hey Del's best race came against straight maidens as a first-time starter! Today he comes back following a layoff. As we have mentioned, a significant trainer/horse form-cycle maneuver concerns the heavily-bet two-year-old coming back after a layoff as a three-year-old for a top trainer.

Track switch/class drop. Peterkin qualifies by this "system." He had run three bad races and now ships and drops. Peterkin is allowed some fair excuses. His first race was competitive, considering the class level, and he ran up against double trouble in his second race before bleeding.

4. Clearly the least likely of these four is Don's Penny. Franbo improved in two dimensions, while Don's Penny's improvement is clearly one-dimensional.
3. Franbo shows no works for two weeks, a serious negative.
2. Peterkin looks terrible, as most track switch/class droppers do. Look at Franbo's improvement under very similar circumstances at 28–1. Peterkin was obviously well bet in his last race, which saw him go on Lasix for the first time.
1. Hey Del is clearly the horse to beat. The only time he was ever in a claiming race cannot count when you evaluate his chances today. In that claimer he ran in the slop and was laid off following the fiasco. This is a classic situation when a horse should run well after a vacation.

	Our Line	Track Odds	Decision
Hey Del	5–2	4–1	Over. Bet.
Peterkin	7–2	11–1	Way over. Bet.
Franbo	5–1	5–2/3–1	Under. No bet.
Don's Penny	6–1	10–1	Over. Bet.

Now we have a problem. Three horses qualify for a wager, but two of them (Hey Del and Don's Penny) offer only a small advantage. If you bet both, the one who is sure to lose will nullify the advantage of the one that may win.

At the same time, Peterkin offers the greatest advantage and clearly must be bet. Between Hey Del and Don's Penny, which is the better investment? Answer: Hey Del, for two reasons:

a. He is our top pick, compared to Don's Penny as a fourth choice.
b. He offers a slightly greater percentage advantage.

	Hey Del	Don's Penny
Our Line	28% (5–2)	14% (6–1)
Track Odds	– 20% (4–1)	– 9% (10–1)
Advantage	8%	5%

This represents my own point of view regarding this type of investment quandary. Other opinions, from respected experts, vary. One says you should use only the horse with the greatest advantage. Another says use the two horses with the highest odds. The decision may seem crucial at the time, but it is not. As long as the player has a positive expectation (advantage), the long-run books will show a profit. In order to avoid spending time and emotions over false controversies, just make sure to be consistent in the way decisions are made.

SECOND RACE **6 FURLONGS. (1.07$\frac{4}{5}$) MAIDEN CLAIMING. Purse $6,500. 3-year-olds. Bred in California. Weight, 118 lbs. Claiming price $12,500.**

Golden Gate

MAY 19, 1988

Value of race $6,500; value to winner $3,575; second $1,300; third $975; fourth $488; fifth $162. Mutuel pool $76,815. Exacta pool $106,664.

Last Raced	Horse	Eqt.	A.	Wt	PP	St	¼	½	Str	Fin	Jockey	Cl'g Pr	Odds $1
7Apr88 ^{2}SA^{10}	Peterkin	b	3	118	5	9	5^{1}	3^{2}	2^{1}	$1^{\frac{1}{2}}$	Maple S	12500	11.30
24Apr88 ^{4}GG^{10}	Exact Image		3	118	11	2	$3^{1\frac{1}{2}}$	2^{2}	1^{2}	$2^{1\frac{1}{2}}$	Martinez O AJr	12500	5.30
28Oct87 ^{6}BM^{8}	Hey Del	b	3	118	8	5	7^{1}	4^{hd}	3^{1}	3^{4}	Baze R A	12500	4.10
17Apr88 ^{1}GG^{6}	Jessa Steele		3	118	2	10	6^{2}	5^{hd}	5^{3}	$4^{\frac{1}{2}}$	Campbell B C	12500	9.30
27Apr88 ^{4}GG^{3}	Man In Charge	b	3	118	12	6	10^{3}	10^{2}	6^{1}	$5^{\frac{1}{2}}$	Hansen R D	12500	10 30
8Apr88 ^{2}GG^{4}	Ewok Wickett		3	118	1	12	11^{1}	11^{2}	10^{3}	6^{hd}	Lambert J	12500	15.30
24Apr88 ^{4}GG^{4}	Franbo		3	118	10	1	2^{hd}	6^{3}	7^{2}	$7^{1\frac{1}{2}}$	Chapman T M	12500	2.90
	B. J.'s Day		3	118	7	11	$9^{1\frac{1}{2}}$	7^{hd}	8^{1}	8^{1}	Diaz A L	12500	7.30
23Dec87 ^{1}BM^{6}	Go Gill		3	118	9	7	12	12	11	9^{1}	Wales H	12500	79.10
24Apr88 ^{4}GG^{12}	Don's Penny	b	3	118	4	3	1^{2}	1^{1}	$4^{1\frac{1}{2}}$	10no	Kaenel J L	12500	10.50
26Mar88 ^{2}GG	He's Beautiful		3	118	6	4	$8^{\frac{1}{2}}$	8^{hd}	$9^{\frac{1}{2}}$	11	Boulanger G	12500	69.60
13Apr88 ^{4}GG	Rhythm Of Silk		3	118	3	8	4^{hd}	$9^{\frac{1}{2}}$	—	—	Hummel C R	12500	49.90

Rhythm Of Silk, Eased.

OFF AT 1:03. Start good. Won driving. Time, :21$\frac{3}{5}$, :45$\frac{1}{5}$, :58, 1:11$\frac{4}{5}$ Track fast.

$2 Mutuel Prices:

5-PETERKIN	24.60	12.40	6.60
11-EXACT IMAGE		8.20	4.40
8-HEY DEL			3.60

$2 EXACTA 5-11 PAID $197.40.

B. g, by Petrone—Cute Piece, by Pretense. Trainer Tate Richard. Bred by The Hat Ranch West (Cal).

PETERKIN, reserved early, moved up on the turn, came out for the drive and closed steadily to wear down EXACT IMAGE. The latter, just off the early pace, loomed a threat in midstretch but could not offer the needed late response. JESSA STEELE lacked the needed rally. MAN IN CHARGE raced wide and showed little. B. J.'S DAY, steadied sharply shortly after the break, lugged well out throughout and was not a threat. DON'S PENNY set the pace for a half mile and stopped suddenly. RHYTHM OF SILK had brief speed, stopped and was eased.

Owners— 1, The Hat Ranch; 2, Lanning C or Lila; 3, Dutton & Eaton; 4, Steele Eileen; 5, Bongi & Delima; 6, Jon-Don Farm; 7, Capehart & Liebau; 8, DeMeo Mr-Mrs J F; 9, Lefort D G; 10, Maniar Dinesh; 11, Schleiger D; 12, Beal & Burns.

Trainers— 1, Tate Richard; 2, Aubuchon Bill; 3, Dutton Jerry; 4, Steele Eileen; 5, DeLima Clifford; 6, Cotton Perry; 7, Offield Duane; 8, Hess R B; 9, Lefort Michel; 10, Morgan Doug; 11, Lippmann Mary; 12, Lonnberg Fred.

Scratched—Dynamic Navajo; Tizzy Duet (27Apr88 ^{4}GG^{2}); Stand Up Guy (28Apr88 ^{1}GG^{6}); Valentino Mio (28Apr88 ^{1}GG^{8}).

ON THE LINE

So concludes the workshop portion of *Thoroughbred Cycles*. The danger of "textbook" examples is that they tend to fit too neatly with the theory they represent. At the same time, real-life manifestations of the same theory will often be cloudy and confusing. For this reason, I have avoided the neat fits and presented cases that demand judgmental and/or creative thinking. I justify this approach because horse-race handicapping is much more an art than a science, and the scientific components of handicapping are not deterministic.

Meteorology and economy are sciences more akin to horse-race analysis than chemistry or algebra. That is why weather experts and economists have often been reduced to bumhood with their forecasts. Weather reports no longer say "rain tomorrow," but rather, "tomorrow, a sixty percent chance of rain."

By having highlighted workshop races that offered more than one scenario or possible outcome, I've tried to make an implicit point that purely mechanical solutions are rare in horse-race handicapping. By having presented form-cycle contenders that lost as well as those that won, the reader is in the position of discovering elimination factors the author might have missed. Most horseplayers who read books on horse racing are critical thinkers who are capable of carrying the ideas beyond the point where the author situates them.

Those are my arguments for minimizing the more obvious, expository examples of form-cycle handicapping from the workshops. With such a stance, I take the risk of misleading the reader into thinking that this methodology will not point out perfect textbook cases in which one horse stands clearly above the rest of the field. Only Art's Angel (Workshop Nine) offered a textbook situation. Please do not be misled: many of the examples in the expository portions of the book became "best bets" of the day.

If I excluded from the workshops races such as the tenth at Golden Gate, May 14, 1988, it was because the obvious analysis took all the work out of the potential workshop. In this race, Soon To Escape

faced a field in which every horse was a recent loser at the $6500 level. At the same time, Soon To Escape fit our form-cycle methodology within two separate major parameters:

1. Track Switch/Class Drop (see Radicals and Revivalists, Chapter 6)
2. Master of a unique trade, high-percentage success rate in northern California, terrible record in southern California (see Craftsmen/Craftswomen, Chapter 4)

His second by a nose at 8–1 (5Feb88, GG) illustrated how the switch of racing circuit had already produced a radical performance revival.

On May 14 Soon To Escape won by five lengths. Before they reached the stretch, he had escaped from the rest of the field. He only paid $5.40 to win, but as an only contender, he would have been 1–2 in our line, making his 8–5 payoff a true bargain. Cases such as this are best left to expository chapters, lest the workshops be converted into a chorus of amens.

While the workshops represent a cross-section of form-cycle situations, in the infinite art of handicapping, the universe of thoroughbred cycles cannot be reduced to a simple structure. Hopefully, the reader has captured the joy of discovery which is the delight of form-cycle analysis.

Above all, this approach allows us to collect big on horses that "don't figure" to the public. Just think, when the race is over and there's a long line to collect, we may not be there; but when the line is short and most of our adversaries are left shaking their heads in disbelief, we are more likely to show up and cash tickets.

Note: After completing the workshops, some readers may wish to reread expository chapters that amplify or clarify concepts illustrated in workshop races. For handy cross-reference, see Addendum C.

Part V

Handicapping
and
Anti-handicapping

CHAPTER 13

Thoroughbred Futures

HANDICAPPING AND ANTI-HANDICAPPING

THROUGH THE WORKSHOP PROCESS we have experienced a methodology in which form cycle is the primary handicapping factor. Among the many possible handicapping persuasions, this represents the "center," a "moderate" format that finds a role for all other handicapping factors.

At the two extremes from our center position are the "conservative" approach, which uses form cycle only as a supporting player, and the "radical" method, which obliterates fundamental factors and elevates form cycle to a totally dominant role. My basic affinity is obvious, having dedicated most of this study to a perspective of balance between traditional and radical styles. However, no perspective that promises profits should be ignored, so here we shall explore both ends of the spectrum. Before we begin, let's review the three perspectives for form cycle in horse-race handicapping.

Conservative. The form-cycle factor is secondary and is used simply as an adjustment, a "variant" to basic factors such as speed, pace, class and trip.

Moderate. Form cycle is the orchestrator of all other factors. In this eclectic approach, all pertinent information is used, with the form factor acting as a foundation.

Radical. Form cycle is an only factor, and all comparative horse-to-horse analysis is rendered irrelevant. Future horse and trainer performance is projected on the basis of past cycles, with no regard for opposing horses.

Both conservative and moderate approaches are here labeled as "horizontal." Imagine a starting gate with relative probabilities standing side by side. The radical approach is said to be "vertical" in that it projects the onward progress of a horse/trainer career with no consideration for other entries in a race. This is most clearly explained in a diagram, in which horse number 5 (or trainer number 5) is being considered. Comparative analysis (conservative and moderate approaches) takes place at the time of the race. "Futures" analysis, the radical approach, was accomplished clearly in advance of this race, which only represents the beginning of a long-term investment.

We call the futures analysis "anti-handicapping" because it literally cuts across the grain of traditional, comparative handicapping.

Let us proceed, then, first with conservative, comparative use of performance cycle as it modifies classical factors, and then with the radical, anti-handicapping approach, which experiments with futures investments.

MOMENTS IN TIME

The following running lines come from the same track, same variant, same time of year:

Horse A	7F	$1^{1\frac{1}{2}}$	$1^{1\frac{1}{2}}$	$1^{2\frac{1}{2}}$	$1^{1\frac{3}{4}}$
		22	44.1		1:21.4
Horse B	7F	$2^{\frac{1}{2}}$	1^{hd}	1^{4}	$1^{5\frac{1}{4}}$
		21.3	43.3		1:21

These two horses meet today at six furlongs. Which one would you choose? (No tricks.) The answer is obvious: Horse B. It has superior early speed and better late speed. Horse B should win by about four lengths, according to these numbers.

The crowd did not see it so clearly. As a matter of fact, they made Horse A 4–5 and Horse B 16–1. The public is not dumb, and must have many reasons for its behavior. In this case, several possible explanations arise as to why the bettors rejected the above numbers. First, B was a filly and A a colt. But Winning Colors was one of many fillies that have beaten the males, and the crowd made her the favorite in the 1988 Kentucky Derby. A second possible explanation is that A was a four-year-old while B was only three; another legitimate reason. However, three-year-olds beat older horses more than just occasionally, and some conditions actually favor younger horses.

Probably the primary reason for the betting public at the 1987 Breeders' Cup, Hollywood Park, to have made the slower Groovy 4–5 against the faster Very Subtle, 16–1, was the fact that the running lines I have highlighted for A (*Groovy*) and B (*Very Subtle*) were not from their most recent races. The lines we have just used came from three months before the Breeders' Cup Sprint, from the month of August at Saratoga.

Now let us examine the lines that represented races immediately prior to the historic November 21, 1987, confrontation between Groovy and Very Subtle.

Groovy	Bel 10Oct87	1^1	$1^{2\frac{1}{2}}$	$1^{3/4}$
		22.4	45.1	1:22.3
Very Subtle	AP 31Aug87	3^1	3^{nk}	$2^{3\frac{1}{2}}$
		22.1	44.2	1:25

I suppose the Breeders' Cup crowd saw two things: (1) Groovy won, while Very Subtle lost to an inferior horse; (2) Groovy had recency, while Very Subtle was coming into the encounter with a nearly three-month layoff. From a pace-handicapping perspective, though, Very Subtle's Arlington Park race might be totally excused, because the second quarter was run just as quickly as the first quarter, a rare occurrence in horse racing, one which is likely to burn out a horse, especially at seven furlongs.

From this analysis I hope to make a point as to how form cycle affects practitioners of other handicapping methodologies, since the form factor was one reason I went back two races instead of one in comparing these two rivals. What good is a perfectly crafted Andrew Beyer speed figure taken from the wrong race of the past performances? What good if an esoteric pace calculation based on the highly successful Sartin Methodology is wasted on the wrong pace line? Only a keen awareness of form cycle allows handicappers of pace, class, or speed persuasions to choose the particular race or period of the past that best projects today's performance level.

The Very Subtle–Groovy confrontation is the classic example where a layoff leads to a sharper race than recency. On the one hand, Groovy's three races prior to the Breeders' Cup event represented a downward trend. Facing essentially the same field each time, including his regular follower, Sun Master, the margin of victory for Groovy was collapsing like a balloon running out of air:

18July87	6½ lengths
23Aug87	1¾ lengths
10Oct87	¾ lengths

On July 18 Moment of Hope was too far behind at the wire to see Groovy's tail, but on October 10 the same rival could have bitten Groovy in the ribs as they crossed the wire. And Sun Master, a horse whose purpose on earth is to make Groovy look good, was getting closer each time.

Very Subtle, on the other hand, figured to do well after a layoff since she had proven she could run fresh, having won as a first-time starter. As we have described, first-time-starter winners belong to the category of horse that has the best race-after-layoff record.

Very Subtle's second-quarter Arlington fraction was more an indication of an improving horse than her finish position was an indication of a declining horse. Therefore, it was fair to use Very Subtle's best effort for our pace line or speed figure. For the declining Groovy, we were giving the benefit of the doubt by going back two races, and conveniently we were left with a *comparable*, a same-distance/same-track/same-variant comparison.

Farmers Almanac

By choosing the Saratoga running lines, we also confront the age and sex issue. Crop cycles of that period (crops of horses) added evidence that Saratoga races offered a legitimate comparison between Very Subtle and Groovy. The *crop* of older male sprinters (the Groovy chasers), led by Sun Master, the Salieri of horse racing, represented a weak harvest season. On the other hand, the fillies that were beaten by Very Subtle at Saratoga came from a fertile field. Up the Apalachee, second by 5¼ lengths to Very Subtle, came right back to win a stakes race next time out. Sacahuista, a distant fifth to Very Subtle, came back to win the Breeders' Cup Distaff against older fillies and mares.

All of this is presented as a case for going back two races in the past performances of Very Subtle and Groovy in order to make a fair *numerical* comparison. At Saratoga, in different races, the filly ran four lengths faster than the colt. The Breeders' Cup Sprint saw Very Subtle beating her more popular rival by . . . exactly four lengths. The carbon copy was worth $34.80 for each $2 invested!

EIGHTH RACE
Saratoga
AUGUST 23, 1987

7 FURLONGS. (1.20⅖) 8th Running THE FOREGO HANDICAP (Grade II). Purse $100,000 added. (Plus $25,000 Breeders' Cup Premium Awards.) 3-year-olds and upward. By subscription of $200 each, which should accompany the nomination; $1,000 to pass the entry box, with $100,000 added. The added money and all fees to be divided 60% to the winner, 22% to second, 12% to third and 6% to fourth. Weights, Tuesday, August 18. Starters to be named at the closing time of entries. A trophy will be presented to the winning owner, trainer and jockey. Closed Wednesday, August 5, 1987 with 15 nominations. Breeders' Cup Fund Awards to: Groovy, Purple Mountain.

Total purse $137,600. Value of race $132,850; value to winner $81,060; second $31,522; third $13,512; fourth $6,756. Nominator Awards $2,250. $2,500 Reverts to Breeders'Cup Fund Mutuel pool $160,939, OTB pool $78,998. Exacta Pool $158,840. OTB Exacta Pool $171,776.

Last Raced	Horse	Eqt.	A.	Wt	PP	St	¼	½	Str	Fin	Jockey	Odds $1
18Jly87 8Bel1	Groovy		4	132	5	1	1½	1½	1½	1¾	Cordero A Jr	.60
11Aug87 9Mth4	Purple Mountain	b	5	113	1	4	2¹	3½	2hd	2¾	Migliore R	8.90
8Aug87 6Sar3	Sun Master		6	118	6	5	5½	4⁴	3½	3²	Romero R P	8.90
1Aug87 11Suf8	Vinnie the Viper	b	4	116	3	3	4hd	6	5	4²¾	Santos J A	12.40
1Aug87 11Suf3	Sunny Feet		4	117	2	2	3½	2hd	4³	5	Thomas D B	19.60
9Aug87 8AP1	Taylor's Special		6	123	4	6	6	5¹	—	—	Day P	2.40

Taylor's Special, Pulled up.

OFF AT 5:37, Start good, Won driving. Time, :22, :44⅘, 1:08⅘, 1:21⅘ Track fast.

$2 Mutuel Prices:			
5-(E)-GROOVY	3.20	2.80	2.20
1-(A)-PURPLE MOUNTAIN		5.00	3.20
6-(F)-SUN MASTER			2.80

$2 EXACTA 5-1 PAID $22.00.

Ch. c, by Norcliffe—Tinnitus, by Restless Wind. Trainer Martin Jose. Bred by Robinson Marshall T (Tex).

GROOVY showed speed from the start, remained well out from the rail while making the pace, settled into the stretch with a good lead and was under lefthanded urging to hold sway. PURPLE MOUNTAIN, close up along the inside early, remained a factor into the stretch and continued on gamely while coming out under pressure during the late stages. SUM MASTER bumped lightly after the start, made a run between horses leaving the turn but weakened during the drive. VINNIE THE VIPER came out after the start forcing TAYLOR'S SPECIAL into SUN MASTER and was finished early. SUNNY FEET raced well out in the track while remaining a factor to the upper stretch and tired. TAYLOR'S SPECIAL, bumped following the start, was racing well out in the track when he stumbled badly nearing the stretch and was pulled up.

Owners— 1, Prestonwood Farm; 2, Wimpfheimer J; 3, Pillar Farms; 4, Lazer II Stable; 5, Murphy J P; 6, Lucas W F.

Trainers— 1, Martin Jose; 2, Sedlacek Woodrow; 3, Lukas D Wayne; 4, Klesaris Robert P; 5, Scanlon Robert N; 6, Mott William I.

EIGHTH RACE
Saratoga
AUGUST 6, 1987

7 FURLONGS. (1.20⅖) 62nd Running THE TEST (Grade III). Purse $150,000 Added. Fillies. 3-year-olds. By subscription of $300 each, which should accompany the nomination; $2,400 to pass the entry box, with $150,000 added. The added money and all fees to be divided 60% to the winner, 22% to second, 12% to third and 6% to fourth. Weight: 121 lbs. Winners of two races of $50,000 since April 15, 3 lbs. additional. Non-winners of a race of $50,000 in 1986-87 allowed 3 lbs.; of a race of $25,000 since April 15, 5 lbs.; of a race of $15,000 in 1987, 7 lbs. Starters to be named at the closing time of entries. Trophies will be presented to the winning owner, trainer and jockey. Closed with 34 Nominations Wednesday, July 22, 1987.

Value of race $193,800; value to winner $116,280; second $42,636; third $23,258; fourth $11,628. Mutuel pool $176,934, OTB pool $196,879. Exacta Pool $167,148. OTB Exacta Pool $316,161.

Last Raced	Horse	Eqt.	A.	Wt	PP	St	¼	½	Str	Fin	Jockey	Odds $1
12Jly87 8Hol4	Very Subtle		3	121	6	4	2½	1hd	1⁴	1⁵½	Valenzuela P A	3.60
19Jly87 8Bel2	Up the Apalachee		3	121	7	5	3½	3⁴	2⁴	2³½	Santos J A	3.10
19Jly87 3Bel3	Silent Turn		3	121	10	11	11³	7½	5½	3hd	Antley C W	f-20.40
6Jun87 7Bel12	Bound	b	3	114	2	14	14	13½	8½	4½	Maple E	13.40
19Jly87 8Hol5	Sacahuista	b	3	121	11	3	5hd	4½	4hd	5hd	McCarron C J	a-6.90
4Jly87 7AP1	Ms. Margi		3	114	5	10	10½	10½	6hd	6³¾	Fires E	f-20.40
19Jly87 8Bel4	Wee Dram		3	116	12	8	9²½	9²	10²	7nk	Bailey J D	26.10
18Jly87 9WO1	Ruling Angel		3	121	4	7	4¹	5¹	9¹	8¹¾	Day P	13.60
6Jun87 7Bel4	Buryyourbelief		3	121	9	12	13¹	11½	11¹	9hd	Velasquez J	17.30
11Jly87 9Mth4	Tappiano		3	121	1	13	7½	8hd	7½	10¾	Cruguet J	6.70
11Jly87 7Bel1	Doubles Partner		3	118	14	2	12hd	12½	12hd	11no	Davis R G	18.70
23May87 8Bel10	Devil's Bride		3	121	13	1	1½	2½	3½	12¾	Vasquez J	7.80
11Jly87 9Mth5	Chic Shirine		3	121	3	9	8hd	14	13²½	13³½	Cordero A Jr	a-6.90
19Jly87 8Bel1	Firey Challenge	b	3	121	8	6	6½	6hd	14	14	Migliore R	16.80

a—Coupled: Sacahuista and Chic Shirine.
f—Mutuel field.

OFF AT 5:19. Start good, Won driving. Time, :21⅗, :43⅗, 1:08, 1:21 Track fast.

$2 Mutuel Prices:			
5-(F)-VERY SUBTLE	9.20	4.60	4.40
6-(G)-UP THE APALACHEE		4.40	4.60
13-(J)-SILENT TURN (f-field)			8.00

$2 EXACTA 5-6 PAID $36.40

Ch. f, by Hoist the Silver—Never Scheme, by Never Bend. Trainer Stute Melvin F. Bred by King J Howard (Ky).

VERY SUBTLE, promising early while saving ground, headed DEVIL'S BRIDE going a half and drew off brisk handling after entering the stretch. UP THE APALACHEE, a factor to the stretch, was no match for the winner while besting the others. SILENT TURN moved up outside horses approaching the stretch but lacked a late response. BOUND, off slowly, finished with good energy while racing very wide. SACAHUISTA raced well out in the track while remaining within striking distance to thestretch and weakened. MS. MARGI split horses during the drive but lacked a rally. WEE DRAM failed to be a serious factor. RULING ANGEL showed some early foot but was finished before going a half. BURYYOURBELIEF was always outrun. TAPPIANO, hustled along after breaking slowly, was finished early. DOUBLES PARTNER was outrun after breaking alertly. DEVIL'S BRIDE was used up vying for the lead with very subtle. CHIC SIRINE was finished early while saving ground. FIERY CHALLENGE tired badly.

Owners— 1, Rochelle B; 2, Simon J M; 3, Diaz D; 4, Claiborne Farm; 5, Beal & French Jr; 6, Cox E A Jr; 7, Pen-Y-Bryn Farm; 8, Sam-Son Farm; 9, Bray D S Jr; 10, Frances A Genter Stable; 11, Oxford Stable; 12, Oak Cliff Stable; 13, Alexander E G; 14, Wootton Mary L.

Trainers— 1, Stute Melvin F; 2, Arceneaux George; 3, Penna Angel; 4, Stephens Woodford C; 5, Lukas D Wayne; 6, Bollero Joseph M; 7, Whiteley David A; 8, Day James E; 9, Barrera Lazaro S; 10, Schulhofer Flint S; 11, Hirsch William J Jr; 12, Gosden John H M; 13, Lukas D Wayne; 14, Dutrow Anthony W.

FIRST RACE
Hollywood
NOVEMBER 21, 1987

6 FURLONGS. (1.08⅘) 4th Running of THE BREEDERS' CUP SPRINT (Grade I). Purse $1,000,000. 3-year-olds and upward. Weights, 3-year-olds, 124 lbs.; older, 126 lbs. Fillies and mares allowed 3 lbs. Value of race $1,000,000. Value to winner $450,000, second $225,000, third $108,000, fourth $70,000, fifth $50,000, sixth $10,000. Nominator Awards: Stallion, winner $25,000, second $12,500, third $6,000; Foal, winner $25,000, second $12,500, third $6,000. Stallion awards will be paid only to the nominators of fully eligible stallions. Owners who supplement horses to Breeders' Cup Day races will be eligible for the Foal Nominator's Award in the case of a 12 per cent supplementary nomination or both the Foal Nominator's Award and the Stallion Nominator's Award in the case of a 20 percent supplementary nomination. in accordance with the Breeders' Cup/European Breeders' Fund cross-registration agreement, nominater's awards will not be paid to horses eligible through the E.B.F. All unpaid nominator's awards will remain the property of Breeders' Cup Limited. Supplementary Nominations: ZANY TACTICS and ZABALETA. 4th DAY. WEATHER CLEAR. TEMPERATURE 73 DEGREES.

Total purse $1,000,000. Value of race $913,000; value to winner $450,000; second $225,000; third $108,000; fourth $70,000; fifth $50,000; sixth $10,000. $87,000 in Foal and Stallion Nominator Awards. Mutuel pool $848,204.

Last Raced	Horse	Eqt.A.Wt	PP	St	¼	½	Str	Fin	Jockey	Odds $1
31Aug87 9AP2	Very Subtle	3 121	11	2	1 ½	1 1½	1 3½	1 4	Valenzuela P A	16.40
10Oct87 7Bel1	Groovy	4 126	1	3	3 2½	2 2	2 1½	2 1¾	Cordero A Jr	.80
16Oct87 8Kee1	Exclusive Enough	3 124	10	6	6 ½	4 ½	4 1½	3 1	Day P	25.10
8Nov87 10BM2	(S)Zabaleta	4 126	7	7	7 1½	5 1	3 hd	4 1	Pincay L Jr	7.90
31Oct87 9Pha1	High Brite	3 124	13	4	4 1	6 1	6 ½	5 1¼	Santos J A	97.10
16Oct87 8Kee5	Taylor's Special	6 126	12	8	8 2½	8 2	8 1	6 nk	Vasquez J	71.30
7Nov87 6Haw4	Slyly Gifted	4 126	2	9	12 ½	9 ½	9 1	7 no	Meza R Q	111.70
31Oct87 1Eng4	Sylvan Express	4 126	9	11	10 2½	11 5	10 1½	8 1¾	Cauthen S	f-66.70
4Nov87 8SA1	(S)Zany Tactics	6 126	3	5	5 hd	7 1½	7 hd	9 nk	Kaenel J L	3.00
4Nov87 8SA2	On The Line	3 124	4	13	9 hd	10 hd	11 5	10 ½	Romero R P	26.40
31Oct87 7Aqu1	Pine Tree Lane	5 123	6	1	2 hd	3 1½	5 ½	11 7	McCarron C J	9.30
25Oct87 4Fra12	Sharp Romance	5 126	8	12	13	12 2½	12 5	12 6	Wigham M	f-66.70
17Oct87 5Eng2	Governor General	4 126	5	10	11 hd	13	13	13	Eddery P	f-66.70

f—Mutuel field.
(S) Supplementary nomination.

OFF AT 11:18. Start good. Won driving. Time, :21⅕, :44, :55⅘, 1:08⅘ Track fast.

Official Program Numbers

$2 Mutuel Prices:

9-VERY SUBTLE	34.80	8.80	5.00
2-GROOVY		3.20	2.60
8-EXCLUSIVE ENOUGH			7.80

Ch. f, by Hoist the Silver—Never Scheme, by Never Bend. Trainer Stute Melvin F. Bred by King J H (Ky).

VERY SUBTLE sprinted to the front before going a quarter after getting away in alert fashion, quickly drew away in the upper stretch and remained well clear through the final furlong while under a drive. GROOVY pressed the early pace along the inner rail after a good start, could not keep pace with VERY SUBTLE in the drive but held on well enough to gain the place. EXCLUSIVE ENOUGH, never far back, came into the stretch four wide and could not gain the necessary ground in the drive. ZABALETA, outrun early after veering out and being jostled and checked in the initial strides, mildly menaced from the inside early in the drive but flattened out. HIGH BRITE, in contention early, lacked the needed response in the last quarter. TAYLOR'S SPECIAL was wide down the backstretch and six wide into the stretch. SYLVAN EXPRESS, devoid of early speed after breaking slowly and being jostled and shuffled back in the opening strides, found his best stride too late. ZANY TACTICS, outrun early, entered the stretch five wide and lacked the needed response when called upon. ON THE LINE bobbled at the start to get away slowly. PINE TREE LANE, off alertly and prominent early, gave way. SHARP ROMANCE broke slowly and was jostled and shuffled back in the initial strides. GOVERNOR GENERAL broke a bit awkwardly and was six wide into the stretch. SABONA (1) WAS WITHDRAWN. ALL WAGERS ON HIM IN THE REGULAR AND DAILY DOUBLE POOLS WERE ORDERED REFUNDED AND ALL OF HIS PICK NINE SELECTIONS WERE SWITCHED TO THE FAVORITE GROOVY (2).

Owners— 1, Rochelle B; 2, Prestonwood Farm; 3, Scharbauer Dorothy; 4, Robert Holmes a' Court; 5, Allen J; 6, Lucas W F; 7, Franks John; 8, Johnson Mrs R A; 9, Brunette Vera C; 10, Klein E V; 11, Young W T; 12, SheikhMohammedAlSabah; 13, Richards R.

Trainers— 1, Stute Melvin F; 2, Martin Jose; 3, Van Berg Jack C; 4, Gosden John H M; 5, Lukas D Wayne; 6, Mott William I; 7, Hronec Philip; 8, Mitchell Philip; 9, Heap Blake; 10, Lukas D Wayne; 11, Lukas D Wayne; 12, Brooks W G A; 13, Ellsworth David R.

Scratched—Sabona (21Oct87 8SA1).

After the fact, both speed and pace handicappers may use these charts to exemplify their crafts. But before the fact, it was a question of knowing which race(s) to use as comparables. Here, form cycle would be a vital tool for the practitioners of those classical methodologies. At the same time, class handicappers needed to consider that their foundation was not frozen in time, that the rigid class structures of the medieval era of kings had no resemblance to the fluid class structures of the sport of kings.

Postscript

At the moment Very Subtle went to post in the 1988 Breeders' Cup Sprint at Churchill Downs, no horse had ever scored back-to-back Breeders' Cup victories. Very Subtle was trying to be the first, and against the boys! This time things did not look good for our heroine. Instead of Groovy, she had to face Gulch, a horse that had defeated her in her home territory. Both Very Subtle and Gulch had gone through various low periods in their performance cycles when forced to run in series of route races, so they shared a common trait in their career histories.

Very Subtle ran a very creditable race at 15–1, finishing fourth, ahead of some very good horses in a field of thirteen, close enough to the leaders to not feel any disgrace. She also collected a salary for her efforts that most human beings would never dream of. The best horse in the race may have been the Canadian, Afleet, who got squeezed back at the start by more than fifteen lengths and closed furiously to finish third.

Later on the same card of races, the Breeders' Cup record that was missed by Very Subtle was reached by the French horse, Miesque. In the Breeders' Cup Mile, Miesque became the first horse to score back-to-back victories in these championship races. Miesque's rival, the English horse Warning, failed to get into contention. Warning's rider blamed the track condition. But a new thoroughbred cycle seemed to be turning. For the past few years the English horses appeared to outclass their French rivals. But the same day in which Miesque outran Warning, thousands of miles away four English horses traveled to Paris to compete in the Prix Perth Handicap, a Grade 3 event frequently dominated by English horses. One of the participants had the best "Time Form" rating of all entrants. None of the four English horses managed to finish in the money.

For U.S. handicappers this cycle is of great importance, since we will frequently be exposed to stakes races in which there will be both English and French horses. For years English horses got extra points; now we give the edge to the French.

CLASS CONSCIOUSNESS

Consider the following chronology for Horse X and fill in the blanks:

Grade 1	15–1	third place
Grade 2	16–1	third
Allowance	2½–1	

Stks level	14–1	second
Grade 1	25–1	second, nk (bobbled)
Allowance	4½–1	

Grade 2	77–1	second, nose (bumped hard start, checked final turn)
Grade 2	60–1	third

Now that you have filled in the blanks, let's start all over again. Does your opinion change at all if I tell you that Horse X is none other than *Schiller*?

The sequence of races above represents all of the in-the-money finishes during a fifteen-month period in Schiller's infamous career. Considering that the two allowance races were not preps, a normal horse—conscious of its "class"—would have won both allowance races. But not Schiller, who finished second at 2½–1 and third at 4½–1. One could say that Schiller possesses a very unique horse "personality"; he is devoid of "class consciousness."

Oblivious to the category of his company, he has the same table manners when eating crepes at Alphonse's as when dining on Big Macs. It might be the ambassador from Switzerland at his side, and he'd still say, "Hey pal, pass me the potatoes." Schiller's uncommon character is an image of his form cycle. His form cycle is the basis of an argument that points out the allowance events and tells class handicappers, "Don't bet because *class is not at issue*." Here's a horse who loves to run, but his principles are opposed to a competitive lifestyle. Some days he wakes up and doesn't feel like going to work. They take him there anyway, put him on the track, he looks around, sees a group that seems too caught up in the rat race, and decides to take the opposite point of view and be uncompetitive. If you've seen an old English movie called *The Loneliness of the Long Distance Runner*, you'll picture what I mean.

Let Schiller serve as the example to class handicappers that a horse's form cycle, as represented by its running personality, will be a vital modifying factor. Schiller loves to run around the track, loves to feel successful existentially, but is not concerned with beating his colleagues. Schiller's behavior is contradictory only to those who view horse society as one-dimensional and dogmatic; but horse society is pluralistic, and each distinct type of lifestyle, which is manifest in a performance cycle, will either modify or transform the projections of speed, class, and pace methodologies. Within his own scheme of things, Schiller's way of living is not at all contradictory.

Is Schiller a nonconformist or does he fit within a particular category of cycle? I wish I had a hundred-race sample to prove my theory, but unfortunately there is a very small colony of horses that live by the "Schiller Principle." It appears that this principle is a product of trainer manipulation. A certain type of trainer runs her/his horses at above their inherent class level, over and over again, until they are no longer intimidated by the nobility. I put the "her" before the "his" because Vivian Pulliam, Schiller's accomplice, is one of those trainers.

One particular trainer who often abides by the Schiller Principle is Jack Van Berg. Several years ago, for example, Van Berg had a horse by the name of Paradies, who was accustomed to finishing in-the-money against the best horses, but when dropped in class, did not improve. Continuing in the same subculture of the Van Berg stable is Vilzak, once second to the great Manila, once third by 1¼ to Snow Chief; yes, the same Vilzak who could only finish in the money, without winning, in allowance races, at 2–3 and 7–5; and yet as a 2 for 27 horse upset Forlitano's dream of winning a Grade 1 event.

Following his failures against lesser horses, Vilzak upheld the Schiller Principle by finishing in the money in stakes races at 12–1 and 40–1. Like his stablemate, Alysheba, who had only won one race prior to the Kentucky Derby, Vilzak entered the Breeders' Cup Turf race with only 2 wins in 26 starts, and the betting public took that record into consideration when making him 147–1. He responded with an amazing fourth-place finish, which in the context of a fourteen-horse field merits being labeled an in-the-money finish.

If Vilzak had dropped in class following that Breeders' Cup fete, I guarantee you he'd have lost. But he found another fourteen-horse field at Grade 1 and won the race. That victory surprised a number of people, including Vilzak, who, at least temporarily, stopped the trend and began to lose again. He still has a chance to become 4 for 49, like Schiller, and make a lot of money at the same time.

The Schiller Principle allows for occasional victories, while its prevailing objective is the destruction of the class structure. This is accomplished by doing reasonably well at high levels while failing in the lower-class neighborhoods. The loss of class consciousness is accomplished by hanging out in the ritzy neighborhoods until the instincts of intimidation that come from horse genes are nullified by the environment.

```
Vilzak                              B. h. 5, by Green Dancer—Zippy Do, by Hilarious
                                    Br.—Bedford & Ford (Cal)                    1987 18  1  2  6        $555,102
 CORDERO A JR                 120   Tr.—Van Berg Jack C                         1986 10  2  1  2         $35,886
Own.—Rosenblum H T                  Lifetime   28  3  3  8  $590,988            Turf 23  3  3  5        $552,338
13Dec87-8Hol  1½Ⓣ:4832:0222:27 fm  14 126  107¼ 73¾ 41½ 1nk  Day P4     Trf Cp Iv   86-16 Vilzak,Forlitano,PoliticalAmbition 14
    13Dec87—Grade I; Shuffled back 1st turn; lugged in late
21Nov87-6Hol  1½Ⓣ:4712:0012:242fm 147 126  59  63½ 34  44½   VelsquzJ 10 Br Cp Trf   95 — Theatrical,Trempolino,VillageStrII 14
    21Nov87—Grade I
8Nov87-8SA    1  Ⓣ:4711:12 1:37 gd  40 115  107¾106¼ 63½ 35  Baze G 3    Cl Kstr H   85-10 DoubleFeint,DeputyGovrnor,Vilzk 10
    8Nov87—Wide into stretch
23Oct87-8Kee  1⅛Ⓣ:4831:1421:523fm  12 126  65  42½ 21½ 31½   BrfldD 7  Kee Brd Cup  77-21 StormOnTheLoos,UptownSwll,Vilzk 9
16Oct87-7Kee  a1⅛Ⓣ          1:55 fm 7-5 114  65  55½ 3½  2½    Day P1      Aw25300     95-04 Mister C., Vilzak, Aggies Best 7
26Sep87-10LaD 1⅜Ⓣ:4821:38 2:134fm  43 113  98½114½ 98½1011   DsrmxKJ9    La D H      86-10 Iades, Ifrad, Great Communicator 12
    26Sep87—Grade III
4Sep87-8AP    1  Ⓣ:50 1:1441:372gd  6½e114  77  75¼ 64½ 46    SthME5  Bud Brd Cup  82-23 PersianMews,MisterC.,VernonCstle 7
18Jly87-9Mth  1 1/16Ⓣ:4641:11 1:413fm 4¼e112 611 63¾ 62½ 55½ McClWH8 OceanportH  91-06 SoverignSong,FlingGlint,Spllbound 8
    18Jly87—Grade III
7Jun87-8Bel   1⅛:47  1:11  1:481ft   8½ 111  58½ 68½ 617 619¾  BaileyJD3 Nssu Cty H  66-22 LcOuimet,FobbyForbes,JohnsTrsur 6
    7Jun87—Grade II
4Jun87-5Bel   1⅜:49  1:381 2:183sy  *2-3 117  25  24  36  312½  Bailey J D1 Aw45000    74-21 Dark Flood, Dance Caller, Vilzak 4
  ●Feb 23 Hol 7f ft 1:274 h          Feb 17 Hol 5f ft 1:024 h
```

BAD TRIPS

Examine the following two trips. In both instances the public reacted to the bad trip by expecting an improved race next time out. As a result, both P and Q were bet more heavily, against the exact same competition, in their next race.

Horse P	8^{11}	7^{4}	$4^{1½}$	$3^{3½}$
	(steadied 5½/crowded ⅜)			
Horse Q	7^{7}	5^{8}	4^{5}	$2^{1¾}$
	(veered out start/checked ⅜)			

Horse P is none other than *Eliminante*, who abides by no social rules except for the Schiller Principle. Like Schiller and Vilzak, Eliminante races in a neighborhood where he doesn't belong and wins smaller prizes at opportune moments. Unlike Schiller, whose advantage is mainly at the beginning of races, Eliminante, as well as Vilzak, tend to "pick up pieces," waiting like a vulture for rivals to be decimated in the early going and then passing in the stretch.

Since Eliminante's running "personality" depends less on his own assets and more on the misfortunes of others, a clean trip tomorrow will not necessarily lead to an improvement over the bad trip of today. In Eliminante's bad trip, outlined above, he finished behind the second-place horse, *Euphrates*. In his good trip the next time out, he finished third once more, again behind the same Euphrates. (The subplot is the same as before. Euphrates is another Eliminante rival who has not been able to win since his duels with the Eliminator.)

Horse Q had the best of excuses in his second-place finish. His bad start was atypical, the only time he'd ever had trouble near the gate. He was forced to check at a most unfortunate moment, precisely as he was making a bold move. But Horse Q, better known as *Freeskate* in Workshop Nine, was at the point of becoming a *declining* horse. The day of Freeskate's bad trip was precisely *the day he was supposed to win*. That was it! His big chance, squandered.

With declining horses as well as with pop-up types, a bad trip today in no way projects an improved race tomorrow. We call on the venerable *Ernie King* to demonstrate the trip factor turned upside down. Observe one of the better sequences in Ernie's up-and-down life history.

4Nov87	wins, *very wide in drive*
17Oct87	second, clean trip
3Sep87	wins, *took up at* ¼
7Aug87	second, clean trip

Ernie King loves old winding roads and hates the freeway. He wins in spite of bad trips and loses in spite of good trips.

We have now seen Very Subtle and Groovy demonstrate how performance-cycle awareness can refine speed and pace analysis. Schiller and Vilzak have illustrated how one type of form cycle requires modifications of fundamental class handicapping. And finally, Eliminante, Freeskate, and Ernie King have demonstrated how trip analysis without a form-cycle foundation may result in a bad trip for the handicapper.

When Very Subtle lost subsequent races out of her specialty, as a sprinter in routes, and when she was beaten by her inferiors when she belatedly returned to her forte, she demonstrated how the class factor is fluid and is subject to adjustments based on form cycle.

FUTURES

The Very Subtle–Groovy conflict is fought within the confines of handicapping tradition. Speed, class, and pace handicappers are using form cycle as a perspective from which to operate.

This would be a comfortable ending to *Thoroughbred Cycles*, concluding that classical methodologies are safe and secure and that the *routine* of seasoned handicappers needs only be subjected to an adjustment in perspective. But in the structures of the past are always found the seeds of radical change.

Can form-cycle handicapping make a total departure from the tenets of Ainslie, Beyer, Davidowitz, Quinn, Quirin, and Sartin? If the *Farmers Almanac* can anticipate future trends, can form-cycle analysis be extended into a similar realm which would open the door to a futures market for thoroughbred bettors?

Nevada casinos offer future betting for big races, but the action is too limited for steady investment and the "vigorish" (take) is so steep that only clairvoyants could be successful in the long run. Future betting on horses is far more precarious than sports' futures; an injured horse is out of the race before they go to post and the money is gone, while an injured football or baseball player can be compensated for by other members of a team.

If there is to be meaningful thoroughbred futures betting, horseplayers must create their own market, removed from the orbit of casino sucker bets. Let's venture out to the fringe, explore new possibilities, keep the form-cycle methodology open-ended, as it should be with the infinite art of horse-race handicapping. That means we will take some chances in this final chapter, leave some ideas with rough edges, leave the chance for the involved and critical reader to write a final chapter. Let's explore.

First step, questions. How do the performance cycles in this book suggest possible futures-market investments?

1. Can horses that won as first-time starters be bet automatically when they eventually race following a layoff? My sample suggests this will be possible if we can incorporate a trainer-intention factor, eliminating obvious prep races, such as those at the wrong distance or on the wrong surface.

2. With a relatively low percentage of winners, and yet with a phenomenal flat-bet profit, is the track-switch/class-drop combination a long-term winner? Eighty percent says yes,

but 20 percent says no. If we can iron out a few wrinkles, we will be able to leave simple instructions with an agent in any town with race-book betting from around the country or at any of the racing circuits with an abundance of shippers.

3. Can lists of horses for courses be arranged in such a way that, at the end of one year's meet, we will already have our potential bets for the next year? I have already had a fair measure of success in this area, but I've had to intervene occasionally on the day of the race with judgmental decisions. It has not yet been entirely mechanical. My research suggests several possible restrictions, but there is always the fear that one restriction too many may hurt more than help, if it eliminates horses that end up winning at the biggest prices. I have found that "systems" with too many requirements will make qualifying horses "look too good" and will seriously reduce the average mutuel by having ruled out precisely the type of horses that systems, better than handicapping, are likely to discover. In this context I rate the various horse-for-course restrictions.

   a. Require the proper distance, perhaps the precise distance, of last year's win(s) . . . *fair, but needs exceptions.*
   b. Require fast track or mud match with last year . . . *fair.*
   c. List only multiple winners from last year . . . *too restrictive* (but multiple winners can receive larger wagers).
   d. Require wins over the course for two consecutive years . . . *too restrictive* (but can receive larger wagers).
   e. Require previous wins over the course to have been at 5–1 or up . . . *fair* (here you're excluding low-priced horses but including potential long shots).
   f. Exclude horses that won at other tracks, since they do not qualify, in the pure definition, as horses for course . . . *fair but may need exceptions.* Horses that have won at tracks other than our target track are more likely to receive public attention and thereby go off at lower prices. Their victories at the target track may be less from affinity for locale and more from horses' own internal performance cycle.

   In the realm of horse for course, another problem arises for the futures bettor: what happens when there are two or more qualifying horses in the same race? The best way to resolve this and the above questions is to establish an odds criteria for distinct types of horses. For example, a horse that last year was only one for three at the target track but paid $100 would require at least 10–1 odds this year, while a proven commodity that was a multiple winner last meet should be worth an investment at 2–1 this time around.

Remember, these are only problems for the futures investor who will be leaving a stake with an agent. Horse-for-course handicapping at the track is simply a question of proper value, and all of the above contradictions are resolved with a reasonably accurate betting line.

4. Can horses Ernie King and Smooth Bid, for example, be "purchased," as when one buys shares of stock, once they have shown signs of having a pari-mutuelly profitable career? This is a most radical proposal, one that demands attention in pages to come. For the moment, let's say that with so many horses yielding a flat-bet profit (17 percent of all horses), all we need to do is identify the characteristics of the potential profit maker. Easier said than done, but we shall make a gallant effort.

5. Can the "masters of their trade," such as Lichi and Auspiciante, be identified in a way that permits futures investment? The prototype of the steady horse excels in its trade for two years, on the average, especially when not overraced. This will allow the futures investor the chance to step in on time and to get off before the trend has subsided. A potential agent would have to be aware that if the odds drop, as they did with Tamtulia, the investment is withdrawn; also, that if the horse is overworked—Far East, for example—the two-year investment period must be drastically reduced. These are the wrinkles that need some light ironing; the foundation still resides in identifying an unusual horse specialty, one which will not become obvious to the public. We are looking for a specialty that is not in the condition book every week, an infrequent type of race that forces our craft specialist to race in less advantageous contexts and thereby hide her/his consistency.

6. Can trainers, such as Brian Mayberry and William Spawr, be invested in over extended periods of time and not just during hot streaks? Although all trainers encounter hot and cold periods, a certain type of trainer will be profitable

in the long run. This subject, too, deserves special attention. Stay tuned.

7. Can trainer short cycles fit within the parameters of futures betting? This is purely a question of form, rather than content. Previous chapters have clearly demonstrated the pari-mutuel power of the trainer short cycle. As we shall see, the futures format will be limited to those infrequent, short events that must be waited for over long periods of time. Short cycles occur infrequently in clusters during short spans of time. Long cycles occur frequently, over extended periods. We shall see, in the case of Canney's Comet, the example that combines the long and the short: long wait, short/few occurrences.

8. Can something as facile and absent of handicapping intervention such as the five-year-old-gelding late-bloomer period be invested in without further modifications? Here, more than ever, the futures mode of investment seems to be an antithesis of handicapping convention. This "factor" resists the intervention of logical adjustments, which only serve to hurt its average mutuel to a greater degree than they increase percentage of winners.

For one moment refer back to the workshops. In the first, third, and fifth workshops, we paid attention to the five-year-old-gelding factor. Workshop Five saw three of these potential late bloomers go to post: Gallant Sailor, Little Red Cloud, and War Debt. The last of these still needed racing. Little Red Cloud took some of our money this time but had already shown a revival typical of this age/sex group. While Gallant Sailor was a noncontender, not fitting the turf surface, he showed four in-the-money finishes at big odds as a five-year-old gelding, including a second at 55–1.

Workshop Three saw us spend money on Dennis D., thus taking one unit away from our winning long shot. Dennis D., too, had clearly displayed improved form as he went into the expected late-bloomer period. But the key figure in this triumphant and yet tragic event was Lonesome Dancer, also a five-year-old gelding. Here was a horse that did not quite fit within conventional handicapping standards. The public sensed this by making Lonesome Dancer 87–1. While yours truly collected triumphantly on Rafael's Dancer, at $39.60, I tragically underestimated the power of the late-bloomer factor. When Lonesome Dancer finished second, he paid more to place than my horse did to win; the calamity (within the good fortune) expands as the minimum $2 exacta involving my choice along with the five-year-old gelding pays $1324.40.

Workshop One saw three five-year-old geldings: Balmondancer, who had already profited by the late-bloomer cycle, as well as contenders Agent Todd and Dishonorable Guest. The latter won, paying $14.60, joining his two rivals as geldings who have found a new lease on life in their fifth year.

In the case of Dishonorable Guest, rather than combine with a traditional handicapping factor, the late-bloomer age/sex factor matched with another wake-up catalyst, the track switch/class drop. In the case of Lonesome Dancer, opportunistic investment procedures should have included the five-year-old gelding; second place in exactas is rarely one's second handicapping choice and is more difficult to predict, because it usually results from more esoteric rationale. What a perfect use of the five-year-old-gelding factor.

However, in the realm of futures betting, none of the above situations could have been anticipated. My suggestion is to not tamper with the factor from a handicapping perspective, but rather, to look for a subset of the subset. Odds is a good nonhandicapping parameter. From my sample, the most vulnerable odds groups are at the bottom and the top. At even money and below, this factor shows a loss. At above 20–1 its percentage of winners plunges. There's still a profit at the high odds because of the two extraordinary payoffs. Those payoffs appear to be atypical for this particular factor. To find out, you'll need a 500-race sample, (a) from your local track, which (b) includes five-year-old geldings exclusively with odds of 21–1 and up. That particular odds group is not a comfortable futures proposition because, even if it is profitable in the long run, it is vulnerable to long losing streaks. By having excluded even money and below as well as 21–1 and up, we have a more sensible futures investment.

This discussion has taken us to the crossroads between handicapping tradition and radically new investment possibilities. This is not a new form of handicapping, nor is it your typical "point system." Rather, it acquires the characteristic of *anti-handicapping*. Hopefully, it will approach the style of a stock-market investment more than the precarious commodities market. Even though our workshops employed some unusual analytical techniques, inspired by various horse and trainer cycles, they remained within traditional handicapping practices in that they employed the comparative approach which measured the relative chances of horses in a field. In thoroughbred futures, horses are bet on with no regard to the ability or level of the competition; they are assumed to be competitive, not by judging the day's card, but by having evaluated the qualifying horse's past history.

The whole concept of cycles suggests the potential for a thoroughbred-futures type of investment. A whole new investment portfolio may be drawn up well in advance of the *Racing Form* past performances, even before the track secretary has written the condition book. The possibilities of this new betting style are enormous. As it stands now, making a living at the track is more time consuming than a full-time job. Thorough handicapping may call for sixteen hours a day, two shifts: first shift, watch the reruns, read the literature, analyze the day's card, attend the races, observe the trips and tote-board trends; second shift, enter the day's records, compile trainer and track-bias statistics, do a preliminary evaluation of the next day's card.

Thoroughbred-futures investment allows horseplayers the luxury of spending time with the family, raising a child or two, jogging a few miles a day, reading an occasional good novel, hiking in the mountains. Most pros don't have family obligations.

Even with no family there is still the number-one threat to competent horseplayers to contend with: burnout. With thoroughbred futures, burnout is no longer an issue. Simply leave your betting guidelines with a trained agent, and while your horses are running, you can be camping in the alpine lakes of Yosemite. As the bankroll grows, you can visit the Alps.

Traditional handicapping is *labor intensive;* that is its greatest limitation, especially for those of us who would like to be well-rounded, three-dimensional human beings who make occasional incursions into the other world, the one that has not seen the glory of horse betting. The fact that we are somewhat isolated from other species of human beings, living on a separate channel of existence, limits our own potential and leaves the world "culturally deprived" of our art. Yet the labor-intensive nature of playing the horses forces us into this cultural ghetto.

Thoroughbred futures, on the other hand, is *capital intensive* and liberates the handicapper/laborer from the daily grind; not to abandon horse racing, but to allow for more time for creative aspects of handicapping research. This is precisely the type of research most crucial for profits, the type of study that is sometimes bypassed by the daily grinder in order to cut corners. Capital-intensive horse wagering also allows time for nonracing activities. Good in themselves, these activities also help keep us *freshened* for our next assault of the pari-mutuel windows.

Thoroughbred futures implies that horseplayers have the insight and technology to foresee future events by understanding the phases and trends inherent to race-horse careers and trainer performance. If astronomers can foresee, through knowledge of orbits, when Jupiter and Mars will be in proximity or when an obscure comet will return, why can't we anticipate this year a few of next year's winners?

No one is suggesting that we abandon the racetrack, only that we have available a type of horse wagering that will allow for vacations from the daily pari-mutuel confrontations. It is better to be there 150 days a year *intensely* than to be there 200 days a year and miss all kinds of great bets because we had no time to do thorough research; to miss an important exacta because of a lapse in concentration caused by overwork.

HORSE FUTURES

Select one hundred horses *at random* and bet an equal amount on each one in its next ten races. Statistically we know ahead of time that in the long run, with an approximately 17 percent take, 83 of these horses should produce a flat-bet loss while 17 should achieve a flat-bet profit. The whole investment should produce a 17 percent loss.

Now examine the 83 losing horses and the 17 winning horses. What characteristics separate the flat-bet winners from the losers? Among the money losers are horses with a high win percentage, who attract action and therefore have such a low average mutuel that they are unprofitable. Also among the money losers are the can't-win horses, the ones whose main function in life is to fill fields and the more talented sorts who manage to finish in the money but are not competitive enough to prevail in the stretch drive.

The flat-bet winners tend to be horses that are, indeed, competitive but do not have a high percentage of victories. They get the job done, but stay out of the spotlight while doing so. They keep a low profile. Like millions of their human counterparts, they produce in excess of the recognition they receive. They are often more competent than some of their peers who receive all the glory. They are like Western artists whose work never makes it to the New York museums and galleries.

For the flat-bet winner, *average mutuel surpasses win percentage* as a primary prerequisite for success. The other prerequisite is the ability to win without gaining recognition, the skill of not attracting attention, the knack of appearing unattractive to the public. For the first time in the history of horse-race handicapping, *name* becomes a factor, as we shall shortly see. You can't find horses with the words "bold" or "royal" in their name who earn a flat-bet profit; in our democratic society, machismo and nobility remain as influential vestiges of medieval times. I challenge you to find a horse with the word "gallant" or "prince" in its name who has earned a profit for its bettors. These horses attract too much action, as the name factor exerts a subliminal influence over many an otherwise competent handicapper.

The Ballad of Fracoza

In southern California many people of Hispanic origin attend the races. In an area where Spanish was the original language and street and city names are often in the Spanish language, many people who are not of Latin origin learn Spanish. The name "Fracoza" is a play on the word "fracaso," which means "failure." Any person who knows Spanish will associate the horse Fracoza with failure.

Fracoza greets the New Year in 1987 with a 2 for 10 record, with double-digit victories. Two for 10 is enough to show competence, not enough to attract a lot of attention. In 1987 this gelding wins four races, paying off at odds of 7½–1, 6½–1, 11–1 and 6½–1. Three of those wins come in succession. Any other horse on a similar binge would have received more betting attention.

On February 21, 1988, Fracoza wins again, this time paying

off at 8–1. He had already shown the form-cycle characteristic of putting three victories together, but in his next race he still goes off at 5–1 for another double-digit victory. He goes for the "hat trick" for the second year in a row, and in his next race he receives even less recognition, racing with odds of 8¼–1. What do you have to do to receive the glory you've earned, Fracoza?

Fracoza wins again. If you'd have invested in him in 1987, you'd have earned a profit of 250 percent. His '88 return is even higher! Certainly other factors must have had some impact in creating such a high average mutuel, but Fracoza's ignoble name earns a big chunk of the credit.

Bad Grammar Leads to Good Profits

At one point in his career, *Core A Apple* ran ten straight races without finishing out of the money. During that stretch he earned his maiden victory at 8½–1 and came right back in an allowance race to win by ten lengths at 5½–1. If his name had been pronounceable, he might have paid less. In a mass demonstration in support of grammatical purism, New Yorkers boycotted Core A Apple at the betting windows.

When this colt completed his tenth race, he had compiled a record similar to that of Fracoza, 2 wins in 10 starts. [At least Core A Apple doesn't make my typewriter beep.]

We pick up Core's career in his thirteenth race. Always in the money, his twelfth race was his debut on the turf, an encouraging third-place finish. So they've brought him back on the grass, and it is logical at the same class level to expect an improvement, now that he's gotten a feel for his new surface. The crowd lets him go to post at 26–1. He takes the lead, in this 1¼ mile event, never quite shaking loose of the second horse. In the stretch he's still got the lead by a neck, and at the wire it's too close to call.

The photo goes against Core A Apple, but considering the odds, it was an effort worthy of horses named "Valiant" and "Noble." This should certainly be enough to convince the crowd to change its mind, or does our hero have to change his name? Bold Core? Or perhaps Gallant Apple.

Core A Apple's next race is in the slop. He had won his allowance race by ten lengths, *in the mud*, so he doesn't lack credentials for today's race.

When the gates open, Core A Apple is last out, while his final

Fracoza — Ch. g. 5, by Messenger of Song—Long Issue, by Long Position
DELAHOUSSAYE E — 116 — Br.—Cozza F (Cal) — 1988 6 3 0 0 $72,650
Own.—Ferguson Mrs J K — Tr.—Richardson Thomas F — 1987 20 4 1 3 $78,150
Lifetime 36 9 2 4 $172,350

15Apr88-7SA 6f :21⁴ :45 1:10 m 6¾ 114 21½ 21½ 51½ 53¾ Pedroza MA 2 Aw55000 84-21 Rconnotrng,Don'sIrshMlody,PsnPt 6
3Apr88-7SA 1 :45³ 1:10³ 1:36²ft 8½ 117 11½ 1½ 1½ 11½ DelahoussyeE 6 100000 86-18 Fracoza, Gorky, Red And Blue 8
23Mar88-7SA 6½f :21² :43⁴ 1:15²ft 5 119 3² 3³ 2³ 1no DelhoussyeE 4 Aw43000 93-18 Fracoza, GallantSailor,RightRudder 5
23Mar88—Off slowly,bumped
21Feb88-6SA 6½f :22¹ :45² 1:16⁴ft 7¾ 117 1hd 2hd 1hd 1² DelhoussyeE 7 Aw35000 86-21 Fracoza,DanceForLee,RedAndBlue 10
7Feb88-5SA 1⅛ :45³ 1:10³ 1:43³ft 14 117 1½ 2hd 43½ 711½ Castanon AL 5 Aw38000 72-16 Fancy Oats, Shigamba,RedAndBlue 9
10Jan88-5SA 7f :22² :44⁴ 1:22¹ft 4½ 116 1¹ 1¹ 2½ 53½ Castanon AL 2 Aw35000 86-15 ReEnter,Fanticola,Buckland'sHalo 10
27Dec87-5SA 6½f :21⁴ :44⁴ 1:16³ft 7½ 117 11½ 1½ 11½ 4² Castanon AL 3 Aw35000 85-17 WndwoodLn,TmForSkrt,RdAndBl 10
13Dec87-5Hol 7f :22 :45 1:22³ft 4½ 115 53½ 54½ 8¹² 916½ Castanon AL 7 Aw36000 74-13 TddyBrHug,OrchrdSong,LoclsOnly 10
25Nov87-7Hol 6½f :21² :43⁴ 1:15³ft 8¾ 116 2hd 2½ 1½ 2½ Castanon AL 2 Aw28000 99-13 Reconnoitering,Fracoz,OrchrdSong 7
8Nov87-5SA 1 :46³ 1:11³ 1:38¹gd 9 1115 1¹ 3¹ 67½ 614½ Gryder A T 8 Aw33000 63-25 Grand Vizier, Captain Valid, Khalil 9
May 10 SA 5f ft 1:01 h — May 3 SA 5f ft :59² h — Apr 25 SA 5f ft 1:00⁴ h — Mar 30 SA 5f ft 1:02 h

Fracoza — Ch. g. 4, by Messenger of Song—Long Issue, by Long Position
GRYDER A T — 1115 — Br.—Cozza F (Cal) — 1987 16 4 0 3 $69,925
Own.—Ferguson Mrs J K — Tr.—Richardson Thomas F — 1986 10 2 1 1 $21,550
Lifetime 26 6 1 4 $91,475

25Oct87-5SA 1⅛ :46 1:10² 1:42³gd 11e 1125 21½ 21 11 32¾ Gryder A T 8 Aw32000 85-19 Light Sabre, Midnight Ice, Fracoza 8
11Oct87-7SA 1⅛ :45¹ 1:09³ 1:42²ft 14 1125 1hd 2½ 3³ 3⁶ Patton D B 8 Aw33000 83-14 NoMarker, Valiant Cougar,Fracoza 9
27Sep87-10Fpx 1⅛ :46 1:10³ 1:43 ft 33 117 11½ 2hd 3³ 45½ FrndAL 3 ⓈC B Aflbgh 90-13 ForignLgion,Rcognizd,LstCommnd 9
7Sep87-9Dmr 1 :44⁴ 1:09³ 1:35 ft 24 116 2¹ 3³ 7⁹ 8¹⁵ Fernandez A L 5 62500 78-14 He'sASaros,IdelQulity,LstCommnd 9
7Sep87—Troubled trip
8Aug87-10LA 6f :21¹ :44² 1:10¹ft 11 119 10²⁴ 10²⁰ 9²⁰ 911¾ Mena F 9 ⓈDn Bnto 80-12 StepSon,Extranix,He'sADncingMn 10
6Jun87-9Hol 1 :44⁴ 1:10¹ 1:37¹ft 16 116 3½ 85½ 8⁸ 816½ Stevens G L 5 80000 61-17 LstCommnd,AmricnLgon,SoctyRod 8
6Jun87—Bumped hard start
29May87-7Hol 6½f :22¹ :45¹ 1:16⁴ft 11 119 52¾ 34½ 35½ 34½ Stevens G L 1 80000 92-16 MyFvoriteMomnt,Hydrosttic,Frcoz 6
29May87—Lugged out final 1/2
16May87-7Hol 7f :22¹ :45¹ 1:22²ft 9 1155 52¾ 75½ 7¹¹ 712¾ Gryder A T 3 Aw25000 79-13 Superoyale,Wtch'nWin,SocietyRod 7
16May87—Lugged out; checked 3 1/2
3May87-5Hol 7f :22 :45 1:23¹ft 6½ 1105 51¾ 4¾ 1¹ 12¾ Gryder A T 2 Aw22000 88-15 Fracoza, Baby Slewy, Mondanite 7
20Apr87-3SA 1⅛ :46¹ 1:10³ 1:44¹ft 11 1115 2½ 2hd 1² 1¾ Gryder A T 5 50000 80-17 Fracoza, Poley, Double Sheng 6
Nov 4 SA 5f sl 1:05³ h — Oct 21 SA 5f ft 1:03¹ h — Oct 17 SA 4f ft :51 h — Oct 7 SA 5f ft 1:02² h

Fracoza — Ch. g. 4, by Messenger of Song—Long Issue, by Long Position
CASTANON A L — 116 — Br.—Cozza F (Cal) — 1987 5 2 0 0 $23,175
Own.—Johnson W R — Tr.—Arena Joseph — $40,000 — 1986 10 2 1 1 $21,550
Lifetime 15 4 1 1 $44,725

3Apr87-5SA 6½f :22 :45³ 1:17²ft 6½ 116 2hd 1½ 1³ 1⁴ Castanon A L 11 25000 83-17 Fracoza, Hurricane Hec, Pegus 11
17Mar87-7SA 1⅛ :46 1:10² 1:42⁴ft 11 117 21½ 3⁴ 6⁹ 714¾ ValenzuelPA 3 Aw31000 73-16 PrinceO'Fire,It'sNotMyJob,Athlone 9
17Mar87—Lugged out.
26Feb87-5SA 1⅛ :45² 1:10² 1:44 ft 5 115 11½ 13½ 2hd 45½ Solis A 8 c25000 76-22 Cold, Exalted Bubble, Julie'sMark 10
7Feb87-9SA 1⅛ :46 1:10³ 1:43³ft 7½ 115 12½ 1² 12½ 12¾ Olivares F 8 16000 83-14 Fracoza, Restage, Tiffani's Toy 9
18Jan87-1SA 7f :22¹ :45¹ 1:24³ft 7 115 95½ 106¾ 98½ 98¾ Olivares F 4 25000 68-19 Bizeboy, Trento, Superb Moment 12
18Jan87—Off slowly, wide
29Nov86-1Hol 6f :22 :45³ 1:10⁴ft 5 117 5⁴ 65½ 65½ 67¾ DelahoussayeE 2 32000 81-12 AnotherBloom,Cbriome,GorgSlptHr 7
29Nov86—Broke in, bumped break, wide 3/8, stretch
9Nov86-5Hol 6f :22 :45¹ 1:10 ft 5¾ 116 53½ 5⁵ 6⁸ 58½ Olivares F 8 40000 84-16 Lans Manus, RosesAreReb,Sebucan 8
31Oct86-6SA 6f :21² :44³ 1:09³ft 8½ 116 63½ 5⁴ 45½ 47½ Olivares F 11 50000 82-16 MischievousMtt,Jimed,RosesArRb 11
8Sep86-3Dmr 6f :21⁴ :45 1:09 ft 3¾ 116 54¾ 68½ 8¹³ 79½ Olivares F 5 62500 83-14 Notoriety,UrbnCowboy,Bo'gerMgic 9
8Sep86—Lugged out badly; took up at 3/16, wide into stretch
15Aug86-3Dmr 6f :21⁴ :45² 1:09³ft *5 116 92½ 3½ 2½ 12½ Olivares F 12 40000 90-12 Frcoz,SprbMomnt,Mybrry'sMdnss 12
15Aug86—Wide 3/8 turn
Mar 28 SA 5f ft 1:00¹ h — ●Mar 10 SA 4f ft :46³ h — Feb 18 SA 4f ft :48¹ h

odds are being computed at 9–1. Eleven lengths out at the half-mile of this 1⅛ mile event, by the six-furlong mark he is thirteen lengths back. Now he is making a bold move and the race caller is obligated to repeat his name without stuttering. In the stretch he has taken the lead and is now attempting to duplicate his previous ten-length win. Maybe then he will gain some recognition. He sloshes across the wire, winning by nine lengths. Core A

THOROUGHBRED CYCLES

Apple, another horse of big pari-mutuel profits who will never be nominated for horse of the year. The racing establishment never gives out awards for horses according to their profitability, thus reducing the chance that good products might get tainted with publicity.

Perfec Travel

The typewriter has beeped again. How do I tell it that bad spelling increases return on investment? Perfec Travel does not fit into the pattern of 2 wins in the first 10 career starts; his career resembles more that of the late bloomer. But because of his name, he becomes a potential member of the same exclusive club of flat-bet-profit horses where Core A Apple hangs out. It is May 7, 1988, Hollywood Park, eighth race, and there are several reasons relating to form cycle why Perfec Travel has a chance to win at 36–1.

1. The horse has won his last race, up at Golden Gate. Twice in his illustrious career, he has put two wins back to back (August 25–September 7, 1985, and October 1–October 11, 1986).
2. He has paid off at huge prices before, including a 7–1 and a 53–1 victory. Whether it's the discouraging name or the ability to win when not looking good in the past performances, it is evident that one long-shot victory can be considered a *credential* for a future big win.
3. Four of his 9 wins come as a shipper; for Perfec Travel, being on the road is a peak experience. He hangs out in the same pool halls as his buddy, Hesa Frequentflyer.
4. He's earned the right to be labeled a late bloomer.

Perfec Travel doesn't quite fit with his colleagues in this chapter but for the fact that the trajectory of his career makes him a horse that must always be considered, regardless of comparative handicapping conclusions. My colleagues Brohamer and Mitchell had more traditional reasons for liking Perfec Travel on this particular occasion, having projected improving pace figures, the same type of ascending numbers that had led to repeat wins twice before.

Perfec Travel paid $74.40 to win and continued with a pari-mutuel profit that far exceeds the percentage of profit of the most powerful multinational corporations. He deserves front-page coverage in *The Wall Street Journal*.

Improvised profits

Dallas Cowboys, "America's Team"; Coca-Cola, America's beverage; jazz, America's art form. The one art form born in the United States that has spread to the rest of the world is jazz music, which in no way approaches the popularity of the Cowboys and Coke. First time I heard a jazz concert on the Fourth of July was in Spain. Coltrane is more of a legend in France and Germany than in his own country. Most people in the United States either ignore jazz or dislike it.

So along comes a horse named *Jazz Player*. He pays off at 7¾–1 as a maiden, and the next time he wins, he pays $100. Like Fracoza and Core A Apple, Jazz Player finishes his tenth career race with a 20 percent win record, 2 for 10. Also like his two colleagues, he has suggested that in the future he will be profitable by having paid off in double figures in his first two races.

But Jazz Player's next win misses double figures by a dollar. His name is supposed to ward off enough bettors to ensure a high average mutuel. He now looks like a formful horse and his odds should go down. But they don't. He comes right back with two more wins, at 4–1 and then at 11–1. Jazz musicians are not heroes in the public consciousness, so Jazz Player gets the job done before a small club of bettors.

The names of these horses seem to tell part of the story, but the statistics they yield place the improvised lines into a full score. Research into horse futures provides encouraging but not conclusive findings.

Concept

1. We want horses that have displayed competence without being sensational. Don't consider can't-win horses.
2. We want horses that have proven to pay big prices, have proven to be underestimated by the betting public.
3. We want a sample of horses from different tracks, different parts of the country, a completely random sample with criteria that are *arbitrary but sensible*.

FIRST RACE
Del Mar
AUGUST 19, 1987

6 FURLONGS. (1.07⅗) CLAIMING. Purse $10,000. 3-year-olds. Weight, 120 lbs. Non-winners of a race since July 1 allowed 2 lbs.; a race since June 1, 4 lbs. Claiming price $16,000; if for $14,000 allowed 2 lbs. (Races when entered for $12,500 or less not considered.) 43rd DAY. WEATHER CLEAR. TEMPERATURE 68 DEGREES.

Value of race $10,000; value to winner $5,500; second $2,000; third $1,500; fourth $750; fifth $250. Mutuel pool $129,833. Exacta pool $111,626.

Last Raced	Horse	Eqt.A.Wt	PP	St	¼	½	Str	Fin	Jockey	Cl'g Pr	Odds $1
30Jly87 3Dmr11	Jazz Player	3 109	2	9	8¹	7¹½	4hd	1½	Cisneros J E5	14000	48.60
5Aug87 1Dmr6	Forcefully	b 3 116	7	7	5¹½	5½	5hd	2½	Delahoussaye E	16000	5.10
15Jly87 5Hol3	Bold Royale	3 118	4	1	5¹½	4²	3¹½	3¹½	Meza R Q	16000	4.40
15Jan87 5SA10	Nicks Irish	b 3 116	10	2	2hd	1hd	1hd	4nk	Stevens G L	16000	4.20
5Aug87 1Dmr2	Chocolate Balls	b 3 116	6	10	10	9¹	8⁴	5¹½	Ortega L E	16000	6.80
5Aug87 1Dmr4	Cremerie	3 109	5	8	9¹½	8¹	7hd	6hd	Gryder A T5	14000	9.80
5Aug87 1Dmr9	Gotta Smoke	3 111	9	5	4²	3²	6¹½	7¹½	Magallon P5	16000	8.00
1Aug87 3Dmr12	Little Paces	b 3 113	1	3	1½	2hd	2½	8¹½	Patton D B5	16000	4.80
15Jly87 5Hol11	Sporting Dan	b 3 116	8	6	7½	10	9²	9⁸	McCarron C J	16000	12.50
17Jun87 2Hol12	Baku Baby	3 116	3	4	3¹½	6½	10	10	Baze R A	14000	18.80

OFF AT 2:02. Start good. Won driving. Time, :22⅕, :45⅘, :58⅘, 1:11⅘ Track fast.

Official Program Numbers

$2 Mutuel Prices:				
	2-JAZZ PLAYER	99.20	30.60	11.80
	7-FORCEFULLY		7.40	4.40
	4-BOLD ROYALE			3.60
	$2 EXACTA 2-7 PAID $626.00.			

B. g, by Pianist—Fancys Pride, by Sir Khalito. Trainer Arena Joseph. Bred by Weiss Mr-Mrs C F (Cal).

JAZZ PLAYER, outrun early, was steadied in midstretch when momentarily blocked, angled out coming to the sixteenth marker, got the lead in the final sixteenth and proved best FORCEFULLY, outrun early, came into the stretch five wide and finished willingly. BOLD ROYALE, within easy striking distance early had a short lead between calls in the final furlong but could not outfinish the top two. NICKS IRISH vied for the lead to midstretch and weakened a bit. CHOCOLATE BALLS trailed early and was unable to gain the needed ground in the drive. CREMERIE was outrun. GOTTA SMOKE, wide while close up early, advanced to engage for the lead leaving the three-eighths pole, entered the stretch four wide and lacked the needed response in the drive. LITTLE PACES vied for the lead to the furlong marker and weakened. SPORTING DAN, wide early, was five wide into the stretch. BAKU BABY vied for the lead for three furlongs, faltered and was not persevered with late when far back.

Owners— 1, Banche Mr-Mrs N C; 2, Korey & Robinson; 3, Layne A F; 4, Belmonte & Gardina; 5, Tinsley Patricia J; 6, Alcrte Sta-Hdig-O'Brdvich; 7, Vee Jay Stable; 8, Beckett J-F-Judy L; 9, Dorfman Mrs C; 10, Felton Ellen Joan.

Trainers— 1, Arena Joseph; 2, Harte Michael G; 3, Layne Arthur F; 4, Mitchell Mike; 5, Tinsley J E Jr; 6, Bell Thomas R II; 7, Johnson Patricia L; 8, Bernstein David; 9, West Ted; 10, Tetzlaff Terri.

Jazz Player * 4
HAWLEY S — **116**
Own.—Bot n' Bob Stable
B. g. 4, by Pianist—Fancys Pride, by Sir Khalito
Br.—Weiss Mr-Mrs C F (Cal) — 1988 2 1 0 1 $17,250
Tr.—Dorfman Leonard $40,000 — 1987 13 3 1 1 $31,375
Lifetime 18 5 1 2 $85,375

28Feb88-9SA 1¹⁄₁₆ :46³ 1:11 1:43⁴gd 4½ 116 31 32½ 43½ 33½ DelahoussyeE6 c32000 78-18 Bananas, Claramount, Jazz Player 8
28Feb88—Bobbled start; crowded 3/8
31Jan88-9SA 1¹⁄₁₆ :46² 1:12 1:45¹ft 11 116 1010 73½ 2hd 1hd DelahoussayeE2 25000 75-21 JazzPlayer,RaceBook,KenaiDancer 12
31Jan88—Wide into stretch
30Dec87-2SA 1¹⁄₁₆ :46⁴ 1:11³ 1:44²m 4 116 1½ 12 12 15½ DelahoussayeE3 20000 79-23 Jazz Player, Precedence, Amatar 11
15Nov87-2SA 1 :46³ 1:11⁴ 1:38³ft 4½ 116 10⁴½ 89½ 67½ 46 DelahoussayeE8 20000 69-18 John Vigors,NomadBoi,SavorFaire 10
15Nov87—Wide into stretch
5Nov87-5SA 1¹⁄₁₆ :47³ 1:12² 1:45²sy 3½ 116 11 1hd 2hd 1½ DelahoussayeE7 16000 74-23 JzzPlyer,Tibon'sTk,Bnny'sBoldBid 11
18Oct87-1SA 6f :21⁴ :45 1:10⁴ft 4½ 116 1111 911 97½ 34½ DelahoussayeE9 16000 77-15 Subito, Punch Bowl, Jazz Player 12
18Oct87—Hopped in air
10Oct87-1SA 6½f :21⁴ :45 1:16⁴ft 15 116 911 89½ 65½ 23½ DelahoussayeE3 20000 82-17 PddyMidoon,JzzPlyr,StndByYorMn 9
10Oct87—Bobbled start
16Sep87-1Dmr 6f :21⁴ :44⁴ 1:10²ft 6½ 115⁵ 79 55½ 68½ 44½ Cisneros J E8 12500 82-14 WellLaDeDa,RreTyson,SuperAdios 10
27Aug87-5Dmr 6f :21⁴ :45¹ 1:10¹ft 18 110⁵ 119½ 108½ 85½ 55½ Cisneros J E8 13000 82-17 HoustonBragg,RreTyson,R::eBook 11
27Aug87—Wide 3/8 turn
19Aug87-1Dmr 6f :22¹ :45³ 1:11²ft 49 109⁵ 87½ 75½ 42 1½ Cisneros J E2 c14000 81-14 Jazz Player,Forcefully,BoldRoyale 10
19Aug87—Bumped start
Mar 17 SA 5f ft 1:01⁴ h Mar 10 SA 5f ft 1:00⁴ h Feb 21 SA 5f ft 1:01³ h Feb 13 SA 5f ft 1:01⁴ h

Core A Apple *
Own.—Friedman H L — **114**
Dk. b. or br. c. 3, by Duns Scotus—Ruckus, by King's Company
Br.—Edwards James F (NY) — 1987 13 3 4 2 $129,870
Tr.—Badgett William Jr — 1986 1 M 0 0 $285
Lifetime 14 3 4 2 $130,155 — Turf 2 0 1 1 $9,340

10Aug87-8Sar 1⅛ :46⁴ 1:11⁴ 1:51²sy 8½ 114 811 513 11 19½ Garcia J A 2 ⓢAlbany 78-19 CorAAppl,VinesCross,JzzirgAround 8
2Aug87-7Bel 1¼ Ⓣ:50² 1:39 2:03²fm 26 112 1½ 1½ 1hd 2no Garcia J A 1 Aw28000 77-19 Patiomat,CoreAApple,I'mEnthused 8
2Aug87—Drifted out
27Jly87-2Bel 1¹⁄₁₆ Ⓣ:49 1:13¹ 1:47⁴gd 4½ 113 53 54½ 35 38 Garcia J A 1 ⓢAw31500 56-27 Musif'sMtch,Finocchio,CoreAApple 8
27Jly87—Forced out
17Jly87-6Bel 1¹⁄₁₆ :47 1:11⁴ 1:43¹ft 3 113 32 31½ 26 28½ Garcia J A 5 ⓢAw31500 77-20 Criscam, Core A Apple, Finocchio 8
17Jly87—Bobbled st.
5Jly87-5Bel 7f :22⁴ :45⁴ 1:24²ft 4 116 80 76½ 57½ 37½ Garcia J A 2 ⓢAw30000 72-24 Proud Guy, Edelnash, Core AApple 9
22Jun87-1Bel 1⅛ :47² 1:11³ 1:50¹m 5½ 109 11½ 1½ 16 110 Garcia J A 3 ⓢAw30500 76-22 CoreAApple,CmpusCop,Roundwood 7
11Jun87-9Bel 7f :23³ :46⁴ 1:25²ft 8½ 114 2½ 2hd 15 16 Garcia J A 12 ⓢMdn 75-23 CoreAApple,EvntfulNshu,I'mAlbrt 12
23Apr87-2Aqu 1⅛ :49 1:14³ 1:54²ft 6½ 112 1hd 1½ 21½ 23 Bailey J D0 M35000 60-24 BnnrCmndr,CrAAppl,Chrst;hrsPpp 9
Jly 23 Bel Ⓣ 4f fm :50¹ b (d) Jly 12 Bel 4f ft :51 b Jly 1 Bel 4f ft :51 b

Requirements

1. Two for 10, first ten career races.
2. Second win at 5–1 or up, or both wins in double figures (4–1 or above).
3. Each horse gets bet an equal amount for each of its next ten races, or for as many races under ten as are available at the time of tabulation.

Results

Number of horses qualifying for investment:	41
Number of "bets":	261
Return:	$616
Invested:	522
PROFIT:	$94 (18%)
Number of winners:	43 (16½%)
Average Mutuel:	$14.32
Profitable horses:	18 (44%)
Unprofitable horses:	23

Analysis

1. The average mutuel tells us that once a horse has proven to pay off at high prices, it tends to maintain its low profile/ high yield.
2. We expected that 17 percent of horses in a random sample would produce a profit, so the fact that the sample conforming to our rules produced 44 percent profitable horses speaks well for our rules.
3. Random betting should produce a 17 percent monetary loss, so our 18 percent profit outperformed random betting by 35 percentage points. Inconclusive, perhaps, but not bad at all.
4. Not bad, especially considering that there was no handicapping intervention. Since we're looking for a futures type of investment, we're assuming the absence of a handicapper. That may be a blessing or a curse. This type of horse tends to win at times when it "looks bad," so it may be better for the handicapper to be absent. On the other hand, objectively, layoff races, wrong-surface races, wrong-

distance races, wrong-jockey races, etc., were all included in the sample.

Without making any extravagant declarations, I think it can be concluded, conservatively, that there is a future for horse futures, that this type of nonhandicapping *projection*-type investment has a good chance to perform better than many good handicappers.

For research purposes it is important to have fixed guidelines, in order to avoid any subconscious fudging. The spirit of the law suggests, though, that a 2 for 11 requirement, or a 2 for 9 rule, should produce similar results. There's nothing magical about the number 10; we just wanted a win percentage that was neither terrible nor sensational. If 2 for 9 had been the criteria, we'd have collected on several monster long shots.

Similarly, the odds requirements should function if slightly altered. My original sample included 42 horses rather than 41. I then discovered that one of the horses had not qualified by the odds parameters, coming short on one pari-mutuel win payoff by *a mere twenty cents.* Her name was Perchance to Dream, and when I DQed her from this research sample, I threw out two wins, a $10 payoff, and a *$74 win mutuel.* Still, it's encouraging to see that the spirit of the law coincides with the letter of the law.

Another horse, by the name of *Threegees,* was excluded from the sample for the opposite reason. Threegees fit the parameters perfectly, having gone 2 for 10 to start his career, with victories well above the odds requirements, at 11–1 and at an amazing *116–1.* A perfect candidate for a futures investment, I thought. I penciled in his name and scanned his record, which went from race eleven through race sixteen.

    Race 11 first, 5–1
    Race 12 third, 11–1
    Race 13 out (he'd switched away from his winning rider, Pedroza, and was racing in the goo)
    Race 14 first, nearly 17–1 ($35.60), with Pedroza back
    Race 15 out
    Race 16 first, 3–1

I was about to add Threegees to the sample, which would have increased the return on investment in the final stats. But something looked wrong. I scanned back at Threegees's record and I thought I saw too many ones. In his first ten races there had been three "ones," the last of which was a disqualification. If that win had counted, he would have been 3 for 10.

Perchance to Dream had qualified by the spirit but not the letter; Threegees made it by the letter but not the spirit of the law. In research it is always better to be conservative and take the *worst-case scenario.* Many systems that seem brilliant would be no more than mediocre if conscious or unconscious "fudging" had not taken place. Threegees told me, in his own way, that I was on the right track; but he never got included in the research.

When I introduced the horse-futures research, I mentioned that I would be going out on the fringe. That didn't mean I would depart from a foundation of rational procedures. The results of the research should assure the reader that "out on the fringe" does not mean "off the deep end."

We now enter the realm of trainer futures, where we will be on very solid footing.

TRAINER FUTURES: THE STABLE INVESTMENT

The foundation for trainer futures is parallel to that of horse futures. Fashionable trainers draw too much action, and the best of them will encounter the inevitable losing streaks. At the other end of the spectrum are the no-win trainers. These guys will come up with an occasional long shot, usually a horse that wins by default against a bad field, but their primary function is to help fill fields.

We are left with the trainers who are consistent and competent but manage to keep a low profile. I have researched this type of trainer and found many with extended periods of flat-bet profit; but they are all eligible for one bad year. One year is a short period in the career of a trainer, but it's long enough to mutilate a bankroll. What's worse, you never know when the best of the trainers will hit the worst of skids.

We need to relate the form (trainer bet) to the content (trainer situation). There are nearly as many trainer situations as there are trainers. Different situations have different duration periods which are fundamental parts of trainer-performance cycles. It is not enough to say that a particular trainer wins 32 percent of the time going from sprint to route, because that 32 percent may be the average of 16 percent one year and 48 percent the next year.

A $7.00 average mutuel with 32 percent winners is profitable, but how would you like to read the statistic and then go bet that trainer situation during his 16 percent phase, when a $7.00 average mutuel turns into a horrendous loss.

For daily handicapping, we have already demonstrated some of the many ways in which sensitivity to trainer trends can translate into significant profits. For trainer futures, we must identify those situations that are the most stable over the most predictable periods of time, which are the least susceptible to the normal fluctuations in the trainer's performance cycle.

In general, the most stable of trainer situations are those with a low rate of frequency. A Mel Stute may be highly proficient with first-time starters, but he gets too many of them for that situation to produce a profit. On the other hand, Mike Mitchell only claims about two or three maidens a year, so he does so with much more critical discipline and much less odds-lowering attention. Whittingham may be a more proficient trainer with foreign imports first time in the U.S., but he gets too many of them with too much public awareness for a pari-mutuelly profitable outcome. On the other hand, Hector Palma only brings back one or two European horses per year, so he's got to be much more selective and discriminating in his choices.

For years now Robert Frankel has allowed his backers to achieve a flat-bet profit if they bet his imports first time in the U.S., allowing for one follow-up bet if the horse fails the first time. Ever since the days of Solva and Aberushka, Frankel has geared his immigrants up for early success. During a particularly weak period in the Frankel trajectory (bottom periods are crucial), which led directly up to the writing of this book, I came across only seven horses that conformed to this highly selective situation:

Art Francais, lost twice
Enbarr, lost twice
Hawaiian Spring, two lengths back at 30–1, lost twice
Solany, won first time, at nearly 7–1 (12Apr87, SA, 3rd)
Point D'Artois, lost once, then won at 3–1 (26Nov87, Hol, 9th)
In Focus, lost once, then won at 10–1 (6Mar88, SA, 7th)
Roi Normand, won first time at 8–5 (25Mar88, SA, 8th)

That's a 4 of 7 success rate. In terms of bets, it means 4 wins in 12 tries. On a flat-bet basis, that's over a 100 percent profit!

The primary fear of trainer-futures bettors will be the specter of a losing streak. Without a proper foundation in time, without a defined context, a trainer trend is likely to be discovered after the fact. The investor may step in just when the trend is winding down. In the worst scenario, the trainer may at the outset of an "0 for" period.

There are reasons for trainer cold streaks, objective, material causes that have nothing to do with the gods of fate. Why do good trainers face bad streaks? The primary reason is simple: bad crop of horses.

When Brian Mayberry's 1987 Santa Anita long-shot binge was about to reach its natural conclusion, I considered, nostalgically, that there must be some way to continue investing in better than competent and underrated trainers such as Mayberry. I reasoned that if Mayberry were to tail off, it would be for lack of the means to replenish his worthy stock. It would be too much to expect that he could recruit another generation of horses that would measure up to the present crop.

On the other hand, the horses he had just won with all had characteristics of the type of thoroughbred that yields a career profit at the pari-mutuel windows. They were not high-percentage winners, so would not attract too much public attention, and they had the proven credentials of long-shot victories. Most important, they were in good hands. If they needed a rest, their trainer would not run them into the ground. If they needed to race at a particular level, he would find that level.

The form is the trainer wager; in this case, Brian Mayberry. The content is this trainer's current stock, one specific generation of horses in his stable. Specifically they are the six 1987 Santa Anita long-shot winners: *Eighty Below Zero, Five Daddy Five, Happy In Space, Hairless Heiress, Live By The Sword,* and *No Double Deal.* Let us place a future bet on Brian Mayberry, on a subset of his stable, and follow the progress of our stock up until the time of this writing:

Eighty Below Zero	3 losses, laid off
Five Daddy Five	19 races, 4 wins at 13–1, 12–1, 3–2, and 3–1
Hairless Heiress	10 races until claimed, 4 wins at 3–2, 8–5, 6–1 and 3–2
Happy In Space	10 races, 2 wins at 9–1 and 7–1

No Double Deal   laid off, claimed in comeback race,
                        1 loss
Live By The Sword   4 losses, laid off

Results

Races bet:	47
Winners:	10 (21%)
Return:	$134
Invested:	94
PROFIT:	$40 (43%)
Average mutuel:	$13.40
Profitable horses:	3
Unprofitable horses:	2 (sixth horse only raced once for Mayberry, claimed, won at big price)

Analysis

If this trainer were to get more than 20 percent winners for several meets, he would surely attract enough attention to lose his value. But only one sector of his stable is winning at that rate, in the same way that a very small sector of the Robert Frankel stable was winning 40 percent of the time. The skill of the trainer-futures investor is to *define* that sector. We are looking for those particular contents of the trainer's stable that are the least susceptible to the ups and downs of trainer performance cycles. The sector of the Frankel stable was made up of newly-arrived foreign immigrants. The sector of the Mayberry stable was defined as proven long-shot commodities.

In trainer futures, as in horse futures, the most important objective statistic is average mutuel, since we do not usually expect a high percentage of winners. The less frequent and more exclusive the type of investment, the more likely we are to demand a higher percentage of winners. Twenty percent winners is great for a heavy-action investment but it's no good for a situation that only arises twice a year.

Epilogue. No Double Deal was claimed from Mayberry after a long and patiently-nurturing layoff. Two races later the horse, still benefiting from the vacation in professional hands, won a race at 65–1 odds. Without taking away from the new trainer Mayberry deserves much of the credit.

Discovering the content or specificity of trainer-futures bets is a creative process that cannot be reduced to a mechanical synopsis. Here is an open-ended, annotated list of various potential trainer-futures situations which the reader may work with when studying trainers at the local racing circuit.

First-Time Starters. Specific workout patterns, particular owners, favorite meets, particular number of workouts, two-year-olds or three-year-olds

Claims. First or second time after claim, for a particular owner, during a special part of the year, waits for end of thirty-day "jail" period and raises in class anyway, claims out of maiden races, trainer claims for self (trainer is owner), claim plus Lasix plus up in class (Francis Campitelli specialty in Maryland)

Trainer Hot Streak with Whole Stable. Trainer gears up for particular meets

Foreign Horses. First or second time in U.S., after layoff, brings horses from a particular country, buys from a well-known supplier, buys for a specific owner, no U.S. workouts, long or short works

Gelded Horses. High percentage winning with horses recently gelded (look for layoffs of approximately one to two months, especially with maidens, when the sex is marked g, and check back to previous race to see if horse was listed as c)

Layoff Specialist. Specific workout patterns, routes or sprints, unique characteristics of this trainer's layoff winners (maidens, younger or older, first-time starter winners, etc.); in Maryland, trainer Cartwright provides a steady profit with layoff horses in spite of the fact that his layoff stats are found in the LaBree Sports Palace computers.

This list is infinite and could include distance switches, surface switches, strange recency patterns such as five-day returns, maidens on turf, class drops, class rises, double jumps or drops, etc.

Usually the handicapper doesn't find these opportunities, but rather, these opportunities find the handicapper. I've watched colleagues go digging into mounds of *Racing Forms* as if they were miners searching for gold. With no leads, they usually come up empty. On the other hand, observant handicappers with open minds will be "struck" by unusual occurrences. These events are leads that should be followed up.

One of my favorite trainer bets, whose specific content relates to jockey switch (remember Mayberry/McHargue) is practically worthless for pure future betting because the politics of jockeys is too unstable; agents change, disagreements arise, riders travel to other tracks and lose mounts. For example, the Mayberry futures situation did not include McHargue, even though that rider had been aboard all of the original winter 1987 long-shot winners. Hot rider/trainer combos make good bets if you are there every day watching the trends, but don't expect the good thing to last for a long time.

Every time something unusual takes place, especially if it results in a big payoff, make a mental note, or if you don't trust your memory, write it down. The best trainer-futures bets will come from your own experience, because you have an intimate relationship with the information you have gathered. It is not the abstract type of knowledge that is accumulated from someone else's trainer study (not easily internalized to the point that it becomes a part of you). I recall, for example, an obscure trainer by the name of William Canney, who suddenly appeared on the scene at the Oak Tree Santa Anita meet in October 1986. Several events made a lasting impression.

CANNEY'S COMET

He won with two first-time starters. He had had no credentials at the time, which made his coup all the more impressive. Helping my memory was the fact that my colleague, Larry Goldstein, was in the process of researching his revolutionary studies on first-time starters. Larry collected on the second of the two Canney winners, a horse by the name of *Chanterella*, which I recall paid about $32.

The strange follow-up to this story is that I cannot recall Mr. Canney ever having any other type of winner. Chanterella became a child-prodigy burnout, losing for the rest of her two-year-old season, zero for two as a three-year-old, and accumulating zeros as a four-year-old while passing into the hands of another unfortunate trainer. Perhaps Canney might have won another race or two, but if he did, I missed it. Here was a guy batting zero or near zero as a trainer of horses that had run before, and simultaneously hitting 1.000 with first timers. Never has a trainer specialty been more clearly defined.

So I am prepared to wait for a long time for Canney's next first-time starter, which will be, of course, an automatic bet. This trainer-futures investment figured to appear infrequently, since the higher the percentage of winners, the less frequent the action. The rest of 1986 passes by and nothing. 1987 goes by, I get older, and still no Canney first-time starters. I expect to see one, maybe in October, since that was the month Canney's obscure orbit appeared over southern California. Nothing.

I feel like an astronomer waiting for Canney's Comet. Then I see it on the horizon. It has come by at a moment when it will draw the least attention, the last day of the year, when most people are getting ready to party. Its name is *Voila*, another filly. Unfortunately for me, she has a 47.2 workout and the best two runners she faces have trainers with a 2 percent win record. Voila, there she is, and the table has been set especially for her.

I'll invest in her at the early betting, since trainer-futures plays are automatic bets, at any price. She's 8–1 in the program, that's fine. Later that afternoon I hear the call of the sixth race and she wins. The price, $8.20. I had not been the only one waiting for Canney's Comet. So this guy is still batting a thousand, and he's now somewhere at the other end of the galaxy. And as I have said, these trainer-futures situations find you, you don't find them. So keep your telescope looking out into the infinite universe of trainer futures.

RIDER FUTURES?

I see little chance that a futures betting method can be built upon the rider factor. If horse-racing futures is at all analogous to the stock exchange or the commodities market, then the role of the trainer would parallel that of the company, while that of the rider comes closer to trader or courier. We have seen how hot trainers can win with cold riders but cold trainers need more than a hot rider to wake up their stables.

And yet, a number of intriguing possibilities remain at issue, and the jockey factor cannot be totally discarded from our possible investment portfolio. Let's put all of the potentially useful information on the table and perhaps we shall move closer to the right combination of ingredients.

1. In Chapter 3 we have seen that *jockey switch* appears in many cases of unexpected short win binges for horses that are normally proven losers.
2. In Chapter 6 the second strongest correlation of factors leading to form reversal was the *class drop/rider switch.*
3. A horse that switches to the rider of its last victory has a better than fair chance of winning. While, in part, such switches are merely reflections of trainer intention, there is no question that certain riders bring out the best in certain horses.
4. When trainers go on binges, they tend to use one jockey in particular. Trainer-rider combos become good bets when part of a short-term trend. In the long run, though, these "teams" change personnel as frequently as Steinbrenner's Yankees. We call this the Billy Martin Syndrome.
5 For years now I have charted the flat-bet performance of jockeys. I am now convinced that certain riders are more likely to show a flat-bet profit. I had the chance to compare my findings with the rider research of a gentleman by the name of Mark Shrager, who developed some very creative measures of jockey proficiency which fortunately included flat-bet profit/loss tabulations. His work studied both New York and California riders and included such esoteric comparisons as won-lost records in photo finishes. Shrager's work confirmed two important concepts:
   a. Most declarations about jockey specialties are myths that have been born from subjective observations
   b. Certain types of riders are more likely to yield a flat-bet profit at the end of a meet, and they are not your "leading jockeys"; the Corderos and Pincays are bet too heavily to be considered an asset to the handicapper/investor

Even in photo finishes, where one would expect the seasoned champs to prevail, lesser riders often had a better percentage of success. These observations don't do justice to Shrager's work, which hopefully will become more ac cessible to the public.

6. There are two types of riders that have the best chance to yield a flat-bet profit:
   a. Proven competent riders who rarely lead in the standings but always figure in the top ten
   b. New arrivals on a racing circuit, either a hot apprentice or a journeyman from another part of the country

   These two categories of riders get less action because, as commodities, they are not as commercial as leading jocks. Their average mutuel is always higher and the percentage of winners is sometimes higher than the first two or three names in the standings. In southern California during the past decade riders such as Meza, Hawley, and Delahoussaye have been able to put together meets and sometimes years of flat-bet-profit riding. For the potential investor the problem is always the same: there is no way to predict when the profitable period will *inevitably* come to an end.

7. The most likely type of jockey to qualify for a futures investment is the *hot apprentice*. With an apprentice rider, it's not always easy to decide when to get on the bandwagon, but it's very simple to know when to get off: when the rider loses his weight allowance. Weight, the most overrated factor in thoroughbred handicapping, becomes the most significant factor in rider-futures investments.

   This unlikely situation is a result of the trainer factor, embedded in the rider factor. I once went to the backstretch to interview trainers, and I asked each one the same question: "What is your opinion about the weight factor?" While many of the trainers questioned, minimized, or discounted the weight factor, more than half thought weight was significant. The reason why this second type of trainer gives mounts to the apprentice is the very same reason he will withdraw those mounts from the apprentice the day there are no more "pounds off."

   It is not as simple to know when to begin an apprentice-futures bet, which would mean an equal amount of money on each and every horse ridden. There are certain standard procedures involved in the important decision. You want to have seen the rider win at big odds with horses that didn't look good; seconds and thirds with long shots are also a good sign. You want to see one or two major trainers begin to give prime mounts to the hot apprentice. You want to see this rider win in confidence-building situations (photos, stakes races). Finally, expect the rider to have shown a certain measure of versatility, winning as a pace setter as well as from behind.

As you can see, I have not arrived at the ultimate formula. It is encouraging to have observed that most apprentices who sustain a winning cycle beyond a few races will maintain the cycle at a peak throughout the "bug" period. Most important, contrary to most futures investments, the hot-apprentice bet has a built-in withdrawal time.

Some of my own jockey investments may be too subjective to qualify for analysis in this study. There have been occasions when I knew "deep down in my heart" that Santos was the right rider; and yet I was not able to explain why. The class-drop/rider-switch pattern has been good to me for years, but I have not been able to totally exclude my interventions as a handicapper, so I don't have a "pure" futures investment.

The final answers may ultimately come from my colleague, Larry Goldstein. I've seen him bet successfully, with automatic rules, on hot apprentices, most recently Corral. I've seen him know when to bet on riders because they are flown across the country to ride in a feature race (Patrick Day was transported across the country to ride the infamous Vilzak in his unexpected Grade 1 victory). And I've watched Larry wager and win because the jockey belonged on the horse. One day Mr. Goldstein may put his research together and prove I am wrong about the rider being a secondary factor.

In the meantime let's not be dogmatic about the jockey factor. Any guy who drives a thousand-pound beast through a small opening, which may shut off at any moment, at forty miles per hour, cannot be considered a nonfactor. If a jockey is merely a passenger on the horse, then I am an observer, sitting here in front of my typewriter, watching these words run across the page.

The jockey factor is probably not the ultimate key to handicapping, but it puts horse racing in an unrivaled position among spectacles. Name another professional sport in which women and men compete in the same events for the same prizes, in which a guy in his fifties named William Shoemaker can compete with a sixteen-year-old apprentice. Find another sport in which athletes of two distinct species coordinate their skills into one courageous image of delicate power.

THE PERSONALITY OF CYCLES II

From a form-cycle perspective, most horse-race betting requires some degree of futures analysis. Numbers from the past help the handicapper, to a certain extent, in projecting performance of the future. But from a total picture of thoroughbred cycles, it is evident that just how a horse responds today to yesterday's numbers is very much a function of its "personality."

Even in automobile races, cars with mechanically-defined performance capabilities achieve varying results from race to race. Since horses are nearer to being human than they are to being machines, it is no wonder that for one horse, the more it races, the sharper it gets, while for another, more work leads to duller performance.

Horse "personality" has much to do with why some competitors pop up occasionally while others win in clusters, why some are consistent while others are irregular, why a class drop to lesser competition will "motivate" some horses while "discouraging" others, why some horses reach their peak when challenged while others produce their highest number when allowed to run alone.

For some thoroughbreds a race of a lifetime will be inspiration for continuing improvement, while for others it will overwhelm them so much that they will bounce in their next race. Some horses will improve by knocking heads with tough company, while others need the feel of being a big fish in a small pond in order to gather competitive spirit.

Consider one of the dumbest animals, the rooster. Probably there is a greater gap in intelligence from a rooster to a horse than there is from a horse to a human being. And yet, even roosters greatly vary in their response to competitive situations. When outclassed in a fight, one rooster will run away while another one will fight it out to his death. If roosters have different attitudes toward life, why not horses?

Some thoroughbreds relish returning after a vacation, while others find it tough to keep their mind on business the first day back on the job. In the spirit of Kerouac, some horses are at home on the road while others can only reach a high when they've gone back to where they belong, West Virginia, Saratoga, Stockton, California.

Will some reader, then, coin a new term for horse personality, a word that can be used in the *Racing Form*, a language that will

be more precise in analyzing why the laid-back Schiller and
Ernie King will occasionally be moved to fire their best shot.
Behind each thoroughbred cycle is a personality. When he fu-
tilely chases Groovy, Sun Master is Salieri finishing behind
Mozart. Hesa Frequentflyer deserves a song about his life written
by Merle Haggard, as this horse comes into new towns like a pool
hustler, cleans up, then leaves through the back door, on the run.

There are the Cyranos of racing, such as Core A Apple and
Fracoza, who, unloved by the public, compensate for their un-
sightly names by becoming warriors on the track and outdueling
their more popular rivals. Then there is the team of *Smooth Bid*
and Joy Scott, both apparently condemned to fill fields; they find
each other, work together with unexpected mastery, achieve
glory in a period of time that is very brief but pari-mutuelly more
sensational than John Henry and Spectacular Bid. And while
these two are separated and each falls from the peak, they will
always have their glorious nostalgia to cling to.

There are the street-gang horses, the ones who are humbled
when away from their habitat but who dominate meets when on
their own turf. Most smaller tracks and some big ones have their
own unique gangs which muscle away the competition, making
life difficult for out-of-towners.

There are the atonal horses, the ones that create a new performance scale, speed figures out of sequence. And from this
dissonance they create a new form, a new orbit of performance:
Little Ignat, whose best races immediately follow his worst ones;
Auspiciante, who loses every time at low odds but is deadly
when over 10–1.

FIRST RACE
Santa Anita
OCTOBER 9, 1987

6 FURLONGS. (1.07⅘) CLAIMING. Purse $12,000. 3-year-olds and upward. Weights, 3-year-olds, 119 lbs.; older, 122 lbs. Non-winners of two races since July 27 allowed 2 lbs.; of a race since September 16, 4 lbs.; since July 27, 6 lbs. Claiming price $10,000. (Races when entered for $8,500 or less not considered). 32ND DAY. WEATHER HAZY. TEMPERATURE 74 DEGREES.

Value of race $12,000; value to winner $6,600; second $2,400; third $1,800; fourth $900; fifth $300. Mutuel pool $168,828.

Last Raced	Horse	Eqt.	A.	Wt	PP	St	¼	½	Str	Fin	Jockey	Cl'g Pr	Odds $1
27Sep87 ^{7}Fpx^{4}	Smooth Bid		6	116	6	1	1^{hd}	1^{hd}	$2^{1\frac{1}{2}}$	1^{nk}	Scott J M	10000	75.80
5Sep87 ^{2}Dmr^{3}	Doodlesack		6	111	8	2	3^{3}	2^{1}	1^{hd}	$2^{3\frac{1}{2}}$	Gryder A T^{5}	10000	1.00
1Oct87 ^{5}Fpx^{1}	Punch Bowl		3	117	3	3	2^{hd}	3^{5}	3^{5}	$3^{1\frac{1}{2}}$	Patterson A	10000	11.50
29Sep87 ^{13}Fpx^{4}	River's Wave		6	116	10	10	10	6^{hd}	5^{hd}	$4^{1\frac{1}{2}}$	Baze G	10000	11.10
29Sep87 ^{13}Fpx^{2}	Piano Player		4	116	9	6	$6^{\frac{1}{2}}$	5^{1}	$6^{1\frac{1}{2}}$	5^{nk}	Stevens G L	10000	4.60
27Sep87 ^{7}Fpx^{1}	Cool'n Scandalous	b	5	120	2	8	4^{1}	$4^{1\frac{1}{2}}$	4^{1}	$6^{1\frac{1}{2}}$	Winick D	10000	4.20
1Oct87 ^{7}Fpx^{3}	Tranzor	b	3	108	5	7	8^{hd}	$7^{3\frac{1}{2}}$	$7^{4\frac{1}{2}}$	$7^{3\frac{1}{2}}$	Magallon P^{5}	10000	12.70
13Nov86 ^{7}Hol^{10}	Miami Dream		4	116	4	4	5^{1}	9^{1}	8^{hd}	$8^{\frac{1}{2}}$	Olivares F	10000	25.50
12Sep87 ^{1}Dmr^{8}	Be Thankful		5	116	7	5	7^{1}	8^{hd}	9^{2}	$9^{2\frac{1}{2}}$	Black C A	10000	45.70
1Oct87 ^{7}Fpx^{8}	Skibi Hancho		3	116	1	9	$9^{1\frac{1}{2}}$	10	10	10	Kaenel J L	10000	71.00

OFF AT 1:01. Start good. Won driving. Time, :21⅗, :44⅘, :57, 1:10⅘ Track fast.

Official Program Numbers

$2 Mutuel Prices:

6–SMOOTH BID	153.60	32.80	18.00
8–DOODLESACK		2.80	2.60
3–PUNCH BOWL			5.80

B. g, by Smooth Stuff—Bid O Win, by Irish Bid. Trainer Wilson Fred S. Bred by White J V & J C (NM).

SMOOTH BID raced head-and-head on the lead from the outset, responded in the crucial stages and outgamed DOODLESACK. The latter was right with the winner from the start and could not quite match strides at the end. PUNCH BOWL forced the issue from the rail and faltered. RIVER'S WAVE finished best of the rest. PIANO PLAYER was no menace. COOL 'N SCANDALOUS was a brief early factor and gave out. TRANZOR bobbled a bit a stride away from the gate and was no menace.

EIGHTH RACE
Hollywood
JULY 5, 1987

1 ⅛ MILES.(Turf). (1.45⅘) 22nd Running of THE BEVERLY HILLS HANDICAP (Grade II). (Chute Start) $100,000 added (Plus $50,000 Breeders' Cup Premium Award). Fillies and mares. 3-year-olds and upward. By subscription of $100 each, which shall accompany the nomination, $1,000 additional to start, with $100,000 added, of which $20,000 to second, $15,000 to third, $7,500 to fourth and $2,500 to fifth. Weights Tuesday, June 30. Starters to be named through the entry box by closing time of entries. Trophies will be presented to the winning owner, trainer and jockey. Closed Wednesday, June 24, 1987 with 16 nominations.

Total purse $159,600. Value of race $127,600; value to winner $64,600; second $33,500; third $19,500; fourth $7,500; fifth $2,500. $30,000 reverts to Association.$2,000 in Foal & Nmntr Awds. Mutuel pool $354,241. Exacta pool $377,746.

Last Raced	Horse	Eqt.	A.	Wt	PP	St	¼	½	¾	Str	Fin	Jockey	Odds $1
30May87 ^{8}Hol^{6}	Auspiciante		6	117	7	8	5^{3}	5^{5}	5^{6}	$4^{1\frac{1}{2}}$	1^{nk}	Valenzuela P A	12.30
24May87 ^{8}Hol^{2}	Reloy		4	120	8	3	$2^{1\frac{1}{2}}$	$2^{1\frac{1}{2}}$	$2^{1\frac{1}{2}}$	$1^{1\frac{1}{2}}$	2^{2}	Shoemaker W	2.20
27Jun87 ^{4}Hol^{1}	Festivity	b	4	114	2	4	$4^{2\frac{1}{2}}$	$4^{3\frac{1}{2}}$	$3^{\frac{1}{2}}$	3^{hd}	$3^{4\frac{1}{2}}$	McCarron C J	8.30
13Jun87 ^{9}WO^{1}	Aromacor		4	112	6	2	3^{2}	3^{hd}	4^{2}	5^{5}	4^{hd}	Solis A	69.70
13Jun87 ^{8}Hol^{3}	Frau Altiva		5	117	5	6	7^{2}	$7^{2\frac{1}{2}}$	7^{2}	$6^{2\frac{1}{2}}$	5^{1}	Pincay L Jr	13.90
17Jun87 ^{8}Hol^{1}	Amongst The Stars		4	116	3	7	8	8	8	$7^{1\frac{1}{2}}$	$6^{2\frac{1}{2}}$	Delahoussaye E	8.90
24May87 ^{8}Hol^{1}	Northern Aspen		5	121	4	1	$1^{\frac{1}{2}}$	$1^{\frac{1}{2}}$	$1^{\frac{1}{2}}$	$2^{\frac{1}{2}}$	$7^{1\frac{1}{2}}$	Stevens G L	1.00
27Jun87 ^{4}Hol^{2}	Stall Cloud		5	115	1	5	6^{1}	$6^{2\frac{1}{2}}$	$6^{\frac{1}{2}}$	8	8	Sibille R	60.40

OFF AT 5:24. Start good. Won driving. Time, :21⅘, :45, 1:08⅘, 1:33, 1:46⅕ Course firm.

$2 Mutuel Prices:

7–AUSPICIANTE	26.60	9.60	5.60
8–RELOY		4.20	3.60
2–FESTIVITY			4.40

$2 EXACTA 7–8 PAID $102.40.

B. m, by Practicante—Auxey, by Right of Way. Trainer McAnally Ronald. Bred by Haras La Biznaga (Arg).

AUSPICIANTE, allowed to settle into stride while being outrun early after breaking a bit slowly, moved up gradually to get closer on the far turn, came through between rivals at the head of the stretch while continuing to gain, found her best stride to close strongly in the last furlong while responding to left-handed pressure and was up in the final yards. RELOY pressed the early pace outside NORTHERN ASPEN after getting away in good order, wrested the advantage nearing the quarter pole, opened a clear lead in the upper stretch, continued with a clear advantage to the last sixteenth then could not quite resist the winner's closing bid. FESTIVITY, never far back, advanced to threaten on the far turn and in the upper stretch but flattened out in the final furlong. AROMACOR, close up to the stretch after an alert beginning, lacked the necessary response in the drive. AMONGST THE STARS was four wide into the stretch. NORTHERN ASPEN broke alertly to take the lead at once, established the early pace inside RELOY, yielded command nearing the quarter pole but remained near the lead to the furlong marker then gave way.

SECOND RACE
Del Mar
SEPTEMBER 3, 1987

7 FURLONGS. (1.20⅘) CLAIMING. Purse $10,000. 3-year-olds and upward. Weights, 3-year-olds, 117 lbs.; older, 121 lbs. Non-winners of a race since July 1 allowed 2 lbs.; of a race since June 1, 4 lbs. Claiming price $10,000. (Races when entered for $8,500 or less not considered.)

Value of race $10,000; value to winner $5,500; second $2,000; third $1,500; fourth $750; fifth $250. Mutuel pool $186,205.

Last Raced	Horse	Eqt	A.Wt	PP	St	¼	½	Str	Fin	Jockey	Cl'g Pr	Odds $1
7Aug87 ^{2}Dmr^{2}	Ernie King	b	7 117	5	10	$11^{1\frac{1}{2}}$	10^{2}	$5^{1\frac{1}{2}}$	1^{1}	Baze R A	10000	6.30
19Aug87 ^{9}Dmr^{9}	Peppy's Consul	b	4 117	7	2	1^{hd}	$1^{\frac{1}{2}}$	1^{3}	$2^{3\frac{1}{2}}$	Stevens S A	10000	6.30
19Aug87 ^{9}Dmr^{4}	Electric Moment	b	6 118	2	7	$8^{1\frac{1}{2}}$	$7^{\frac{1}{2}}$	6^{hd}	3no	Simpson B H	10000	5.50
17Aug87 ^{10}LA^{1}	Ever Brilliant		5 116	8	1	3^{1}	4^{2}	2^{hd}	4^{1}	Patton D B^{5}	10000	6.80
17Aug87 ^{10}LA^{4}	Axopet		6 112	4	9	$10^{1\frac{1}{2}}$	8^{hd}	$7^{\frac{1}{2}}$	5^{nk}	Comber J^{5}	10000	76.10
17Aug87 ^{6}LA^{6}	Johns Tomorrow	b	4 112	3	5	6^{3}	$6^{\frac{1}{2}}$	4^{1}	$6^{1\frac{1}{2}}$	Gryder A T^{5}	10000	28.60
26Aug87 ^{2}Dmr^{5}	Tigerillo	b	4 112	9	3	$4^{\frac{1}{2}}$	2^{hd}	$3^{1\frac{1}{2}}$	$7^{\frac{1}{2}}$	Bringhurst AD^{5}	10000	7.60
19Aug87 ^{5}LA^{1}	Buddy Rich		3 117	1	8	7^{hd}	11^{4}	8^{1}	8^{nk}	Stevens G L	10000	5.20
22Aug87 ^{11}LA^{5}	Summers Hitter	b	4 117	6	6	5^{hd}	5^{3}	9^{1}	9^{hd}	Patterson A	10000	78.80
13Aug87 ^{1}Dmr^{3}	Serious Play		4 117	12	4	9^{hd}	$9^{\frac{1}{2}}$	$10^{2\frac{1}{2}}$	10^{6}	Black C A	10000	3.20
21Aug87 ^{5}LA^{7}	Blizzard Comin	b	6 117	11	12	$2^{\frac{1}{2}}$	3^{hd}	11^{4}	11^{6}	Pedroza M A	10000	20.70
19Mar87 ^{9}SA^{10}	The Last Dragon	b	4 117	10	11	12	12	12	12	Wellington H	10000	37.90

OFF AT 2:36. Start good for all but BLIZZARD COMIN. Won driving. Time, :22⅘, :45⅘, 1:11, 1:24 Track fast.

$2 Mutuel Prices:				
	5-ERNIE KING	14.60	6.40	4.80
	7-PEPPY'S CONSUL		6.40	4.40
	2-ELECTRIC MOMENT			5.20

B. g, by Cougar II—Sweet Swede, by Fleet Nasrullah. Trainer Richardson Donald P. Bred by P L C Investments (Ky).

ERNIE KING, devoid of early speed, was checked sharply when lacking room leaving the three eighths pole, came into the stretch five wide, closed with a rush to overtake PEPPY'S CONSUL in deep stretch and proved best. The latter, a pace factor from the start, drew well clear in the upper stretch but was unable to resist the winner's late charge. ELECTRIC MOMENT, outrun early, was fanned six wide into the stretch and was unable to gain the necessary ground in the drive. EVER BRILLIANT forced the pace to the stretch and weakened. TIGERILLO forced the pace to the stretch and gave way. BUDDY RICH was outrun. SUMMERS HITTER, in contention early, lacked the needed response when called upon and was four wide into the stretch. SERIOUS PLAY lacked early speed, was fanned seven wide into the stretch and lacked the necessary rally. BLIZZARD COMIN stumbled at the start, pressed the issue early and faltered.

There are the bullies, such as Eliminante, who hang out in neighborhoods where they don't belong, not for their own benefit, but to the detriment of others. But there are also the heroes. Very Subtle, who is not intimidated by male competition. Great Communicator, who went to the major leagues before he was ready, got back up each time he was knocked down, until one day he began to defeat the same guys who used to beat him easily. Lichi, who regularly got the job done, with artistry, while never getting fair recognition for her craft.

And there are the antiheroes, the Willy Lomans who are forced by the economic structure of the racing industry to labor under unfair working conditions, in impossible jobs, filling fields to increase the handle for others, battling back after each setback.

To know these horse personalities is to discover unique lifestyles which are sometimes realistic images, other times metaphors of the ups and downs of thoroughbred cycles. A collection of the prototypes of these personalities becomes the format for a handicapping methodology. This methodology stresses change over continuity and views past performances not as static moments in time but as horse histories in movement.

Numbers in the past performances become graceful and dynamic images of living beings who defiantly resist becoming racing machines by not "running 'em alike." Old *Racing Forms* acquire new significance as they contain information about the childhood behavior of these athletes which may give clues as to their performance as mature competitors. The human partners of these beings have their own histories, with more ups and downs, to add dimensions to a complex system of orbits. When all these moving factors converge in a particular race, a whole new galaxy appears in the expanding universe of horse racing.

The handicapper of thoroughbred cycles is both psychologist and astronomer as each new race is a new clash of personalities within a fresh convergence of orbits. This is the type of infinite puzzle that the human mind was made for.

Suppose that there were only ten possible horse cycles. In an evenly matched eight-horse field, there would be 100 million possible combinations of cyclical relations between the eight horses. But we know that, given the tremendous variation in horse personalities—running styles, frequency and wavelength of ups and downs, class consciousness, seasonal, and spatial preferences—many more than ten cycles exist.

Now add to the equation trainer and rider cycles, which exert distinct pulls on the horse orbits, and each and every race becomes a unique puzzle of astounding dimensions. Our original 100 million combinations now look like one large barrel of sand dumped in the Nevada desert.

For this reason the thoroughbred-cycles methodology cannot be reduced to one model or procedure. Consider final-time handicapping, an apparently lineal procedure, which requires the adjustments of a number of variants—notably, track, pace, form, and trip. Expand this to form-cycle handicapping and graph the chronological progression of horses' speed/pace ratings; we are now in two dimensions instead of one. But by having expanded from one to two planes, the need for variants grows geometrically. The existence of distinct horse-behavior traits will mean that even the same record of performance cycles for two horses may lead in different directions. The value of graphs is thus largely illustrative and symbolic, with limited use for handicapping.

There are two basic approaches to confronting this astonishing complexity: *head on*, complexity vs. complexity (comprehensive handicapping), or with guerrilla tactics, simplicity vs. complexity (anti-handicapping). If we decide on the comprehensive approach, we must understand in advance that our process will never be capable of matching the complexity of the situations we confront. And if we decide oι anti-handicapping, the futures mode, we must be aware that our method will never completely elude the superior depth of the "confusion" we wish to sidestep.

That people around the world have opted to engage in deciphering the past performances, instead of finite mental activities with simpler and safer solutions, says a lot about the spirit of horseplayers. Many students and colleagues, successful in their livelihoods, have confided that they would gladly give up their professions or business in exchange for mastery of the art of handicapping. One of my students, owner of a successful business, once said with profound emotion: "If at the races I could earn a third of what I now make in my business, I'd willingly give up many of my material comforts in exchange for the satisfaction of horse racing."

This gentleman has made a spiritual statement. For him, return investment has a completely different meaning than for the banker or corporate magnate. It represents a measure of his skill in an art that he loves. I am sure that most readers share these sentiments. We all have this in common. We have chosen this immense challenge as a very significant part of our lives.

Addenda

A. PRIMARY RESEARCH, CROSS-REFERENCE BY CHAPTER

Theme	Chapter
Beaten Favorites	1
Proven Losers at Peak	1
Winners After Layoff	2
Second Race After Layoff When Comeback Race Was a Peak Effort	2
Sudden Win Cluster for Proven Losers	3
Breeders' Cup Juvenile Horses at Kentucky Derby Time*	5
The Five-Year-Old Gelding	5, 13
Form Reversal Winners	6
Track Switch/Class Drop	6
Horses for Courses (Del Mar)	7
Hot Trainer Streaks (Mayberry and Spawr)*	8
First-Time Starters (Matlow)*	9
Annual Cycles (M. Whittingham, Gosden)*	9
Flat Bet Profit Horse Careers	13
The Stable Investment*	13
Foreign Imports: Frankel*	13
The Schiller Principle*	13

*Denotes small-sample illustrative research, as opposed to research of larger, universal samples

B. FEATURED HORSE HISTORIES:

An Alphabetical Index with Chapter(s) Where They Appear
(*Note:* Horses from workshops excluded from this list)

C. CYCLES OF MAJOR IMPACT FROM WORKSHOPS:

Cross-Reference with Corresponding Expository Chapters

Workshop	High-Impact Cycle	Chapter
1	Five-Year-Old Gelding	5
	Track Switch/Class Drop	6
	Trainer Total Dictatorship	8
2	Horse for Course	7, 10
	Ascending Numbers	1
3	Trainer/Horse Partnership	10
	Proven-Loser Win Cluster	3
	(forced labor above level)	
4	Turn Takers	1
	When Good Horses Bounce	2
5	Trainer/Horse Partnership	10
	Horse for Course	7
6	Master of Trade	4
	Trainer/Horse Partnership	10
7	Child Prodigy	5
	Ascending Numbers	1
8	Partial Trainer Dictatorship	9
	Layoff Winners	2
9	Proven Losers	1, 3
	Ascending and Descending	
	Numbers	1
10	Proven Losers	1, 3
	Track Switch/Class Drop	6

D. SYSTEMS?

Concepts with *Defined Rules* Which Resulted in Flat-Bet Profits in Research Samples

1. The Five-Year-Old Gelding, chapters 5, 13
   Bet five-year-old geldings in all races, no restrictions
2. Track Switch/Class Drop, chapter 6
   a. Out-of-money, more than 2 lengths behind, in last 3 races
   b. Drop in class
   c. Ship to different track
   d. Minimum odds, 4–1

3. Horse Futures, chapter 13
   a. Invest in horses that have 2 wins in first 10 career starts
   b. Second of those 2 wins must be 5–1 or up, or both wins must be 4–1 or above
   c. Qualifying horses receive an equal unit bet in their next 10 races

E. METHODS:

Profitable Concepts Without Mechanical Rules, with Clear Guidelines, but Requiring Judgmental Intervention of Handicapper

1. Late Bloomer. Previously mediocre horse, wins with improved pace and speed figures, gets claimed while going up in class ....Chapter 5
2. Horse for Course. Alphabetical listing of last year's winners at short meets. When last year's win condition materializes this year (sloppy track, specialty distance, etc.), invest. List can be limited to less usual types of winners; for example, specialty distance, 5–1 or up win, multiple winner at target track, specialty surface ....Chapter 7
3. Hot Trainer Bets. Bet on trainers who are recent multiple winners with two of the three following characteristics: winners at 5–1 or up, with form reversals, outside of the trainer's normal specialty.....................................Chapter 8
4. Long and Short Trainer Cycles. Pattern of prior victory is repeated in today's pps ....Chapters 9, 10, 13
5. Layoff Winners. Horse won as first-time starter or shows prior win following layoff.....................................Chapter 2
6. Maiden Comebacker. Raced once or twice as two-year-old, heavily bet, ran poorly, laid off, comes back today ....Chapter 11

7. Other Concepts with Broader Guidelines and More Judgmental Handicapping. Ascending numbers (Chapters 1, 13), masters of a trade (Chapters 6, 13), proven-loser win cluster (Chapter 3), taking turns (Chapter 1), and third race after layoff, bounced in second race back (Chapter 2)
8. Variation of Horse for Course: the Three-year-Old Head Start Cycle. Apr./May meet switch, only one horse in field has head-start win at target track, has positive form indications, in three-year-old field..........................Chapter 10, Workshop Two

F. BIBLIOGRAPHY

The recommended survey that contains the best critical commentary on the literature of thoroughbred handicapping is found in James Quinn's *The Best of Thoroughbred Handicapping* (William Morrow & Co., 1987). This volume covers the work of Ainslie, Beyer, Davidowitz, Quinn, Quirin, Sartin, Scott, Ziemba, and many other notables. To the authors covered by Quinn, add the work of Tom Brohamer, Barry Meadow, and Dick Mitchell, whose recent contributions are destined to join the classics.

Off Broadway

To qualify for the Off Broadway Bibliography, the following contributors to handicapping knowledge must: not have published a book on thoroughbreds; fit the description of a mad scientist; have contributed to the concept that horse-race handicapping should be rated on a par with progressive jazz, abstract expressionism, and the modern novel as a major art form of the twentieth century. Entries are listed by name, specialties, and general whereabouts.

ANDERSON, ANDY. Exactas. San Francisco Bay Area.
ANGELO, JOHN. "Saratoga Scorecard." Research. Manchester, New Hampshire.
BEDERSON, JACK. Research on recency. Southern California.
COTOLO, FRANK. Fiction and contradiction. Exact whereabouts unknown. Look for him at the large transaction window. Split personality: harness and thoroughbreds

GOLDSTEIN, LARRY. Best research ever on first-time starters. Southern California.

MARTIN, STEVE. Not the actor. Once an opera singer, he made the natural transition from opera to horse-race handicapping. Esoteric, Renaissance mentality. East and West coasts.

McCORMICK, DAVID. Foreign horses. Listens to the English races on ham radio. Best research on foreign imports as first-time starters in U.S. Southern California.

McMANNIS, M. SCOTT. Speed figures. In spite of his higher education, he talks straight. Greater Chicago area.

MURRAY, GENE. Computer expert, currently working on horse-race data base. This guy can figure out the place and show payoffs in his head faster than I can do it with a preprogrammed calculator. Southern California.

OLMSTED, BILL. Eclectic, pace/speed figures. "Thoroughbred Speculator." Maryland.

OWENS, BOB. Research. San Diego.

RICHARDS, JAY. Always something new. Las Vegas, Nevada.

ROBLIN, RONALD. Harness racing. Methodology for handicapping snowy surfaces. Buffalo, New York.

SHRAGER, MARK. Unusual jockey research and other subjects. Southern California.

STOFF, RICK. Trainers. Art appreciation: takes nonhorseplayers to the track to expose them to the fine art of handicapping. Southern California.

G. THOROUGHBRED CYCLE HANDICAPPING APPLIED TO HUMAN BEINGS:

Baseball Pitcher Predictions for 1988 Season

This horse-race handicapper predicted a successful 1988 season for the following pitchers who had had terrible or underachieving 1987 seasons:

Won-Lost Record

	1987	1988
D. Jackson	9–18	23–8
Candiotti	7–18	14–8
Knepper	8–17	13–5
E. Show	9–16	14–11
Hurst	15–13	18–6

We were wrong in projecting an underachieving year for Voila and a good year for Valenzuela, but these were the only notable misses. We were right about big years for Browning and Rasmussen and a dull year for D. Darwin. The point is, in the realm of *cycles, similar handicapping techniques can be applied to horses and human beings.*

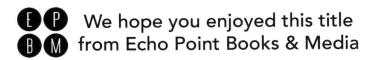 We hope you enjoyed this title
from Echo Point Books & Media

Before Closing this Book, Two Good Things to Know

1. Buy Direct & Save

Go to www.echopointbooks.com (click "Our Titles" at top or click "For Echo Point Publishing" in the middle) to see our complete list of titles. We publish books on a wide variety of topics—from spirituality to auto repair.

Buy direct and save 10% at www.echopointbooks.com

DISCOUNT CODE: EPBUYER

2. Make Literary History and Earn $100 Plus Other Goodies Simply for Your Book Recommendation!

At Echo Point Books & Media we specialize in republishing out-of-print books that are united by one essential ingredient: high quality. Do you know of any great books that are no longer actively published? If so, please let us know. If we end up publishing your recommendation, you'll be adding a wee bit to literary culture and a bunch to our publishing efforts.

Here is how we will thank you:

- A free copy of the new version of your beloved book that includes acknowledgement of your skill as a sharp book scout.
- A free copy of another Echo Point title you like from echopointbooks.com.
- And, oh yes, we'll also send you a check for $100.

Since we publish an eclectic list of titles, we're interested in a wide range of books. So please don't be shy if you have obscure tastes or like books with a practical focus. To get a sense of what kind of books we publish, visit us at www.echopointbooks.com.

If you have a book that you think will work for us,
send us an email at editorial@echopointbooks.com

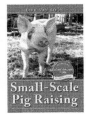  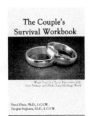  

Printed in the USA
CPSIA information can be obtained
at www.ICGtesting.com
LVHW022034091223
766037LV00005B/427